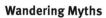

Wandering Myths

Wandering Myths

Transcultural Uses of Myth in the Ancient World

Edited by
Lucy Audley-Miller and Beate Dignas

DE GRUYTER

ISBN 978-3-11-071008-3
e-ISBN (PDF) 978-3-11-042145-3
e-ISBN (EPUB) 978-3-11-042151-4

Library of Congress Control Number: 2018935090

Bibliographic information published by the Deutsche Nationalbibliothek
The Deutsche Nationalbibliothek lists this publication in the Deutsche Nationalbibliografie;
detailed bibliographic data are available on the Internet at http://dnb.dnb.de.

Contents

Beate Dignas and Lucy Audley-Miller
Preface
Wandering Myths: Transcultural Uses of Myth in the Ancient World —— **VII**

Robin Lane Fox
Introduction
Travelling Myths, Travelling Heroes —— **XXXIII**

Part I: **Changing Cultural and Mythical Landscapes in Anatolia**

Ian Rutherford
Kingship in Heaven in Anatolia, Syria and Greece
Patterns of Convergence and Divergence —— **3**

Catherine M. Draycott
Making Meaning of Myth
On the Interpretation of Mythological Imagery in the Polyxena Sarcophagus and the
Kızılbel Tomb and the History of Achaemenid Asia Minor —— **23**

Tanja S. Scheer
Myth, Memory and the Past
Wandering Heroes between Arcadia and Cyprus —— **71**

Part II: **Reception and Innovation of Mythological Programmes
between Greece and Italy**

Nancy T. de Grummond
From Mezntie to Mezentius?
The Stratigraphy of a Myth in Etruria and Rome —— **95**

Luca Giuliani
Pots, Plots, and Performance
Comic and Tragic Iconography in Apulian Vase Painting —— **125**

Katharina Lorenz
Distributed Narrative
A Very Short History of Juxtaposing Myths on Pompeian Walls —— **143**

Barbara E. Borg
No One is Immortal
From Exemplum Mortalitatis to Exemplum Virtutis —— **169**

B. C. Ewald
Attic Sarcophagi
Myth Selection and the Heroising Tradition —— **209**

Part III: **Wandering East, Wandering South**

Martin West
Gilgāmeš and Homer: The Missing Link? —— **265**

Rana Sérida
Myth, Memory, and Mimesis
The Inaros Cycle as Literature of Resistance —— **281**

Luke Pitcher
Death on the Nile: The Myth of Osiris and the Utility of History in Diodorus.
Egypt In Greco-Roman Historiography —— **309**

Rachel Wood
Wandering Hero, Wandering Myths?
The Image of Heracles in Iran —— **327**

Katherine M. D. Dunbabin
The Transformations of Achilles on Late Roman Mosaics in the East —— **357**

Robert Parker
Epilogue —— **397**

Index —— **405**

Beate Dignas and Lucy Audley-Miller

Preface

Wandering Myths: Transcultural Uses of Myth in the Ancient World

Greek myths[1] occupied a central place in the thought-worlds of ancient people over considerable time and space. This fact, together with the interpretative potential that has been demonstrated by important recent studies on the ancient uses and resonances of these myths,[2] justifies adding to the large body of work that has been produced on myth in the ancient world. The current volume seeks to contribute to this field a specific focus on a transcultural perspective. The multicultural nature of the ancient Mediterranean and its interconnections with the Near East, the differing cultural traditions and continuous changes within and between these areas pose tremendous challenges to such a focus, but also enormous possibilities. It is not difficult to see that ancient societies were linked by their creation and understanding of mythological narratives, from the Ancient Near East to Rome and beyond. It is much harder to discern and describe any patterns in this shared understanding, or to examine how myths came to "move" and to become locally resonant in disparate places in different ways. The authors in this volume take up the challenge and show that this approach offers the opportunity to see links between cultures as well as modes of adaptation and reception that would not otherwise be visible and which fundamentally characterised ancient perspectives and identities.[3]

---

1 Myth is a term that is notoriously difficult to define and the editors of this volume shrink from the task of attempting it here. A range of different definitions have been proposed but there is, perhaps, something to be said for Dowden and Livingstone's bold assertion that "we know a Greek myth when we see one and have need of no definitions, guidance, or code of practice to identify it as such" (Dowden and Livingstone 2011, 3). We use the term "Greek Myth" above, and elsewhere, to refer to the most notable tellings of these narratives in the works of figures such as Homer and Hesiod and in order to broadly situate the volume, but agree with criticism that it is unhelpful to use this term to express cultural exclusiveness or opposition (a point raised by various scholars, see for example Beard 1993, 50; Junker 2005 (translation 2012), xiii; Newby 2016, 10–4). As others have shown elsewhere, and the authors in this volume clearly demonstrate, myths were subject to continuous redefinition to suit new contexts and this process could lead to their adoption and indigenisation far away from Greek contexts.

2 For a few examples, from the many possible, see: De Angelis and Muth 1999; Zanker and Ewald 2004; Junker 2005 (translation 2012); Patterson 2010; Smith 2012; Giuliani 2013; Woodard 2013; Hall 2013; MacSweeney 2014; Lorenz 2016; Hawes 2017.

3 Although this concept has come to be regarded as problematic by some (see e.g. Niethammer 2000 and, when applied to the ancient world, as potentially anachronistic, e.g. Hölscher 2008, esp. 52–4; Hölscher 2011, 60; see also Brooks 2011 on individual identity as a concern that is particular to a post-Enlightenment world). We use the term here because, like many scholars, we believe it is useful, if

https://doi.org/10.1515/9783110421453-001

The study of myths has few competitors when it comes to a history of scholarship that is imbued with conflicting theories.[4] Much is gained from looking at the genesis of each and the relationship between these theories, much from testing each on specific examples. Most is probably achieved by not settling on one theory but by acknowledging that the complexity of the phenomenon escapes single interpretation. This is particularly true when we address "cross-cultural transferences of myth", and the reasons for this are manifold. While "theorising" is not primarily a matter of "filling the gaps", it is precisely our growing knowledge of the mythologies, the languages, the bodies of texts, and ultimately the interaction between Greek and other ancient cultures that questions the veracity of one specific mode of interpretation. Although it has taken an extremely long time for the "paradigm of Greek myth" to disappear (and some theories of myth were rather developed to keep it tenaciously alive), comparison across cultures and thinking about the notion or modes of diffusion have become a must in any study of myth.

The intellectual stimulus of the discovery of oral poetry and transmission has transformed the study of archaic epic, and the same is happening with regard to the increasingly studied body of Near-Eastern texts – if we think this further and develop new insights into cross-cultural story-telling we further add to a multi-layered understanding of mythical stories. As some of the contributions of this volume are going to show, the intricate web of similarities and differences can make all the difference to the notion of what myth is and does, and even more so the proposals and conclusions we generate about the communication between individuals and groups, via every possible medium and in every possible setting. It is most welcome that this thought process has been set into motion also in the study of other periods, genres and geographical settings, and this not only in the context of "empire" and cultural dominance.[5] Inevitably, critically and constructively thinking about ideas of "culture"[6] and "cultural diffusion", or the movement of cultural forms from one society to another, becomes a crucial aspect of our task. The extremely rich and scholarly discourse on "Hellenisa-

---

treated as a dynamic, i.e. part of a continuous overlapping process of self-definition performed in relation to varied situations, group identifications, social relationships, and socio-culturally defined values (e.g. Bauman 1996; Hall 1996, 1–17; Kuper 1999, 226–247; Diaz-Andreu and Lucy 2005, 1–13; Revell 2009).

4 For excellent overviews see the concise introduction in Dowden 1992, 22–34, and the key publications on myth by Graf 1993; especially poignant: Graf 2004.

5 See especially Whitmarsh and Thomson 2013, who do this with remarkable persuasion for the study of the ancient novel ("imaginative texts written (mostly) in Greek between 400 BCE and 200 CE", 2).

6 Misgivings against using this charged term are closely related to those regarding "identity". See note 3 above.

tion",[7] "Romanisation",[8] hybridity,[9] globalisation[10] and indigenisation provided part of the stimulus for our project.[11] Not expounding the benefits of one of the developed models but rather contributing to our understanding of these processes, the authors of this volume consistently focus on the agency of those deploying myths, and they show the range of ways in which these narratives could be adjusted to serve the specific needs of different contexts.

With regard to more recent scholarship on myth, likewise, this focus on case-specific agency keys into broader trends. There is no longer a desire to "test" myth for its truth content or the question of whether ancient users "believed" in their myths but rather a careful investigation of what triggered the surfacing and adaptation of myths in local contexts. While studies of kinship and foundation myths loom large and are indeed fruitful, insights go well beyond the claim that Greek identity guaranteed cultural status in non-Greek, Hellenistic or Roman imperial contexts.[12] Looking at the notorious and important relationship between myth and ritual, already Burkert introduced a more "accommodating" discussion, suggesting a variety of possible links and stepping back from one rigid and genetically determined one.[13] Again, we think that the cross-cultural perspective is reason to embrace this approach and to look at "ritual" in a fresh way. This should not *a priori* go against a "constructivist" model but new considerations surface. Mythological narratives make important charged statements about the gods and their relationships with mortals, about human origins and about society and its institutions, and changing societal conditions must therefore evoke an adjustment of myths if these are to survive and remain relevant.[14] Successful myths are often those that adapt easily as an inadvertent response to changes within their (human) setting. Regardless of how fluid our concept of "culture" is and how reluctant we are to use the term "cultural identity", transposing a story into a new cultural

---

7 For key discussion of this term, see Zanker 1976; Wallace-Hadrill 2008; Prag and Quinn 2013.

8 A term which has been particularly reviled as deemed to be rife with colonialist assumptions and baggage (e.g. Barrett 1997; Mattingly 2002; Mattingly 2004; Mattingly 2006, 14–17). More recently some scholars have observed that the term does at least have the merit of referring to the contact culture in question in a way that "cultural change" does not, and suggest that perhaps the term can be useful if carefully defined (e.g. Wallace-Hadrill 2008, 28; Mullen 2013, 9–10).

9 E.g. Webster 2003 (on "creolised" modes of hybridity in the Roman period).

10 For parallels between Roman cultural change and "globalisation" see Witcher 2000; Hingley 2005; Hitchner 2008; Alexandridis 2010, esp. 253–9. For discussion of economic parallels see Geraghty 2007; Morley 2007, 90–107.

11 On the movement of goods and practices involving "hybridisation, interpretation, translation, manipulation, mutation and 'indigenisation'", see Hingley 2005, 111.

12 The contributions by Scheer, Draycott and Sérida in this volume illustrate this approach nicely, but see also, Clarke 2008; Patterson 2010; Dignas 2012; Thomas 2014.

13 Burkert 1979. Burkert's relationship with ritualist theories is complex and cannot be set out in detail here; for a succinct summary of the history of scholarship see, e.g., Segal 2015, 49–65, and Csapo 2005, especially 132–80.

14 Graf 1993, esp. 3–4.

setting would make the need for adaptation even greater. If, however, myth and ritual were often connected, such as in the form of aetiological stories that explained or were performed as part of a recurring ritual or festival, a deliberate and striking lack of adjustment is also possible and the question of meaning has a very different dimension. The question as to whether a myth may or may not have travelled along with ritual opens up a myriad of added possibilities.[15]

The relationship between an existing or non-existing spatial fluidity of myth and a cross-cultural dimension is a fascinating one, and one that requires further attention given valuable recent work on the physical setting of myth. Hawes' volume *Myths on the Map* brings together an array of casestudies and important general conclusions.[16] Specificity of location is highlighted, for example, in Minchin's intriguing diachronical analysis of the story of Hero and Leander, in which the Hellespontine setting is not optional, regardless of how other central aspects of the story, its appeal as a narrative of love and loss, determine its success and survival.[17] Myth, here, is not only anchored by location but also expresses and creates collective memory that determines the evolution of the myth in time. This example shows nicely how the study of myth is both embedded in and transcends two strong trends in recent historical scholarship, namely that towards environmental history[18] and that towards memory studies[19] , in themselves concerns that benefit immensely from a cross-cultural perspective.

Finally, we wish to emphasise our acknowledgement that this cross-cultural line of enquiry into the study of ancient myth is not entirely novel. Indeed, recent scholarship has been particularly fruitful in this area and has shown that it warrants further investigation. This work served as the impetus for this book. Examples that show the potential for such an approach can be found in a wide range of disciplines, and our contributors have helpfully situated their own work within the discourse of each of their fields, making a lengthy introduction to current research in their various areas superfluous here. At the risk of repeating some of their discussion, one example will hopefully adequately serve the purpose of this preface, namely the study of Greek myth in Roman visual culture. Roman society and its art had traditionally been viewed as relatively lacking in terms of its own "original" myths,[20] having been "sat-

---

15 This is potentially a very different process, and its investigation a very illuminating one, where the retelling of a story may have been linked to its aetiological motif for different reasons than early theories would have postulated.

16 Hawes 2017.

17 Ch. 4 in Hawes 2017.

18 See for example Bekker-Nielsen 2014.

19 For an overview of recent scholarship and altogether an excellent collection of individual studies see Galinsky 2016; with much relevance also Bommas 2013 and 2014.

20 On Roman lack of myth, see Wissowa 1912; Latte 1926; such theories together with contemporary argument against this view are succinctly and helpfully overviewed in Beard et al. 1998, esp. 171–81; Kearns and Price 2003, xi–xii. On "Roman myths" see also Grant 1973; Wiseman 2004.

urated" with references to "Greek" ones.[21] Nineteenth-century scholarship was initially interested in using such images to reconstruct lost Greek artworks or texts, but the depiction of Greek myths later came to be viewed as less significant than forms that seemed more "Roman".[22] However, there has been an increasing interest in how Greek myths were adapted and selectively employed and a related move away from exploring "Greek" myths in polar distinction to those that were local to Rome. A range of relationships with Greek myth have been explored, from absorption, transformation, to references that consciously allude to the Greek origins of these narratives and iconographies.[23] The depiction of Greek myths in Rome has ceased to be interpreted straightforwardly in terms of their ability to elevate through reference to classical culture.[24] Instead, new interpretations and questions have been raised to explore the ways by which Greek mythology became locally resonant. These include hypotheses regarding how Greek mythology was used and responded to in different ways by different socioeconomic levels within Roman society.[25] New insights have been gained into cultural change by examining shifts in the representations of Greek myth in Roman art over time.[26] The use of Greek myths in Rome has been explored in a range of contexts, from the funerary sphere,[27] to domestic contexts,[28] with an emphasis upon examining what the ways of depicting these narratives can reveal.[29] This important work has traced the manner in which these myths were adjusted to serve varied needs and has offered considerable cultural insights through this process. The present book explores

---

21 Newby 2016, 1–19 uses this term "saturated" to refer to images of Greek myths in the Roman visual environment and offers a good recent summary of the earlier scholarship. The history of approaches to Greek myths on Roman sarcophagi is also overviewed in this volume in Borg's contribution, and earlier scholarship on Greek myths in Roman wall painting is discussed here by Lorenz.

22 In 1987, Hölscher could write that Greek mythological images were a comparatively neglected field in the study of Roman art. As Elsner makes clear already in his Foreword to the English translation of 2004, this is certainly no longer the case (Hölscher 2004).

23 These and other such relationships are outlined in Newby 2016, 10–9.

24 On mythology as conveying classicism and education, see, for example, Nock 1946, esp. 163. His emphasis upon "worldly" paideia was advanced against Cumont's eschatological interpretations of mythological sarcophagi (Cumont 1942).

25 For example, Mayer argued that this was not simply a "top down" fashion but instead identified some uses of mythology in houses and tombs which he identified as specific to the social values of the "middle classes" (Mayer 2012, 100–212). On the problems associated with using the term "middle classes" to explore Roman culture, see Wallace-Hadrill 2013.

26 Newby 2011; Newby 2016.

27 E.g. Fittschen 1992; Koortbojian 1995; Zanker and Ewald 2004; Newby 2014.

28 E.g. Bergmann 1994; Bergmann 1999; Muth 1998; Muth 1999; Trimble 2002; Hales 2003a, esp. 135–66; Hales 2003b.

29 On playful ways of visualising Greek epic, including miniaturisation, see Squire 2011. On the importance of using close "reading" of the iconography to interpret specific resonances of the images in their various Roman contexts, see Dunbabin, Lorenz, Borg and Ewald in this volume.

and expands not only upon some of these particular Roman case studies,[30] but it also seeks to gain broader insights by moving across disciplines and presents these themes in a wider range of temporal, spatial and cultural contexts.

Formally, the volume brings together and interprets the research presented at three workshops and an international conference that were held in Oxford between January and April 2014. The aim of these events was to advance our understanding of the mechanisms by which mythological tales were disseminated and made locally resonant in the ancient world, and to do so by investigating both wider geographic circulations of mythical themes and local transformations of myth within individual regions. From the outset, this project has been deeply interdisciplinary, aiming to explore the register of ways through which myths were made present in the lives of ancient people. Discussion centered on a range of case studies with a particular focus on Anatolia, the Near East, and Italy. Beyond their specific themes, all contributions formulated and responded to general questions that aimed to enhance our under-standing of the factors that guided the processes of reception and steered the facets of local interpretation. The resulting volume does not present a singular consensus view, but rather proposes a series of different ways of examining these questions together with both overlapping and different interpretations. All contributions stand alone as studies on how and why myths wandered – read alongside each other, we believe, they yield greater understanding of a complex phenomenon.

The book commences with Robin Lane Fox's challenging and provocative intro-duction that sets out the questions in straightforward terms and postulates almost easy explanations to account for the emergence and dissemination of myth at large: "creative linguistic misunderstandings" paired with "sex" in the contexts of "con-quest" and "mission". This contribution deploys varied examples with regard to space, time and cultural perspective, and Lane Fox's views of why and how myths did or did not travel draw heavily on his wide ranging scholarly opus. His examples include that ongoing creator of myth, Alexander the Great, who is used here to illus-trate forcefully the author's proposed mechanisms for transmission and adaptation. In addition, following on from his much-acclaimed *Travelling Heroes* (2008), Lane Fox explores the Mediterranean travels of the archaic Euboean heroes, who travelled both West, as in the Bay of Naples and other parts of south Italy and Sicily, and East, in particular the very north-eastern corner between Turkey, Cyprus and Syria. In this context, Lane Fox looks not only at what facilitated the dissemination of myths but also at why myths may not have travelled. His findings in both regards consistently em-phasise travelling people, rather than travelling myths: so that, for example, Euboean travellers did not transfer their own specifically local myths but strongly enhanced the travelling of panhellenic heroes, such as Heracles, or produced their own mythical creations that were inspired by their travels to far-away-places. Their contacts with

---

30 See Borg, Dunbabin, Ewald, and Lorenz in this volume.

the heritage of Anatolian civilisations brought Near-Eastern myths into the Euboean travellers' thought-world, but only their further travelling in the Mediterranean facilitated the emergence of various local appropriations of these myths. Inevitably, the retelling of such myths in the Hesiodic Theogony according to Lane Fox depended heavily on the poet's Euboean connections, above all manifest in his performance at the funeral games for Amphidamas in Chalcis.

In the general context of the present volume it is not so much the precise identity of such myth-carrying travellers as Euboeans that will alert a critically minded reader. More importantly, there is the assumption that the all-important (Euboean) travellers formed an entirely novel impetus to local storytelling, which would indeed turn them into travelling heroes of the dissemination and creation of myth. Surely, there pre-existed stories that stemmed from cultic, cultural or socio-geographical local idiosyncrasies and facilitated the reception of the mythological material brought by any travellers? Last but not least Lane Fox struggles to fit the paramount Homeric epics into his picture of Euboean travelers: why do they not feature centrally in poems contemporary to the Hesiodic ones, and how does their tradition as oral poetry bear on their reception of Near-Eastern and Anatolian mythological themes? Lane Fox's elegant solution is spelled out in the remarks that conclude his introduction here: the Trojan myths and the dispersed Trojans were in essence the "perfect" travellers. The idea is both obvious and attractive but one wonders to what extent an almost inevitable blur between travelling archaic "heroes" and "travelling mythological heroes" treats the wide range of concrete as well as metaphorical meanings of "travelling" too lightly. There is no doubt, however, that the focus on the Homeric epics and their wandering heroes deserves crucial space in the discussion, and along the lines of the author's emphases we are bound to ask whether and how "travelling heroes" were "travelling myths" or "travelling people"? Lane Fox's challenging hypotheses and "big" statements ache for case studies, analysis, and a critical response, which the contributions in the following chapters offer in a multi-facetted way. Their interdisciplinary nature and the ease with which the study of textual material is intertwined with, preceded and followed by that of material culture highlights the pervading nature of the phenomenon, as well as its attraction and complexity.

Part I, "Changing Cultural and Mythical Landscapes in Anatolia", looks at a region that has a rich local mythological topography and can, arguably, be seen as one of the keys to understanding patterns of cross-cultural exchange throughout antiquity. Ian Rutherford's comparison of Greek and Near-Eastern myths about "Kingship in Heaven" does not take for granted Lane Fox's straightforward "diffusion" as the reason for similar story-patterns. Instead, he reminds us that substantial background work is needed to find a "critical mass" of parallels in order to establish that narratives are truly related. Rutherford's careful and detailed comparisons support the view that the Hesiodic succession myth can almost certainly be linked to the Hittite mythical narrative of the "Song of Going Forth" and most probably illustrates a borrowing from East to West. Beyond this, and very importantly, we also learn of other traditions and complex earlier interactions that formed part of the process. The links between other Near-Eastern and Greek myths are traced with even more difficulty (for example, transmission via a Luwian/Anatolian route appears as plausible as via a Syrian/Levantine one), which appears to be a direct effect of the multi-facetted and often long-distance connectivity of the relevant areas. Rutherford's work demonstrates that the more we understand the linguistic, religious, and economic nature of this connectivity, the more complex the emerging picture becomes.

Cathie Draycott's study looks at such factors of connectivity, exploring the regional dynamics that emerged in two specific areas in Anatolia at a time of social change ushered in by the Achaemenid Empire. The author also shifts our attention to the complex hermeneutic difficulties and opportunities involved in interpreting mythological scenes in visual culture. Her analysis centres on the puzzling and open-ended features of two spectacular tombs: the Polyxena sarcophagus with its carefully selected mythological imagery and the Kızılbel Tomb with its wide-ranging programme. Confronted with the task of filling the gaps and open to ideas such as social constructionism, the modern viewer is reminded that there was no singular historical "meaning" for all, rather, Draycott emphasises the agency of the viewers in interpreting these images and making meanings. As well as presenting persuasive new interpretations, this author explores the potential resonances of these images from a range of perspectives and shows it is unnecessarily limiting, and potentially problematic, to read them only in terms of presumed gender or ethnic identity. This contribution examines the role of these mythological images in expressing consolation for the bereaved, potentially acting as forms of visual elegy, but also in creating social distinction for the patron, by evoking different sorts of connection and knowledge at a time when the region was resounding with greater access to materials and ideas. Her analysis charts significant micro-local variation in the uptake of mythological images and explores what this might indicate in terms of different circles of contact as well as different local agendas and ideas about how high social distinction was best expressed. The adaptation of myths examined here offers considerable insights into the appearance of new modes of self-representation at a time of transformation in two differently connected regions in early Achaemenid Anatolia.

The examination of uses of myth through an Anatolian lens is concluded with Tanja Scheer's "Wandering Heroes between Arcadia, Asia Minor and Cyprus". Scheer examines a number of issues raised by Lane Fox's bold introduction, above all the differentiation between "wandering heroes" and "wandering myths". Myths that feature wandering protagonists, i.e. Lane Fox's "perfect dispersed Trojans", were common in antiquity because reconstructing one's own past tended to be linked to ideas of migration as well as genealogies of mythical heroes. Scheer warns us not to map the two realms of historical colonisation and foundation myths onto each other but rather asks about the contexts and initiators that were interested in creating and highlighting the wandering heroes. She explores this process in terms of "channeling local historical memory into familiar themes of mythology" and "setting a myth in motion". Her specific example illustrates this approach beautifully, highlighting myth as the cultural currency that forged and navigated international networks. She observes that few literary sources emphasise the story of Agapenor and the Arcadians as dispersed heroes of the Trojan War who ended up in Cyprus. Only the city of Paphos claimed connections to Agapenor and even here tales about the pre-Greek Cypriot king Kinyras and his descendants were much more prominent than the Arcadian connection. Exceptional interest in a link with Agapenor arose in first half of the second century BC, at a time of Ptolemaic control and strong economic and cultural interest in the island, and specifically a long-term governor named Ptolemaios of Megalopolis, who is also attested as a man with literary ambitions. For Scheer the mutual convenience of a Homeric foundation myth that evoked Arcadian kinship is evident and serves as a powerful explanation for its "activation".

Several significant conclusions emerge: wandering heroes may wander long after their travels depending on political and cultural contexts. The motif was so prominent because foundation myths were always closely linked to ideas about colonisation and kinship, which those "responsible for the local memory culture" used to advance the image and political ties of the community. Scheer reinforces the creative nature of this process that allows for the entirely new "wandering" of heroes, even back to their origins, with the help of another example, a dedication to Aphrodite Paphia at Tegea by a certain Laodike, a descendant of Agapenor. What is fascinating is that the evidence that Scheer (or indeed Pausanias) uses to reconstruct the creation and wandering of myths reveals that the mediators and their media did not necessarily have to travel themselves: sending a cult image or votive could actually take place without Laodike having undertaken the journey from Paphos to Tegea.

Part II takes us to the West, primarily to Italy, one of the preferred destinations of Lane Fox's Euboean travellers. The five contributions demonstrate the necessity of focusing upon specific case studies and addressing issues of genre in order to approach the complexities of the volume's central questions. In tracing movement in the uses of myth over time, space and medium, they also illustrate, powerfully, the potential for idiosyncratic local interpretation. Nancy De Grummond's intriguing interpretation of a bronze Etruscan mirror now held in the Villa Giulia in Rome warns us against dismissing the presentations of myths that, at first sight, seem unorthodox to our eyes. Rather than assuming mistakes by those trying to reproduce standard canons of Greek culture, such as scribes mislabelling characters, she proposes that images like the Villa Giulia mirror are the physical products of vigorous local oral narrative traditions and gain their resonance through reference to a form of transmission that inevitably led to variation. De Grummond sees pieces like the Villa Giulia mirror as artefacts of this process. She invites us to explore the shifts in narratives that occurred as wider stories were adjusted to suit different local needs, and she proposes that through careful examination of texts and material culture we can gain insights into the local "stratigraphies" that developed in myth. Her diachronic analysis charts a relationship between a real historical individual, the story shown in the Villa Giulia mirror and the famous

depiction of Mezentius in Virgil's Aeneid. De Grummond demonstrates that mythological narratives did not possess a special appeal because they evoked a known and
"correct" original version, but because they had the potential to be adapted to different contexts at different times and thus to suit a very specific local audience.

Also interested in the dynamics of reception and local reinterpretation, Luca Giuliani explores references to the plots of Attic drama in the richly varied body of images
preserved in Apulian vase painting. The author's answers as to how and why myths
wandered through space and from one medium to another envisage on the one hand
a looser relationship between "pots and plays" than has often been proposed, and
on the other hand a vigorous absorption and appropriation of Athenian drama and
its specificities on stage. The study starts from the commonly observed contrast between comic images that regularly include clear reference to theatrical performance
and the larger group of images depicting "serious" mythological scenes without such
reference. Giuliani examines what drove the disparity between the treatment of these
genres and what it reveals about the interest Apulian painters had in Attic narratives.
Theatrical elements are seen here to receive new meanings or functions when depicted
on vases that were distinct from their resonance on the stage. For example, rather than
"signalling" that the image related to the performance of a play, the long-sleeved costume worn on stage by all figures, together with a mask, became used on vases as
a distinctive marker to identify the subjects as kings, men of exotic origin or pedagogues. Giuliani further suggests that comic costumes need not suggest comic performance, but helped with comic effects in their own right, creating an emphasis on the
difference between the actual and the pretend, whereas such performance elements
would have undermined the resonance of a tragic scene and turned the protagonists
into "mere actors". The picture here emphasises the cultural transformations wrought
through the process of cultural transference, including reference to dramatic elements
in scenes that were in themselves neither dramatic nor narrative in character. Apulian
artists are seen here to have been deeply inspired by Attic drama, with all its idiosyncrasies of place and genre, but to have vigorously absorbed, adjusted, and adapted
theatrical elements according to the artist's needs regarding medium and message.

Katharina Lorenz' contribution focuses on the display of myth in Pompeian
homes, tracing significant shifts in Roman practices of visual story-telling. She focuses on the thematic connections between wall paintings and concentrates on the
effects the conscious juxtaposition of mythological images had on the ancient viewer,
who was invited to compare and contrast tales, and to draw analogies thereby par-
ticipating in practices that articulated and informed the social configuration of the
house. The spectrum of decorative decisions attested at Pompeii shows that it is inadequate to simply argue that the patrons of wall paintings picked the designs for their
houses from pattern books and that this is how this iconography "wandered" to and
within the settlement. While pattern books may have potentially provided a portfolio
of material from which Pompeian customers chose; this shared pool of motifs was laid
out according to highly individualised arrangements. Lorenz' new contribution to this

field traces the origins and developments of viewers' interaction with images of myth in a comprehensive diachronic way. She looks at changes in how mythological images were placed together and the ensuing differences in meaning production that they inspired in their viewers. A movement towards increasingly complex forms of exegesis on the part of the viewer is traced here through significant differences outlined in the ways that mythological scenes were interrelated and displayed. Lorenz also observes how the broad and well-documented style changes that have been long observed in wall painting relate to these shifts in the contemporary use of mythological narrative. In looking at how mythological scenes were adapted and adjusted to meet the needs of domestic display, through meticulous discussion of case studies Lorenz reveals significant innovation in visual presentations of myth, in modes of interpretation, and the role of the viewer.

How this constantly shifting and reciprocal interaction between presentation, context, and a viewer's background informed the resonance of mythical stories is also the emphasis of Barbara Borg's work. Here, it is the medium of metropolitan Roman sarcophagi that is explored, with a particular focus on the second century. Showing again that there was never any one singular "true" version of a myth, she explores how the resonances of the stories were informed by the viewer's "horizon of experience" and expectations, which in the case of sarcophagi are not best understood by a straightforward correlation between image and the most famous known literary versions, but by exploring carefully the content and style of the images themselves and considering the funerary context in which these images were viewed. Roman artists and patrons, so Borg observes, drew upon myth not by using it as visual allegory, but as *exampla* that worked by analogy. The scope of differing *exempla* that resulted from iconographic adjustment to the same myth was wide, ranging from *exempla virtutis* to *exempla mortalitatis* or *exempla maeroris*. As in Lorenz' contribution, Borg is able to show some striking temporal shifts in the ways that myths were used: here moving from an emphasis on *exempla mortalitatis* or *exempla maeroris* in second-century sarcophagi, to an increasing focus on using myths as *exempla virtutis* especially from the late Antonine period onwards to the third century when this developed into the principal role of myth, particularly in cases with the addition of portrait features to mythological protagonists. The inevitable openness and overlap of these forms of *exempla* were narrowed by the parameters of specific ancient viewing, and Borg gives fascinating and surprising examples that show how different the patterns of analogy were from our expectations. What emerges is a picture of utmost creativity employed by artists and patrons in using myths as *exempla* in a dynamic and changing way to commemorate the dead and comfort the bereaved.

Sharing the focus on uses of myth on sarcophagi from the Roman period, Björn Ewald looks at *wandering myths* by way of geographical comparison, juxtaposing the reading and understanding of Attic sarcophagi with their counterparts in Rome. In contrast with Borg, Ewald examines Roman sarcophagi in terms of allegory, but in other aspects there is much methodology in common between these two authors' readings of the visual material to gain broader historical insights. Ewald demonstrates that these two centres of production shared "open and related mythospheres" and that we can gain real social insights through a close textured analysis of which mythological themes wandered between Athens and Rome, and which did not. The actual geographic wandering of myths on Attic sarcophagi reflects a broad consumer demand by elites around the Mediterranean world, which adds further complexity to their uses and adaptations. We are shown here Athenian sarcophagus workshops that marketed elements of Greek "cultural identity" in a way that was particularly suited to elite status display around the Mediterranean in the Roman imperial period. As Draycott and others in this volume also demonstrate, Ewald shows how trade in antiquity amounted to more than the circulation of objects, and instead implied and served as a conduit for a conscious exchange of ideas, values, and knowledge. Ewald's comparison between Athens and Rome yields fascinating similarities and differences. While there was certainly iconographic exchange and a shared frame of reference between the two, Attic sarcophagi emphasised in an exceptional way timeless, almost anachronistic, heroic myth and a focus on the male body beautiful. Ewald interprets this as offering a form of heroisation, that chimes with the widening contemporary practice in the Greek East of referring to tombs as *heroa* and the deceased as "hero". He shows how such practices resonated with the cultural tenets of the so-called second sophistic and can also be linked to earlier heroising traditions of the Greek East. Masculine heroic behaviour appears to have been employed to commemorate women or even young girls, in a manner that finds broad parallels with some of the gender flexibility encountered with Borg's *exempla*. Ewald shows that these mythological sarcophagi served as potent forms of symbolic capital, offering a form of "*arete* for sale" that served to "naturalise" the social status of elite clients.

While readers travel further afield within the ancient world in Part III, many of the themes raised in Lane Fox's introduction and the other two sections resonate and find examples and explanation in each of the contributions. Martin West's "Gilgāmeš and Homer" takes up Ian Rutherford's questions of how to reconstruct wandering myths through the comparison of Greek and Near-Eastern literature. While Rutherford offered a cautious "perhaps" with regard to the reception of many Hittite myths and even more so with regard to the mediators and channels of this reception, West boldly presents an argument that proposes concrete channels by which the greatest Mesopotamian mythological poem, the Standard Babylonian Gilgamesh, leaves such striking traces in each of the two Homeric poems.

Beyond speculating vaguely about "bilingual poets", no-one has tried to work out in detail what the process of transmission from Gilg. SBV to the *Iliad* and *Odyssey* would look like. The missing link, West proposes, is a "Gilgamising" elaborate *Herakleia* composed by a bilingual poet. West's thought experiment allows us to not have to rely on a plurality of Akkadian-Greek (or Phoenician-Greek, or Aramaic-Greek) bilingual poets of the early archaic period to posit an intervening stage whereby Mesopotamian literary works were received or translated into Greek and were then accessed by the historical Greek poets whose work is known to us. While speculative and vulnerable to objections – and West was well aware of this – his idea to envisage the reception of Gilg. SBV into Greek hexameter poetry as having taken place at a pre-historical stage in the context of Heracles-mythology is ingenious and has attractive features: the number of references to Heracles-mythology in the Homeric epics as well as Hesiod and Archilochus points to a plethora of existing Heracles poems, accounts of single adventures as well as an extended telling of a series of labours imposed on the hero by Eurystheus. As West's analysis shows, there are significant similarities (if at times only palpable with a minute knowledge of both narratives) between Heracles and Gilgamesh. Moreover, the *Iliad* can be held to signal a source in Heracles-mythology at two key points where it most strikingly resembles the Gilgamesh epic, namely in the context of Diomedes' wounding of Aphrodite (*Il.* 6.392ff), corresponding to Gilgamesh "wounding" Ishtar's pride (Gilg. SBV VI), and in the context of Patroclus' death bringing Achilles' mortality home to him (*Il.* 18.117ff), corresponding to the effect of Enkidu's death on Gilgamesh (Gilg. SBV X and XII). The latter parallel presupposes a telling of the death of Heracles' companion Iolaos in our hypothetical poem as well as an explanation for the lack of knowledge about this in later Heracles poems. West has to imagine an oral poem that went out of circulation and was forgotten. It is left to the reader, of course, whether to accept West's idea and his audacious reconstruction of a vanished oral Heracles epic – there is no doubt, however, that the paper is of immense value in provoking thought on a vitally important issue.

Rana Sérida's paper focuses on the opposite direction of transmission and looks at the influence of Greek epic material in the demotic Inaros Cycle from Greek and Roman Egypt. Well beyond asking about channels of transmission, though, she discusses the purpose and effect of the appropriation of myth as a means towards forging a collective identity, cultural pride and legitimacy, very similar to the thrust of Scheer's earlier contribution, albeit in a different cultural context and via different media and mediators. Owing to the fragmentary state of the manuscripts and a plethora of further philological challenges that present themselves to their editors, the heroic narratives about Inaros, a native Egyptian king during the seventh century BC when Nubians and Assyrians rivalled over the control of Egypt and faced uprisings by the local vassal princes in the northern Delta, have neither been published in their entirety nor examined systematically. Sérida gives us an excellent overview regarding themes and protagonists and interprets them as stories of resistance, composed and preserved by the Egyptian priesthood, who created a myth of an ideal Egyptian king by imitating the tools of Greek epic on various levels.

The criteria that invite comparison range from the significance of personal armour and the demeanour of duelling combatants, to the wider set of beliefs underlying heroic description. Given the themes of the narratives one wonders how surprising it is that, altogether, the "epic formula" of the Homeric poems fits the Inaros stories so well, and it is almost as intriguing to explore differences such as the absence of the tragic death of the hero in the Egyptian narrative tradition or different manners of conflict resolution. Ultimately, Sérida adopts the perspective of the challenged Egyptian priesthood under Roman rule, which means that she looks back at many centuries of a narrative tradition that was shaped by many factors, not least the "epic" conquest and figure of an Alexander the Great, and the similarities between the *Posthomerica* of Quintus Smyrnaeus and stories in the Inaros Cycle raise the crucial question of mutual influence. If, as the author proposes, the fact that the stories were transmitted exclusively in the demotic language and script points to an entirely Egyptian audience, the idea of a "literature of resistance" is indeed compelling. With regard to the conditions that made myths travel, the force of a multi-facetted yet focused cross-cultural epic formula is equally compelling.

Luke Pitcher keeps the focus on Egypt to explore the use and utility of mythology in Greco-Roman historiography. He notes that – in contrast to the popularity of the theme in other genres – our extant historians, including Herodotus, tend to be rather silent when it comes to Egyptian mythology and the early history of Egypt. Interestingly, the only exception to this is Diodorus, who opens his universal history precisely with a lengthy account of the early history of Egypt, justified by the explanation that "Egypt is the country where mythology places the origin of the gods" (Diod. 1.9.6). Putting aside the question of Diodorus' sources and their specific interests in the theme, Pitcher explores what the Egyptian material meant to Diodorus himself, and he does so by relating it to the immediately preceding general statements on the (moral) utility of history expressed in the preface to Diodorus' work. According to the historian, subtly but not entirely different from Polybius' views, history provides useful experience, and it either spurs on to immortal glory or warns against infamy. The career of Osiris as a culture hero and *protos heuretes* forms the backbone of the following narrative in Book One, and it is easy to see how the Egyptian god and king, and indeed his wife Isis, exemplify the kind of individuals that the writing and study of history creates. The myth of Osiris, or, as Pitcher emphasises, the multiple "Osirises" in Diodorus' narrative is complex and not straightforwardly mapped onto the preface. It is not his exemplary achievements that gain Osiris his immortal honours but in fact Isis' deceit and pact with the Egyptian priesthood, and the same lack of ultimate but not immediate results applies to comparable figures or even couples in Diodorus' history, such as Ninos and Semiramis in Book Two – here, again, it is not Ninos' desire to be the architect of an eternal city that achieves his memorialisation but the burial mound raised by his wife for him, and her own ambition for fame expressed in founding Babylon (that would later decline) ultimately only succeeded because it was commemorated in Diodorus' work. Pitcher's careful analysis, therefore, sees the myth of Osiris as well as other such myths employed because they offer vibrant illustration of the historian's generalised utilitarian concepts of his profession, as well as of the complexities of this utility in the concrete.

A much more obvious and prototypical wandering hero, much along the lines initially presented by Robin Lane Fox, is Rachel Wood's "Heracles", whose appearance and transformation she investigates in the region of modern Iran, from the period after the Macedonian conquest to the establishment of the Sasanian Empire. While at first sight these seem case studies of a transmission of the specific mythological narrative of the Greek hero, these are by no means examples of an easy and straightforward "reception" – even, so Wood argues, when an accompanying text emphatically identifies the figure as the Greek hero. Employing Heracles iconography when e.g. representing local divinities formed part of a complex process that involved close interaction with local audiences and traditions. To give but one example: while the presence of a nude figure wrestling a lion may suggest that part of the mythological narrative had been retained and referred to Heracles fighting the Nemean lion, this is not necessarily so because the iconography of "lion wrestling" had a longstanding local resonance of its own for royal and divine subjects. In many cases Heracles came to be "plucked out of his mythological canon" and locally reconfigured in a wide range of ways. The striking selectivity in the process of adopting Heracles' image into Iranian art suggests that the persistence of myths was achieved by something more than the movement of people and local predispositions for a subject – an observation that may introduce another moment of pause into Robin Lane Fox's tour de force of wandering myths.

With a broadly comparable geographical and temporal scope to Wood's contribution, but showcasing a different hero, Katherine Dunbabin's paper explores a remarkable flourishing of imagery drawn from the Achilles saga in the art of the later Roman Empire, focusing particularly on mosaics produced for domestic contexts in the eastern half of the Empire. Like Ewald, Dunbabin employs regional comparison to reveal striking local variation both in the uptake of certain narratives and in the iconographies employed to embody them. The Eastern mosaics reveal attitudes to Achilles which are sometimes surprising. They rarely represent Achilles in scenes relating to his warrior role in the *Iliad* and usually depict the hero's relations with women, or relate to themes such as his childhood or education. Dunbabin demonstrates clearly that it is inadequate to interpret the continuing popularity of Achilles subjects as due to the ongoing importance of Homeric epics in the educational canon. On the contrary, they indicate an audience familiar with all sorts of versions of the Achilles saga, drawing on more contemporary literature, other images and more ephemeral media, such as pantomime performances on the stage. She shows that as long as a central core element was preserved to make the allusion intelligible, images of this multi-faceted hero were selectively adapted to meet different local needs in the patron's domestic display. Artists are again shown here as creatively seeking new ways to present the familiar, as emphasising and juxtaposing particular characteristics in the hero, making interpretive selections, or offering alternative versions of the narratives, as well as visually interplaying with other media, for example, villa sculptural decoration. The paper traces the appeal of Achilles in some surprising contexts, including Christian Edessa where, far from being a display of adhesion to foreign culture, his presence is shown to be internalised and acclimatised into local culture over a considerable span of time. Dunbabin demonstrates how Achilles images became an articulate part of a common cultural heritage, used to express a wide range of concerns to both pagan and Christian viewers. The complexity of the wanderings of the hero are traced here not simply to reveal geographical engagements with particular myths, but to draw wider conclusions about precisely how and why they were actively reshaped to suit differing cultural needs and agendas.

The above overview of the volume should leave no doubt that the contributions in all three sections of the book critically address and respond to Robin Lane Fox's challenges in an equally challenging way. This is not, then, a book seeking to make bold statements about definitive origins, versions or clearly discernible developments of myths. Rather, our aim is to explore *how* stories "wandered" and were subject to ongoing redefinition. Broader comparison is used in order to gain greater analytical traction into the sorts of cultural processes at play. Robert Parker's *Epilogue* makes this even clearer when reflecting on and contrasting the "wanderings of myths" according to the criterion of "importing" and "exporting" myths, and in their varying degrees of requiring guesswork with regard to contexts and recipients. Here, it is the image of "myths that have arrived and undergone naturalisation" that leads Parker to thinking about "travel between cultures". It lies in the nature of the subject that at the very end of our study Parker suggests core motivations that do not contradict but complement those proposed by Lane Fox at the beginning. Underlying both, and all other contributions, is the recognition of what Parker calls the "profound human need and craving for narrative", and this is what makes the cross-cultural wandering of myths a given at all times.

As always, using style conventions that are both reader-friendly and consistent has been a challenge. We have latinised Greek names and places where these forms are at all familiar but have kept to a transliteration of the Greek where Latin forms are rarely or not at all used. For the ease of readers who are not familiar with them, we have not abbreviated the titles of academic journals or series in the bibliographies. The two notable exceptions to this are the "Realencyclopaedie der klassischen Altertumswissenschaft" (RE) and the "Lexicon Iconographicum Mythologiae Classicae" (LIMC).

For the reader's ease of reference, we have commissioned the production of a small number of maps. These are far from all-encompassing in nature. Depicting the wanderings of myths with the help of conventional maps is fraught with difficulty – there are anachronisms, and the potential for false emphases on spatial dimensions or even directions of movements, assumptions of local or regional identities and the implication of causal factors. Nonetheless, in spite of these problems, the present volume has included them to support and (to a limited extent) to collate its individual contributions. We believe that they also serve as a tool that points to the wide range of examples that inform the study; suggest something of the way in which myths bridge time and space (without any blunt assumptions of self-explanatory continuities); and also indicate how physical space and landscape are dynamic and can be redefined in multiple ways, very much like the myths that inhabit and create these entities.

We would like to take this opportunity to extend our sincere thanks to a number of people and organisations. The workshops and symposion would not have been possible without the assistance of Nicholas Ollivère and the financial support of the following: The Classical Association, The Classics Conclave and Roger Michel, The Craven Fund, The Hellenic Society, The John Fell OUP Research Fund, Oxford University's Faculty of Classics, The Oxford Research Centre in the Humanities, Somerville College. We would like to express our deep gratitude to them, to all who attended and participated in the conference, to the authors of this book, and to the critical and encouraging peer readers of those contributions which did not fall within the expertise of the editors: Bruno Currie, John Tait, Sibylle Haynes, Michael Shenkar, Vesta S. Curtis; to Bert Smith for his contribution to the conference and ongoing support before and after. We also wish to thank Nick West for his work on a gallery trail at the Ashmolean Museum that was associated with this project and to thank the Ashmolean for their help in providing the image on the front cover of this book. We are deeply indebted to Betty Smith for her invaluable assistance at the conference, to Malcolm Nicholson and Juliane Zachhuber for their support in preparing the volume, and to Michelle de Gruchy for producing the maps. We very much hope that the readers of *Wandering Myths* will spend a satisfying and enjoyable time with the resulting volume.

As readers have seen from the summary of his argument above, the present volume presents a paper by Martin West, who participated in and contributed to our Somerville conference in April 2014. Martin died a week after he submitted his manuscript to us and it is with gratitude that we include one of his last works in our publication. Martin did not get a chance to revise his contribution, which stands as he handed it to us, with its characteristic ingenious and powerful argument. This book is dedicated to his memory.

Bibliography

Alexandridis A. Neutral Bodies? Female Portrait Statue Types from the Late Republic to the Second Century CE, in: *Material Culture and Social Identitites in the Ancient World*, edited by S. Hales and T. Hodos (New York, 2010), 252–279.

Assmann J. *Cultural Memory and Early Civilization: Writing, Remembrance, and Political Imagination* (Cambridge, 2011).

Barrett J. C. Romanization: a Critical Comment, in: *Dialogues in Roman Imperialism: Power, Discourse, and Discrepant Experience in the Roman Empire*, edited by D. J. Mattingly (Portsmouth, Rhode Island, 1997), 51–66.

Bauman Z. From Pilgrim to Tourist or a Short History of Identity, in: *Questions of Cultural Identity*, edited by S. Hall and P. du Gay (London, 1996), 18–36.

Beard M. Looking Harder for Roman Myth: Dumézil, declamation and the problems of definition, in: *Mythos in mythenloser Gesellschaft. Das Paradigma Roms. Colloquium Rauricum 3*, edited by F. Graf (Stuttgart; Leipzig, 1993), 44–64.

Beard M. et al. *Religions of Rome* (Cambridge, 1998).

Bekker-Nielsen T. (ed.) *Space, Place and Identity in Northern Anatolia* (Stuttgart, 2014).

Bergmann B. The Roman House as Memory Theater: the House of the Tragic Poet in Pompeii. *Art Bulletin* 76 (1994), 225–256.

Bergmann B. Rhythms of Recognition: mythological encounters in Roman Landscape Painting, in: *Im Spiegel des Mythos. Bilderwelt und Lebenswelt*, edited by F. De Angelis and S. Muth (Wiesbaden, 1999), 81–107.

Bommas M. (ed.) *Cultural Memory and Identity in Ancient Societies* (New York, 2013).

Bommas M. *Memory and Urban Religion in the Ancient World* (New York, 2014).

Brooks P. *Enigmas of Identity* (Princeton; Oxford, 2011).

Burkert W. *Structure and History in Greek Mythology and History* (Berkeley; London, 1979).

Clarke K. *Making Time for the Past. Local History and the Polis* (Oxford, 2008).

Csapo E. *Theories of Mythology* (Oxford, 2005).

Cumont F. *Recherches sur le symbolisme funéraire des Romains* (Paris, 1942).

De Angelis F. and S. Muth (eds.) *Im Spiegel des Mythos. Bilderwelt und Lebenswelt. Lo specchio del mito: immaginario e realtà. Symposium, Rom, 19.–20. Februar 1998* (Wiesbaden, 1999).

Diaz-Andreu M. and S. Lucy. Introduction, in: *The Archaeology of Identity*, edited by M. Diaz-Andreu, S. Lucy and S. Babić (London, 2005), 1–13.

Dignas B. Rituals and the Construction of Identity in Attalid Pergamon, in: *Historical and Religious Memory in the Ancient World*, edited by B. Dignas and R. R. R. Smith (Oxford, 2012), 119–144.

Dowden K. *The Uses of Greek Mythology* (London; New York, 1992).

Dowden K. and N. Livingstone (eds.) *A Companion to Greek Mythology* (Oxford, 2011)

Fittschen K. Der Tod der Kreusa und der Niobiden. Überlegungen zur Deutung griechischer Mythen auf römischen Sarkophagen. *Studi Italiani di Filologia Classica* 10 (1992), 1046–1059.

Galinsky K. (ed.) *Memory in Ancient Rome and Early Christianity* (Oxford, 2016).

Geraghty R. M. The Impact of Globalization in the Roman Empire, 200 BC–AD 100. *The Journal of Economic History* 67:4 (2007), 1036–1061.

Giuliani L. *Image and Myth: A History of Pictorial Narration in Greek Art* (Chicago, 2013).

Graf F. *Greek Mythology: An Introduction* (Baltimore; London, 1993).

Graf F. Myth. *Religions of the Ancient World*, edited by S. Iles Johnston (Cambridge, MA, 2004), 45–58.

Grant M. *Roman Myths* (Harmondsworth, 1973).

Hales S. The Houses of Antioch: A study of the domestic sphere in the imperial Near East, in: *Roman Imperialism and Provincial Art*, edited by S. Scott and J. Webster (Cambridge, 2003a), 171–191.

Hales S. *The Roman House and Roman Social Identity* (Cambridge, 2003b).

Hall E. *Adventures with Iphigenia in Tauris. A Cultural History of Euripides' Black Sea Tragedy* (New York; Oxford, 2013).

Hall S. Introduction: Who Needs "Identity"?, in: *Questions of Cultural Identity*, edited by S. Hall and P. du Gay. (London, 1996), 1–17.

Hawes G. (ed.) *Myths on the Map: The Storied Landscapes of Ancient Greece* (Oxford, 2017).

Hingley R. *Globalizing Roman Culture: Unity, Diversity and Empire* (London; New York, 2005).

Hitchner B. Globalization Avant la Lettre: Globalization and the History of the Roman Empire. *New Global Studies* 2 (2008), 1–12.

Hölscher T. *The Language of Images in Roman Art* (Cambridge, 2004).

Hölscher A. The Concept of Roles and the Malaise of "Identity": Ancient Rome and the Modern World, in: *Role Models in the Roman World: Identity and Assimilation*. S. Bell and I. L. Hansen. (Ann Arbor, 2008), 41–56.

Hölscher T. Myths, Images, and the Typology of Identities in Early Greek Art, in: *Cultural Identity in the Ancient Mediterranean*, edited by E. S. Gruen (Los Angeles, 2011), 47–65.

Junker K. *Interpreting the Images of Greek Myths: an Introduction* (Cambridge, 2005 [translation 2012]).

Kearns E. and S. Price (eds.) *The Oxford Dictionary of Classical Myth and Religion* (Oxford, 2003).

Koortbojian M. *Myth, Meaning, and Memory on Roman Sarcophagi* (Berkeley; London, 1995).

Kuper A. *Culture: The Anthropologists' Account* (Cambridge, MA; London, 1999).

Lane Fox R. *Travelling Heroes* (London, 2008).

Latte K. Über eine Eigentümlichkeit der italischen Gottesvorstellung. *Archiv für Religionswissenschaft* 24 (1926), 244–258.

Lorenz K. *Ancient Mythological Images and their Interpretation: An Introduction to Iconology, Semiotics and Image Studies in Classical Art History* (Cambridge, 2016).

MacSweeney N. (ed.) *Foundation Myths in Ancient Societies. Dialogues and Discourses* (Philadelphia, 2014).

Mattingly D. J. Vulgar and Weak 'Romanization', or Time for a Paradigm Shift? *Journal of Roman Archaeology* 15 (2002), 536–540.

Mattingly D. J. Being Roman. Expressing Identity in a Provincial Setting. *Journal of Roman Archaeology* 17 (2004), 5–25.

Mattingly D. J. *An Imperial Possession: Britain in the Roman Empire, 54 BC–AD 409* (London, 2006)

Mayer E. *The Ancient Middle Classes: Urban Life and Aesthetics in the Roman Empire, 100 BCE–250 CE* (Cambridge, Mass.; London, 2012).

Morley N. *Trade in Classical Antiquity* (Cambridge, 2007).

Mullen A. *Southern Gaul and the Mediterranean: Multilingualism and Multiple Identities in the Iron Age and Roman Periods* (Cambridge, 2013).

Muth S. *Erleben von Raum – Leben im Raum: Zur Funktion mythologischer Mosaikbilder in der römisch-kaiserzeitlichen Wohnarchitektur* (Heidelberg, 1998).

Muth S. Hylas oder "Der ergriffene Mann": zur Eigenständigkeit der Mythenrezeption in der Bildkunst, in: *Im Spiegel des Mythos. Bilderwelt und Lebenswelt*, edited by S. Muth and F. De Angelis (Wiesbaden, 1999), 109–129.

Newby Z. Myth and Death: Roman mythological sarcophagi, in: *A Companion to Greek Mythology*, edited by K. Dowden and N. Livingstone (Chichester, 2011), 301–318.

Newby Z. Poems in Stone: Reading mythological sarcophagi through Statius' Consolations, in: *Art and Rhetoric in Roman Culture*, edited by J. Elsner and M. Meyer (Cambridge, 2014), 256–287.

Newby Z. *Greek Myths in Roman Art and Culture: Imagery, Values and Identity in Italy* (Cambridge, 2016).

Niethammer L. *Kollektive Identität: Heimliche Quellen einer unheimlichen Konjunktur* (Reinbeck bei Hamburg, 2000).

Nock A. D. Sarcophagi and Symbolism. *American Journal of Archaeology* 50 (1946), 140–170.

Patterson L. E. *Kinship Myth in Ancient Greece* (Austin, 2010).

Prag J. and J. Quinn (eds.) *The Hellenistic West: Rethinking the Ancient Mediterranean* (Cambridge, 2013).

Revell L. *Roman Imperialism and Local Identities* (Cambridge, 2009).

Segal R. A. *Myth. A Very Short Introduction*, 2nd edition (Oxford, 2015).

Smith R. R. R. Defacing the Gods at Aphrodisias, in: *Historical and Religious Memory in the Ancient World*, edited by B. Dignas and R. R. Smith (Oxford, 2012), 283–326.

Squire M. *The Iliad in a Nutshell: Visualizing Epic on the Tabulae Iliacae* (Oxford, 2011).

Thomas R. The Greek *polis* and the Tradition of *polis* History: local history, chronicles, and the patterning of the past, in: *Patterns of the Past. Epitedeumata in the Greek Tradition*, edited by A. Moreno and R. Thomas (Oxford, 2014), 145–172.

Trimble J. Greek Myth, Gender, and Social Structure in a Roman House: two paintings of Achilles at Pompeii, in: *The Ancient Art of Emulation: Studies in Artistic Originality and Tradition from the Present to Classical Antiquity*, edited by E. K. Gazda (Ann Arbor, 2002), 225–248.

Wallace-Hadrill A. *Rome's Cultural Revolution* (Cambridge, 2008).

Wallace-Hadrill A. Trying to Define and Identify the Roman 'Middle Classes'. *Journal of Roman Archaeology* 26 (2013), 605–609.

Webster J. Art as Negotiation, in: *Roman Imperialism and Provincial Art*, edited by J. Webster and S. Scott (Cambridge, 2003), 24–53.

Whitmarsh T. and S. Thomson *The Romance between Greece and the East* (Cambridge, 2013).

Wiseman T. P. *The Myths of Rome* (Exeter, 2004).

Wissowa G. *Religion und Kultus der Römer* (Munich, 1912).

Witcher R. E. Globalisation and Roman Imperialism: perspectives on identities in Roman Italy, in: *The Emergence of State Identities in Italy in the First Millennium BC*, edited by E. Herring and K. Lomas (London, 2000), 213–225.

Woodard R. *Myth, Ritual and the Warrior in Roman and Indo-European Antiquity* (Cambridge, 2013).

Zanker P. (ed.) *Hellenismus in Mittelitalien. Kolloquium in Göttingen vom 5. bis 9. Juni 1974* (Göttingen, 1976).

Zanker P. and B. J. Ewald *Mit Mythen leben: Die Bilderwelt der römischen Sarkophage* (Munich, 2004).

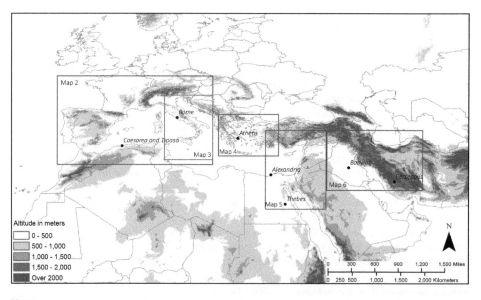

Map 1

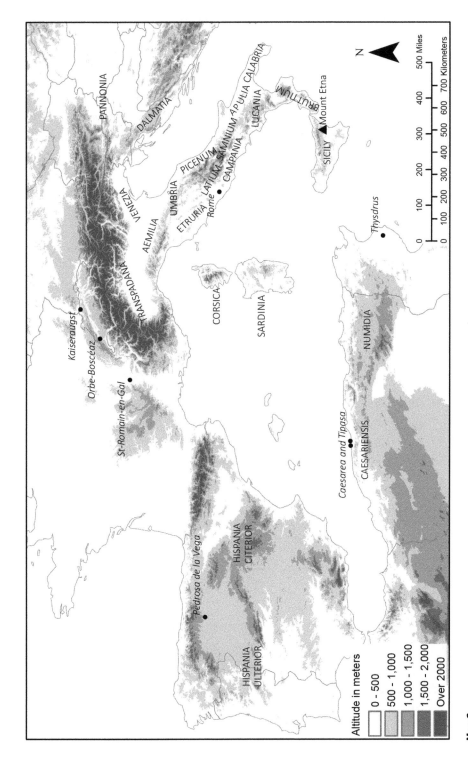

Map 2

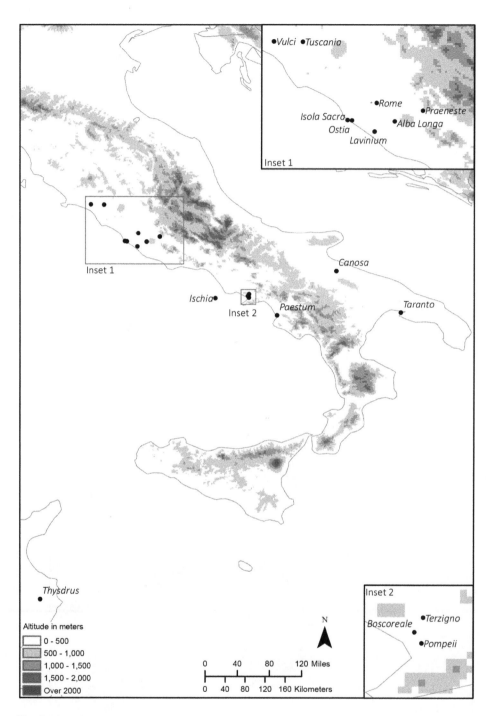

Map 3

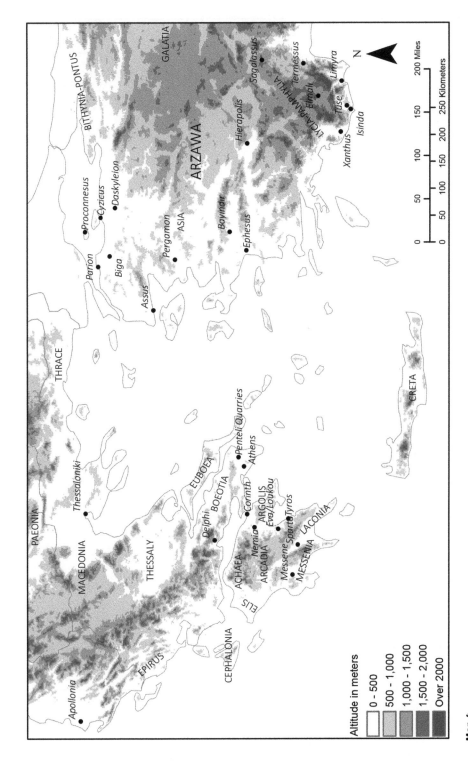

Map 4

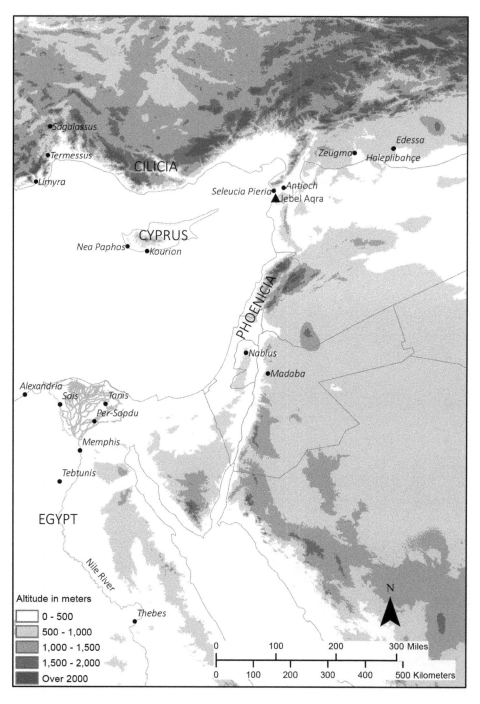

Map 5

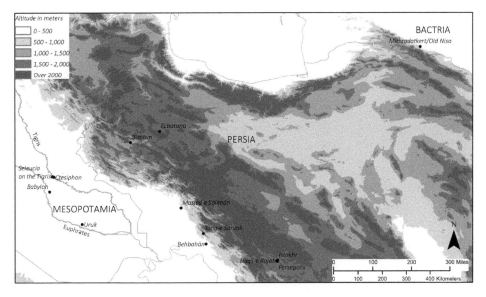

Map 6

Robin Lane Fox

Introduction

Travelling Myths, Travelling Heroes

Aristotle once remarked that as he was on his own and a loner, he had become more fond of myths (*philomuthos*).[1] Those who meet, confer and discuss also become more fond of myths, as this volume and its underlying Conference testify.

What do we mean by a "myth", that much-discussed concept? Nobody nowadays would agree with Freud that myths are the redirected dreams of primitive peoples. For classicists, the most-cited recent definition is Walter Burkert's: myths are "traditional tales applied, with secondary, partial reference to something of collective importance."[2] His definition has not escaped criticism and is not comprehensive. It does not fit the stories, surely myths, about many items in the ancients' natural world, those tales of metamorphosis, for instance, which were attached to trees and flowers and which were not of collective, as opposed to aesthetic or topographic, relevance.[3] I hesitate to define myths, as they are protean entities, but I would categorise them as stories with no known authors but with a currency in a social group and told about fictional persons who, unlike many protagonists in folk-tales, are named. We may talk loosely of the "myth" that Cleopatra once dissolved a pearl in vinegar and drank it in Mark Antony's presence or the "myth" that Caesar Augustus ordered all the world to be taxed during Quirinius' governorship of Syria, but this use of myth is secondary and derivative.[4] It means only a widely-held belief which is in fact untrue.

If myths are necessarily current in a social group, how do they travel? In 1979, the question was sharply posed by Tom Stinton, in disagreement with his former Oxford pupil John Henderson. In a vigorous article on Phaedrus and his fables, Henderson appeared to be implying that a study of the structures of story-types helps to explain their travels.[5] Stinton acutely replied that the structural variables which we may list in a story cannot explain its diffusion. If a myth is to travel, it must either surface in separate places because it is a part of deep cognitive structures of the human mind or is somehow revealed by a supernatural power, or else it simply travels with a person and by personal contact, what Henderson had called "the historico-geographic method".[6]

---

1 Arist. F668 (Rose).
2 Burkert 1979, 23.
3 Bremmer 1987, 1–9, esp. 7, proposing a refined definition of myth as "traditional tales relevant to society", but Forbes Irving 1990 studies many counter-examples among myths of metamorphosis.
4 Macrob. *Sat.* 3.17.14–17; *Gospel of Luke* 2.1–5.
5 Stinton 1979, 432–5, answering Henderson 1977, 17–31.
6 Stinton 1979, 435; Henderson 1977, esp. 24.

https://doi.org/10.1515/9783110421453-002

Since Stinton wrote, cognitive science has in no way established that deep structures, generative of identical stories, are somehow embedded in the human mind. The theory that such structures exist remains, as Stinton tartly observed, "mysticism". He argued that the historico-geographic approach is therefore the best we have. I would argue, more firmly, that it is the right one. Within it, it is quite untrue that myths can take root only in societies with a social structure similar to the one in which they originate. Myths from the Greek *poleis* were taken up and adapted in the very different social structures of early Rome and Etruria.

The problem, implicit in my working definition of myth, is that we cannot trace the origin of a particular myth to a particular person, place and time. I know of only one possible exception, but on closer inspection it turns out to be apparent, not real. It concerns what has become one of the most potent myths of all. In late 1540, as good Spanish sources testify, the tale of a gilded man, living in a kingdom so rich that gold was used as body-décor, was first heard in Quito.[7] For once, we know a "myth's" origin: it was first told by Spanish conquistadors who had newly returned to the town from Bogota. One of them was bringing a captured Indian boy, later baptised as Roderigo. Perhaps, across the language barrier, they had misunderstood Roderigo's words.[8] Nearly thirty attempts to locate El Dorado were then made on the strength of the story, costing thousands of human lives. However, the first tellers, I presume, and the first explorers, certainly, believed that El Dorado existed. To them he was not a myth at all. He became a myth, but only when nobody found him and the legend was too potent to disappear.

As the El Dorado story reminds us, at the root of every myth somebody, somewhere first told it, whether it was a story about Perseus or Jason. What Stinton called the "historico-geographic approach" also involves people: it requires that myths travel only because of people on the move and the contacts which they make. We cannot identify the first teller of any ancient myth, but we can sometimes identify the agents involved in a myth's travels. They include individual artists, travelling craftsmen, mosaicists armed with pattern books, unstoppable poets performing and competing on the network of Greek festivals, diplomats, antiquarians, and that overlooked category, old bores with time and money to travel. Travelling myths are not often dependent on travelling rituals in order to move around. Studies of "myth and ritual" are seldom relevant to them.

The presiding genius of the historico-geographic approach was not in Stinton's mind, but he stands at the head of what I wish to say. He is, of course, Louis Robert. His *Hellenica* are only one part of his work, but they neatly frame our subject, beginning in *Hellenica* volume 1 with the "Homeric school" of Nysa in Caria and their location of Homer's boggy "Asian meadow" in the grassy uplands of the mountain above

---

7 Ramos Perez 1973 is still the fundamental study.
8 Hemming 1978, 97–109.

their home city and ending in *Hellenica* 13 with Argive Perseus' location in Cilicia, especially Aegae, and the castrated Attis' location at Dokimeion in Phrygia where the violet-purple streaks in the marble-quarries were presented by local observers as the blood shed by Attis, causing Attis to be shown on Dokimeion's coins.[9]

Within the category of myth, the criteria for a travelling myth are straightforward. There has to be a myth and it has to travel from one place or culture to another. The interesting questions are the channels of transmission and the impulses behind them, questions which historians can sometimes answer. Within the framework of the historico-geographic approach, I will give examples of three types of contact: conquest, sex, and the travels of those social misfits, missionaries. I will then re-visit and expand a model of travel and transfer which I set out in my book *Travelling Heroes* in 2008. I will conclude with a cluster of myths which travelled reassuringly with "people like us".

The most interesting transmissions are those between two cultures and two languages. They are characterised by what I call "creative misunderstanding", whether of uncaptioned objects, misinterpreted out of context, or of words and languages, "lost in translation". Momigliano once declared rather sweepingly that linguistic ineptitude was the "fault of the Greeks", who, in his view, were the Mediterranean's only monoglots.[10] Even where that fault was in evidence it was not always unfruitful. There is room for a history of fertile mistakes.

More than anything else, conquest brings previously separate linguistic groups into contact, never more so than during the far-flung conquests of Alexander, already called "Great" in his lifetime.[11] He is the locator of travelling myths whom we can best follow in action. It was he himself, his historians claimed, who located Dionysus in modern Tadjikistan, thanks to the sight there of ivy.[12] In memorable style, he approved a similar location of a myth to Acuphis' kingdom beyond modern Peshawar, where the mythical Nysa, nursery of the god Dionysus, at last seemed to have been discovered.[13] In the *Bacchae*, in lines first performed in Macedon, Euripides had merely traced Dionysus' subsequent travels west from Bactria.[14] Alexander and his men had gone further east and found Dionysus' starting-point. Recently, Brian Bosworth explained the relocation of such myths as a cynical ploy, to encourage the failing morale of the Macedonian army.[15] However, Alexander's manner of reasoning, from analogies of the slenderest kind, was nothing of the sort. It was shared by those around

---

9 Robert 1940, 144–8; id. 1965, 108 and 122–3.

10 Momigliano 1975, 9–19: for the most recent counter-evidence, Mayor, Colarusso and Saunders 2014, 447–94.

11 Ephippus *FGrHist*. 126 F2.

12 Curt. 7.9.15; Bosworth 1995, 207.

13 Arr. *Anab* 5.1.1–2; Bosworth 1995, 197–213; Lane Fox 2008, 190–1, on the local vines as well as ivy.

14 Eur. *Bacch*. 15.

15 Bosworth 1996, 140–66; Bosworth 1995, 207 and 213–8 on doubters, already in antiquity.

him, and as we can see elsewhere was an innocent part of their and Alexander's own way of thinking. In the last year of his life, it was Alexander himself, we are assured by the eyewitness Aristobulus, who commanded that a newly-reported island in the Persian Gulf be called "Ikaros".[16] We know, though Aristobulus appears not to, that the local name of this island, attested in cuneiform texts, was Akarum.[17] An argument from analogy also underlay Alexander's order. His sea captains reported that there was a shrine of a wild hunter-goddess on the island who was honoured by offerings of goats. Alexander and his Macedonians no doubt assumed that she was Artemis Tauropolos, the hunter-goddess whom they knew back home at Amphipolis.[18] They surely also knew, or were told by accompanying historians, that this Artemis had a cult on the island of Ikaria in the Aegean, whose name had caused the island to be related to travelling Ikaros's fall.[19] Alexander thus named the new find "Ikaros" for two types of reason, a misunderstanding of its non-Greek name and an analogy between its cult and a cult known in the Greek world at a place connected with the same mythical traveller. Nowadays we may smile at this sort of reasoning, but it is one which we maintain. We know the island as Failaka, but this name for it is a corruption of the Greek word Phylake, or guard post, referring to the island's Hellenistic function.

In a neglected passage in Pliny, deriving, I believe, from his court-historian Callisthenes, we can observe Alexander doing the same in Egypt. According to Pliny, Alexander was shown at Memphis a tree called a persea.[20] He therefore ordered that wreaths of it should be given as prizes to athletic victors because it was the tree of Perseus. It was indeed at Memphis in 331 that Alexander staged the first Greek games to be held in Egypt.[21] As Callisthenes's history publicised, Alexander had just been rivalling the travelling hero Perseus by making a journey to the Siwah oracle.[22] On his return the tree and its name seemed to fit wondrously with the Perseus-mood of the moment. Modern botanists classify the "persea" as a Mimusops, but to Alexander it sounded like Perseus' very own plant, confirming the hero's travels through Egypt.

Alexander was not alone in this sort of reasoning. In 330 BC, two Thessalian officers in his army, the noble Medius of Larissa and Cyrsilus of Pharsalus, went west from Ecbatana into Armenia and convinced themselves from the inhabitants' style of dress, and much else, that they were Thessalians, no less, by origin.[23] The Thessalian Jason, the mythical hero, even seemed to have been there before them because they discovered that there were Iasonia, or Jason shrines, in Armenia. As Marquart long ago

---

16 Arr. *Anab.* 7.20.3–5.
17 Bernard 1995, 352–408, esp. 395 n. 93.
18 Diod. Sic. 18.4.5; Liv. 44.44.4; Bernard 1995, 396–7.
19 Green 2004, 40–6.
20 Plin. *HN* 15.45–6, also noticed by Amigues 2002, 141–7, esp. 145–7.
21 Arr. *Anab.* 3.5.2.
22 Callisth. *FGrHist.* 124 F14A.
23 Str. 11.14.13–14.

explained, these "Iasonia" were probably Greek misunderstandings of a west Iranian word Iayezana, meaning "places of worship".[24] To explain these traces which seemed to link their compatriots to the Armenians the two Thessalians postulated a new Thessalian hero, Armenos, as the Armenians' founding father. They assumed that he had travelled into this land as a Thessalian companion of travelling Jason.

Further east, India became an even more prolific source of mythical misunderstanding. Alexander's belief that he was on the tracks of Dionysus and Heracles is well known. In south India he encountered the Sibai whose cattle were branded with the symbol of a club, surely a clear trace of their relationship with club-bearing Heracles.[25] Again he was not alone in this type of thinking. Within ten years of his death, Megasthenes claimed that in India, in towns which can be located near Delhi, girls become fertile from a very young age, ever since Heracles, travelling there, had engaged in the ultimate act of incestuous child-abuse and impregnated his daughter Pandaia when she was only seven.[26] Megasthenes's visit to India occurred as early, it now seems, as c. 315 BC.[27] His story had no previous roots in anything claimed about Heracles in previous Greek myth-making and so it arose from a Greek's contact, surely his own, with Indian stories. In 1829 Colonel James Tod pointed to an Indian tale about a royal guardian near Delhi, no less, who had sex with his young ward, Pandaia, his half-sister.[28] In the Rig Veda, the Creator god Prajapati actually has sex with his own young daughter.[29] There is no question here of a Greek influence back onto Indian tradition. Quite separately from existing Greek myths about Heracles, the name Pandaia and the theme of under-age incest in Megasthenes' aetiological myth were Indian themes. Megasthenes therefore talked to Indians, surely Brahmins, who knew a story about a divinity, perhaps Indra, in which these various themes had become entwined. They were oral stories, because writing was not practised in India, even in 315 BC. In 1993, Sherwin White and Kuhrt suggested that Megasthenes was writing with a political agenda to glorify India and thereby "legitimate its non-conquest" by his master, Seleucus.[30] On the contrary, Megasthenes misunderstood tales which Sanskrit-speakers told to him and his interpreters. He wrote them up not for imperialist reasons but because he was amazed, as any Greek would be, by the India he saw and thought he heard.

Despite the modern post-colonial chorus, Alexander and his associates were not imposing these myths for reasons of power or colonial exploitation. Touchingly, they rested on their assumption that non-Greek places and peoples were much more

---

24 Marquart 1930, 131–216.
25 Arr. *Ind.* 5.12, *Anab.* 5.3.4.
26 Arr. *Ind.* 9.1–8.
27 Marquart 1930, 530–51.
28 Tod 1894; Stoneman 2017.
29 Dahlquist 1962, 110–2, citing Rig Veda 61.5–10.
30 Sherwin-White and Kuhrt 1993, 93–7.

like Greeks than they really were. Armenians and Acuphis' kingdom were not being "othered" as aliens. They were being "samed" as "people like us". Geoffrey Lloyd once picked out the role of polarity and analogy in early Greek thought, but his book stopped with Aristotle.[31] Analogy continued to flourish importantly in Hellenistic thinking.

So, in thought and action, did sex. In the ancient world, sexual partners were much more likely to transmit myths than diseases. Under the stars or in each others' arms there was much time to tell each other stories, in an era when no TV's or i-pads were to hand as a distraction. It was through females that the myth of Adonis began to travel in the Greek world. Adonis' name was based on Greek observers' misunderstanding of the cry "My Lord", or "Adonai", uttered by Tammuz's female worshippers from the Levant. The myth of Adonis, himself a creative misunderstanding, then travelled, first, I have argued, into Cyprus, specifically to Golgi and Arsos, and then across the Aegean.[32] It must have travelled with females, because they were the new demigod's only worshippers. Those females travelled either because of sex, as brides, or simply for it, as slaves and *hetairai*.

Females were crucial in generating, but males were more active in diffusing the ultimate travelling myth, Amazons. Much about their travels has recently become clear and exciting thanks to Adrienne Mayor's brilliant study of the subject.[33] She has brought to classicists' attention a Caucasian epic, Nart Saga 26, translated from Circassian and made available by J. Colarusso in 2002, in which the leader of warrior women is called Amezan.[34] These epics were collected and written down only in the 1850s but there is no sign anywhere else in them that "Western" influence, let alone classical Greek mythology, had shaped their oral content. "Amezan" may be a further clue to the "Amazon" name. If Greeks heard it before the later eighth century BC, it could have been lost in translation and in Greek, become "A-mazon". In the Nart Saga 26, Queen Amezan looks down from her saddle and realises in despair that the warrior she has killed is her beloved man. A cry filled her throat, "My sun has set for ever...".[35] In Greek myths Amazons did not kill their own beloved. They themselves were killed by men, none more memorably than Penthesilea by Achilles. His loving gaze fixed on her as she died.

Meanwhile, as Mayor excellently demonstrates, up on the broad steppe lands from Bulgaria right across to the borders of China and Mongolia, real warrior women were active and galloping to a degree which classicists have not yet recognised. What were first published in this zone as "warrior chieftain burials" by male archaeologists have recently been submitted to DNA testing of their bones. Under kurgans near Greek

---

31 Lloyd 1966.
32 Lane Fox 2008, 249–50.
33 Mayor 2014.
34 Colarusso 2002, 129–31; Mayor 2014, 17 and 87–8, giving other derivations.
35 Mayor 2014, 17.

Tyras, beneath mounds in the Thracian kingdom, at the mouth of the river Borysthenes, from the Caspian Sea to Kazakhstan and beyond, up to 37 % of the so-called "chieftains" in famous individual graves or grave-clusters have turned out to be females.[36] All over the steppe land, while the Greek *polis* was emerging in male political control, female warrior-leaders were galloping freely on horses with their bows and quivers.

Already for Homer in the mid to late eighth century there were *Amazones antianeirai*, Amazons "like men", not "opposed to men".[37] Greeks had already been visiting the southern shores of the Black Sea in Homer's lifetime and from the seventh century BC onwards some of them settled in the Crimean peninsula.[38] On arrival they surely heard through imported slaves and local sexual partners of the existence of these female viragoes just to the north of their male selves. Already a Greek had misunderstood the name "Amezan" as Amazon. Now Greek settlers learned that what seemed to be real-life Amazons were active just beyond their own horizons.

In the wake of this knowledge, locations of outlying Amazons occurred in the real world. Amazons were validated near the Black Sea by Xenophon and the Ten Thousand who saw their characteristic axes (or *sagareis*), and then by Pompey's troops and embedded historians near the Amazonian mountains, leading up to the mouth of the Thermodon river in that southern Black Sea delta whose many watery arms were described exactly by Apollonius Rhodius and re-emphasised in 1980 by Louis Robert.[39] Believing resulted in seeing.

Once again, Alexander and his travelling army were susceptible. In late summer 330, just by the west end of the Caspian Sea, all except Alexander's most sober officer-historians insisted that an Amazon queen arrived in his camp with "300" female companions and had 12 days of sex with him in his tent because she wished to become pregnant. She was called Thalestris.[40] At the very least the location suited the claim, because Alexander was encamped not far south of the lands in which we now know that female warriors on horseback were prominent. Maybe one of them did indeed come as an envoy to him and was categorised by gossip in camp as a visiting Amazon. That very thing was alleged (though not by competent eyewitnesses) to have happened six years later. In 324 BC the satrap of western Media, Atropates (whose name still lives on in our "Azerbaijan"), sent female cavalry to join Alexander's army. His Macedonians were said to have thought that these paradoxical riders were travelling Amazons. The story even claimed that their right breasts were indeed smaller than their left ones and were exposed in battle. Alexander was said to have sent them away,

---

36 Mayor 2014, 63–84, esp. 63–4.
37 Hom. *Il.* 3.189, 6.186; Blok 1995, 156–67.
38 Boardman 1980, 238–64.
39 Apoll. Rhod. 2.970–85, with Robert 1980, 192–201; Mayor 2014, 346–7, for Pompey's troops and Amazons.
40 Diod. Sic. 17.75–7; Curt. 6.5.24–32; Plut. *Alex.* 46; Baynham 2001; Mayor 2014, 319–38.

fearing mass rape, and returned them to their queen near, once again, the Caspian Sea with a message that otherwise he would come and make her pregnant.[41] Perhaps behind this story, too, lay some female nomad cavalrywomen, sent by their satrap as recruits for Alexander's army.

To later historians, women on horseback were such a transgression of Greek norms that they could only be classified as Amazons. A forerunner, however, has now been suggested within Philip's Macedon itself. The front chamber of King Philip's double Tomb at Aegae-Vergina was closed as the last resting-place of the bones of a royal female, wrapped in her purple robe and laid in a fine gold *larnax*. On the floor were about 70 Scythian arrowheads as well as a superb gold arrow-case, or *gorytos*, whose exact pair is known up on the Danube near the Black Sea.[42] The discovery of yet more bones from this woman's skeleton, carefully bagged and labelled by their finder, Manolis Andronicos, has allowed further osteological analysis. The big surviving piece of her pelvic bone has convinced her most recent analysers, led by Theodore Antikas, that she was aged between 25 and 35.[43] Most importantly, her leg-bones are of differing lengths, matching the two greaves of differing lengths which were found propped up against the tomb-chamber's doors. Antikas suggests that the *gorytos*, the many arrows and perhaps even the greaves may be explained as the lady's own possessions, a princess, therefore, with a warrior background from or near the Scythian steppes. If we follow this suggestion, the obvious identification of the princess is Meda, the wife whom Philip acquired from that area late in his reign. Antikas's further suggestion is more tenuous, that the worn state of her hip bone is to be explained as evidence of her persistent riding since early childhood. Nonetheless, like other women in her homeland, she may well have been a horsewoman. Tales of an Amazon were certainly known to Philip, whether or not Meda related to them. On the inside of Philip's superb ceremonial shield, found in his tomb-chamber, the image of Achilles looks down lovingly at the dying Amazon Penthesilea. It was made, in my view, near the end of his life, by which time he was married yet again, to the Macedonian Cleopatra.[44] Whether or not Philip, in his early forties, had married a horse-riding warrior woman, it was not completely fanciful for people in Alexander's camp to credit Alexander with a sexual fling with an Amazon if a horse-riding female warrior rode down from the nearby steppes and stayed with him briefly in 330BC. Amazons were not at all the virginal man-haters exalted by one wing of modern wishful thinking.[45] Myths presented them as heterosexually avid, and it was easy for gossip to ascribe this trait to Alexander's reported visitor near the Caspian.

---

41 Arr. *Anab*. 7.13.2–4 with Brunt 1983, 493–5.
42 Andronicos 1991, 175–97; Lane Fox 2011, 25–7.
43 Antikas and Wynn-Antikas 2016.
44 Andronicos 1991, 134–40; Kottaridi 2013, 273 and 276.
45 Mayor 2014, 129–41.

Once again, this way of locating what, to us, is a wandering myth did not die out after antiquity. In the sixteenth century, Spanish conquerors, who had long been aware of the Amazon myth, relocated Amazons even further away, out on the South American river which they discovered and duly called the Amazon. On its banks they must have seen prominent women, perhaps armed. They jumped to conclusions and believed they had found the elusive Amazon females.[46] In the 1620s, the remarkable Irish adventurer, Bernard O'Brien, described how he went upstream and met the Amazon Queen herself. She was called, he writes, by an Inca word and indeed it is one which means "princess". He gave her a shirt, he said, which she much liked, and it was absolutely clear that one of her breasts was stunted like a man's but the other was big and broad like a woman's. Perhaps she undressed while bending forwards to put on the shirt. O'Brien was remarkable for his soldiering prowess, his learning of local languages and his hard-headed practical career, but for him, as much as for any hardened Macedonian infantryman, believing was seeing.[47]

No more than Alexander were these people making myths travel by random fantasy. They had found evidence, a similar-sounding word and a bevy of real warrior females. Examples seemed to be present before Macedonian, Spanish or Irish eyes. Creative misunderstanding, not structural analysis of the myths themselves, is what explains their remarkable wanderings and re-location.

Creative misunderstanding is also frequent in the cross-cultural communication of religious teachings. In antiquity none wandered further than the legend, to modern eyes a myth, of Barlaam and Jehoshaphat. It arose from a misunderstanding by polyglot missionaries. The legend arose precisely in the third to fourth century AD with Manichaean missionaries who were active in Bactria and in lands beyond the Oxus.[48] Jehoshaphat was the missionaries' linguistic misunderstanding of the word Bodhisattva, or manifestation of Buddha. The Manichaeans regarded themselves as the true Christians and it was they who invented the story that this Jehoshaphat was converted to Christianity, albeit to the "true" Christianity, their own. In due course, whether by Manichaean "Christians" in Syria or by other Christians there, Jehoshaphat's converter was given the well-known Christian monastic name, Barlaam. Cantwell Smith's explanation of the story's origin has become even more compelling since the recent preliminary report of stories about Mani at the court of the Persian kings, preserved in the Coptic codex of early Manichaean "chapters", or traditions, now in the Chester Beatty Library in Dublin. In it, Mani himself is said to have refuted one "Iodasphes", again a Bodhisattva.[49] Conversion or refutation of Buddha, we now see clearly, was a claim which Manichaeans in the fourth to early fifth century were much concerned to make. In parts of western India, in Bactria and also Sogdia, their

---

46 Hemming 1978, 90–1 and 119–22.
47 Hemming 1995, 227–79 and 2009, 50–2.
48 Cantwell-Smith 1981, 7–10 with important endnotes.
49 Gardner 2014, 81–4.

first missionaries, including Mani himself, were confronted with a strong local Buddhist presence and their stories of "Jehoshaphat"'s conversion were their response to it. The tale of Barlaam and Jehoshaphat then travelled through Islamic Asia and into the medieval West.[50] The mythical protagonists are still visible among the sculptures on the rose-pink stone of Parma's baptistery in north Italy.

In *Travelling Heroes* I was concerned with an even bolder type of transfer and travel, one of myths which were encountered by Greeks in a foreign language at identifiable places and times in the Levant and then located in yet more detail by fellow-Greeks at the other end of the not-so-small Greek world. As a result, items from these myths travelled and were located at specific places in Italy, Sicily and the north Aegean. Their carriers and locators were above all Euboeans, travelling north, east and west in the eighth century BC. More finds and work since 2008 have added to the scope of this contention.

First, a skeletal summary of the argument of my book.[51] In and around the modern Jebel Aqra, that great mountain of the gods in north Syria, the ancient Mount Hazzi or in Greek, Mount Kasios, localised myths of the struggles between the gods in heaven were sung and combined with rituals, as is known above all from Hittite texts of the Late Bronze Age. Even after the upheavals at the end of that era, the mountain and its weather persisted, and so, I argued, did the songs and stories which related to it, remaining current for Greeks who revisited the region in the ninth to eighth century BC. It is now even clearer that Hittite cults and myths of this type did indeed live on locally after 1150 BC. The stone reliefs of a local ruler beside the storm god Tarhunta, found in the god's temple on Aleppo's citadel, have now been published: the relief of the ruler, at least, is dated to the eleventh century BC.[52] They show that the cult of Tarhunta and, surely, its accompanying myths indeed persisted after the ending of the Late Bronze Age. Newly-read Luwian neo-Hittite inscriptions found at the site testify to a King Tahta. Yet more such inscriptions, recently found at Arsuz on the coast, testify to a King Suppiluliuma (a royal personal name well known in earlier Hitttite texts). These texts and others have allowed both David Hawkins and Mark Weeden to establish that in the eleventh and tenth centuries BC, kings, neo-Hittite in culture, were ruling a realm which turns out to have been called Palestin-Walestin.[53] This "Palestin" (the first attested "Palestine") turns out to have been the heartland for much which I discussed in the Near-Eastern sections of my book. "Palestin" included the old land of Unqi, now in the Hatay province of modern Turkey but in antiquity in northern Syria. Its urban centre was Patina, the modern Tell Tayyinat, where a line of neo-Hittite kings indeed persisted. The remarkable find in 2012 of a statue and

---

50 Schulz 1981, 131–43.

51 The review in *The Classical Review* 61 (2011), 505–7 did not address the main subject of the book (pp. 175–380), so I summarise it again here.

52 Kohlmeyer 2011.

53 Hawkins 2011; Weeden 2013.

inscription of King Suppiluliuma at Tell Tayyinat takes a neo-Hittite presence there down into the mid-ninth century. Assyrian evidence then attests a certain "Lubarna" there in 829 BC and if this word reflects the old Hittite title "Lubarna", the neo-Hittite presence comes right down to adjoin the arrival of Greeks from the Aegean. Tell Tayyinat is on the river Orontes, just up from its mouth, the site of Al Mina, the place where a much-discussed concentration of Greek, especially Euboean, pottery in its lowest levels points to a Greek, specifically Euboean, presence in the early to mid-eighth century, arguably from c. 820–780 BC onwards.[54] Unqi and especially Al Mina lay at the very foot of the great Jebel Aqra mountain, Mount Hazzi, scene of the battles of the gods and the songs about them. My claim that the localised Hittite songs about the gods, attested in the Late Bronze Age, surely persisted on and around the mountain into the 800s BC and were heard there by newly-arrived Euboeans no longer looks like a leap across intervening time. Kings of a "neo-Hittite" culture were indeed still active in the area.

There is no doubt, pottery apart, that Greeks were making contact with north Syria in this mid-eighth century era. Evidence lies in the manifest impact of north Syrian (not "Phoenician") objects and craftsmanship on objects made and found in the mainland Greek world. Aramaeans and north Syrians did not bring them personally, because they were not seafarers.[55] The case for making Euboeans the most prominent visitors to the arc of coastline between the Levant and east Cilicia in this period rests especially on the preponderance of their pottery among such Greek pottery as is found in the area and also on their close relation to the origins of the alphabet, learned outside Greece, albeit from a Phoenician, not an Aramaean.[56] In 2008, I was most concerned with Euboeans and their travels because I had also noticed how it was at or near Euboean points of settlement in the west Mediterranean and north Aegean that locations of items in myths attested in and around Mount Hazzi could be identified. Of course Euboeans were not the only people in the Greek-speaking world to have the chance of such "Near-Eastern" contact. I said less about these myths' travels to nearby Crete and Cyprus because neither Cypriots nor Cretans could be shown to have located any items from them as far away as Ischia or the straits of Messina, although Cypriots had certainly been travelling there long before Euboeans settled in the West.[57] Nearer home, Hesiod's *Theogony*, c. 710 BC, contains evidence that deities on both Cyprus and Crete had already become attached to the old core of myths about the succession of the gods in heaven which were told on and around Mount Hazzi. The goddess Aphrodite is presented as born from the god Heaven's castrated private parts and sperm and as then being washed to Cyprus.[58] New-born Zeus is presented

---

54 Lane Fox 2008, 99–113; Lauinger 2012, 91; Harrison 2009.
55 Dunbabin 1957, 36–42; Boardman 2005, esp. 285.
56 Kenzelmann Pfyffer, Theurillat and Verdan 2005; Marek 1993.
57 Lane Fox 2008, 126–7 and 132.
58 Hes. *Theog.* 193–200.

as being taken and protected in a cave on Crete where the Kouretes drowned his cries while his father Kronos was left with only a mouthful of rock.[59] Cypriots lived near to the Orontes river-mouth and the Jebel Aqra directly behind it and were the obvious Greek-speakers to have encountered the Hittite myths of these combats, independently of any Euboeans. As well as hearing these myths on their eastward travels to north Syria, they could also hear about them through Phoenician visitors and residents on their island. As Jacqueline Karageorghis has now made admirably clear, the goddess Aphrodite was indeed a new creation on Cyprus, where she emerged only c. 1000 BC in its post-Bronze Age.[60] She then became connected with the old Hittite story of Heaven's castration. On Crete, as Martin West explained in 1965, the local Cretan god was the young Kouros, a god of herds and fertile nature, but he too became connected to the Hittite Succession stories, to the tales of a younger god's birth and eventual succession to power after struggles in heaven.[61] Archaeologists have held whole conferences on Iron Age Crete and Cyprus without looking sideways from pottery and metal-working to this striking evidence of the religious and mythical contacts of the two islands.[62] In the tenth to ninth century, I believe, the myths of both Cypriot Aphrodite and Cretan Zeus became connected into the old myths of the gods' succession struggles. Cypriots heard them while visiting north Syria and so perhaps did Cretans, but Cretans may also have heard them from Cypriot visitors in an era when contacts between the two islands are evident or even from Phoenicians whose presence on Crete in the ninth and eighth centuries is also now clear.[63] The myth of child-devouring Kumarbi, in Greek, Kronos, was then applied by Greeks to explain the child-sacrifices which were conducted by the Phoenicians around them. As Louis Robert well put it, Kronos became "le grand dieu phénicien, mangeur des enfants". In real life, Baal was another.[64]

As I also argued, Euboeans, some of them the very Euboeans from these Levantine adventures, headed west and rediscovered items known from the neo-Hittite songs in what was, to them, a faraway new world. These rediscoveries are attested at sites of specifically Euboean foundation. As a result, myths of Typhon, the sickle of Kronos and the mouldering corpses of the defeated Giants were located on Ischia, behind Cumae and on east Sicily. The bodies of the rebellious Giants were also located near Mende in Chalcidice, another long-standing Euboean point of contact.[65] I wish to revisit these travelling myths beside two more recent studies, each with a Euboean focus.

---

59 Hes. *Theog.* 470–80.
60 Karageorghis 2005, 227–8.
61 West 1965.
62 Karageorghis and Stampolidis 1998 is a recent example.
63 Lane Fox 2008, 163.
64 Robert 1939.
65 Lane Fox 2008, 319–32.

In 2010, in his fine book *La Patrie de Narcisse*, Knoepfler used evidence from Strabo and epigraphy to locate the mythical young hero Narcissus at Eretria, specifically at the temple of the huntress-goddess Artemis at Amarynthos.[66] We can hope here for much new information now that this sanctuary has been located, the last great one to be found in Greece, in 2007 by Sylvian Fachard and the Swiss School's teams.[67] As Strabo confirms, Narcissus's tomb was not shown in Eretria. It was sited on the other side of the Euboean gulf, but still in Eretria's orbit, near Oropus.[68]

Knoepfler traces Narcissus' subsequent local history in nearby Boeotia, above all at Thespiae in what he nicely calls "la résidence secondaire".[69] Like British Members of Parliament, travelling heroes, even young ones, always have second homes. Narcissus' tomb lay in the territory called Graia, the name of which has been well argued to have been carried out west by Euboeans and which led to them and their fellow Greeks being known there as *Graeci* when they first touched on Italy.[70] For our purposes, the interesting point, which Knoepfler had no reason to emphasise, is that unlike the name Graia, Narcissus never travelled west in Euboean company to become located in or around one of their new settlements. Some myths travel, but others do not.

In Chalcidice, since 2007, M. Tiverios has been emphasising evidence for local myths at, for instance, the mouth of the gold-bearing river Echedoros, the likely source, we might add, for much of the gold used by Protogeometric craftsmen in Euboean Lefkandi.[71] Tiverios proposes that the cults of the Echedorian nymphs here go back to early Euboean settlers. He suggests a similar origin for the myth of Heracles' fights with the hostile local Cycnus in the same region. Heracles is indeed a major presence at Eretria, amply attested from the later archaic age, and Euboeans may well have involved him in a local myth of conquest and supremacy which seemed relevant to their own successful settlement in this northern region.[72] However, neither the Euboean myth studied by Knoepfler nor the northern Euboean myths postulated by Tiverios are travelling myths in the full sense of the phrase. Narcissus never travelled except across the gulf to Graia, a place which was under Eretrian influence. Heracles travelled up to the Chalcidice, but the myth in which he became involved there was a specific local invention and never travelled anywhere else. In general, Euboeans did not relocate myths which were strongly localised in their own home territory. What they caused to travel were either a great traveller in panhellenic myth, Heracles, or

---

66 Knoepfler 2010, 73–158.
67 Knoepfler, Karapaschalidou, Fachard et al. 2014, for progress at the site since its discovery in autumn 2007.
68 Str. 9.2.10; Knoepfler 2010, 74–100.
69 Knoepfler 2010, 53–72.
70 Mazarakis-Ainian 1998, esp. 210; Lane Fox 2008, 171–2.
71 Tiverios 2008, relevant to Lemos 2002, 134.
72 Tiverios 2013, 97–110.

items in myths which they had met far from home, in Cilicia and north Syria, in a foreign tongue. "Non-travelling myths", therefore, are ones which are already deeply rooted in a home settlement's local terrain and identity. Nobody ever relocated the daughters of Cecrops from Athens's acropolis nor did any of the local mythology about the Athenian royals travel elsewhere. Narcissus was very strongly rooted in Eretria. He had a local festival there and a tomb just across the water. He gave his name, we now know, to one of the six tribes at Eretria which were instituted c. 500 BC in the wake of the new ten tribes at Athens which Cleisthenes had introduced in 508.[73] How could he be discovered by Eretrians anywhere else? As an exception, which nonetheless proves the rule, we can contrast the young Hyacinthus. He too was strongly localised in one place, Sparta, and yet Hyacinthia festivals appear in fellow-Dorian *poleis* on Crete or Thera and in Dorian Asia Minor.[74] The reason, I assume, is that Hyacinthus' festival had given its name to a month in the calendar, one which was then exported very early through Dorian Greek communities.[75] By contrast, Narcissus' festival did not become one of the Ionic calendar's month-names and so it never travelled outside Eretria.[76] Narcissus and Hyacinth, flower-heroes still visible in the springtime of the year, are symbols of travelling and non-travelling heroes.

Can the model which *Travelling Heroes* identified be applied elsewhere, to myths other than the old succession struggles in heaven which were picked up from one culture and then extended by misplaced discoveries into the landscapes of another? There are no doubt many examples in the cultures and landscapes of what we westerners call the Far East. One obvious one is the transfer of Daoist myths about the Islands of the Immortal Gods from Tang China across to the Japanese archipelago. Thereupon, Japanese scholars concluded that the Immortal islands about which they were hearing were their very own islands of Japan. Unlike eighth-century Euboeans, they even replicated their new discovery in the landscape: they laid out gardens to represent the floating islands of the gods.[77]

In what we call the "Near East", the model neatly fits the westward spread of Christianity into the Gentile world, what Tolkien once described to C. S. Lewis as "a myth that is true". It was picked up from the Aramaic language at similar points in the Levantine "triangle" to those which Euboeans had visited many centuries before. Greek-speakers took the new myth from Antioch (in the former land of Unqi), across first of all to Cyprus and then in due course to the north (Macedonia) and the West (Sicily and Italy).[78] Again, there was creative misunderstanding. As Greek speakers, many of its

---

73 Knoepfler 2010, 104–23, 219–24 and also in *Bulletin épigraphique* 2011, 403–4; 2013, 493 and 2014, 477–8 with further bibliography.

74 Knoepfler 2010, 175–6, 188–9 and *Bulletin épigraphique* 2007, 300; Moreno Conde 2008.

75 Knoepfler 2010, 189, with Trümpy 1997.

76 Knoepfler 2010, 189, updating Knoepfler 1989.

77 Attlee 2010, 90 on the Ryogen-in garden.

78 *Acts* 11.19–25, 13.1–12, 16.9–10.

first Gentile hearers could not understand what a Messiah, in Greek *Christos*, really was. When the new Christianity then spread in Greek and Latin across the West, it located items which its Gospel stories had left unlocated. After touching down in Croatia and the Italian Marches on its travels, the Virgin Mary's miraculous house ended up in England at Walsingham. Joseph of Arimathea arrived unexpectedly at Glastonbury Tor.

In the more immediate wake of my travelling Euboeans, there is still scope for seeing if my model fits myths attested in Rome and Italy. Elizabeth Gebhard has acutely proposed that the stories of Ino-Leucothea and Melicertes were transferred to Rome and Italy by travelling Corinthians and then resurfaced there in the cult and legends of Mater Matuta.[79] Ino-Leucothea (but perhaps not Melicertes) are considered to have originated as Greek transfers from the Near East, Leucothea being present also at Pyrgi, that Etruscan meeting point of East and West.[80] Other examples to explore are, of course, the whole cluster of stories around visiting Greek heroes from the East, especially Odysseus, which were then reinterpreted in Latin and relocated in Latium and even in Rome.

There is also the cult at Nemi, a long-running fascination for scholars. It has no discernible link to myths originating in the Levant but it certainly became linked with myths travelling from the Greek-speaking world. In Jacques Heurgon's opinion it was as early as c. 500 BC that it became connected with the story of migrant Orestes and his protection by Artemis, with whom the goddess at Nemi was identified.[81] Also, Nemi's local cult-hero Virbius became understood to be Hippolytus, raised from the dead after his premature death near Troezen and wondrously transferred to Nemi, yet again by Artemis.[82] The cult's connection with Orestes may have arisen through the sort of westward-travelling myths which we can read in the mid-sixth century in Stesichorus' poems. To explain the connection with travelling Hippolytus, the impact of classic Greek drama is, I think, important. In nearby Cumae, as elsewhere in the Greek-speaking West, Euripides' plays were known and admired, perhaps even performed. The wild Diana cult at Nemi was already understood as a cult of Artemis, and like the wild Taurian Artemis in Euripides' play about Iphigenia, Nemi's Artemis was credited with a contact with the wandering hero Orestes. Greek visitors to Nemi then found that horses, most unusually, were banned from the goddess' sanctuary. The reason, no doubt, was that they were only allowed in as yearly offerings to the goddess.[83] Puzzled by this ban, Greek visitors, I suggest, reasoned that Artemis must have banned horses out of her love for horse-loving Hippolytus, thrown to death from his horse-

---

79 Gebhard 2005.

80 Bonnet 1988, 63–6 and 284–6 (on Leucothea at Pyrgi), but at 388–90 she does not accept a link between Ino's son Melicertes and Melqart.

81 Heurgon 1942, 305–7; Coarelli 2012; Pairult 1969, esp. 446–7.

82 Callim. Fr.190 (Pfeiffer); Hyg. *Fab.* 49.251; Verg. *Aen.* 7.767–77.

83 Str. 5.3.12; Paus. 3.16.7; Verg. *Aen.* 7.777–9; Ambr. *De Virg.* 3.2.6 for the annual rite.

drawn chariot. By 350 BC mythographers had already begun to claim that Hippolytus was no longer dead at Troezen, but had been brought back to life and taken off westwards.[84] Either as a response to them or perhaps as their inspiration, fans, I suggest, of Euripides' Hippolytus came to Nemi or heard about it locally and assumed that they had discovered Hippolytus' new home because horses were banned from the temple, the animals which had reared up and killed Hippolytus in his former life in the Peloponnese.

Myths, here, wandered through the creative misunderstandings of "people like us", lovers of Greek drama with their heads stuffed full of classical learning. To pursue the parallel, I will end with a cluster of supreme travelling myths, those concerning Trojans. After Troy fell, many of the Trojans were eventually said to have reached Italy. First, however, some of them reached the Chalcidice where the polis of Aineia claimed, from its analogous name, to be the very site visited by Aeneas while still carrying Anchises. The claim was already being made in the sixth century BC.[85] The name Aineia supported it, but it is also relevant, I suggest, that nearby Scione was claiming to have been founded by Protesilaos on the way to Troy.[86] These claims, like similar claims on Cyprus, are not real echoes of a Bronze Age past. They grew from inter-polis rivalry in the post-Homeric age. Inland, north–west of Aineia, the Macedonian Argead kings claimed to have come from Argos and to rule an Argos Orestikon,[87] surely the reason why the nearby Paeonians, still at odds with Macedon, claimed in rivalry to be Trojans by origin.[88] Before long, Epirus' nearby royal houses joined in the competition and claimed to be descended both from Achilles, through his son Neoptolemus-Pyrrhus, and Trojans, through Priam's son Helenus and Andromache's son Pergamus.[89]

Travelling Trojans had several advantages for those who claimed descent from them. Nobody knew where most of the Trojans had gone when holy Ilion fell. Also, Trojans were not Greek, so they were ideal ancestors for settlements with no credible claims to Greek ancestry, especially if the settlements wished to keep up with Hellenic claimants nearby. Over in south Italy, Epeios, carpenter of the Trojan Horse, was claimed as a travelling founder by the non-Greek Oenotrians at their urban centre Lagaria and also by their neighbouring rivals at Metapontum.[90] Brilliantly, Marianne Kleibrink has now explained this amazing claim by adducing the remarkable non-Greek wooden architecture of the region. She argues, decisively, that the Trojan carpenter was claimed as a visitor because his presence and handiwork allowed this

---

84 Apollod. 3.10.3, citing the Hesiodic *Naupaktia* which may be earlier than c. 400BC.
85 Erskine 2001, 93–8.
86 Thuc. 4.120.1; Hill 1926 for the coin-type c. 480 BC; Hornblower vol. 2 1996, 377–8.
87 Hdt. 5.22.
88 Hdt. 5.13.2.
89 Hammond 1967, 384–9 and 412–4.
90 Lycoph. *Alex.* 930–50; Ps.-Arist. *MirAusc.* 108; Just. *Epit.* 20.2.1; Erskine 2001, 140.

distinctive local woodwork to be related to the networks of Greek myth.[91] In Sicily, Elymian Segesta adopted Trojan ancestry as a counter, surely, to her neighbouring Greeks and Phoenicians.[92] So then, did Rome, merely one more Italian community to do so. However, Rome's Trojan legend clashed hopelessly with her non-Greek myths of the she-wolf and the twins, a point which was vigorously made by the Aetolians when they protested against Rome's Trojan "kinship" in the early 230s, a protest which is surely historical although only attested in Justin's *Epitome of Trogus*, Book 28.[93] It was not, then, only for literary or aesthetic reasons that the first surviving Latin poet Livius Andronicus translated the *Odyssey*, which had very complimentary lines about Trojans in Book 18. Like Naevius, he also wrote a majority of his poems on Trojan themes. At the time, Trojan myths were of contemporary, contested relevance. As Rome became powerful in the Greek world, others hurried to flatter the Trojan-Roman connection. On Chios, the much-discussed monument representing Romulus and Remus may be a pro-Roman dedication made in the 180s BC.[94] Similar sculptures can be traced in the following decades in the Adriatic, on Cephallenia and then Leucas, islands previously linked with the myths of Aphrodite and travelling Aeneas. In 189 and 167 respectively, they were brought into political alignment with Rome.[95]

Flattery by antiquarian learning is still a classic skill in academic life. However, the erudite location of travelling Trojans is essential to understanding great poetry, two books of Virgil's *Aeneid* which otherwise still perplex purely literary readers. From Troy, in Book 3, Virgil's Trojans go first to coastal Thrace. Then they travel all the way down to Crete. Then they are to be found near the site of Buthrotum (Butrint) and eventually in Sicily at the future site of Egesta which Virgil wrongly considers to have been beside the sea.[96] The explanation of these particular destinations lies in pre-Virgilian locations of wandering myths. At the future site of "Ainos" on the Thracian coast, a place-name fit for a visit by "Aeneas", Aeneas encounters the tomb of Trojan Polydorus whose death and burial there was not a myth shown on the city-coinage, but nonetheless one with pre-Virgilian roots.[97] Thence, differing from previous Aeneas-traditions, Virgil's Trojans go down to Crete because a local place named "Pergamon" existed there near Cydonia and was known to Virgil through previous scholarship. This Cretan "Pergamon" is first attested for us in the work of Pseudo-Scylax in the mid-fourth century.[98] Next they go to Buthrotum where also lived "Pergamioi", attested in

---

91 Kleibrink 2006 with Zachos 2013 on related traditions about Epeios.

92 Thuc. 6.2.3 with Erskine 2001, 188–93.

93 Just. *Epit.* 28.2.8–11 with Erskine 2001, 188–93 for the debate about its historicity.

94 Derow and Forrest 1982, 179–92.

95 Hammond 1967, 413 and 647–8; Erskine 2001, 194: Milena Melfi has helped me with her important work, as yet unpublished, on the chronology and the sculptors involved.

96 Verg. *Aen.* 3.13–68, 3.104–34, 3.293–355, 5.35, 5.700–61.

97 Verg. *Aen.* 3.19–68; Eur. *Hec.* 3–10, 767–82; Williams 1962, 57–9.

98 Ps.-Scyl. 47; Plut. *Lyc.* 31.7; Plin. *HN* 4.59; Robert 1940, 99 n. 2.

a fragmentary Hellenistic inscription (brilliantly recognised by Louis Robert) and surrounded by wandering Trojan myths and topography. At Buthrotum, Virgil's Aeneas, much moved by what he sees, is duly taken to see the local mini-Troy, a copy of the great Pergamon, and its dry riverbed called Xanthus. He even kisses the posts of the local Scaean Gate. It was probably just before Virgil wrote these lines that the antiquarian Varro visited Buthrotum and reported that all these names had been verified by him on location, perhaps during one or other of the Triumviral campaigns.[99] The fugitive Trojan Helenus was said to have settled at Buthrotum, the person whom Virgil shows ensconced contentedly in this new Troy while he tries to persuade the Trojans with Aeneas to give up their journey and join him. As for the site of Egesta, its claim to a "Trojan" origin had already been accepted by Thucydides and had been exploited to mutual profit by Egesta and Rome during the First Punic War. A fellow-travelling Trojan, Acestes, meets Aeneas and his crews there and in due course Virgil ascribes Egesta's first foundation and organisation to Aeneas: he leaves behind on site the weary Trojan mothers and stragglers who had despaired of any more voyaging.[100]

In Homer's *Odyssey*, Odysseus' travels home soon take him into "Neverland", one which Homer is likely to have imagined in part from the stories of pre-"colonial" Greek voyagers. Odysseus' encounters in it are nowhere fixed by Homer in the real world.[101] Between Homer's great epic and Virgil's, however, myths had travelled to exact locations for the sorts of reasons we have been studying. Scholarly poets, mythographers and schoolteachers had pinned them down in space and time: Virgil's magpie mind was their heir. Without previous locators of the unlocatable, *Aeneid* Books three to five would look very different.

In his *Small Greek World*, Irad Malkin recently remarked, "For a social *histoire de mentalité*, cult is more significant than myth ... a myth, explicit as it may be, might reflect only the concerns of erudite circles, poets, and mythographers ... cult signifies a living reality relevant to the community at large."[102] My paper has aimed to modify this claim. From Alexander and his fellow officers to their Amazon–hungry un-erudite troops, from my boatloads of travelling Euboeans to Cypriot and Cretan Iron age priests, from Greek visitors at un-Greek Nemi to Greek communities coming into contact with an increasingly powerful Rome, I have discussed people who caused myths to travel not because they had an eccentric individual view but because they were making sense, they believed, of things heard and seen and which then passed into their community's self- image and discourse, fit to be linked to diplomacy, foundation-stories or cities' obsequious claims to favours. Those claims worked in the real world because they spoke for communities at large, not just for a few learned

---

99 Robert 1940, 95–105; Verg. *Aen.* 3.344–55; Varro, ap.Serv.ad *Aen.* 3.349; Teucer *FGrHist.* 274 F1; Hammond 1967, 385.
100 Thuc. 6.2.3; Zon. 8.9, with Erskine 2001, 181–2 and Cic. *Verr.* 4.72.
101 Lane Fox 2008, 180–3; Murray 1988, 1–17.
102 Malkin 2011, 133.

freaks. The study of them is not only a search for exact details of localised understanding, relished by all who read the best of Louis Robert, nor is it a tussle only for a moment of smug understanding when we, the knowing historians, can see the creative error behind an island called Ikaros or a one-breasted Amazon. It is itself a travel into the "mentalité" of members of a *polis* or *ethnos* or army and is a continuing discovery that sweeping generalisations about a "post-classical death of myth" are remarkably untrue. Paul Veyne has asked if "the Greeks believed in their myths".[103] The study of their travels is not only a bravura exercise in local topography, foreign words misunderstood and broken inscriptions restorable with wondrous secondary learning, the rarer the better. It is a continuing answer to Veyne's question.

Those wandering Trojans had been losers, yet they wandered on westwards and northwards to become the "founders" of the royal houses in much of post-antique Europe, from France to Scandinavia. They even provided the legendary first rulers in the dark abyss of early British history. Behind the diffusion of these Trojan myths and their use by poets, including Chaucer, we can point, as often in antiquity, to a named individual. Guido delle Colonne was a prominent Sicilian in Messina, educated in Latin, himself a lawyer but misled by acquaintance with those two historical fakes, Dictys and Dares, supposedly the embedded war-correspondents during the Trojan War.[104] Thanks to erudite misunderstanding, our kings, our queens and most of the classicists in this volume became descended from wandering losers.

Bibliography

Amigues, S. *Études de botanique antique* (Paris, 2002).

Andronicos, M. *Vergina: The Royal Tombs and the Ancient City* (Athens, 1991).

Antikas, T. G. and L. K. Wynn-Antikas. New Finds From The Cremains in Tomb II at Aegae. *International Journal of Osteoarchaeology* 26 (2016), 682–692.

Attlee, H. *The Gardens of Japan* (London, 2010).

Baynham, E. Alexander and the Amazons. *Classical Quarterly* 51 (2001), 115–126.

Benson, C. D. *The History of Troy in Middle English Literature; Guido delle Colonne's Historia Destructionis Troiae in Medieval England* (Woodbridge, 1980).

Bernard, P. Une légende de fondation hellénistique: I. Apamée sur l'Oronte d'après les Cynégétiques du Pseudo-Oppien. II. Paysages et toponymie dans le Proche-Orient hellénisé. *Topoi* 5 (1995), 53–408.

Blok, J. H. *The Early Amazons: Modern and Ancient Perspectives on a Persistent Myth* (Leiden, 1995).

Boardman, J. *The Greeks Overseas* (London, 1980).

Boardman, J. Al Mina: notes and queries. *Ancient West & East* 4 (2005), 278–291.

Bonnet, C. *Melqart: cultes et mythes de l'Héraclès tyrien en Méditerranée* (Leuven, 1988).

Bosworth, A. B. *A Historical Commentary on Arrian's History of Alexander, volume 2* (Oxford, 1995).

---

[103] Veyne 1988.

[104] Benson 1980.

Bosworth, A. B. *Alexander and the East* (Oxford, 1996).

Bremmer, J. *Interpretations of Greek Mythology* (London, 1987).

Brunt, P. A. *Arrian's Anabasis of Alexander, Books V–VII* (Cambridge, Mass., 1983).

Burkert, W. *Structure and History in Greek Mythology and History* (Berkeley; London, 1979).

Cantwell-Smith, W. *Towards a World Theology* (London, 1981).

Coarelli, F. Le sanctuaire de Diana Nemorensis. Nouvelles découvertes. *Comptes rendus des séances de l'Académie des inscriptions et belles-lettres* (2012), 555–569.

Colarusso, J. *Nart Sagas from the Caucasus* (Princeton, 2002).

Dahlquist, A. *Megasthenes and Indian Religion* (Uppsala, 1962).

Derow, P. S. and W. G. Forrest. An Inscription from Chios. *Annual of the British School at Athens 77* (1982), 179–192.

Dunbabin, T. J. *The Greeks and Their Eastern Neighbours* (Oxford, 1957).

Erskine, A. *Troy Between Greece and Rome* (Oxford, 2001).

Forbes Irving, P. M. C. *Metamorphoses in Greek Myths* (Oxford, 1990).

Gardner, I. The Final Ten Chapters, in: *Mani at the Court of the Persian Kings: Studies in the Chester Beatty Kephalaia Codex*, edited by I. Gardner, J. Be Duhn and P. Dilley (Leiden, 2014), 75–97.

Gebhard, E. R. Rites for Melikertes-Palaimon in the Early Roman Corinthia, in: *Urban Religion of Roman Corinth: Interdisciplinary Approaches*, edited by D. Schowalter (Boston, Mass., 2005), 165–204.

Green, P. *From Ikaria to the Stars* (Austin, 2004).

Hammond, N. G. L. *Epirus* (Oxford, 1967).

Hammond, N. G. L. The Royal Tombs at Vergina: evolution and identities. *Annual of the British School at Athens* 86 (1991), 69–82.

Harrison, T. P. Neo-Hittites: the land of 'Palistin'. Renewed investigations at Tell Tay'yinat on the plain of Antioch. *Near East Archaeology* 72 (2009), 132–147.

Hawkins, J. The Inscriptions of the Aleppo Temple. *Assyriological Studies* 61 (2011), 35–54.

Hemming, J. *The Search for El Dorado* (London, 1978).

Hemming, J. *Red Gold: The Conquest of the Brazil Indians* (London, 1995).

Hemming, J. *Tree of Rivers: The Story of the Amazon* (London, 2009).

Henderson, J. G. W. The Homing Instinct. A Folklore Theme in Phaedrus. *Proceedings of the Cambridge Philological Society* 23 (1977), 17–31.

Heurgon, J. Recherches sur l'histoire, la religion et la civilization de la Capoue préromaine (Paris, 1942).

Hill, G. F. Protesilaus at Scione. *British Museum Quarterly* 1 (1926), 24.

Hornblower, S. *A Commentary on Thucydides, volume 2: books IV–V.24* (Oxford, 1996).

Karageorghis, J. *Kypris: the Aphrodite of Cyprus. Ancient Sources and Archaeological Evidence* (Nicosia, 2005).

Karageorghis, V. and N. Stampolidis. *Cyprus, Dodecanese, Crete. 16th–6th century BC* (Athens, 1998).

Kenzelmann Pfyffer, A., T. Theurillat and S. Verdan. Graffiti d'époque géometrique provenants du sanctuaire d'Apollon Daphnephoros à Érétrie. *Zeitschrift für Papyrologie und Epigraphik* 151 (2005), 51–84.

Kleibrink, M. *Oenotrians at Lagaria Near Sybaris: a Native Proto-Urban Settlement* (London, 2006).

Knoepfler, D. Le calendrier des Chalcidiens de Thrace: essai de mises au point sur la liste et l'ordre des mois eubéens. *Journal des Savants* (1989), 23–59.

Knoepfler, D. *La Patrie de Narcisse* (Paris, 2010).

Knoepfler, D., Karapaschalidou A., Fachard S. Amarynthos 2013. *Antike Kunst* 57 (2014), 127–133.

Kohlmeyer, K. Building Activities and Architectural Decoration in the 11th c B.C. The Temples of Taita, King of Palasatani/Palestin in Aleppo and 'Ain Dara', in: *Empires after the Empire in Anatolia, Syria and Assyria after Suppiluliuma* II, Eothen 17, edited by K. Strobel (Florence, 2011), 255–281.

Kottaridi, A. *Aigai. The Royal Metropolis of the Macedonians* (Athens, 2013).

Lane Fox, R. *Travelling Heroes* (London, 2008).

Lane Fox, R. Introduction: Dating the Royal Tombs at Vergina, in: *Brill's Companion to Ancient Macedon*, edited by R. Lane Fox (Leiden, 2011), 1–30.

Lauinger, J. Esarhaddon's Succession Treaty at Tell Ta'yinat: text and commentary. *Journal of Cuneiform Studies* 64 (2012), 91–127.

Lemos, I. S. *The Protogeometric Aegean* (Oxford, 2002).

Lloyd, G. E. R. *Polarity and Analogy* (Cambridge, 1966).

Malkin, I. *A Small Greek World: Networks in the Ancient Mediterranean* (Oxford, 2011).

Marek, C. Euboia und die Entstehung der Alphabetenschrift bei den Griechen. *Klio* 75 (1993), 27–44.

Marquart, J. *Südarmenien und die Tigrisquellen nach griechischen und arabischen Geographen* (Vienna, 1930).

Mayor, A. *The Amazons* (Princeton, 2014).

Mayor, A., J. Colarusso and D. Saunders. Making Sense of Nonsense; Inscriptions Associated with Amazons and Scythians on Athenian Vases. *Hesperia* 83 (2014), 447–494.

Mazarakis-Ainian, A. Oropos in the Early Iron Age, in: *Euboica: Euboia e la presenza euboica in Calcidica e in Occidente*, edited by M. Bats and B. D'Agostino (Naples, 1998), 179–215.

Momigliano, A. *Alien Wisdom: Limits of Hellenisation* (Cambridge, 1975).

Moreno Conde, M. *Regards sur la religion laconienne: les Hyacinthia* (Madrid, 2008).

Murray, O. Omero e l'etnographia. *Kokalos* 34–5 (1988–89), 1–17.

Pairault, F.-H. Diana Nemorensis, déesse latine, déesse hellénisée. *Mélanges d'archéologie et d'histoire de l'École française de Rome* 81 (1969), 425–472.

Ramos Perez, D. *El mito del Dorado: su genesis y processo* (Caracas, 1973).

Robert, L. Inscriptions grecques de Phénicie et d'Arabie, in: *Mélanges syriens offerts à René Dussaud* (Paris, 1939), 729–738 = Robert, L. *Opera Minora Selecta* 1 (Amsterdam, 1969), 603–605.

Robert, L. *Hellenica* 1 (Limoges, 1940).

Robert, L. *Hellenica* 13 (Paris, 1965).

Robert, L. *À travers l'Asie Mineure* (Paris, 1980).

Sherwin-White, S. and A. Kuhrt. *From Samarkhand to Sardis. A New Approach to the Seleucid Empire* (London, 1993).

Schulz, S. A. Two Christian Saints? The Barlaam and Josaphat Legend. *India International Quarterly* 8 (1981), 131–143.

Stinton, T. C. W. Phaedrus and Folktale: an old problem restated. *Classical Quarterly* 29 (1979), 452–455.

Stoneman, R. How the Hoopoe Got his Crest, in: *Ancient Historiography on War and Empire*, edited by T. Howe, S. Mueller, R. Stoneman (Oxford, 2017), 188–199.

Tiverios, M. Greek Colonisation in The Northern Aegean, in: *An Account of Greek Colonies and Their Settlement Overseas*, volume 2, edited by G. R. Tsetskhladze (Leiden, 2008), 1–154.

Tiverios, M. The Presence of Euboeans in the North Helladic Region and the Myths of Heracles, in: *Studies in Ancient Art and Civilization* 17, *Dedicated to Professor Ewdokia Papouci-Wladyka*, edited by J. Bodzek (Krakow, 2013), 97–110.

Tod, J. N. *Annals* and *Antiquities of Rajast'han* (Calcutta, revised ed., 1894).

Trümpy, L. *Untersuchungen zu den altgriechischen Monatsnamen und Monatsfolgen* (Heidelberg, 1997).

Veyne, P. *Did the Greeks Believe in Their Myths? An Essay in Constitutive Imagination* (Chicago; London, 1988).

Weeden, M. After the Hittites: the kingdoms of Karkamish and Palistin in northern Syria. *Bulletin of the Institute of Classical Studies of the University of London* 56:2 (2013), 1–20.

West, M. L. The Dictaean Hymn to the Kouros. *Journal of Hellenic Studies* 85 (1965), 149–159.

Williams, R. D. *Virgil: Aeneid III* (Oxford, 1962).

Zachos, G. A. *Epeios* in Greece and Italy: two different traditions on one person. *Athenaeum* 101 (2013), 5–24.

Part I: **Changing Cultural and Mythical Landscapes in Anatolia**

Ian Rutherford

Kingship in Heaven in Anatolia, Syria and Greece

Patterns of Convergence and Divergence

Introduction

Anyone who studies mythology in different ancient cultures will sooner or later be struck by similarities between them, and wish to understand how such similarities come about. There are three general ways of explaining similar story-patterns in different cultures:

1. as coincidence;
2. as common cultural patterns that go back very early in human pre-history; and
3. as diffusion, either long-term over several millennia (3a) or more recently (3b).

A recent proponent of position 2 is the Harvard indologist Michael Witzel who in *The Origins of the World's Mythologies* (2012) argues that many of the similarities between the mythologies of different cultures can be traced back to the period before the human migrations of the late Stone Age. He makes a primary distinction between features shared by cultures of Eurasia and the Americas (for which he uses the geological term "Laurasia"), and those of Africa and Australasia on the other (for which the analogous geological term is "Gondwana") which in his view diverged around 40,000 BC. For Witzel some diffusion may have taken place subsequently, but for the most part parallels are to be explained by movements of people rather than of myths.

Scholars of early Greek literature and myth have for the most part had a more limited focus. In recent decades they have been concerned particularly with two types of diffusion. One is cross-cultural diffusion from the Ancient Near East (ANE), either in the Late Bronze Age (1400–1200 BC) (LBA) or the "Orientalising Period" (eighth century BC).[1] The other is linguistic and cultural diffusion associated with speakers of Indo-European languages who are believed to have spread from a common homeland, probably around the Black Sea.[2] The problems posed by the two cases are slightly different, but one thing they share is that there exists widespread disagreement about how significant diffusion actually was.

To take the case of the purported diffusion from the ANE, some have argued for widespread and comparatively recent diffusion from East to West, given archaeologi-

---

[1] Burkert 1992; West 1997.
[2] West 2007; Watkins 1995.

https://doi.org/10.1515/9783110421453-003

cal evidence for the movement of material culture, and textual evidence for the existence of similar patterns in different cultures.[3] For others trying to pinpoint borrowing is futile given the limitations of our knowledge, and the most we can reasonably do is make comparisons.[4] Witzel's work serves as a warning that diffusion is not the only way of explaining shared cultural patterns. If we are to make a convincing case for it, we have to show that it is more likely than the other hypotheses. One way of doing that might be to point to the existence of parallel names in narratives in two different traditions. Another might be to demonstrate a critical mass of parallels between narratives in two different traditions. It is also important to be able to present a persuasive narrative about how it comes about.

The Succession Myth and the Near East

The strongest case for diffusion between the Near East and Greece (and one that convinces Witzel)[5] is that of the Divine Succession Myth as we find it in Hesiod's *Theogony*. Myths about the origin of the gods and their early battles are found in various cultures of the Near East, including Babylon and Ugarit, but the best parallel for Hesiod's version, as has long been known, is a Hittite narrative, known now as the "*Song of Coming Forth*", the surviving text of which, like those of other Hittite myths, comes from the archives of the Hittite capital at Boghaz-Köy in central Anatolia. Along with at least two other narratives it forms a sequence charting the origins of the Storm god and his early battles with monstrous challengers. These texts seem to have a background in the narrative literature and religion of the Hurrians of North Syria, with whom the Hittites had strong cultural links from the early sixteenth century BC. The Hurrian language (which was neither Indo-European not Semitic) is still imperfectly understood, and we have little independent information about their literature, although we know they had themselves absorbed the elements of the earlier cultures of Syria and Mesopotamia, and at an earlier point, when they lived further to the East, they seem to have been in contact with Indo-Iranians. The Hittite versions of the myths have sometimes been thought to be translations from Hurrian ones, but the more recent thinking is that they should be seen as loose adaptations.[6]

Hittite religion and poetry were in fact deeply multicultural. They had taken over central Anatolia from an earlier "Hattic" culture (another non Indo-European language) whose religion and mythology they continued to use. They also absorbed elements of another culture or group of cultures, the Luwians (Luwian was another Indo-

---

3 Burkert 1992; West 1997.
4 Haubold 2013.
5 Witzel 2012, 73.
6 Archi 2009; Corti and Pecchioli Daddi 2012.

European language closely related to Hittite), who occupied parts of southern and western Anatolia. The Hittite archives contain texts translated from Hattic and Hurrian (as well as original versions), and in addition ritual texts collected from as far away as Arzawa in the west of Anatolia and Babylon. The Hittites were in diplomatic contact with Ahhiyawa (Mycenaean Greece), and one text from about 1300 BC gives us the startling information that the deities of Ahhiyawa and Lazpa (surely the island of Lesbos) were somehow present in the Hittite capital.[7]

The Hittite archives preserve about twenty narrative-myths, a fairly small proportion of all Hittite texts of which there are many hundreds.[8] Four major classes of narrative texts are:

- narratives about the gods' conflict with the snake Illuyanka (Hoffner 1); see below §6.
- narratives relating to vanishing gods (Hoffner 2–8); these resemble Greek myths of disappearing gods, such as that of Demeter, but it is impossible to prove influence either way.[9] A feature of the vanishing god narratives, as well as of the Illuyanka narratives, is that the texts supply information about the ritual context of their performance, something which tends to be absent from Greek myths and which scholarly ingenuity has long tried to supply.
- narratives relating to the theme of kingship in Heaven, adapted from Hurrian (Hoffner 14–18);
- other translations and adaptations: of the Babylonian epics of Gilgamesh and Atrahasis;[10] and of an Ugaritic tale, Elkunirsa and Ashertu (Hoffner 21); an early Hittite tale, the story of the queen of Kanesh and her thirty sons and thirty daughters (Hoffner 19). The most recent addition has been a bilingual Hurrian and Hittite text called "The Song of Release", which includes narratives involving both gods and humans (Hoffner 18a). Most of these narratives involve cultural translations of one sort or another; even the vanishing god narrative and the Illuyanka narratives may be translated from the "Hattic" sphere.

---

7 AhT20§24.

8 I follow here the convenient enumeration in Hoffner 1998. Many of the Hittite myths now appear in Lopez-Ruiz 2013, with translations by M. Bachvarova.

9 See e.g. Burkert 1979a, 127; Bernabé 1988. One specific parallel between Demeter's disappearance in the *Homeric Hymn* and the Hittite myths is that a powerful goddess is involved in saving the situation: just as the goddesses Hannahanna and Kamrusepa play a part in restoring order in the Anatolian myths, so in the *Homeric Hymn* the abduction of Persephone by Hades is seen only by Hekate and the Sun, and it is Hekate who informs Demeter about what happened, though she claims not to know that the perpetrator was Pluto. Hekate has an even bigger role in a version of the myth attributed to the Hellenistic poet Callimachus (fr.466) who makes her a daughter of Zeus and Demeter and has her sent to the Underworld in search of Persephone. Less well known is the Argive myth-ritual of the disappearance of Dionysus, who vanished into Lake Lerna and was summoned back with trumpets: Dionysus disappearing in the water; cf. Hanhana and Kasha ritual: "he has disappeared".

10 See Haas 2006, 272–9.

Remarkable as the Hittite narratives are, they are unlikely to have been unique in this period. A significant corpus of narratives has also been found at Ugarit (see below §5), and it seems likely that similar myths were composed, performed and archived in many parts of the Ancient Near East. For example, it has been recently argued that there was an early Levantine myth narrating the battle of the Storm-god with the Sea-deity, which had a deep influence on the Hurrian-Hittite tradition (see below). Mythical narratives seem to have wandered easily from one culture to another at this time. Their movement is particularly easy to observe within what we might call the zone of cuneiform culture (from Mesopotamia, Syria, Anatolia), but Syrian and Mesopotamian narratives even reach Egypt.[11] They might well have reached the Aegean as well, or indeed moved from the Aegean to Anatolia and Syria;[12] Hittite influence extended to areas where Greeks may well have encountered it, especially the West of Anatolia (known in the Late Bronze Age as "Arzawa"), but also the South-East ("Kizzuwatna") and even the Black Sea coast;[13] in the case of Syrian and other Near-Eastern myths the contact zone could have been the Levant or Cyprus.

Why might such myths wander? One facilitating factor is probably that different states had shared ideas about the gods, who are thus "translatable" (cf. M. S. Smith 2008). Walter Burkert in the 1980s argued for the importance of wandering ritual practitioners in cultural transfer (and cosmogonies are known to have been recited during rituals).[14] Another context for wandering might be festivals, attended by travelling singers,[15] and official delegates from different states.[16] A further key factor could have been political ideology, which myth supports: a letter from Mari (eighteenth century BC) transmits a message to King Zimri-Lim purporting to come from the god Addu of Aleppo, saying that he had sent him the weapon with which he had battled the Sea (the first evidence for the existence of that myth), a piece of information which would obviously have been useful propaganda for Zimri-Lim.[17] Similarly, in neo-Assyrian royal inscriptions the king may be presented as following in the footsteps of the victorious storm god Marduk, smiting his enemies.[18]

---

11 The Egyptian "Astarte and the Sea" (COS 1.35–36) may adapt Ugaritic "Baal and the Sea" or even the Hurrian-Hittite "Song of Ullikummi": cf. Helck 1983. The Amarna Letters (fourteenth century BC) include some mythological narratives (EA356–9).

12 Diffusion from the Aegean to Anatolia is not out of the question, and indeed it has sometimes been suggested that religious practices in Western Anatolia might reflect contemporaneous Greek practice. See e.g. Faraone 1987, 277.

13 Zalpa on the Black Sea near Samsun was an important religious centre for the Hittites: see Forlanini 1984.

14 Cf. Lopez-Ruiz 2010.

15 Travelling singers in Mari archive: Ziegler 2007.

16 Bachvarova 2016, 225–6.

17 See Durand 1993; Ayali-Darshan 2015, 40.

18 Pongratz-Leisten 2014; ead. 2015, 311; also Crouch 2013. For the tendency of rituals related to royal authority to be borrowed, see Kristiansen and Larsson 2005. Note also that the ancient Greek word "turannos" (tyrant) may go back to Luwian tarwani- : cf. Giusfredi 2009.

Hurrian-Hittite Myths: The *Song of Coming Forth* and the Tarpanalli-Narratives

Three Hittite mythical narratives which chart the early history of the gods seem to belong together.[19] The first is the *"Song of Going Forth"* (*"SÌR parā-kan pāwar"*; see Corti 2007), previously known as "Song of Kumarbi", of which only the first tablet survives. This describes the origin of the present generation of gods, especially the Storm god (sumerogram IM), whose normal Hittite name was Tarhunt (Hurrian Tessub); he seems also to be referred to by a second Sumerian writing KA.ZAL, whose Hittite rendering might be *muwatalli* ("mighty") or *walliura* ("proud").[20] Their origin comes about via conflict between two lines of older gods: Alalu rules first, and is deposed by Anu ("sky"), who is then in turn deposed by Alalu's son Kumarbi who bites off Anu's genitals. This results in the former becoming pregnant with the latter's children, and subsequently the gods "come forth" from his body. He spits the semen of Anu onto Mt Kanzura, from where the god Tasmisu/Suwaliyat arises. Then Kumarbi visits Nippur where he gives birth to the Storm god, who emerges from the head (the "good place"), and the Tigris River, who emerges from somewhere else. Immediately after giving birth Kumarbi demands the Storm god back, so that he can eat him, but the gods give him a stone instead.[21] The tablet ends with the young Storm god exalting in his glory and the earth on the point of giving birth to twins. Only the first tablet survives, and it is unclear how many tablets might have followed.

Significant new information has now become available in another text whose modern title is *"Ea and the Beast"*. In this, the coming of the Storm god is narrated in the form of a prophecy delivered by the "Beast" in conversation with the god Ea.[22] If the reconstruction is right, the long fragment consist of two sections:

1. (col.ii): the triumph of the Storm god, who will drive down his enemies to the underworld, and keep them defeated with strings. He will judge the gods. The earth will produce a *"tarpalli"* (presumably the same as a *tarpanalli*: see below), described apparently as "the snake (mus*illuyanka*) of the mountains, rivers, sea".
2. (col.iii): apparently a flashback: the creation of the earth and the installation of someone (presumably the Storm god) as king by the fate-deities; then apparently the theme of Kumarbi's giving birth to the various gods, though a different set from that in the *Song of Coming Forth*.

---

19 Full survey: Haas 2006, 130–75; Archi 2009; see also van Dongen 2012; Ayali-Darshan 2015.
20 See Corti and Pecchioli Daddi 2012.
21 §13: the Storm-god wonders how to get out of Kumarbi's body, and chooses the "good places", which is apparently the skull. "He split him like a stone. He left him, namely Kumarbi. The divine Muwatalli(?), the valiant king, came up out of his skull"; then in §14 Kumarbi demands the child back, so that he can eat him, and the gods give him a stone instead. See Beckman 2011.
22 Archi 2002; Rutherford 2011.

Two other narratives provide a sequel to the *Song of Coming Forth*. *The Song of Hedammu* (Hoffner 17), a very fragmentary text, narrates the story of the sea monster Hedammu, child of Kumarbi and a daughter of the Sea god, who is described as a "*tarpanalli*" ("substitute" or "challenger") against the Storm gods. It seems that the gods deal with the threat by having the goddess Sauska/Ishtar seduce it, a motif that Nora Ayali-Darshan (2015) has recently argued is borrowed from an earlier narrative of the Storm god's conflict with the Sea, which originated somewhere in the Levant. *The Song of Ullikummi* (Hoffner 18), the longest of the extant texts in three cuneiform tablets, narrates a further conflict between the gods and a blind and deaf stone giant, Ullikummi son of Kumarbi. Ullikummi, whose name means "Destroy Kummiya" (the home of Tessub), is also described as a *tarpanalli*. Kumarbi has the infant Ullikummi planted on the shoulder of Ubelluri, a sort of Atlas figure who supports the heaven and earth (§16, §61). The Sun god sees him growing in the sea (§22–3: "it was standing like a shaft with the sea coming up to its knees") and reports to the gods, who go to Mt Hazzi (Mons Kasion) to observe. They initially try having Sauska seduce it again, but a great wave of the sea points out that this is futile (§36) (This motif clearly presupposes the *Song of Hedammu*). Then the Storm god and the gods drive their chariots against him but they fail. Hebat, watching the battle, wonders whether her husband is dead (§44–5). Eventually, Tasmisu/Suwaliya advises Tessub to visit Ea in Apzuwa (the Mesopotamian Apsu, the subterranean waters). Ea in turn visits Ubelluri and persuades the Primeval gods to release the copper cutting tool that was originally used to separate earth and sky (a detail heard about only here) in order to detach Ullikummi from the ground (§63). This is done. Ea is apparently shocked at seeing the dead in the Underworld (§65). When the text breaks off, we may be in the middle of the final battle.

According to Ayali-Darshan, the *Song of Ullikummi* too incorporates material from a Syrian tradition about the battle with the Sea. One borrowed feature would be the role of Mt Hazzi, also found in the Ugaritic narrative about Yamm (see below).[23] The abortive seduction of the Sea also seems to come from that tradition. If the original setting of Ullikummi is rocky central Anatolia,[24] perhaps we can see the Ullikummi story as an early wandering myth, Mediterraneanized by contact with Syria, just as Ullikummi himself is born inland and transplanted to the shoulder of Ubelluri, from where he grows up through the Mediterranean Sea.

The Luwian term "*tarpanalli*" is applied to both Hedammu and Ullikummi and the snake in *Ea and the Beast* is called a *tarpalli*, presumably the same thing. In ritual contexts "*tarpalli*" means a substitute, referring to a sacrifice made in place of someone else, e.g. the king, a common Near-Eastern practice. Possibly the idea behind it is that the monster replaces the Storm god temporarily as ruler of the universe but is

---

23 Ayali-Darshan 2015, 46 n. 77.
24 Haas 2006, 157.

fated (cf. Ullikummi §48) to be destroyed/sacrificed in the same way that a king in the Ancient Near East was replaced temporarily by a human substitute if there was reason to think that his life was in danger.[25]

Other narratives may belong in the same sequence:[26]

- the *Song of LAMMA* (Hoffner 15), also very fragmentary, is named after the deity designated by the Sumerian sign LAMMA, which implies that he is one of a broad class of Anatolian deities known as the "tutelary" deities. Volkert Haas suggested that it was Kurunta, a Luwian deity represented as a stag (the name could in fact mean "horned").[27] At the start of the narrative he had for some reason defeated Tessub, and is allowed by Kumarbi and Ea to assume leadership of the *kosmos*. His rule ushers in a sort of Golden Age, a consequence of which is that no one feeds the gods. Kubaba (his spouse?) urges him to go talk to the Primeval gods. He refuses, so they depose him.
- The *Song of Silver* narrated the story of Silver, another son of Kumarbi, who seems to have assumed the rule of heaven for a brief while.[28]
- Another fragment has recently been published featuring a period of rule by another primeval deity, Eltarra.[29]
- There was probably also a narrative narrating a conflict between the Storm god and the Sea, along the lines of the Ugaritic narrative of Baal and Yamm, and probably originating in a much earlier Syrian or Levantine version.[30]

Traces of some of these narratives survive in Hurrian as well,[31] though the Hurrian stage was not the original one. Hurrian religion underwent early influence from Mesopotamia and Syria (see Archi 2013), and the narratives will have been influenced in the same way. Most of the details are beyond our understanding at present, but one case where Mesopotamian influence shows clearly is the figure of Ea, Mesopotamian god of wisdom, who seems to play a crucial part in the action of

---

25 See Corti and Pecchioli Daddi 2012, 617. On substitute rituals, see Huber 2004.

26 Bachvarova 2016, 27 is sceptical about whether the *Song of LAMMA* and the *Song of Silver* belong in this sequence.

27 Haas 2003. Archi 2009, 218 suggested that Kurunta is the Luwian form of LAMMA, corresponding to Karhuha, the deity of Carchemish, where he believes that poem originated. Haas suggested that the end of the myth of LAMMA where the god is killed can thus be seen as a sort of precursor to the Greek myth of Actaeon, the man who is transformed into a stag and torn apart by hunting dogs.

28 Recently compared to the Greek story of Phaethon by James and van der Sluijs 2012.

29 Polvani 2008; Dijkstra 2011, 70–72.

30 See Rutherford 2001 and Dijkstra 2011, who explores links with the Hedammu myth and the Ugaritic material; Ayali-Darshan 2015 studies the evolution of the Sea-myth.

31 Edited in Salvini and Wegner 2004.

the some of narratives, initially supporting the rebels, but later on working with the Storm god.[32]

Ugaritic and Phoenician Myths

An already complex situation is complicated still further by the evidence for a related narrative tradition from Syria and the Levant. The best evidence comes from Ugarit (Late Bronze Age), but we have indirect evidence for Mari on the Euphrates (Middle Bronze Age) and also Phoenicia (first millennium BC).[33]

Ugarit was an important kingdom in the Late Bronze Age, destroyed around 1180 BC at the same time the Hittite kingdom itself vanished from the record. Excavations there in the 1930s yielded a corpus of previously unknown narrative poems, including one group concerned with Baal of Mt Ṣapanu (Mt Kasion, just North of Ugarit). Surviving narratives deal with Baal's combat against his adversaries Yamm (the Sea) and Mot (Death). The combat with Yamm is a sort of proem, followed by Baal's building his palace on Mt Ṣapanu; the combat with Mot is more complex, divided into two sections, the first of which concludes with the temporary death of Baal. Although no Ugaritic divine succession myth has been found, there may be a trace of Hurrian-Hittite myth in the fact that Baal has two different fathers, Dagan (usually) and El (see below).

The narrative of the battle between Baal and Yamm is a general resemblance of the Egyptian Astarte narrative and the Hittite-Hurrian *Song of the Sea* and one specific point they have in common is that all three have an episode where the Sea demands tribute from the gods. It seems likely that behind all of them is an older narrative about the Storm god and the Sea which originated in the Levant.[34]

No narratives in Phoenician survive at all. However, a Greek writer from the early Imperial period, Philo of Byblos, claimed to have access to an otherwise lost work by the Phoenician author Sanchuniathon.[35] Sanchuniathon's *Theogony* as reported by Philo is long and complex, and it includes Egyptian elements such as the god Thoth (not necessarily a sign of inauthenticity, since there actually was a lot of Egyptian influence in the Levant in the Late Bronze Age). One subnarrative in it was devoted to a sequence of three or four generations of gods:

---

32 See Hoffner 1998, 41–2. Ea's position in Hesiod's *Theogony* has something in common with that of Gaia, also a primordial chthonic figure, whose wise advice is critical to Zeus' success, although she acts against Zeus when she gives birth to Typhon: Strauss Clay 2003, 26–7. Another case of Syrian influence may be the myth of the Storm god and the Sea, for which see below.

33 For Mari see above. For even earlier evidence from Ebla (third millennium BC) see Bachvarova 2016, 257.

34 Ayali-Darshan 2015; Dijkstra 2011.

35 See the edition of Baumgarten 1981.

Generation 1: Elioun (Most High) and Berouth (in Byblos).
Generation 2: Ouranos (Sky), whose original name was "terrestrial autochthon", and Earth.
Generation 3: Elos/Kronos, Baitylos, Dagon/grain and Atlas. These are the Titans.
Generation 4? Demarous.

Ouranos is deposed by Elos/Kronos because he maltreats Earth. Ouranos has a concubine, who is pregnant with Demarous (apparently Zeus, also called Adados, i.e. Hadad, the god of Aleppo). He gives her to Dagon as wife, so Dagon becomes the stepfather of Demarous. At a later point Kronos castrates Ouranos.

It is possible that this is a piece of Hellenistic or Roman local history, a pastiche from earlier mythological elements including some from Hesiod (the inclusion of the castration of Ouranos towards the end looks suspicious), constructed to give Phoenicia a privileged place in the origin of the *kosmos*.[36] A similar local theogony involving Titans is known from Adana in Cilicia, possibly going back to the philosopher Athenodorus of Cana (first century AD).[37] However, in recent decades scholars have begun to appreciate that Greek historiography about the Ancient Near East (such as Berossos' *Babyloniaca*) is far from being completely unreliable, and often contains authentic material.[38]

One episode in Philo that may well point back to the Bronze Age is Ouranos' giving his concubine, who is pregnant with Demarous, to Dagon so that Dagon brings him up; Dagon clearly corresponds to Dagan, an ancient Semitic deity, attested already in the third millennium BC, often identified with Kumarbi in Hittite texts.[39] Thus this episode could be construed as a faint echo or rationalisation of Kumarbi's acting as parent of Anu's child in the *Song of Coming Forth*, except without the sexual violence.[40] Kumarbi's role seems to have been divided in two: the supplanter of Anu (Elus/Kronos) and the surrogate father of his child (Dagon).

There may be intimations of this in Ugaritic texts, in which both El and Dagon are said to be the father of Baal; as we saw, that may reflect the dual paternity of the warrior god in the Hurrian tradition.[41] Some deity-lists from Late Bronze Age Ugarit preserve a similar sequence of gods: Ilu (El), Dagan and Baal Ṣapanu (i. e. Baal of Mt Ṣapanu).[42] It

---

36 Baumgarten 1981, 6 and 261–68 takes this view; for bibliography see now Metcalf 2015, 179.
37 The entry for Adana in the lexicon of Stephanus of Byzantium states that Adana was founded by Adanos and (the river) Saros, and then gives a genealogy: ἔστι δὲ ὁ Ἄδανος Γῆς καὶ Οὐρανοῦ παῖς, καὶ Ὄστασος καὶ Σάνδης καὶ Κρόνος καὶ Ῥέα καὶ Ἰαπετὸς καὶ Ὄλυμβρος (Adanos is son of Earth and Heaven, along with Ostasos, Sandes, Kronos, Rhea, Iapetos and Olumbros). Three of the children (Kronos, Rhea, Iapetos) are Hesiodic Titans. On this see Rutherford 2017, 89–90.
38 See Dillery 2015.
39 Feliu 2003, 106.
40 Lopez-Ruiz 2010, 99–100.
41 See the important article of Ayali-Darshan 2013 on this.
42 Lopez-Ruiz 2010, 102; Pardee 2002, 30 etc.

is thus possible that there is some degree of continuity from a narrative parallel to the *Song of Coming Forth*, but we cannot be sure that there was an act of violent copulation between two male divinities in the Ugaritic or proto-Phoenician myths: it is possible that what comes through the Semitic tradition is simply the bipaternity of the Storm god, for which Sanchuniathon provides an explanation consistent with the grammar of genealogy.

Hesiod's *Theogony* and the *Song of Coming Forth*

On the Greek side, the standard source for the creation myth is the *Theogony*, composed probably in the late eighth century BC by Hesiod of Ascra in Boeotia whose family came from Cumae in W. Anatolia. The *Theogony* charts the history of the universe from the beginnings to the present cosmic. There are two phases:

1. The generations of the gods, with greatest emphasis on the most recent four generations and the transitions between them. The generations are first, that of Ouranos (Sky) and Ge (Earth); second, Kronos and the Titans; third, Zeus and his siblings; and fourth, Zeus' children. Ouranos suppresses his children, the twelve Titans, but Kronos overthrows him by castrating him when he comes to penetrate Ge. The blood of Ouranos falls on Ge and engenders the Erinyes, the Giants and the Meliai-Nymphs, and the genitals fall in the sea, from where Aphrodite is born. Kronos tries to prevent his own overthrow by swallowing his children, but Zeus tricks him into swallowing a stone instead, and he disgorges the rest, which lead to the current regime of gods. Zeus is warned by Ouranos and Gaia that any son he has by the Titaness Metis will be more powerful than himself. So he swallows Metis, and the goddess Athena is born from his head.

2. Challengers to the cosmic order: first, the Titans, whom the gods defeat with the help of the Hundred-Handers; and then Typhon (820–68).

A third theme in the poem is the relationship of gods to men, and here we have the episode of Prometheus, son of the Titan Iapetos, who tricked Zeus in the first sacrifice, and when Zeus withheld fire from men, stole it, in retaliation for which the gods created the first woman, Pandora, a disaster for men (the position of Pandora in the story seems roughly parallel to that of Eve in Genesis).[43]

Hesiod's other surviving poem, *Works and Days*, contains no cosmogonic material, though it does present an anthropogenic myth, the "myth of the races", the golden race, the silver race, the bronze race, the race of heroes and the present iron race. The period in which the golden race lived was a golden age, presided over by Kronos,

---

43 See the treatment of the myth by Vernant 1980.

where the crops grew of their own accord. *Works and Days* has a second account of the creation of Pandora, but neither poem gives an account of the origin of man.[44]

Over the last eighty years many similarities have been observed between Hesiod's *Theogony* and the Hittite narratives, almost all of them concerning the *Song of Coming Forth*.[45] These include:

- there are three stages (generations in the Greek but not in the Hittite), from rule by Sky to the present stage, with something else in between;
- the transition from stage 1 to stage 2 comes about via the emasculation of Sky;
- the gods of stage 3 grow from inside a member of stage 2;
- a god swallows a stone thinking that it is another god;
- a god gives birth to another god through his head (the Storm god from the head of Kumarbi; Athena from the head of Zeus);
- a god is born from the semen of another god (Kumarbi spits Anu's semen onto Mt Kanzura, from where the god Tasmisu/Suwaliyat was born; Ouranos' semen lands in the sea and Aphrodite is born).[46]

There are also some differences. In the *Song of Coming Forth* there are originally two families, not one, and three stages with two generations, not three: Kronos emasculates his father, but Kumarbi emasculates the god who deposed his father. The Hittite-Hurrian Storm god is the son of the Sky, whereas Zeus is his grandson. Kumarbi's role is much more transgressive than that of Kronos, since Kumarbi inadvertently becomes the mother of Sky's children. In Hesiod it can be argued that the castration of Ouranos is the moment of final separation between Sky and Earth, allowing the Titans to come forth, but in the Hittite tradition, as we learn from the *Song of Ullikummi*, the separation of Earth and Sky was carried out with the copper cutting tool, apparently a separate event from the battle between Kumarbi and Anu, and long before it.

The question also arises whether there are parallels or differences between Hesiod's succession myth and Ugaritic or Phoenician myths. This is impossible to answer, since so little survives.[47]

---

44 On that see Bremmer 2008, 19.

45 First in Forrer 1936; followed by Barnett 1946, and Lesky 1950.

46 On the role of aetiology in this context see Metcalf 2015, 179–82.

47 Lopez-Ruiz 2010, 115–29 makes a good case for a parallels between the depiction of Baal's father El in Ugaritic narratives and Greek ideas about Kronos (equated with Elos by Sanchuniathon). However, the Ugaritic tradition seems to be different, both because Baal has two fathers, each of whom seems to correspond to Kumarbi, and because there is no trace of the violent succession narrative. On this, see Dijkstra 2016, 127; Dijkstra also has much to say about El, his chthonic associations and his resemblance to Kronos.

Typhon and the East

How do the rest of the Hittite myths of this sequence compare with Hesiod and Greek mythology? Hedammu and Ullikummi resemble Typhon only in a very general way. Typhon is not the son of Kronos in Hesiod (although he has that role in one anonymous source).[48] Typhon differs from Hedammu because he is not a sea-monster and he differs from Ullikummi both in his form, and in the way he is defeated. Other Greek monsters are a better match for Ullikummi, such as the giant Aloeadae Otus and Ephialtes who attempted to storm heaven by piling one mountain on top of another.[49] The scene where the Sun deity catches sight of Ullikummi rising from the waves perhaps has a resonance in a completely different Greek text, Pindar's Victory Ode for Diagoras of Rhodes (lines 62–3), where Helios claims the island of Rhodes for himself after he sees it rising from the sea.

Slightly better parallels are now provided by *Ea and the Beast*, in which, as we saw, Tessub seems to have driven his enemies down to the earth and bound them (like Hesiod's Titans),[50] and then to have fought a snake, Illuyanka or an *illuyanka* (like Typhon?).[51] The enemies driven down to the underworld seem to correspond to the Titans in Hesiod, and it is quite possible that these events were also told in the lost continuation of the *Song of Coming Forth*.[52]

The *Song of LAMMA* does not seem to resemble anything in Hesiod either, though it is worth observing that LAMMA's revolution against the divine order has one parallel with Greek literature: the idea that the gods are deprived of sacrifice occurs in Aristophanes' comedies, for example in his *Birds*, where the gods are starved out of heaven because their access to the savour of the cooking sacrificial meat is cut off.[53] Perhaps some common myth-ritual pattern underlies this.

The snake called Illuyanka, who features in *Ea and the Beast*, is also the focus for the Illuyanka-narratives, from the Hittite homeland (probably pre-Hittite), apparently associated with the Purulli-festival at Nerik, an important state-festival. There are two versions:

---

48 A scholion on Homer reports that Typhon's father was Kronos (i.e Kumarbi), the product of one of two eggs, buried in Cilicia (Σ on *Il.* B.783; ed. Dindorf III 148–9).

49 See Burkert 1979b for another parallel with Greek mythology.

50 Cf. *Ea and the Beast* ii.10–11; also in the Purifying a House Ritual (CoS 1.171§33). "He takes three birds and offers two of them to the Anunnaki deities, but the other bird he offers to the Pit and he says as follows: 'For you, Oh primordial deities, cattle and sheep will not be forthcoming. When the Storm god drove you down to the Dark Underworld he established for you this offering.'"

51 *Ea and the Beast* ii.27.

52 Notice that for Solmsen 1989 the Hesiodic themes of kingship in heaven and driving the Titans down to the underworld came from distinct Near-Eastern traditions; we now know they were both present in the Hittite version.

53 Aristoph. *Av.*188–93, 1514 etc.; cf. id. *Plut.*1113–20.

Version 1: The Storm god is defeated by Illuyanka, who is in turn tricked by the goddess Inara, the Storm god's daughter, and the mortal Hupasiya, who feast him and get him drunk. Hupasiya ties him up and the Storm god kills him.

Version 2: The Storm god is defeated by Illuyanka, who takes the heart and eyes of the Storm god; meanwhile, the Storm god has a son by the daughter of a poor man; the son marries Illuyanka's daughter and demands the heart and eyes as the brideprice. The Storm god recovers, does battle with Illuyanka, but kills his son in the process.

Parallels have been observed between these and the Greek myth of Typhon, though not the Hesiodic version. Further details about him are preserved by later sources:

1. The mythographer Apollodorus (first century AD?) (1.6.3) says that Zeus chased Typhon as far as Mt Kasion (Mt Hazzi), attacking him with thunderbolts and a sickle (*harpe*). But Typhon stole his sinews ("*neura*"), imprisoned Zeus in the Corycian Cave in Cilicia, along with the sinews, which were hidden in a bearskin, guarded by the she-dragon Delphyne. But Hermes and Aigipan (apparently a form of Pan) restored them to Zeus, who chased him to Thrace and finally imprisoned him under Mt Etna.

2. The poet Oppian (second century AD) in his *Halieutica* (3.15–28) situates the conflict at Corycus in Cilicia, where Pan saved Zeus by luring Typhon from his undersea lair with a banquet of fish. Pan is said to be the son of Hermes.

3. The poet Nonnus (fourth century AD) (*Dion.*1.481ff.) has an elaborate account in which Typhon steals first Zeus' thunderbolts, and then, after attacking heaven, steals his sinews as well. The mortal Cadmus, with the help of Pan, disguises himself as a shepherd and challenges Typhon to a musical competition. He retrieves the sinews by asking Typhon for them so that he can string his lyre. Meanwhile, Zeus steals back his thunderbolts and after some violent resistance Typhon is defeated.

At least some of this may be much earlier than the Hellenistic period. Oppian was a Cilician, and his version could be a local Corycian version rooted in Luwian tradition;[54] but Typhon is already associated with Cilicia in the fifth century BC, so it is possible some Corycian version was already known to Greeks at that time.[55] Parts of #1 may also go back to some early source, perhaps the Titanomachia,[56] and it is conceivable that this version actually predates Hesiod (as Joseph Fontenrose thought).[57] A work

---

54 See Houwink ten Cate 1961, 206–15; Lytle 2011, 371–3; Hicks 1891, 241.

55 Pind. *Pyth.* 1.17 and Ps. Aesch. *PV* 353. Homer and Hesiod both associate Typhon with a people or place called Arimoi, the location of which is unknown: but see Bonnet 1987, 133–4; Lane Fox 2008, 280–301.

56 Argued for by Tsagalis 2013 and Ogden 2013, 74, but see D'Alessio 2015.

57 Fontenrose 1959, 70–6.

attributed to the Cretan seer Epimenides (possibly fourth century BC) may have contained the detail that Typhon succeeded in storming Zeus' palace because Zeus was asleep,[58] and Robert Fowler has suggested that this version may also have referred to Mt Kasion.[59]

Versions 1 and 2 have parallels with the Illuyanka stories. In 1930 Walter Porzig pointed out that the detail reported by Apollodorus that Typhon steals Zeus' sinews (*"neura"*) roughly resembles Illuyanka 2. And in 1962 Houwink ten Cate observed that Oppian's version in which the deception of Typhon happens at a feast has a parallel in Illuyanka 1 (208–9). Illuyanka 1 also anticipates Nonnus' version in giving a critical role to a mortal. Perhaps Illuyanka 1 survived at Corycus where Luwian traditions were particularly well preserved down to the Greco-Roman period.[60]

These parallels are not particularly precise (which matters, since dragon-slaying myths are common in all cultures). But if there is anything in them, the *prima facie* consequence is that early Greek cosmogony draws on two different strands of Anatolian mythology: Hesiod's divine succession myth on the Hittite-Hurrian *Song of Coming Forth* and the non-Hesiodic Typhon myth on Hattic-Hittite mythology as we find it in texts relating to Nerik (Hesiod's version of the Typhon myth does not look particularly Anatolian at all). We should be aware, however, that the impression of distinct traditions of Hittite mythology may be an illusion generated by the limited evidence that happens to survive. In fact, Anatolian mythology may have been a lot more mixed up than that (as the religious system itself was), and it is perfectly possible that what we call the Hurrian-Hittite tradition also had Illuyanka-narratives of this sort, just as the Hattic-Hittite tradition might have had a myth of divine succession.

Typhon has also been linked to the Levant. The Hesiodic Typhon has a vague resemblance to Yamm, because he seems to be associated with the sea, although, as Peter Haider shows, there are also resemblances to a range of Ancient Near-Eastern mythical monsters, including the Sumerian Anzu-bird.[61] It has even been suggested that the name "Typhon" points eastwards, if it is connected to Mt Ṣapanu, the Semitic name for Mt Hazzi.[62] This was the seat of Baal who was known as Baal Ṣapanu, a deity whose cult was widely disseminated in the Mediterranean (often under the Greek

---

58 *FGrHist*. 457F8, VS3B8; Epimendes 10 in Fowler 2000–13, 1, 97. Contrast Ps. Aesch. 360 who says that Zeus struck Typhon with an "unsleeping missile" (Ogden 2013, 74), perhaps an indication that this detail is earlier.

59 See previous note.

60 Lytle 2011. Houwink ten Cate 1961, 128–9 has argued, on the basis of nomenclature, that the deity Runtas (supposed to be a later version of Kurunta, a Luwian tutelary deity) must have still been worshipped in the area, and that he should be identified with Hermes who assists Zeus in Oppian's version of the Typhon Myth (see now Lytle 2011, 370–9).

61 Haider 2005, 321; there is a resemblance to the seven headed Sea-deity Litan whom Baal is said to have fought in the Baal Cycle: see Parker 1997, 141–3.

62 Bonnet 1987, 133; Gruppe 1889, 487, cites even earlier literature.

name Zeus Kasios).[63] From the point of view of phonetics that seems fine (the Greek *tau* may correspond to Phoenician *Ṣade* as in the case of the Greek Turos and the Phoenician Ṣor), but on the semantic level we need an explanation for how the seat of the Storm god came to be reinterpreted as the name of his adversary.[64] It suggests an adversarial form of borrowing, in which a foreign myth was flipped over so that its hero is reinterpreted as its anti-hero.[65]

Conclusions

The Hesiodic succession-myth and the *Song of Coming Forth* share so many motifs (a "critical mass", as I called it in the introduction) that it seems likely they are connected, at least indirectly. In theory, influence could have happened in either direction; Greek influence on Near-Eastern texts is not out of the question even at an early date (did early Greek myths wander to Hattusa along with the deities of Ahhiyawa and Lazpa perhaps?).[66] Nevertheless, the probability is very much in favour of the borrowing being from East to West.

This was only a late stage in a much longer process, however: just like the generations of gods, the myths had even earlier stages. As well as moving from the Hurrians to the Hittites, they had been influenced at some point by Mesopotamian traditions. No doubt the real situation was even more complex.[67]

The case for a borrowing of the Typhon myth is less straightforward: different clues point toward the Hittite Illuyanka poems, local traditions at Corycus, and the Weather god of Mt Hazzi/Ṣapanu/Kasion, and the hypothetical proto-Syrian myth of the Storm god and the Sea is likely to have been a factor as well.

The northeast corner of the Mediterranean had long been a region of intense cultural interaction. In the LBA there was trade between Ugarit and Hittite-controlled Ura,[68] which must have been somewhere in Rough Cilicia, and the religion of Kizzuwatna in this period seems to have been a mixture of Luwian, Hurrian and Syrian

---

63 See Koch 1993; Fauth 1990.

64 See Lopez-Ruiz 2010, 112. Gruppe 1889 had thought that Hebrew zephon could mean "North wind".

65 One possibility is that this could have happened in Egypt: a secondary cult of Baal Ṣapanu is known to have existed in northeast Egypt near Pelusium, presumably introduced by immigrants in the mid second millennium BC: see Fauth 1990, 110–6. There he was identified with the Egyptian god Seth, who also defended the cosmos against a monstrous threat, in this case the snake Apophis, but came increasingly to be seen as the destructive adversary of Osiris and Horus: see Velde 1967, 138–51.

66 For possible Hesiodic influence on the Hebrew Bible see Louden 2013 (on the relation between Iapetos and Japheth).

67 Egyptian influence may have been underestimated: cf. on possible Egyptian influence Faraone and Teeter 2004. On possible Indo-European influence see Rutherford 2009, 9–14, esp. 13.

68 Haider 1995.

elements. Similarly, in the Iron Age, the Phoenicians are known to have been active in Cilicia. In the same way, Hurrian-Hittite, Hittite and Syrian narrative traditions were probably already somewhat mixed up in the LBA, and that probably continued in the immediately following. It thus becomes impossible to say for sure whether transmission is via a Luwian/Anatolian route or Syrian/Levantine one.

At any rate, it seems possible that the myths reached Greece from there, crossing to Cyprus and Crete (both important places in Hesiod), or along the southern coast of Turkey, and round to Ionia. This could have happened in the LBA or in the early decades of the first millennium. If we assume transmission in the first millennium, it might have come about in the area of Corycus, where indigenous Luwian culture still flourished in the first millennium BC. (Thus, the god Sandas was associated particularly with Tarsos, who continues the LBA Luwian deity Santas).[69] Greek colonisation in Cilicia starts in the eighth century BC.[70] Alternative, Hittite ideas might have been preserved in Neo-Hittite kingdoms of North Syria, such as the recently discovered kingdom of Taita in Palistin near Aleppo, perhaps in the context of cultic activities at Mt Kasion.[71]

However, it may be a mistake to infer from the various pieces of evidence that link the myths to Cilicia and the Levant that the Greeks must have encountered them in the vicinity. There is another possibility, namely that they reached Greece via Western Anatolia. Connectivity was very good across Anatolia in the Hittite period, and indeed it had been since the early second millennium BC, when we know of trading links between Assur and central-west Anatolia and beyond.[72] In the LBA the Storm god was worshipped throughout Anatolia, and the canonical myths about his rise to power and early conflicts could have been widely known and widely performed. In the mid second millennium BC there were powerful states in the West, especially Arzawa, which we can infer from theophoric royal names had a Storm god.[73] Mycenaean Greeks were already operating in Western Anatolia in the LBA, and it seems perfectly possible that they encountered these myths then. A similar argument could be made for the first millennium BC, when Lydia might have played a key role in transmission, either because it inherited religious traditions from the previous millennium or because it had close contacts with the kingdoms to the East.[74] As well as its association with

---

69 Rutherford 2017.

70 Some think the existence of a polity called Hiyawa in east Cilicia, now attested for the tenth century BC, suggests an even earlier Greek presence: see Jasink and Marino 2007 and now Dinçol et al. 2015.

71 See Strauss Clay and Gilan 2014; for Mt Kasion see Rutherford 2001.

72 See Barjamovic 2011. For religious links: Cammarosano 2015.

73 Tarhundaradu of Arzawa (fourteenth century BC), Tarhunaradu of the Seha-River Land (thirteenth century BC). Notice that Mason 2008 has suggested that the capital of Lesbos, Mytilene, might owe its name to the Hittite adjective *muwatalla* ("mighty"), which was the name of a Hittite king of the early thirteenth century BC and also perhaps one of the names of the Storm-god (see above).

74 For Lydia as a route for the passage of Anatolian myth to the Greeks see Bremmer 2008, 87. The recent argument of Arnaud 2015 for a cuneiform Lydian theogony does not seem convincing to me.

Corycus, the Typhon-myth served as an aetiology for the Katakekaumene area of Lydia, and this could well go back to an indigenous Anatolian myth about the Storm god and a snake.[75] Since myths of this sort could have existed all over Anatolia for a very long period, it would be sensible to keep an open mind about where and when they passed to the Greeks.

Bibliography

Archi, A. Ea and the Beast. A Song Related to the Kumarpi Cycle, in: *Silva Anatolica. Anatolian Studies Presented to Maciej Popko on the Occasion of his 65th Birthday*, edited by P. Taracha (Warsaw, 2002), 1–10.

Archi, A. Orality, Direct Speech and the Kumarbi Cycle. *Altorientalische Forschungen* 36:2 (2009), 209–229.

Archi, A. The West Hurrian Pantheon and Its Background, in: *Beyond Hatti: a Tribute to Gary Beckman*, edited by B. J. Collins and P. Michalowski (Atlanta, 2013), 1–21.

Arnaud, D. Une cosmologie lydienne en langue babylonienne: BM 74329. *Aula Orientalis* 33 (2015), 5–20.

Ayali-Darshan, N. Baal, Son of Dagan: in search of Baal's double paternity. *Journal of the American Oriental Society* 133:4 (2013), 651–657.

Ayali-Darshan, N. The Other Version of the Story of the Storm-god's Combat with the Sea in the Light of Egyptian, Ugaritic, and Hurro-Hittite Texts. *Journal of Ancient Near Eastern Religions* 15 (2015), 20–51.

Bachvarova, M. R. *From Hittite to Homer. The Anatolian Background of Ancient Greek Epic* (Cambridge, 2016).

Barjamovic, G. *A Historical Geography of Anatolia in the Old Assyrian Colony Period* (Copenhagen, 2011).

Barnett, R. D. The Epic of Kumarbi and the Theogony of Hesiod. *Journal of Hellenic Studies* 45 (1946), 100–101.

Baumgarten, A. I. *The Phoenician History of Philo of Byblos: a Commentary* (Leiden, 1981).

Beckman, G. Primordial Obstetrics, in: *Hethitische Literatur: Überlieferungsprozesse, Textstrukturen, Ausdrucksformen und Nachwirken: Akten des Symposiums vom 18. bis 20. Februar 2010 in Bonn*, edited by M. Hutter and S. Hutter-Braunsar (Münster, 2011), 25–33.

Bernabé, A. Himno a Deméter 43–46. Adaptación de un motivo anatolio. *Emerita* 56 (1988), 87–93.

Bonnet, C. Typhon et Baal Saphon, in: *Studia Phoenicia V. Phoenicia and the East Mediterranean in the First Millennium BC*, edited by E. Lipiński (Leuven, 1987), 101–143.

Bremmer, J. N. *Greek Religion and Culture, the Bible and the Ancient Near East* (Leiden, 2008).

Burkert, W. *Structure and History in Greek Mythology and Ritual* [Sather Classical Lectures 47] (Berkeley, 1979a).

Burkert, W. Von Ullikummi zum Kaukasus: Die Felsgeburt des Unholds. Zur Kontinutät einer mündlichen Erzählung. *Würzburger Jahrbuch für die Altertumswissenschaft* NF 5 (1979b), 253–261, reprinted in: *Orientalia*, edited by M. L. Gemelli Marciano (Göttingen, 2003), 87–95.

Burkert, W. *The Orientalizing Revolution: Near Eastern Influence on Greek Culture in the Early Archaic Age* (Cambridge, Mass.; London, 1992).

---

75 See Fontenrose 1959, 111 n. 36; Str. 12.8.19, 13.4.6; Nonnus *Dion.*13.474–8.

Burkert, W. Kronia-Feste und ihr altorientalischer Hintergrund, in: *Karnevaleske Phänomene in antiken und nachantiken Kulturn und Literaturen*, edited by S. Döpp (Trier, 1993), 11–30.

Cammarosano, M. Foreign Gods in Hatti. A New Edition of CTH 510. *KASKAL* 12 (2015), 199–244.

Corti, C. The so-called "Theogony" or "Kingship in Heaven". The name of the Song. *Studi Micenei ed Egeo-Anatolici* 49 (2007), 109–121.

Corti, C. and F. Pecchioli Daddi. The Power in Heaven: Remarks on the So-Called Kumarbi Cycle, in: *Organization, Representation, and Symbols of Power in the Ancient Near East, Proceedings of the 54th Rencontre Assyriologique Internationale at Würzburg, 20–25 July 2008*, edited by G. Wilhelm (Winona Lake, Ind., 2012), 611–618.

Crouch, C. L. Ištar and the Motif of the Cosmological Warrior: Assurbanipal's adaptation of Enūma eliš, in: *"Thus Speaks Ishtar of Arbela": Prophecy in Israel, Assyria and Egypt in the Neo-Assyrian Period*, edited by R. P. Gordon and H. M. Barstad (Winona Lake, Ind., 2013), 129–141.

D'Alessio, G. B. Theogony and Titanomachy, in: *The Greek Epic Cycle and its Ancient Reception*, edited by M. Fantuzzi and C. Tsagalis (Cambridge, 2015), 199–212.

Dijkstra, M. Ishtar Seduces the Sea-serpent. A New Join in the Epic of Ḫedammu (KUB 36, 56 + 95) and its Meaning for the Battle Between Baal and Yam in Ugaritic Tradition. *Ugarit-Forschungen* 43 (2011), 53–83.

Dijkstra, M. El-Kunirsha in Anatolia, the Levant and Elsewhere, in *Études Ougaritiques* IV, edited by V. Matoian and M. al Maqdissi (Leuven; Paris; Bristol 2016), 119–138.

Dillery, J. *Clio's Other Sons: Berossus and Manetho. With an Afterword on Demetrius* (Ann Arbor, 2015).

Dinçol, B., Dinçol, A., Hawkins, J. D., Peker, H. and A. Öztan. Two New Inscribed Storm-God-Stelae from Arsuz (Iš kenderun): ARSUZ 1 and 2. *Anatolian Studies* 65 (2015), 59–77.

Durand, J.-M. Le Mythologeme du combat entre le Dieu de l'orage et la Mer en Mésopotamie. *Mari annales de recherches interdisciplinaires* 7 (1993), 41–61.

Faraone, C. A. Hephaistos the Magician and Near Eastern Parallels for Alcinous Watchdogs. *Greek, Roman and Byzantine Studies* 128 (1987), 257–280.

Faraone, C. and Teeter, E. Egyptian Maat and Hesiodic Metis. Mnemosyne 57 (2004), 177–208.

Fauth, W. Das Kasion-Gebirge und Zeus Kasios. Die antike Tradition und ihre vorderorientalischen Grundlagen. *Ugarit-Forschungen* 22 (1990), 105–118.

Feliu, L. *The God Dagan in Bronze Age Syria* (Leiden, 2003).

Fontentose, J. *Python. A Study of Delphic Myth and its Origins* (Berkeley; Los Angeles, 1959).

Forlanini, M. Die "Götter von Zalpa". Hethitische Götter und Städte am Schwarzen Meer. *Zeitschrift für Assyriologie und vorderasiatische Archäologie* 74 (1984), 245–266.

Forrer, E. Eine Geschichte des Götterkönigtums aus dem Hatti-Reiche, in: *Mélanges Franz Cumont* (1936), 687–713.

Fowler, R. L. *Early Greek Mythography*, 2 volumes (Oxford, 2000–13).

Giusfredi, F. The Problem of the Luwian Title *Tarwanis. Altorientalische Forschungen* 36 (2009), 140–145.

Gruppe, O. Typhon-Zephon. *Philologus* 48 (1889), 487–497.

Güterbock, H. G. *Kumarbi. Mythen vom churritischen Kronos aus den hethitischen Fragmenten zusammengestellt, übersetzt und erklärt* (Zurich; New York, 1946).

Haas, V. Betrachtungen zu CTH 343, ein Mythos des Hirschgottes. *Altorientalische Forschungen* 30 (2003), 296–303.

Haas, V. *Die hethitische Literatur: Texte, Stilistik, Motive* (Berlin; New York, 2006).

Haider, P. Ura – eine hethitische Handelsstadt. *Münstersche Beiträge zur antiken Handelsgeschichte* 14 (1995), 70–107.

Haider, P. Von Baal Zaphon zu Zeus und Typhon, in: *Von Sumer bis Homer*, edited by R. Rollinger (Münster, 2005), 303–337.

Haubold, J. *Greece and Mesopotamia. Dialogues in Literature* (Cambridge, 2013).

Helck, W. Zur Herkunft der Erzählung des sog. 'Astartepapyrus', in: *Fontes atque Pontes. Eine Festgabe für Hellmut Brunner (= Ägypten und Altes Testament (ÄAT) Bd. 5)*, edited by M. Görg (Wiesbaden, 1983), 215–223.

Hicks, E. L. Inscriptions from Western Cilicia. *Journal of Hellenic Studies* 12 (1891), 225–273.

Hoffner, H. A. *Hittite Myths*[2] (Atlanta, 1998).

Houwink ten Cate, P. *The Luwian Population Groups of Lycia and Cilicia Aspera During the Hellenistic Period* (Leiden, 1961).

Huber, I. Ersatzkönige in griechischem Gewand: Die Umformung der sar puhi Rituale bei Herodot, Berossos, Agathias und den Alexander-Historikern, in: *Von Sumer bis Homer*, edited by R. Rollinger (Münster, 2004), 339–397.

James, P. and M. A. van der Sluijs. "Silver": A Hurrian Phaethon. *Journal of Ancient Near Eastern Religions* 12 (2012), 237–252.

Jasink, A. M. and M. Marino. The West Anatolian Origins of the Que Kingdom Dynasty. *Studi Micenei ed Egeo-Anatolici* 49 (2007), 407–426.

Koch, K. Hazzi-Safon-Kasion. Die Geschichte eines Berges und seiner Gottheiten, in: *Religionsgeschichtliche Beziehungen zwischen Kleinasien, Nordsyrien und dem Alten Testament. Internationales Symposion Hamburg 17. -21. März 1990*, edited by B. Janowski et al. (Freiburg; Göttingen, 1993), 171–223.

Kristiansen, K. and T. Larsson. *The Rise of Bronze Age Society: Travels, Transmissions and Transformations* (Cambridge, 2005).

Lane Fox, R. *Travelling Heroes: Greeks and Their Myths in the Epic Age of Homer* (London, 2008).

Lesky, A. Hethitische Texte und griechischer Mythos. *Anzeiger der Österreichischen Akademie der Wissenschaften, Phil.-hist. Klasse*, 9 (1950), 137–159 (= *Gesammelte Schriften* [Bern, 1966], 356–371).

Lopez-Ruiz, C. *When the Gods Were Born: Greek Cosmogonies and the Near East* (Cambridge, Mass., 2010).

Lopez-Ruiz, C. *Ancient Mediterranean Myths: Primary Sources from Ancient Greece, Rome and the Near East* (New York; Oxford, 2013).

Louden, B. Iapetus and Japheth: Hesiod's *Theogony*, *Iliad* 15.187–93, and Genesis 9–10. *Illinois Classical Studies* 38 (2013), 1–22.

Lytle, E. The Strange Love of the Fish and the Goat: regional contexts and Rough Cilician religion in Oppian's Halieutica 4.308–73. *Transactions of the American Philological Association* 141:2 (2011), 333–386.

Mason, H. J. Hittite Lesbos?, in: *Anatolian Interfaces: Hittites, Greeks and Their Neighbours*, edited by M. Bachvarova et al. (Oxford, 2008).

Metcalf, Ch. *The Gods Rich in Praise. Early Greek and Mesopotamian Religious Poetry* (Oxford, 2015).

Mondi, R. Greek Mythic Thought in the Light of the Near East, in: *Approaches to Greek Myth*, edited by L. Edmunds (Baltimore; London, 1990), 142–198.

Ogden, D. *Drakōn: Dragon Myth and Serpent Cult in the Greek and Roman Worlds* (Oxford, 2013).

Pardee, D. *Ritual and Cult at Ugarit* (Atlanta, 2002).

Parker, S. B. (ed.) *Ugaritic Narrative Poetry* (Atlanta, 1997).

Polvani, A. M. Temi di mitologia anatolica tra Oriente e Occidente: il dio scomparso, in: *La questione delle influenze vicino-orientali sulla religione greca: stato degli studi e prospettive della ricerca. Atti del colloquio internazionale, Roma, 20–22 maggio 1999*, edited by S. Ribichini et al. (Rome, 2001), 413–420.

Polvani, A. M. Relations between Rituals and Mythology in Official and Popular Hittite Religion, in: *Offizielle Religion, lokale Kulte und individuelle Religiosität. Akten des religionsgeschichtlichen Symposiums "Kleinasien und angrenzende Gebiete vom Beginn des 2. bis zur Mitte des*

1. Jahrtausends v. Chr." (Bonn, 20.–22. Februar 2003), edited by M. Hutter and S. Hutter-Braunsar (Münster, 2004), 369–376.

Polvani, A. M. The God Eltara and the Theogony. *Studi Micenei ed Egeo-Anatolici* 50 (2008), 617–624.

Pongratz-Leisten, B. The Mythology of the Warrior God in Text, Ritual and Cultic Commentaries, and the Shaping of Marduk's Kingship. *Journal of the Canadian Society for Mesopotamian Studies* 7 (2014), 13–18.

Pongratz-Leisten, B. *Religion and Ideology in Assyria* (Boston, 2015).

Rutherford, I. The Song of the Sea (*SA* A-AB-BA SIR^3).Thoughts on KUB 45.63, in: *Akten des IV. International Kongresses für Hethitologie, Würzburg, 4.–8. Oktober 1999*, edited by G. Wilhelm (Wiesbaden, 2001), 598–609.

Rutherford, I. Hesiod and the Literary Traditions of the Near East, in: *Brill's Companion to Hesiod*, edited by F. Montanari et al. (Leiden, 2009), 9–35.

Rutherford, I. Ea and the Beast. The Hittite Text and its Relation to the Greek Poetry, in: *Hethitische Literatur: Überlieferungsprozesse, Textstrukturen, Ausdrucksformen und Nachwirken: Akten des Symposiums vom 18. bis 20. Februar 2010 in Bonn*, edited by M. Hutter and S. Hutter-Braunsar (Münster, 2011), 217–226.

Rutherford, I. Sandas in Translation, in: *Hittitology Today: Studies on Hittite and Neo-Hittite Anatolia in Honor of Emmanuel Laroche's 100th Birthday/L'hittitologie aujourd'hui : études sur l'Anatolie hittite et néo-hittite à l'occasion du centenaire de la naissance d'Emmanuel Laroche. IFEA, ed. by A. Mouton (Istanbul, 2017), 81–100.

Salvini, M. and I. Wegner. *Die mythologischen Texte [Corpus der hurritischen Sprachdenkmäler 6]* (Rome, 2004).

Smith, M. S. *God in Translation: Deities in Cross-Cultural Discourse in the Biblical World* (Tübingen, 2008).

Solmsen, F. The Two Near Eastern Sources of Hesiod. *Hermes* 117 (1989), 413–422.

Stamatopoulou, Z. *Hesiod and Classical Greek Poetry. Reception and Transformation in the Fifth Century BCE* (Cambridge, 2016).

Strauss Clay, J. *Hesiod's Cosmos* (Cambridge, 2003).

Strauss Clay, J., Gilan A. The Hittite "Song of Emergence" and the Theogony. *Philologus* 158: 1 (2014), 1–9.

Tarenzi, V. Patroclo θεράπων. *Quaderni urbinati di cultura classica* 80 (2005), 25–38.

Tsagalis, C. Typhon and Eumelus' *Titanomachy*. *Trends in Classics* 5 (2013), 19–48.

van Dongen, E. The 'Kingship in Heaven'-Theme of the Hesiodic *Theogony*: origin, function, composition. *Greek, Roman and Byzantine Studies* 51 (2011), 180–201.

van Dongen, E. The Hittite Song of Going Forth (CTH 344): a reconsideration of the narrative. *Die Welt des Orients* 42 (2012), 23–84.

Velde, H. te. *Seth, God of Confusion: a Study of his Role in Egyptian Mythology and Religion* (Leiden, 1967).

Vernant, J. P. The Myth of Prometheus in Hesiod, in: *Myth and Society in Ancient Greece* [tr. J. Lloyd] (Brighton, 1980), 168–185.

Versnel, H. S. Greek Myth and Ritual: the case of Kronos, in: *Interpretations of Greek Mythology*, edited by J. Bremmer (London, 1987), 121–152.

Watkins, C. *How to Kill a Dragon* (New York, 1995).

West, M. L. *The East Face of Helicon* (Oxford, 1997).

West, M. L. *Indo-European Poetry and Myth* (Oxford, 2007).

Witzel, M. *The Origins of the World's Mythologies* (Oxford, 2012).

Ziegler, N. *Les musiciens et la musique d'après les archives de Mari (Florilegium Marianum IX)* (Paris, 2007).

Catherine M. Draycott
Making Meaning of Myth

On the Interpretation of Mythological Imagery in the Polyxena Sarcophagus and the Kızılbel Tomb and the History of Achaemenid Asia Minor

This paper concerns the interpretation of mythological images decorating two tombs dating to the later sixth and early fifth century BC in Asia Minor and their meaning for understanding the cultural and social history of the peninsula following its incorporation into the Achaemenid Persian Empire in the 540s BC.[1] It has two overlapping aims. One is methodological: to wrestle with how one might use mythological images as valuable historical evidence while still appreciating the hermeneutic problems that affect interpretation – an issue which intersects with much broader debates about how one "makes meaning" of visual, and other, evidence. The other is historical: to show how important attention to the content of these tomb images is for grasping regional dynamics that emerged in one part of the Achaemenid Empire's vast territories – a "satellite view" approach that can allow one to transcend sticking points in iconographic interpretation to still draw useful historical conclusions.

The two tombs concerned – the richly sculpted marble Polyxena Sarcophagus from the Granicus Plain in northwest Turkey and the painted tomb chamber at Kızılbel in southwest Turkey – are unusual for the time in their employment of extensive mythological narrative imagery. Asia Minor was the locus of many ancient myths known from Greek sources – not least the Trojan War – and although local literature is lacking, one imagines that such myths or versions of them were as widely shared here as they were among the predominantly Greek-speaking parts of the Mediterranean. Certainly we know that founder stories, epic myth histories and hero cults were embraced by various groups seeking to make their mark, and this only seems to have increased after the Achaemenid conquest.[2] Yet the display of mythological imagery is not abundant. Besides in the Greek temples on the coasts (most notably in the frieze of the temple of Athena at Assus), it may also have been seen in architectural terracottas

1 I am indebted to Lucy Audley-Miller and Beate Dignas for their invitation to prepare this paper, to those who gave feedback at the conference and to colleagues at the British Institute at Ankara and Durham University, especially Sophie Moore and Pam Graves. I would also like to express my indebtedness to Peter Stewart, whose writing and whose bestowal on me of his teaching at The Courtauld Institute of Art in 2011–12 stimulated thinking that fed into this paper. Naturally, however, only the author is responsible for infelicities or errors.

2 Rose 2008; Dusinberre 2013, 222–5; MacSweeney 2013; Draycott 2015. Association of tumuli in the Troad with Greek (and other) fallen heroes: Cook 1973, 159–65 and 87, fig. 9; Rose 1998; 2013, 61–3; Rose and Körpe 2016.

https://doi.org/10.1515/9783110421453-004

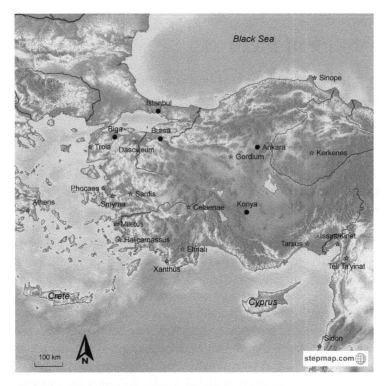

Fig. 1: Map of Asia Minor. By author using Stepmap.com.

adorning buildings; a handful known so far bear mythological-looking themes. The clay painted Clazomenian sarcophagi used in Ionia on the west coast include some myths among the subjects shown, but otherwise there are mostly limited examples of mythological creatures (sphinxes, siren-like creatures and gorgon heads). Only the Tatarlı Tomb near Celaenae in southwest Phrygia (Fig. 1), of the middle of the fifth century BC – later, then, than the two tombs considered here – also seems to have contained at least one mythological narrative (Heracles stealing the cattle of Geryon) alongside other non-mythological themes.[3] Myth may have been most frequently encountered on imported Attic painted pottery, which, as it happens, increased at some sites in the wake of the Persian conquest.

Even if other tombs with mythological imagery come to light, this would not necessarily shift the impression that the Polyxena Sarcophagus and the Kızılbel Tomb were then something of a novelty in their environs, and novelties which have something to do with the kind of economic and social changes ushered in with the Achaemenid Empire, including the above-mentioned pottery importation. The Polyxena Sarcoph-

---

3 Summerer and von Kienlin 2010, 144–50.

agus has been the subject of a great deal of discussion concerning its sculptures and their meaning in political context, but questions concerning identification of its subjects and owners still affect its interpretation. The earlier Kızılbel Tomb, excavated in the 1970s, has not received as much attention, especially recently. Discussions have tended to focus on identification of subjects – particularly problematic here – and on the relevance of the images to death and/or the self-representation of the deceased, with little in the way of historical conclusions.

Here the primary concern is historical conclusions and the methods by which one can reach these with any success. In what follows, I first provide an overview of issues surrounding interpretation that are implicit in any attempt to use imagery, especially mythological imagery, as historical evidence, before moving on to discuss each of the tombs and their thematic packages. Within those sections some new ideas about the identification of certain subjects are included. The main *foci*, though, are how far one can reconstruct meanings that particular themes may have had in their sepulchral and local contexts, and how the phenomenon of these unusual displays allows insights into the history of Achaemenid Asia Minor that might otherwise be overlooked.

Myth, Meaning and Method

Myths do not mean anything by themselves. Of course, they do not exist, God-like, by themselves either, as if they preceded their rendering. They are entirely the product of human imagination. This is just as true for their making as for their understanding, both in the past and now, millennia after the first elements of what they would come to be were uttered. Both utterance and reception are necessary for myths to wander through time and space, and integral components for their transformation through cycles of making/telling, understanding, and respinning. The acts of making and receiving are thus paired; a maker receives information and expresses an understanding of it on some level in their work, whether consciously and coherently or not. A recipient of this expression makes sense of it, as best they can, referring to conventional ideas with which they are familiar, or digging and doing conscious research. They may themselves go on to make a new expression: an imitation; a retelling; a translation; an explanation.

Scholars of the ancient world are receivers of myths, whether in textual or pictorial form, and makers of explanations. And our explanations are particular to the kinds of stories that we want to tell. In this sense, we make myth mean particular things according to our needs. This is not quite the same thing as "making sense" of myth, although to a certain extent this is semantic word play. "Making meaning", as opposed to "making sense", simply acknowledges our agency in the production of explanations, allowing for the imposition of our particular *foci*, how this might tailor our understandings, and point us in certain directions.[4] This is totally different from saying that we wilfully make things up. It is rare for someone engaged in scholarship to make things up; it is obvious that scholars, like others, take certain angles on things, look at things through particular lenses – whatever metaphor one wants to use.

A main kind of narrative that scholars of the ancient classical world tend to want to produce nowadays concerns social and cultural history, reconstructing not so much past events, but attitudes, understandings and mindsets. Social significance had been considered in earlier studies of classical art, particularly in studies of symbolic meanings of tomb and religious images, but the kind of socio-cultural history of which I speak – *histoire des mentalités* – is really indebted to the French structuralist approaches that spread from the "semiotic turn" in linguistics through the anthropology associated with Claude Lévi-Strauss and into multiple other fields, including ancient history (the *Annales* school), classics and classical archaeology in the second half of the twentieth century.[5] Influenced by this, studies of myth focused not on determining origins – the etymology – of the stories, but on semiotic meanings and importantly their function within and for society (*social functionalism*).[6] Studies of classical (and other) art took similar approaches, the term "visual culture" coming to be preferred to "art history", which some see as loaded with concepts of connoisseurship and excluding the full range of visual materials, some of which might not usually be considered "art".[7] Further work nuancing structuralist approaches especially associated with Michel Foucault, sometimes classed as post-structuralist, directed special attention to variations and changes in contextual meaning (*relativism*), and above all to the construction of power and identity (*social constructionism*). The plethora of works appearing in the later twentieth century, far beyond merely the study of classical art, incorporating phrases such as "Art and Society", "Power and Image" or "Identity and Art" in their titles is testament to the influence of these approaches.[8] The tenets of the approach are to look for evidence outside the monument or image itself in order to

---

4 For use of similar phrasing see Elsner 2016. On methods in interpretation of mythological images see Junker 2012, esp. 14–5 for thoughts related to making of meaning (although importantly he does not use that term); Lorenz 2016, which I have unfortunately not been able to take full advantage of as it appeared after the production of this paper.

5 For some earlier interpretative approaches to Roman funerary art, esp. the work of Franz Cumont and Arthur Nock's criticisms of it, see e.g. Elsner 2010; Zanker and Ewald 2012, 1–55, esp. 18–21; Elsner 2016; also Junker 2012, 161–3.

6 For Greek myth see especially Vernant et al. 1990.

7 Fundamental on conventional meanings of art in historical contexts: Panofsky 1955; on structuralism in classical art, especially Greek vases, inter alia: Bérard 1989; Lissarrague 2001, with comments by Robin Osborne 1991; summarising structuralist approaches, especially to images on Greek vases: Stansbury-O'Donnell 2011. Again, for overviews: Stewart 2008; Junker 2012; and now Lorenz 2016, who usefully compares Panofsky's iconological approach with the semiotic (structural) approach.

8 For a good and accessible discussion, which brings in "self-representation" as discussed below, see Stewart 2008, 39–76.

narrow down not only aspects of physical and temporal context, but for the thought worlds of which the monuments were once a part, often employing ancient literature as a major tool for this.

Although not usually referred to as such, a school of work along these lines has arisen, led by German scholars such as Paul Zanker and Klaus Fittschen, and in Anglophone scholarship by R. R. R. Smith, with a primary focus on analysing constructions of visual identities in ancient art, especially in portraiture and memorials.[9] Within these two areas this can be referred to as "self-representation" (*Selbstdarstellung* in German) – a term which does not mean "self-portraiture", *per se*, and indeed may not even comprise human figures. Rather, the term conveys the idea that images functioned to meet the needs of consumers rather than how they conveyed ideas attributable solely to their makers.[10] Further, in ancient "self-representation", images selected for display are usually not taken to represent *individual* personality traits as much as *social personae* – types of persons that one could be or aspire to be within one's society, within an often constrained and conservative range.[11] Concerning the use of mythological imagery, with which this paper is concerned, one can cite above all studies of its use in the rich reliefs adorning Roman sarcophagi, where tales of heroism or virtue, for instance, might allude to qualities intended to be attributed to the deceased, and sometimes do this directly through the inclusion of portrait heads on protagonists.[12] Such studies also, though, admit meanings less directly linked to constructions of social identity and "self-representation"; tales of unfortunate death and loss, for example, although relevant to the memory of the deceased may be more meaningful in terms of the grief felt by survivors than in terms of the persona of the deceased.[13]

Whether close analysis of the narrative nuances and the semiotics of visual language in individual works, or observations of broader chronological and spatial patterns, this kind of historical, contextual approach to imagery has made profound contributions to our understanding of the past, illuminating much that is not available

---

9 E.g. inter alia Fittschen and Zanker 1983–2014; Smith 1988; Zanker 1988; 1995; Smith 2002; Smith et al. 2006. Barbara Borg's work is also very significant here (see e.g. her article in this volume), as well as Tonio Hölscher, several of whose works are referred to further below (e.g. n. 11).

10 See Smith 2002; again, see Stewart 2008 as per n. 8 above.

11 This idea of "social personae" has similarities to the concept of social "roles" as outlined by Hölscher 2008, esp. 52–4, where, however, he pits this against "identity", which he sees as too loaded with modern values. Cf. also on mythological themes Hölscher 2011, where the problem with "identity" seems mostly with uncritical assumptions about expressions of group (ethnic, cultural, national) identity, and where he is more ambivalent about the utility of the term. This ambivalence can be further compared to his concern about the extent of meaning attributable to mythological themes in architectural sculpture: Hölscher 2009; see n. 20 below.

12 Most obviously see Zanker and Ewald 2012.

13 Cf. the expansive discussion of how myth on Roman sarcophagi could function as various kinds of *exempla*, including exemplary deaths and grieving, by Barbara Borg in this volume.

from textual sources. Indeed, much more than supplying "extra" information, this work shows how fundamental attention to art and archaeology is for any endeavour to comprehend the past, for visual and material culture was very pervasive, spread through the whole of society, bound up in the practices and experiences of a huge proportion of ancient populaces. The historical approach to ancient art has not escaped some criticism, however. Despite the fact that it moves away from the intentions of the maker, it tends to incorporate, or does not distance itself from, notions of intentional meanings. French post-structuralist thinking, this time associated most with the *deconstructionism* of Jacques Derrida, has stressed the vagaries of communication and the problems of locating meaning, which may not be clearly formulated by the utterer and may at the other end be received and interpreted variously.[14] Context, which one tends to think of as exerting control over understanding, is, to some extent anyway, individually constructed – a part of the whole field of constructing meaning rather than an external, reliable constant. In that sense, at its farthest extreme one might argue that fixing an originally intended meaning or normal understanding of an utterance, a story, an image, *in context* is a futile endeavour.

The impact of these concerns, which have been more pronounced in other areas of archaeology and art history, are seen in another school of approach to classical art which privileges the viewer over consumer as a locus of meaning.[15] This work is not deconstructionist, abandoning the idea of finding meaning, but draws attention to the slippery and ambiguous nature of images, and greater varieties of what one might think of as "portable" contexts dependent on differing viewer backgrounds (class, gender, ethnic affiliations, religious beliefs), which may have generated different categories of meaning.[16] In this work *historicism* can be represented negatively. One might say, however, that it is the *quality* of historicism which is really at issue. It would not be fair to say that all work that might be classed as "historicist" insists that the meanings derived (or better, reconstructed) were *intended*, exactly, or that the viewer's share in creating meaning is rejected. Within the above-mentioned studies of Roman sarcophagi, for example, one often finds admission that the power of the depictions of mythological stories lies in part in their capacity to stimulate the imaginations and discussion of viewers, necessarily therefore admitting some level of

---

14 E.g. Derrida 1988.

15 Most prominently Elsner 1995; 2007. Other work on viewing and response in classical archaeology, inter alia: Osborne 2000; Stewart 2003; Barringer 2008; for an overview see Stewart 2008, 123–42. More generally on the meaning of art in terms of its affective nature rather than content: Freedberg 1989; Gell 1998. Cf. also Jordanova 2012, 154–87 on what she terms "audiences" and responses. For influence of deconstructionism in post-processual archaeology, inter alia: Shanks and Tilley 1987a; 1987b; Bapty and Yates 1990; Tilley 1991; Whitley 1998. See now also Davis 2015. Summaries of the archaeological theory: Johnson 1999, esp. 98–115; Wylie 2002, 171–8.

16 Cf. especially Elsner 2015, 56–7, 59 and 63–70.

subjectivity.[17] On the other hand, while questioning intentionality, and accepting levels of ambiguity and subjectivity, more recently a "post-reception" reaction from some scholars points out that meanings and understandings were (and are) not unlimited.[18] The real bugbear is not necessarily the idea of intended or conventionally understood meanings, *per se*, or the notion that one might be able to control at least some *probabilities* of these, but the idea of *specific* meanings, in particular that images can be read as kinds of symbolic, encoded *messages*, often political or religious messages. This is an issue long discussed in the interpretation of mythological images in architectural sculpture, where there are cases that remain notoriously difficult to understand (one thinks of the friezes of the Siphnian Treasury or the centauromachy on the temple of Zeus at Olympia).[19] Two main poles that might be called "strong"/"maximal" and "soft"/"weak" interpretations tend to be perceptible, the one extreme being speculative, the other including proposals that at least some of the figured sculptural programmes from the ancient world may have been more decorative than didactic.[20]

To say they might be decorative is not to dispute that imagery is historically meaningful, however. In the first place, things need to be judged on a case-by-case basis. It is clear that some images were carefully contrived to convey particular ideas, even if not everyone (or anyone) really understood them. Other images were not so carefully chosen. But even imagery that was not intended to be strictly meaningful in terms of didactic, symbolic messages can be placed into broader patterns in order to gain a sense of qualities of behaviour. The same in fact needs to be done even where one feels able to narrow down probabilities of intended or conventionally understood meanings; arguably it is only by placing this into broader patterns of behaviour that one can draw historical conclusions. It is toward this end that this paper now proceeds: it considers probabilities of intended meanings/common understandings (not quite the same thing) of the themes shown on the Polyxena Sarcophagus and the Kızılbel Tomb, but also emphasises how the use of myth in these tombs can be made meaningful by appreciating it more generally as a particular strategy of distinction – a strategy that, seen within broader geo-economic contexts, reveals regional dynamics that are important additions to the history of Achaemenid Asia Minor, and which, it should be stressed, would go unnoticed *without* attention to the art.

---

17 E.g. Junker 2012, 117–8, and especially 187–96, where he discusses seeing images of myth as having a "reflective" capacity; at 188, however, he explicitly *rejects* the notion that they are "polysemic"; Zanker and Ewald 2012, 26–7, 31, 37 and 49, where they speak of "openness" of the images but at the same time advocate main intended meanings; see also Borg in this volume; on themes on public architecture see Ridgway 1999, 9–10, acknowledging Freedberg 1989 and Schneider 2016, passim.

18 See e.g. Stewart 2008, 125; Junker 2012, as noted in n. 17 above, and 122–3; Audley-Miller 2016, 554, citing Stewart 2007, 166–75; Tanner 2007, 82–3 and 91; Borg in this volume. One can add here Elsner 2015, where he discusses the necessity, but also the problems associated with using images as empirical evidence toward histories, with further references to Robin Osborne's work.

19 Buitron-Oliver 1997; Ridgway 1999; Schultz and von den Hoff 2009.

20 Hölscher 2009, noted in John Ma's review: Ma 2011.

The Polyxena Sarcophagus and the Granicus Plain

The Polyxena Sarcophagus was an astonishing find made after reports of tomb robbing in the Granicus (modern Biga) River Plain in 1994.[21] This area of northwest Anatolia (Fig. 2) was high traffic and complicated in its political geography. Strabo, writing in the early Roman Empire, names multiple groups living in the area in his day, among them Mysians, Phrygians, Bithynians and various Thracian groups (Str. 12.1.3, 12.4–6, 12.8.2–7, 13.1.1, 13.1.8). He places the Biga Plain in the Troad, separated from Mysia to its east by the Aisepus River (Str. 12.4–6), but the area may have been part of "Mysia" in earlier periods.[22] It is also often associated with Hellespontine Phrygia – a term usually applied to the whole of an Achaemenid Persian satrapy with a seat at Daskyleion, but which may have referred to an earlier northwest Phrygian-speaking polity.[23] The use of Daskyleion as a Persian administrative centre may have started not long after the conquest of Anatolia, but there seems to have been a new period of activity and building at that site in the period after the Persian War battles of 480 and 479, when a dynasty of satraps is attested.[24] Along the coastline were Greek colonies including the nearby cities of Cyzicus and Parion, and Greek nobles are known to have held estates in the area.[25] There may, in fact, have been a generally Greek-identifying settlement group in the Biga River delta area between Cyzicus and Parion: the remains of a pair of small (c. 2 m high) Ionic columns thought to date to the late sixth or early fifth century found at Biga, one with a boustrophedon dedicatory inscription in Ionic Greek mentioning a temple committee and *temenos* income, imply an organised Ionian community.[26] The Polyxena Sarcophagus itself was found near a site thought to have been ancient Didymateiche (or Didymon Teichos – Double Wall). The name is found in the later fifth-century Athenian Tribute Lists, indicating the town joined the Delian League, a point raised in support of a majority Greek-speaking populace.[27] Since the name "Daskyleion" also appears in those lists and the Lycians certainly joined the League, however, one might be cautious about leaping to conclusions about an exclu-

---

21 Sevinç and Rose 1996; Rose 2014, 72–103. Neer 2012 is crucial for references to flourishing literature on the sarcophagus.

22 Xenophon notes recalcitrant Mysians in the mountains of the Troad during the later fifth century BC (*Hell.* 10–15): Ma 2008.

23 On "Mysia" and "Hellespontine Phrygia" inter alia: Osborne 1975; Carrington 1977; Schwertheim 1988; Bakır 2001; Trachsel 2002; Fiedler 2003, 29–31; Maffre 2007. Also comments in Draycott (forthcoming).

24 In Xenophon's *Cyropaedia* (8.6.7) Cyrus gives the satrapy already to Pharnuchos. On the possibility that the satrapal seat was not fully established before c. 480 BC see Kaptan 2002, esp. 5–8 and 211.

25 Greeks holding estates: Austin 1990; Briant 2002, esp. 561–3.

26 Robert and Robert 1950, 78–80; 1951, 186 no. 87; Koenigs 1989.

27 Didymateiche, identified with Dimetoka in the area of the Granicus tumuli: Leaf 1923, 71 and map (uncertain about identification); Robert 1937, 195; Meritt et al. 1939, 481; Neer 2012.

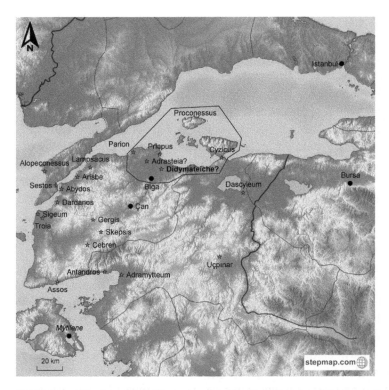

Fig. 2: Map of Northwest Asia Minor showing sites in the Troad and Hellespontine Phrygia. Modern Turkish province boundaries shown. Potential networked area exploiting the Proconessian marble quarries between Cyzicus, Proconessus, Parion and the Biga Plain outlined. By author using Stepmap.com

sively Greek political and linguistic zone. Greek-speakers were clearly living in the Biga area, but there may have been other languages spoken, and the idea that these different groups should be distinguishable through material and visual culture, or practices, may be particularly confounded in this diverse area.

This is to say that the ethno-linguistic identity of the owners of the Polyxena Sarcophagus is unclear – a point to which I shall return. The sarcophagus itself was found under one of a number of tumuli scattered through the landscape of the Biga Plain, which seem to have proliferated in the wake of the Persian conquest of Asia Minor in the 540s BC.[28] Unlike some of the other tumuli, which contained stone built tomb chambers similar to those found in other areas of Asia Minor, especially Lydia, the aptly named Kizöldün (Dead Girl) Tumulus did not contain such a chamber, but only two sarcophagi: a smaller and plainer one found in an upper layer which was used

---

28 Survey of the valley and tumuli: Rose, et al. 2007; Rose and Körpe 2009; Rose 2014; Rose and Körpe 2016. Burials in Lydia: Roosevelt 2009.

for a child, and the Polyxena Sarcophagus, which sat at ground level in the centre of the mound, clearly the original deposition on this spot.[29] The Polyxena Sarcophagus is anything but plain. About the height of an average human, it is lavishly decorated with an imitation gabled, tiled roof, Ionic egg and dart mouldings, and dentils. All four sides of the main chest are finely carved with large archaic-Greek-style figurative relief sculptures including the death of the eponymous Trojan princess, Polyxena (Fig. 3). The sculptural style has suggested to some a date in the late sixth century BC, although there are similarities to the archaic-style reliefs on the chest at the top of a large pillar-type tomb from Lycia: the Harpy Monument, which (although with some debate) is often dated to around 480 BC.[30] There is even some possibility that it could be later: despite the clear frontal eyes and silhouette of the figures, which recall Greek sculptures of the second half of the sixth century BC, the dress style, in particular the *sakkos* headdress shown on many of the women in the reliefs, is most prevalent in Attic vase paintings of the first half of the fifth century BC. Some have argued, too, that the dentils included in the architectural decoration are canonical in the fifth century, not before.[31] Precision on dating therefore is difficult, but generally the monument can be placed in a half century, c. 510–460 BC. This seems to have been a period when settlements and smaller groups in the area increasingly exploited the marble quarries on Proconnesus for monumental building, and one might posit that this was first dominated by a network between the Greek colonies of Cyzicus and Parion (Fig. 2) before the marble was brought in for satrapal building projects at Daskyleion.[32]

The relief sculptures on the sarcophagus have been the topic of much discussion not only because of their extent and quality, but for the rarity of the themes and especially for the preponderance of women in them. Running along two sides of the sarcophagus, usually prioritised through their labelling as Sides A and B, is a continuous scene of the sacrifice of the Trojan princess Polyxena over the grave of Achilles – an episode of the Trojan cycle known from the *Ilioupersis* attributed to Arctinus of Miletus, and fifth-century BC works such as Euripides' *Trojan Women* and *Hecuba*, and a lost play on Polyxena herself by Sophocles.[33] The composition is tripartite over the two

---

29 One chambered tomb: the Dedetepe Tumulus, near Çeşmealtı: Sevinç and Rose 1998; Rose 2014, 117–28. Similar tumulus burials with chamber tombs have been found around Daskyleion and further east: Bakır 1991; Bakır and Gusmani 1993; Kütük 1995; Kökten Ersoy 1998; Kökten 1998; Bakır, et al. 2002. An unusual "tholos" type chamber near Çan, further inland along the Biga River, contained the Hunt sarcophagus: Sevinç et al. 2002; Ma 2008; Rose 2014, 129–42. The Child's Sarcophagus above the Polyxena Sarcophagus: Sevinç and Rose 1999; Rose 2014, 104–15.
30 Harpy Monument, London, British Museum B 287: Rudolph 2003; Draycott 2007.
31 Ateşlier and Öncü 2004.
32 Biga columns and tombs already mentioned, but also fifth-century buildings and tombs at Daskyleion associated with the satrapal dynasty there (see n. 24, above): Ateşlier 1999; 2001; Aytekin 2007; Karagöz 2007; Karagöz 2013.
33 *LIMC* 7, s.v. "Polyxene" (Touchefeu-Meynier); Calder 1966; Neer 2012, esp. 99 n. 7 for references to poetic fragments.

Fig. 3: The Polyxena Sarcophagus. From Rose (2014), 80, fig. 3.7 (Troia slide 19937). Reproduced with the kind permission of C. Brian Rose.

sides: on the left end of the long Side A is a file of mourning Trojan women (Fig. 4). On the right end the princess is shown being held horizontally by several males distinguished by their short *chitons* and short or bound hair. One, by tradition Neoptolemus, the son of Achilles, grabs her hair and drives a sword into her throat while she struggles, legs kicking and torso twisting. On the far right is a large tumulus with a tripod before it: the tomb of Achilles.[34] The edge of the tumulus overlaps onto the left corner of the short Side B, where an old woman who would be Polyxena's mother Hecuba is shown seated on the ground under a leafless tree, two further Trojan women behind her.[35]

This episode is rare in art. It could be mistaken for the sacrifice of Iphegenia, the daughter of Agamemnon, whose death was demanded to bring the winds enabling the Greeks to sail to Troy in the first place.[36] Polyxena's death brackets this at the end of the war; it was demanded by the ghost of Achilles in order to bring winds to sail back home. The compositions usually differ for both princesses, the girls being led to the altar/tomb, or being shown kneeling before it; only one sixth-century Tyrrhenian

---

34 Hedreen 2001, 132–6, suggests that the tripod could refer to the burial of Achilles in a place sacred to Apollo, like his son, who according to tradition was buried at Delphi.

35 On the leafless tree as a pathetic fallacy: Neer 2012, 100.

36 *LIMC* 5, s.v. "Iphigenia" (Kahil and Icard).

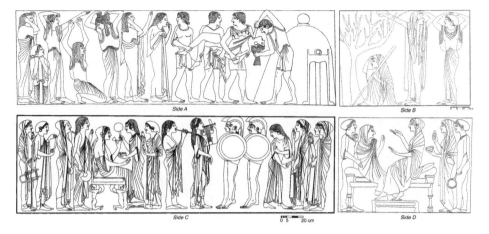

Fig. 4: Compilation of line drawings of reliefs on the four sides of the Polyxena Sarcophagus, by Kate Clayton after Nurten Sevinç. Reproduced from Rose (2014), 80, fig. 3.8, 84, fig. 3.12, 89, fig. 3.15, 92, fig. 3.18, with the kind permission of C. Brian Rose.

amphora shows a similar composition with the girl held horizontally, there with labels clearly identifying it as the sacrifice of Polyxena.[37]

Although the two other sides of the sarcophagus, labelled C and D (Fig. 4), tend to be seen as of secondary importance in the programme, they are central to interpretive questions concerning this tomb. Also organised in a tripartite division, the long side (Side C) shows on the left a seated woman surrounded by a large entourage of ladies in waiting. On the right is shown a group of four armed dancers flanked by a female playing a *kithara*, another female playing an *aulos*, a dancer with castanets and on the far right a group of female onlookers. The short side (D) shows two females seated on a *kline* (couch) flanked by attendants holding drinking implements.

The subjects of these two sides have been variously interpreted. Most scholars see non-mythological, idealised events in the life (and/or death) of a high status woman. The excavators initially proposed funerary celebrations, and Brian Rose upholds this interpretation based on the nature of the objects brought to the seated woman on Side C, which he sees as funerary.[38] In this sense, both sets of reliefs could refer to the deaths of princesses, juxtaposing mythological and historical. Others have seen the juxtaposition as one of death versus life. Very attractive is Carola Reinsberg's pro-

---

37 Tyrrhenian amphora, London, British Museum 1897.7–27.2, attributed to the Timades Painter, c. 570–60 BC: *LIMC* 7, s.v. "Polyxene" (Touchefeu-Meynier), 26*; *ABV* 97.27; *BAdd*[2], 26; Beazley Archive Pottery Database number 310027; Neer 2012, 100, who notes that interestingly some of the male figures bear Trojan names. Cf. a proto-Attic pot fragment showing a similar composition, which could also depict Polyxena, since there is no known example of Iphigenia being shown in such a prone position: *LIMC* 5, s.v. "Iphigenia" (Kahil and Icard), 2 (drawing in text).
38 Sevinç and Rose 1996; Rose 2014, 98.

posal that what is shown are preparations for a wedding (the *proaulia*), the bedecking of the bride on the left, the young bride reassured by her mother on the night before the wedding on the short side, the armed dancers part of an associated rite, perhaps to Artemis.[39] The nadir of death versus the pinnacle of life that is a wedding is a thematic opposition that would make sense as a programmatic response to grief.[40] The juxtaposition is known elsewhere, most notably for the archaic period in the inscription of the *kore* of Phrasiklea from the Attic countryside (*CEG* 24): "I am forever to be called *kore* (virgin/unmarried girl), in place of marriage this is the name the gods allotted me."[41]

Embedded in assumptions about the relevance of such a theme, however, is the idea that it is particularly relevant to a woman. This is, beside ethno-linguistic identity, the other major problem with the identity of the owners of this tomb, for surprisingly examination of the bones has concluded that its occupant was a male in his forties.[42] As Richard Neer has aptly stated, this is an "inconvenient truth".[43] Many would solve this apparent incongruity by imagining that the monument was originally made with a woman in mind, but eventually used, for whatever reason, for the burial of a man.[44] Neer explores, alternatively, how the imagery might be relevant to male identity. One possibility is that Polyxena's death may be, in part, a device to present the tomb of Achilles, a nearby landmark in the Troad, to which the grand burial of a "heroic" man might be likened.[45] As well, it is not just Polyxena who is the protagonist of the scene, but Neoptolemus, also known as Pyrrhus. Neoptolemus/Pyrrhus' eyes, Neer notes, meet those of the princess he is slaughtering in a manner recalling the locked gazes of Achilles and the Amazon queen Penthesilea as shown on a famous Attic vase painted by Exekias.[46] For Sides C and D, which are more difficult to reconcile, Neer's solution is that there may be another Pyrrhus connection: Neoptolemus/Pyrrhus was the inventor of the Pyrrhic armed dance – a choral armed dance which is the closest in style to that shown on the sarcophagus. The seated woman and musicians in particular have some parallels with a fragment of Sappho (fr. 44) that speaks of the arrival of Andro-

---

39 Reinsberg 2001; 2004. Interpreting a wedding see also: Ateşlier and Öncü 2004; Şare 2005. Rose feels the objects offered are unlike those seen in images of weddings on Attic vases: Rose 2014. See also Neer 2012 for comments and further references.

40 Şare 2005.

41 For themes bringing together marriage and death on Roman sarcophagi: Zanker and Ewald 2012, 76–77; Junker 2012, 164.

42 Sevinç et al. 2002.

43 Neer 2012, 108.

44 Neer 2012, 103–4; Rose 2014, 95–7.

45 Neer 2012.

46 Attic black-figure amphora by Exekias, London, British Museum B210: *CVA* London, British Museum 4, IIIHe.4, pl.(194) 49.2A-C; *ABV* 144.7, 672.2, 686; *Paralipomena*, 60; *BAdd*², 39; Beazley Archive Pottery Database number 310389.

mache for her wedding to Polyxena's heroic brother, Hector, the bride bedecked with finery and celebrations:

> the sweet-sounding pipe and cithara were mingled and the sound of castanets, and maidens sang clearly a holy song, and a marvellous echo reached the sky...and everywhere in the streets was ...bowls and cups...myrrh and cassia and frankincense were mingled. The elder women cried out joyfully, and all the men let forth a lovely high-pitched strain calling on Paean, the Archer skilled in the lyre, and they sang in praise of the godlike Hector and Andromache.[47]

Neoptolemus, Neer reminds us, traditionally took Andromache as his concubine after the fall of Troy. The armed dancers, taken as males rather than females *à la* Reinsberg's interpretation, could then mirror the four Greek youths, including Pyrrhus/Neoptolemus himself, shown on the other side of the sarcophagus, alluding, albeit obliquely, to him.

The meaning of the armed dancers has proved one of the most difficult aspects of the tomb's reliefs to determine and Neer's proposal would make sense of them. There is, after all, some clever compositional mirroring on this tomb. Unlike the mothers on the short sides (Hecuba, Side B, and the larger figure on the *kline*, Side D) and the princesses on the long sides (Polyxena and the seated woman), however, the armed dancers are not spatially opposite the four Greek men on the other side (one needs to imagine the sarcophagus in 3D rather than laid out as in the drawing in Fig. 4). Although one cannot exclude the *possibility* that such a connection could have been intended and/or understood, it seems perhaps too oblique to be considered highly *probable*. This borders on special pleading to make the armed dancers meaningful in the context of a male burial, and indeed to support the claim that the tomb was *intended* for a male. This is not certain.

Very intriguing in Neer's careful discussion of the long Side C, though, is the relation to the fragment of Sappho, for this opens up the possibility that Sides C, and perhaps D too, could also be mythological, depicting the wedding of Andromache – an *epitome* of a wedding known, as Sappho's fragment shows, in archaic poetry. As Neer notes, the scene includes almost all of the elements indicated in the fragment – with the exception of the armed dancers. They could, however, complement such a theme rather than detract from it, adding to the grandiosity of *royal-level* festivities. They might even add a Phrygian touch: as well as rites to Artemis, pointed out by Reinsberg, the Phrygian Corybantes were well-known armed dancers. The rendering of what looks like a Pyrrhic dance might not specifically identify it as that, rather than a formal armed dance in general. And one need not see a specific rite as much as a general nod to Phrygian musical and performance practices that might suit Troy, imagined as a Phrygian-related (if not exactly Phrygian) city.[48]

---

47 Trans. Campbell 1990, 88–91; cf. Neer 2012, 108.
48 Homer does not say that the city was Phrygian itself, but had Phrygian allies.

Without a clear male protagonist, such a mythological/legendary wedding might still seem best suited to the memorial of a female. The preponderance of women shown on the tomb, including female protagonists, and the fact that the seated woman on Side C (perhaps Andromache) can be seen as a very grandiose version of the "mistress and maid" formula, usually unquestioningly associated with women's memorials, supports this.[49] Assumptions of gendering in memorial practices might be confounded by, for instance, women being buried with items such as weaponry, but the analogy is not sound;[50] there are no good comparanda for men being memorialised *deliberately* with such female-rich imagery. The Mourning Women's Sarcophagus from Sidon is different, as the women on the sides of that tomb are shown lamenting – a traditional female role which has no bearing on the gender of the person within the tomb.[51]

If one assumes that the sexing of the bones found in the sarcophagus is correct, however, then clearly the tomb *was* used for the burial of a man.[52] Resistance to the idea that such a monument could have been made for a woman and then used by a man seems to stem in part from an underlying idea that this is a *problem*, both in terms of a woman powerful enough to commission such a grandiose tomb and in terms of gender specific iconography. Although unusual, this need not be a problem. It is known that there were powerful women in Anatolia. In fact, one such woman, Mania, inherited rule of the Dardanos (Troad) itself from her husband in the fourth century BC (Xen. *Hell.* 3.1.10–26). The Polyxena Sarcophagus could well have been made for a woman of very high status, then, but used for a male burial due to its exceptional quality, iconographic relevance being a relatively minor consideration. Although geographically and temporally distant, that this is not culturally inconceivable is suggested by the fifteenth-century AD chapel of Anne Herlyng at East Harling in Norfolk, England, in which her husband, who predeceased her, was buried, while she went on to marry again, being buried elsewhere.[53] If one needs to have a man as commissioner, it is also possible for a husband to commission a grand tomb *for* a very high status/

---

49 The mistress and maid theme on Attic white *lekythoi*, with possibilities they are related to wedding imagery: Kurtz 1988; Reilly 1989; Sabetai 1994; Oakley 2000. On classical Attic grave stelai for women: Stears 1995; Leader 1997. Similar scenes on stelai taken as women's from the Black Sea area: Akurgal 1955; Akyüz 2013; Laflı and Meischner 2015. One from Daskyleion: Polat 2007. Two other stelai from inland western Anatolia, one in Afyon museum, the other from Lydia: Uçankuş 2002, 4–85, bottom left (Afyon Stele); Roosevelt 2009, cat. 18.1B, fig. 6.24 (Lydia stele).

50 Women buried with weapons: Arnold 1995.

51 Mourning Women sarcophagus from Sidon, now in Istanbul Archaeological Museum: Fleischer 1983.

52 N.B. a report has not been published, and sexing of bones can be very problematic, so what specifically led to the identification of a male here would be a welcome addition to the literature. Rose simply states that the bones are "unquestionably male": Rose 2014, 95. Bias in sexing of bones: Weiss 1972; Dennison 1979; Morris 1992, 81–2; Parker Pearson 1999, 95–6.

53 Graves 2000, 77–83.

highly-valued wife. If he predeceased her this may have led to his being buried within, while his wife was eventually buried elsewhere, for whatever reason.

There is also the possibility, though, that the iconography of the Polyxena Sarcophagus need not have been designed with explicit relevance for gender identity in the first place. This is not to say that there are no examples of gendered iconographies; as noted above, the pattern of usage of the "mistress and maid" scheme suggests that there were, and in most of the (admittedly few) cases in which bones have been found in decorated tombs in archaic and classical Asia Minor and identified as male the themes include such traditionally male spheres as hunting and battle, with male protagonists.[54] But given the exceptional nature of the Polyxena Sarcophagus, it could be a special case in which themes epitomising lamentation of death and celebration of life were selected with less concern for gender than modern and perhaps even other ancient viewers might expect. Although not a perfect parallel, Roman sarcophagi bearing myths involving female protagonists offer examples of how themes that might seem gendered could be used for single male or multi-gender burials.[55] And without needing the Pyrrhus-Pyrrhic dance connection, one could see how even the wedding of Andromache could swing both ways, the death and loss of Hector (and plenty of tragedy besides) intimately bound up in the theme.

The themes, then, could have been intended to resonate not primarily in terms of gender, but in other ways. One other way, as recognised by most, is through strong relevance to the locality. As noted above, Strabo placed the Biga Plain in the Troad – the territory of Troy. Whether or not the site of Hısarlık associated with Homer's Ilion later on was already recognised as such at this point, its connection with the Hellespontine area would have been alive. By the fifth century BC, if not earlier, tumuli and hillocks were identified as the tombs of Greek heroes such as Achilles and Patroclus, and as Rose points out in the vicinity of the Biga plain, the Ethiopian hero Memnon.[56] The Polyxena relief not only shows the tomb of Achilles, a local landmark, but an event (perhaps events) in the myth-history of the area.

As indicated above, another difficulty of narrowing down meaning of the images on this tomb is whether they had particular relevance for different groups living in the area. Scholars tend to be divided over whether the tomb was intended for and used by a Greek family or a "native" Anatolian family, perhaps Mysians or Phrygians. Concerning "native Anatolians", there were traditions of the survival of Trojan princes taken as founders of later communities.[57] Neer points out that the Teukrians at Gergis further inland in the mountains (the seat of the above-mentioned Mania and her husband),

---

54 As noted by Rose 2014, 96.
55 See examples especially concerning tragedy of death (Niobe and her children) and marriage and death (Medea sarcophagi) in Zanker and Ewald 2012. This is also discussed by Borg in this volume.
56 See n. 2 above.
57 Carrington 1977.

considered themselves descendants of Troy.[58] The use of Trojan myths could be seen as part of intensifying ethnogenesis in an area with increasingly high traffic, changing occupancies and threats to land ownership under the Achaemenid Empire, perhaps especially around the time of the Ionian Revolt and Persian Wars. On the other hand, however, there were also Greek-speakers living in the Biga Plain area. As Neer has pointed out, the myth(s) employed here could be "read" from a Greek perspective too, since not only was the Trojan War one in which the Greeks were victorious, but there are references to Greek heroes and, in particular, to the tomb of Achilles, with which our tomb might be compared. Sarcophagi were used in Ionia, for instance on the island of Samos, so the burial custom itself is not necessarily "native" Anatolian, and there is nothing inherently Achaemenid about the iconography which might suggest some kind of Persian cultural affiliation opposing Greek culture – quite the opposite in fact, considering that items such as the typically Achaemenid tall incense burner with stepped lid *could* have been included.[59] One such burner is shown on a stele showing a seated woman from Daskyleion.[60]

A difficulty with the idea of different ethnic perspectives on the iconography of the Polyxena Sarcophagus is that it assumes that these were necessarily different. Different ethno-linguistic groups did indeed define themselves in terms of lineage and culture, and increasingly so in the time of the Persian Empire, when new obligations and pressures were interfering with traditional alliances and relationships. But it is not clear that this has to apply to the Polyxena Sarcophagus, where the basic relevance of the myth(s) to the context of death and to the locality and its prestigious history may have been shared.[61] At any rate, we do not *know* which ethnic group used this tomb, and so while the images *could* be meaningful in terms of ethnic identity, we do not have the information necessary to determine this kind of political intent. The possibilities can be mooted, and that there are those possibilities is important to recognise, but to insist on determining one or another meaning not only goes beyond what the evidence can actually support, but seems predicated on the idea that this is the only method of making meaning of myth.

Rather than dwelling on that sense of meaning, one might register possibilities and then zoom back out and look at the phenomenon of the appearance of myth and its relationship to the locality more generally. The ability to situate this tomb within display habits in this region is hampered by the fact that only a few tumuli have been excavated. So far, though, the Polyxena Sarcophagus stands out for the centrality of myth in its decoration compared to relief-decorated stelai from nearby Daskyleion and the overall low use of mythological imagery in monumental decoration in Asia Minor

---

58 Neer 2012, 114 with references in nn. 70–1.

59 Samian sarcophagi: Hitzl 1991. Cf. Rose on Achaemenid influence: Rose 2014, 93 and 95.

60 See n. 49 above. This stele is noted by Rose 2014, 93–94.

61 Cf. here Hölscher 2011 for concerns regarding the extent to which myths might resonate for particular group identities depending on historical (primarily political) contexts.

around this time. As noted early on in this paper, then, this monument may have been a real novelty. Having taken some time to make, and needing to be in place before deposition, it is reasonable to think that the monument was set up on the spot of the burial for some time before it occurred – a process which would have created some commotion and elicited interest in the area. The tomb then would have become a local landmark itself, and moreover a staged spectacle of unusual and exciting visual renderings of perhaps familiar stories, with a limited time opportunity for viewing before it was covered up.[62] Myth itself, arguably more open to interpretation than some other images, could be particularly useful for intriguing viewers, engaging their imaginations and offering them scope to think and talk about its meaning. The talk that something like the Polyxena Sarcophagus would ignite, spreading the news about the monument, could ensure a legacy reaching far beyond the time it was covered with earth, as well as a trajectory beyond the control of its makers and owners.

This act can be situated in the political history of Anatolia following the Achaemenid Persian conquest in the 540s BC. Looked at as "messages" and solely in terms of political ideology, one can *make* the myth(s) employed here meaningful as an assertion of power based on local legacy, opposing or resisting Persian threats to landownership and autonomy. Certainly, the kind of imagery that went into the Polyxena Sarcophagus contrasts with more "Persianising" imagery found in reliefs on tombs around Daskyleion, where trappings associated with the Persian court can be found in images of battle, hunt, banquets and even the stele depicting a woman noted above. But it is not necessary to see the sarcophagus' programme only in terms of political ideology. One can also see the unusual employment of myth as part of the economic enablement of this region under the Achaemenid Empire, when imported Attic pottery increased at Daskyleion and elsewhere, and when, as already noted, the Proconnesian quarries seem to have been increasingly exploited, opening up new possibilities for achieving distinction.

This does not mean that any old myth would do. In the same way that any old myth could not be used for Pindar's odes, the myths here were tailored. The design of the reliefs participates in a known trope of juxtaposing negative and positive, as found in the depiction of the city at war and peace on the Shield of Achilles where, it might be noted, a wedding is also included (Hom. *Il.* 18.478–608).[63] Polyxena's death and the weight given to the mourning Trojan women – the quintessence of lamentation – is

---

62 This notion of creating a scene during construction has been mooted in an as yet unpublished paper on "Building Sites", delivered by Rolf Schneider in Oxford in 2011, but also touches on themes of agency (Gellian technologies of enchantment), materialities and place-making that can be further explored and consolidated, e.g. variously Gell 1992; 1998; Graves 1989, esp. 312–6 (citing Evans 1988); Mukerji 1997; Thomas 2001, esp. 177–81; Snickare 2012; Harmanşah 2013a; 2013b; 2014; Osborne 2014, and to some extent Turnbull 2002; Swenson 2015, esp. 700 on the notion of powerful persistence; Farmer and Lane 2016.
63 Shield of Achilles: Byre 1992.

clearly relevant to a sepulchral function. Also, of course, that myth, and perhaps the other sides if taken as referring to Andromache's wedding, were part of local myth-history, making this monument particularly resonant in this area, and indeed elevating it to a landmark that drew on and competed with the tombs of the great heroes of the Trojan War that dotted the countryside. Putting on a special show of well-chosen myth, and presumably importing the sculptors to carry this out, was one possible avenue for distinction. While the myth(s) chosen here could relate to the identity claims of one or another polity in this area, or one or another gender, then, one need not force decisions on that in order to appreciate the relevance and meaning of the subjects selected. And, importantly, a broader view of the use of myth itself as a phenomenon is another way of making it meaningful, in the sense of discerning regional dynamics in play in the provincial histories of the Achaemenid Empire.

The Kızılbel Painted Tomb and the Milyad

Regional dynamics of this kind are more pronounced in the case of the Kızılbel Tomb, located in what is often called "North Lycia" (Fig. 5). In contrast to the Polyxena Sarcophagus, this is a stone built tomb chamber, the interior walls of which were covered in a myriad of paintings, friezes of differing sizes depicting varied subjects (Fig. 6).[64] It is earlier than the Polyxena Sarcophagus, the style of the paintings indicating a date around 530 BC – not long, then, after the Achaemenid conquest. Located on an isolated hill overlooking a plain where once there was a lake, the tomb also precedes another famous painted tomb from this area located on the other side of Elmalı: the Karaburun II Tomb, the paintings of which show strongly Persian-oriented themes and are stylistically datable to around 470 BC.[65] Bones found in both of the tombs have been attributed to males, the one from the Kızılbel tomb having died in his late 40s.[66]

Although often called "North Lycia", sometimes the "Lycian Highlands", this upland plateau, or *yayla*, was known as the Milyad in antiquity.[67] It is only in the fourth century BC that rock-cut tombs similar to those used on the coast of Lycia and, importantly, Lycian inscriptions, are found in the *yayla*.[68] Before then, the cultural and

---

64 Mellink 1998.

65 Karaburun II Tomb, not yet fully published: Mellink 1970; 1971; 1972; 1973; 1974; 1975; Miller 2010. The banquet painting from this tomb was robbed in 2010. Reconstructed tomb now housed in the new Elmalı Museum.

66 Kızılbel bones, 70 fragments, sex indicated by general size and thickness, bony rims suggest age: Mellink 1998, 71 (Lawrence Angel). Full report plus Karaburun II bones: Mellink 1973, Appendix 303–7 (Lawrence Angel). The excavators imply that the death may have been related to a significant knee injury exacerbated by regular horse riding.

67 Coulton 1993; Kolb 2009; Momigliano and Aksoy 2015.

68 Lockwood 2006; Kolb 2009; Lockwood 2011.

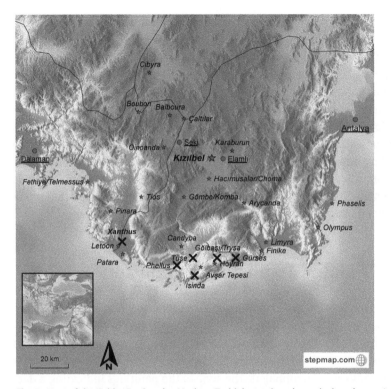

Fig. 5: Map of the Tekke Peninsula. Modern Turkish province boundaries shown. Lycian sites with significant early pillar tombs marked with X. By author using Stepmap.com.

linguistic identity may have been quite distinct from the mountainous Lycian coast: only a few of a cluster of 100 tumuli at Bayındır, very near the later Karaburun II Tomb, have been excavated, but those were found to contain wooden chambers resembling those at Phrygian Gordium in central Anatolia, and vessels within bear wax labels with Phrygian inscriptions.[69] Even in the Roman period, Arrian calls the Milyad a part of Phrygia controlled by Lycia (*Anab.* 1.24.5). Following the Persian conquest, when the Kızılbel Tomb was built, nucleated settlement seems to have diminished considerably; although this may change with further investigation in the area, so far there is a gap in sherd scatters and evidence at the mound of Choma (Hacımusalar).[70] A similar drop off in the Seki Plain, another *yayla* just to the west, has prompted the suggestion that there was a change to pastoral agriculture in the Persian period.[71] If so, the Kızılbel Tomb would be the landmark tomb of a so-called pastoral lord in the Milyad.

---

69 Dörtlük 1988; Börker-Klähn 2003; Işık 2003; Şare 2010.
70 Özgen 1998; 2006.
71 Momigliano et al. 2011; Coulton 2012.

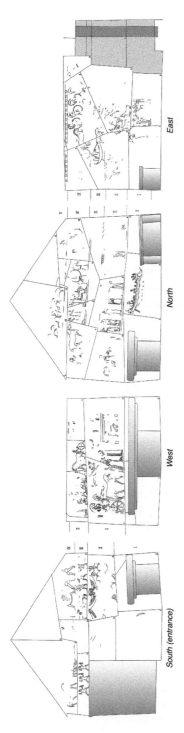

Fig. 6: Compilation of drawings showing paintings on the walls of the Kızılbel Tomb. After Mellink (1998), drawing sheets A-D, with the kind permission of Bryn Mawr College.

The tomb represents, then, an opportunity to characterise a "pastoral lord" through material and visual culture. Already the stone-built tomb chamber, in contrast to the earlier wooden chambers at Bayındır, resembles types that flourish in the wake of the Persian conquest in other areas of Asia Minor, especially Lydia and the Hellespont, and indicates new connections and new material acquisition as well as skills (the quarrying of and building with stone). The tomb paintings, which have not occasioned the perplexity concerning gender encountered with the Polyxena Sarcophagus, represent around twenty subjects, scattered in a much less tightly controlled compositional scheme. Included are a high number of males, especially warriors, and the themes form a spectrum from those which appear to be non-mythological, such as hunts, often taken as biographic or idealised activities pertaining to the deceased, to some which are clearly known myths. In between are a large number of paintings, including the warrior images, which appear to be mythological or what one might broadly call "epic", but which resist immediate identification.

One of the obviously mythological subjects, shown in relatively large scale on the South (entrance) wall of the chamber (Figs. 6 and 7), is the beheading of Medusa by Perseus.[72] The hero himself is not preserved, but is assumed to have been shown fleeing on the left to the door of the tomb, note the quadruple-winged, gruesome sisters of Medusa pursuing him, while Medusa herself was shown collapsing on the right hand side (Figs. 8 and 9). From her neck emerge her sons by Poseidon, the horse Pegasus (here his wings, signalling his divinity, are not clear) and the humanoid hero Chrysaor (see Hes. *Theog.* 278–83).

Although easily identifiable, determining the meaning of this painting has proved troublesome. The scholarship, so far, has concentrated largely on two main possibilities for its relevance: eschatological symbolism and local myth history. Mellink, for instance, noting the use of the theme with emphasis on Pegasus and Chrysaor on the foot of a sarcophagus of about 470 BC from Golgi on Cyprus, thought that the theme could allude to rebirth.[73] Others have concentrated on the potential local, *Lycian* relevance of Pegasus and Chrysaor.[74] Pegasus, for instance, was ridden by Bellerophon, who according to tradition sought supplication with the king of Lycia, by whom he was charged with slaying the Chimera.[75] Having succeeded, the hero married the Lycian king's daughter and begat a line of descendants. It is known that he was considered a hero and was shown on later Lycian tombs.[76] Chrysaor himself was not specifi-

---

[72] Mellink 1998, 35–6, 57. Cf. similar compositions: *LIMC* 4, s.v. "Gorgo, Gorgones" (Krauskopf and Dahlinger) and *LIMC* 7, s.v. "Perseus" (Jones Roccos).

[73] Mellink 1998, 57. Golgi sarcophagus: Wilson 1972; *LIMC* 7 s.v. "Perseus" (Jones Roccos), 169*.

[74] Metzger 1983; Metzger and Moret 1999.

[75] *LIMC* 7, s.v. "Pegasos" (Lochin); Schmitt 1966.

[76] Bellerophon on the Heroon of Perikles at Limyra and the Heroon at Trysa, as well as man on winged horse versus panther outside a rock-cut tomb at Tlos, man on winged horse in relief on rock-cut tomb at Pinara and a charioteer versus a chimera on the sarcophagus of Merehi at Xanthus (all late fifth to

Fig. 7: Photo of Southwest corner of the interior of the Kızılbel Tomb showing on the South wall the beheading of Medusa and the ambush of Troilus, and on the West wall the departure of "Amphia-raus" and an arming scene in the top register. Mellink (1998), pl. 37, with the kind permission of Bryn Mawr College.

cally linked to Lycia, and his depiction is rare, but another Lycian founder hero of the same name (apparently a great-grandson of Bellerophon) is known from later Lycian inscriptions; Henri Metzger has therefore suggested that the son of Medusa could have resonated for someone who knew of his namesake, even if they were not conflated.[77] The theme of Perseus beheading Medusa is itself also known from later Lycian tombs, such as a fragmentary *acroterion* from the *heroon* tomb of the fourth century Lycian dy-

fourth century BC): Borchhardt 1976; Metzger 1983; Metzger and Moret 1999, 295–301; Şare 2013. Also on Bellerophon see Keen 1998, 211–2.

77 Metzger 1983, 363–7; Metzger and Moret 1999, 305–13 (with references to the inscription).

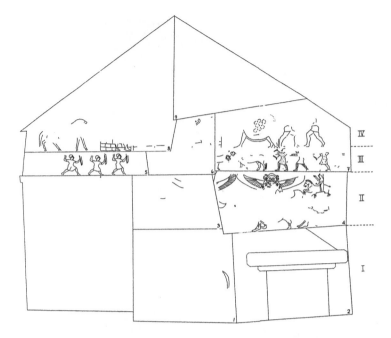

Fig. 8: Drawing of the paintings on the South (entrance) wall of the Kızılbel Tomb, showing the beheading of Medusa (II), a lion hunt (III) and the abush of Troilus (IV). Mellink (1998), drawing sheet D, with the kind permission of Bryn Mawr College.

nast Perikles at Limyra. Attempts to interpret this later use of the theme have tended to derive political messages, either pro-Persian (the Persians being descended from Perses, the son of Perseus: Hdt. 7.61), or anti-Persian, the Persians once having been ruled by a Greek hero.[78] Perseus' association with Lycia is also indicated by his commissioning of the Cyclopes of Lycia to build the walls of Argos.[79]

Apart from the difficulty of assuming a Lycian identity on the part of a tomb-owning group in the Milyad, this is a good example of attempts to derive intentional political ideological messages from tomb decoration. Given that Perseus was shown on tombs in (coastal) Lycia later on, and that there is a connection to the hero in another of the tomb's paintings (as argued below), one could speculate that there were claims to genealogical descent from Perseus circulating in southwest Asia Minor. If the Persian genealogy that Herodotus recounts was already circulating in this period (some 100 years before he was writing, but in a post-conquest period in which such ideas could have emerged) descent from Perseus could feasibly enable claims of brotherhood (*filia*) with the Persians, which could confer some political and economic

---

78 Pro-Persian: Borchhardt 1976, 123; Keen 1998, 158. Anti-Persian: Özgen and Özgen 1988, 53. See discussion in Şare 2013, 60.
79 Barringer 2008, 190–6.

Fig. 9: Painting of the gorgons on the South (entrance) wall of the Kızılbel Tomb (SII). Two sisters pursue Perseus (not shown), while Medusa collapses on the right, Pegasus and Chrysaor emerging from her neck. Mellink (1998), pl. XXVIIa, with the kind permission of Bryn Mawr College.

benefits on local polities, whether kin or larger groups. But the relevance may be far less clear-cut. Perseus might generally be seen as an apt exemplum for the memorial of a man. The composition and emphasis of the painting makes much of the monstrousness of the gorgons, rather than presenting Medusa as a maiden, which might have drawn attention to her as a victim of death herself.[80] This monstrousness and the prominence of the sisters could indicate that the stress here lay on the heroic defeat of monsters – something which could be supported with reference to menacing beasts on other tombs in Western Anatolia, including gorgon heads, sphinxes, siren-like bird women and the chimera. The birth of Pegasus *and* Chrysaor is also rather prominent, and it is possible that this had local resonance or even resonated in terms of life emerging from death, as Mellink suggested.

It is difficult without good external evidence to make choices *between* these, and it may be that none of them were precisely intended. But neither need the paintings be merely decorative. Rather than allegory or a kind of visual *eulogy*, one might see this painting (one of many in the tomb) as *elegy* – part of a vibrant collection of "visual songs" performed at a memorial, which need not be directly relevant to the social

---

80 Medusa as a maiden and victim of death: Topper 2007; 2010.

identity of the deceased, but create an impression, in this case one of high drama and action, excitement and escape. It is through such *feelings*, then, rather than *messages*, that the man buried here would be remembered, Perseus being relevant without having to connote anything too particular.[81]

Another painting on the same South wall may be appreciated in the same light, although in that case is it easier to narrow down more focused potential meanings. Above a thin frieze depicting a lion hunt, are the traces of what has been identified as the ambush of the young Trojan prince Troilus (the brother of Polyxena) by Achilles (Figs. 8 and 10).[82] On the left side of the frieze, just about visible, are the legs of a horse and a pair of ankles and feet in front of an ashlar masonry wall. On the other side of the masonry wall are the lower legs of a larger figure shown crouching and holding a large round shield. These elements fit known depictions of Achilles' ambush of Troilus as related in the *Cypria* – a prequel to the *Iliad*: the prince was attacked by Achilles as he watered his horses at a fountain outside of Troy's walls.[83] This is a very widely depicted theme in ancient Greek vase painting and its use in funerary contexts is also known from a Clazomenian sarcophagus and, most prominently, in the roughly contemporary Tomb of the Bulls in Etruria.[84] Some paintings on Greek vases of the theme include Polyxena, who by some traditions accompanied her brother to the fountain. A variant of the story has this as the point Achilles falls for the princess, which leads ultimately to her sacrifice at his tomb later on. A badly preserved patch in the centre of the wall could be an embellishment of the fountain or another figure, perhaps Polyxena.[85]

By the Roman period, Troilus can be depicted as a hero of the Trojan War and, having survived it, an ancestor of Anatolian groups. Earlier versions, however, concentrate on the tragedy of the death of a mere youth, slain before his time – an event that was nonetheless key to the Trojan War since his murder in the sanctuary of Apollo led to that god eventually slaying Achilles.[86] Mellink suggested that the Kızılbel painting might have been meaningful for the tomb owners in terms of general allusion to the great "historic" event of the Trojan War, in which ancestors of the Lycians had participated.[87] The name Troilus is found in a range of Roman period inscriptions from the

---

81 Cf. Junker 2012, 161–9, esp. 169, on the broad spectrum of themes in Roman chamber tombs with multiple sarcophagi.

82 Mellink 1998, 38, 58.

83 *LIMC* 8, s.v. "Troilos" (Kossatz-Deissman) and *LIMC* 1, s.v. "Achilleus" (Kossatz-Deissman); Metzger and Moret 1999, 313–15.

84 *LIMC* 1, s.v. "Achilleus" (Kossatz-Deissman), 277 (Clazomenian sarcophagus in Izmir Mus. 3619); Tomb of the Bulls/Tomba dei Tori: Steingräber 1986, 350–1, no. 120, pls. 157–65, esp. pls. 157–8. On relationships between tomb paintings in Anatolia and Etruria more generally: Paschinger 1985; Steingräber 2010.

85 Mellink 1998, 38; Metzger and Moret 1999, 314–5 (who feels there could be an "oriental" element inserted).

86 Smith and Hallett 2015.

87 Mellink 1998, 58.

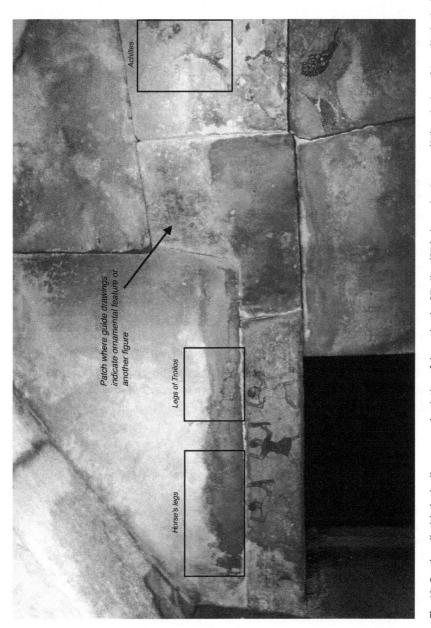

Labels on image: Achilles; Patch where guide drawings indicate ornamental feature or another figure; Legs of Troilos; Horse's legs

Fig. 10: South wall with the badly preserved painting of the ambush of Troilus (SIV) above the Gorgons (SII) and a hunt frieze (SIII). The lower legs of the prince and his horse are just about visible above the door, while on the far right are patches of the shield, cloak and leg of Achilles. In the centre is a badly preserved patch of painting that could have shown an embellished fountain spout or another figure, such as the sister of Troilus, Polyxena. Cf. Fig. 8. Mellink (1998), pl. XXIXa, with the kind permission of Bryn Mawr College, with annotations by author.

Roman province of Lycia and Pamphylia, including the mountainous Pisidia, and it is possible that the deceased was an earlier namesake, even if his primary language was not Greek (*or* Lycian).[88]

The depiction of Troilus as a young boy, though, has no direct connection to the age of the person buried in the tomb, nor to his death specifically. One could think therefore that it was Achilles who was intended as an *exemplum*, rather than Troilus, but the Kızılbel painting makes no attempt to glorify that hero's chase and capture of the mounted prince on foot. Unless it is a groom rather than Troilus, it is the young prince's feet that are shown before the horses. He was unmounted then, and Achilles' size is clearly differentiated. Clearly the boy stood no chance.

Such a death might seem rather "unheroic", but it could also serve as an epitome of a *blameless* death. As highlighted by Neer in his discussion of the Polyxena Sarcophagus, "blameless" was a trope in ancient literature, used to describe the tomb of Achilles ("a great and blameless tomb": Hom. *Od.* 24.80–4).[89] The term suits even better the unfortunate death of Troilus (as well as his sister), however – all the more so since they perished at the hands of the greatest of heroes. As Barbara Borg points out in the case of some poignant myths on Roman sarcophagi, both Polyxena and Troilus would in this sense serve as *exempla mortalitatis* and *exempla pietatis*.[90] If one speaks of representation of the deceased, then, it is this concept of a blameless death, packaged in a theme which, given its appearance on other tombs, may have been widely understood to symbolise that idea that may be relevant, rather than a character comparison or a simple local link.

Another painting on the West wall could have similar resonance. Here there is a question of whether the theme is mythological, strictly speaking. The largest and best preserved in the tomb, and consequently the most widely known and discussed, it depicts a warrior stepping into a chariot (Fig. 11). The warrior, shown in hoplite-style armour, turns to a female figure behind him. A charioteer of smaller scale than the protagonist stands at the ready, and before the chariot is shown a group of three people: an old man seated on the ground, holding a staff, his hand raised up before him, and two women, one of whom holds a young child that Mellink identifies as a boy.[91]

The iconography and composition is very similar to the departure of the hero Amphiaraus in Greek vase paintings, most obviously the Amphiaraus Crater, a late Corinthian crater of c. 560 BC, where the figures are labelled.[92] The hero was one of

---

88 Troilus as name: Milner 2012, 103–4, no. 18, IBb20, 05–6, no. 20, IBb37, 15–6, no. 31, IDg1, 23–4, no. 40, IKh3, with further examples listed by Coulton on 420.

89 Neer 2012.

90 Borg, this volume. Cf. here Junker 2012, 164–5 on the resonance of *mors immatura*, not necessarily restricted to memorials for particular genders or age groups.

91 Mellink 1998, 22–4.

92 Amphiaraus crater, formerly Berlin, Antikensammlung 1655 (the vase disappeared after WWII): *LIMC* 1, s.v. "Amphiaraos" (Krauskopf), 7*; Wrede 1916.

Fig. 11: Painting of the chariot with warrior (Amphiaraus?), woman (Eriphyle?) to the left and elder seated on the ground to the right, the winged figure above the horses. West wall, above the *kline* (WI). Two other women, one with a child, is shown behind the seated elder. Mellink (1998), pl. VIb, with the kind permission of Bryn Mawr College.

the Seven against Thebes, who according to later literary sources was persuaded by his wife Eriphyle to join that battle despite knowing he would perish; she herself was bribed to do this with the gift of the necklace of Harmonia, clearly shown on the Crater. It has been pointed out, though, that some vase paintings and the Kızılbel painting deviate from the Crater in various ways, above all in the lack of the necklace. In the Kızılbel painting the elder male is shown seated on the ground, unlike his counterpart, the seer Halimedes on the Crater, and he does not hold his hand to his head in a gesture of dismay, but out before him in a gesture that Mellink saw as one of "well-wishing".[93] Metzger has also pointed out that while Amphiaraus is shown with an angry expression on his face in the Berlin Crater painting, this too is lacking in the Kızılbel painting.[94] The most striking difference in the Kızılbel painting, however, is the appearance of a very distinctive, long-haired, bearded winged figure over the horses pulling the chariot.

---

93 Mellink 1998, 59.
94 Metzger 1983, 361; Metzger and Moret 1999, 317.

It has been suggested that the vaguer vase paintings could depict a more generic "departure of the warrior", drawing on a well-known iconographic formula, and that this could be the case for the Kızılbel painting as well.[95] A scene of arming shown in the register above (Figs. 6 and 7) – a trope in literature and featured often on Athenian painted vases – could be related.[96] A further suggestion is that there was an adjustment here first to make the painted warrior more clearly allude to the deceased (Mellink saw the painting as biographical), and second to make it express the idea of his final journey, not just to battle but to the afterlife.[97] According to this, the winged figure would be an addition emphasising the eschatological connotations of the painting.[98]

Argument over whether the painting is mythological or not may be a red herring. As Metzger implied, even the more generic images of departure in this vein could be seen as dependent on the Amphiaraus model, with a related allusion to the death of the man buried in the tomb as brought upon him by forces outside his control rather than by his own failings: again, *blameless*. Such ideas could resonate particularly well as an epitome within a visual elegy for an elite man, working in the way that Pindar drew on heroic models, Amphiaraus included, for his odes. In this sense, there could have been some tailoring to direct the viewer away from Amphiaraus and increase the connection to the deceased more specifically, which if so is an important interference. But it is hard to know if this is over interpreting intention here, and one still needs to admit the strong mythological basis in the painting.

The addition of the winged figure is an important interference, though. Such a figure is unknown in any of the other depictions of Amphiaraus or the related departure compositions. One can imagine it enhancing the fatalism of the painting, suited to the tomb context. But this is not the only reason it is important. It also suggests something about the connectivity of the *yayla*, which is quite telling. The form recalls winged figures sometimes shown in Laconian vase painting, some archaic depictions of *nikai* and divine figures (and sometimes monsters), but the hairstyle, especially the beard, and the lotus, described as "oriental" by most, make one think of Egypt, or perhaps even more so Syria, the Levant or Cyprus. The opposite of what has been argued for some Cypriot art such as the "Master of Animals" and the Cypriot "Heracles", where iconographies related to those known in the Greek world were used to enhance a lo-

---

95 Wrede 1916; Metzger 1983, 361–2; Metzger and Moret 1999.

96 Mellink 1998, 25–6, 52, 61–2. Departure of the warrior trope: Yalouri 1971; Shapiro 1990; Oakley 2004; Matheson 2005.

97 Paschinger 1985, esp. 5, sees most of the paintings in the tomb as "narrative" as opposed to "symbolic", which seems to mean historical narrative rather than mythical; Mellink 1998, 51–4.

98 Paschinger 1985, 20–41, esp. 36, argues that the lotus carried by the figure is a symbol of death. Mellink 1998, 51–4, saw the figure, which she identified as female despite its beard, as "auspicious". Metzger sees an oriental insertion to localise the story or perhaps to enhance the eschatological aspect: Metzger 1983, 367–8; Metzger and Moret 1999, 315–8.

cal idea, this would be the insertion of a "foreign" motif into more standard Greek iconography, which could enhance the connotations of the heroic warrior (whoever he is) as understood by certain circles.[99] Whether this would have been the circles of the painters or the circles of the tomb owners depends on to whom one attributes the design. Either way, this one insertion suggests that people in this *yayla* shared some imaginative links with groups in the Eastern Mediterranean.

Finally I turn to those paintings in this tomb that seem mythological, but which have proved hard to identify. Such are the plentiful images of warriors, including the arming scene on the West wall mentioned above, a cavalcade and march of hoplite figures, which could all be "generic", but could all easily belong to mythological heroic stories. The line between the two is very fuzzy here. Also difficult to identify, but tempting to see as mythical episodes of some sort are three paintings on the North wall, including from top to bottom a supplication, apparently in a court ambient; a procession of figures behind a seated female; and a ship (Figs. 12 and 13). The "supplication" scene includes on the far left an elderly man seated seer-like on the ground with a pair of horses before him and a file of figures before that, while on the right there is a file of hoplite-style warriors processing right. In the centre is a seated elder, before whom crouches a youthful figure, presumed to be male, his hands held to the knees of the elder. The whole suggests some epic narrative, but so far specific identification has proved elusive. Mellink suggested that this may be a "Lycian" myth, unknown in literary sources.[100] It may be, however, that the subject is known, but unrecognisable because it was rarely depicted, or depicted quite differently. One suggestion has been Priam begging for the return of the body of Hector, but apart from the lack of a body the ages of the protagonists in the centre are reversed.[101] Other possibilities mooted by Mellink include someone (Kassandra?) begging Priam not to admit the Trojan horse; the arrival of Odysseus at the court of Alkinoos; or the arrival of Bellerophon at the court of the Lycian king.[102] The combination of elements suggests supplication with possible provision of military aid, but also the possibility of doom indicated by the seer.

The ship shown on the bottom of the same North wall has been seen as biographical by some, but could also very well belong to the world of epic myth, perhaps even a related one.[103] The type of ship and the waves underneath it are similar to ships shown on the sides of Attic craters and *dinoi*, which may play on the Homeric notion of sailing on the wine dark sea, but the occupants of the ship are not paralleled elsewhere. They

---

99 As Metzger and Moret 1999, 317–8. Master of animals and Cypriot Heracles: Counts 2008; Counts and Arnold 2010.

100 Mellink 1998, 58.

101 Priam's supplication to Achilles: Metzger and Moret 1999, 301–5 (Moret).

102 Mellink 1998, 29, 58.

103 Biographic: Paschinger 1985, 4, 16–7 and 44–7. "Lycian" myth: Mellink 1998, 52, 53 (where she moots the idea that the figure in the bow of the boat may be the suppliant) and 58.

Fig. 12: North wall showing paintings *in situ*. Cf. Fig. 13. Mellink (1998), pl. 31, with the kind permission of Bryn Mawr College, with annotations by author.

Fig. 13: Drawing of paintings shown on the North wall, opposite the entrance to the tomb. Note the length of the entourage in the second frieze from the bottom (NII), here identified as the exposure of Andromeda to the *Ketos*/Kraken. Mellink (1998), drawing sheet B, with the kind permission of Bryn Mawr College.

include several rowers and other crew, as well as a dark-haired bearded man shaded by a parasol shown seated near the stern and two figures in the castle at the bow, one pointing forward, the other turned back and gesturing toward the other figures in the ship. One thinks of possibilities including Paris abducting Helen, which could link to a return of Paris to Priam and the resulting Trojan War (the subject of the warrior and supplication paintings?). In that case, however, the identity of the parasol-shaded man, who should be a ruler of some kind, would remain a question – unless he should be Paris, with Helen and another woman in the bow. The possibilities are tantalising, and research that could turn up identifications has not been exhausted.

As indicated at the start of this paper, a new identification of one of the paintings in this tomb is offered here, and this supports the idea of known myths rendered in unfamiliar ways. The long frieze across the middle of the North wall shows a procession and a seated woman on the far left. The focus has so far been on the seated woman, who is confronted by some kind of beast with scales (just about visible) and a roaring, apparently feline face (Figs. 13 and 14). Mellink, suggesting a connection between all the images on the North wall, proposed that what may be shown is Bellerophon presenting the Chimera, the beast the Lycian king demanded he slay, to the Lycian

Fig. 14: Detail of the far left of the second frieze from bottom (NII) (cf. Fig. 12 for location), showing from right to left: horses, woman standing, seated woman, what has been interpreted as a small feline head at face level of the seated woman, and patches of scales. Mellink (1998), pl. XVIa, with the kind permission of Bryn Mawr College, annotations by author.

queen.[104] Surprisingly little attention has been paid to the entourage, which after all makes up most of the frieze (Figs. 12 and 13). Included are several female attendants, many with one arm bent, hand up by their heads. They may have been shown carrying goods on their heads, or performing a gesture of dismay.[105] Behind them are traces of other figures, including, importantly, a group of naked males painted in dark blue, their genitals left white. The positions of their arms, bent and raised to their heads, suggested to Mellink that they too may have been shown bearing items on their heads.[106]

These blue men are absolutely key. Who are they? Blue figures are known in Etruscan wall painting, most obviously the paintings in the Tomb of the Blue Demons, where they are clearly demons.[107] The Kızılbel figures do not have any demonic attributes and their colour is notably darker. A distinct possibility is that they represent black men – Nubians or Ethiopians. Black people are shown as enemies or subjects in Egyptian tomb paintings, and on Greek painted vases they are stereotyped as "others", with pronounced facial features and genitals.[108] A known myth fits the appearance of black men here: the exposure of the Ethiopian princess Andromeda to the *Ketos* or Kraken. She is shown on later Attic red-figure vases together with black attendants who indicate her Ethiopian origin (although not race – she is not herself shown as black).[109] In vase paintings she is most often shown standing, tied to posts or being rescued by Perseus, but she can be shown seated on some red-figure vases and on Etruscan urns from Volterra.[110] The *Ketos* is usually shown as a dragon or serpent, but sometimes it is only the head which is shown, as on the earliest known rendition of the myth on a late Corinthian vase, where Perseus is shown fending off the beast (Fig. 15).[111] This would suit the scales visible to the left of the supposed feline head (Fig. 14), which could actually be the snout of the beast. It is possible that Perseus was shown grappling with the beast. His rescue of Andromeda is popular in art from around this time, but the painting is not well-preserved enough to distinguish his figure if so.

---

104 Mellink 1998, 52 and 58. This possibility was entertained by Metzger too, who eventually opted for an unknown related Lycian story: Metzger and Moret 1999, 295–301.

105 Mellink 1998, 52, perceived a faint curve of an item above the head of the third standing female.

106 Mellink 1998, 32. For a colour photo see Mellink 1998, pl. XVIII c.

107 Tomb of the Blue Demons/Tomba dei Demoni Azzuri: Krauskopf 1987; Haynes 2000, 238–9; Krauskopf 2006.

108 Snowden 1970; 1983; Bérard 2000, 390–412; Bindman et al. 2010.

109 *LIMC* 1, s.v. "Andromeda I" (Schauenburg), 2* (= red-figure pelike in Boston MFA 63, 2663), 3* (= red-figure hydria in London, BM, E 169); Phillips 1968; Bérard 2000, 402–6.

110 *LIMC* 1, s.v. "Andromeda I" (Schauenburg) e.g.: 16* (= red-figure oinochoe in Bari Arch. Mus. 1016), 28* (= Volterra urn in Florence Arch. Mus. 78.486); Phillips 1968, pl. 13 fig. 39, pl. 14 fig. 43, pl. 15 fig. 44. See also *LIMC* 7, s.v. "Perseus" (Jones Roccos).

111 Berlin, Staatliche Museen F 1625: *LIMC* 1, s.v. "Andromeda I" (Schauenburg), 1*; Phillips 1968, pl. 1 fig. 1. See also the Volterran cist, Volterra Museum 331, *LIMC* 1, s.v. "Andromeda I" (Schauenburg), 27 and 28*; Phillips 1968, pl. 15 fig. 44. Further: *LIMC* suppl., s.v. "Ketos" (Boardman).

Fig. 15: Corinthian amphora showing Perseus, Andromeda and the *Ketos*, from Cerveteri/Caere, 575–550 BC. Berlin, Staatliche Museen F 1652, h. 34.8 cm. Photo by Ingrid Geske (bpk, Antikensammlung, SMB, photo number 00089850).

Such a theme brings us back to the difficulty encountered with the painting of Perseus beheading Medusa: how is this meaningful in this context? Perseus was often shown rescuing Andromeda, so there is a connection, but since he is not emphasised in the painting one might consider how the exposure of Andromeda itself may have been resonant. Again, rather than direct didactic eulogising of the deceased, the subject of a girl offered up to death would not be unsuited to a broader funeral elegy. Such a theme could also resonate in terms of hubris and ensuing tragedy, a motif of mythic punishment known to have been the subject of some Hellenistic period public statue groups.[112] Andromeda's exposure was due to her mother Cassiopeia's having boasted of her beauty, in a way similar to the boasts of Niobe, whose children are shown being slain in punishment on Roman sarcophagi.[113] In that case, though, the grief of Niobe over her loss is prominent. Another possibility is that this is a version of a trope of the sacrifice or attempted sacrifice of a daughter, which could allude to the sacrifices a good leader must face.[114] Or, the choice may have been predicated on the desire to include tales of exotic foreign lands and peoples, especially given the space accorded to the entourage and the prominence of the unusual blue men. Among the above one might see what are perhaps more *probable* ways that this subject could have been

---

112 Smith 1991, 356–8.

113 Hubris, sacrilege and punishment themes: Smith and Hallett 2015, 161, and see also Smith in n. 55, above. Niobe sarcophagi, see n. 55 above.

114 On sacrifice to save the city: Kearns 2002.

relevant (a link to Perseus; the jaws of death), but it is difficult to determine with any certainty what was intended.

And again, precise meaning may be beside the point. Rather than didactic or decorative, imagining that these paintings functioned in an elegiac sense would allow more flexibility in how they could work, neither imposing meaning nor implying it was entirely free. One can also appreciate more generally how the use of myth in this tomb would have fit into the dynamics of this region. Unlike the Polyxena Sarcophagus, this tomb was not open to the air, so there was limited time for viewing and this may have been possible only for a limited crowd of admirers, creating and reinforcing power structures in the area. Privileged visitors, both before and at the burial ceremony, would have been presented with a visual show, not only impressing them with novelty, but inviting them to participate in interpretation. Even those who could not see the paintings would still hear of them, disseminating and further diversifying potential interpretations, but at the same time multiplying the power of the landmark as it was transmitted through the imaginations of the local populace and beyond.

Although not exactly intended consciously, the theme of "exotic, foreign lands" noted above is something worth returning to. The ship painting also makes allusions to travels and overseas contact, whether biographical or not. This is important in grasping the imaginative world of elites in this inland, rural *yayla*. This imaginative world speaks of highly cultivated contacts: well-known iconographies and innovative new renderings indicate an influx of stories and the skills needed to depict them in the upland plain. Even though imports of image-rich Attic pottery did increase at Gordium after the Persian conquest, one suspects that the transmission of such stories came not from old connections to central Anatolia, but from the Lycian coast to the south. There, while the inland Milyad was becoming less nucleated, urban monumentality as well as importation of Attic pottery was on the increase – at least at Xanthus.[115] Metzger has suggested that travelling Greek poets of the kind that composed dedications in Greek verse for the later, fourth century BC Lycian dynast Arbinas may have been responsible for the uptake of myth in the Kızılbel tomb.[116] But, as he also notes, the unusual insertions such as the winged figure in the "Amphiaraus" painting, may have been drawn from other Eastern sources, suggesting multiple connections in the *yayla*. Robin Lane Fox has suggested that a major transmission route for stories and ideas was not so much (or only) itinerant poets, but sailors and traders who exchanged their own tales for those foreign to them.[117] The unusual elements in the Kızılbel paintings suggest what one might well imagine – that such bearers of stories may include people other than Greeks. Unusual renderings such as the proposed Andromeda myth may also suggest drawing on versions of stories more frequently encountered in Eastern

---

[115] Metzger 1972; Draycott 2015.
[116] Metzger and Moret 1999, 299 and n. 9.
[117] Lane Fox 2008 and this volume.

Mediterranean circles than in the Aegean, or other parts of the Mediterranean, and therefore depicted in unfamiliar ways.

This new *yayla* connectivity is all the more striking for the contrast it forms with the Lycian coast – or more particularly the western and central Lycian coast. While the *yaylas*, in the period following the Persian conquest, see a decrease in settlement density and monumental urbanism, as noted above there is a corresponding increase along the coast. It is at this time that a series of monumental stone built tombs – the pillar tombs of Lycia – start to be erected at various sites. Some of the earliest of these tower-like tombs, from Xanthus, Isinda, Tüse, Gürses and Trysa for example (sites marked with an X in Fig. 5), carried relief sculptures around their tops. Apart from the later Harpy Monument (c. 480 BC), which includes siren-type figures abducting young girls, and a few "eastern-style" figures stabbing rampant lions on one or two of the earlier tombs, the reliefs include plenty of hoplite style warriors, but are devoid of the kind of myths shown in the Kızılbel paintings.[118] This is confusing, since it is at places such as Xanthus that an increase in Attic pottery imports is notable, and an early fifth-century BC cup foot from the acropolis of that city even carries a Greek hexameter.[119] Both coast and *yayla* were ostensibly under Achaemenid administration at the time. One infers, however, that such different display patterns stem at least in part from different circles of contact, and indicate differing regional dynamics in operation along the western and central coast of Lycia, separated as it was from the inland Milyad by rugged mountains. The Milyad may have been in contact with the Mediterranean through the Arycandus River valley in eastern Lycia, still the easiest route between plain and coast, or through Pamphylia to its east. So far only a little is known of archaic Limyra, at the mouth of the Arycandus River, but further investigation of these levels may help to shed light on its relationship to the Milyad and the Mediterranean.[120]

Conclusions and Reflections

Both of the tombs considered here offer different possibilities for narrowing down some reasons why the mythological images they bear may have been chosen. The Polyxena Sarcophagus presents a case of carefully selected and controlled imagery: a juxtaposition of epitomes of death and grief through the murder of Polyxena and the mourning of the Trojan women (also important protagonists in that sense), and life through what may well be a wedding, and more specifically as proposed here the wedding of Andromache – a wedding which not only complements a Trojan-oriented package, but which was a topic of archaic period poetry. The subjects seem female-

---

118 See Draycott 2007; 2008.
119 Metzger 1972, no. 386, pl. 85 (A18–1482); Metzger and Moret 1999, 299 n. 9.
120 Limyra early phases: Gebauer 2012a; 2012b; Marksteiner 2012.

oriented, and even though a man may have been buried in the sarcophagus, the idea that it was designed for a woman need not be considered a problem. But on the other hand it is not necessary to *force* a decision about whether it was only meaningful in terms of one or another gender, especially if it was, as the sexing of the bones indicates, used for a man.

Neither is it necessary to see the iconography as strictly meaningful for a "native" Anatolian group or for Greeks – at least not in the sense that one can identify the group through their iconographic choices. One suspects that in the high traffic Hellespontine area ethno-linguistic identity may have been important, and there is every chance that the sarcophagus was made to be meaningful on that level, or, if not intended, that viewers could make that of it. The staging of this sarcophagus with its innovative depictions of mythological stories – all the more innovative if one does take Sides C and D as a rare pictorial rendition of the wedding of Andromache – would have been a major local event, pulling in viewers and allowing them to form opinions, perhaps even *inciting* ethnic identification. As we cannot know the ethnicity of the group who had the tomb made, however, one need not insist on it having to be read one or another way. It is also possible to view the tomb more generally as a visual event, drawing attention, making a landmark and in doing so revising local social relations with the community and establishing hierarchic power through private possession of such a wonder. One can in this way appreciate the relevance of the programme and also allow for subjective receptions and meanings – and indeed appreciate that as a part of what makes it work.

What is most striking is that this was a method of social distinction that is located in the Achaemenid Empire period, not just because it can be seen as an identity response on a political level, but because it emphasises the enrichment of its provinces, set abuzz with greater abilities to obtain materials and ideas, and to create and become new things. This is all the more clear in the case of the Kızılbel tomb. There, the programme seems far less controlled. With some of the paintings, such as the ambush of Troilus and the allusion to, if not *the* departure of Amphiaraus, it is relatively easy to appreciate how they could have resonated in context as epitomes or *exempla* of blameless deaths, in two different ways. With others, such as the beheading of Medusa and the painting here identified as the exposure of Andromeda, immediate relevance is harder to pin down, and may not have been the point. Rather than self-representation in the sense of conveying the identity of the deceased in any direct way, eulogising him, or functioning as allegories, it has been suggested here that one might think of these paintings as parts of an elegy – a medley celebrating the deceased without dictating meanings about death or him as a person.

How unexpected it is for myth to be used in this fashion in the Milyad in this period is something which has not been highlighted in the literature, and indeed the social structure and connections of the Milyad in this period are generally not very well-known. The influx of this visual range and the innovative creation of what appear to be bespoke (and thus difficult to identify) paintings in an area which had previously shown connections with central Anatolia imply the emergence of cultural and economic links with new areas. The mythological themes in general as well as the painting of the ship suggest that the Mediterranean was now an important imaginative reference point. Themes with far off lands and the unusual winged figure in the "Amphiaraus" painting hint at interactions with the Eastern Mediterranean. The contrast with the themes that prevail on the contemporary pillar tombs in Lycia along the south coast augments and expands the impression from the tomb architecture, both indicating how much the two areas differed in priorities and perhaps connections, even if the *yayla* was now more Mediterranean-oriented.

None of this undermines the value of considering the relevance of the particular mythological subjects adorning these tombs. One should not underestimate the sophistication that went into their creation, selection of themes and the rendering of complex narratives visually, which are important parts of understanding mindsets and behaviours of people in the past. It is not just what one can glean from the subjects chosen and their rendering that matters, though, but also the fact that epic language is being chosen as a method of attraction at all.

Often, when tombs like this are set into historical context the concentration lies on political history, using literary sources for political geography and event history and taking images as responses or expressions of political ideologies, especially "Greek versus Persian" politics that tend to dominate discussions of Achaemenid Asia Minor.[121] The emphasis here has been more on discerning economic and connectivity patterns, which might be missed without attention to "art" and the imaginative sphere. In the second section of this paper it was noted that "making meaning" is a term intended to acknowledge modern-day scholarly agency in the production of explanations. The concepts of economy and connectivity should therefore be admitted as central to the kind of historical explanation offered here. Whether this complements or conflicts with the kinds of meanings and the kinds of histories that others want to make is something this paper opens for discussion.

Abbreviations

ABV   Beazley, J. D. *Attic Black-figure Vase-painters* (Oxford, 1956).
BAdd[2]   Carpenter, Th. H., Th. Mannack and M. Mendonça. *Beazley Addenda*, second edition (Oxford, 1989).
CVA   *Corpus Vasorum Antiquorum*.
LIMC   *Lexicon Iconographicum Mythologiae Classicae* (Zurich, 1981–1997).
Paralipomena   Beazley, J. D. *Paralipomena. Additions to Attic Black-figure Vase-painters and to Attic Red-figure Vase-painters* (Oxford, 1971).

---

121 Cf. again Hölscher 2011, on meaning of myth for group identities in contexts of conflict such as the Persian Wars.

Bibliography

Akurgal, E. *Zwei Grabstelen vorklassischer Zeit aus Sinope* (Berlin, 1955).

Akyüz, U. Samsun-Kurupelit'de Ele Geçen Bir Grup Mezar Steli ve Çakalca-Karadoğan Höyük Üzerine Bir İnceleme. *Kubaba. Arkeoloji – Sanat Tarihi – Tarih Dergisi* 22 (2013), 33–50.

Arnold, B. "Honorary Males" or Women of Substance? Gender, status and power in Iron Age Europe. *Journal of European Archaeology* 3 (1995), 153–168.

Ateşlier, S. *Daskyleion Buluntuları Işığında Batı Anadolu'da Akhaemenid Dönemi Mimarisi.* PhD thesis, Ege Üniversitesi (1999).

Ateşlier, S. Observations on an Early Classical Building of the Satrapal Period at Daskyleion, in: *Achaemenid Anatolia. Proceedings of the First International Symposium on Anatolia in the Achaemenid Period, Bandırma 15–18 August 1997*, edited by T. Bakır (Leiden, 2001), 147–168.

Ateşlier, S. and E. Öncü. Gumuşçay Polyksena Lahiti Üzerine Yeni Gözlemler: Mimari ve iconografik açıdan bakış. *Olba* 10 (2004), 45–87, pls. 4–12.

Audley-Miller, L. The Banquet in Palmyrene Funerary Contexts, in: *Dining and Death: Interdisciplinary Perspectives on the "Funerary Banquet" in Ancient Art, Burial and Belief*, edited by C. M. Draycott and M. Stamatopoulou (Leuven, 2016), 553–590.

Austin, M. M. Greek Tyrants and the Persians, 546–479 BC. *Classical Quarterly* 40 (1990), 289–306.

Aytekin, E. Remarques sur les constructions architecturales de la période achéménide à Daskyléion, in: *The Achaemenid Impact on Local Populations and Cultures in Anatolia (6th–4th Centuries B.C.). Symposium in Istanbul, 21–22 May 2005*, edited by A. Dinçol and İ. Delemen (Istanbul, 2007), 177–194.

Bakır, T. A Phrygian Inscription Found at Daskyleion. *Museum* 4 (1991), 60–61.

Bakır, T. Die Satrapie in Daskyleion, in: *Achaemenid Anatolia. Proceedings of the First International Symposium on Anatolia in the Achaemenid Period, Bandırma 15–18 August 1997*, edited by T. Bakır (Leiden, 2001), 169–180.

Bakır, T. and R. Gusmani. Eine neue phrygische Inschrift aus Daskyleion. *Epigraphica Anatolica* 18 (1993), 157–164.

Bakır T., G. R. Gürtekin-Demir and C. Tanrıver. Daskyleion 2001. *KazıSonuçlarıToplantısı* 24.1 (2002), 491–500.

Bapty, I. and T. Yates. *Archaeology after Structuralism: Post-structuralism and the Practice of Archaeology* (London, 1990).

Barringer, J. M. *Art, Myth, and Ritual in Classical Greece* (New York, 2008).

Bérard, C. (ed.) *A City of Images: Iconography and Society in Ancient Greece* (Princeton, 1989).

Bérard, C. The Image of the Other and the Foreign Hero, in: *Not the Classical Ideal. Athens and the Construction of the Other in Greek Art*, edited by Beth Cohen (Leiden, 2000), 390–412.

Bindman, D., H. L. Gates and K. C. C. Dalton (eds.) *The Image of the Black in Western Art* (Cambridge, Mass., 2010).

Borchhardt, J. *Die Bauskulptur des Heroon von Limyra: Das Grabmal des lykischen Königs Perikles* (Berlin, 1976).

Börker-Klähn, J. Tumulus D. von Bayındır bei Elmalı als historischer Spiegel, in: *Licia e Lidia prima dell'ellenizzazione. Atti del convegno internazionale, Roma, 11–12 ottobre 1999*, edited by M. Giorgieri, M. Salvini, M. C. Trémouille and P. Vannicelli (Rome, 2003), 69–105.

Briant, P. *From Cyrus to Alexander: A History of the Persian Empire (= Histoire de l'empire perse, 1995)* (Winona Lake, 2002).

Buitron-Oliver, D. (ed.) *The Interpretation of Architectural Sculpture in Greece and Rome* (Washington, 1997).

Byre, C. S. Narration, Description, and Theme in the Shield of Achilles. *The Classical Journal* 88.1 (1992), 33–42.

Calder, W. M. A Reconstruction of Sophocles' Polyxena. *Greek, Roman and Byzantine Studies* 7 (1966), 31–56.

Campbell, D. A. *Greek Lyric, Volume 1: Sappho, Alcaeus* (Cambridge, Mass., 1990).

Carrington, P. The Heroic Age of Phrygia in Ancient Literature and Art. *Anatolian Studies* 27 (1977), 117–126.

Cook, J. M. *The Troad: an Archaeological and Topographical Study* (Oxford, 1973).

Coulton, J. J. North Lycia before the Romans, in: *Akten des II. internationalen Lykien-Symposions*, edited by J. Borchhardt and G. Dobesch (Vienna, 1993), 79–85.

Coulton, J. J. *The Balboura Survey and Settlement in Highland Southwest Anatolia* (London, 2012).

Counts, D. B. Master of the Lion: representation and hybridity in Cypriote sanctuaries. *American Journal of Archaeology* 112.1 (2008), 3–27.

Counts, D. B. and B. Arnold (eds.) *The Master of Animals in Old World Iconography* (Budapest, 2010).

Davis, W. The Deconstruction of Intentionality in Archaeology. *Antiquity* 66 (2015), 334–347.

Dennison, J. Citrate Analysis as a Means of Determining the Sex of Human Skeletal Material. *Archaelogy and Physical Anthropology in Oceania* 14 (1979), 136–143.

Derrida, J. Signature Event Context, in: *Limited Inc* (Evanston, Il., 1988).

Dörtlük, K. Elmalı Bayındır Tümülüsleri Kurtarma Kazısı. *Kazı Sonuçları Toplantısı* 10 (1988), 171–174.

Draycott, C. M. Dynastic Definitions: differentiating status claims in the archaic pillar tomb reliefs of Lycia, in: *Anatolian Iron Ages 6: The Proceedings of the Sixth Anatolian Iron Ages Symposium held at Eskişehir-Turkey, 16–19 August 2004*, edited by A. Sagona and A. Çilingiroğlu (Leuven, 2007), 103–134.

Draycott, C. M. Bird-women on the Harpy Monument from Xanthos, Lycia: sirens or harpies?, in: *Essays in Classical Archaeology for Eleni Vassiliou, 1977–2007*, edited by D. C. Kurtz, C. Meyer, D. Saunders, A. Tsingarida and N. Harris (Oxford, 2008), 145–153.

Draycott, C. M. "Heroa" and the City. Kuprlli's New Architecture and the Making of the "Lycian Acropolis" of Xanthus in the Early Classical Period. *Anatolian Studies* 65 (2015), 97–142.

Draycott, C. M. Activating the Achaemenid Landscape. The Broken Lion Tomb (Yılan Taş) and the Phrygian Highlands in the Achaemenid Period, in: *The Phrygian Lands over Time (from Prehistory to the Middle of the 1st Millenium AD)*, edited by G. R. Tsetskhladze and M. Bilge Baştürk (Leuven, forthcoming).

Dusinberre, E. R. M. *Empire, Authority, and Autonomy in Achaemenid Anatolia* (Cambridge, 2013).

Elsner, J. *Art and the Roman Viewer: the Transformation of Art from the Pagan World to Christianity* (Cambridge, 1995).

Elsner, J. *Roman Eyes: Visuality and Subjectivity in Art and Text* (Princeton, 2007).

Elsner, J. Introduction, in: *Life, Death and Representation. Some New Work on Roman Sarcophagi*, edited by J. Elsner and J. Huskinson (Berlin, 2010), 1–20.

Elsner, J. Visual Culture and Ancient History: issues of empiricism and ideology in the Samos Stele at Athens. *Classical Antiquity* 34 (2015), 33–73.

Elsner, J. Review of Janine Balty, Jean-Charles Balty (ed.), Franz Cumont. Recherches sur le symbolisme funéraire des Romains. Bibliotheca Cumontiana – Scripta Maiora (BICUMA), 4 (Turnhout, 2015). *Bryn Mawr Classical Review (2016.06.38)* (2016), (http://bmcr.brynmawr.edu/2016/2016–06–38.html).

Evans, C. Acts of Enclosure: a consideration of concentrically-organised causewayed enclosures, in: *The Archaeology of Context in the Neolithic and Bronze Age: Recent Trends*, edited by J. C. Barrett and I. Kinnes (Sheffield, 1988), 85–96.

Farmer, J. L. and M. F. Lane. The Ins and Outs of the Great Megaron. Symbol, Performance, and Elite Identities around and between Mycenaean Palaces. *Studi micenei ed egeo-anatolici* 2 (2016), 41–79.

Fiedler, G. *Le monde phrygien du Xe s. au IVe s. avant notre ère: culture matérielle, territoires et structures sociales.* PhD thesis, Université de Provence, Aix-Marseille I (2003).

Fittschen, K. and P. Zanker. *Katalog der römischen Porträts in den kapitolinischen Museen und den anderen kommunalen Sammlungen der Stadt Rom 1–4* (Mainz am Rhein; Berlin, 1983–2014).

Fleischer, R. *Der Klagefrauensarkophag aus Sidon* (Tübingen, 1983).

Freedberg, D. *The Power of Images: Studies in the History and Theory of Response* (Chicago, 1989).

Gebauer, J. Prehellenistic Ceramics of the 2002–2005 Excavations at Limyra. The Banded and Waveline Pottery, in: *Uluslararası Genç Bilimciler Buluşması, 1. Anadolu akdenizi, sempozyumu 4–7 kasim 2009, Antalya. Sempozyum bildirileri/International Young Scholars Conference, 1. Mediterranean Anatolia, 4–7 November 2009, Antalya. Symposium proceedings*, edited by K. Dörtlük (Antalya, 2012a), 123–130.

Gebauer, J. Die archaische und klassische Fundkeramik der Weststadtgrabung 2002–2005. Ein Überblick, in: *40 Jahre Grabung Limyra. Akten des internationalen Symposiums Wien 3.–5. Dezember 2009*, edited by M. Seyer (Vienna, 2012b), 169–178.

Gell, A. The Technology of Enchantment and the Enchantment of Technology, in: *Anthropology, Art and Aesthetics*, edited by J. Coote and A. Shelton (Oxford, 1992), 40–66.

Gell, A. *Art and Agency: an Anthropological Theory* (Oxford, 1998).

Graves, C. P. Social Space in the English Medieval Parish Church. *Economy and Society* 18.3 (1989), 297–322.

Graves, C. P. *The Form and Fabric of Belief: an Archaeology of the Lay Experience of Religion in Medieval Norfolk and Devon* (Oxford, 2000).

Harmanşah, Ö. (ed.) *Of Rocks and Water: an Archaeology of Place* (Oxford, 2013a).

Harmanşah, Ö. *Cities and the Shaping of Memory in the Ancient Near East* (Cambridge, 2013b).

Harmanşah, Ö. *Place, Memory and Healing: an Archaeology of Anatolian Rock Monuments* (London, 2014).

Haynes, S. *Etruscan Civilization. A Cultural History* (London, 2000).

Hedreen, G. *Capturing Troy. The Narrative Functions of Landscape in Archaic and Early Classical Art* (Ann Arbor, 2001).

Hitzl, I. *Die griechischen Sarkophage der archaischen und klassischen Zeit* (Jonsered, 1991).

Hölscher, T. The Concept of Roles and the Malaise of "Identity": Ancient Rome and the modern world, in: *Role Models in the Roman World: Identity and Assimilation*, edited by S. Bell and I. L. Hansen (Ann Arbor, 2008), 41–56.

Hölscher, T. Architectural Sculpture: Messages? Programs? Towards rehabilitating the notion of "decoration", in: *Structure, Image, Ornament: Architectural Sculpture in the Greek World*, edited by P. Schultz and R. von den Hoff (Oxford, 2009), 54–67.

Hölscher, T. Myths, Images, and the Typology of Identities in Early Greek Art, in: *Cultural Identity in the Ancient Mediterranean*, edited by E. S. Gruen (Los Angeles, 2011), 47–65.

Işık, F. *Die Statuetten vom Tumulus D bei Elmalı* (Antalya, 2003).

Johnson, M. *Archaeological Theory, an Introduction* (Oxford, 1999).

Jordanova, L. J. *The Look of the Past: Visual and Material Evidence in Historical Practice* (Cambridge, 2012).

Junker, K. *Interpreting the Images of Greek Myths: an Introduction* (Cambridge, 2012).

Kaptan, D. *The Daskyleion Bullae. Seal Images from the Western Achaemenid Empire* (Leiden, 2002).

Karagöz, Ş. Neue Ansichten zu freistehenden Grabmonumenten aus Daskyleion, in: *The Achaemenid Impact on Local Populations and Cultures in Anatolia (6th–4th Centuries B.C.). Symposium in Istanbul, 21–22 May 2005*, edited by A. Dinçol and İ. Delemen (Istanbul, 2007).

Karagöz, Ş. *Kleinasiatisch-gräko-persische Kunstwerke im Archäologischen Museum von Istanbul* (Tübingen, 2013).

Kearns, E. Saving the City, in: *The Greek City from Homer to Alexander*, edited by O. Murray and S. R. F. Price (Oxford, 2002), 323–346.

Keen, A. G. *Dynastic Lycia: a Political History of the Lycians and their Relations with Foreign Powers, c. 545–362 B.C.* (Leiden, 1998).

Koenigs, W. Zwei Säulen aus Biga. *Istanbuler Mitteilungen* 39 (1989), 289–295, pl. 32.

Kökten Ersoy, H. Two Wheeled Vehicles from Lydia and Mysia. *Istanbuler Mitteilungen* 48 (1998), 107–133.

Kökten, H. Conservation and Reconstruction of Phrygian Chariot Wheels from Mysia, in: *Thracians and Phrygians: Problems of Parallelism. Proceedings of an International Symposium on the Archaeology, History, and Ancient Languages of Thrace and Phrygia, Middle East Technical University, Ankara, Turkey, 2–6 June 1995*, edited by N. Tuna, Z. Aktüre and M. Lynch (Ankara, 1998), 131–146.

Kolb, F. Die Entstehung der Landschaft Lykien. Historische Geographie und archäologischer Befund, in: *Kulturraum und Territorialität. Archäologische Theorien, Methoden und Fallbeispiele. Kolloquium des DFG-SPP 1171, Esslingen 17.–18. Januar 2007*, edited by D. Krausse and O. Nakoinz (Rahden, 2009), 131–141.

Krauskopf, I. *Totengötter und Todesdämonen im vorhellenistischen Etrurien* (Florence, 1987).

Krauskopf, I. The Grave and Beyond in Etruscan Religion, in: *The Religion of the Etruscans*, edited by N. Thompson de Grummond and E. Simon (Austin, 2006), 66–89.

Kurtz, D. C. Mistress and Maid. *Annali di archeologia e storia antica* 10 (1988), 141–149.

Kütük, S. Balıkesir Üçpınar Tümülüsü. *Arkeoloji ve Sanat* 69 (1995), 17–22.

Laflı, E. and J. Meischner. Eine frühklassische Stele aus Samsun-Amisos. *Istanbuler Mitteilungen* 65 (2015), 63–81.

Lane Fox, R. *Travelling Heroes: Greeks and their Myths in the Epic Age of Homer* (London, 2008).

Leader, R. E. In Death not Divided: gender, family, and state on classical Athenian stelai. *American Journal of Archaeology* 101 (1997), 683–699.

Leaf, W. *Strabo on the Troad: Book XIII, Cap.1* (Cambridge, 1923).

Lissarrague, F. *Greek Vases: the Athenians and their Images* (New York, 2001).

Lockwood, S. Reading a Fourth-century B.C. Sepulchral Relief in Northern Lycia: iconography, influence and identity, in: *3. Likya sempozyumu 7–10 Kasım 2005 Antalya: sempozyum bildirileri/The 3rd Symposium on Lycia: 07–10 November 2005, Antalya: Symposium Proceedings*, edited by K. Dörtlük, B. Varkıvanç, T. Kahya, J. des Courtils, M. Doğan Alparslan and R. Boyraz. (Antalya, 2006), 409–423.

Lockwood, S. *Aytas Mevkii/Islamlar in the Elmali Basin, Turkey: a Multi-period Sepulchral Site in Northern Lycia*. PhD thesis, University of Cincinnati (2011).

Lorenz, K. *Ancient Mythological Images and Their Interpretation. An Introduction to Iconology, Semiotics and Image Studies in Classical Art History* (Cambridge, 2016).

Ma, J. Mysians on the Çan Sarcophagus? Ethnicity and Domination in Achaimenid Military Art. *Historia* 30 (2008), 1–16.

Ma, J. Review of Peter Schultz, Ralf von den Hoff (ed.), Structure, Image, Ornament: Architectural Sculpture in the Greek World. Proceedings of an International Conference Held at the American School of Classical Studies, 27–28 November 2004. (Oxford: Oxbow Books, 2009). *Bryn Mawr Classical Review* (2011.03.48) (2011), (http://bmcr.brynmawr.edu/2011/2011–03–48.html).

MacSweeney, N. *Foundation Myths and Politics in Ancient Ionia* (Cambridge, 2013).

Maffre, F. Example of the Persian Occupation in the Satrapy of Phrygia through the Study of the Population from the Asian Provinces in the Achaemenid Empire (Semites/Iranians), in: *The Achaemenid Impact on Local Populations and Cultures in Anatolia (6th–4th Centuries B.C.).*

Symposium in Istanbul, 21–22 May 2005, edited by A. Dinçol and İ. Delemen (Istanbul, 2007), 225–246.

Marksteiner, T. Die Siedlungsgeschichte der ostlykischen Polis Limyra. Ein wissenschaftlicher Essay, in: *40 Jahre Grabung Limyra. Akten des internationalen Symposiums Wien 3.–5. Dezember 2009*, edited by M. Seyer (Vienna, 2012), 199–209.

Matheson, S. B. A Farewell with Arms: departing warriors on Athenian vases, in: *Periklean Athens and Its Legacy: Problems and Perspectives*, edited by J. M. Barringer and J. M. Hurwit (Austin, 2005), 23–35.

Mellink, M. J. Excavations at Karataş-Semayük and Elmalı, Lycia, 1969. *American Journal of Archaeology* 74 (1970), 245–259.

Mellink, M. J. Excavations at Karataş-Semayük and Elmalı, Lycia, 1970. *American Journal of Archaeology* 75 (1971), 245–255.

Mellink, M. J. Excavations at Karataş-Semayük and Elmalı, Lycia, 1971. *American Journal of Archaeology* 76 (1972), 257–269.

Mellink, M. J. Excavations at Karataş-Semayük and Elmalı, Lycia, 1972. *American Journal of Archaeology* 77 (1973), 293–307.

Mellink, M. J. Excavations at Karataş-Semayük and Elmalı, Lycia, 1973. *American Journal of Archaeology* 78 (1974), 351–359.

Mellink, M. J. Excavations at Karataş-Semayük and Elmalı, Lycia, 1974. *American Journal of Archaeology* 79 (1975), 349–355.

Mellink, M. J. *Kızılbel: an Archaic Painted Tomb Chamber in Northern Lycia* (Philadelphia, 1998).

Meritt, B. D., H. T. Wade-Gery and M. F. McGregor. *The Athenian Tribute Lists* (Princeton, 1939).

Metzger, H. *Fouilles de Xanthos 4: les céramiques archaïques et classiques de l'acropole lycienne* (Paris, 1972).

Metzger, H. Sur quelques emprunts faites aux art d'"Occident" par l'imagerie lycienne des périodes archaique et classique, in: *Beiträge zur Altertumskunde Kleinasiens: Festschrift für Kurt Bittel*, edited by R. M. Boehmer (Mainz, 1983), 361–368, pls. 74–75.

Metzger, H. and J.-M. Moret. Observations sur certaines des peintures tombales de Kızılbel en Lycie du Nord-Est. *Journal des Savants* July-December (1999), 295–318.

Miller, S. G. Two Painted Chamber Tombs of Northern Lycia at Kızılbel and Karaburun, in: *Tatarlı. Renklerin Dönüşü/The Return of Colours/Rückkehr der Farben (ex. cat.)*, edited by L. Summerer and A. von Kienlin (Istanbul, 2010), 318–329.

Milner, N. P. The Remaining Inscriptions from the Balboura Survey Project, in: *The Balboura Survey and Settlement in Highland Southwest Anatolia*, edited by J. J. Coulton (London, 2012), 83–127.

Momigliano, N. et al. Settlement History and Material Culture in Southwest Turkey: report on the 2008–2010 survey at Çaltılar Höyük (northern Lycia). *Anatolian Studies* 61 (2011), 61–121.

Morris, I. *Death-ritual and Social Structure in Classical Antiquity* (Cambridge, 1992).

Mukerji, C. *Territorial Ambitions and the Gardens of Versailles* (Cambridge, 1997).

Neer, R. "A Tomb Both Great and Blameless". Marriage and Murder on a Sarcophagus from the Hellespont. *Res. Anthropology and Aesthetics* 61–62 (2012), 99–115.

Oakley, J. H. Some "Other" Members of the Atheniean Household: maids and their mistresses in fifth century Athenian art, in: *Not the Classical Ideal. Athens and the Construction of the Other in Greek Art*, edited by B. Cohen (Leiden, 2000), 227–247.

Oakley, J. H. *Picturing Death in Classical Athens. The Evidence of the White Lekythoi* (Cambridge, 2004).

Osborne, J. F. *Approaching Monumentality in Archaeology:/IEMA Proceedings, Volume 3* (Albany, NY, 2014).

Osborne, M. J. The Satrapy of Mysia. *Grazer Beiträge* 3 (1975), 291–315.

Osborne, R. Whose Image and Superscription is This? (Review article on A City of Images). *Arion* 1.2 (1991), 255–275.

Osborne, R. Archaic and Classical Greek Temple Sculpture and the Viewer, in: *Word and Image in Ancient Greece*, edited by N. K. Rutter and B. A. Sparkes (Edinburgh, 2000), 228–246.

Özgen, E. and İ. Özgen. (eds.) *Antalya Museum* (Ankara, 1988).

Özgen, İ. Survey and Preliminary Excavations at Hacımusalar (Ancient Choma) near Elmalı in Northern Lycia, in: *Light on Top of the Black Hill: Studies Presented to Halet Çambel/Karatepe'deki İşik: Halet Çambel'e sununlan yazılar*, edited by G. Arsebük, M. J. Mellink and W. Schirmer (Istanbul, 1998), 603–609.

Özgen, İ. Elmalı ovası ve Hacımusalar, in: *3. Likya sempozyumu 7–10 Kasım 2005 Antalya: sempozyum bildirileri/The 3rd Symposium on Lycia: 7–10 November 2005, Antalya: symposium proceedings*, edited by K. Dörtlük, B. Varkıvanç, T. Kahya, J. des Courtils, M. Doğan Alparslan and R. Boyraz. (Antalya, 2006), 537–555.

Panofsky, E. *Meaning in the Visual Arts: papers in and on art history* (Garden City, 1955).

Parker Pearson, M. *The Archaeology of Death and Burial* (Stroud, 1999).

Paschinger, E. Zur Ikonographie der Malereien im Tumulusgrab von Kızılbel aus etruskologischer Sicht. *Jahreshefte des österreichischen archäologischen Instituts in Wien* 56 (1985), 1–47.

Phillips, K. M. Jr. Perseus and Andromeda. *American Journal of Archaeology* 72 (1968), 1–23.

Polat, G. Daskyleion'dan yeni bir Anadolu-Pers steli/A New Perso-Anatolian Stele from Daskyleion, in: *The Achaemenid Impact on Local Populations and Cultures in Anatolia (6th-4th Centuries B.C.). Symposium in Istanbul, 21–22 May 2005*, edited by A. Dinçol and İ. Delemen (Istanbul, 2007), 215–224.

Reilly, J. Many Brides: "mistress and maid" on Athenian lekythoi. *Hesperia* 58 (1989), 411–444.

Reinsberg, C. Der Polyxena-Sarkophag in Çanakkale. *Olba* 4 (2001), 71–99, pls. 23–26.

Reinsberg, C. Der Polyxena-Sarkophag in Çanakkale, in: *Sepulkral- und Votivdenkmäler östlicher Mittelmeergebiete (7. Jahrhundert v. Chr.–1. Jahrhundert n. Chr.): Kulturbegegnungen im Spannungfeld von Akzeptanz und Resistenz. Akten des Internationalen Symposiums Mainz, 1–3 Nov 2001*, edited by R. Bol and D. Kreikenbom (Mainz, 2004), 199–217.

Ridgway, B. S. *Prayers in Stone. Greek Architectural Sculpture ca. 600–100 B.C.E.* (Berkeley, 1999).

Robert, J. and L. Robert. *Hellenica 9: Inscriptions et reliefs d'Asie Mineure* (Paris, 1950).

Robert, J. and L. Robert. Bulletin épigraphique. *Revue des études greques* 64 (1951), 119–216.

Robert, L. *Études anatoliennes* (Paris, 1937).

Roosevelt, C. H. *The Archaeology of Lydia, from Gyges to Alexander* (New York, 2009).

Rose, C. B. Troy and the Historical Imagination. *The Classical World* 91 (1998), 405–413.

Rose, C. B. Separating Fact from Fiction in the Aiolian Migration. *Hesperia*, 77 (2008), 399–430.

Rose, C. B. *The Archaeology of Greek and Roman Troy* (New York, 2014).

Rose, C. B. and R. Körpe. The Tumuli of Troy and the Troad, in: *Tumulus as Sema: Space, Politics, Culture and Religion in the First Millenium BC*, edited by O. Henry and U. Kelp (Berlin, 2016), 373–385.

Rose, C. B. and R. Körpe. The Granicus River Valley Survey Project, 2007. *Araştırma Sonuçları Toplantısı* 26: 2 (2009), 343–356.

Rose, C. B., B. Tekkök and R. Körpe. Granicus River Valley Survey Project, 2004–2005. *Studia Troica* 17 (2007), 65–150.

Rudolph, C. *Das 'Harpyien-Monument' von Xanthos: Seine Bedeutung innerhalb der spätarchaischen Plastik* (Oxford, 2003).

Sabetai, V. Aspects of Nuptial and Genre Imagery in Fifth-Century Athens: issues of interpretation and methodology, in: *Athenian Potters and Painters*, edited by J. H. Oakley, W. D. E. Coulson and O. Palagia (Athens, 1994), 319–335.

Şare, T. *Marriage to Death on the Polyxena Sarcophagus*. MA thesis, Rutgers University (2005).

Şare, T. An Archaic Ivory Figurine from a Tumulus near Elmalı: cultural hybridization and a new Ana-
    tolian style. *Hesperia* 79:1 (2010), 53–78.
Şare, T. The Sculpture of the Heroon of Perikles at Limyra: the making of a Lycian king. *Anatolian
    Studies* 63 (2013), 55–74.
Schmitt, M. L. Bellerophon and the Chimaera in Archaic Greek Art. *American Journal of Archaeology*
    70 (1966), 341–347.
Schneider, R. M. Context Matters. Pliny's Phryges and the Basilica Paulli in Rome, in: *The Archae-
    ology of Greece and Rome: Studies in Honour of Anthony Snodgrass*, edited by J. Bintliff and
    K. Rutter (Edinburgh, 2016), 402–434.
Schultz, P. and R. von den Hoff. (eds.) *Structure, Image, Ornament: Architectural Sculpture in the
    Greek World. Proceedings of an International Conference Held at the American School of Classi-
    cal Studies, 27–28 November 2004* (Oxford, 2009).
Schwertheim, E. Studien zur historischen Geographie Mysiens. *Epigraphica Anatolica* 11 (1988),
    65–78.
Sevinç, N. and C. B. Rose. A New Sarcophagus of Polyxena from the Salvage Excavations at
    Gümüşçay. *Studia Troica* 6 (1996), 251–264.
Sevinç, N. and C. B. Rose. The Dedetepe Tumulus. *Studia Troica* 8 (1998), 305–327.
Sevinç, N. and C. B. Rose. A Child's Sarcophagus from the Salvage Excavations at Gümüşçay. *Studia
    Troica* 9 (1999), 489–509.
Sevinç, N., C. B. Rose, R. Körpe, M. Tombul, D. Strahan, H. Kiesewetter and J. Wallrodt. A New
    Painted Graeco-Persian Sarcophagus from Çan. *Studia Troica* 11 (2002), 383–420.
Shanks, M. and C. Y. Tilley. *Social Theory and Archaeology* (Cambridge, 1987a).
Shanks, M. and C. Y. Tilley. *Re-constructing Archaeology: Theory and Practice* (Cambridge, 1987b).
Shapiro, H. A. Comings and Goings. The Iconography of Departure and Arrival on Attic Vases. *Métis* 5
    (1990), 113–126.
Smith, R. R. R. *Hellenistic Royal Portraits* (Oxford, 1988).
Smith, R. R. R. Review of Bernard Andreae, Laokoon und die Gründung Roms (Mainz, 1988). *Gnomon*
    63 (1991), 351–358.
Smith, R. R. R. The Use of Images: visual history and ancient history, in: *Classics in Progress; Essays
    on Ancient Greece and Rome*, edited by T. P. Wiseman (Oxford, 2002), 59–102.
Smith, R. R.R and C. H. Hallett. Troilos and Achilles: a monumental statue group from Aphrodisias.
    The Journal of Roman Studies 105 (2015), 124–182.
Smith, R. R.R, S. Dillon, C. H. Hallett, J. Lenaghan and J. Van Voorhis. *Roman Portrait Statuary from
    Aphrodisias* (Mainz, 2006).
Snickare, M. How to Do Things with the Piazza San Pietro: performativity and Baroque architecture,
    in: *Performativity and Performance in Baroque Rome*, edited by P. Gillgren and M. Snickare
    (Farnham, 2012), 65–86.
Snowden, F. M. *Blacks in Antiquity: Ethiopians in the Greco-Roman Experience* (Cambridge, Mass.,
    1970).
Snowden, F. M. *Before Color Prejudice: the Ancient View of Blacks* (Cambridge, Mass., 1983).
Stansbury-O'Donnell, M. *Looking at Greek Art* (Cambridge, 2011).
Stears, K. Dead Women's Society: constructing female gender in classical Athenian funerary
    sculpture, in: *Tradition and Society in Greek Archaeology. Bridging the Great Divide*, edited
    by N. Spencer (New York, 1995), 109–131.
Steingräber, S. *Etruscan Painting. Catalogue Raisonné of Etruscan Wall Painting* (New York, 1986).
Steingräber, S. Etruscan Tomb Painting of the Archaic Period and its Relationship to the Painting
    in Ionian Asia Minor, in: *Tatarlı. Renklerin Dönüşü/The Return of Colours/Rückkehr der Farben
    (ex. cat.)*, edited by L. Summerer and A. von Kienlin (Istanbul, 2010), 355–366.
Stewart, P. *Statues in Roman Society. Representation and Response* (Oxford, 2003).

Stewart, P. Gell's Idols and Roman Cult, in: *Art's Agency and Art History*, edited by R. Osborne and J. Tanner (Oxford, 2007), 158–178.

Stewart, P. *The Social History of Roman Art* (Cambridge, 2008).

Summerer, L., A. von Kienlin. (eds.) *Tatarlı. Renklerin Dönüşü/The Return of Colours/Rückkehr der Farben (ex. cat.)* (Istanbul, 2010).

Swenson, E. The Materialities of Place Making in the Ancient Andes: a critical appraisal of the ontological turn in archaeological Interpretation. *Journal of Archaeological Method and Theory* 22 3 (2015), 677–712.

Tanner, J. Portraits and Agency: a comparative view, in: *Art's Agency and Art History*, edited by R. Osborne and J. Tanner (Oxford, 2007), 70–94.

Thomas, J. Archaeologies of Place and Landscape, in: *Archaeological Theory Today*, edited by I. Hodder (Cambridge, 2001), 165–186.

Tilley, C. Y. *Material Culture and Text: the Art of Ambiguity* (London, 1991).

Topper, K. Perseus, the Maiden Medusa, and the Imagery of Abduction. *Hesperia,* 76 (2007), 73–105.

Topper, K. Maidens, Fillies and the Death of Medusa on a Seventh-century Pithos. *The Journal of Hellenic Studies* 130 (2010), 109–119.

Trachsel, A. La Troade. Entre espace littéraire et paysage historique. *Appunti romani di filologia* 4 (2002), 41–53.

Turnbull, D. Performance and Narrative, Bodies and Movement in the Construction of Places and Objects, Spaces and Knowledges. The case of the Maltese megaliths. *Theory, Culture & Society* 19 (2002), 125–143.

Uçankuş, H. T. *Ana Tanrıça Kybele'nin ve Kral Midas'in Ülkesi Phrygia (Kültür Rehberi)* (Ankara, 2002).

Vernant, J. P., P. Vidal-Naquet and J. Lloyd. *Myth and Tragedy in Ancient Greece* (New York, 1990).

Weiss, K. M. On Systematic Bias in Skeleton Sexing. *American Journal of Physical Anthropology* 37 (1972), 239–250.

Whitley, D. S. *Reader in Archaeological Theory: Post-processual and Cognitive Approaches* (London, 1998).

Wilson, V. A. *The Cesnola Sarcophagi. Studies in Cypriot Iconography and Sculpture.* D. Phil. thesis, Oxford (1972).

Wrede, W. *Kriegers Ausfahrt in der archaisch-griechischen Kunst* (Mainz, 1916).

Wylie, A. *Thinking from Things: Essays in the Philosophy of Archaeology* (Berkeley, 2002).

Yalouri, A. A Hero's Departure. *American Journal of Archaeology* 75 (1971), 269–275.

Zanker, P. *The Power of Images in the Age of Augustus* (Ann Arbor, 1988).

Zanker, P. *The Mask of Socrates: the Image of the Intellectual in Antiquity* (Berkeley, 1995).

Zanker, P. and B. C. Ewald. *Living with Myths: the Imagery of Roman Sarcophagi* (Oxford, 2012).

Tanja S. Scheer

Myth, Memory and the Past

Wandering Heroes between Arcadia and Cyprus

Myths and heroes do not wander by themselves. Myths require media to transport them from one place to another. They need mediators. Such mediation may be provided by the story-teller or the rhapsode who recites the tales. Or else, the mediators may be the people who communicate the myth, again with the help of media: written texts, pictures or objects, which make the mythical stories visible and durable. After all, mythical subject matters are preserved and passed on for a reason. They require occasion and opportunity to "start moving", they wander within historical contexts, always with a cause. Studying wandering myths requires us, then, to direct our attention to a range of periods of Greek history as well as places and forms of mythical testimonials. Following this approach, the key question for the modern historian's methodology cannot be whether "mythology" or even a specific myth relates historical truths in absolute terms, or whether it contains memories of historical facts.[1] Instead, the question to focus on is where, when and why particular mythical tales manifest themselves in different places. Who lets them wander, sets them in motion, recounts them at different times and in different places?[2] Furthermore, a number of mythical tales feature protagonists who "wander" around. Ancient authors reveal a concept of reconstructing the past, which conceives of their own early history as a series of migrations:[3] in this, the names and genealogies of mythical heroes form focal points to put this tradition in concrete terms, pinpoint it chronologically and ennoble its content.

This paper examines the mythical story of Arcadian wanderers, who are said to have come to Cyprus after the Trojan War. Who told the story of Arcadian founders on Cyprus in antiquity and what media gave it shape there? In what period of Greek history was this myth considered important and how did it function within the context of its immediate testimonial?

---

1 Cf. Malkin 1998, 5.

2 On the function of local mythologies cf. Price 2005, 115; on the meaning of the fruitful misunderstanding in communicating with and about myth see Scheer 1993, 341 and Lane Fox 2008, 103.

3 Cf. Malkin 1998, 3–5.

Note: This study would not have been possible without the support provided by the *Deutsche Forschungsgemeinschaft* as part of the project Sche 421/3–1 "Wo liegt Arkadien? Arkadienbilder in der klassischen Antike" ("Where is Arcadia? Images of Arcadia in Classical Antiquity"). The final draft of this chapter was completed in August 2015; later publications e.g. John Franklin's *Kinyras: The Divine Lyre* (Washington, 2015) could not be taken into consideration.

https://doi.org/10.1515/9783110421453-005

Colonising Cyprus: Agapenor and the Arcadians

In his eighth book, Pausanias gives an account of a special relationship between Arcadia and Cyprus:[4]

> Agapenor, the son of Ancaeus, the son of Lycurgus, who was king after Echemus, led the Arcadians to Troy. After the capture of Troy the storm that overtook the Greeks on their return home carried Agapenor and the Arcadian fleet to Cyprus, and so Agapenor became the founder of Paphos, and built the sanctuary of Aphrodite at Palaepaphos (Old Paphos). Up to that time the goddess had been worshipped by the Cyprians in the district called Golgi.

The myth of Agapenor and the Arcadians on Cyprus evidently sounded plausible to an ancient Greek audience. For one thing, the story inserted itself into the tradition and the claim to authority of the Homeric epics.[5] The Trojan War was accepted as historical fact, as the central event of a common Greek past.[6] According to Thucydides the Greeks' return from Troy was to blame for revolts, civil wars and migrations, while exiles "founded other cities".[7] This background provided a neat framework for the story of how Agapenor and the Arcadians ended up in Cyprus. Traditions of failed homeward journeys explained "why peoples moved about."[8]

Ancient recipients thus generally believed the tradition of Agapenor's arrival on Cyprus, while modern scholars saw Agapenor and his shipwrecked Arcadians as part of the still controversial debate about the Hellenisation of Cyprus in the early Iron Age. The mythical tradition was drawn on to confirm archaeological signs of Cyprus' Hellenisation. However, depending on how this Hellenisation was reconstructed, the same myths acted as historical memory of very different courses of historical events, connected merely by the same keyword of "migration". The extent of this broad range of interpretations is revealed by Sabine Fourrier's highly useful overview of the rather convoluted history of scholarship.[9] The tradition of Agapenor and his Arcadians received special attention in this context[10]: in 1944, Gjerstad already wrote that the

---

4 Paus. 8.5.2: Ἀγαπήνωρ δὲ ὁ Ἀγκαίου τοῦ Λυκούργου μετὰ Ἔχεμον βασιλεύσας ἐς Τροίαν ἡγήσατο Ἀρκάσιν. Ἰλίου δὲ ἁλούσης ὁ τοῖς Ἕλλησι κατὰ τὸν πλοῦν τὸν οἴκαδε ἐπιγενόμενος χειμὼν Ἀγαπήνορα καὶ τὸ Ἀρκάδων ναυτικὸν κατήνεγκεν ἐς Κύπρον, καὶ Πάφου τε Ἀγαπήνωρ ἐγένετο οἰκιστὴς καὶ τῆς Ἀφροδίτης κατεσκευάσατο ἐν Παλαιπάφῳ τὸ ἱερόν· τέως δὲ ἡ θεὸς παρὰ Κυπρίων τιμὰς εἶχεν ἐν Γολγοῖς καλουμένῳ χωρίῳ.
5 On Agapenor as Arcadian leader in epic: Hom. *Il.* 2.603–14, esp. 609.
6 Thuc. 1.9.1–4; cf. Hornblower 1991, 31; Malkin 1998, 3; Scheer 2003, 217.
7 Thuc. 1.12.1–2; cf. Hornblower 1991, 36–7.
8 Malkin 1998, 3; Finkelberg 2005, 150.
9 Fourrier 2008, 103–17.
10 Gjerstad 1944, 110, 114; cf. n. 13 below; see e.g. Maier 1973, who, however, later revises his position: cf. Maier 1986, 311–320; cf. e.g. also Vanschoonwinkel 1991, 301, 306: Agapenor's foundation as "refondation d'une ville préexistante".

historicity of this myth of the Arcadians was substantiated by "strong linguistic evidence".[11] Gjerstad's argument referred to the Arcadocypriot dialect of ancient Greek, itself a label that suggests a close connection between Cyprus and Arcadia. As has been emphasised frequently, Arcadocypriot is the Greek dialect which displays the closest relationship with Mycenaean Greek.[12] This does indeed indicate that Cyprus was inhabited comparably early on by speakers of an early Greek dialect.[13]

Less clear, however, is the connection between the dialectal evidence and the mythology. Two possibilities may present themselves: the story of the arrival of Agapenor and his Arcadians returning from Troy and arriving on Cyprus might indeed be based on local historical memory of the gradual migration by Peloponnesian Greeks. In this case, however, this "memory" would have distorted historical reality almost beyond recognition, channelling it instead – whenever this may have happened – into the familiar themes of mythology (theme: return journeys from Troy).[14] This sort of tradition would only be of limited value for reconstructing historical events. Alternatively, the connection between the Cypriot and the Arcadian dialect may already have been recognised as peculiar in antiquity: to explain it, one would have resorted to the widespread explanatory model of "migration", linking this to Trojan mythology: if epic had portrayed Agapenor as leader of Homeric Arcadians, who must have sailed around the Mediterranean, it would have seemed logical to connect similarities between Arcadians and Cypriots with his person.[15] Yet the surviving ancient sources neither think it worth mentioning the striking peculiarities of the Cypriot syllabary – illegible for anyone arriving from the Greek motherland – nor the strange linguistic habits of the Cypriots, postulated by modern scholarship to have

---

11 Gjerstad 1944, 111.

12 Cf. Ventris and Chadwick 1973, 68; Morpurgo-Davies 1992, 422; Finkelberg 2005, 126.

13 The oldest textual evidence identified as Greek on Cyprus is the inscription of a name O-pe-le-ta-u in the "Arcadian genitive" on the much discussed *obelos* from grave 11 of the necropolis of Palaepaphos-Skales (1050–950): Masson 1983, 414; Iacovou 2008a, 255; Iacovou 2008b, 650; Egetmeyer 2010 I, 396–7; Steele 2013, 42: "generally accepted to be the earliest Greek inscription from the island (indeed the earliest surviving Greek inscription following the Mycenaean texts)". That these early Greeks arrived on Cyprus with an "Arcadian sense of identity" is rather difficult to imagine. More plausible is the theory, similar to the one put forward by M. Voyatzis, that in Cyprus and Arcadia, both relatively remote regions, in different ways, an archaic dialect, similar to Mycenaean, could survive until the classical period, or develop itself in linguistically similar ways: Voyatzis 1985, 157–8: "each retaining similar elements of the eastern dialect in the historic period"; cf. also Colvin 2007, 31–2; Vanschoonwinkel 1991, 303 who draws attention, correctly, to the fact that the Cypro-Arcadian genitive is attested on the entire island, not just in Paphos.

14 Scheer 2003, 217.

15 Cf. Pirenne-Delforge 1994, 329.

existed at least until the fourth century BC:[16] nor does any ancient source ever refer to Arcadians and Cypriots recognising each other based on their common dialect.[17]

Agapenor's Story and Ancient Literature

In view of the prominence enjoyed by the mythical example of the Arcadians on Cyprus in modern scholarship, we may distinctly ask what meaning and significance Agapenor's story had in our ancient sources. Cyprus was known to the epic authors: in the *Iliad*, Agamemnon received his armour from the Cypriot king Kinyras,[18] and his brother Menelaus travelled "over Cyprus and Phoenicia" before arriving in Egypt on his journey home.[19] It is tempting to hypothesise that Agapenor's fate might have been mentioned in the "Nostoi", but later sources bear no signs that the Arcadians appeared in this epos.[20]

Writing in the fifth century, Herodotus is the earliest ancient author even to speak expressly of a connection between Cyprus and Arcadians: "These are their tribes: some are from Salamis and Athens, some from Arcadia, some from Cythnus, some from Phoenicia, and some from Ethiopia, as the Cyprians themselves say."[21] Herodotus does not tell us what caused this mix of populations on Cyprus. Nor is it clear whether his source citation, "as the Cyprians themselves say", refers only to the final group, the Ethiopians, or to the entire tableau.[22] At any rate, the Cyprian "Arcadians", who fight alongside the Persians, are mentioned in second place, after those originating from Athens, and form only one of a series of ethnic groups. The hero Agapenor is not referred to by name. That Herodotus was familiar with the myth of Agapenor can only be hypothesised but not proved.[23]

Aside from Herodotus' brief mention we must look all the way to Lycophron's mythological poem *Alexandra* for the next reference to Arcadians on Cyprus, around

---

16 Iacovou 2008a, 234: until the fourth/third century, the dialect "remained hopelessly antique", similarly Iacovou 2008b, 633; Reyes 1994, 11. On the end of the syllabary and the dialect's antiquity in Hellenism see Mitford 1980, 1308; Iacovou 2008a, 256.

17 Ventris and Chadwick 1973, 68–9, 73–5. Cf. Macan 1908, comm. Herodotus 7.90: "It must have been the observation of resemblances between Kypriote and Arcadian dialects ... that suggested to the Logographi a direct connexion between Kypros and 'Arkadia'."

18 Hom. *Il.* 11.21; Hom. *Od.* 18.443. West 1997, 628.

19 Hom. *Od.* 4.83–4. On allocating the epic 'Cypria' to Cypriot poets see West 1997, 628; Lane Fox 2008, 181.

20 This conjecture in Gjerstad 1944, 112; sceptical: Pirenne-Delforge 1994, 327.

21 Cf. Hdt. 7.90: τούτων δὲ τοσάδε ἔθνεα εἰσί, οἳ μὲν ἀπὸ Σαλαμῖνος καὶ Ἀθηνέων, οἳ δὲ ἀπ' Ἀρκαδίης, οἳ δὲ ἀπὸ Κύθνου, οἳ δὲ ἀπὸ Φοινίκης, οἳ δὲ ἀπὸ Αἰθιοπίης, ὡς αὐτοὶ Κύπριοι λέγουσι.

22 Macan 1908, comm. on the passage wants the statement to refer only to the last group.

23 Cf. Fourrier 2008, 116.

c. 190 BC.[24] Although it describes Agapenor's fate, his name again fails to appear. This is typical of Lycophron, whose narrator Alexandra tends to prefer complex and cryptic circumscriptions of a mythical character to directly referring to them by name.[25] The readers are expected to solve the riddle of this "landsman's" origin themselves. Accordingly, the poet lists an entire series of stereotypes, connected to Arcadia in the Hellenistic period.[26] The newcomer himself is characterised as a successful copper miner. Yet Lycophron tells us neither where this "miner" settled nor does he identify him as founder of a city or a sanctuary. Nevertheless, the scholia to Lycophron suggest that he was able to lean on Hellenistic specialist literature regarding Cyprus. As regards the excursus on Arcadians, Eratosthenes has been considered a particularly likely source.[27]

Apart from this, the first time Agapenor is linked with a foundation story is a source from the Augustan period. Strabo who credits the hero with founding New Paphos, yet explicitly separates this foundation from Old Paphos and its "old" and famous temple of Aphrodite.[28] Nor does Agapenor's story feature prominently in Apollodorus' mythological handbook. One mere fragment from the *Codex Sabaiticus* briefly refers to Agapenor, who came to Cyprus.[29] Lastly, we find one epigram for Agapenor of Tegea, the "king of the shield-bearing Paphians" among the funerary epigrams for

---

24 Lycoph. *Alex.* 479–93: ὁ δεύτερος δὲ νῆσον ἀγρότης μολών,/χερσαῖος, αὐτόδαιτος, ἐγγόνων δρυὸς/λυκαινομόρφων Νυκτίμου κρεανόμων,/τῶν πρόσθε μνήμης φηγίνων πύρνων ὀχὴν/σπληδῷ κατ᾽ ἄκρον χεῖμα θαλψάντων πυρός,/χαλκωρυχήσει, καὶ τὸν ἐκ βόθρου σπάσει/βῶλον, δικέλλη πᾶν μεταλλεύων γνύθος.
"The second, a hunter, comes to the island,/A landsman, earth-nourished, one of the sons of the oak,/Who took the shape of wolves after they cut Nyktimos to pieces;/They were older than the moon, and warmed their food of acorn-mast/In the ashes of their fires at dead of winter./He will dig for copper, and will wrench the clods/From out of the pit, mining the whole shaft with his mattock" (Translation: Hornblower 2015, 231); on the date cf. Hornblower 2015, 37.
25 Fraser 1979, 333.
26 Jost 1989, 290 emphasises, without going further into the specifically Cypriot context, that Lycophron conveys a rather gloomy and simultaneously conventional picture of Arcadia, which surely does not stem from autopsy.
27 Cf. Hornblower 2015, 229 comm. Lycoph. *Alex.* 484; Geus 2002, 269, n. 51; Pirenne-Delforge 1994, 327; Fraser 1979, 336.
28 Str. 14.6.3 p. 683: "Then to ... Palaepaphus, which last is situated at about ten stadia above the sea, has a mooring-place, and an ancient temple of the Paphian Aphrodite... Then to Paphus, which was founded by Agapenor, and has both a harbour and well-built temples. It is sixty stadia distant from Palaepaphus by land" (εἶτα ... Παλαίπαφος, ὅσον ἐν δέκα σταδίοις ὑπὲρ τῆς θαλάττης ἱδρυμένη, ὕφορμον ἔχουσα καὶ ἱερὸν ἀρχαῖον τῆς Παφίας Ἀφροδίτης: ... εἶθ᾽ ἡ Πάφος, κτίσμα Ἀγαπήνορος καὶ λιμένα ἔχουσα καὶ ἱερὰ εὖ κατεσκευασμένα: διέχει δὲ πεζῇ σταδίους ἑξήκοντα τῆς Παλαιπάφου).
Pirenne-Delforge 1994, 327, has suggested that Strabo's information on Paphos should also be traced back to Eratosthenes. Cf. also Fraser 1979, 341.
29 Apollod. *Epit.* 6.15: "After their wanderings the Greeks landed and settled in various countries ... and some settled also in Cyprus ... Agapenor in Cyprus" (Ὅτι πλανηθέντες Ἕλληνες ἄλλοι ἀλλαχοῦ κατάραντες κατοικοῦσιν ... εἰσὶ δὲ οἳ καὶ Κύπρου ᾤκησαν .... Ἀγαπήνωρ ἐν Κύπρῳ).

mythical characters in the (undated) pseudo-Aristotelian *Peplos*.[30] On top of this, the iconographic tradition of Agapenor has so far remained silent – not just on Cyprus.[31]

Even considering the accidental character of the extant sources, it becomes evident that comparatively few literary sources were concerned with the mythological theme of the Arcadians stranded on Cyprus.

Constructing Mythical Cyprus: The Context of Agapenor's Story

Generally speaking, the story of Agapenor forms quite a small part of Cyprus' "cabinet of curiosities" of Greek traditions and foundation myths. Menelaus was not alone in supposedly having stopped over on Cyprus on his homeward journey from Troy; Agamemnon was even said to have conquered the entire island with his men after the fall of Troy, in punishment for the treachery of the local king Kinyras.[32] Discussing each of the numerous Greek foundation myths on Cyprus would go beyond the scope of this paper.[33] If we regard the Agapenor-tradition within the Cypriot context, we can see how the myth of wandering heroes arriving from Arcadia to Cyprus via Troy, is exclusively linked to Paphos. No other Cypriot city claims connections to Agapenor or to his Arcadians.

Even Paphos has no purely Arcadian profile within the mythical context. The traditions concerning Kinyras – as a pre-Greek Cypriot king of legendary wealth, or king of Paphos – seem to overshadow the myth of Agapenor and his Arcadians[34]: Kinyras became the *heros eponymos* for the royal family of Paphos. The local significance of the Kinyras-tradition is demonstrated by the information that Kinyras and his descendants were buried in the sanctuary of Aphrodite.[35] Later, the Kinyrads are still described by Tacitus as acting priests in the sanctuary[36]: significantly, Pausanias relates that the Cypriot king Euagoras of Salamis in the early fourth century was also descended from Kinyras and a daughter of Teukros of Salamis. According to this ver-

---

30 Ps. Aristoteles, *Peplos* (= Anthol. Lyrica (ed. Hiller-Crusius) p. 368 no. 30: Ἀρχὸς ὅδ' ἐκ Τεγέης Ἀγαπήνωρ, Ἀνκάιου υἱὸς| κεῖτη' ὑπ' ἐμόι Παφίων πελτοφόρων βασιλεύς.

31 Cf. the lack of an entry in the *Lexicon Iconographicum Mythologiae Classicae*.

32 Menelaus: Hom. *Od.* 4.83–4; Lycophr. *Alex.* 824; Agamemnon: Theopompos of Chios *FGrHist.* 115 F103.

33 For the material see Engel 1841, 210–229, Gjerstad 1944; Hermary 2002, 275; Ulbrich 2008, 291, 331, 359, 370, 417, 452; Lane Fox 2008, 180–1; Hornblower 2015, 218–55.

34 Evidence for the Kinyras tradition in Näf 2013, 18; Baurain 1980, 277–308; Engel 1841, 203–9.

35 Ptolemaios of Megalopolis *FGrHist.* 161 F1.

36 Tac. *Hist.* 2.3. See Maier 1971, 4; Iacovou 2008b, 649. Baurain 1980, 283 n. 26 points out that the Kinyrads never appear in Cyprus' syllabic script; West 1997, 57 sees Kinyras as the "mythical eponymous ancestor of the Kinyradai, the guild of temple musicians, who controlled the Paphian cult".

sion, Teukros as a hero of the Trojan War and Greek founder of Salamis, the rival city of Paphos, received the hand of the local king Kinyras' daughter in marriage – rather than Agapenor of Paphos.[37]

Wealth and oriental refined luxury are central to the image of Cyprus, in mythology but also elsewhere. The description of the highly luxurious and effete lifestyle of an anonymous *basileus* of Paphos can be traced back to Clearchus of Soloi, a Cypriot[38], and student of Aristotle.[39] In the fourth century, Middle Comedy evokes the picture of a prince, also from Paphos, who reclines his perfumed body on the softest cushions, while live doves fan him.[40]

If we look at Cyprus as a mythological landscape, searching for common traditions or cultural similarities with Arcadia, it is difficult to draw a special connection. Whereas Arcadians were known for primordial age, cultural simplicity and a strong bodily appearance, hard fighters venerating Zeus and Athena, Cypriots are seen rather as culturally refined, effeminate orientals, venerating Aphrodite.[41] While the Paphian kings were said to lie on soft bedding, being fanned by doves, the cities of the Arcadians were called windswept as early as the Homeric epics.[42] Locating myths in Cyprus and Arcadia may have been a convenient solution based on the perceived antiquated character of both landscapes. The sources, however, never state this expressly.

From a Cypriot perspective the mythical story of Arcadian colonisation did not form a major tradition marking the whole island's awareness of its past. A similar impression is given at the other geographical pole of the story: in Arcadia, the myth of Agapenor on Cyprus was also no major tradition. Pausanias recounts a whole series of traditions of Arcadian heroes journeying around the Mediterranean in various contexts, between Crete, Italy, the Black Sea and Asia Minor. The story of Agapenor forms a single example among several.[43] So we may finally ask ourselves whether we can discern specific times, places and historical contexts, within which this myth was set in motion – beyond the interest of learned mythographers. Who might have been interested in activating such a myth and in transforming it into a "wandering myth"?

---

37 Teukros and Kinyras' daughter: Paus. 1.3.2; on Euagoras' descent claim Isoc. 3.28, 9.18; cf. also Paus. 2.29.4.

38 Tsitsiridis 2013, 1–3.

39 Clearchus fr. 19b Wehrli = Ath. 6.255e; Tsitsiridis 2013, 120–1; Reyes 1994, 25. On dating the text to the final quarter of the fourth century cf. Tsitsiridis 2013, 129.

40 Antiphanes K.-A. fr.200 = Ath. 6.257d-e.

41 Scheer 2010, 287–9.

42 Evidently the Hellenistic Cypriots were also aware of the climatic differences: cf. the poem on Pan composed by Kastorion of Soloi and passed down by Clearchus of Soloi (Clearchus, Περὶ γρίφων fr. 88 Wehrli = Ath. 10. 82 p. 454f.): σὲ τον βολαῖς νιφοκτύποις δυσχείμερον/ναίονθ' ἕδραν, θηρονόμε Πάν, χθόν' Ἀρκάδων... ("You Pan, master of animals/you who inhabit/the place hard-pressed/in winter/by snow-storms/the land of the Arcadians"); Tsitsiridis 2013, 152; cf. also Jost 1989, 290.

43 Scheer 2010, 276–8.

A Wandering Myth: When, Who and – Above All – Why?

It is difficult to ascertain to what extent Greek myths – and, more specifically, foundation myths – played a role in Cyprus before the fifth century. It has been postulated repeatedly that the Cypriot kingdoms of the archaic period had already bolstered themselves with these stories, but so far there is almost no evidence to support this.[44] Cyprus' mythical past was evidently activated in the fifth and fourth centuries, when traditions of Teukros "wandered" against the background of the Persian Wars and the Delian League between Athens and Cyprus: This was surely based on the homonymy of Cypriot Salamis and the island of the same name, lying adjacent to the coast of Athens.[45] In this period, there was a demonstrable emphasis on genealogical traditions joining the Cypriot kings of Salamis with Athenian heroes.[46] So far there is no trace of the Arcadia-tradition being used actively in this period.

The myth of the wandering hero Agapenor was set in motion in a different historical phase: in the second century BC. In 1961, T. B. Mitford published 2 new votive inscriptions from Palaeopaphos, which had been fixed to a base for two statues.[47] Based on the letterforms, Mitford suggested a date around c. 160 BC for both. The first inscription reads as follows:

> Echetime, daughter of Agapenor dedicated (the statue) of her daughter Euagoratis to Aphrodite Paphia.

The second inscription refers to the same family:

> Echetime, daughter of Agapenor dedicated (the statue) of her son Agapenor to Aphrodite Paphia.

These inscriptions from the old sanctuary of Aphrodite so far form the only known evidence for Agapenor's story being actively taken up in Paphos. In the second century BC a family thus becomes visible, whose wealth allows them to dedicate statues by and also for female family members. Names from the Arcadian foundation myths feature over several generations. The father of the dedicant is called Agapenor, her son was

---

44 This idea appears for instance in Fourrier 2008, 116; Iacovou 2008b, 648; Rupp 1988, 218–9. The evidence of the Cypriot syllabary has so far delivered no references to the foundation myths: Reyes 1994, 122; Hermary 2002, 275 on the absence of relevant textual evidence for early history and on the meaning of the iconographic material, which also lacks references to foundation myths. On the lack of Cypriot sources on identity cf. Mavrojannis 2006, 153–4. Also sceptical: Lane Fox 2008, 181.

45 Plausibly argued in Gjerstad 1944, 119; Mavrojannis 2006, 161; Schollmeyer 2009, 45.

46 See above n. 37.

47 *JHS* 9 (1888), 236, nos. 36a and 36b; Mitford 1961a 24 n. 61; *SEG* XX 1964, 57, 201: 201 c. 160. Mitford 61 a: [Ἐχετ]ίμ[η Ἀγα]πήνορος/[τὴν α]ὐτῆς θυγατέρα/['Εὐα]γοράτιν/['Αφροδ]ίτηι Παφίαι. Mitford 61 b: Ἐχετίμη ['Αγαπήνορος]/'Αγαπήνορα [τὸν αὐτῆς υἱὸν]/'Αφροδίτηι Πα[φίαι].

also called Agapenor, after his maternal grandfather.[48] If we follow Mitford in dating the dedication to around 160 BC, this would put the older Agapenor's birth in the late third or early second century, based on an estimated marital age of 30 for men and 15 for women.

The naming of female family members in the inscriptions is also revealing. The dedicant and her daughter bear names which clearly appeal to Cyprus' royal traditions: Echetime, the feminine form of Echetimon, can be associated with a king of Paphos whose name, Echetimon, is attested in the Paphian syllabic inscriptions of the fourth century.[49] Her daughter's name, Euagoratis, functions as the feminine form of Euagoras, linking it to this royal name.[50]

Within which political and cultural contexts should we locate these inscriptions? The foundation of New Paphos possibly falls in the reign of Nikokles, the last king of Paphos. According to Strabo, this city was founded at a distance of approximately 11 km from the old town[51], whose harbour no longer proved sufficient. Yet the old town, including its ancient sanctuary of Aphrodite, continued to exist.[52] After the fall of the Paphian kings, "New-Paphos" became the seat of the new ruler, the Ptolemaic strategos.[53] From 295, Cyprus found itself firmly under Ptolemaic control, constituting one of the most important outposts of the Ptolemaic kingdom due to its wealth and its mineral and timber resources. The change entailed significant consequences for the families of the Cypriot elite. Its members were forced to reassure their standing amongst their peers as well as towards the new power.[54]

Cyprus' importance for Egypt further meant that the island generally found itself the focus of Ptolemaic interests: Alexandrian scholars became (were made?) aware of Cyprus and had the means, in the context of the Library of Alexandria, to collect and systematise the traditions of this island, so long considered rather marginal from a Greek perspective.[55] Already around the fifth century Hellanicus had composed a work "About Cyprus".[56] Theopompus of Chios, who presumably spent the final years of his life in Alexandria in the final quarter of the fourth century, told of Agamemnon conquering Cyprus in his *Philippika*.[57] Whether Callimachus, whose interest in

---

48 Michaelidou-Nicolaou 1976, 30, A6 and 7: Agapenor; ibid., 60, E 28: Euagoratis; ibid., 61, E 53: Echetime; ibid., stemma: 131, E 53, dated mid second century.

49 Masson 1961, 113–5, 115 no. 17: Echetimon cautiously dated to 370–350. Masson and Mitford 1986, 39; Maier 1996, 129.

50 See above n. 37.

51 Str. 14.6.3 p. 683.

52 Arr. *Succ.* 15.15–24, 6; Maier 1971, 5; Ulbrich 2008, 394; Papantoniou 2012, 118, 126.

53 Bagnall 1976, 61; Ulbrich 2008, 394.

54 See Papantoniou 2012, 128; Iacovou 2008a, 251, 256.

55 Fraser 1979, 328–43.

56 Hellanicus *FGrHist.* 4 F57; Engel 1841, 5.

57 Theopompus of Chios *FGrHist.* 115 F103.

Arcadian traditions is well attested[58], included Cypriot traditions in his lost work on the foundation myths of islands and cities is unclear. He did however visit the island of Cyprus himself.[59] In the third century BC, several of his contemporaries and his students engaged with Cyprus including its mythological traditions: thus, for instance, Philostephanos of Cyrene, compatriot and contemporary of Callimachus, derived the island's name from Kypros, a daughter of Kinyras and Aphrodite, in his work *Περί νήσων* or *Περί Κύπρου*.[60] Also according to Callimachus' student Istros, himself from Paphos, the goddess Aphrodite was mother to this daughter Kypros.[61] In the historical and geographic work (*Περί νήσων*) of Xenagoras – albeit no Alexandrian – Cypriot foundation myths also played a role.[62] In his poem *Hermes*, Eratosthenes of Cyrene referred directly to the myths of Paphos' foundation and that of the sanctuary of Aphrodite.[63] Fraser's idea that the court of the Ptolemies may have featured "a generally accepted Ptolemaic version of the history and antiquities of the island accessible to all these authors" seems highly attractive, especially in view of the historical background of Ptolemaic rule over Cyprus.[64] Lycophron's *Alexandra* certainly refers back to the Alexandrian authors of the third century: Callimachus, Philostephanos, and especially Eratosthenes.[65] As a result, Fraser ascribed Lycophron's excursus on Cyprus to an "Alexandrian and not epic, cyclic or tragic" background.[66]

In addition, Madeleine Jost has emphasised how interested third century Alexandrian authors were in Arcadia:[67] she traces the picture of Arcadia painted by Lycophron back to an Alexandrian "poets collective", emphasising in particular Callimachus and Apollonius Rhodius.[68] No matter whether one follows Jost in dating Lycophron to the third century or prefers, like Fraser and Hornblower, to locate him in the early second century, it can be perceived that in the period of the third and second centuries Alexandrians were interested in both Cypriot and Arcadian traditions. This interest is reflected in corresponding works. Within the context of the Library of Alexandria, it would also be plausible that local scholars such as Callimachus, who was interested in Arcadian and Cypriot themes, or Eratosthenes, who engaged with

---

58 Callim. *H. Iov.* 4–41.
59 Suda s.v. "Καλλίμαχος" (3, p.19 Adler); Wilamowitz-Moellendorff 1962², 181, 197.
60 Philostephanos *FGrHist.* 334 F45: Gjerstad 1944, 112 assumes that Philostephanos based his work on local traditions: "oral or preserved in logographic works".
61 *FGrHist.* 334 T1; Näf 2013, 13; Steph. Byz. s.v. "Κύπρος"; Istros FHG I 423.
62 Xenagoras *FGrHist.* 240 F1B; Steph. Byz. s.v. "Χύτροι".
63 Parsons 1974 = *Pap.Oxy.* XLII, 3, no. 3000; Fraser 1979, 338, 340; Geus 2002, 114; see also Pirenne-Delforge 1994, 327; Hornblower 2015, 445.
64 Fraser 1979, 338.
65 Fraser 1979, 333–4, 337. Hornblower 2015, 217–9.
66 Fraser 1979, 340.
67 Jost 1989, 286, 290–1.
68 Jost 1989, 291.

issues of dialect in his grammatical works, may have noticed connections between the Cypriot and Arcadian dialects.[69] Evidence for this is, however, still lacking.

An Arcadian Strategos for Cyprus: Ptolemaios of Megalopolis

Nikokles, the last king of Paphos, had still presented himself as a descendant of Kinyras in Paphia's local sanctuary in Ledra.[70] A few generations later, the kingdom of Paphos was a thing of the past and Paphos itself had become the seat of the Ptolemaic governor. Around 160 BC, Echetime, daughter of Agapenor and mother of a homonymous son, dedicated statues of her children in Aphrodite's temple in Paphos. The inscription of the Agapenorids is our first indication that the Arcadian foundation tradition played a role also in Paphos itself.

Our surviving sources do not, however, reveal whether or to what extent Echetime's family was connected to the Kinyrads. In the late fourth century, Paphos' royal family, equated in our sources with the Kinyrads, was almost wiped out in a catastrophic mass suicide.[71] Yet later sources inform us that members of this family held the priesthood of Aphrodite: Tacitus still assumes that the Kinyrads are the ones to turn to in the sanctuary of Paphos.[72]

Accordingly it is not unlikely that certain branches of the family survived the catastrophe.[73] The so-called "Agapenorids" of the second century may even have formed part of such a branch: evidence for this may be provided by the familial names in the female line, which refer to the kings of Paphos. Whether Agapenor, Echetime and Agoratis held a religious office in the cult of Aphrodite cannot be ascertained directly from the dedications. But the Agapenorids' dedicatory practice turns out to have been conspicuously similar to that of the Kinyrads. Demokrates, archon of the Kinyrads, and his wife Eunike also dedicated a statue for their daughter Aristion in the temple of Aphrodite; in addition, the same Eunike is attested as the sole dedicant of statues of her two sons in other inscriptions.[74]

---

69 Geus 2002, 295; cf. above n. 17.

70 Mitford 1961b, 136–137, no. 36; *SEG* XX, 1964, p. 36, 114. Fourrier 2008, 116.

71 Cf. Diod. Sic. 20.21.1–3; Polyaenus 8.48; see Papantoniou 2012, 106; on the relevant scholarly discussion cf. Miller 1988, 153–4, n. 7.

72 Tac. *Hist.* 2.3; Hesych. s.v. "Κινυράδαι"; on the Kinyrads' continuing status as a priestly family in Paphos cf. Mitford 1961b, 136–7, no. 36 (Nikokles); Mitford 1961a, 13, no. 32: (221–205) Demokrates, Archos of the Kinyrads (ἀρχὸς τῶν Κινυραδῶν). See also Maier 1971, 4.

73 Cf. the peculiar anecdote in Plut. *Mor. de fort. Alex.* 8.340c-d.

74 Cf. above n. 73; Mitford 1961a, 13 no. 32; see ibid. no. 33; *SEG* XX 1964 no. 191.

The question remains, however, why the Agapenor-tradition surfaces when it does, namely in the second century BC. Around the same time when Echetime's family was utilising the name Agapenor the island of Cyprus was being governed by a *strategos* with roots in Arcadia and literary interests: Ptolemaios of Megalopolis.[75] This man appears to have held the highest office on Cyprus from 197 until the end of Ptolemy V's reign.[76] His first name Ptolemaios suggests that he himself was already born in Egypt and that his father Agesarchos was in the service of the Ptolemies.[77] The latter originated from Arcadia's recent foundation Megalopolis.[78] We may accept the Arcadian roots as fact: the historian Polybios, himself from Megalopolis, reports "Ptolemaios of Megalopolis" succeeding Polykrates of Argos as *strategos* of Cyprus around 197/6.[79] Not much is known about Ptolemaios of Megalopolis' immediate activities on Cyprus because only two (disputed) inscriptions refer to his presence.[80] The strategos' daughter seems to have held an important position in the Ptolemaic ruler cult,[81] while the incumbent himself, in the role as *archiereus*, supervised all of the island's cults.[82] Ptolemaios of Megalopolis is, however, known to have been a man of literary ambition and historical and cultural interests. As a contemporary of Philostephanos of Cyrene and the younger Lycophron, the former strategos composed a history of Ptolemy IV's reign, during the last years of his life.[83] Ptolemaios of Megalopolis also expressed interest in the mythology of his new place of residence, Cyprus: he provides us with the information on the graves of the Kinyrads in the temple of Aphrodite at Paphos.[84] Considering his own Arcadian roots, the tradition of Paphos' foundation by Arcadians may have appealed to him on a personal level. Establishing a connection to Agapenor and the Arcadians in the Paphian sanctuary now became useful for both sides: for the Paphian elite and for Ptolemaios as the representative of the new power on Cyprus. During the rule of the Ptolemies the temple of Aphrodite at Paphos was a venue for prominent families to cultivate their public image, by dedicating statues of their children to the goddess. After the fall of the local royal dynasty this sanctuary also became a place for local dignitaries to ingratiate themselves with the *strategos* in particular, through honorary statues and dedications.[85] In the context of

---

75 Cf. Pros. Ptol. 15068, 16944; Michaelidou-Nicolaou 1976, 103, Π 59.

76 Bagnall 1976, 256; Anastassiades 2013, 230.

77 Cf. Bagnall 1976, 255.

78 Pol. 15.25.14; Michaelidou-Nicolaou 1976, 30 A 10.

79 Pol. 18.55.8. On Polybius' particular interest in Ptolemaios see Jacoby's commentary at *FGrHist*. II b on 161, 592.

80 For the discussion see Bagnall 1976, 255.

81 Bagnall 1976, 46.

82 Bagnall 1976, 48; Anastassiades 2013, 230; Papantoniou 2012, 134.

83 Jacoby *FGrHist*. 161; Bagnall 1976, 255.

84 Jacoby *FGrHist*. 161 F1: Πτολεμαῖος ... λέγει ἐν τῷ τῆς Ἀφροδίτης ἱερῷ Κινύραν τε καὶ τοὺς Κινύρου ἀπογόνους κεκηδεῦσθαι.

85 Bagnall 1976, 47; Papantoniou 2012, 154.

local rivalries, the Paphians may have found it particularly important to be able to call on a Homeric foundation myth, just like Salamis. In this case, the Paphian Arcadian tradition was more useful than the story of Kinyras, who was connected to several different origins but certainly did not come from Greece. The possibility of emphasising a personal kinship connection to the longstanding governor would have been particularly attractive for the urban dignitaries. If Ptolemaios of Megalopolis visited the graves of the Kinyrads, a follow-up question about the graves of the Agapenorids would surely have suggested itself for a man of Arcadian origin. It is doubtful but not impossible that Ptolemaios really was shown a grave of Agapenor in Paphos. The funerary epigram attested in the pseudo-Aristotelian *Peplos* indicates that Agapenor's grave had been located at Paphos – whenever this might have happened.[86]

It is certainly plausible to assume that the presence of an Arcadian governor would have quickened the local upsurge of the Agapenor-tradition, to which the Paphian elite started to refer. For the Ptolemies and their representatives it was surely beneficial to join themselves to the important island of Cyprus by emphasising common ties.[87] This may indeed have resulted in an island-wide surge of Greek foundation myths. Here, then, we are discovering a context in which myths were set in motion and in which "free floating poetic and erudite articulations" acquired "historical force".[88]

Wandering Back to Arcadia: Laodike in Tegea

There are various indications that Agapenor's myth was revived in the Hellenistic period in places other than Cyprus. The mythical Agapenor had always remained in Cyprus but in the Hellenistic period he virtually wandered back home.

Here too Pausanias is our essential source. Shortly after recounting the myth of Agapenor founding Paphos, the periegete reports on later contacts between Tegea and distant descendants of Agapenor:[89]

> Afterwards Laodike, a descendant of Agapenor, sent to Tegea a robe as a gift for Athena Alea. The inscription on the offering told as well the race of Laodike: –
> "This is the robe of Laodike; she offered it to her Athena,
> Sending it to her broad fatherland from divine Cyprus."

---

86 Ps.-Aristotle, *Peplos* (= *Anthol. Lyrica* [ed. Hiller-Crusius] p.358 no. 30): cf. above n. 30; Pirenne-Delforge 1994, 327 n. 97: pseudo-épigramme funeraire; Mavrojannis 2013, 110: at least a honorary monument for Agapenor in Paphos.

87 Cf. Price 2005, 116.

88 Malkin 1998, 8.

89 Paus. 8.5.3: χρόνῳ δὲ ὕστερον Λαοδίκη γεγονυῖα ἀπὸ Ἀγαπήνορος ἔπεμψεν ἐς Τεγέαν τῇ Ἀθηνᾷ τῇ Ἀλέᾳ πέπλον· τὸ δὲ ἐπὶ τῷ ἀναθήματι ἐπίγραμμα καὶ αὐτῆς Λαοδίκης ἅμα ἐδήλου τὸ γένος· Λαοδίκης ὅδε πέπλος· ἑᾷ δ' ἀνέθηκεν Ἀθηνᾷ | πατρίδ' ἐς εὐρύχορον Κύπρου ἀπὸ ζαθέας.'

Later on in the text, while describing the city of Tegea, Pausanias again refers to the woman who dedicated the *peplos*, and thereby to the contacts between Tegea and Cyprus:[90]

> There is also at Tegea a temple ... of Aphrodite called Paphian. The latter was built by Laodike, who was descended, as I have already said, from Agapenor, who led the Arcadians to Troy, and it was in Paphos that she dwelt.

Who was Laodike, and when did her present reach Tegea? If we assume that Pausanias took Laodike for a daughter of the mythical Agapenor,[91] the Tegeans would thus lay a claim to possessing a votive offering dating from the first generation after the Trojan War. This object could have been interpreted as real evidence for memories of earliest contacts between Tegea and Cyprus.[92] Alternatively, we follow Gjerstad in assuming that the Tegeans equipped an anonymous old votive offering with mythical origins.[93] Pausanias' formulation: χρόνῳ δὲ ὕστερον, "in later times" indicates – as has been emphasised more recently – that the periegete rather considered Laodike to be a "descendant" of Agapenor.[94] This throws open the possibility of dating the votive dedication much later. James Roy has offered a very interesting solution in this context[95]: For literary reasons, he estimated the epigram's date to fall quite late,[96] pointing out that the epigram itself makes no reference to a relationship between Agapenor, Paphos and Laodike.[97] Thus the votive offering may be considered an authentic dedication by a historical Laodike.[98] Whether Pausanias himself saw it remains doubtful. Following this, the dedicant would presumably be a woman from Tegea, who, having migrated to Cyprus in the Hellenistic period, honoured both her native goddess Athena in Tegea and the dominant goddess of her new home, Aphrodite Paphia, with votives; the mythological reference to Agapenor was only established derivatively, by Pausanias – or by the Tegeans.[99]

---

90 Paus. 8.53.7: ἔστι ... ναός ... Ἀφροδίτης καλουμένης Παφίας: ἱδρύσατο αὐτὴν Λαοδίκη, γεγονυῖα μέν, ὡς καὶ πρότερον ἐδήλωσα, ἀπὸ Ἀγαπήνορος ὅς ἐς Τροίαν ἡγήσατο Ἀρκάσιν, οἰκοῦσα δὲ ἐν Πάφῳ.
91 Daughter: Engel 1841, 226; Gjerstad 1944, 107; Vanschoonwinkel 1991, 301; similarly still in Iacovou 2008b, 649.
92 Stoll 1894–97, 1829–30 s.v. "Laodike 4".
93 Gjerstad 1944, 111.
94 Roy 1987, 194; Pirenne-Delforge 1994, 328 n. 103; cf. also Jost 1998, 167: "Laodiké est donnée pour une 'descendante' d'Agapénor, non pour sa fille, et l' expression 'par la suite' peut impliquer plusieurs siècles."
95 Roy 1987.
96 Roy 1987, 196, also points out that it was not common before the third century BC to put the dedicant's name in the genitive in this sort of context.
97 Roy 1987, 196.
98 Also Pirenne-Delforge 1994, 328.
99 Roy 1987, 198, 200: in view of the complete lack of other evidence it is "entirely possible" that a connection between Agapenor and Laodike was first forged in Tegea.

Whether Pausanias himself saw Laodike's *peplos* in Tegea cannot be ascertained[100]: but we may postulate that the *periegete* received local information while visiting.[101] Even if the *peplos* – potentially consisting of perishable material[102] – no longer existed, one can imagine its ongoing presence, for instance in an inventory of old votive offerings.[103] Such inventories may have served as aides-mémoire for those responsible for the local memorial culture, that is, the guides, whom Pausanias depended on. The tradition of Laodike from Paphos seemed significant enough to Pausanias to mention it twice: the double reference may indicate how eager the Tegeates were in telling the story, demonstrating the continued importance still attached to the relationship with Cyprus in the imperial period.[104]

But who was this Laodike from Paphos, whose name was still familiar to tour guides of the imperial period? A Paphian Laodike is otherwise not directly known.[105] Yet it is evident that this personal name carried prestige for Greeks, and, particularly in the Hellenistic period, was associated with royal status. Laodike was a popular name for royal women among the Seleucids, but also in other dynasties.[106] In addition, royal daughters in various mythical contexts had been called Laodike. In the *Iliad*, Priam and Hekabe[107] as well as Agamemnon and Klytemnestra are said to have a daughter of this name.[108] Apollodorus' *Library* even refers to a Cypriot Laodike from mythical times. Unfortunately there is no hint of a direct connection with Agapenor's Cypriot family.[109] Nor is anything said about Agapenor's wife and children in Cyprus in our mythological sources: accordingly, Pausanias is the only source ever to link the name of Laodike with Agapenor. He mentions "Laodike of Paphos" in two separate contexts: she dedicates the *peplos* and she venerates Aphrodite Paphia in Tegea. Pausanias' expression "ναόν … πλησίον δὲ Ἀφροδίτης καλουμένης Παφίας· ἱδρύσατο αὐτὴν Λαοδίκη" has usually been taken to refer to a cultic foundation.[110] Roy, however, has correctly pointed out that the formulation should be understood as referring to the dedication of a statue.[111] Accordingly, Laodike would have erected an image of Aphrodite Paphia, that is, financed a statue. Due to Laodike's origins the goddess bore the epithet Paphia, which is highly unusual on the Greek mainland. Presumably

---

100 On this discussion cf. Roy 1987, 198–9; Pirenne-Delforge 1994, 328, Jost 1998, 167.
101 Pirenne-Delforge 1994, 328.
102 Roy 1987, 199; Mavrojannis 2013, 109.
103 Cf. the Milesian textile inventory in Günther 1988, 215–37; Scheer 2000, 55–6.
104 Roy 1987, 199.
105 Roy 1987, 194.
106 A royal Laodike of the second century BC is found for instance in Stirpe 2001, 232.
107 Hom. *Il.* 6.252; Lycoph. *Alex.* 316; Paus. 10.26.7.
108 Hom. *Il.* 9.145, 287; *LIMC* 6 (1) (1992), 192.
109 Apollod. 3.9.1.
110 On the previous understanding of the text: Roy 1987, 194.
111 Roy 1987, 195 with Pirenne-Delforge 1994, 328.

the statue would have been set up in an existing temple of Aphrodite.[112] The epithet may then have continued to be used in such an "older" Tegean Aphrodite cult;[113] and through it, old mythical links between Cyprus and Tegea would have been attested.

In either case, Laodike's dedicatory activity suggests substantial financial resources. That any Tegean woman who somehow ended up in Paphos – perhaps as the wife of a mercenary – would have such surplus funds at her disposal is at least questionable. Against the background of Pausanias' information that a certain Laodike from Agapenor's line dedicated the *peplos*, a connection between the dedicant and the Hellenistic Agapenorids of Paphos suggests itself in many respects. Female members of this family seem to have been given names with royal claim. Laodike would fit into this concept as much as Echetime and Euagoratis. It was moreover evidently customary for female family members in Hellenistic Paphos to assume responsibility for costly dedications in sanctuaries: Echetime, daughter of Agapenor of Paphos, dedicated statues of her children in the sanctuary of Aphrodite of Paphos. Laodike, of the house of Agapenor, "who was resident in Paphos", had a statue of Aphrodite Paphia erected in Tegea. Whether such a dedication reveals a competitive stance against the priestly family of the Kinyrads, who are attested in literary and epigraphic evidence, or whether the Agapenorids themselves formed a branch of this family, cannot at present be ascertained on the basis of our surviving sources.

Tegea, Pergamon and Cyprus: Wandering Heroes, Wandering Myths

There are further arguments for dating Laodike and her gifts to the context of the second century BC. In this period, i. e. when Ptolemaios of Megalopolis was *strategos* and when the Agapenorids erected statues in the sanctuary of Aphrodite, not only Paphos was keenly interested in a past imprinted with links to Arcadia.[114] Tegea, the starting point of Agapenor's mythical wanderings, also demonstrates mythological ambitions in the first half of the second century BC: "international" contacts were sought keenly and reference to wandering heroes of the mythological past formed a central tenet within such a policy.[115] This is demonstrated by an inscription discovered in Pergamon and dated to this period.[116] Tegean envoys had come to Pergamon to exchange *isopoliteia* with this important Hellenistic metropolis. They based their argu-

---

112 Roy 1987, 195; Gjerstad 1944, 111; on the epithet Paphía in Paphos in the Hellenistic period: Maier 1996, 123.
113 Pirenne-Delforge 1994, 271–2.
114 Cf. Papantoniou 2012, 158 with an assumption of "changes in memorial patterns".
115 Scheer 1993, 146–7; Scheer 2003, 225.
116 Fränkel 1890, 156; Gawantka 1975, 212 no. 28: prior to 159 BC.

ments both on ancient mythical kinship *as well as* on cultic links. In this case it was the connection through the hero Telephus (an "earlier relative" of Agapenor) and his mother, the Tegean princess Auge. Telephus was considered to be the founder of Pergamon.[117] Cultic relations were a significant element in substantiating tight, familial ties between cities, in this context as elsewhere. The stele attesting the kinship between Tegea and Pergamon was to be erected in the Pergamene sanctuary of Athena, ἣν ἱδρύσατο Αὔγη: which Auge, priestess of Athena and daughter of the Arcadian king Aleas of Tegea had founded.[118]

The decisions regarding the common past of Pergamenes and Tegeans were expressly declared to be remembered for eternity[119]: evidently both sides valued the ancient kinship, the Tegeans, who had sent the embassy, as well as the Pergamenes, who set up the inscription in one of their sanctuaries. On this level, myth appeared as the "desirable commodity" described by Malkin, and it was its "mediating function"[120] in particular that was called upon when myths of wandering heroes were set in motion, becoming wandering myths. The Tegeans' *isopoliteia* embassy and Laodike's dedications to Tegea imply a similar milieu: contexts in which mythical stories were activated and wandered with people who communicated through them or through objects associated with them (cult images, statues, votive offerings). In addition, the Tegeans had good reason to remember Laodike's votive offerings: for Agapenor was not "firmly connected with Tegea" from the beginning, as Gjerstadt thought, but rather the general leader of the Arcadian contingent at Troy.[121] Tegea had to lay a claim to this Homeric leader, important for Arcadia as a whole.[122] The dedications that Laodike, a descendant of Agapenor, sent to Tegea, could be seen as a signal to the outside world by way of strengthening the mythological-historical claim of the Tegeans to this Homeric hero.

How did Laodike's gifts reach Tegea? Pausanias leaves no doubt that Laodike sent (ἔπεμψεν) the *peplos* (to Athena). Apparently his informants were certain that she herself never came to Tegea. Nor did the second act attributed to her – the dedication of a statue to Aphrodite Paphia – require her presence: she may simply have provided the funds to commission a Tegean sculptor or sent an "aphidryma" from Cyprus.[123] Presumably Laodike's gifts reached Tegea in the hands of envoys from Cyprus. Hellenistic

---

117 Scheer 1993, 71–95; Scheer 2003, 223.
118 Fränkel 1890, 156 l.25. Note the identical choice of wording in the Pergamene inscription and in Pausanias on the dedication of Auge and of Laodike in Tegea: ἱδρύσατο Αὔγη/ἱδρύσατο αὐτὴν Λαοδίκη. See Scheer 2003, 224.
119 *IvP* 156, ll. 22–3.
120 Malkin 1998, 5.
121 Gjerstad 1944, 112.
122 Cf. Apollod. 3.7.5; for a later "appropriation" of Agapenor see Pirenne-Delforge 1994, 329 with n. 110.
123 Scheer 2000, 246–7.

inscriptions attest Cypriot kings and envoys in the Greek motherland as dedicating objects or granting presents. On these occasions, kinship ties were also emphasised.[124] Following the end of the Cypriot kings' reigns, it seems that the representatives of the new powers were integrated into the "kinship net" of the changing "memorial patterns"[125] as well.[126] That there were efforts on the Cypriot side to forge connections to Arcadia, home of Ptolemaios of Megalopolis, is accordingly not unlikely.[127] We might reconstruct a plausible setting of an embassy sent from Paphos to Tegea in the second century BC, tasked with calling attention to the ancient ties, perhaps seeking confirmation of the *asylia* of the temple of Aphrodite or securing *isopoliteia*: votive offerings sent by a descendant of Agapenor substantiated these claims and ambitions nicely. The Tegeans of the Hellenistic period, who had themselves tried to forge ties with descendants of Telephus in Pergamon, would have welcomed such an embassy from Cyprus with open arms: the integration of the votive offerings into local tradition demonstrates this beyond any doubt.

As to the question of who delivered the initial impetus in the Hellenistic period to make the myth wander, this cannot be ascertained. Was it Tegea, perhaps sending out further embassies in the second century BC, trying to follow the footsteps of their wandering heroes?[128] Or instead envoys from Paphos, tasked with reviving memories of Homeric times? So far no *isopoliteia* decree is known between Tegea and Paphos. It is Laodike's *peplos*, still known to Pausanias in the second century AD, which became a medium, an object by means of which the myth was crystallised as "history", forming part of the "self emergent process of the creation of mythical, quasi historical, and historical networks of collective imagination".[129]

In the Homeric epics Agapenor left Arcadia never to return. Centuries later his descendant's votive offerings returned, confirming his arrival on distant shores. Both *peplos* and statue affirmed ties of ancient royal kinship between Tegea and Cyprus, ties which proved beneficial to both geographical focal points of the story and demonstrated, once again, that "Greek mythology was the cultural currency of even the re-

---

124 This is demonstrated for instance by the statue that King Nikokreon of Salamis on Cyprus received in the late fourth century BC after he had donated copper for shields in a competition to his "metropolis", Pelasgian Argos: *IG* IV 583 (Argos, 331–307) = Kaibel *Ep.Gr.* 846.

125 Cf. also Papantoniou 2012, 158.

126 Aupert 1982, 275 n. 36 has drawn attention to the Argive descent of the Cypriot *strategos* Polykrates (late third century – 197), who was the immediate predecessor to Ptolemaios of Megalopolis (see also Bagnall 1976, 254). The Ptolemaic dynasty and a number of Cypriot cities still appear in Argos as benefactors in the second century BC (168–4): Aupert 1982, 275–6.

127 On the concrete advantages arising from such efforts see Price 2005, 121–2.

128 A Nemean list of *theorodokoi* (323 BC) shows that Peloponnesian *theoroi* came to Cyprus, where Nikokles of Salamis as well as his compatriot Teukros, son of Akestokreon functioned as *theorodokoi*: cf. Miller 1988, 149, 153. Hermary 2002, 276.

129 Malkin 2011, 121.

motest corners of the Greek world."[130] Tegea had formed part of an international network since its earliest days, as well as being part of the Homeric tradition. Its royal past would additionally have placed it in a position worthy of communicating with contemporary kings. As for Cyprus, the memory of Agapenor made good sense in this period: in the second century BC the previous political system of Cyprus, the independent city kingdoms, had ceased to exist. With the Ptolemies, new rulers were established. Cities and families had to think anew how they adapted to the current order of things. This might have been yet another reason why myths, cults and heroes started to wander again.

Bibliography

Anastassiades, A. The Strategos as High Priest and the Royal Cult in Ptolemaic Cyprus: some observations, in: *Epigraphy, Numismatics, Prosopography and History of Ancient Cyprus. Papers in Honour of Ino Nicolaou*, edited by D. Michaelides (Uppsala, 2013), 227- 234.

Aupert, P. Une donation lagide et chypriote à Argos. *Bulletin de correspondance hellénique* 106 (1982), 263–277.

Bagnall, R. S. *The Administration of the Ptolemaic Possessions outside Egypt* (Leiden, 1976).

Baurain, C. Kinyras. La fin de l'Âge du Bronze à Chypre et la tradition antique. *Bulletin de correspondance hellénique* 104 (1980), 277–308.

Cameron, A. *Greek Mythography in the Roman World* (Oxford, 2004).

Colvin, S. *A Historical Greek Reader: Mycenaean to the Koine* (Oxford, 2007).

Egetmeyer, M. *Le dialecte grec ancient de Chypre*, vol. 1: Grammaire; vol. 2: *Répertoire des inscriptions en syllabaire chypro-grec* (Berlin; New York, 2010).

Engel, W. H. *Kypros. Eine Monographie*, vol. 1 (Berlin, 1841).

Finkelberg, M. *Greeks and Pre-Greeks. Aegean Prehistory and Greek Heroic Tradition* (Cambridge, 2005).

Fourrier, S. Légendes de fondation et hellénisation de Chypre. Parcours historiographique. *Cahiers du centre d'études chypriotes* 38 (2008), 103–117.

Fraenkel, M. *Die Inschriften von Pergamon* (AvP 8) I (Berlin, 1890).

Fraser, P. M. Lycophron on Cyprus. *Report of the Department of Antiquities Cyprus* (1979), 328–343.

Gawantka, W. *Isopolitie. Ein Beitrag zur Geschichte der zwischenstaatlichen Beziehungen* (Munich, 1975).

Geus, K. *Eratosthenes von Kyrene. Studien zur hellenistischen Kultur-und Wissenschaftsgeschichte* (Munich, 2002).

Gjerstad, E. The Colonization of Cyprus in Greek Legend. *Opuscula Archaeologica* 3 (1944), 107–123.

Günther, W. 'Vieux et inutilisable' dans un inventaire inédit de Milet, in: *Comptes et inventaires dans la cité grecque*, edited by D. Knoepfler (Neuchatel, 1988), 215–237.

Hermary, A. Les ascendances légendaires des rois chypriotes: quelques messages iconographiques, (Hommage à Marguerite Yon). *Cahiers du centre d'études chypriotes* 32 (2002), 275–288.

Hornblower, S. *A Commentary on Thucydides* (Oxford, 1991).

---

130 Cameron 2004, 221.

Hornblower, S. *Lykophron, Alexandra. Greek Text, Translation, Commentary and Introduction* (Oxford, 2015).

Iacovou, M. Cyprus. From Migration to Hellenisation, in: *Greek Colonisation. An Account of Greek Colonies and other Settlements Overseas* vol. 2, edited by G. R. Tsetskhladze (Leiden; Boston, 2008a), 219–288.

Iacovou, M. Cultural and Political Configurations in Iron Age Cyprus: the sequel to a protohistoric episode. *American Journal of Archaeology* 112 (2008b), 625–657.

Jost, M. Image de l'Arcadie au III s. av. J.-C. (Lycophron, Alexandra, V. 479–483), in: *Mélanges Pierre Lévêque. Tome II: Anthropologie et société*, edited by M.-M. Mactoux and E. Geny (Paris, 1989), 285–293.

Jost, M. (ed.) *Pausanias. Description de la Grèce. Tome VIII. Livre VIII. L' Arcadie* (Paris, 1998).

Karageorghis, V. *Palaepaphos-Skales: an Iron Age Cemetery in Cyprus* (Konstanz, 1983).

Lane Fox, R. *Travelling Heroes. Greeks and Their Myths in the Epic Age of Homer* (London, 2008).

Macan, R. W., Herodotus: the Seventh, Eighth, and Ninth Books. vol. 1.1 (London, 1908).

Maier, F. G. Alt-Paphos auf Zypern. *Antike Welt* 2:3 (1971), 2–14.

Maier, F. G. Evidence for Mycenaean Settlement at Old Paphos, in: *The Mycenaeans in the Eastern Mediterranean*, edited by V. Karageorghis (Nikosia 1973), 68–78.

Maier, F. G. Kinyras und Agapenor, in: *Cyprus Between the Orient and Occident*, edited by V. Karageorghis (Nikosia, 1986), 311–320.

Maier, F. G. History From the Earth: the Kingdom of Paphos in the Achaemenid period. *Transeuphratene* 12 (1996), 121–137.

Malkin, I. *Myth and Territory in the Spartan Mediterranean* (Cambridge, 1994).

Malkin, I. *The Returns of Odysseus* (Berkeley, 1998).

Malkin, I. *A Small Greek World. Networks in the Ancient Mediterranean* (Oxford, 2011).

Mavrogiannis, T. L'identité chypriote de la révolte Ionienne à Éuagoras (499–374 avant J.-C), in: *Identités croisées en un milieu méditerranéen, le cas de Chypre (Antiquité – Moyen-Âge)*, edited by S. Fourrier and G. Grivaud (Mont-Saint-Aignan, 2006), 153–163.

Mavrogiannis, T. Η Ετυμολογία του ονόματος Κύπρος και η Αρκαδικὴ καταγωγή των Κυπρίων in: *Epigraphy, Numismatics, Prosopography and History of Ancient Cyprus. Papers in Honour of Ino Nicolaou*, edited by D. Michaelides (Uppsala, 2013), 103–117.

Masson, O. *Les inscriptions chypriotes syllabiques: recueil critique et commenté.* Études chypriotes I (Paris, 1961).

Masson, O. Les objects inscrits de Palaepaphos-Skales, in: *Palaepaphos-Skales: an iron age cemetery in Cyprus*, edited by V. Karageorghis (Konstanz, 1983), 411–415.

Masson, O. and T. B. Mitford. *Les inscriptions syllabiques de Kouklia-Paphos* (Konstanz, 1986).

Michaelidou-Nicolaou, I. *Prosopography of Ptolemaic Cyprus* (Göteborg, 1976).

Miller, S. G. The Theorodokoi of the Nemean Games. *Hesperia* 57 (1988), 147–163.

Mitford, T. B. The Hellenistic Inscriptions of Old Paphos. *The Annual of the British School at Athens* 56 (1961a), 1–41.

Mitford, T. B. Further Contributions to the Epigraphy of Cyprus. *American Journal of Archaeology* 65 (1961b), 136–137.

Mitford, T. B. Roman Cyprus. *Aufstieg und Niedergang der römischen Welt* II 7.2 (1980), 1285–1384.

Morpurgo-Davies, A. Mycenaean, Arcadian, Cyprian and Some Questions of Method in Dialectology, in: *Mykenaika*, BCH Suppl. 25, edited by J.-P. Olivier (Athens, 1992), 415–432.

Näf, B. *Testimonia Alt-Paphos* (Darmstadt; Mainz, 2013).

Papantoniou, G. *Religion and Social Transformations in Cyprus: from the Cypriot "basileis" to the Hellenistic "strategos"* (Leiden, 2012).

Parsons, P. J. (ed.) *The Oxyrhynchos Papyri XLII* (London, 1974).

Pirenne-Delforge, V. *L'Aphrodite grecque*. Kernos Supplément IV (Athens; Liège, 1994).

Price, S. Local Mythologies in the Greek East, in: *Coinage and Identity in the Roman Provinces*, edited by C. Howgego, V. Heuchert and A. Burnett (Oxford, 2005), 115–124.

Pros. Ptol. = Peremans, W. and E. Van't Dack. *Prosopographia Ptolemaica* I–VI (Louvain, 1950).

Reyes, A. T. *Archaic Cyprus. A Study of the Textual and Archaeological Evidence* (Oxford, 1994).

Roy, J. Paus. 8.5.2–3 and 8.53.7. Laodike, Descendant of Agapenor, Tegea and Cyprus. *L' antiquité classique* 56 (1987), 192–200.

Rupp, D. W. The Seven Kings of the Land of Ia', a District of Ia-ad-na-na: Achaean Bluebloods, Cypriot Parvenus or Both?, in: *STEPHANOS. Studies in Honor of Brunilde Sismondo Ridgway*, edited by K. J. Hartswick and M. C. Sturgeon (Philadelphia, 1988), 210–222.

Scheer, T. S. *Mythische Vorväter. Zur Bedeutung griechischer Heroenmythen im Selbstverständnis kleinasiatischer Städte* (Munich, 1993).

Scheer, T. S. *Die Gottheit und ihr Bild: Untersuchungen zur Funktion griechischer Kultbilder in Religion und Politik* (Munich, 2000).

Scheer, T. S. The Past in a Hellenistic Present: myth and local tradition, in: *A Companion to the Hellenistic World*, edited by A. Erskine (London, 2003), 216–231.

Scheer, T. S. They that Held Arkadia. Arkadian Foundation Myths as Intentional History in Roman Imperial Times, in: *Intentional History: Spinning Time in Ancient Greece*, edited by L. Foxhall, H. J. Gehrke and N. Luraghi (Stuttgart, 2010), 275–298.

Schollmeyer, P. *Das antike Zypern. Aphrodites Insel zwischen Orient und Okzident* (Mainz, 2009).

Steele, P. *A Linguistic History of Ancient Cyprus* (Cambridge, 2013).

Stirpe, P. Dalla Laodice omerica alla Laodice moglie di Perseo? Su Lycophr. 316–322 e 495–503. *Hespería* 14 (2001), 227–236.

Stoll, H. W. Laodike, in: *Ausführliches Lexikon der griechischen und römischen Mythologie II.2*, edited by W. H. Roscher (Leipzig, 1894–97), 1829–1830.

Tsitsiridis, S. *Beiträge zu den Fragmenten des Klearchos von Soloi* (Berlin; Boston, 2013).

Ulbrich, A. *Kypris. Heiligtümer und Kulte weiblicher Gottheiten auf Zypern in der kyproarchaischen und kyproklassischen Epoche* (Münster, 2008).

Vanschoonwinkel, J. *L'Égée et la Méditerranée orientale à la fin du deuxième millénaire, témoignages archéologiques et sources écrites* (Louvain-la Neuve, 1991).

Ventris, M. and J. Chadwick. *Documents in Mycenaean Greek* (Cambridge, 1973).

Voyatzis, M. Arcadia and Cyprus. Aspects of Their Interrelationship between the 12th and 8th Centuries B.C. *Report of the Department of Antiquities Cyprus* (1985), 155–163.

West, M. L. *The East Face of Helicon. West Asiatic Elements in Greek Poetry and Myth* (Oxford, 1997).

Wilamowitz-Moellendorff, U. von. *Hellenistische Dichtung in der Zeit des Kallimachos* (Hildesheim, 1962²).

Part II: **Reception and Innovation of Mythological Programmes between Greece and Italy**

Nancy T. de Grummond
From Mezntie to Mezentius?

The Stratigraphy of a Myth in Etruria and Rome

A bronze Etruscan mirror in the Museo Nazionale Etrusco di Villa Giulia, Rome, dated ca. 300 BC, depicts a 5-figure mythological scene inscribed with names that may be read tentatively as Achle, Uhuze, Velachtra, Ethun and Mezntie. It is argued that this is a representation of a story involving two characters known from Greek myth (Achilles and Odysseus), two from Etruscan myth (Ethun and Velachtra) and one known primarily from Roman myth, Mezentius. The mirror seems to show an otherwise unknown story in which Mezntie is grieving and Achle is strapping on armour to go off to battle. This study includes a review of the evidence for a legend/myth of Mezentius in Italy, beginning with a real individual named Laucie Mezentie, whose name appears inscribed on a vessel of the seventh century BC (Paris, Louvre), and ending with the famous depiction of Mezentius in Virgil's *Aeneid* that has conditioned modern perceptions of this figure.

The astonishing variations in the myth of Mezentius are scrutinised by means of three theoretical approaches. First, the scene on the mirror may be analysed as a mythologem, a term introduced by C. Kerényi[1] to refer to a complex of individual motifs that combine to indicate the type of scene represented. Second, it is possible to construct a stratigraphy of the story, in which the typology of the narrative can be observed to change against the context in which it is found, from reality to ritual needs and ultimately to literary purposes. An identical pattern may be seen in the myth of the Vipinas (Vibenna) brothers and Cacu (Virgilian Cacus), known from a famous Etruscan mirror in the British Museum. Third, the "wandering" of the stories of Mezntie and Cacu relates directly to the process by which most myths in Etruria, it is argued, were disseminated: oral transmission.

This article addresses a problematic bronze Etruscan mirror in the Villa Giulia Museum in Rome (Figs. 1–2), thus far studied only in a very limited way.[2] It dates to around

---

[1] Kerényi 1969. This term is more fully defined and explored later in this paper with discussion of the Villa Giulia mirror.

[2] De Grummond 2006, 205–7. J. P. Small, "Mevntie", *LIMC* 6 (1992), 566. I. Krauskopf, "Ethun", *LIMC* 4 (1988), 38. G. Camporeale, "Achle", *LIMC* 1 (1981), 209 (no. 164). Height of mirror: 27.8 cm. Diam. of disc: 14 cm. The mirror was first recorded in the accessions of the Villa Giulia, inv. 56135, for the year 1931–32, as acquired from a certain Comm. Ugo Sandolo and was first published in Buonamici 1938, 312–4. See also Vetter 1955, 65. No precise provenance is recorded for it, but I suggest it may have come from the area of Orvieto. The disc is damaged, and seems to have been intentionally hammered out of shape on the obverse reflecting side, perhaps indicating a ritual common around Orvieto (de Grummond 2009). I thank Francesca Boitani for the courtesy of allowing me to consult the archives at the Villa Giulia

https://doi.org/10.1515/9783110421453-006

Fig. 1: Bronze Etruscan mirror. Museo Nazionale Etrusco di Villa Giulia, inv. 56135. Provenance unknown. Ca. 300–275 BC. Photo: Soprintendenza Archeologia del Lazio e dell'Etruria Meridionale.

300 BC and is of unknown provenance, but the overall geographical context involves southern Etruria and Latium, an area where there was a ferment of exchange among Etruscans, Romans, Faliscans, Praenestines and Greeks (especially from Magna Graecia). It shows, I argue, an astonishing assemblage of mythological figures from Etruscan, Roman and Greek myth, in a story that is otherwise not known. Before presenting the argument, it is useful to discuss some basic questions about the issues and methodology for interpreting Etruscan representations of myth.

and to examine the mirror in person. Lorenzo Galeotti assisted me in the study of the mirror and in the acquisition of photos made after the mirror had been cleaned (Figs. 1–2). I am grateful to other friends who have tried to help me as I sought answers to the difficult questions posed by the mirror: Giovanna Bagnasco Gianni, Larissa Bonfante, Domenique Briquel, Francesco De Angelis, Maria Stella Pacetti, Charlotte Potts, Francesca Serra Ridgway, Rex Wallace.

Fig. 2: Detail of medallion. Bronze Etruscan mirror. Museo Nazionale Etrusco di Villa Giulia, inv. 56135. Provenance unknown. Ca. 300–275 BC. Photo: Soprintendenza Archeologia del Lazio e dell'Etruria Meridionale.

Setting the Scene: Greek Myths in Etruria

First, let us look at a few Etruscan depictions that are generally regarded as showing Greek myths. A remarkable scene on an Etruscan mirror of similar style and of the same date as the Villa Giulia mirror shows a horse being worked upon (Fig. 3).[3] While this bids to be a representation of the making of the Trojan horse, it is remarkable that the horse is labelled Pecse, the Etruscan equivalent of the Greek name Pegasos.

---

3 *ES* 2, 235.2; Rebuffat-Emmanuel 1973, 252–8; R. Lambrechts "Etule", *LIMC* 4 (1988), 39 (no. 1). For the inscriptions see *ET* OA S. 4.

Fig. 3: Bronze Etruscan mirror. Sethlans and Etule labor over the horse Pecse. Inscription on right: *hlins*. Paris, Bibliothèque Nationale. Probably from the area of Orvieto. Third century BC. After *ES* 2, 235.2.

The figure on the left is labelled as Sethlans, the Etruscan craftsman god who is often equated with Hephaestus, though in fact he is beardless and in Etruria is usually not crippled. He seems to be applying clay to the neck of the horse, though this would be at odds with the repeated references in ancient literature to the Trojan horse as made of wood. He is assisted by Etule, otherwise unknown, who is dressed not as a Greek, but as a Trojan with long sleeves and an oriental cap. He plies a hammer. The horse is evidently alive, since it appears to be chained up by its front leg. To the back leg is attached a strange box or sign that reads *hlins*, perhaps referring to Greeks. Very little in the scene fits with the written Greek version of the story of the Trojan horse. Besides what has already been indicated, in Homer's *Odyssey* (8.493) Epeios[4] is the craftsman who creates the horse, and he does so with the help of Athena, not Hephaestus. Roman Virgil cites the same personnel, Pallas (Athena) and Epeios (*Aen.* 2.15 and 264). Representations in Greek and Roman art, which normally feature some of the warriors involved in the story, provide no convincing parallels for the Etruscan scene.[5] Thus we are unable to explain this mixture of motifs and characters by reference to any known text or representation.

The Etruscans depicted on another mirror a story about a creature with the body of a man and the head of a bull Thevrumines (Fig. 4), literally "the bull of Minos," a

---

4 Another Epeios, not the one who made the horse, had a brother named Aetolos. According to Rebuffat-Emmanual 1973, 477, this could be the source for the name Etule.

5 Sparkes 1971. The images closest to the scene are one of Athena applying clay to a horse, which has been rejected as a scene of the Trojan horse and instead interpreted as showing Athena as a sculptress (Sparkes 1971, 60), and a scene of Athena supervising a workman applying a hammer and chisel to a normal-sized horse in the presence of onlookers (Sparkes 1971, 60 and pl. 2b).

designation that has usually been equated with the Minotaur.[6] On the far left is Mine, next to him the goddess Menrva, and on the right is the veiled female figure Ariatha. This constitutes a shocking deviation from standard Greek myth in that the slayer of the Minotaur is not Theseus, but a man identified by label as "Hercle". That this is not a casual mistake but actually represents the way the story was sometimes told in Etruria is made more likely by the fact that there is at least one other representation of Hercle killing the Minotaur,[7] and furthermore that the assistant of Hercle is even included in this scene. He is called Vile in Etruscan, a name that is agreed to come from Iolaus, the nephew of Heracles, though in Etruria Vile was probably the twin of Hercle.[8] Recently Ambrosini has made a brilliant argument that the scene represented is actually Hercle having defeated the Cretan bull (it would be fair to call it "the bull of Minos"), and the other characters may thus be justified as present in the scene.[9] The fact that the creature in question is part human tends to fit better with the identification of the Minotaur, but in any case the point is rather that the Etruscans were

Fig. 4: Bronze Etruscan mirror. Hercle (far right) with the dead Thevrumines (= Minotaur) at his feet. From left to right, Mine, Menrva, Vilae, Ariatha. Rome, Museo Nazionale Romano. From Civita Castellana (Falerii). Ca. 300 BC. After Brommer 1981, fig. 10.

---

6 Found at Civita Castellana and contemporary with the Villa Giulia mirror. Brommer 1981; F. Jurgeit, "Ariadne/Ariatha", *LIMC* 3 (1986), 1070–1071 (no. 4); de Grummond 2006, 186. *ET* Fa S.2 for the inscriptions. Ambrosini 2010 reveals that the mirror is no longer to be considered "lost," as so often repeated, but is actually in the Museo Nazionale Romano, Rome.

7 Etruscan black-figure amphora, Paris, Musée du Louvre, inv. 11069, late sixth century BC. Torelli 2000, 435, 608 (cat. no. 215). See the discussion by Bruni 2002, 10–2, where Hercle and the Minotaur are recognised on Late Etruscan ash urns from Volterra.

8 M. Pipili, "Iolaus/Vile", *LIMC* 5 (1990), 700 (no. 30; "Vile and Herakles wrongly associated with the Minotaur"); de Grummond 2006, 184–6.

9 Ambrosini 2010, 11–2.

telling their own version of a deed of Hercle. Completely Etruscan, as far as can be seen, is the figure of a child in the upper exergue, who holds a scroll and interacts with a bird, an obviously prophetic motif that would have resonated in Etruria.[10] In sum, the combination of elements suggests that there is no specific Greek text or image that explains this mythological scene; it is an Etruscan variant that probably arose through oral transmission.

A very large mirror from Vulci, dated around 325 BC, depicts two different scenes (Fig. 5).[11] The bottom register shows in the middle an enthroned Elinai, reaching out to clasp hands with Achmemrun. Menle stands in a tranquil pose between them. On the left, a nearly naked youth, Elchsntre (= Alexander, i.e. Paris) is crowned by Mean, the Etruscan goddess of Victory. Aevas (= Ajax) looks on in awe and on the right an Etruscan spirit Lasa Thimrae dips perfume from a bottle. The astounding scene seems to show harmony and friendship among the principals of the Trojan War, and includes Etruscan spirits mingling with the Greek figures.[12] In the top register Hercle stands with the child Epiur before Tinia, the Etruscan counterpart of Zeus, as Turan (counterpart to Aphrodite) on the left and Thalna on the right look on. Thalna and the story of Epiur are unknown in Greece and Rome.[13] There are other representations of Epiur and Hercle in Etruria, but thus far no enlightenment from classical texts or Greek and Roman art.

It is also appropriate to look at scenes from engraved bronze mirrors from Praeneste, often studied along with Etruscan mirrors due to the similarity of techniques and the geographical proximity. An equally rich and challenging body of engravings of mythological scenes occurs on cistae from Praeneste, often inscribed with the names of the participants. The inscriptions, however, are not Etruscan but a dialect kin to Latin.[14] A typically Praenestine pear-shaped mirror of the fourth century BC shows a scene in which the labels reveal that Luqorcos is attempting to kill Pilonicos, the child of Taseos, but is stopped by Taseos (Fig. 6).[15] The story is quite unknown, but some

---

10 The scene is rife with prophetic motifs, utilising gestures that I have argued are recurring vocabulary for eliciting of a prophecy (the upturned fingers of Hercle); for explaining a prophecy (the raised finger of Mine); and the reception of a prophetic message (the strange humanlike "hand" of the bull raised up in an otherwise unexplained gesture). See de Grummond 2002, esp. 73, and de Grummond 2011, esp. 328.

11 De Grummond 2006, 61–3, 66; Rebuffat-Emmanuel 1973, 52–64, 521–6; I. Krauskopf, "Alexandros", *LIMC* 1 (1981), 521 (no. 106); Domenici 2009, esp. 229, ET Vc S. 24.

12 The scene has been explained as the Greek myth of Helen on the island of Leuke, where she married Achilles, a bizarre alternate to the more traditional ending in which she returned to Menelaus. But Achilles is not present, and in fact, even the Menelaus figure seems to have a secondary role, as Elinai joins hands with Achmemrun. Rebuffat-Emmanuel 1973, 524–5.

13 On Thalna, G. Camporeale "Thalna," *LIMC* 7 (1994), 900–2; de Grummond 2006, 152–6. For Epiur, E. Mavleev, "Epiur," *LIMC* 3 (1986), 810–2. In depth treatment by Domenici 2009, 197–231.

14 De Grummond 2006, 237.

15 De Puma 1980, 20. A. Parrini, "Pilonicos Taseio filios", *LIMC* 7 (1994), 410 (no. 1).

Fig. 5: Bronze Etruscan mirror. Turan, Hercle with Epiur, Tinia, Thalna. Aevas, Mean, Elchsntre, Elinai, Menle, Achmemrun, Lasa Thimrae. Paris, Bibliothèque Nationale. From Vulci. Ca. 325 BC. After *ES* 2, 181.

Fig. 6: Bronze Praenestine mirror. Luqorcos attempts to kill Pilonicos, the child of Taseos, but is stopped by Taseos. Paris, Louvre. From Praeneste. Fourth century BC. After *ES* 5, 108.

scholars have thought the artist just made a mistake[16] and mislabelled the story of Telephus threatening to kill Orestes, being stopped by Agamemnon, since the general composition resembles Greek representations of that story. If there were no labels, we would no doubt assume that the mirror indeed depicted the story of the wounding of Telephus, but the inscriptions seem to be very specific, including the information that Pilonicos is the child of Taseos. Here we have a rather surprising case of motifs used in one context transferred to tell another story.

Another case of a Praenestine composition with the "wrong" story is on an engraving from a bronze Praenestine cista (Fig. 7).[17] It shows Alixentr (Alexander = Paris), with three ladies, but this is not the usual depiction of the judgment of Paris. It may well be a beauty contest, judging from the preening poses of the naked females, but the story is not known from written texts. From left to right, the ladies are named Ateleta, Alsir and Helena. Atalanta and Helen may well be the counterparts of Ateleta and Helena, but no one knows of Alsir, nor of the youth with his back to Alixentre, named Alses. The image should not simply be assumed to constitute a misunderstanding or a mistake just because it deviates from the versions of the story that we are familiar with. Like the other examples I have presented, this is surely evidence for a locally transmitted story.

On another Praenestine cista (Fig. 8), Aciles puts on greaves as Victoria hands him a helmet, and a character named Micos leads up a pair of horses. The context is remarkable, with Ajax balancing Aciles on the other side of the cista (Fig. 9), being aided in his arming by a personification whose name has been read as Iuventus,

---

16 A. Farnoux, "Lykourgos I", *LIMC* 6 (1992), 312 (no. 17).
17 Bordenache Battaglia and Emiliozzi 1990, 1.1, 64–5, and pl. 73.

Fig. 7: Engraved bronze Praenestine cista. Alixentr encounters Ateleta, Alsir and Helena. Alses stands on the left. From Praeneste. Berlin, Staatliche Museen. Third century BC. After Bordenache Battaglia 1990, I.1. pl. 73.

Fig. 8: Bronze Praenestine cista with arming of heroes and weighing of souls. Micos, Aciles, and Victoria. Vatican, Museo Gregoriano Etrusco. Third century BC. After Bordenache Battaglia 1990, I.2. pl. 462.

Fig. 9: Bronze Praenestine cista with arming of heroes and weighing of souls. Hercles, Diesptr, Ivno, Mircurios, Iacor, Ajax and Iuventus (?). Vatican, Museo Gregoriano Etrusco. Third century BC. After Bordenanche Battaglia 1990, I.2. pl. 462.

Youth, or Veritus (i.e. *Virtus*, Courage).[18] In between the two heroes Mircurios plies a scale presumably to weigh their fates and ascertain the future as the surprising combination of Iuno, Diesptr, Hercles and an unknown warrior named Iacor look on. It seems that we have a double arming scene and fate will decide which of the warriors is successful. It is noteworthy that abstract personifications, frequent on Etruscan mirrors,[19] attend the heroes, Victoria for Aciles and Iuventus or Virtus for Ajax.

Error or Local Agency?

Examples could be multiplied. There are many, many scenes in Etruscan and Praenestine engraved art that have what are considered problematic combinations of mythological figures, some known from elsewhere and others unknown apart from the one scene where they are presented. How can all this be explained? Quite commonly, scholars have concluded that the artist really meant to depict an authentic Greek myth, and somehow he or the scribe confused the names. It is by no means argued here that in Italy artists or scribes (who may have been different from the artists) never made mistakes. Surely at times they did (just as artists or scribes may have done in

---

18 Bordenache Battaglia and Emiliozzi 1990, 1.2, 320. The name has also been read as Vepitus (= Veritus or Virtus).
19 Examples are numerous. See esp. Cristofani 1985.

any culture), but each case should be considered on its own terms, as well as against the general background offered here – that it is so common to find bizarre departures from Greek myth in Etruria indicates that we should not assume that all of them are simply misunderstandings or errors regarding Greek culture.

A second explanation often offered is that these are Greek myths for which no full narrative has survived, and so it is legitimate methodology to find different Greek texts and weave them together to explain the story. This procedure can indeed give clues, but can also be misleading. And since no text perfectly suits the story, a certain amount of guesswork is involved, and often is based on what ought to happen in Greece rather than Italy. Thus, a story that is not recorded in any literary text is often conjectured to be from one of the numerous lost Greek plays.[20] On the other hand, it is frequently acknowledged that there is evidence of the existence of Etruscan plays, from Varro's mention of a certain Volnius, *qui tragoedias Tuscas scripsit* (*De Lingua Latina* 5.55), and it has been noted that the presence of "very deformed proper names" from Greek myth written on Etruscan mirrors and paintings suggests that scribes were writing down what they had heard said aloud in Etruscan versions of the myths.[21]

A third approach is to admit that the story itself is strange, and we may never know what the narrative was, but we can at least speculate why the particular theme was chosen for Etruria or Praeneste. One may argue for social, political or cultural values or for ritual purposes.[22] This methodology can be effective, and has the positive value of starting inside Italy rather than beginning by imposing Greek culture on Etruscans and others in Italy. This stance can be used in combination with a fourth approach, namely the argument that a great many of these stories were transmitted orally. Oral transmission can lead to a number of variants. Under this argument, there is no original, there is no standard correct version, but each story is meaningful at its face value. Artists are not illustrating particular texts, but rather evoking a story that is circulating as common property.[23]

---

20 Heurgon 1964, 244–5. This explanation has been made regarding scenes on mirrors by Bonfante 1980, 152 (n. 27) and Bonfante 2003, 121 (n. 43) and 129 (n. 56). Regarding ash urns from Volterra, where the setting sometimes looks stage-like and costumes can be recognised, see van der Meer 1977, for a review of the bibliography and theories. Pairault Massa 1977, 160 and n. 145 ff. stresses Greek themes as transmitted in "Pergamene tragic style" and in the nascent theatre of Rome.

21 Heurgon 1964, 245–7.

22 E.g. Pfiffig 1975, who integrates deviations into his reconstruction of aspects of Etruscan religion, e.g. liver divination (118), lightning (130–1), the Underworld (323–36). Domenici 2009, 46–9, reviews the intellectual background and examples of this stance. Pairault Massa 1992 stresses political connections, but almost always tries to justify the Etruscan narratives by citing Greek connections.

23 Small 2003, esp. ch. 6, "There is No Original!". Interestingly, this approach is completely valid for the study of Greek and Roman myth in art, which have their own surprising departures from the canonical versions of the stories, e.g. Small 2003, 12 and 180 n. 15 (the charioteers in the funeral games of Patroclus are all but one different from those in Homer; the victor is different), 143–53 (numerous

The dynamics of oral transmission were summarised succinctly by Werner Kelber in a quite different context, in regard to the Gospels. He noted that oral transmission manifested a "multiplicity of tendencies", with motifs and themes migrating from one context to another, dropping out or being added, and sequences often changing; variants are constantly being developed.[24] Albert Lord famously recognised such tendencies in his studies of oral poetry and Homeric epic. He noted that we seem to find it necessary "to construct an ideal text or an original, and we remain dissatisfied with an ever-changing phenomenon... . From one point of view performance is an original. From another point of view it is impossible to retrace the work of generations of singers to that moment when some singer first sang a particular song."[25] T. P. Wiseman notes that this situation was understood by M. Finley as long ago as 1964: "Every time the tale was told, it was told to a particular audience on a particular occasion and their expectations and preconceptions changed over time with the changing circumstances of the community. Oral tradition does not transmit what has become obsolete or irrelevant."[26] He also noted the creativity involved in the variants.

Though classical scholars have a tradition of interpreting myths in art on the basis of their similarity to or difference from texts, there is an increasing awareness of the importance of oral tradition, of stories that were "in the air", of shared material that was perhaps never written down or at least was read by very few. More and more scholars are willing to acknowledge the importance of public performances that transmitted a myth, especially in the theatre, but also in songs, poems or narratives delivered to account for or to support a ritual in a religious context.[27] Without doubt stories about gods and heroes were told in the home or on travels and simply in daily conversation.[28] Travellers like Herodotus collected from oral sources tales relevant for myth, legend and history. It is especially important to recognise oral transmission in the case of Etruria, where only a small percentage of the populace will have been literate. The Etruscan mirror has often been taken as evidence of Etruscan literacy, suggesting for example that this instrument showed that Etruscan women, who were often the users, could read. Statistics indicate, however, that only about 11 % of Etruscan mirrors fea-

---

discrepancies between the text of the *Aeneid* and its "illustrations" in the Vatican Vergil Codex Latinus 3225); Woodford 2003, 201–3 (the abduction of Deianeira by the centaur Dexamenos; Thetis arming Menelaus).

24 Kelber 1997, 29.

25 Lord 2000, 100. S. Lowenstam, following Lord, utilised the term "multiform" in discussing representations in art, to refer to a body of related myths having variants rather than being based on some fixed "original" text. Discussed by Muellner 2012.

26 Wiseman 2008, 17.

27 Small 2003. Woodford 2003. Wiseman 2008. For a brilliant review of the importance of song for the Romans, see Horsfall 2003, esp. 12–3 and 96–7 (where he gives useful references but at the same time retreats from the idea that myth was thus transmitted).

28 Paradigmatic is the reference in Plato to the custom of mothers and nurses telling stories to children: Pl. *Resp.* 377. Cf. the discussion by Graf 1996, 4.

tured inscriptions.[29] Naturally scholars tend to privilege these, since they provide precious clues about subject matter. But many individuals probably could not read, and would have interpreted mythological scenes, whether inscribed or not, through storytelling.

Looking at Myth through the Villa Giulia Mirror

With this background in mind, let us turn now to examine the myth represented on the reverse of the Villa Giulia mirror (Fig. 2). There is a group of five figures in a setting that combines conventional elements of landscape and of architecture. The medallion is surrounded by a rich hybrid vine with various types of leaves and flowers[30] and a hint of architecture is given at the top of the medallion, where triangular shapes extend along a curved line, below which is at least one column capital with a volute shape.

Around the rim are inscriptions naming the figures. Starting on the right, with the least controversial character on the mirror, we see the label for *aχle* (Achle),[31] whose Greek counterpart would be Achilles, an identification that is consistent with the image we see. He is a youth, characterised as a warrior by the shield leaning against a support behind him, the baldric with sword at his chest and the action he is carrying out. The pose is that of a warrior putting on his greaves, a motif known in both Greece and Italy and which in fact we have already seen on the Aciles on the Praenestine *cista*.[32] The greaves are only vaguely indicated, but the action is unmistakable. He also wears a cape that is appropriate for a warrior. The hair is long, with no covering, and the face is beardless.

Scenes of the arming of Achilles are known in Greece, Magna Graecia and Etruria, especially on painted vases and engraved mirrors.[33] It is often said that there were

---

29 De Grummond 2002, 309. Though exceptions may occur, most of the evidence for ownership or usage of Etruscan mirrors, based on tomb groups, inscriptions and images of mirrors in use, suggests that the instruments were primarily used by women: de Grummond 2002, 309–10. For a sensitive reading of the evidence from tomb groups and the possible exceptions, see Carpino 2008.

30 So far I detect no connection between the scene in the medallion and a winged female in a tiered garment represented on the transition piece between disc and handle.

31 For the inscriptions on this mirror, see Buonamici 1938, 313–4; Rix, *ET*, OI S 22. In citing Etruscan inscriptions it is considered more accurate to use the letter χ instead of the transliterated *ch*. In this article, in observance of practicality in typography, the letter will be transliterated as *ch* unless an actual inscription is being cited. Similarly, it is usual to use θ instead of *th* in Etruscan inscriptions; the policy for transliteration will be the same.

32 A. Kossatz-Deissmann, "Achilleus", *LIMC* 1 (1981), 70 (no. 187). Von Bothmer 1990, 178–80. Zazoff, 1968, 61 (no. 77). *ES* 2, 227. For discussion see *CSE* Great Britain 3. 5 (N. de Grummond).

33 A. Kossatz-Deissmann, "Achilleus", *LIMC* 1 (1981), 70–1 (definitely Achilles: nos. 187–9, 191, 197, 199, 201, 203, 204, 205; identity not certain: 190, 193–6, 198, 202). G. Camporeale, "Achle", *LIMC* 1 (1981), 206–7 (nos. 96–117).

two episodes of arming the hero, but there also seems to be a third, which will be described below. The first, obliquely referenced in *Iliad* 11.765–803, takes place when Achilles starts out from his homeland in Phthia and is given armour in the presence of his mother Thetis and an older man who is interpreted as his father Peleus or Nestor. Odysseus may also be present. The second time is when his armour has been lost at the death of Patroclus and Thetis commissions spectacular new armour from Hephaestus; in such scenes Thetis and her Nereid sisters carry the new armour for him, while other individuals may be present such as Phoenix, his mentor, taking the place of Peleus.[34] The Hephaestian armour is referenced in Homer (*Il.* 19.1–39), where no one but Thetis bestows the armour, though Odysseus and Diomedes appear soon after, when Achilles summons a council. A third type of scene seems to take place when Achilles is in hiding at the court of Lycomedes, but is found out by an embassy led by Odysseus and Phoenix, who offer him weapons and armour. Besides the women of the court of Lycomedes, Achilles' son Neoptolemus may be present.[35] As will become clear, none of these three possibilities fits with the scene of the arming of Achilles represented here.

Next to Achle is an older man, bearded and somewhat stooped, leaning upon a knotted staff and wearing an unusual pointed hat that looks to have a feather inserted in it. He wears a long dress and his left arm is completely concealed by the drapery wrapped around it. He seems to meditate as he leans upon the staff. In iconography he most resembles the elder who appears in Greek scenes of the arming of Achilles such as Peleus, Nestor, or Phoenix, but the inscription above his head naming him starts with the letter *u*, which would not support the identification of any of those

Fig. 10: Cornelian carved gem, cast. Odysseus as old beggar. New York, Metropolitan Museum of Art. Fifth century BC. After *LIMC* 6 (1992), pl. 638, Odysseus 212.

---

34 A. Kossatz-Deissmann, "Achilleus", *LIMC* 1 (1981), 123–7 (nos. 506–41; no. 508 has the name of Phoenix inscribed; see also 124, no. 521).
35 A. Kossatz-Deissmann, "Achilleus," *LIMC* 1 (1981), esp. 65–6 (nos. 176–81). *CSE* USA 4. 2 (R. De Puma).

Fig. 11: Carved gem. The myth of Tages and Tarchon (?) London, British Museum. Fourth century BC. Photo: Trustees of the British Museum.

figures. I suggest that the figure may be Odysseus, whose name occurs in Etruscan as *uθuze, uθste, utuse, utzte,* and other minor variants[36] and who was in one way or another connected with all three known types of arming scenes. He therefore seems to have taken over the role of the senior mentor.

The iconography is not inconsistent with other representations in art of Odysseus. In fact a stooped bearded man with a pointed hat leaning on a cane compares well with images from Greek glyptic identified as Odysseus (Fig. 10).[37] Achilles and Odysseus are found together on one other Etruscan mirror, along with Thetis, although there is no presentation of the armour there, and are also found on two inscribed gems that show the departure of Achilles.[38] Another point of interest is that the pose of the bearded figure here resembles not only the elder in other scenes of the arming of Achilles, but

---

36 De Simone 1968, I, 124–6. De Simone lists only two other Greek figures whose name starts with *u: urφe* (= Orpheus) and *uφstie* (equivalent unknown). The only two other mythological male figures possible are Etruscan Usil (the sun god) and Umaele, a prophetic figure who is never represented with a beard.

37 O. Touchefeu-Meynier, "Odysseus", *LIMC* 6 (1992), 943–70, esp. 966 (no. 212).

38 *CSE* USA 3.18 (L. Bonfante). On the mirror again Odysseus is bearded and Achilles is beardless and more youthful. For the two inscribed gems, which show the armed *aχele* moving away from the seated figure of *utuse*, see 1) sardonyx scarab, fifth century BC, from Bolsena: Furtwängler 1900, pl. 16, no. 28; *ET* Vs G. 1; Zazoff 1968, 144 (no. 301); G. Camporeale, "Achle", *LIMC* 1 (1981), 209 (no. 157), De Simone 1968, I, 32 (no. 2) and 124 (no. 1); and 2) cornelian scarab, fifth century BC, Philadelphia, University Museum; *ET* OI G. 42. Zazoff 1968, 144 (no. 303); G. Camporeale, "Achle", *LIMC* 1 (1981), 209 (no. 161); De Simone 1968, I, 33 (no. 8a) and 124 (no. 3a); Zazoff 1968, 144, lists several other examples, including a lost specimen from Vulci (no. 302; Furtwängler 1900, pls. 16, 26) that shows the Odysseus figure seated, leaning on a staff or spear and with head bent forward as on the Villa Giulia mirror. Almost certainly it shows the same story as on the mirror, but without the three figures on the left of the mirror.

also recalls various meditating figures in Etruscan prophecy scenes, which perhaps gives a clue of interpretation. A well-known mirror from Tuscania, for example, shows the figure of Avl Tarchunus in a meditative posture, leaning on his staff as he observes divination carried out by Pava Tarchies.[39] A gem in the British Museum shows one of the numerous scenes of a talking prophetic head (Fig. 11), observed and meditated upon by a senior figure leaning upon a staff.[40] We shall return to this possibility.

The inscription above the bearded elder on the mirror is unfortunately highly problematic. Buonamici has noted in general the irregularities in the writing on this mirror, observing variations in size and spacing of the letters and even that one letter (*m*) is "fatta male."[41] In short, the scribe here seems inexperienced. For this word, after the first letter *u*, there is a great deal of uncertainty. The second letter may be an *h*; Buonamici regarded it as perhaps a combination of *i* and *e* (with the e written backwards), but more likely *h*. Next occurs a gap (no letter was ever written in the space).[42] The complete absence of a letter in the middle of the word suggests that the scribe may have been copying the inscription from a preliminary version and simply missed one letter in so doing. If this inscription is indeed intended to be the Etruscan name of Odysseus, the letter may have been *u*. After that there is another letter, which has been read as a *digamma*, but which could possibly be understood as a *zeta*, again reflecting the known forms of the Etruscan name of Odysseus. An alphabet from Vulci shows precisely this form for a *zeta*.[43] Alternatively it should not be ruled out that the scribe was uncertain what letter he was writing.[44] Since *digamma* and *zeta* are side by side in the alphabet and each features a vertical line intersected by two lines sloping downward toward the left, it is easy to see how they might get interchanged. Could this combination of letters be understood as *uh(u)z* or even *uh(u)z(e)*? Perhaps another letter was omitted at the end of the word, an *e*, because the first letter of the next

---

39 De Grummond 2006, pl. 2.2.

40 De Grummond 2006, 27.

41 Buonamici 1938, 313–4. In autopsy I also noted that the *l* in *aχle* has a double strike at the base.

42 Conclusion reached through personal examination of the mirror.

43 Pandolfini and Prosdocimi 1990, 38 (n. II.3), dating to the sixth century BC, relevant geographically but not ideal in chronology for our purposes. An alphabet of the fourth century BC found near Mantua also has precisely this form for *zeta*, but written from left to right: Pandolfini and Prosdocimi 1990, 79 (n. III.31).

44 Cf. Pfiffig 1964 and 1977, reviewing nearly 200 scribal mistakes in Etruscan. See esp. 1977, 7–9, where he discusses mistakes in which one letterform is swapped for another. For example, *digamma* and *epsilon* are sometimes mixed up, and likewise *zeta* and *tau*. Pfiffig does not cite any specific exchange between *digamma* and *zeta*, but since the two letters are side by side in the alphabet and each features a vertical line intersected by two horizontal or slightly sloping lines, it is easy to see how they might get confused. Pfiffig's study is by no means exhaustive. He drew largely from ash urns and did not include bronze mirrors in his survey. I am grateful to Rex Wallace for pointing out Pfiffig's studies to me.

name is an *e*. All of this would yield the name Uhuze, which comes very close to the known names for Odysseus in Etruscan.

The next figure is a standing youth with the inscribed name *eθun*, unknown apart from this mirror.[45] His head turns toward the figures of Achle and the older man. He is nearly nude, with boots (only one is visible), a baldric and a diadem, and possibly in addition a wreath. On his proper left shoulder is a curious loop, which seems to attach to a collar-like accoutrement and has a point that approaches his hair. His right arm is not shown, and his left arm seems to be wrapped in drapery.

To the left of Ethun is a standing female figure, almost completely nude except for boots (only one is showing), a bit of drapery around her proper left leg, a bracelet on her proper left arm, a torque and a wreath. She turns toward the left side of the mirror as if to offer sympathy to the seated figure next to her. Her right arm is not visible but perhaps we are to think that she has placed it on the back of the seated figure. Her name was read as *zelaχtra* by Buonamici.[46] He noted that the letters in this word varied considerably in size and that the word as a whole featured letters much larger than those of the next word, further evidence of the uncertainty of the scribe. The form of the letter he identified as *zeta* is not identical to the one posited above in the name of Uhuze. If that is indeed a *zeta* is it possible the scribe made the swap of letters complete, and chose this form for *digamma*? If so, that would mean that the name intended was not *zelaχtra*, but *velaχtra*.

It is worth noting that the suffix *-tra* has been recognised as having a deictic usage, meaning "da parte di", i.e.[47] "on the part of" someone, in this case Zelach or Velach.[48] This is the only place in Etruscan writing where this name occurs (whether Zelachtra or Velachtra), and so far it does not seem possible to identify her beyond her role on this mirror. It is worth noting that both Ethun and this figure are nude, suggesting that they are not ordinary mortals in the narrative. Perhaps they are personifications, as seen earlier on the Praenstine cista and on many Etruscan mirrors, closely tied to the enthroned figure and the group as counsellors.

On the far left is a figure seated in an elaborate throne, labelled with an inscription read in the past as *mevntie* by Buonamici (followed by Rix and others).[49] The mirror was published by J. P. Small in *LIMC* as a unique instance of this character, whom

---

45 Buonamici 1938, 314; Rix ET OI S 22. I. Krauskopf, "Ethun", *LIMC* 4, 1988, 38.

46 Buonamici 1938, 314. Followed by Rix, ET OI S 22. There is no article on Zelachtra in *LIMC*.

47 De Simone 1991.

48 Note the many names in Etruscan that have the combination of *vel, vela, velc, velca, velχ*. For the reading of *zelaχtra*, there are no such parallels. On the other hand, an argument could be made that *zelaχ* – is another form of *zilaθ*, the Etruscan title for a high official. There is abundant evidence of the interchangeability of *i* and *e* in Eruscan. Further, the combining form is written as *zilaχ* -. In that case one would have to consider that the wreathed lady is someone official, perhaps of high counselling status. But this would be a rather rare situation.

49 Buonamici 1938, 314; Vetter 1955, 65; *ET* Vs S.5.

she, following Buonamici and others, identified as female.[50] But the ending of the name indicates that the figure is male, and the other elements that were thought to be characteristic of a female – the dress and hair – may be easily justified as male. The long hair of the enthroned figure is very similar to that of the nude male standing figure of Ethun in the centre of the composition, and the garment, a dress with long sleeves, may be seen worn by a bearded male on a well-known mirror in the Louvre which is stylistically similar to the Villa Giulia mirror and is probably contemporary. It shows a figure of a king in an almost identical dress. The dress is theatrical and may be found on figures of kings and rulers represented in South Italian vase painting.[51]

The inscription is again problematic, with the letters uneven in size and in spacing. The form of *m* is strange, but could hardly be identified as anything else.[52] Considering the irregularities already noted in the inscriptions of the mirror and the possibilities of the swapping of letters it may be argued that the letter previously read by other scholars as a *v (digamma)* is here, as in the conjectured Uhuze meant to be a *zeta*. The name then becomes Mezntie. Based on this conjecture, we may explore the possibility that this name may relate to the character Mezentius, king of Etruscan Caere, known in Latin legend and myth, especially in Virgil's *Aeneid*. He is indeed regal, seated upon an elaborate throne, and resting his right hand on a staff. His hair is bound with a diadem. In short, all the characteristics – throne, sceptre, clothing and diadem – are quite consistent with the identification of this figure as a king. The attitude of the king is subdued, and he seems to incline his head to rest it upon his hand, which is raised to the face in a gesture best interpreted as showing dismay or grief. We shall return to the reasons for dismay.

His throne is very elaborate, featuring several tiers of decoration. It is hard to find very good comparisons in Etruscan art,[53] but there are several parallels in Apulian vase painting of the fourth century BC, where we find the high back and the elaborate arms, most often in scenes that probably again reflect theatrical performances. Often the enthroned figure is a king.[54]

---

50 J. P. Small, "Mevntie", *LIMC* 6 (1992), 566.

51 King Oeneus on a mirror with Meleager and Atalanta: *CSE* France 1.1.14 (D. Emmanuel-Rebuffat). Cf. Priam on a mirror with his family: *ES* 5.118. South Italian vases: e.g. Phineus, king of Thrace: Trendall, 1989, fig. 19. See also the discussion by Giuliani in this volume.

52 Further, there is a somewhat wide space after the second letter (not wide enough for another letter, as in the inscription above the Odysseus figure). It is difficult to tell whether it is due to a crack in the mirror at that point (which may have been there from the beginning, but more likely occurred when the mirror was mutilated; see note 1) or to some problem with the copying of the inscriptions.

53 Steingräber 1979, 22–34, identifies six throne types and their subtypes, and not one of these compares closely with the throne on the Villa Giulia mirror. See also note 55.

54 Apulian examples: Taplin 2007, 184 (no. 63), 235 (no. 92), 246 (97), 249 (no. 99). See also the representation of Uni, the Etruscan counterpart of Hera, being released by Sethlans and an otherwise unknown helper Tretu from the infamous ensnaring throne; it has the high straight back and tooled legs, though not the multiple rungs: de Grummond 2006, VI.30, with bibliography.

Fig. 12: Apulian red-figure volute krater. Detail of "Isolated Head." Attributed to the Ganymede Painter. Basel, Antikenmuseum. Fourth century BC. Photo: museum

An unusual head appears on one of the rungs of the throne in the mirror. This motif on a throne is extremely rare and does not seem to appear on any other mirror. A possible parallel appears on a terracotta seat from Aricia, where a Medusa head is placed just below the armrest of a throne with a curved back of a type popular in Italy for centuries.[55] This head is easily construed, however, as an apotropaic accessory for the goddess who sits upon the Aricia throne,[56] while the head on the Villa Giulia mirror seems to have a different significance. It appears to emerge amid sprigs of vegetation. For a parallel again we are drawn to South Italian vase painting, where literally thousands of examples have been identified of the "isolated head" that pops out of vegetation or comes out of the ground or is set into its own framework.[57] The one on the Villa

---

[55] Haynes 1975, 261 and pl. 80.2; Richter 1966, 85–6, figs. 427–31. The only comparable detail cited by Steingräber (1979, 265, no. 366) occurs on a mirror representing a throne of Helen, in which there is a depiction on the arm rest of a scene of two figures struggling (Ajax and Cassandra?). The scene is quite different from the head representation and the rest of the throne is totally different from the throne on the Villa Giulia mirror.

[56] Similarly, the feline head on the throne of Elinai on the mirror from the Bibliothèque Nationale (Fig. 5) may be apotropaic.

[57] Heuer 2011. So far, however, I have not found a throne with such a head.

Giulia mirror bears an interesting resemblance to some of these, in the three-quarter tilt of the head and the sprigs of vegetation that appear around it (e.g. Fig. 12). Heuer concludes that such heads in South Italian vase painting are much more than decoration, and relates them to an iconography of death and the funeral. She explores the possibility that such heads may be thought of as speaking and delivering a message.[58] To add to this argument, it is worth noting that many of the heads in those vase paintings show an open mouth.[59] Elsewhere I have argued that isolated heads in Etruscan art may represent a voice of prophecy, whether coming out of the ground or the sky or the landscape in general.[60] It is concluded here that the head on the throne represents such a message, perhaps conceived as coming from the throne itself. As a parallel, the small head represented on the ship Argo on a Greek red-figure column *krater* (ca. 460 BC) indicates the capability of the ship to speak and prophesy, because it contained oak wood from the oracle at Dodona.[61]

If there is a prophecy being delivered, many of the elements of the scene begin to link up. The king must be in dismay because of the ominous news; the elder leaning on a staff is meditating on the prophecy and may interpret its meaning. The youthful courtiers next to the king listen to the news and perhaps offer counsel. The warrior strapping on his armour may be the subject of the prophecy or else may be reacting to it. Thus we could refer to the representation as a mythologem,[62] a mythological account in which several key motifs combine to construct an overall scene type. This term was introduced by C. Kerényi to refer to the basic components or complex of motifs of a mythological narrative, carrying a deeper significance than designations such as "stock theme," or "stock narrative" or "myth type." The concept comes very close to the term "archetype" used by C. Jung, which refers, however, to a single figure or motif, while the mythologem refers to a broader context of multiple components of a recurrent myth.[63]

In this case we have the particular units – speaking prophetic head, grieving king, counsellors, seer and arming warrior – of the mythologem of the warrior's departure and fate. Using this concept, it is here argued, we can understand the scene at a certain level without using names at all. Given that the inscriptions are so problematic, this result provides some satisfaction and also prepares the way for further study of the scene in comparison with other examples of arming and departure in a prophetic context. The probing of the meaning of the scene would then be placed within a quite extensive inquiry into mythological narratives of the arming of the hero occurring in classical literature and in art, encompassing numerous references in Greek epic and drama and

---

58 Heuer 2011, 245.
59 For example, Heuer 2011, pls. 92, 93, 108, 112, 226, 227, 234, 235, 244.
60 De Grummond 2011.
61 Carpenter 1991, fig. 278. Apollonius Rhodius, *Argonautica*, 4.580–91.
62 Kerényi 1969, 2–4, 22, 27, 30, 107, 118, 145, for examples of Kerényi's use of the term mythologem.
63 Jung 1969, written as a pendant to Kerényi's essay on the primordial child.

also drawing from comparative mythology (e.g. the arming of Marduk against Tiamat in the *Enuma Elish*).[64]

Of course, we may also approach the mythologem using the names that have been proposed here in a speculative and provisional manner. We should ask if there is anything in the other evidence for Mezntie or his Virgilian counterpart Mezentius that can help us to confirm the argument for identifying the figures in the mirror. A remarkable inscription in the Louvre was recognised and published in 1989 by Briquel and Gaultier, as making a dedication in the name of Laucie Mezentie.[65] Convincingly dated to the seventh century and hypothesised to have come from Caere on stylistic grounds (the find spot is unknown), the vessel may be described as a small chalice. The inscription should not be burdened with excessive interpretation, as noted by Briquel, but it may reveal a startling forerunner of the figure of Mezentius, showing that there was indeed at Caere an aristocratic or royal family with this name in a very early period. Recent discussions argue that his name may in fact be a variant on an Italic title, such as used for a magistrate or governor.[66]

Fig. 13: Roman fresco. Mezentius and Ascanius make peace. From the columbarium near the Tomb of the Statilii, Esquiline Hill, Rome. Rome, Museo Nazionale Romano. Photo: After *LIMC* 6 (1992), pl. 309, Mezentius 1.

---

64 For the relevant text see Dalley 1989, 251 (arming of Marduk).
65 Briquel 1989; Briquel and Gaultier 1989a and 1989b.
66 De Simone 1991.

Apart from this inscription, the only other material evidence for this legendary figure seems to be a scene in the cycle of paintings related to the founding of Rome created for a columbarium on the Esquiline Hill often associated with the household of the Statilii, dated to the second half of the first century BC.[67] The heavily damaged paintings have yielded a sequence that includes Aeneas fighting against the Rutulians, the founding of Lavinium, the battle of the Numicus River, a truce between Ascanius and Mezentius, the founding of Alba Longa, the story of Rhea Silvia, and the birth and youth of Romulus and Remus. The figure of Mezentius is identified on the basis of an inscription once recorded beneath the figure, MC.ENT (Fig. 13). The identification of Ascanius is less certain and is based on literary sources (to be reviewed below), while the nearby river god is almost certainly the Numicus. To the right of this group is a battle scene that has been interpreted as part of the ten-year war between the Rutuli, led by Turnus and Mezentius, against the allied forces of Trojans and Latins, led by Aeneas and Ascanius. It is recorded that Aeneas died or disappeared when these forces were in combat by the River Numicus. So if we are reading from right to left, we have the Battle of the Numicus, then this scene in which Mezentius and Ascanius make peace. They have their spears pointed toward the ground, and they join right hands.

Narrative Stratigraphies

There are many versions of the story of King Mezentius that were in fact written down. Their amazing variety is in line with the idea that they were probably transmitted orally and then happened to get recorded. In these stories there are many substitutions and inversions, with compressions and expansions of the material, and changes of chronological sequence.

The major known variants can be organised into a broadly chronological chart (Tab. 1). Cato recorded a story in which Aeneas and Turnus die, and Ascanius kills Mezentius. Cato also included a story in which Mezentius lives, but haughtily demands tribute from the Rutuli, in the form of their first fruits. They give the first fruits to Jupiter instead and found the festival of the Vinalia. The story is told by Dionysius as well, as a prelude to peace between Ascanius and Mezentius. Here Mezentius demands first fruits from the Latins, but they pledge them to Jupiter instead. In the ensuing battle, Lausus, the son of Mezentius, is evidently killed, and Mezentius in remorse relents and makes a treaty of friendship. The first fruits go to Jupiter. A similar version to the scenario in the columbarium near the Tomb of the Statilii is found in Livy and Dionysius of Halicarnassus, thus contemporary with the columbarium paintings of the second half of the first century BC. Aeneas dies, and Turnus, too, leaving Mezentius and Ascanius. Peace is made between the Latins and Mezentius. In the *Fasti* of Ovid, Mezentius

---

67 Holliday 2005, 98. For the image of Mezentius, see J. P. Small, "Mezentius", *LIMC* 6 (1992), 567, no. 1.

Tab. 1: Variants of the Myth of Mezentius.

1. Aeneas and Turnus die; Ascanius kills Mezentius	Cato, *Origines*, frg. 9–11
2. Mezentius lives, demands offerings of first fruits from the Rutulians; they refuse and give their offerings to Jupiter and start the festival of the Vinalia	Cato, *Origines*, frg. 12
3. Mezentius demands first fruits from the Latins; his son Lausus is killed and Mezentius relents; first fruits given to Jupiter for the first festival of the Vinalia.	Dionysius Hal. *Ant. Rom.* I.65.5
4. Aeneas and Turnus die; Mezentius becomes a friend to Ascanius and they live in peace	Livy I.2–3, Dionysius Hal. *Ant. Rom.* I.65.5
5. The Latins vow their new wine to Jupiter. Mezentius is killed by Aeneas and the Latins start the festival of the Vinalia	Ovid, *Fasti* 4. 885–900
6. Aeneas kills Lausus and then Mezentius. Mezentius is a cruel tyrant, but is ennobled by his love for his son and his passion in battle.	Virgil, *Aeneid* 10. 817–820; 907–908.

is killed by Aeneas, and at last we have the version that appears in Virgil, except that it is here connected with the Vinalia.

In the great and well-known tale of Virgil about Mezentius, he is *contemptor divum* (*Aen.* 7.648), arrogant and scornful of the gods, among the greatest warriors fighting against Aeneas. He is described as fighting with sling and spear, and brandishing a torch, and is likened in heroic fashion to a boar, a lion, and to the mighty hunter Orion (*Aen.* 9.522, 586; 10.689–768). He is a brutal and treacherous king hated by his own people. This part is not incompatible with versions told by Cato, Dionysius and Ovid, who have him demand the tribute that leads to the founding of the Vinalia.[68] Mezentius' cruel acts are described, involving tying a living man to a dead man, but the overall picture of him, how he fights and his appearance, how his noble death offsets his other villainous deeds (*Aen.* 8.485–488; 10.900–908) – all of this seems to be constructed for the poem of Virgil. He is a very sympathetic figure when he loses his son. In Virgil both Lausus and Mezentius die at the hands of Aeneas. Of the other authors, only Ovid has Mezentius die at the hands of Aeneas, and in that story Lausus is never mentioned. The powerful originality and art of the epic poet Virgil are frequently acknowledged.[69]

Can any of this material from Roman times help us with the Etruscan Mezntie? Perhaps. It is important to note that before the second century BC, there is no evidence

---

68 Though in the Virgilian version, there is no reference to the Vinalia.
69 Briquel 1989, 81, with references.

of the cruel tyrant Mezentius.[70] Even in the first century there are variants in which Mezentius may be other than the vicious character created by Virgil; for example, he is able to relent and make a peace treaty, according to the account of Dionysius, and even become a "constant friend" to the Latins (Dion. Hal. *Ant. Rom.* 1.65.5).

But one's first impression on returning to the mirror is that it is breathtakingly unlike the other versions. The names, if correct, and the story they seem to convey are indeed astonishing. Could Mezentius of fame in early Italy interact with the two Greek heroes Achilles and Odysseus, in the company of two purely Etruscan mythological figures? An interesting parallel is found in a bronze mirror from Città della Pieve (near Chiusi), dating probably to the third century BC, in which the Etruscan founder hero Tarchon sits down in a gathering with Trojan Priam and Paris and Etruscan Menerva.[71] Achle appears on other Etruscan mirrors in startling circumstances and novel company. One warrior spears another on a mirror from Tarquinia: the victor is labelled *amphiare* (Amphiaraus) and the surprising victim is *aχle* (Achilles).[72] On a mirror in Providence, R.I., he appears with Thetis and the Etruscan personification figure of Achuvisr. All three are naked and dancing with arms intertwined, in front of a basin for bathing.[73]

Conclusions

In summary, what can we say about the story of Mezntie on this mirror? Of the five figures, only Mezntie has a vague resemblance to the figure in the Roman myths of a later period. He is indeed a king, and he seems to be disturbed by something that has to do with warfare since Achle is arming in his presence. Within the story his consternation might be as a result of his grieving over the death of his son Lausus. Zelachtra and Ethun stand by as advisors, perhaps even personifications, like the attendants of Aciles (Victoria) and Ajax (Iuventus) on the Praenestine cista. Achle may have been preparing to go out on the battlefield to avenge the death of the son of Mezntie. Judging

---

70 Several scholars argue that Mezentius should be linked with the historic cruel deed at Caere after the battle of the Sardinian Sea ("Battle of Alalia"), c. 540–535 BC, when the Caeretans stoned their prisoners to death. But no literary source mentions Mezentius in connection with this battle; further, the Caeretan inscription with the name Laucie Mezentie dates at least 100 years earlier. For the fullest statement of the argument see Gras 1985, esp. 446–53.

71 *CSE* Great Britain 2.17, mirror now in Cambridge (R. V. Nicholls). Maggiani 2005, 71 (no. 145) identifies the Latin sibyl Albunea on an Etruscan mirror from Chiusi in the company of other figures with Greek, Etruscan and Latin names.

72 *ES* 5, 123. *ET* Ta S.2.

73 *CSE* USA 4. 49. R.D. De Puma notes (67): "Although Achilles and Thetis are frequently depicted on Etruscan mirrors, they are never shown together nude and embracing in a seemingly erotic encounter. ... The figure of Achuvisr is even more problematic."

Tab. 2: Stratigraphy of the Myth of Mezntie/Mezentius

1st cent. BC	Virgil, Ovid: vicious tyrant exiled from Caere, killed by Aeneas.
	Ovid: Demands tribute from Latins
1st cent. BC	Livy, Dionysius, Columbarium fresco: king who makes peace with Ascanius
2nd cent. BC	Cato, Origines: king of Caere who demands tribute, killed by Ascanius
300–275 BC	Mirror with Mezntie, Achle, Uhuze: dismayed king, connected with Achle, Uhuze; prophecy
680/675–650/640 BC	Impasto vessel: Mi Laucie Mezenties; historical person of status at Caere

from the mood of the characters on the mirror, the outcome may be dire. A prophetic head may be delivering a message about this, and Uhuze, in the role of a seer, seems to meditate the prophecy, perhaps to interpret it for the others.

Many questions are still unanswered and probably will remain so. Meanwhile, I propose looking at the myth or story of Mezntie in ancient Italy from another perspective, by creating a kind of stratigraphical chart, arranged so that the earliest datable material is at the bottom of the column (Tab. 2). We can see for now, at least, his starting point as a real historical person, of high status at Caere. By the late fourth or early third century, he is depicted as a king, somehow allied with Achle and Uhuze, in a troubling situation that involves battle and probably a prophecy. In the second century BC he behaves in a tyrannical and arrogant manner and ends up killed by Ascanius, though we find variants in the first century, as he lives and makes peace with Ascanius. Finally we have the spectacular poetical version of Virgil, in which he emerges as a powerful and monstrous tyrant, killed by Aeneas.

Fig. 14: Bronze Etruscan mirror. Cacu, with Artile, attacked by Caile and Avle Vipinas. London, British Museum. 300–275 BC. After Bonfante 1990, fig. 18.

The whole sequence is remarkably like that for the well-known Etruscan sacred story of Cacu and Avle and Caile Vipinas (Fig. 14).[74] Cacu appears on a mirror of exactly the same time as the Mezntie mirror. He is a beautiful, youthful prophet shown with his assistant Artile. They are being approached as they practise divination, to be seized by the warriors Avle and Caile Vipinas, who want to learn their prophecy. There is a good bit of evidence that Avle Vipinas was a real person, including a dedicatory inscription on a bucchero vessel from Veii (600–550 BC), where his name is written as *avile vipiiennas*.[75]

Tab. 3: Stratigraphy of the Myth of Cacu/Cacus

1st cent. BC	Virgil: Monster killed by Hercules in Rome
2nd cent. BC	Gnaeus Gellius: Cacus the warrior, imprisoned by Tarchon, defeated by Hercules; connected with Megales, a prophet
300–275 BC	Mirror with Cacu and the Vipinas brothers: prophet attacked by the Vipinas brothers
600–550 BC	Bucchero vessel: mine muluv(an)ece avile vipiiennas at Veii

Thus in the stratigraphy (Tab. 3), we have an archaic inscription from the early sixth century that refers to a real historical person of high status, i.e. Avle Vipinas, in a situation very similar to that of Laucie Mezenties. Then at exactly the same time as the Mezntie mirror we have the clearly articulated story on the mirror of the warrior brothers Vipinas catching the prophet. The next step is an amazing and bizarre story preserved from the annalist Gnaeus Gellius (see below), roughly parallel to the stories of Mezentius as a tyrant demanding the first fruits but able to make peace with Ascanius. The latest thing in the column is again a powerfully creative version by Virgil – of a fire-breathing monster (*Aen.* 8.194–267), so different that it has nothing to do with the Vipinas Brothers, and little to do with Cacu apart from the theme of captivity and the name of the captive.

A closer look at the Gellius story about Cacus will help make an important point concerning the Mezntie myth and the development of myth in Etruria. Here is the way the story was summarised by E. Richardson:

---

74 Small 1982. *ET* Vs S4; de Grummond 2006, 27–9; Domenici 2009, 109–71.
75 Buranelli 1987, 234 (no. 95, by F. Boitani). I omit from the discourse here the interesting but highly problematic cup inscribed *avles vpinas naplan* that once belonged to Rodin: Buranelli 1987, 234–5 (no. 94, by F. Gilotta).

... a certain Cacus ... was sent with a Phrygian companion, Megales, as an envoy to Tarchon the Tyrrhenian by Marsyas, the Phrygian king of the Marsi in central Italy. Tarchon imprisoned Cacus, but he escaped and returned whence he had come and with the help of a great host founded a kingdom for himself on the Volturnus in Campania, but because he had dared to lay hands on territory belonging by rights to the Arcadians, he was overthrown by Hercules. Megales fled to the Sabines, who gave him refuge and learned the science of augury from him.[76]

Richardson called this "a fine mishmash", a humorous description, but one which could also be applied to the tangle of characters and themes on the Villa Giulia mirror. The story shows that Gellius' myth of Cacus was quite alive and evolving. In fact it stands rather neatly in between the two radically different versions of the purely Etruscan story and that of the *Aeneid*. Here Cacu, now Cacus, turns into a warrior (substituting for the Vipinas brothers, who drop out), but he still gets captured and taken prisoner. He is a respectable general rather than a revered prophet, but the prophet role has been transferred to Megales. Hercules enters the story at this time and defeats Cacus, and he will stay around for the Virgilian version in which Cacus turns into a really nasty creature.[77]

So the two myths on contemporary Etruscan mirrors, of Mezntie with Achle and of Cacu with the Vipinas brothers, show novel stories, many of the details of which we do not know and most likely never will. They belong to a remarkable narrative sequence in which we see an historical personage referred to in an inscription; a dramatic myth featuring prophetic motivation; and a brilliant literary creation by a great poet. I suggest that we can access their strange wanderings by setting up a stratigraphical model, which shows how the characters and their stories can vary through time, especially if we keep in mind that these narratives, though represented in art and sometimes written down, experienced a dynamic life of growing, changing and evolving in a context of oral transmission.

Abbreviations

CSE *Corpus Speculorum Etruscorum*
ES E. Gerhard, G. Klügmann and G. Körte, *Etruskische Spiegel*, 5 vols. (Berlin, 1840–1897).
ET H. Rix and E. Meiser, *Etruskische Texte*, 2 vols. Editio minor. (Tübingen, 2014).

---

76 Richardson 1964, 222. The narrative comes from Solinus 1.8–9, quoting Gellius. See also Small 1982, 5–6 and 77.
77 For several other variant details, see Domenici 2009, 160 (from Livy, Dionysius of Halicarnassus, Propertius and Ovid).

Bibliography

Ambrosini, L. Raffigurazioni e didascalie in etrusco sugli specchi di età ellenistica; alcuni casi-studio. *Bollettino di Archeologia On Line Roma 2008, International Congress of Classical Archaeology* (2010).

Bonfante, L. An Etruscan Mirror with "Spiky Garland" in the Getty Museum. *Getty Museum Journal* 8 (1980), 147–154.

Bonfante, L. Etruscan, Reading the Past, (London, British Museum, 1990).

Bonfante, L. *Etruscan Dress* (Baltimore, 2003).

Bordenache Battaglia, G. and A. Emiliozzi. *Le Ciste prenestine*, I.1–2 (Città di Castello, 1990).

Briquel, D. A propos d'une inscription redécouverte au Louvre: remarques sur la tradition relative a Mézence. *Revue des études latines* 67 (1989), 78–92.

Briquel, D. Lausus fils de Mézence et le Laucie Mezentie de l'inscription du Louvre, in: *Corollari: scritti di antichità etrusche e italiche in omaggio all'opera di Giovanni Colonna*. Studia erudita 14 (Pisa; Rome, 2011), 14–18.

Briquel, D. and F. Gaultier. L'iscrizione arcaica di Lucio Mezenzio, in: *Miscellanea Ceretana* 1 (Rome, 1989a), 41–44.

Briquel, D. and F. Gaultier. Réexamen d'une inscription des collections du Musée du Louvre: un Mézence à Caeré au VIIe siècle av. J. C. *Comptes rendus des séances de l'Académie des inscriptions et belles-lettres* (1989b), 99–115.

Brommer, F. Theseus und Minotauros in der etruskischen Kunst. *Mitteilungen des Deutschen Archäologischen Instituts, Römische Abteilung* 88 (1981), 1–12.

Bruni, S. *Nugae de Etruscorum fabulis*. Ostraka 11 (2002), 7–28.

Buonamici, G. Rivista di epigrafia etrusca. *Studi etruschi* 12 (1938), 312–315.

Buranelli, F. (ed.) *La Tomba François di Vulci* (Rome, 1987).

Carpenter, T. H. *Art and Myth in Ancient Greece* (London, 1991).

Carpino, A. Reflections from the Tomb: mirrors as grave goods in Late Classical and Hellenistic Tarquinia. *Etruscan Studies* 11 (2008), 1–33.

Cristofani, M. Faone, la testa di Orfeo e l'immaginario femminile. *Prospettiva* 42 (1985), 2–12.

Dalley, S. *Myths from Mesopotamia. Creation, the Flood, Gilgamesh and Others* (Oxford, 1989).

de Grummond, N. T. Mirrors, Marriage and Mysteries. *Journal of Roman Archaeology, Supplement* 47 (2002), 63–85.

de Grummond, N. T. Etruscan Mirrors Now. *American Journal of Archaeology* 106 (2002), 307–311.

de Grummond, N. T. *Etruscan Myth, Sacred History and Legend* (Philadelphia, 2006).

de Grummond, N. T. On Mutilated Mirrors, in: *Votives, Places and Rituals in Etruscan Religion*, edited by H. Becker and M. Gleba (Leiden, 2009), 171–182.

de Grummond, N. T. A Barbarian Myth? The Case of the Talking Head, in: *The Barbarians of Ancient Europe*, edited by L. Bonfante (Cambridge, 2011), 313–346.

De Puma, R. D. A Fourth Century Praenestine Mirror with Telephos and Orestes. *Mitteilungen des Deutschen Archäologischen Instituts, Römische Abteilung* 87 (1980), 5–28.

De Simone, C. *Die griechischen Entlehnungen im Etruskischen*. 2 vols. (Wiesbaden, 1968).

De Simone, C. *Etrusco Laucie Mezentie: Archeologia Classica* 43 (1991), 559–573.

Domenici, I. *Etruscae fabulae: Mito e rappresentazione* (Rome, 2009).

Furtwängler, A. *Die Antiken Gemmen*. 3 vols. Repr. 1964–65 (Amsterdam, 1900).

Graf, F. *Greek Mythology: An Introduction* (Baltimore, 1996).

Gras, M. *Trafics tyrrhéniens archaïques* (Rome, 1985).

Haynes, S. Eine Bronzeattasche in Form eines Frauenkopfes. *Mitteilungen des Deutschen Archäologischen Instituts, Römische Abteilung* 82 (1975), 257–261.

Heuer, K. E. *The Development and Significance of the Isolated Head in South Italian Vase-Painting*, Ph.D. Dissertation, New York University (2011).

Heurgon, J. *Daily Life of the Etruscans* (London, 1964).

Holliday, P. J. The Rhetoric of *Romanitas*: the Tomb of the Statilii frescoes reconsidered. *Memoirs of the American Academy in Rome* 50 (2005), 89–129.

Horsfall, N. The Culture of the Roman Plebs (London, 2003).

Jung, C. G. The Psychology of the Child Archetype, in: *Essays on a Science of Mythology: the Myth of the Divine Child and the Mysteries of Eleusis* (Princeton, 1969), 70–100.

Kelber, W. H. *The Oral and the Written Gospel: the Hermeneutics of Speaking and Writing* in *the Synoptic Tradition, Mark, Paul and Q* (Bloomington, 1997).

Kerényi, C. Prolegomena. The Primordial Child. Kore, in: *Essays on a Science of Mythology: the Myth of the Divine Child and the Mysteries of Eleusis* (Princeton, 1969) 1–69, 101–155.

Lord, A. *The Singer of Tales.* Second Edition, edited by S. Mitchell and G. Nagy, *Harvard Studies in Comparative Literature*, 24 (Cambridge; London, 2000).

Maggiani, A. La divinazione in Etruria. *Thesaurus cultus et rituum antiquorum* 3 (2005), 52–78.

Muellner, L. Grieving Achilles, in: *Homeric Contexts: Neoanalysis and the Interpretation of Oral Poetry*, edited by F. Montanari, A. Rengakos and C. Tsagalis (Berlin; Boston, 2012), 197–220.

Pairault Massa, F.-H. Ateliers d'urnes et histoire de Volterra, in: *Caratteri dell'ellenismo nelle urne etrusche*, edited by M. Martelli and M. Cristofani, *Prospettiva*, Suppl. 1 (Florence, 1977), 154–167.

Pairault Massa, F.-H. *Iconologia e politica nell'Italia antica. Roma, Lazio, Etruria dal VII al I secolo a.C.* (Milan, 1992).

Pandolfini, M. and A. L. Prosdocimi, Alfabetari e insegnamento della scrittura in Etruria e nell'Italia antica (Florence, 1990).

Pfiffig, A. J. Verschreibung und Verbesserung in etruskischen Inschriften. *Studi Etruschi* 32 (1964), 183–205.

Pfiffig, A. J. *Religio etrusca* (Graz, 1975).

Pfiffig, A. J. *Fehler und Verbesserung in etruskischen Inschriften* (Vienna, 1977).

Rebuffat-Emmanuel, D. *Le miroir étrusque d'après la collection du Cabinet des Médailles.* 2 Vols. (Rome, 1973).

Richardson, E. H. *The Etruscans: Their Art and Civilization* (Chicago, 1964).

Richter, G. M. A. The Furniture of the Greeks, Etruscans and Romans (London, 1966).

Small, J. P. *Cacus and Marsyas in Etrusco-Roman Legend* (Princeton, 1982).

Small, J. P. *The Parallel Worlds of Classical Art and Text* (Cambridge, 2003).

Sparkes, B. A. The Trojan Horse in Classical Art. *Greece & Rome* 18.1 (1971), 54–70.

Steingräber, S. *Etruskische Möbel* (Rome, 1979).

Taplin, O. *Pots and Plays: Interactions between Tragedy and Greek Vase-Painting of the Fourth Century B.C.* (Los Angeles, 2007).

Torelli, M. (ed.) *Gli etruschi* (Cinisello Balsamo, 2000).

Trendall, A. D. *Red Figure Vases of South Italy and Sicily* (London, 1989).

Vetter, E. Literaturbericht 1938–1953, Etruskisch. *Glotta* 34 (1955), 47–66.

van der Meer, L. B. La trasmissione degli archetipi nei rilievi mitologici delle urne volterrane, in: *Caratteri dell'ellenismo nelle urne etrusche*, edited by M. Martelli and M. Cristofani, *Prospettiva*, Suppl. 1 (Florence, 1977), 146–149.

von Bothmer, D. (ed.) *Glories of the Past* (New York, 1990).

Wiseman, T. P. Unwritten Rome (Exeter, 2008).

Woodford, S. *Images of Myths in Classical Antiquity* (Cambridge, 2003).

Zazoff, P. *Etruskische Skarabäen* (Mainz, 1968).

Luca Giuliani
Pots, Plots, and Performance
Comic and Tragic Iconography in Apulian Vase Painting

Apulian vase painters of the fourth century BC have produced an extraordinary narrative imagery, the wealth and variety of which remain without parallel in the horizon of ancient Greek arts and crafts. It is worthwhile noting that this imagery is based on stories that were *not* of Apulian origin: particularly often the painters referred to plots of Attic drama. Myths certainly *do* wander: not only through space, from Athens to Apulia, but also from one medium to the other, in our case from the theatrical stage (or from dramatic texts) into vase painting. Such a transfer never goes without deep transformations: in this paper, I am going to concentrate exactly on this process of transformation. I shall thereby examine two very different classes of images. The first class is constituted by comic images that regularly depict figures in costumes and masks, acting on a stage: their relation to the theatre is perfectly obvious. To the second, much larger class belong images depicting serious myths: here we find no such reference to theatrical performance. This absence is all the more noteworthy, as we have strong reasons to assume that the vast majority of such images were actually inspired by the plots of Attic tragedies. But if both classes of images, the comic as well as the serious ones, are connected to the theatre, why then is there such an insistence on the concrete dimension of theatrical performance only in comic images and not in serious, i.e. tragic iconography? An attempt to answer this question might lead to us understand what kind of interest Apulian vase painters had in Attic tragedy in the first place.

Allow me to start with a very brief remark: The best book one can read today about tragic and comic iconography on Apulian vases is Oliver Taplin's *Pots and Plays*, published in 2007.[1] Before 2007, the best book on the subject was Taplin's *Comic Angels*, which appeared in the early 1990s.[2] Since then, for more than twenty years now, any contribution about the relationship between theatre and vase painting in southern Italy has inevitably centred on Taplin's work.[3] I myself have greatly profited from his writings as well as from conversations we have had; they gave me the opportunity to revise some opinions and to correct certain mistakes. Taplin and I happen to be interested in very much the same kind of problems; between our approaches I see plenty of agreement with only marginal divergences. Nevertheless in the present paper, in

---

1 Taplin 2007a.
2 Taplin 1993.
3 Taplin's views have been the subject of a series of seminars organised between 2011 and 2012 by the *Centro studi classicA* at the Iuav (= Istituto universitario di architettura Venezia), the contributions of which have recently been published: Bordignon 2015; the volume also offers a useful bibliography.

https://doi.org/10.1515/9783110421453-007

order to stimulate a focused discussion, I shall indulge in the narcissism of small differences, concentrating on one minor point where Taplin and I do not seem to agree with each other (at least until now).

Taplin has forcefully argued that Attic tragedies of the fifth century must have actually been re-performed throughout the fourth century in the cities of Apulia: this might not be quite a hundred per cent certain, but it is nevertheless "extremely likely: perhaps ninetynine percent? Indeed it is almost inconceivable that they were not."[4] I can only agree, and I also agree that there is no possible doubt about the impact that Attic tragedies have had on Apulian vase painting. Starting from here I would like to ask a simple question: what was it exactly about Attic tragedy that Apulian vase painters were interested in? Was it the play – or was it the plot? Was it the play as theatrical performance? Or was it the plot – something that could also be easily summarised in a few sentences, without any staging whatsoever?

I would like to begin with two volute kraters by the Ilioupersis painter, one of the first Apulian artists who had a marked predilection for subjects that can be related to Attic tragedies. Both kraters can be dated to around 360 BC: one is in Vicenza (Fig. 1),[5] the other one in Naples (Fig. 2).[6] The krater in Naples shows a scene from Euripides' *Iphigenia in Tauris*: Orestes is sitting on the altar on which he expects to be sacrificed; to the left you see Pylades; approaching from the right we have Iphigenia as a priest (the names of all three are inscribed). The krater in Vicenza, on the other side, shows the murder of Neoptolemus in Delphi, as it is told in Euripides' *Andromache*; we see Neoptolemus kneeling on an altar, deadly wounded; the attack has been plotted by Orestes, who is stealing away to the right (again, the names are inscribed). In both vases there is a clear division between a lower register, where the drama unfolds, and an upper register, where onlookers have taken their seats. Both scenes are in a sanctuary; there is an altar in three-quarter view; in the background stands a temple with its door open. In Tauris there is a laurel tree growing next to the altar; in Delphi we see a palm tree and an elaborate depiction of the *omphalos*, the sacred navel of the earth. In Tauris the onlookers are Apollo and Artemis, in Delphi it is Apollo alone, accompanied by the priest who, in this case, has no part in the human drama.

The similarities between the two images are evident. But are the texts to which the images refer also similar? If we focus on the passages that are actually relevant an interesting difference emerges. What is shown on the krater in Naples corresponds closely to the action in the second episode of the drama, after Orestes and Pylades have been captured and escorted to the sanctuary (456ff.), but before Iphigenia and Orestes recognise each other as brother and sister (769ff.). As regards the death of Neoptolemus, the situation is quite different. In the *Andromache*, the action is in Thessaly, at

4 Taplin 2007a, 14.
5 Vicenza, Collezione Banca Intesa Sanpaolo (formerly Ruvo, Coll. Caputi, then Milan, Coll. H. A.): RVAp 193, 8/4; Sena Chiesa and Starazzi 2006, vol. 2, 306–9, no. 110; Taplin 2007a, 139, no. 43.
6 Museo Archeologico H 3223; RVAp 193, 8/3; Taplin 2007a, 150, no. 47.

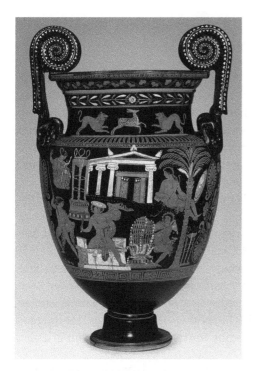

Fig. 1: Apulian Volute krater, ca 360: Neoptolemus murdered in Delphi. Vicenza, Coll. Intesa Sanpaolo.

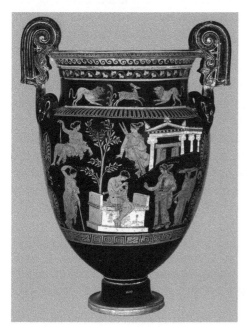

Fig. 2: Apulian Volute krater, ca. 360: Orestes and Iphigenia in Tauris. Su concessione del Ministero dei Beni e delle Attività Culturali e del Turismo – Museo Archeologico Nazionale di Napoli.

the court of King Neoptolemus; the king himself is absent, he is in Delphi; and there he is murdered in a plot organised by Orestes, who then quickly travels back to Thessaly; the killing itself is reported by a messenger (1085–1165).

One krater depicts an action that, in the drama, happens on stage, the other shows something that happens far off and is merely reported; in the latter case, the vase painter could not rely on what he might have seen during a performance. For the structure of the pictures, this difference seems to be of no relevance whatsoever: in both cases, the painter organises his images in accordance with the possibilities and the conventions of his own medium. What we see is the product of a vase painter, and not the reflection of what a theatre director might have put on stage.[7]

Even though the painter does not simply mirror a stage performance, some of the elements in his images could nevertheless reflect theatrical reality. In the *Iphigenia*, the action takes place in the sanctuary of Artemis and the stage building might easily have shown the front of the temple. In the *Andromache*, the temple of Apollo was definitely not visible; its appearance on the krater in Vicenza could nevertheless have been inspired by a theatrical stage, and this theatrical element could have been used as a signal to denote the origin of the depicted story as a whole, as if the painter wanted to tell the beholder: "Don't forget, behind this image there is a tragedy and this tragedy has been performed on stage." Such a signalling function is possible – but is it also plausible?

We shall come back to this question later. But first I would like to have a look at two famous volute kraters attributed to the Underworld Painter, who was active about one generation later than the Ilioupersis Painter.[8] Both kraters were found in the same chamber tomb in Canosa and are now in Munich. The first krater displays on its belly an image referring to the tragedy of Medea (Fig. 3).[9] At the centre of the scene we find a building very similar to the ones we have just seen, even though it is slightly more elaborate and we can see it in full height, from the *crepis* up to the tip of the pediment; nevertheless, there is a difference: the building on the Medea krater is not to be interpreted as a temple anymore, but as a palace. The front of a palace is of course what the audience could expect to see at the back of the stage in most performances of a tragedy: on our vase this could be a theatrical reminder.[10] The roof of our building is carried by six columns; there are no walls, and this is convenient, because what is

---

7 This is exactly what Taplin has stressed in *Pots and Plays*: "The vases are not [...] 'banal illustrations,' nor are they dependent on or derived from the plays. They are informed by the plays: they mean more and more interest and depth for someone who knows the play in question" (Taplin 2007a, 25). "Whatever it was that viewers wanted from the mythological paintings, it was clearly not pictures of plays and not pictures of tragic performances" (ibid., 26).

8 Munich, Staatliche Antikensammlungen 3296 and 3297. For the provenance from the chamber tomb Monterisi-Rossignoli see Mazzei 1992.

9 Antikensammlungen 3296: RVAp 533, 18/283; Taplin 2007a, 255–7, no. 102.

10 This is what Taplin calls a portico (interpreting it as a theatrical signal): Taplin 2007a, 38–9.

happening inside the building is an essential part of the plot. We see Creon, the king of Corinth, with his collapsing daughter Kreonteia; Kreonteia's death, as we know, is caused by magic worked by Medea, whom we see at the bottom left of the image, about to kill one of her children; next to her *Oistros*, the personification of frenzy, is waiting in a chariot drawn by snakes, ready to drive Medea away. It is not easy to identify the tragedy to which the krater refers. Nikolaus Himmelmann has made a highly sophisticated (I think ultimately unconvincing) attempt to show that the action depicted would be compatible with Euripides' *Medea*.[11] Taplin argues, far more plausibly to my mind, that the image relates to another tragedy, the plot of which had been influenced by the Euripidean play, but with significant differences: Euripides' Medea famously kills both of her children; on the Munich krater, one of them seems to be escaping death.[12] What is beyond dispute, however, is the relation of the vase to a tragedy in the first place. Taplin points out that three of the figures wear long-sleeved garments that perfectly match what we know about 'tragic costumes':[13] these are Creon, Medea, and Medea's father Aietes, who is present as a ghost; a very similar costume is finally worn by a pedagogue, who in this specific case "may well have played the part of a messenger".[14] So we have a building that could possibly resemble a stage prop and some figures wearing tragic costumes: both elements could easily be interpreted as theatrical signals. But is this interpretation convincing? I think it is not.

Let us just cast a glance at the main image of the twin krater, also in Munich, coming from the same Apulian workshop and from the same chamber tomb at Canosa, where the two vases obviously constituted a pair. This second krater offers a particularly elaborate depiction of the Underworld (Fig. 4).[15] Again we have a building at the centre of the scene: in this case it is the palace of Hades, the king of the Underworld; we also have several figures wearing a 'tragic costume': this is true of Hades himself, of Orpheus, of Tantalus, and of one of the three judges of the dead that are commonly identified as Minos, Rhadamanthys and Aiakos (or Triptolemus).[16] Some of the inhabitants of the Underworld depicted here have names (and stories), others do not. But even where there would be stories to tell, this krater does not focus on stories at all: what it offers is a descriptive panorama of the Underworld as a whole. I would like to stress that *no* scholar has ever attempted to relate this vase to any kind of theatrical performance. It seems evident that neither the building nor the costumes in themselves have to be interpreted as signals of theatricality. But then, why should we consider the very same elements as theatrical signals on the other krater, depicting Medea, Creon, Kreonteia, & Co.?

---

11 Himmelmann 1994, 143–4, n. 62.

12 Taplin 2007a, 257.

13 Taplin 2007a, 38; see also Wyles 2010.

14 Taplin 2007a, 256.

15 Antikensammlungen 3297: RVAp 533, 18/282.

16 J. Boardman, "Aiakos", *LIMC* 1 (1981) 311–12.

Fig. 3: Apulian Volute krater, ca 320: Medea's revenge. Staatliche Antikensammlungen und Glyptothek München, Photo: Renate Kühling.

Comparing the two kraters in Munich (which an ancient beholder could readily compare in Canosa) we are drawn to the conclusion that the painter has made no effort whatsoever to distinguish between an image that relates to theatre and an image that does not; on the level of iconography, this difference simply did not seem to matter. With this in mind, it is worthwhile having one more look at the garments with long sleeves. They are indisputably of theatrical origin; but this origin is of little help if we want to understand their meaning in vase iconography. The difference between theatrical performance and the iconography on vases is obvious: On stage the long-sleeved costume is worn by *every* figure (and every figure also wears a mask); on vases, on the contrary, the same garment is used for very few figures in order to distinguish them from all the others (who are usually naked); this distinctive feature is used as a marker for: a) kings (like Creon, Tantalus, Minos), b) some men of exotic origin (Orpheus, e.g., came from Thrace) and c) pedagogues. As early as 1899, Walter Amelung pointed out the difference between the theatrical *origin* of this type of garment and its new distinguishing *function* within iconography: the origin, he made clear, does not determine the function; function is independent from origin. Amelung argued *against* the possibility of using the garment as a signal for theatricality:[17] he did so vigorously,

17 W. Amelung, 1899, 2206–17.

Fig. 4: Apulian Volute krater, ca 320: The Underworld. Staatliche Antikensammlungen und Glyptothek München, Photo: Renate Kühling.

convincingly and (if we consider the recent literature on the subject) with no success whatsoever. This lack of success notwithstanding, the argument was and remains perfectly sound.

What I said about the long-sleeved costume could also be said about the figure of the pedagogue that is found on dozens of Apulian vases since the middle of the fourth century.[18] The theatrical origin of this figure, which on the vases appears always more or less in the same attire, is beyond doubt. But to accept this is one thing; it is quite another thing to claim that "la présence du pédagogue oblige à évoquer le theatre";[19] that "the presence of the *paidagogos* on a vase is a means of saying 'this is a scene from a play'" or even – one step further – that it is "a way of pointing to the fact that it is a scene from a particular play, one the reader of the image knows or should know."[20] The latter claim is based on the assumption that behind the image there was a "particular

---

18 For the "little old man (*paidagogos* figure)" see Taplin 2007a, 40.
19 Chamay and Cambitoglou 1980, 38; for a general analysis of the figure of the pedagogue see 40–3.
20 Green 1999, 49.

play" in which the pedagogue had an essential part; the pedagogue in the image would then be nothing but the reflection of the pedagogue that had been seen on stage.

This assumption is perfectly unwarranted and it can easily be proven wrong. What the authors of the quoted statements neglect is simply the capacity of vase painters to adopt a given figure (whatever its origin might be) as a standard motif of their repertoire, using it for their own purposes. Let us consider two volute kraters by the Dareios Painter: one in St. Petersburg (Fig. 5),[21] the other one Taranto (Fig. 6).[22] Both depict the departure of Amphiaraus for the expedition of the Seven against Thebes. Amphiaraus had the capacity to foresee the future; he knew that the enterprise was doomed to fail and that he would not return home alive; nevertheless he joined the expedition, because his wife Eriphyle, who had been bribed by the Seven, forced him to do so. The two kraters show Amphiaraus bidding farewell to his two sons (Eriphyle being conspicuous by her absence): on the krater in St. Petersburg the two boys are accompanied by a pedagogue in distress; on the krater in Taranto the younger boy is talking to an old nurse sitting above him. How is this discrepancy to be understood? Why do we see a pedagogue on one krater and an old nurse on the other? If we understand the two figures as mirroring what had been seen on stage, we are obliged to relate the two kraters not to one but to *two* different tragedies: the first of which featured a pedagogue, the second one a nurse. I take this conclusion to be absurd: it seems obvious that both kraters refer to one and the same plot. Pedagogue and nurse[23] are simply functional equivalents and therefore largely interchangeable. Vase painters bring them into play whenever children have an important role in the story depicted. Children, by the way, are frequently among the participants of tragic plots, and I would perfectly agree with the claim that our two kraters are most likely to have been inspired by such a plot. What I'm saying is that neither the pedagogue nor the nurse is in itself to be understood as a *signal* pointing to such a source of inspiration.

I would like to go one step further. Oliver Taplin discusses several elements that he interprets as "traces of theatrical realities", as "signals" as he calls them; he thereby comes to the conclusion that none of them is really "infallible proof of the theatrical connection":[24] as a signal, none of them seems to be reliable. But is this lack of reliability really compatible with the function of a signal? Let me clarify the problem with a trivial example. A traffic light functions as a signal only because there is a general agreement, in this context, about the meaning of green and red; if we were not sure

---

21 Erémitage B 1710; RVAp 490, 18/21; Aellen 1994, cat. 37.

22 Museo Archeologico Nazionale Inv. 194763 (formerly Cleveland Museum of Art); RVAp 496, 18/41; Aellen 1994, cat. 41; Taplin 2007a, 237–8 no. 93.

23 Cf. Taplin 2007a, 40: "The nurse is a common figure both in tragedy and on the vases; but it would be unwise to claim her as a strong signal, since nurses appear in other forms of narrative as well."

24 Taplin 2007a, 37; besides the porticoes, the tragic costume and the pedagogue, Taplin discusses the presence of Furies and related figures, the rocky arch as well as supplication scenes. For a very similar catalogue of signals see Trendall 1989, 262.

Fig. 5: Apulian Volute krater, ca 330: Departure of Amphiaraus. St. Petersburg, Erémitage.

Fig. 6: Apulian Volute krater, ca 330: Departure of Amphiaraus. Su concessione del Ministero dei Beni e delle Attività Culturali e del Turismo – Museo Archeologico Nazionale di Taranto – Archivio Fotografico.

that red always means "stop" and never means "proceed", if the meaning was ever so slightly ambiguous, the traffic light would increase – instead of reducing – the risk of accidents, and its signalling function would collapse. Obviously our painted vases are, in function and meaning, infinitely more complicated then traffic lights. Nevertheless, as the traffic lights, they have been made in order to be used as meaningful objects for the purpose of communication. As historians, we are confronted with the task to recover and to understand the meaning of their images. If in these images we find elements the meaning of which is *not* reliable, then this in itself looks like a most reliable sign that the elements in question were actually *not* meant to function as signals. The reason why the signals of theatricality discussed by Taplin turn out to be unreliable is quite simple: none of these elements was actually *intended* to function as a signal. Modern scholars of ancient theatre might have a comprehensible interest in distinguishing images that were based on dramatic sources from images that were not: for the ancient vase painters and their audience this difference seems definitely *not* to have been of primary relevance. For this attitude of the painters there are specific reasons, to which I shall return at the end.

But first let us have a look at comic iconography, as it has been analysed most prominently, again, by Taplin himself. Here the theatrical elements are so obvious that it would be almost absurd to call them signals. A classic example is provided by a bell krater in Boston.[25] On the front of the krater two figures are standing on what is clearly meant to signify a stage (Fig. 7). Each of the two wears a comic mask as well as a tight costume that reaches down to his wrists and ankles, simulating naked skin; a large phallus is part of the costume, and belly and bottom are abundantly padded. It is important to stress the deeply paradoxical character of this attire: the costume imitates nakedness; at the same time, it is wrinkled, pointing to the fact that what we see is actually not skin, but a textile. The resulting message is twofold: the costume carefully aims at creating an illusion of nakedness and, at the same time, perfectly succeeds in destroying such an illusion. On the reverse of the krater (Fig. 8), we have again two figures: but here the two are walking on the ground line of the image; there is no stage and no costumes; and nakedness, here, is *real* nakedness: no textile mimicking naked skin. Coming back to the front, the comedy is easy to understand. The scene appears to play in a gymnasium. On the left stands a young athlete who has laid down his clothing and his oil bottle on a herm pillar; on the right is a short old man, with a fat posterior and a bent back, perhaps a slave; at any rate he is returning from the market, where he has purchased two full baskets. This fits what we know about contemporary comedy, in which eating was often a central theme and the cook one of the main roles. On our image, the old man takes his time: he has set down his burden (which is perhaps urgently awaited at home) and is about to engage in sports. He is in

---

25 Boston, MFA 69.951: RVAp 100, 4/251; Taplin 1993, 32–4, 41–2, 44 pl. 11.3; Padgett 1993, 68–70, no. 13 pl. V.13.

Fig. 7: Apulian Bell krater, ca 380: A: Scene of comedy. Boston, Museum of Fine Arts.

Fig. 8: Apulian Bell krater, ca 380: B: Two revellers. Boston, Museum of Fine Art.

the act of pouring oil into his left hand, to the utter astonishment of the young athlete. The viewer, of course, is asked to remain aware of the costume the figure is wearing and to concretely imagine what would happen if someone clothed in such a garment would try to oil himself. This breach of the illusion is itself a (very effective!) means of producing a comical effect. If the artist had avoided illusion-destroying components, a large part of the humour would be lost: we would see merely two men in a gymnasium and a basket of food beside one of them – nothing very funny. The theatrical props fulfil a very precise function that could not easily be renounced: they stress the difference between stage play and the depicted action, between the actor and his role; and a large part of the comic quality lies precisely in this difference.

The Boston krater belongs to a large class of vases with comic images, often referred to as Phlyax vases.[26] As Taplin has written, such images "openly flaunt their theatricality, and they delight in the indecorousness and everyday clutter of comedy."[27] I will draw on just one more example, a calyx krater in an Italian private collection, formerly in Bari (Figs. 9–10).[28] Again we see a scene on stage, whose participants are conspicuously depicted as actors. Two dancers wearing festive wreaths are performing a double-flute duet in a sanctuary, as indicated by the altar and the suspended skull of a sacrificed cow. To the left, an old man listens to the music with a gesture of enjoyment (he appears to be a connoisseur). But that is not the entire reality yet. For to the right, squatting behind a tree and thus hidden from the listener, is a flute player without mask or costume: he is thus no actor, but part of the theatrical machinery behind the scenes. In reality, the music comes from him; we see this not least because of the *phorbeia* that reduces the tension of his cheeks. And after a little thought it occurs to us that the broad mouth opening of a comic mask would make it utterly impossible to produce any sounds at all from such an instrument. So this image offers us two different perspectives: if we remain within the horizon of fiction we see two flute players making music; stepping out of this horizon and into the real world we see the actual flute player, with the two dancing farce actors performing a pantomime; the flute player is hiding behind a tree which is growing from underneath the stage: it is therefore a real tree, not just a stage prop! Fiction and reality are juxtaposed to make the contrast between them evident; and it is exactly this contrast that produces the comic effect.

Let me now turn back to vase paintings of tragic episodes. My last example is a monumental amphora that used to be in Boston; it was returned to Italy some years ago and is now in Taranto.[29] I would like to concentrate only on the upper frieze,

26 Trendall 1967.

27 Taplin 1993, 32.

28 Formerly in the Collezione Malaguzzi-Valeri, Bari, now allegedly in Venice or Padua (information Soprintendenza, Taranto): RVAp 400, 15/28; Trendall 1991, 162–3; Taplin 1993, 70, 76, 113.

29 Taranto, Museo Archeologico, Inv. 194765; formerly in Boston, Museum of Fine Arts, FA 1991.437: RVAp Suppl. 2, 148. 492, 18/47b; Padgett 1993, 42, 115–118, pl. XI,42; Aellen 1994, no. 10 pls. 16–17; Nostoi 2007, 182–3, no .50; Taplin 2007a, 241–3, no. 95; 289, n. 61; Taplin 2007b, esp. 180–3, 195–6.

Fig. 9: Apulian Bell krater, ca 350: Scene of comedy. Private Collection. Photo: R. Arciuli.

Fig. 10: Apulian Bell krater, ca 350: Scene of comedy. Private Collection. Photo: R. Arciuli.

which depicts the murder of Atreus, king of Mycenae (Fig. 11). We see Atreus (the name is inscribed) mortally struck, toppling headlong from his throne; from the right, a Fury rushes forward (her inscription reads *[P]oine*: revenge). Atreus' brother *Thyestes* strides with drawn sword to the left, his glance turned backward; next to him, also with sword drawn but in his left hand, stands the young *Aigisthos*, the son of Thyestes. Beside him, at the left end of the image, is *Pelopeia*, who covers her face and turns away from the gruesome event. Pelopeia is tragically connected to all the men involved in the action, as she is Thyestes' daughter, with whom Thyestes has generated Aegisthus; she is therefore at the same time Aegisthus' mother and his sister; finally, she has become the wife (and in this very moment the widow) of Atreus.

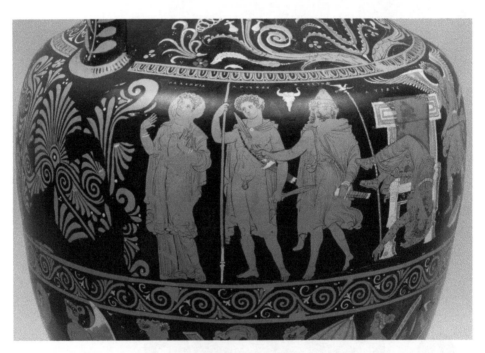

Fig. 11: Apulian Amphora, ca 340: Death of Atreus. Su concessione del Ministero dei Beni e delle Attività Culturali e del Turismo – Museo Archeologico Nazionale di Taranto – Archivio Fotografico.

Atreus wears the garment with long sleeves that we have just discussed: it serves to identify him as a king (together with the throne and the sceptre). Thyestes wears a *chiton* and a cloak, Aegisthus only a cloak around his shoulders. In the entire picture, of course, there is no trace of masks or any other theatrical prop. Not a single component indicates the concrete circumstances of a dramatic performance. And yet the image is, as Taplin has made clear, most likely derived from the plot of a tragedy: interfamilial murders, incest, the central significance of revenge, the fateful entanglement of the generations – these are all typical elements of a tragedy.[30] Nevertheless, the painter's interest was obviously *not* directed toward the dramaturgical reality of tragedy, not to what happens on stage, but toward the tragic action itself: toward the plot. In the context of the tragic plot, all stage elements, costumes, or masks would be not only superfluous, but downright counterproductive, for they would counteract the aesthetic illusion. Depicting costumes or masks, the painter would have signalled that the picture does *not* want to show the myth itself, but its reproduction on a stage, and that the figures of the myth are merely embodied by actors; that actually no one dies and only theatre blood flows.

The Tarentine amphora is of course only one out of hundreds of examples. When Apulian vase painters have to deal with serious subjects, they strictly avoid theatrical connotations: no stage, no costumes, no masks. Theatrical costuming is displayed only in the context of farce – and it is easy to understand why: the contrast between the actor and his role, between actual and pretended nudity, between two figures pretending to play a flute and a real flute player who actually produces the music, between the beholder's reality and the reality he sees on stage – this contrast is in itself a comic element. We therefore find such a contrast regularly exploited in comic imagery, but of course only there; whenever we are dealing with a serious subject, any contrast of this kind would be completely counterproductive. As Taplin has rightly stated: serious pictures "show a mythological story as a mythological story: they are paintings of a myth, not paintings of a play".[31] I could not agree more. But for exactly this reason, I would claim, the vase painters never made use of signals specifying the theatrical origin of some of the stories depicted.

By this I do not mean to reduce the importance of Attic tragedy for Apulian iconography. This importance can hardly be exaggerated. But this had nothing to do with the *theatricality* of tragedy: it had to do with its *plots*. It is worthwhile remembering that among the thousands of Apulian vases we do not find two that are quite alike: on the level of luxury ware, the vase painters and their audience were not interested in replicas, they were interested in variations. Within the workshops producing narrative images this created a constant need for new stories. Vase painters could derive such stories also from epic poetry – and we actually know they did. But epic poetry was a genre that had come to a close: the old epic poems were performed over and over again, but no new variations were produced. For tragedies, the contrary is true. In Athens, the annual competitions produced constantly new tragedies varying the traditional myths and inventing new plots. In Attic tragedy the constant variation was an essential part of the game. The Apulian painters focused on Attic tragedy not be-

---

30 Taplin 2007b, 183: "The family violence, the gender tension, the centrality of vengeance – all are highly characteristic of tragedy. And Aegisthus, with his incestuous life story, might well be regarded as the archetypal figure of a certain kind of tragedy of unnatural family relations."
31 Taplin 2007a, 28.

cause it was a theatrical genre, but because it was a most powerful cultural engine generating a constant output of new plots.

Let me briefly sum up. I perfectly agree with Oliver Taplin about the huge impact Attic tragedy had on Apulian vase painting. I also agree with his claim that there are several elements that have been diffused from the sphere of theatre into the iconography: "There are", as Taplin writes, "quite a range of features that may 'leech in' from the painters' and viewers' familiarity with the visual dimension of theater."[32] "Leeching in" is, to my mind, a most appropriate term. Indisputably, people in Apulia felt a strong fascination for theatre, which they might have considered as the culminating point of Greek culture. As a result of this, the iconographic output of Apulian workshops often turns theatrical. Again and again, elements of theatrical origin diffused into Apulian vase imagery; but this diffusion was certainly *not* limited to images whose plot depends on theatrical sources: it concerns Apulian iconography *as a whole*. We might therefore find elements of theatrical origin even in a panorama of the Underworld, which has nothing whatsoever to do with theatre. Taplin is perfectly right in his claim that the influence of theatre on Apulian iconography has been overwhelming. But exactly for this reason we should not take any theatrical element in any specific image as a signal that the story represented had been derived from a tragedy. Apulian painters took over elements from the theatre and used them for their own purpose, in all sorts of images: in pictures that actually *were* related to the plot of a tragic drama as well as in pictures that *were not*, being related to a literary source that was not dramatic, or having no narrative character at all (as the depictions of the Underworld). In a nutshell: there are hundreds of Apulian images that have been inspired by Attic tragedies; and Apulian vase painters use, again and again, iconographic elements of theatrical origin: but the two phenomena are *not* concurrent. An image can be derived from a tragic plot and show no theatrical element; or it can show plenty of such elements, without any connection to a tragic plot.

Since the nineteenth century modern scholars interested in Attic tragedies, the texts of which are lost, have been using Apulian vase iconography as a source. The focus of Oliver Taplin's research is different. He is less interested in the reconstruction of lost Athenian tragedies than in the actual theatre performance in Magna Graecia; nevertheless, he remains perfectly aware that the iconography of vases follows its own rules and is never a faithful mirror of what happened on stage. Taplin's writings have profoundly enriched our understanding of western Greek culture, demonstrating the importance of tragic plots for Apulian narrative imagery and the impact of theatrical aesthetics on the iconography as a whole. But the two phenomena, I would claim, are largely independent from each other. In Apulian vase iconography, elements of theatrical origin are to be found everywhere, but they are not meant to function as theatrical signals; only in comic iconography the painters make use of signals in order

---

32 Taplin 2007a, 37.

to make clear that what is depicted is a staged performance, with masked actors in costumes pretending to be what in reality they are not. Tragic images, on the contrary, want to be taken seriously. What they depict are not illusionary performances, but the real events of myth: Atreus tumbling to death or Medea about to kill her child. One specific quality of Apulian tragic iconography lies precisely in the absence of theatrical signals. I suggest we stop searching for them.

Acknowledgment: For improving my English text, I would like to thank Lucy Audley-Miller. For their help in obtaining pictures of the vases (and the permission to publish them) my thanks go to Svetlana Adaxina, Emanuele Arciuli, Michele Coppola, Eva Degl'Innocenti, Zhanna Etsina, Laura Feliciotti, Astrid Fendt, Federica Giacobello, Paolo Giuglierini, Valeria Sampaolo, Phoebe Segal and Anna Trofimova.

Abbreviations

RVAp Arthur, D. Trendall and Alexander Cambitoglou. *The Red-Figured Vases of Apulia* (Oxford, 1978–1982).
RVAp Suppl. 2 Arthur, D. Trendall and Alexander Cambitoglou. *Second Supplement to the Red-Figured Vases of Apulia* (London, 1991–1992).

Bibliography

Aellen, Ch. *À la recherche de l'ordre cosmique* (Kirchberg, 1994).
Amelung, W. Cheiridotos chiton in *RE* 3, 2 (1899) 2206–17.
Bordignon, G. (ed.) *Scene dal mito. Iconologia del dramma antico* (Rimini, 2015).
Chamay, J., Cambitoglou A. La folie d'Athamas par le peintre de Darius. *Antike Kunst* 23 (1980), 35–43.
Green, J. R. Tragedy and the Spectacle of Mind: messenger speeches, actors, narrative and audience imagination in 4th century BCE vase painting, in: *The Art of Ancient Spectacle*, edited by B. Bergmann (New Haven, 1999), 37–63.
Himmelmann, N. *Realistische Themen in der griechischen Kunst der archaischen und klassischen Zeit*. Jahrbuch des Deutschen Archäologischen Instituts, Ergänzungsheft 28 (Berlin, 1994).
Mazzei, M. *Ipogeo Monterisi Rossignoli*, in: *Principi imperatori vescovi. Duemila anni di storia a Canosa. Catalogo dell'Esposizione (Bari 27 gennaio – 17 maggio 1992)*, edited by R. Cassano (Bari, 1992), 163–175.
Nostoi 2007: L. Godart and S. De Caro. (eds.) *Nostoi. Capolavori ritrovati:* Catalogo della Mostra, Roma, Palazzo del Quirinale, 21.12.2007–2.3.2008 (Rome, 2007).
Padgett, J. A. (ed.) *Vase Painting in Italy. Red-Figure and Related Works in the Museum of Fine Arts* (Boston, 1993).
Sena Chiesa, G. and F. Starazzi. *Ceramiche attiche e magnogreche Collezione Banca Intesa*. Vols. 1–3 (Milano, 2006).

Taplin, O. *Comic Angels and Other Approaches to Greek Drama through Vase-Painting* (Oxford, 1993).

Taplin, O. *Pots & Plays. Interactions between Tragedy and Vase-painting on the Fourth Century B.C.* (Los Angeles, The J. Paul Getty Museum, 2007a).

Taplin, O. A New Pair of Pairs, in: *Visualizing the Tragic. Drama, Myth and Ritual in Greek Art and Literature: Essays in Honour of Froma Zeitlin*, edited by C. J. Kraus (Oxford, 2007b), 177–196.

Trendall, A. D. *Phlyax Vases* (London, 1967).

Trendall, A. D. *Red Figure Vases of South Italy and Sicily. A Handbook* (London, 1989).

Trendall, A. D. Farce and Tragedy in South-Italian Vase-Painting, in: *Looking at Greek Vases*, edited by T. Rasmussen and N. Spivey (Cambridge, 1991), 151–182.

Wyles, R. The Tragic Costumes, in: *The Pronomos Vase and its Context*, edited by O. Taplin and R. Wyles (Oxford, 2010), 231–253.

Katharina Lorenz
Distributed Narrative

A Very Short History of Juxtaposing Myths on Pompeian Walls

The ancients were not at all keen to present in freely juxtaposed pictures temporally closely related facta, in which one would, as it were, constitute the continuation of the other. Such proximity would curtail the suggestive in the broadest sense and trap it within confines too narrow. The only exceptions were those comprehensive cyclical displays. Otherwise, they rather chose to combine narrative moments that were distant from each other, that would relate to each other as if beginning and end, or cause and effect; they even preferred sometimes when choosing pendants to pick elements from different mythological cycles and so contrast one scene with a poetic-mythological analogy from another cycle.

Heinrich Brunn[1]

Heinrich Brunn was among the first scholars to pick up on the distribution of mythological scenes on the walls of Pompeian houses, noting how their juxtaposition and alignment facilitate comparative viewing and shape narratives fuelled by analogy. Brunn was followed by Adolf Trendelenburg who published the first study on the combination of mythological pictures in Pompeian houses in 1876.[2] Notwithstanding the waves of scepticism against this type of interpretation of Pompeian juxtapositions of myths, this approach is now fully accepted in scholarship, not least because of the important contributions by Richard Brilliant and Bettina Bergmann who demonstrated some of the key mechanisms of the Pompeian juxtaposition of myths and their rootedness in Roman aesthetics.[3] These studies proved that Pompeian frescos did not serve merely as quotations of famous Greek panel paintings but rather were designed specifically for their individual contexts, fulfilling a range of functions within the social configuration of the Roman domestic sphere.

---

1 Trans.: author. Quoted after Schefold 1952, 32: "In frei einander gegenübergestellten Bildern liebten es die Alten keineswegs, zeitlich sich so nahe berührende Fakta darzustellen, daß das eine gewissermaßen die Fortsetzung des anderen bildete. Denn das Beziehungsreiche im weitesten Sinne wird durch eine solche Nachbarschaft beschränkt und in zu enge Grenzen eingeschlossen. Nur ausführliche Zyklen bilden hier eine Ausnahme. Lieber wählten sie entweder weiter voneinander abliegende Momente, die sich verhielten wie Anfang und Ende, Ursache und Wirkung, oder sie zogen selbst bei solchen Parallelbildern nicht selten vor, die Gegenstände nicht aus einem Mythenkreis zu wählen, sondern der einen Szene eine poetisch-mythische Analogie aus einem anderen Kreis gegenüberzustellen."
2 Trendelenburg 1876.
3 Brilliant 1984, 53–89; Bergmann 1994.

https://doi.org/10.1515/9783110421453-008

My discussion examines an aspect of the Roman practice of juxtaposing pictures which has received little attention in earlier scholarship: that is, the possible origins of these forms of distributed narrative in pendant compositions and their historical development, specifically focusing here on the period from the late Republic until the Vespasianic era (and the destruction of Pompeii).[4] Such a diachronic exploration is key to a better understanding of the display of myth in the Roman domestic context and Roman practices of visual story-telling more broadly because it provides us with an understanding of the formal and iconographic templates that the Romans appropriated and the protocols of viewing and meaning production to which they aspired.

Mythological Painting in Roman Culture

Three types of material evidence have been identified as antecedents for Roman figural painting: first, the Hellenistic palaces of mainland Greece and possibly also Egypt.[5] Second, the tomb decorations from the north and south of Italy, including the tomb paintings from Paestum of the fourth century BC; the Etruscan paintings from the tombs of Vulci and Tarquinia, such as the François Tomb of the later fourth century BC and the Conference Tomb of the second or first century BC; and the paintings from the tombs on the Esquiline Hill from the third and second centuries BC.[6] Third, the

---

4 Brilliant 1984, 66 argues for this practice to derive from the artistic production of Hellenistic Alexandria; the Cyzicene *stylopinakia* might offer an example of this legacy: according to the lemma in the *Anthologia Palatina* III, these epigrams accompanied a series of mythological reliefs in the temple for Queen Apollonis of Pergamon at Cyzicus of the first half of the second century BC. For the *stylopinakia*, see Brilliant 1984, 35–7; Looy and Demoen 1986; Stupperich 1990. Generally, the combination of myths in classical Greek architectural sculpture and paintings such as in the Stoa Poikile present, in Brilliant's view, earlier antecedents for this epideictic practice.

5 For the difficulties of mapping this legacy, see Fittschen 1976, esp. 540–4. Other potential influences have been considered too, such as the domestic decorations found on Sicily where the evidence from sites such as Morgantina, Monte Iato or Solunto provides us with glimpses of developments in wall-painting on the Italian peninsula during the Hellenistic period. For an overview, see the contributions in La Torre and Torelli 2011. The implicit assumption in these studies that this type of wall-painting is to be classed as Italic constitutes a movement away from the research trajectory of the 1970s and 1980s, where great pains were taken to abolish the dichotomy between Greek and Roman art and instead map the Roman emulation of Greek art – the context in which Klaus Fittschen had developed his ideas on the emergence of the Second Style in Roman wall-painting (see Fittschen 1976, 539). Zanker 1976 is the milestone publication of this earlier trajectory; for a lucid assessment of the intentions of this approach, see Hölscher 1990, 73–4.

6 For an overview of the development of Etruscan and Roman painting during the Middle and Late Republic see Rouveret 2012 and Bragantini 2012; see also Ling 1991, 5–11; Croisille 2005, 23–6. Etruscan culture exerted a noticeable influence on Pompeii during the archaic period, as documented in the famous passage in Strabo (5.4.8) and by the Italic character of the temple (for Minerva and Heracles) on the Triangular Forum, the Apollo Temple (see De Caro 2007, 73–81), and the presence of Etruscan buc-

large numbers of Greek panel paintings which flooded Rome during and after the period of the conquest of Greece from the second century BC onwards, when many Greek paintings (and painters) found their way to Rome. The literary sources, above all Pliny the Elder,[7] report extensive collections of masterpieces of Greek figural panel painting including mythological subjects, put on display for the public to enjoy in places such as the *Saepta* on the *Campus Martius*, the *Porticus Octaviae* and the Library of Asinius Pollio in Rome, as well as in the houses of the aristocracy.

Literary works are seen as another inspiration for Pompeian mythological frescos, especially the works of Virgil, Horace and Ovid:[8] the paintings are often interpreted as illustrations of literary accounts, in particular Ovid's *Metamorphoses*. However, there is little evidence that the depictions were designed as illustrations beyond the fact that myths which occur in Ovid also feature on Pompeian walls.[9] Given that, usually, the pictures show little similarity to Ovid's account, it is far more plausible to consider them a fully independent media operating within a cultural sphere that shared access to the same narrative pool as literary production, rather than assuming that images merely copied texts.

The Pompeians and their Myths

The range of thematic choices made for mythological pictures depicted on Pompeian walls may seem another, robust way of establishing their potential antecedents. However, attempts at capturing statistically these thematic choices throw up a range of problems. The existing quantifications are heavily reliant on the definitions of the categories within which the individual frescos are counted; we need to ask what understanding really can be gained, for example, by ordering scenes according to the "Trojan" or "Theban" cycle in light of the range of differing accentuations in which individual episodes from these cycles are featured on the walls.[10]

The mere counting of episode titles also fails to account for the fact that the display of mythological themes undergoes significant stylistic changes which impact the

chero pottery, including also Etruscan writing (Carafa 2007, 65; Bellelli 1995, 9–10). This influence had long ended in the Augustan period, and since the third century BC onwards was overlaid by interaction with Samnite culture.

7 Plin. *HN* 35.1.5–10.34–41.

8 See Colpo 2011 and Knox 2014 for relatively recent examples of this type of approach; Karl Schefold famously discussed the potential influence of Horace on the mythological pendant pictures of the Third and Fourth Styles (Schefold 1952, 87–95); for Virgil's potential role in the shaping of Roman wall-painting, see Simon 1998b, 20–2.

9 Hodske 2007, 34 asserts that 41 % of Pompeian mythological topics also feature in Ovid.

10 For the problems with statistical analysis of mythological depictions, see Zanker 2005, 243 no. 1.

content of the individual panels and the way in which viewers engage with them.[11] In the late Second Style, during the second half of the first century BC, mythological scenes are displayed within vast landscape settings as megalographies or set within painted *aediculae*. The paintings of the Third Style, spanning the first decades of the Julio-Claudian principate, may continue to feature mythological landscapes, but those are not presented as if extending beyond the wall of the room; these paintings are now unmistakably characterised as affixed to the central section of the wall. Fourth Style painting emerges during the Claudian period and presents quadratic mythological panels that are reduced in size compared to the rectangular versions of the Third Style; these scenes focus primarily on individual characters and their relationship, without much elaboration of their surroundings.

Notwithstanding the vagaries of quantitative analysis, it is noticeable that across the Third and Fourth Styles around 70 % of mythological panels in Pompeii centre upon the presentation of lovers:[12] the largest proportion focuses on romantic encounters; smaller segments deal with abandoned lovers or those depicted on their own. Fourth-Style frescos are especially concerned with individuals such as Narcissus or the abandoned Ariadne; here, we also find depictions which cannot be allocated to a specific mythological storyline, such as scenes of Venus fishing. The remaining 30 % display complex mythological narratives: some are taken from the Homeric epics (covering both the first and second Trojan Wars), others present Bellerophon, episodes from the Argonautica with Jason or Hylas, and scenes with Pentheus or Lycourgus. The absence of topics which otherwise enjoy popularity in the early empire is notable: there are only a few Roman myths on display; the myths depicted are almost exclusively Greek, with the exception of some select scenes of the Roman foundation myth.[13]

Myths on Display: the Concept of Juxtaposition

The juxtaposition of mythological scenes in individual rooms is a key characteristic of the display of myths in Roman domestic contexts. Engagement with these modes of display is crucial for developing an understanding of the choices made by Pompeians

---

11 Nearly 75 % of all known Pompeian mythological pictures are from Fourth-Style decorations; almost 25 % form part of Third-Style decorations (Second-Style mythological panels only account for 1 % of all preserved frescos): Hodske 2007, 33; his calculations are based on 760 paintings.
12 These figures are based on an analysis of 560 mythological panels; see Lorenz 2008, 32–3.
13 Three panels have sometimes been interpreted as the sacrifice of Sophoniba, the Carthaginian heroine who killed herself rather than let herself be displayed in a Roman triumph (Liv. 30.12–15); this interpretation is not convincing. See Brendel 1935, 564–8.

regarding their use of myth.[14] Across Pompeii, the set of scenes chosen for such combinations was only very rarely repeated exactly.[15] This high level of variation demonstrates the individual decisions taken by those in charge of the decorative designs. This spectrum of decorative decisions also demonstrates how inadequate it is to rely on the traditional argument that the patrons of the decorations picked the designs for their houses from pattern books, or: *Musterbücher*.[16] The evidence suggests that pattern books may have provided a portfolio of material from which Pompeian customers chose; but the evidence of the interior decoration tells us that the choices made from this shared pool of motifs led to highly individualised arrangements.

When probing into the origins of these picture combinations, we find similarities in Etruscan tomb decorations where juxtaposition is employed to frame correspondences and facilitate meaningful connections between individual scenes. The decoration of the Tomba François offers a striking example of such storytelling through pendants. The *megalographia* friezes that adorn the internal walls of the hypogeum contrast scenes of Greek epic with Etruscan history; name labels facilitate identification of all the figures on display.[17] For example, along the long walls of the tomb's *tablinum* section, a scene of Achilles sacrificing the Trojan prisoners at the tomb of Patroclus is juxtaposed with scenes of the legendary exploits of the city of Vulci against the Romans and her Etruscan allies. In the scene at Troy, Achilles is shown cutting the throat of a prisoner,[18] with Ajax and Agamemnon standing nearby. Opposite, Aulus Vibenna and two companions each slaughter an opponent in similarly gruesome fashion, whilst the fourth pair shows Aulus' brother Caelius being freed from imprisonment.

Peter Holliday described this type of visual narrative as deductive and extractive:[19] the viewers are invited to isolate individual elements from the extended cyclical de-

---

14 The corpus of studies on the picture combinations in Pompeian houses has rapidly increased in recent decades. See Trendelenburg 1876, Schefold 1952, 87–151, Thompson 1960 and Brilliant 1984, 59–89 for early explorations in this field. Bettina Bergmann investigated the principles underlying the combinations: Bergmann 1994; for a comprehensive analysis of Pompeian combinations of mythological scenes and the narratives they shape, see Lorenz 2008; cf. Lorenz 2014, 183–8 for a discussion of the influence of rhetorical principles on Pompeian picture combinations.
15 A notable exception are the Fourth-Style decorations of Room (15) in the Casa del Poeta Tragico (VI 8,3–5) and Room (h) in the Casa di L. Cornelius Diadumenus (VII 12,26–27); in both rooms pictures of Ariadne abandoned (in the former, Theseus is shown as leaving; in the latter, his ship has already departed), Artemis and Callisto, and the cupid's nest are combined. For the decoration in the Casa del Poeta Tragico: *PPM* IV 566–81; for the Casa di L. Cornelius Diadumenus: *PPM* VII 571–81.
16 For Roman *Musterbücher*, see the summary of recent debates in Schmidt-Colinet 2009; for a comprehensive survey of modes of transmission, see Ghedini 1997, esp. 834–5.
17 For a detailed analysis of the tomb's decoration see Holliday 1993; see now also Rathje 2014.
18 Note the creolisation attested here by showing Achilles accompanied by Vanth and Charun, the two Etruscan demons of death.
19 Holliday 1993, 175, referring to Brilliant 1984, 23.

signs of the friezes and so turn them into pendants. By comparing and contrasting these pendants, the viewers are able to synthesise the content on display and thereby create new meaning. Holliday rightly argues that this juxtaposition – full of parallels in composition and in content – produces a rhetoric of *comparatio* and *amplificatio* in which Greek myth – and specifically Greek epic – is here employed to underpin, legitimise and to place Etruscan historical legend on a par with it:[20] "The Greek material functioned as a complementary analogue to the political struggles of the Etruscan present."

For Roman Campania one of our earliest examples of juxtaposing mythological scenes are those from the walls of exedra (13) in Villa 6 at Terzigno in the environs of Pompeii. The precise date of the Second Style decorations of this room is debated, with a date in the third quarter of the first century BC the most convincing proposition.[21] A predecessor of the execution of the figural *megalographia* frieze that sits in the central zones of the three walls of the room is surely the decoration from room (H) in the Villa of Fannius Synistor at Boscoreale, where the figural scenes also extend beyond the painted columns of the decoration.[22]

The Terzigno frieze is organised in three sections, each occupying one wall. There is consensus in scholarship that the section on the back wall, itself subdivided into three panels, shows Venus in its central panel, possibly in the Genetrix type because she seems to hold her mantle up; she is flanked by a cupid on a pedestal on each side.[23] The two side panels of the back wall each show a female attendant busy with sacrificial activities. The identity of the figures in the sections shown on the side walls is less clear.

Volker Michael Strocka has argued that the section on the left depicts Dido mourning the departure of Aeneas, while the opposite section features the building of the walls of Troy, with Apollo and Poseidon at the court of King Laomedon.[24] According to Strocka, the room's decoration was thematically channelled to map out the road towards the foundation of the city of Rome – a road, as these pendants pictures would like to have it, paved by the demise of others, that is: the Trojans and the Carthaginians, and regulated by the ancestral mother of the *Gens Iulii*, Venus. Eric Moormann

---

20 Holliday 1993, 192.

21 For an overview of the controversy, and with a detailed proposal for the chronological placing, see Strocka 2005, 82–6, esp. 82; he argues for a date after the decorations of the villa at Oplontis (60/50 BC) and before the House of Augustus on the Palatine in Rome (30 BC); contra Cicirelli 2013.

22 Strocka 2005, 82. For the decorations in this room, see most recently Barbet 2013; see also Müller 1994; Smith 1994; Torelli 2003; Bergmann 2010.

23 Strocka 2005, 87–8, with reference to earlier scholarship.

24 Strocka 2005, 89–95; cf. the interpretations by Sampaolo 2005 and Moormann 2005; Sampaolo identified the scene on the left as Phaedra, the one on the right as a depiction of Laomedon, Apollo and Poseidon; Moormann interpreted the scene on the left as Helen at Sparta and the scene on the right as Paris with Trojans. See Moormann 2013, 227–33 for a summary.

has recently presented a convincing argument that this type of political interpretation has no foundation in the pictorial evidence.[25]

Notwithstanding the precise interpretation of the two scenes on the long walls of exedra (13), the symmetry in the composition of both sides is notable. Each section shows the same number of figures: four in the central panel, two in each side panel, and a further figure in the section adjoining the back wall. The gender of the actors in the central panel is complimentary: on the left, four women; on the right, four men. The theme of the Trojan War also clearly seems to underpin the design: I would agree with Strocka and Sampaolo that on the right we see Apollo and Poseidon at Laomedon's court. For the scene on the left, I would concur with Strocka that the woman on the throne shows an iconography otherwise associated with Dido;[26] but the rest of the scene appears closer to depictions of Paris at Sparta, suggesting instead that the subject is Helen.[27]

The Terzigno display of myth presents a type of juxtaposition that differs from the strategies at play in the Tomba François. The three scenes do not amplify each other's content or stimulate extraction. Instead, two diverging mechanisms are at play: first, the frieze format puts emphasis on the consecutive relationship of all the presented action; this curtails the potential for *comparatio* between the two scenes on the long sides and their distribution of genders. Second, the bracketed presentation of Venus turns her into a ready-made extract; her figure serves as a reference point for the two scenes of epic to the sides, which might stimulate deduction regarding the outcomes of those episodes. This dual approach to transmission, combining consecutive and referential strategies, finds a parallel in the positioning of the Circe scene as the narrative hub of the contemporary Esquiline Odyssey landscapes, notwithstanding the otherwise unambiguous claims of the design to visualise a continuous landscape.[28]

---

25 Moormann 2013, tackling also the politics-focussed *megalographia* interpretations of Esposito 2008. For a discussion of the difficulties concerning the interpretation of Roman megalographies, see Allroggen-Bedel 2008.

26 Three representations of Dido abandoned exist in Pompeii: ACCADEMIA DI MUSICA (VI 3,7.25.26); Third Style. *PPM* IV 285–7. CASA DEI AMANTI (I 10,10–11), Room (8), West-wall, in situ. Fourth Style. *PPM* II 476–7. CASA DI MELEAGRO (VI 9,2.13), *atrium* (2), North-wall, in situ. Fourth Style. *PPM* IV 677. See Lorenz 2008, 122–4, 237–45; Hodske 2007, 249.

27 Cf. CASA DEGLI AMORINI DORATI (VI 16,7.38), *tablinum* (e), West-wall, in situ. Third Style. *PPM* V 738.

28 Cf. Lorenz 2013, 227. For the Odyssey landscapes see most recently O'Sullivan 2011, 116–49 with further bibliography.

The Casa del Citarista, Room (20): a Trinity of Myth

In the Augustan period, probably a few decades after the Terzigno decorations were executed,[29] the presentation of myths on Roman walls changed significantly – a change that in scholarship is only discussed for its formal properties, not for the way in which this change signals shifts in the use of mythological narrative. One of the earliest Campanian examples of this new type of mythological display comes from the Casa del Citarista in Pompeii (I 4,5.25.28), one of the most splendid Pompeian residences, which covers a substantial part of an entire insula, with rooms arranged around three peristyle courts (Fig. 1).

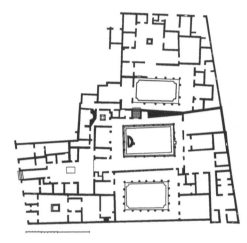

Fig. 1: Pompeii, Casa del Citarista, ground plan. Drawing: Author.

In Room (20), one of the reception rooms leading off from the middle *peristylium* (17), the decoration from the early Third Style includes three large mythological panels (Fig. 2).[30] The panel that has received most attention in scholarship is that from the North-wall (Fig. 3).[31] It shows a woman seated on the left; she embraces a man seated on the right. With his right arm around her shoulders he lifts her mantle away from her body. The woman has turned her unveiled upper body both to her partner and to the viewer of the picture; assorted pieces of jewellery underline her beauty further. He is depicted in the nude, with a sword around his torso, and a dog in front of him – polysemous attributes indicating he might be a warrior, a hunter or even a shepherd.

---

29 Bragantini 2012, 318–9 is right to remind us that the chronology of Roman wall-painting has to be handled with care.

30 The first comprehensive discussion of the room's decoration is Elia 1937, 6–10; see most recently Bergmann 2014, 76–7, 81: her discussion is based on the newly cleaned panels and supported by excellent digital reconstructions of the house and its decoration.

31 Naples, Museo Archeologico Nazionale inv. 112282. Third Style. H 2.53 m, W 1.5 m.

Fig. 2: Pompeii, Casa del Citarista, Room (20), digital reconstruction of the view into the room. Digital reconstruction. Courtesy of James Stanton-Abbott.

The scene is set in a vast landscape; behind the couple rises a block-like votive pillar, and further in the distance, filling the whole background, appears a mountain with flattened top. The couple are accompanied on the right by a sleeping figure who is shown wearing hunting boots and a sun hat, with the left hand raised to support the chin. Further to the right stands a man dressed in a cloak. Finally, from the top right of the picture a cupid floats in carrying a torch. The identification of the figures in the scene has caused much controversy, especially regarding the central male protagonist. As is the case with the Terzigno friezes, there are iconographic parallels only for individual elements of the composition, not for the overall scene.

The Citarista Couple: Iconographic Excursus

Dido and Aeneas.[32] The identification of the figures in the scene in the Casa del Citarista as Dido and Aeneas is supported by Virgil's account of their encounter in front of a grotto.[33] Iconographically, it rests on comparison with a mostly destroyed fresco in House Regio IX 6, d-e, which preserves just the toes of three pairs of feet along with the tips of two spears held together (Fig. 4). One pair of feet is booted and rendered in the same way as those of the figure seated next to the couple in the picture from the Casa del Citarista; the accompanying name labels identify the other two pairs of feet as belonging to Dido and, underneath the spears, Aeneas.[34] Whilst this motif of feet is pervasive across Pompeian representations of seated figures, the motif of the two spears bears rather more significance as a male attribute – an attribute that is conspicuously absent from the scene in the Casa del Citarista, where no reference to

---

32 *PPM* I 151–4; Provenzale 2008, 17–56, 76–7, 123–33; Bergmann 2014, 77.

33 Verg. *Aen.* 4.129–172.

34 *PPM* I 151–4. See also *PPM* IX 730–1 fig. 15.

Fig. 3: Naples, Museo Archeologico Nazionale inv. 112282. From: Pompeii, Casa del Citarista, Room (20), North-wall: Venus and her consort. Third Style. Courtesy of Museo Archeologico Nazionale, Naples.

Fig. 4: Pompeii, House IX, 6, Room (e): the panel with labels for Dido and Aeneas. Third Style. Courtesy of German Archaeological Institute, Rome, neg. no. 53.589.

this type of weapon is made, despite the fact that the dog in the picture might allude to a hunting context.

Venus and Adonis.[35] The absence of such spears also speaks against identification of the male character as Adonis, whose trademark weapons these are. This reservation stands despite the iconographic similarities to other Pompeian frescos of that myth, which show Venus turning to, and embracing, her consort in a way similar to the depiction from the Casa del Citarista. Moreover, these scenes of Venus and Adonis lack the reciprocity of action between the protagonists which we can observe here.[36]

Mars and Venus.[37] The main reason for arguing against an identification of the scene as a depiction of Mars and Venus is the compositional relationship of the two figures in the Casa del Citarista: that is, the fact that the female character is embracing the male. Furthermore, the male figure lacks the helmet that is the key defining attribute of Mars in around thirty Pompeian depictions of the two gods (Fig. 5), who are the most popular mythological couple on Pompeian walls and appear from the Augustan period until the end of Pompeii.[38]

However, there are also some iconographic parallels with the Pompeian depictions of the divine couple: the motif of lifting the woman's dress in an outdoor setting is featured in the pyramidal type, the most popular form of presenting Mars and Venus in Fourth-Style decorations.[39] Both gods are seated and Venus leans on Mars while he

---

35 As such identified in Lehmann 1953, 38–81.

36 Hodske 2007, 148–9 solves the discrepancy by proposing a second iconographic strand of Adonis depictions, to which he allocates the scenes in the Casa del Citarista along with three other scenes to be discussed below. This interpretation fails to offer an explanation why Adonis, the hunter, would be shown without spears.

37 Helbig 1868, 83 no. 323.

38 For the myth of Mars and Venus on Pompeian walls, see Strocka 1997; Lorenz 2008, 149–85. The inspiration for these Pompeian iconographic types seems not to come from Augustan state art, where the paternal Mars Ultor and the modest Venus Genetrix prevail, but from Etruscan mirrors and Campanian ware pottery of the Hellenistic period which show the romantic encounter of the two youthful gods. See, for example, Campanian ware bowl. London, British Museum Coll. E. Piot 1890 199. Third century BC. *LIMC* 2 (1984), s.v. "Aphrodite" no. 1315.

39 For this type, see Strocka 1997, 130; Lorenz 2008, 158–66. The pyramidal type emphasises especially that Mars is putting aside all his equipment: helmet, spear, shield and sword. Two or more cupids accompany the couple; they hold the gods' attributes or play with Mars' weapons, a symbol of the power exerted by Venus. This aspect is not present in the depiction from the Casa del Citarista.

Fig. 5: Naples, Museo Archeologico Nazionale inv. 9256. From: Pompeii, Casa di Meleagro (VI 9,2.13), *tablinum* (8), North-wall: Mars and Venus in the pyramidal type. Fourth Style. Courtesy of German Archaeological Institute, Rome, neg. no. 63.2201 (H. Felbermeyer).

is holding her from behind, lifting her mantle; she either holds a necklace behind her head or helps to lift her dress – either action enhances the effect of his approach to unveil her nude body fully to the viewer. Venus wears jewellery, including on occasion a venus chain, which also adorns the female in the Casa del Citarista; Mars is clean-shaven and wears a mantle.

The *lectus* type, an iconographic strand only documented in Third-Style decorations of *tablina*, offers in parallel with the fresco from the Casa del Citarista a cupid and bystanders, albeit in a different action scheme.[40] In two frescos, Mars and Venus have gathered next to an oversized *lectus*, which gives this iconographic strand its name: she is seated, fully dressed, whilst Mars, helmet on his head, stands behind and touches her. The other personnel are arranged standing or sitting around the bed in a domestic setting indicated by a colonnade and a door. Only in the panel from the Casa del Amore Punito does the couple appear within a sacral landscape with a votive pillar at the back; here the number of attendants is reduced to two: a maid to the left, and the cupid, floating with an *iynx* wheel to the right.

The sacral atmosphere evoked in the fresco from the Casa del Amore Punito also reoccurs in a couple of domestic cult images of the two gods.[41] In the fresco in the Casa dell'Efebo Mars and Venus are depicted sitting next to each other in front of a votive pillar in an outdoor space whilst a cupid holds a parasol over their heads. Similar to the picture from the Casa del Citarista, Venus embraces Mars and she is adorned with

---

40 For this type, see Strocka 1997, 130–1; Lorenz 2008, 151–8. The frescos come from the following houses: Casa annessa alla Casa dell'Efebo (I 7,19), *tablinum* (c), North-wall, in situ. *PPM* I 766–7. Casa di M. Lucretius Fronto (V4a), *tablinum* (7), North-wall, in situ. *PPM* III 1016–8; Peters 1993, 213–9. Casa del Amore Punito (VII 2,23), *tablinum* (f), South-wall, now: Naples, Museo Archeologico Nazionale inv. no. 9249. *PPM* VI 674–5.

41 Strocka 1997, 130; Lorenz 2008, 166–70. Two frescos constitute this strand: Casa dell'Efebo (I 7,10–12), Porticus (19), West-wall, in situ. Fourth Style. *PPM* I 698–701. Casa di Re di Prussia (VII 9,33), *viridarium* (2), West-wall, in situ. Third Style. *PPM* VII 355–7.

a venus chain. However, in contrast to the Citarista fresco, Mars is characterised by his helmet and in this picture refrains from lifting Venus' dress.

Venus and Anchises. As proposed by Erika Simon, the male character that matches the characteristics of the figure in the Casa del Citarista scene most closely, at least in principle, seems to be Anchises, the noble Trojan and father of Aeneas, who is seduced by a love-stricken Aphrodite on Mount Ida while working as a shepherd.[42] However, the relationship of Aphrodite/Venus and Anchises is difficult to capture iconographically.

Fig. 6: Paris, Musée du Louvre 1035/Br 1723: Etruscan mirror with Anchises and Venus. Around 300 BC. After Gerhard (1867), 64–5 pl. 326.

---

42 Simon 1998a, 136–7.

Potential parallels come from late-Classical and Hellenistic art. A bronze mirror from Epirus shows two figures seated next to each other in a composition similar to the scene in the Casa del Citarista:[43] Aphrodite/Venus is turned towards her consort, and towards the viewer. Her partner is dressed in Phrygian costume; rather than touching her, he has raised his arm behind his head in a motif reminiscent of the Apollo Lykeios and so presents his body to the viewer too. The couple is accompanied by two cupids and a dog. The Phrygian dress and the dog would not be out of place in a depiction of another Trojan shepherd who is seduced by Aphrodite/Venus: namely, Paris; but the lack of other figures characteristic of judgement scenes (such as Hermes, Athena and Hera) renders an identification as Anchises possible. On an Etruscan mirror from around 300 BC the identification of Anchises is unambiguous because of the name label Anchas defining the figure (Fig. 6); however, his youthful iconography bears no specific characteristics other than that he is accompanied by Thalna, a companion of Turan, the Etruscan goddess of beauty.[44] Thalna is characterised in the scene by toying with the *iynx* wheel, the symbol of the fickle nature of love and, possibly, a pointer to the Homeric story.

The Citarista Couple: Mythological Iconographies in Flux

The difficulties concerning the iconographic identification of the scene in the Casa del Citarista are perhaps explicable when we consider that we are dealing with an iconography in flux, similar to the situation in Terzigno. Despite the difficulties in identifying the precise subject, it does seem clear that this iconography is shaped by Hellenistic Greek, Etruscan and Italic templates for the depiction of romantic relationships. Whilst the identity of the figures in the scene in the Casa del Citarista might remain a mystery, its further development and the range of potential accentuations can be traced in three Pompeian frescos from the Third and Fourth Styles which display some significant similarities to the scene in the Casa del Citarista, with the caveat that all three panels are only preserved in drawings of the eighteenth and nineteenth centuries.[45]

---

43 London, British Museum 1904.7–2.1; from Paramythia/Epirus; previously Collection Hawkins, Bagnor Park. Mid-fourth century BC. Michaelis 1882, 212 no. 1; Vermeule 1955, 130.

44 Paris, Musée du Louvre 1035/Br 1723. Gerhard 1867, 64–5 pl. 326.

45 Casa di Virinius Modestus (IX 7,16), Room (c), West-wall; lost in situ [drawing by G. Discanno]. Third Style. *PPM* IX 803–4. – Casa delle Vestali (VI 1,6.7), Room (23), West?-wall. Fourth Style. Helbig 1868, no. 316 [Ares and Aphrodite]; *PPM* IV 21–2. – Casa di Sirico (VII 1,25.47), Room (34), South-wall; lost in situ [facsimile by G. Abbate]. Fourth Style. Helbig 1868, no. 317 [Ares and Aphrodite]; *PPM* VI 349.

In all three pictures the compositional arrangement is parallel to that seen in the Casa del Citarista (Fig. 3): a seated woman turns around to embrace the man next to her. In the Fourth Style pictures from the the Casa di Sirico (Fig. 7) and Casa delle Vestali (Fig. 8) her upper body is nude, he has a sword strap around his torso and the scene is set outdoors in front of a rocky outcrop and next to a votive pillar; in the Third-Style picture from the Casa di Virinius Modestus she is fully dressed, he wears a mantle, but carries no weapons and the scene is set indoors. In all three pictures a dog is at the man's side and a cupid is present in the picture; in the Casa di Sirico and the Casa di Virinius Modestus he carries one or two torches and, in the former, he is airborne as is the cupid in the Casa del Citarista; in the Casa delle Vestali he flies in carrying a helmet towards the man.

The drawing of the fresco in the Casa delle Vestali shows the male figure with helmet, which given the defining role of this attribute in Pompeian iconographies of Mars suggests that this compositional type had come to be used for representation of Venus and Mars[46] at least by the time of the Fourth Style. Naturally, the Casa delle Vestali cannot be taken as evidence that the scene in the Casa del Citarista necessarily depicts Mars and Venus, but the example does demonstrate how Pompeian figure painters might amend or specify the iconography of individual scenes for specific purposes. It also shows how the iconographies for Mars and Venus chosen by the Pompeians kept to the Hellenistic templates for Ares and Aphrodite: they favoured the athletic, clean-shaven warrior and the beautiful goddess in a state of undress, not the types so popular in Augustan state art: the paternal Mars Ultor and the more modest patroness of the *gens Iulii*.

Fig. 7: Pompeii, Casa di Sirico (VII 1,25.47), Room (34), South-wall: Venus and consort. Fourth Style. Watercolour by G. Abbate. Courtesy of German Archaeological Institute, Rome, neg. no. 58.1911.

---

46 Cf. Provenzale 2008, 76–7.

Fig. 8: Pompeii, Casa delle Vestali (VI 1,6.7), Room (23), West-wall: the helmet identifies Venus' consort unambiguously as Mars. Fourth Style. Courtesy of Museum für Abgüsse klassischer Bildwerke, Munich.

Room (20): the Couple in Context

This iconographic survey demonstrates that an unambiguous identification of the scene on the North-wall cannot be reached on the basis of the iconographic evidence that we have; this constitutes a problem that applies equally to the other two mythological panels in the room.[47] However, the presentation of Venus and her consort in juxtaposition with these other frescos offers some clues regarding the potential role of the scene in this particular setting.

The fresco on the South-wall opposite the Venus panel shows Leda as a veiled woman in the centre, accompanied by two maids and identified by the presence of a proportionally diminutive swan next to her and the eagle approaching from the skies, both of whom embody Zeus (Fig. 9).[48] The scene is set in a sanctuary context, with the detailed rendering of a temple in the background and votive statues and sacrificial objects littering the ground around Leda who has opened her mantle, possibly to offer the swan refuge from the eagle. The fresco differs significantly from the other Pompeian depictions of this myth that all come from the Fourth Style.[49] These show

---

47 Cf. Bergmann 2014, 79 who rightly emphasises that these pictures might be purposefully designed as "open", to offer their audiences the opportunity to explore different interpretations.
48 Naples, Museo Archeologico Nazionale inv. 120034. Third Style. H 2.8 m, W 1.6 m.
49 Hodske 2007, 219–21; Lorenz 2008, 195–7.

Fig. 9: Naples, Museo Archeologico Nazionale inv. 120034. From: Casa del Citarista, Room (20), South-wall: Leda with the swan. Third Style. Courtesy of Museo Archeologico Nazionale, Naples.

Leda in differing stages of undress either struggling against or actively embracing the swan; they are set within an interior context, not an outside sanctuary space.

On the central East-wall of the room, two men are standing to the side of a third, who is dressed in oriental clothes and seated on a throne in front of a tent, with soldiers in the background (Fig. 10).[50] The central group of three men follows the same iconographic template as the depiction from Terzigno, albeit providing more detail regarding the setting. This is possibly another depiction of Apollo and Poseidon at the court of Laomedon, with the figure on the left characterised by a laurel wreath and branch, regardless of the fact that the figure to the right holds a staff, not a trident. Except for the Terzigno example, the iconography is once again unique in Campania: the only other, much later version of this episode depicts the two gods at the actual building site, with no reference to Laomedon and his army.[51]

---

50 Naples, Museo Archeologico Nazionale inv. 111472. Third Style. H 1.89 m, W 1.13 m.

51 Casa di Sirico (VII 1,25.47), Room (10), West-wall; in situ. Fourth Style. Helbig 1868, no. 1266; *PPM* VI 294–6. – In Room (h) of the Casa di Octavius Quartio (II 2,2) the episode is implicit in the Fourth-Style depiction of the First Trojan War, but not made explicit: Lorenz 2013, 230, 242.

Fig. 10: Naples, Museo Archeologico Nazionale inv. 111472. From: Casa del Citarista, Room (20), East-wall: Laomedon with Apollo and Poseidon. Third Style. Courtesy of Museo Archeologico Nazionale, Naples.

The walls surrounding the mythological frescos are decorated in a manner that is characteristic of the Third Style: the sections are arranged in vertical and horizontal axis with the figure scenes painted in dark red. This makes the mythological panels with their vibrant colours, framed by painted *aediculae*, stand out strikingly, drawing in the eye; the effect is enhanced by the bright yellow colour that adorns the remainder of the walls. Whilst the setting puts each panel on display in a similar way, the tone of each picture differs in colour, background and action scheme. The central panel in the back with Laomedon in front of his tent presents darker figures in front of a lighter background, with an emphasis on the built environment. This is first of all the depiction of a military context charged with notions of *officium* and *virtus* in the way in which the regal figure is surrounded by his entourage and receiving visitors.

The depiction of Leda in the south also highlights a public setting, but of a different kind: the focus is on sacrificial activity and *pietas*; a difference also highlighted by the predominantly light colours of the panel and the contrast in gender of the human actors in the scene who are all female. Opposite, the picture of Venus and her consort puts lighter figures in front of a dark background and, in contrast to the other two frescos, displays them within a vast landscape setting. Thematically, the panel stands out because of its focus on explicit male-female interaction which is lacking from the other two frescos. The cupid with torch elevates the romantic nature of this interaction to the level of another set of Roman virtues: that is, *matrimonium* and *concordia*.

Across all three pictures, the articulation of these values is achieved by selecting specific elements from the underpinning mythological narrative and staging them in complementary environments: the meeting in the military camp emphasises Laomedon's regal status, not his unreliability as a business partner; Leda's offer of asylum in the sanctuary to the swan underscores her piety more than it draws attention to her union with Zeus; Venus and her consort, whoever he may be, celebrate marital union more than female seduction. In their combination, therefore, the three frescos in the Casa del Citarista reflect on different spheres of life emulating a rhetoric similar to the one employed on the commander sarcophagi of the second century AD, for example on the Mantua sarcophagus which shows the general in scenes of marital union and pre- and post-combat to highlight his *pietas, concordia, virtus* and *clementia*.[52]

This focus on the selective display of individual values communicated via the genre of myth differentiates the decoration of Room (20) from the paintings in Villa (6) at Terzigno, notwithstanding the parallels that may exist between the two in terms of thematic choice.[53] The format chosen for the Terzigno display – the continuous frieze, and the juxtaposition of two scenes of epic narrative with the tableau of Venus and her consorts – at once facilitates a narrative sequence between the two epic episodes and presents Venus as the cardinal reference point for the room's decoration. In contrast, the display in the Casa del Citarista lacks such hierarchy; and the framing of each individual panel pushes into the background any cyclical connections that might be drawn between the three topics on display.

At the other end of the scale, we find that the decoration of Room (20) is aligned with the practices of decoration to be found in three-room groups of a later date, those configurations of representative spaces for entertainment situated in the peristyle area of many Pompeian houses.[54] The mythological decorations of these three-room groups transmit content in different shades across the configuration of rooms. The main themes presented in the central room of these configurations, the main entertainment space, are often taken from an epic context or set in a regal or divine setting, with episodes such as the Judgement of Paris, Orestes and Pylades at the court in Tauris and Dionysus with his entourage discovering Ariadne; these depictions are primarily focused on male virtues such as *virtus, dignitas* and *auctoritas*.[55] Meanwhile, the rooms to the sides of the central reception room are usually decorated in a more

---

52 Mantua, Palazzo Ducale c. AD 160. Muth 2004, esp. 269–70. On the predilection in sarcophagus studies for focusing on these so-called cardinal virtues, or: *exempla*, see Gessert 2004, 218–9. For the individual virtues as personified: R. Vollkommer, "Pietas", *LIMC* 8 (1997); T. Hölscher, "Homonoia/Concordia", *LIMC* 5 (1990); T. Ganschow, "Virtus", *LIMC* 8 (1997); T. Hölscher, "Clementia", *LIMC* 3 (1986).
53 Volker Michael Strocka has only recently aligned these two contexts in this sense: Strocka 2005, 95–6.
54 For this configuration of rooms, see Dickmann 1999, 30–3, 321–3.
55 For mythological scenes in three-room groups, see Lorenz 2008, 361–79.

playful manner; in the Fourth Style, scenes of lovers or individual figures such as Narcissus within pleasant outdoor settings are put on display here.

However, there are examples of Fourth-Style decorations in which these two trajectories of content are mixed together in the central room of the architectural configuration in the same way as occurs in the mythological display in Room (20) and the other rooms with mythological decoration that constitute the three-room group off *peristylium* (17) in the Casa del Citarista.[56] In Room (62) in the Casa di Fabius Rufus (VII 16,22) where a ceremonious scene of Phaeton and Aphrodite at the court of Apollo in the central position is combined with more playful and erotic depictions of Poseidon and Dionysus to the sides, each god is depicted with a woman about to straddle him: Amymone on the left, Ariadne on the right.[57]

We can conclude that in decoration such as that found in Room (20) the type of continuous display characteristic of the Villa of Terzigno has been abandoned in favour of a more selective, episodic and abstracted form of visual presentation – a display that prefigures the forms of content transmission at play in the three-room groups of the Fourth Style.

Distributed Narratives: a Historical Perspective

The distributed, highly referential form of "pendant" narrative that first emerges in decorations such as in the Casa del Citarista shaped the transmission of mythological content in the domestic contexts of the early Empire. In the course of the first century AD, comparative viewing was the governing mode for the reception of these displays along with a strong interest in the juxtaposition of extracts from mythological storylines. Remarkably, this drove even decorations that in their form seemingly adhere to the consecutive compositional principles at play in Villa (6) at Terzigno.

The Fourth-Style decorations of the Vespasianic period in Room (h) in the House of Octavius Quartio exemplify this (Fig. 11). The display combines two friezes running on top of each other around the walls of the room.[58] The smaller frieze below shows scenes from the *Iliad*; the larger frieze above displays episodes from the life of Her-

---

56 The state of preservation of these rooms limits our ability for analysis. See Bergmann 2014, 77–80 on the decoration of these rooms, Rooms (19) and (21), differentiation through the overall decorative schema (but not the choice of mythological juxtaposition) and the intricate play of "analogia" more generally that unfolds in the different rooms with mythological decoration across the Casa del Citarista.

57 Leach 1991; Lorenz 2008, 299–302.

58 For the house: Baldassare, Lanzillotta and Salomi 1991, 42–108; Spinazzola 1953, 1026–7; see also Zanker 1979. For the decoration of Room (h): Aurigemma 1953; Brilliant 1984, 60–2; Croisille 1985, 203–7; Coralini 2001a, 165–73; Coralini 2001b; Clarke 2007.

Fig. 11: Pompeii, Casa di Octavius Quartio (II 2,2). Room (h), East-wall. Heracles and Iliad friezes: Heracles and Laomedon & the Funeral Games for Patroclus. Fourth Style. Courtesy of German Archaeological Institute, Rome, neg. nos 57.873 & DAIR 57.874 (F. X. Bartl).

cules, including his involvement in the First Trojan War and his apotheosis.[59] Each frieze has its distinct sequence, which means that the viewer has to follow different directions to make sense of each. However, the two friezes interplay with each other at various points. This is achieved by means of compositional similarities and through the deployment of narrative elements relevant for both friezes.

The central element in this double-platform narration is the opening scene of the *Iliad* frieze in the south-west corner of the room, the first image seen by audiences entering the room. It shows Apollo spreading the plague in the Achaean camp, a moment crucial to the further course of the *Iliad*. Equally, it is not without relevance for the Hercules frieze: Hercules' rescue of Hesione is obviously only necessary because of Laomedon's obliviousness towards Poseidon and Apollo, causing the former to send the sea monster, while the latter inflicts a bout of plague on Troy. The motif of Apollo sending the plague, therefore, serves to connect the two friezes, welding together their storylines around an element of divine punishment, which is visually accentuated here.

The narrative coherence generally associated with a cyclical design is continuously challenged in Room (h): viewing the friezes results in breaking up their individual sections into pendants of the type we also find in the Casa del Citarista. This is both similar and opposed to the situation in the Tomba François and at Terzigno. In the Etruscan tomb decoration *comparatio* through juxtaposition is employed as a narrative technique to provide Etruscan historical events with an epic veneer. This is the function of picture combination in the Casa di Octavius Quartio too, where the life of Hercules gains an epic underpinning through combination with the Iliad scenes. But the design in the Tomba François facilitates no actual narrative slippage between the content in the way in which in the Pompeian house individual events in one frieze

---

59 This argument is based on the interpretation of the room's decoration presented in Lorenz 2013.

gain a narrative function in the other, as is the case with the figure of Apollo who sends the plague.

The decoration of Room (h) in the Casa di Octavius Quartio may appear cyclical in the same way in which the Terzigno decorations operate, not least because both share an interest in the prelude to the First Trojan War with their depiction of Poseidon and Apollo at the court of Laomedon. However, where the Terzigno design is geared towards bringing three different scenes into interaction and shaping a cycle, the juxtaposition in the Casa di Octavius Quartio results in an active deconstruction of the cyclical narrative. The display provides a ready-made deduction and extraction of the content and so shapes truly exegetic viewing on the part of the audience.

This principle of ready-made extraction characterises the Roman practice of mythological display from the early imperial period; it facilitates those forms of narrative slippage and analogy which drive a discourse around values and behavioural ideas that orchestrate the domestic sphere. Interestingly, this is not achieved by means of updating the depiction to include contemporary Roman *realia* or insignia of office, as is the case in Roman historical depictions, but by zooming in on particular aspects of a myth and juxtaposing those with other stories whilst keeping each distinct within its own frame.

This survey has shown that we can locate the beginning of this practice at some point between the decorations of Villa (6) at Terzigno and the Casa del Citarista. This new exegetic design puts a different set of affordances on the part of the viewer: not deduction and extraction, as in contexts such as the Tomba François and Terzigno, but the synthesis of diverse contents and, with it, more complex forms of exegesis. This constitutes a real innovation in visual story-telling. It remains to be examined in what ways this innovation grows gradually out of the narrative traditions of Etruscan and Hellenistic Italy or presents a break with those earlier forms of visual story-telling.

Abbreviation

PPM *Pompei. pitture e mosaici.*

Bibliography

Allroggen-Bedel, A. Megalographien in der römisch-kampanischen Wandmalerei. Überlegungen zu ihrer Interpretation. *Bonner Jahrbücher* 208 (2008), 29–44.

Aurigemma, F. Tre nuovi cicli di figurazione ispirate all'Iliade in Case Della Via dell'Abbondanza in Pompei, in: *Pompei alla luce degli scavi nuovi di Via dell'Abbondanza*, edited by V. Spinazzola (Rome, 1953), 865–1008.

Baldassare, I., T. Lanzillotta, and S. Salomi. (eds.) PPM (Rome, 1990–2000)

Barbet, A. Reconstitution et restitution des peintures de Boscoreale: principes et méthode. Le péristyle de la villa de Publius Fannius Synistor, in: *La villa romaine de Boscoreale et ses fresques*, Vol. 2, edited by A. Barbet and A. Verbanck-Piérard (Arles, 2013), 149–163.

Bellelli, V. Anomalie Pompeiane. *Prospettiva 77* (1995), 2–15.

Bergmann, B. The Roman House as Memory Theater. The House of the Tragic Poet in Pompeii. *The Art Bulletin 76.2* (1994), 225–256.

Bergmann, B. New Perspectives on the Villa of Publius Fannius Synistor at Boscoreale, in: *Roman Frescoes from Boscoreale: The Villa of Publius Fannius Synistor in Reality and Virtual Reality*, edited by Bergmann, B., S. De Caro, J. R. Mertens and R. Meyer (New York, 2010), 11–32.

Bergmann, B. Blick und Betrachter. Das Bildprogramm der Casa del Citarista, in: *Pompeji: Götter, Mythen, Menschen: Eine Ausstellung des Bucerius Kunst Forums mit Werken aus dem Archäologischen Nationalmuseum Neapel. Bucerius Kunst Forum, Hamburg, 27. September 2014 bis 11. Januar 2015 [anlässlich der Ausstellung Pompeji. Götter, Mythen, Menschen]*, edited by V. Sampaolo, A. Hoffmann, B. Bergmann and M. Philipp (Munich, 2014), 72–83.

Bragantini, I. Roman Painting in the Republic and Early Empire, in: *The Cambridge History of Painting in the Classical World*, edited by J. J. Pollitt (Cambridge; New York, 2012), 302–369.

Brendel, O. Archäologische Funde. *Archäologischer Anzeiger* (1935), 519–595.

Brilliant, R. *Visual Narratives: Storytelling in Etruscan and Roman Art* (Ithaca, 1984).

Carafa, P. Recent Work on Early Pompeii, in: *The World of Pompeii*, edited by J. J. Dobbins and P. W. Foss (London; New York, 2007), 63–72.

Cicirelli, C. Terzigno, in: *Città vesuviane: antichità e fortuna. Il suburbio e l'agro di Pompei, Ercolano, Oplontis e Stabiae*, edited by P. G. Guzzo and P. Seu (Rome, 2013), 104–112.

Clarke, J. R. *The Houses of Roman Italy, 100 B.C.–A.D. 250: Ritual, Space, and Decoration* [reprint] (Berkeley, 2007).

Colpo, I. Tutte Le Arianne Di Ovidio. *Eidola 8* (2011), 65–78.

Coralini, A. *Hercules Domesticus: Immagini di Ercole nelle case della regione Vesuviana: I secolo a.C.-79. d.C.* Studi della Soprintendenza Archeologica Di Pompei 4 (Naples, 2001a).

Coralini, A. Una stanza di Ercole a Pompei. La sala del doppio fregio nella casa di D. Octavius Quartio (II 2,2), in: *Iconografia*, edited by I. Colpo, I. Favaretto and F. Ghedini (Rome, 2001b), 331–343.

Croisille, J.-M. La frise d'Heraklès de la maison de Loreius Tiburtinus et la tradition épique, in: *Hommages à Henry Bardon*, edited by M. Renard (Brussels, 1985), 89–99.

Croisille, J.-M. *La peinture romaine* (Paris, 2005).

De Caro, S. The First Sanctuaries, in: *The World of Pompeii*, edited by J. J. Dobbins, P. J. Foss (London; New York, 2007), 73–81.

Dickmann, J.-A. *Domus frequentata: Anspruchsvolles Wohnen im pompejanischen Stadthaus*, vol. 1. Studien zur antiken Stadt 4 (Munich, 1999).

Elia, O. *Le pitture della Casa del Citarista*. Pompei, fasc I. Monumenti della pittura antica scoperti in Italia 3 (Rome, 1937).

Esposito, D. Filosseno, il Ciclope e Sesto Pompeo. Programmi figurativi e 'propaganda' politica nelle domus dell'aristocrazia pompeiana della tarda età repubblicana. *Mitteilungen des Deutschen Archäologischen Instituts, Abteilung Rom 123* (2008), 51–99.

Fittschen, K. Zur Herkunft und Entstehung des Zweiten Stils – Probleme und Argumente, in: *Hellenismus in Mittelitalien: Kolloquium in Göttingen vom 5. bis 9. Juni 1974*, edited by P. Zanker. Abhandlungen der Akademie der Wissenschaften in Göttingen, Philologisch-Historische Klasse. 3rd series, no. 97 (Göttingen, 1976).

Gerhard, E. *Etruskische Spiegel*. Vol. 4 (Berlin, 1867).

Gessert, G. Myth as Consolatio: Medea on Roman sarcophagi. *Greece & Rome 51* (2004), 217–249.

Ghedini, F. Trasmissione delle iconografie. *Supplementum* 5. *Enciclopedia dell'arte antica* 2 (Rome, 1997), 823–837. http://www.treccani.it/enciclopedia/trasmissione-delle-iconografie_(Enciclopedia-dell'-Arte-Antica)/.

Helbig, W. *Wandgemälde der vom Vesuv verschütteten Städte Campaniens* (Leipzig, 1868).

Hodske, J. *Mythologische Bildthemen in den Häusern Pompejis: Die Bedeutung der zentralen Mythenbilder für die Bewohner Pompejis*. Stendaler Winckelmann-Forschungen, Vol. 6 (Ruhpolding, 2007).

Holliday, P. J. Narrative Structures in the François Tomb, in: *Narrative and Event in Ancient Art*, edited by P. J. Holliday (Cambridge, 1993), 175–197.

Hölscher, T. Römische nobiles und hellenistische Herrscher, in: *Akten des XIII. Internationalen Kongresses für Klassische Archäologie, Berlin 1988*, edited by Deutsches Archäologisches Institut (Mainz, 1990), 73–84.

Knox, P. E. Ovidian Myths on Pompeian Walls, in: *The Handbook to the Reception of Ovid*, edited by J. F. Miller and C. E. Newlands (Chichester, 2014), 36–54.

La Torre, G. F. and M. Torelli (eds.) *Pittura ellenistica in Italia e in Sicilia: linguaggi e tradizioni. Atti del convegno di studi (Messina, 24–25 settembre 2009)*. Archaeologica 163 (Rome, 2011).

Leach, E. W. The Iconography of the Black Salone in the Casa di Fabio Rufo. *Kölner Jahrbücher für Vor- und Frühgeschichte* 24 (1991), 105–112.

Lehmann, P. *Roman Wall Paintings from Boscoreale in the Metropolitan Museum* (Cambridge, MA 1953).

Ling, R. *Roman Painting* (Cambridge; New York 1991).

Looy, H. van and K. Demoen. Le Temple en l'honneur de la reine Apollonis à Cyzique et l'énigme des Stylopinakia. *Epigraphica Anatolica* 8 (1986), 133–144.

Lorenz, K. *Bilder machen Räume: Mythenbilder in pompeianischen Häusern*. Image & Context, v. 5 (Berlin; New York, 2008).

Lorenz, K. Split Screen Visions: Heracles on top of Troy in a Pompeian house, in: *Epic Visions: Visuality in Greek and Latin Epic and its Reception*, edited by H. Lovatt and C. Vout (Cambridge; New York, 2013), 218–247.

Lorenz, K. Rhetoric on the Wall? The House of Menander and Its Decorative Structure, in: *Art and Rhetoric in Roman Culture*, edited by J. Elsner and M. Meyer (New York, 2014), 183–210.

Michaelis, A. *Ancient Marbles in Great Britain* (Cambridge, 1882).

Moormann, E. M. Der römische Freskenzyklus mit grossen Figuren in der Villa 6 in Terzigno, in: *Otium: Festschrift für Volker Michael Strocka*, edited by T. Ganschow (Remshalden, 2005), 257–266.

Moormann, E. M. Did Roman Republican Mural Paintings Convey Political Messages? The megalography of Terzigno and other second style paintings, in: *La villa romaine de Boscoreale et ses fresques*, edited by A. Barbet and A. Verbanck-Piérard (Arles, 2013), 227–235.

Müller, F. G. J. M. *The Wall Paintings from the Oecus of the Villa of Publius Fannius Synistor in Boscoreale*. Iconological Studies in Roman Art 2 (Amsterdam, 1994).

Muth, S. Drei statt vier. Zur Deutung der Feldherrnsarkophage. *Archäologischer Anzeiger* (2004), 263–274.

O'Sullivan, T. M. *Walking in Roman Culture* (Cambridge; New York, 2011).

Peters, W. J. Th. (ed.) *La Casa di Marcus Lucretius Fronto a Pompei e le sue pitture*. Scrinium 5 (Amsterdam, 1993).

Provenzale, V. *Echi di propaganda imperiale in scene di coppia a Pompei: Enea e Didone, Marte e Venere, Perseo e Andromeda*. Antenor Quaderni 10 (Rome, 2008).

Rathje, A. Self-Representation and Identity-Creation by an Etruscan Family: the use of the past in the François Tomb at Vulci, in: *Attitudes Towards the Past in Antiquity. Creating Identities: Proceedings of an International Conference Held at Stockholm University, 15–17 May 2009*, edited by B. Alroth and C. Scheffer. Stockholm Studies in Classical Archaeology 14 (Stockholm, 2014), 55–65.

Rouveret, A. Etruscan and Italic Tomb Painting, c. 400–200 B.C., in: *The Cambridge History of Painting in the Classical World*, edited by J. J. Pollitt (Cambridge; New York, 2012), 238–287.

Sampaolo, V. In margine alle pitture del salone 13 della Villa di Terzigno, in: *Storie da un'eruzione: in margine alla mostra. Atti della tavola rotonda, Napoli, 12 Giugno 2003*, edited by P. G. Guzzo (Pompeii, 2005), 113–125.

Schefold, K. *Pompejanische Malerei. Sinn und Ideengeschichte* (Basel, 1952).

Schmidt-Colinet, A. 'Musterbücher' statt 'Meisterforschung'. Zum Verständnis antiker Werkstattstrukturen und Produktionsprozesse; review article of 'Antike Musterblätter. Wirkkartons aus dem spätantiken und frühbyzantinischen Ägypten.' *Journal of Roman Archaeology* 22 (2009), 787–792.

Simon, E. Ungedeutete Wandbilder der Casa del Citarista zu Pompeji, in: *Römische Kunst. Ausgewählte Schriften* II (Mainz, 1998a), 132–140.

Simon, E. Vergil und die Bildkunst, in: *Römische Kunst. Ausgewählte Schriften* II (Mainz, 1998b), 18–28.

Smith, R. R. R. Spear-won Land at Boscoreale: on the royal paintings of a Roman villa. *Journal of Roman Archaeology* 7 (1994), 100–128.

Spinazzola, V. *Pompei alla luce degli scavi nuovi di Via dell'Abbondanza* (Rome, 1953).

Strocka, V. M. Mars und Venus in Bildprogrammen pompejanischer Häuser, in: *I temi figurativi nella pittura parietale antica: IV sec. a.C.-IV sec. d.C.. Atti del VI convegno internazionale sulla pittura parietale antica*, edited by D. Scagliarini Corlàita. Studi e scavi 5 (Imola, 1997), 129–143.

Strocka, V. M. Troja – Karthago – Rom: Ein vorvergilisches Bildprogramm in Terzigno bei Pompeji. *Mitteilungen des Deutschen Archäologischen Instituts, Abteilung Rom* 112 (2005), 79–120.

Stupperich, R. Zu den Stylopinakia am Tempel der Apollonis in Kyzikos, in: *Mysische Studien*, edited by E. Schwertheim (Bonn, 1990), 101–109.

Thompson, M. L. *Programmatic Painting in Pompeii. The Meaningful Combination of Mythological Pictures in Room Decoration* (New York, 1960).

Torelli, M. The Frescoes of the Great Hall of the Villa at Boscoreale: iconography and politics, in: *Myth, History and Culture in Republican Rome: Studies in Honour of T. P. Wiseman*, edited by D. Braund and T. P. Wiseman (Exeter, 2003), 217–256.

Trendelenburg, A. Die Gegenstücke in der campanischen Wandmalerei. *Archäologische Zeitung* 34 (1876), 1–8, 79–83.

Vermeule, C. C. Notes on a New Edition of Michaelis: ancient marbles in Great Britain. *American Journal of Archaeology* 59:2 (1955), 129–150.

Zanker, P. (ed.) *Hellenismus in Mittelitalien: Kolloquium in Göttingen vom 5. bis 9. Juni 1974*. Abhandlungen der Akademie der Wissenschaften in Göttingen, Philologisch-Historische Klasse. 3rd series, no. 97 (Göttingen, 1976).

Zanker, P. Die Villa als Vorbild des späten pompejanischen Wohngeschmacks. *Jahrbuch des Deutschen Archäologischen Instituts* 94 (1979), 460–523.

Zanker, P. Zur Veränderung mythologischer Bildthemen auf den kaiserzeitlichen Sarkophagen aus der Stadt Rom, in: *Lebenswelten: Bilder und Räume in der römischen Stadt der Kaiserzeit. Symposium am 24. und 25. Januar 2002 zum Abschluß des von der Gerda Henkel Stiftung geförderten Forschungsprogramms "Stadtkultur in der römischen Kaiserzeit,"* edited by R. Neudecker and P. Zanker. Palilia 16 (Wiesbaden, 2005), 243–252.

Barbara E. Borg
No One is Immortal

From Exemplum Mortalitatis to Exemplum Virtutis

To Klaus Fittschen for his 80th birthday

Mythical images started to appear on Roman sarcophagi around the turn of the first and second centuries AD, and decorated entire sarcophagus fronts in increasing numbers from the Hadrianic period onwards before their production ceased again almost completely around the middle of the third century.[1] Yet admiration for these caskets has never fully subsided, and many items were re-used for burial, as fountain basins, or as display pieces through the centuries and into the modern age.[2] From the later nineteenth century onwards, they have also attracted the interest of scholars, who explored an array of different questions.[3] Among these, the relationship between Greek and Roman elements dominated the debate for a considerable time. After all, the stories depicted on the vast majority of mythical sarcophagi are Greek in origin, and many of the iconographic patterns employed to depict these narratives also derive from Greek models.

In this paper, I would like to offer some general reflections on the Romans' use of Greek myths in the funerary sphere, and, more specifically, on sarcophagi of the second century AD.[4] In the first part of this paper, I discuss a number of conceptual and methodological concerns around the way Greek myths worked and were actualised in a Roman (funerary) environment. In the second part, I want to show the implications of these general considerations for the interpretation of Roman sarcophagi with

---

1 There is a final revival in the Tetrarchic period, but from the early fourth century onwards, no further caskets with traditional myths were produced. On the cessation of mythical images see Borg 2013, 162–3, 177–8.

2 Zanker and Ewald 2012, 1–17.

3 For an overview of the scholarly debates see Turcan 1978; Koch and Sichtermann 1982, 6–20; Zanker and Ewald 2012, 18–21; Bielfeldt 2005, 16–25; Russenberger 2015, 3–9; Elsner and Hung 2012, esp. 1–12; Newby 2016, 273–4, with ample recent bibliography in nn. 1–2.

4 Sarcophagi from the third century have received much attention over the years, and I have presented my own thoughts in Borg 2013, 161–211, and Borg 2014; see also Newby 2011b.

Note: This paper was submitted in September 2015, before Zahra Newby and Katharina Lorenz' important books on Greek myths in Roman art and culture (Newby 2016; Lorenz 2016) and a few other publications had appeared or become available to me. I have therefore only been able to add references to these works in the footnotes.

https://doi.org/10.1515/9783110421453-009

narrative mythological images. I would like to stress from the outset, however, that I am neither claiming nor attempting to discuss the chosen examples exhaustively. This paper is intended to propose some rather general lines of thought, along which these images are likely to have been interpreted by their patrons, which, if found convincing, may then be fleshed out elsewhere.

Methodological Considerations

When scholarship on Roman sarcophagi started in the nineteenth century, the fact that the myths depicted on the caskets were Greek constituted their main attraction. Research was not really interested in the sarcophagi and their Roman patrons, but rather aimed at reconstructing either lost Greek artworks on which the reliefs were allegedly modelled, or Greek literature, especially lost tragedies, for which the same dependency was assumed. This approach has very few followers today, after the focus shifted from art-historical and literary concerns to enquiries around the meaning that these images held for those who produced and viewed them.[5] The Greekness of the myths was still very present in earlier studies, but it had moved from being the main research interest to being the background against which an increasing "Romanisation" of the stories was studied. In 1992, Peter Blome published an influential article that, at the time, was not necessarily methodologically revolutionary, but spelled out the way Greek myths were seen to be adapted to their new Roman environment.[6] Initially, these myths contained few, if any, genuinely Roman elements, and followed known Greek narratives relatively closely, thus maintaining, so he claimed, their "inherent symbolism" (*inhärente Eigensymbolik*). Later on the stories were increasingly manipulated, and Roman elements, such as portraits or certain props, added to them. He conceded that the early images could be related to the individual bereavement by way of analogy,[7] although he refused to take speculations very far. The later images with their "more intensive *interpretatio Romana*", however, strongly focused on Roman themes such as the praise of virtues and deification of the deceased.[8] Independently of whether or not we agree with his readings of individual sarcophagi, there are valid observations in this paper. That the second-century myths convey their message by analogy will be explained further below, and scholars today agree that the

---

5 Cumont 1942, who proposed eschatological interpretations for the sarcophagi, and the ensuing review by Nock 1946, were essential for the shift in interest, although it took several more decades until the interpretation of sarcophagi as Roman objects became a majority interest. Pioneering studies in this regard are Fittschen 1970, Fittschen 1975, Blome 1978.

6 Blome 1992.

7 Here following Turcan 1978, 1729–33.

8 Blome 1992, 1071–2.

third century saw an increasing focus on the praise of virtues. But with regard to the earlier sarcophagi, he still succumbed to the fundamental misunderstanding, shared also by some prominent predecessors and contemporaries, that there once was an autonomous, ultimately enigmatic Greek myth, onto which an *interpretatio Romana* was gradually imposed, a process which, in the end, destroyed the myth.[9]

Others saw more clearly that an autonomous (Greek) myth never existed, and that the traditional stories we call myths used to be manipulated and adapted from the very beginning, always in relation to the special interest of an individual or group, and with changing focus over time.[10] This meant that a Roman interpretation had to be found for the early mythical sarcophagi as well, a task that was hampered by the absence of any written sources that comment on sarcophagi, or on the meaning of the specific myths depicted on them. Many scholars thus looked for guidance to those images that contained the most Roman elements such as portrait heads, with which some gods and heroes were fitted out, and attributes and iconographies known from non-mythological Roman images. These often pointed, as Blome had already observed, to the use of myths for praise of the deceased, with portrait identifications suggesting that the deceased claimed similar character features for themselves as the heroes or divinities possessed.[11] These images, which had generally been manufactured later in the history of sarcophagus production, were now considered to convey only more clearly a meaning – the *interpretatio Romana* – that the myths had possessed all along in the Roman funerary realm, namely to provide *exempla virtutis* for the deceased.[12] While some stories resisted the attempts of even the most persistent hunters for Roman virtues, in the end, not only figures such as Hercules (Fig. 1), Hippolytus (Fig. 2), and Meleager (Fig. 3), who are depicted carrying out their heroic deeds, were identified as *exempla virtutis*, but also some less obvious characters and their actions:[13] Adonis, who is shown fatally wounded by the boar and is dying in the arms of Aphrodite

---

9 Esp. Sichtermann 1966, 80–7; still in 1992, he claimed that the "real Greek myth", which he identified on some sarcophagi, is ultimately impossible to interpret ("*letztlich unausdeutbar*"): Sichtermann 1992a, 53. Similar ideas guided the study of mosaics: see e.g. Raeck 1992, who concluded: "Der Mythos, der zuvor unveräußerliches und unveränderbares Gemeingut war, wird jetzt [i.e. in late antiquity] zur individuellen Aneignung und Nutzung freigegeben." (ibid. 159). For a critique of his approach see Muth 1998, 284–8 and passim.

10 For scholars focussing on images cf. e.g. Hölscher 1993; Koortbojian 1995, 3; Muth 1998, 287–8; Zanker 1999, 132, 134; Junker 2012, 30–63; Russenberger 2015, 8–9.

11 Ditto already Wrede 1981, yet with eschatological interpretation added on.

12 Zanker 1999 was particularly influential, concluding that not only on the Tetrarchic sarcophagus, from which he took his departure, both Hippolytus and Phaedra were meant as role models for the deceased, but that also on second-century sarcophagi "Phädra artikuliert demnach nicht nur Trauer und Verzweiflung, sondern umschreibt gleichzeitig in poetischer Weise ein weibliches Rollenideal": ibid. 138 and passim; more recently e.g. Birk 2013, 14, and Linant De Bellefonds 2013. There is a certain irony in this approach, given that it originally started from the premise that myths change over time according to needs; for a critique see Newby 2011b; Borg 2013, 164–78; Borg 2014.

13 For a summary see Zanker and Ewald 2012, esp. 179–243.

Fig. 1: Sarcophagus showing the labours of Hercules. Mantua, Palazzo Ducale. Photo: D-DAI-ROM-62.141.

Fig. 2: Hippolytus sarcophagus. Uffizi, Florence. 3593. Photo: G. Singer, neg. D-DAI-ROM-72.142.

Fig. 3: Meleager-hunt sarcophagus. Rome, Palazzo Doria Pamphilj. Photo: G. Singer, neg. D-DAI-ROM-71.1474.

(Fig. 6);[14] Phaeton falling from the sky;[15] Achilles dragging the body of Hector around the walls of Troy or the tomb of Patroclus;[16] Phaedra, who had caused her beloved stepson's death (Fig. 2),[17] and even Orestes, who slaughtered his mother and stepfather in revenge for their killing of his father,[18] and Medea, who killed Creusa and her own two children.[19]

With this line of interpretation, the relationship between Greek and Roman was no longer essential to the understanding of these myths, and so in recent years, this relationship has mostly been discussed in different terms, namely how exactly the mythical narratives relate to the real-life situation on which they are said to bear.

Visual Rhetoric

From the 1990s, sarcophagus decoration was increasingly understood as a visual rhetoric, and compared to speeches delivered at funerals: while these orations praised and lamented the deceased in words, the mythological images did the same in visual form.[20] The vocabulary often used to describe the role of myth – such as symbol, metaphor, allegory, etc. – was based on rhetorical technical terms, though mostly used in a casual, fuzzy way. The main point was often to raise awareness that images do indeed talk – albeit in a language of their own.[21] Yet two concepts have been theorised to some extent, those of allegory and analogy.

---

14 Documentation in: Koch and Sichtermann 1982, 131–3; Grassinger 1999, 70–90, 211–21 cat. 43–67; for interpretations including the *virtus* aspect: Koortbojian 1995, 23–62, esp. 32, 34–5, 38; Zanker and Ewald 2012, 207–12. For further discussion see below.
15 Robert 1919, 332–42, 344–9; Koch and Sichtermann 1982, 180–3; Zanker and Ewald 2012, 372–4. Critical of Phaeton as *virtus* paradigm now Russenberger 2015, 200; see also below for literary references to Phaeton.
16 Giuliani 1989, esp. 37; Grassinger 1999, 50–7 with cat. 27, 29–33; ambivalent about this particular scene: Zanker and Ewald 2012, 287–91.
17 See n. 12.
18 Bielfeldt 2005, esp. 285–8. Contra: Newby 2011a, 307–8; Russenberger 2015, 195–7.
19 Koortbojian 1996, 435–6, but so far nobody seems to have followed him; cf. the explicit rejection in Gessert 2004, 229–30, although I find her own interpretation as negative *exemplum* (also suggested by Galinier 2013, 83–6, for this and a few other myths) equally unconvincing. Koortbojian 1995, 8–9, is more balanced in suggesting that Medea, like Phaedra, exemplifies the human condition that is "inextricably bound to the omnipotence of Fate." For a different attempt at finding virtues in Creusa/ Medea sarcophagi see Junker 2006, 180–1.
20 Giuliani 1989; Müller 1994; Koortbojian 1995; Zanker 2002; Zanker 2003; Zanker and Ewald 2012, 103–5; Elsner 2014; Newby 2014; Newby 2016, 273–319; for the rhetorical character of Christian sarcophagi see Elsner and Huskinson 2011.
21 But see Newby 2014, for a close comparison between Statius' rhetorical strategies and sarcophagi, who identifies several similarities that have so far been overlooked, and now Newby 2016, 273–319, with an approach similar to my own but different conclusions. For Statius as a guide to understanding

Allegory

In an influential paper, Luca Giuliani (adopting Quintilian's definition at *Inst.* 8.6.47–8) proposed the idea that mythical sarcophagus images be considered in terms of an *allegoria apertis permixta* that mixes factual, straightforward elements with allegorical ones.[22] The traditional mythical elements would constitute the allegory, while contemporary Roman elements such as the typically Roman *lectus* on which the Greek hero is lying in state, are the non-allegorical elements of the "mix". The concept has recently been seized by Katharina Lorenz in a programmatic article.[23] Yet, as Ruth Bielfeldt had already observed, in many cases where the term is used, including Giuliani's and Lorenz's, there is little if anything that calls for an allegorical interpretation.[24] Speaking allegorically means "saying something differently" or "saying something else" (i.e. than what is really meant), thus separating the level of what is *apparently* said from the (hidden) *actual* message.[25] In Quintilian's example (which he took from Cicero), the *tempestates et procellas* (tempests and storms) that Milo had to weather refer to the turmoil in public assemblies; the description of a weather condition "really" meant the heated debates and confrontations the politician had to face in these meetings. Such instances of allegorical expression are, however, rare on Roman sarcophagi. Achilles mourning Patroclus is not an allegory for the Roman mourning over a dead friend or relative, but another instance of a particular situation, an analogy, here used as exemplum,[26] a term first proposed as a main principle of how sarcophagus images work by Robert Turcan and later Frank Müller.[27]

---

sarcophagi see also Kathleen M. Coleman's contribution to the forthcoming Sarkophag-Studien vol. 6 (ed. C. Hallett), which she kindly shared with me.

22 Giuliani 1989, 38–9.

23 Lorenz 2011, where her "Image in Distress" is "torn between providing an allegorical layer of mythical reflection and documenting real-life situations" (p. 313). Explicit approval also by Ewald 1999, 78–9.

24 Bielfeldt 2005, 377–8 with n. 810.

25 For a full discussion of the term see Borg 2002, 13–35, 41–8, 83 n. 237, with bibliography.

26 On analogy see Lloyd 1966, esp. 172–420; Koortbojian 1995, 3–9. To be sure, myths were allegorised in antiquity, but hardly any of the readings of sarcophagus myths in more recent scholarship fulfils the required criteria (although e.g. Cumont's did). For the difference and visual examples see Borg 2002, for literary examples the index of Dowden and Livingstone 2011, and esp. chs. 10, 15, and 17. Admittedly, as allegories as well as exempla are based on analogies, the distinction between exemplum and allegory is not always entirely clear-cut. On sarcophagi, one might argue that the image of rape could be both an allegory of death or a paradigm, depending on the protagonists. Persephone is raped by Hades and taken to the underworld; as he is essentially Death himself, little translation is needed for an understanding of the "real" significance of the story. In contrast, the rape of the Leucippidae may be seen as allegory since, according to the story, they lived on with the Dioscuri, who were no divinities of the underworld either.

27 Turcan 1978, 1729–33; Müller 1994, 87–100, 144–5; Gessert 2004; now Newby 2014; Newby 2016, 273–319; Koortbojian 1995, 3–9, 34–7, goes in a similar direction but mainly speaks of analogy. Fittschen

Exemplum

Exempla or *paradeigmata*, including mythical exempla, were a key element of any ancient speech ever since Homer, ranging from the formal public oration to the more casual conversation or written communication. They are often part of an exhortation, suggesting that one should either emulate the individuals and actions of the exemplum, or else avoid such emulation.[28] But they can also be used more generally as illustration, and to confirm general principles, statements, and inferences, without necessarily implying moral judgement or inviting imitation.[29] In all cases, they are meant to support and reinforce the statement or argument by inviting conclusions from analogy. They draw their persuasive power from the fact that the characters or situations referred to are in some way superior to those of the humble present, thus suggesting that these conclusions, statements, etc. are natural, self-explanatory, and quite simply true (cf. Quintilian, *Inst.* 5.11). Even where they serve merely as rhetorical embellishment, they heighten the tone through their reference to a superhuman sphere of beings, to a time when the gods still took an interest and intervened in human life, and to stories ennobled by antiquity or the name of their narrators.[30]

Highly irritating to a modern audience is the fact that the stories chosen as *paradeigmata* can be manipulated, often substantially so, in order to fit a given situation, without challenging the truth status of the story or compromising the exemplum's impact. This practice goes back at least to the *Iliad*. In order to convince Priam, who had come to ransom his son's body, to join him for a meal, Achilles tells the story of Niobe who allegedly enjoyed eating again after having lost not one but "many" children (Hom. *Il.* 24.599–620). The origins of the story are not exactly known, but at least two details are highly suspicious of having been Achilles' (or Homer's) invention:[31] Firstly, the Niobids are said to have lain in their blood for nine days since Zeus had turned "the people" into stone, preventing them from burying the children. Not only is this an awkward and otherwise unknown element of the story, in which normally Niobe is turned into stone, but there is now a closer parallel with Hector, who had been denied burial for the same number of days, and equally lay in his blood. Secondly, that Niobe started eating again is also unknown from other accounts, but is at the heart of

---

1992 argued already along similar lines but did not reflect on the rhetorical use of analogy or exemplum.

28 Cf. Willcock 1964; Nagy 1992. The literature on exempla is vast. On exempla in funerary contexts see esp. Kassel 1958; Griessmair 1966, 85–91; Müller 1994, 91–8; Newby 2014; Newby 2016, 273–319, and 320–47 on Roman exemplarity more generally.

29 For Homer's use of myth as *paradeigma* see Willcock 1964; Létoublon 2011, esp. 40; Livingstone 2011, 126–9.

30 For the general idea see Coleman 1999, on Statius.

31 For a full discussion of this passage see Willcock 1964, 141–2; Schmitz 2001.

Achilles' exhortation. It is thus highly likely that these two details had been invented on the spot to fit the purpose of Achilles' speech.

Similar manipulations have been observed for the even more extended exemplum of Meleager that is used by Nestor to convince Achilles to return to battle (Hom. *Il.* 9.524–605):[32] While the well-known background to the war between the Curetes and the Aetolians is summarised only briefly, and the reason for his mother's curse not mentioned at all, the detailed parts of the narrative are those matching the present situation: the hero's withdrawal from battle in anger, prolonged attempts to make him return, and the offering of gifts. None of these details are ever mentioned elsewhere, where Althea's anger over Meleager's killing of her brothers leads immediately to the hero's death.[33]

Arguably, serving as exempla was one of the main, if not *the* main purpose(s) of myths, which also prevented them from developing any canonical forms.[34] It is therefore misleading to try and set *the* Greek myth and its significance or meaning – or their absence – off against a single *interpretatio Romana*,[35] or against a specifically Roman way of treating myths that is characterised by its manipulation of Greek myth.[36] The traditional stories we call myth were constantly in flux ever since they were first created, and until the present day, with parts of them dismissed or ignored, altered, or added, to make them fit the occasion and the message they were meant to illustrate or support. Homer's account of the events before Troy may therefore be better literature than some later texts, but in terms of content it is not intrinsically "better" or more "correct" than those of, say, Statius' *Achilleïs*, the accounts of Dares and Dictys, Benoît de Sainte-Maure's *Roman de Troie*, or indeed Wolfgang Petersen's film *Troy*. For that reason, both individual heroes or mythical figures and their actions could also be evaluated very differently at different times and depending on different contexts. Even remaining in the ancient world, Achilles could be the greatest of heroes, but also *Achill das Vieh* (Achilles the monster) or a ludicrous love-stricken figure,[37] the sack of Troy the greatest victory or a sacrilege.[38] The very notion of *interpretatio Romana* is there-

---

32 Willcock 1964, 147–53.

33 Willcock 1977, for Homeric inventions in general; cf. Nagy 1992, for some valid qualifications, although in insisting that there were no on-the-spot inventions but just choice from pre-existing variants he fails to explain why myths did change over time, and is unconvincing in our examples.

34 Cf. Walter Burkert's conclusions adopted by Nagy 1992, 313, that "Myth is *applied* narrative." Livingstone 2011. For summaries of attitudes to and uses of myths see e.g. Dowden and Livingstone 2011; Junker 2012.

35 As the scholars cited nn. 8 and 9 did.

36 This idea still implicit in e.g. Bielfeldt 2005, 21–22: "Auch diese frühe Sarkophagkunst ist demnach bereits bestimmt von einem singulären Spannungsverhältnis zwischen mythologischem Sinn und seiner Realisierung durch eine *interpretatio romana*."

37 Hoff 2005, borrowing his title from Christa Wolf's characterisation of the hero; Fantuzzi 2012, 267–79, and passim.

38 Ferrari 2000.

fore highly problematic as it suggests a unity of interpretation by "the Romans" or "in the Roman period" that never existed.

Modes of Reading

Bearing this in mind has obvious implications for our attempts at understanding the significance of a mythical story, here on Roman sarcophagi. Yet, as Zahra Newby has succinctly observed, understanding that the myths worked as exempla and thus by analogy does not in itself help with identifying the meaning(s) of an individual image.[39] While some figures and events may have been more ambiguous than others, we cannot take for granted the meaning and evaluation of a hero in every context he appears in. So far, the inclusiveness of most modern scholars with regard to the range of possible readings is adequate and welcome. The interpretation of myths on Roman sarcophagi as illustrations of a Roman value system, often reduced to the "cardinal" virtues of *virtus*, *pietas*, and *concordia*,[40] has frequently given way to a more open-minded approach that allows for a range of readings depending on the physical and social context of a sarcophagus and the varied dispositions of its viewers. Zanker and Ewald's *Living with Myth* is a masterpiece in demonstrating the wide range of potential readings a mythical image could induce.[41]

However, there is a danger of going to the other extreme and adopting an anything goes approach. To be sure, strictly speaking, anything *does* go – after all, the human mind can take strange directions, and our very own scholarly interpretations sometimes testify to the fact. But I would still hold that there are more and less *likely* ancient readings.[42] It is not inherently wrong to speculate about any individual's potential interpretation, but from a socio-historical and anthropological point of view general trends may be more instructive. Such likely readings are determined by both the visual clues provided by the iconography, the "rhetoric" of the images, and by what the literary theorist Hans Robert Jauss termed the *Erfahrungshorizont* or "horizon of experience", the accumulation of experiences one has gathered in the past.

---

39 Newby 2011a, 303.
40 Rodenwaldt 1935, who identified the virtues of Augustus' *clipeus virtutis* as the subject of a range of second- and early third-century commanders' sarcophagi, has been highly influential here. Perhaps the most dogmatic form of reading myths in this way is found in Grassinger 1994, and elsewhere, but see also Gessert 2004, who believes that "(c)ertainly some conceptual contact was understood between the deceased and the figure of Medea" (p. 231), Bielfeldt 2005, on Orestes, or Lorenz 2016, 71–88 on Althaea and Meleager.
41 Zanker and Ewald 2012; see also Ewald 2012, esp. 53–4, for a critique of the "'reading for virtue' model" of interpretation, but see Newby 2016, 281–97, and Lorenz 2016, 71–88, for recent revivals of the "cardinal virtues paradigm".
42 Ditto Birk 2013, 14.

This "horizon" or, as I would prefer, background of experience in turn generates expectations regarding the assessment of what one might encounter in any given text or image, with which one is newly confronted (what he termed *Erwartungshorizont* or "horizon of expectation").[43] These ideas are, of course, not fundamentally new. They summarise what cognitive psychologists have long established as the way we come to grips with, and make sense of the world surrounding us. There will also be few scholars nowadays who would not embrace them, although most would use a different terminology. They will acknowledge that the context in which an image is viewed impacts on its reading, and that familiarity with specific iconographic formulae will guide a viewer in his or her interpretation.[44] What I like about Jauss' terminology is its open and – in theory – all-encompassing concept of past experience, which invites reflection on the range of contexts that may have been relevant in any given case, while the term "expectation" avoids any too schematic conclusions of how this past experience may impact reaction to a new situation or image.

Both these factors, the visual rhetoric and the horizon of experience and expectation are equally important, although it is not always easy to reconcile them. To take the by now largely abandoned or at least marginalised eschatological interpretation of Roman sarcophagi as an example,[45] it has been argued that, according to the story as we know it from literary texts, Persephone was eventually permitted to return to the upper world for half of the year, and so the choice of the story for sarcophagi would reflect the patron's hope for an afterlife (Fig. 4). A similar case has been made for Adonis sarcophagi (Fig. 6). As these stories were very well known, one may argue that they formed part of the background of experience and thus influenced the reading of the sarcophagus imagery. But at closer inspection this argument is problematic. On the one hand, the background of experience is shaped at least equally if not more urgently by texts from the same context as the sarcophagi such as the consolatory

---

43 First explained in his famous inaugural lecture in 1967; Jauss and Benzinger 1970; Jauss 1982, 3–45; cf. Holub 1984, 53–82, esp. 58–63. Jauss has been criticised for limiting his *Erfahrungs-* and *Erwartungshorizont* – against his own aspiration – to the literary and aesthetic qualities of texts, and for a range of other failures. I am here using his terms and explanation more as inspiration than as ready-made model.

44 Programmatically so already Müller 1994, 86–100; Koortbojian 1995, 9–18 and *passim*; Russenberger 2015, 10–11 and passim; focussing on the context of the tomb: Zanker 2000; for a summary see e.g. Junker 2012, 140–58; the contextual paradigm explored in Lorenz 2016, *passim*.

45 For the debate see Harkness 1899; Cumont 1942; Nock 1946. More recent summaries of the debate include Esteve-Forriol 1962, passim, esp. 147–8; Brandenburg 1967, 242–4; Turcan 1978; Wrede 1981; Koch and Sichtermann 1982, 583–617; Müller 1994, 98–106; Pekáry 1994; Zanker and Ewald 2012, 20–1, and elsewhere; Hope 2007, 211–47; Hope 2009, 97–120. Revivals of Cumont's or Cumont-style interpretations such as Mucznik 1999; Turcan 1999; Balty 2013 (on which see Russenberger 2015, 519 n. 14), and Balty and Balty 2015 (on which see Elsner 2016) are still exceptions, but it is noticeable that many recent studies consider the interpretation of some myths in eschatological terms as one possibility (e.g. Platt 2011, 335–93; Birk 2013).

literature and epitaphs. In these, Persephone's return is conspicuously absent, and the story is used consistently to lament the merciless, irreversible fate of death.[46] On the other hand, the eschatological interpretation privileges the (or one) background of experience while ignoring the images themselves. Not only is Persephone almost invariably desperately struggling to avoid her fate, but among a total of some 90 sarcophagi there is not a single one that depicts her return from Hades although it would have been easy to include the scene had the intended message been about return to life. To be sure, this does not exclude the possibility that an individual who nurtured some vague hopes for an afterlife may have drawn comfort from the thought that Persephone returned to the upper world for part of the year. But given the general scepticism of the Romans in this regard, the rhetorical common place of the rape by Hades as a metaphor for death, often lamented as cruel fate, and the lack of any visual hint at the heroine's return, it is probably safe to assume that such a reading was neither intended by those who designed the images, nor a typical and majority one.[47]

Fig. 4: Persephone sarcophagus. Florence, Uffizi. Photo: G. Singer, neg. D-DAI-ROM-72.120.

For the reconstruction of any likely ancient reading of mythological sarcophagi the horizon of experience and expectation must include, and, in cases of conflict give preference to, similar contexts as the ones in which the images were viewed;[48] and secondly, the creativity of the artists to find images that actually express the proposed message well, should not be underestimated: we should take the images and their own rhetoric seriously and not dismiss them without very good reason.

---

46 Cf. Borg 2016, 267–8; for epitaphs using this metaphor see e.g. Brelich 1937, 20–1; Lattimore 1942, 147–9.

47 Accordingly, Newby places the Persephone sarcophagi in her category of caskets thematising "death and destruction": Newby 2011a, 305–6. But I would like to draw a distinction between this subject and the Niobids or Creusa, for instance, since the rape by a god holds some consolation: Borg 2016, 279–80.

48 Thus also the argument of Cumont's critics here n. 45; see also Zanker 2000. While few would disagree today (but see Mucznik 1999, who seems to be unaware of all of this), it is remarkable how often the principle is ignored in practice.

Exempla in the Funerary Realm

Based on these premises, we can now explore the background of experience that is likely to have guided a Roman viewer in his or her reading of a mythological sarcophagus image. For obvious reasons, it is impossible to speculate over idiosyncratic experiences, and within the scope of the present paper, even common experiences cannot be considered comprehensively. I shall focus here on the way exempla, and mythical exempla in particular, were used in texts pertaining to the funerary realm, and which I shall call collectively consolatory texts,[49] to explore the principles according to which the rhetoric of the images was likely to work as well.

In 1992 Klaus Fittschen observed that "the importance of these texts has repeatedly been pointed out in recent times .... But one only looked for exact thematic parallels, not for general attitudes to death."[50] Here, he referred specifically to epitaphs, but the same could be said for consolatory texts at large. The range of attitudes towards death found in these texts, so he suggested, are likely to be expressed among the diverse imagery on Roman sarcophagi. Discussing Creusa/Medea and Niobid sarcophagi, he demonstrated against the then current eschatological interpretations that they depict the inescapability of death, its horrors, and the lament it causes, themes that are all found in epitaphs.

This line of thought was explored further by Frank Müller and, most recently, by Zahra Newby who used Statius' *epicedia* to identify general ideas and rhetorical strategies of consolation.[51] Müller found that mythical exempla in the consolatory literature and in epitaphs mostly, albeit not exclusively, serve as *exempla mortalitatis*. The consolation consists in the insight that death simply is the fate of mortal men; that even the greatest and the heroes of old could not escape it; and that others have suffered more terrible losses than the present bereaved. The general strategy of consolation is already mocked in a fragment from Timocles (fr. 6 in: Athenaeus 6.223 c–d; transl. S. Douglas Olsen), an Attic comedian of the fourth century BC:

> One guy, who's a pauper, finds out that Telephus was poorer than he is, and immediately he has an easier time putting up with his own poverty. The man who's a bit unstable thinks of Alcmaeon. Someone has an infected eye; Phineus' sons are blind. Someone's child has died; Niobe cheers him up. Someone's crippled; he sees Philoctetes. An old man's down on his luck; he finds out about Oineus. Because when a person considers all the bad luck even worse than his own that's hit other people, he complains less about his own troubles.

---

49 Equally, when I speak of consolatory literature, I am referring to all literary genres with a funerary context, not just to *consolationes* proper. Bielfeldt 2003, 22–3, has cautioned against the use of such sources, but focussed only on the formal *laudatio funebris*, which may have been the privilege of the upper classes. But while we do not know what exactly "ordinary" Romans said at the tombs of their loved ones, taking the various types of utterances in different media together, patterns become apparent, which, I am arguing, can be assumed to have been widely accepted and used.

50 Fittschen 1992, with quote p. 1058 n. 12 (my transl.).

51 Müller 1994, 88–90, based on Griessmair 1966, 85–91; Newby 2014; now Newby 2016, 273–319.

In consolatory texts, however, the psychological effect is used in all sincerity. The universality and inevitability of death is a recurring motif of consolation in all sorts of texts, and Lattimore concludes that, in epitaphs, the idea that death is common to all is the consolation *par excellence*.[52]

These *exempla mortalitatis* come in two variations. In the majority of literary exempla, the focus is not so much on the deceased as on the bereaved.[53] Their grief is compared to a range of mythological mourners, some more obvious than others. Müller calls such exempla "*exempla mortalitatis* by implication", although I prefer to call them *exempla maeroris*.

In his *consolatio ad Liviam*, for instance, (allegedly) consoling Augustus' wife for her son Drusus Nero's death, Pseudo-Ovid first cites examples of bereavement from Augustus' and Tiberius' families, and continues then with references to mythical mothers, wives, and sisters lamenting the death of their sons, husbands and brothers in order to demonstrate the ubiquity of death and grief (106–18: Procne, Alcyone, Meleager's sisters, Clymene, and Phaeton's sisters; 317–22: Andromache and Euadne).[54] In his elegy on the death of Tibullus, Ovid compares his grief with that of Eos over Memnon and Thetis over Achilles (*Am.* 3.8.1). Statius, on the occasion of his father's death, recalls the laments of Erigone, Andromache, Phaeton's mother and sisters, and Niobe over their children, husband and brother (*Silv.* 5.3.74–79; 85–7).[55] In a rare epigraphic example, Philomela, Alcyone, Echo, and Zeus share into the laments of a man over the death of his wife and child.[56]

Exempla mortalitatis proper are much rarer and serve to demonstrate that no one is immortal; they remind us that all humans are bound to die, be they young and innocent (in which case death is particularly tragic), strong and powerful, of high birth, or even the son of a god. The earliest example of such an *exemplum* goes straight back to the *Iliad*, where Achilles, before he kills Lycaon, reminds him that not only Patroclus, who was better than he, had to die, but that also Achilles himself will not escape this fate (*Il.* 21.107–13). Propertius, in his elegy on the occasion of Marcellus' death, notes:

> What availed him his lineage, his worth, the best of mothers? What availed him his union with the house of Caesar, or the rippling awnings of the theatre but now so thronged and all that his mother's influence had procured? He is dead, beauty saved not Nireus, nor his might Achilles, nor Croesus the wealth produced by Pactolus' stream (3.18. 11–15, 27–8, transl. G. P. Gould).[57]

---

52 Lattimore 1942, 250–6 §71; cf. Brelich 1937, 55–6; Russell and Wilson 1981, 161–5; Esteve-Forriol 1962, 150–1 §60.

53 Cf. the overview in Esteve-Forriol 1962, 154–5, and now Newby 2014, 268–71, on Statius.

54 For this *consolatio* see Schoonhoven 1992.

55 For a fuller list of examples in literature see Esteve-Forriol 1962, 154–5.

56 Courtney 1995, 176–7, 387–8 no. 187 = *CIL* VI 25063.

57 Cf. Hor. *Carm.* 1.28.7–10 quoting Tantalus, Tithonus, Minos and Euphorbos. For the motif in Greek epitaphs cf. Peek 1960, 208–11 no. 360 (Hylas, even though he is the best of heroes and beautiful like the gods = fourth century inscription [not a sarcophagus, as Peek has it] from Nea Isaura); 236–7 no. 417

On sarcophagi, these two strands normally converge in that the death of a hero serves as paradigm of the present death while the ensuing lament is paradigmatic of the grief of the bereaved. This has long been recognised for some stories. Ever since Fittschen's 1992 article, scholars have identified these motifs as the main message of the above-mentioned sarcophagi depicting the death of the Niobids, that of Creusa and Medea's children, of the women and children at the sack of Troy, and several others.[58] It has also been acknowledged that this is part of the message of those sarcophagi that are otherwise claimed as *exempla virtutis*. After all, the two notions are by no means mutually exclusive. But as Müller observed, mythological *exempla virtutis* are extraordinarily rare in epitaphs and other consolatory texts. Moreover, they are limited to Greek, metric texts, and almost exclusively used for the praise of children, adolescents, and women.[59] Given the rarity of mythological *exempla virtutis* in consolatory texts, arguably resulting in little expectation to find such a message on sarcophagi, how likely is it that they were as ubiquitous as is often claimed?

Exempla Virtutis

To be sure, there is an encomiastic potential even in the plain *exempla mortalitatis*. At least implicitly, they are meant to let the glorious past, upon which they draw, rub off on the more mundane present, to elevate the present by suggesting a relationship of similarity with the heroic past,[60] and perhaps also supplement in some cases, the "bourgeois" and sober content and style of prose inscriptions.[61] Moreover, even lament and grief must be earned. It is the exceptional character of the deceased that caused the deepness of sorrow – and rendered it acceptable. Lament and mourning for an undeserving, average, or even inherently base character would just be ridiculous and reflect badly on those who cannot adequately control their emotions. Lament, thus, is a form of honour the deceased needs to merit. This is consistent with the general strategy of elegies, funerary orations, and consolations, where encomiastic parts are interwoven with lament, and the bereaved's grief is justified by the loss of an outstanding friend or relative.[62] The comparison of situation also invites a more specific comparison between the deceased and the mourners of both the mythical past and the

---

(Achilleus, who is strong and the son of a goddess = funerary altar from Thera, *IG* XII 3, 870). I have not found a Latin epitaph with the same motif.

58 Zanker and Ewald 2012, 57–84; Newby 2014, 268–85, drawing on Statius for comparison; Newby 2016, 297–301.

59 This becomes clear from the overview in Esteve-Forriol 1962 (for literary texts), Lattimore 1942, Peek 1960, and others. On Statius' use of mythical figures as *simile* see Newby 2014, 264–7.

60 This is the strategy applied by Statius in many contexts: Bright 1980, esp. 18; Coleman 1999.

61 E.g. Zanker 2003, 345–6; Zanker and Ewald 2012, 240–2; Muth 2005, 264.

62 Esteve-Forriol 1962, 127 §27 for examples.

present. But this is not the same as claiming that any such exemplum is also suitable for identification with the protagonists; that it is automatically an *exemplum virtutis*. In other words: an exemplum is not necessarily an exemplar.[63] The latter assumes not only the general similarity of a situation, fate, or reaction to it, but entails a value judgement and proposes a positive assertion that the character or his or her actions are exemplary. The implicit invitation to extend the comparison, to turn the exemplum into an exemplar, may therefore be frustrated by elements of the story that render any closer identification with the characters and their actions undesirable – as is the case in the examples given above.

So again: to what extent are we permitted to read the mythological images as *exempla virtutis* and reflections of a Roman value system? There is no simple answer to this question, but I would argue that, where there is a lack of a corresponding horizon of expectation it would need very strong visual incentives to support such a reading, such as portrait features given to mythical figures. One criterion must surely be that the alleged virtue is also visually present in the image and not just implicit in our "knowledge" of the characters; another one, that any behaviour present in the image that is not acceptable according to what we know about Roman values should count as discouragement of such a reading.

The following cases are meant as examples for how I think an argument based on the methodological premises outlined above could be constructed. I would like to stress that I am not suggesting that sticking a label such as *exemplum mortalitatis* or *exemplum virtutis* onto an image is equivalent to an interpretation. Sophisticated readings that take into account the details of each story, and the way it is being depicted, are needed to gain a fuller understanding of the significance of these sarcophagi for their patrons. Moreover, to state that a hero such as Hippolytus or Heracles is an *exemplum virtutis* only suggests in the most general terms the excellence of the patron(s) of the casket, but not what this excellence may consist of. In addition, as Björn Ewald has reminded us most forcefully, there are elements that are related to such interpretations only in an oblique way, and relate to the Roman value system in a much less reflected way, such as the changing focus on physicality and levels of emotionality transmitted by the style of the images.[64] What I want to outline is how considering the kind of exemplum we are looking at can be a helpful starting point and guide further analysis.

---

63 Nagy 1992, 326, drawing also on the Roman lexicographical tradition as in Paulus ex Festo 72.5.
64 Ewald 2012. This excellent paper presents a more sophisticated approach to the phenomena than e.g. Zanker 2002; Zanker 2003; Ewald 2005; Muth 2005; Russenberger 2011; Zanker and Ewald 2012, 203–15; for some qualifications of the views presented in these earlier discussions see Borg 2015.

Hercules

Hercules and his labours are a popular subject, shown on 30 Roman caskets (Fig. 1), as well as six Attic and Asiatic ones from Rome.[65] Explanations of this choice have either taken Hercules as *exemplum virtutis* or as a prefiguration of the casket's patron's apotheosis, an *exemplum deificationis*, if you want, or a combination of the two. Both readings could be supported by the stories around this hero, who was not only famous for his labours but also rewarded by joining the Olympian gods after his death. On the other hand, already in the *Iliad* Achilles, facing his own death, states: "For not even the mighty Heracles escaped death, albeit he was most dear to Zeus, son of Cronus, the king" (Hom. *Il.* 18.117–8), and we find him to be a popular *exemplum mortalitatis* elsewhere.[66] Given the general rarity and vagueness of expressions of hope for an afterlife in Roman consolatory texts, and the absence of mythical exempla illustrating such ideas,[67] we would need strong visual incentives to read the images as an eschatological message. Significantly, neither his death nor his entrance into Olympus are ever depicted on the caskets, which is hard to explain had the main significance been eschatological. Moreover, his adventures with Cerberus and the Hesperids, which both have the potential of serving as symbols or allegories of overcoming death, are depicted, with a single exception, only on the secondary short sides, if at all. We thus have to conclude that these events were less relevant to the sarcophagus patrons, who were not interested in Hercules' relation to death and the afterlife.

In contrast, there is ample evidence suggesting that a viewer's first reaction would have been to read the images as an encomiastic comment on the deceased, even when the hero received portrait features only twice in the third century – notably without any further changes to the iconography.[68] Comparisons of men with Heracles are well known since classical times when individuals and entire dynasties claimed descent from the hero, and sometimes even styled themselves as a new Heracles; Alexander is the most famous example.[69] In Rome, Hercules started his career as a god of victory and triumph, who was credited for his support by victorious military commanders, and to whom they erected temples and altars. His epithet "Victor" stayed with him into late antiquity. In the early imperial period, due to Mark Antony's close connection with the hero, his career floundered, but only temporarily so, and from Trajan onwards, he returned prominently onto the political stage,

---

65 Koch and Sichtermann 1982, 148–9; Jongste 1992, for the most complete list; Grassinger 2007.
66 Müller 1994, 107–9, with further examples.
67 For Hercules as *exemplum deificationis* in non-consolatory texts see Borg forthcoming, ch. 4, with further discussion.
68 Grassinger 2007, who points out that some sarcophagi show the hero aging over the course of his deeds, so that we are presented with a kind of *curriculum vitae*; for the caskets with portraits see Wrede 1981, 139 cat. 136–7; Jongste 1992, cats. F5–6.
69 See the summary in Rawlings 2005, 164–6, with bibliography.

Fig. 5: Portrait statue of a man posing as Hercules. Rome, Palazzo Barberini. Photo: H. Schwanke, neg. D-DAI-ROM-77.1730.

becoming the favoured god of many emperors.[70] Commodus' portraits with the lion scalp are just the most well-known visual proof.[71] Small children were depicted as baby Hercules strangling the deadly snakes sent by Hera[72] and compared to the hero in epitaphs,[73] and in rare cases grown up men imitated Alexander and Commodus' habit by posing with the lion skin (Fig. 5).[74] Used to such encomiastic comparisons

---

70 For Hercules' career in Rome see Ritter 1995; Rawlings 2005; Hekster 2005; and Rees 2005, for his career under the empire. His other main significance in Rome since the second century BC was that of patron of trade and commerce (Ritter 1995). There is nothing in the sarcophagus images that hints at this aspect, but it is possible that, given the choice, merchants preferred him as *exemplum virtutis* over other options.

71 Fittschen and Zanker 1994, 85–90 cat. 78 pls. 91–4.

72 Wrede 1981, 238–40 cat. 121, 124, 125 pls. 17.1–2.

73 E.g. *IG* XIV 2126 = Peek 1960, 190–1 no. 323.

74 Wrede 1981, 239–42 cat. 122, 126, 127 pls. 15.1–2, 16.1–4.

both in and outside the funerary sphere, a viewer will surely have been encouraged to read the sarcophagus images along similar lines as Cicero. Speaking of the everlasting fame of the great men of Rome such as Brutus, Camillus, the Scipios etc., he evokes the exemplum of Hercules to illustrate that "the body of a brave and great man is mortal, yet the impulses of the mind and the glory of virtue are eternal".[75] Here, as on the sarcophagi, it is not Hercules, who achieves immortality, but the glory won by his deeds, a message that fits in very well with the scepticism regarding an individual afterlife and the prominence that commemoration of the dead had in ancient Rome. The afterlife that most people hoped for was in the memory of future generations.[76]

Hippolytus

Another obvious candidate for an *exemplum virtutis* is Hippolytus (Fig. 2).[77] His hunt occupies a major part of the sarcophagus fronts. The hero is shown on horseback attacking the huge boar and just about to deliver the fatal blow. As if this was not clear enough, the hero is even accompanied by the personification of Virtus herself. His departure from Phaedra is often depicted in an iconography similar to a Roman *profectio*, and celebrates his beautiful athletic body. His death, on the other hand, is marginalised – only hinted at by Phaedra's grief. Moreover, there is nothing in the image that contradicts an unambiguously positive reading of this character, and might discourage from identifying with the hero more directly. It is therefore no surprise that his iconography was deemed suitable for "real-life" hunting sarcophagi, which replaced the Hippolytus theme in the third century.[78]

---

75 Cic. *Sest.* 143, quoted by Grassinger 2007, 116. Heracles is also listed by Menander Rhetor among those heroes an orator delivering a *logos epitaphios* may refer to for comparison (Soffel 1974, 151; Russell and Wilson 1981, ca. 176–7); cf. Müller 1994, 109–10 n. 452; Grassinger 2007, 115.
76 Cf. Lattimore 1942, 241–6 §67–8; Esteve-Forriol 1962, 150 §56. It must be admitted, though, that Cicero does use Hercules as a model for someone achieving apotheosis through superior deeds and benefactions to humanity: cf. Cole 2013, and Borg forthcoming, ch. 4. The point here is that any such speculation would need to come to this imagery from an existing predisposition, and is not obviously encouraged through the imagery.
77 Robert 1904, 198–217 nos. 161–76; Koch and Sichtermann 1982, 150–3.
78 Andreae 1980, esp. 17–32; Borg 2013, 178–82.

Adonis

This is quite different from Adonis sarcophagi (Fig. 6).[79] To be sure, the images of his departure as well as the fact that he dared to face the boar indicate that he was a brave young hunter. Yet, as Russenberger has correctly observed, he is not actually shown hunting, but rather as the victim of his prey.[80] He is falling or fallen to the ground fatally wounded, no longer capable of raising his spear, or disarmed altogether. In most cases, he faces the deadly boar with alarm, even fear, sometimes even causing Aphrodite to rush onto the scene in panic and despair.[81] Lateral images show him dying in the arms of his lover. The measures of *virtus* and death are obviously inversely proportional to those in Hippolytus sarcophagi, suggesting that Adonis is primarily an *exemplum mortalitatis*. The message is: even a beautiful, brave hero like Adonis, loved by the goddess of love herself, had to die. His beauty and accomplishments are background knowledge and alluded to, but not the main subject of the present discourse.[82]

This interpretation is also consistent with the observation that, in the unique case where Adonis – and also Aphrodite – received portrait features in the third century, the iconography was profoundly changed by adding a rather regal and unprecedented scene in the centre (Fig. 7).[83] Adonis is obviously injured but this does not seem to affect him very much. With Aphrodite to his left, he is enthroned rather than just sitting, not leaning on her shoulder breathing his last breath but looking rather confident next to his similarly behaved partner. Except for his nudity, the two look entirely like a couple, or maybe rather: mother and son, of some distinction ready to receive some guests

---

79 See above n. 14.

80 Russenberger 2015, 199–200, 365–6.

81 Koortbojian 1995, 32, for a different reading.

82 The famous Rinuccini sarcophagus provides no counter argument, as is often suggested (already Blome 1990; Brilliant 1992; and still Zanker and Ewald 2012, 44–6; Stilp 2013, 61–2; Newby 2016, 287–91). True, the death of Adonis on the right is here combined with two scenes known from *vita romana* sarcophagi, the *concordia*-marriage and the general's formal sacrifice, which praise the deceased's achievements and virtues. But the standard sequence of the scenes has been changed on the Rinuccini sarcophagus, so that there is no need to equate the Adonis scene with the battle scene that sometimes appears at the far left end of the *vita romana* caskets. Moreover, as Muth 2004 has shown, the *vita romana* sarcophagi do not actually focus on the canon of virtues suggested by Rodenwaldt 1935, and which has influenced sarcophagus studies so much, but on the offices and very tangible achievements of the sarcophagus patron. Given the difficulties discussed above, I prefer to see the mythical image as an attempt to include in the range of messages expressed by the reliefs the notion of death through an *exemplum mortalitatis*. That it is the death of a hero makes the story suitable for the deceased (and his wife), but does not distract from the message of achievement. That death is here illustrated by a mythical image distances the notion of death and "defeat" from the sarcophagus patron, and leaves his confident self-representation untinged.

83 On this sarcophagus: Blome 1990, esp. 54–5 fig. 22; Koortbojian 1995, 50–3 fig. 7; Grassinger 1999, 74 no. 65 fig. 7 pls. 47.2, 49.3, 52.2, 53.2, 55–7, 59, 63.1; Zanker and Ewald 2012, 210–1, 301–3 no. 6 fig. 189; for the interpretation suggested here see Borg 2013, 169–70 fig. 87; Borg 2014, 249–50 fig. 7.10.

Fig. 6: Adonis sarcophagus. Mantua, Palazzo Ducale. Photo: H. Koppermann, neg. D-DAI-ROM-62.138.

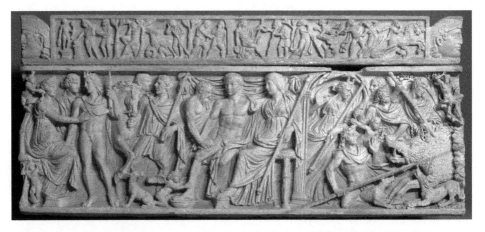

Fig. 7: Adonis sarcophagus. Vatican, Musei Vaticani, Museo Gregoriano Profano 10409. Photo: G. Singer, neg. D-DAI-ROM-71.1762.

or clients. Only the couple in this image is equipped with portrait heads while the protagonists in the two flanking, traditional scenes showing the hero's departure and death respectively, are generic figures, who are also depicted in smaller size, detaching the deceased from Adonis and Aphrodite's more passionate and dramatic moments of love and death. As in other examples where problematic stories previously used as *exempla mortalitatis* or *maeroris* are getting encomiastic overtones by the introduction of portraits, the aspects of death and drama were marginalised, and the story became an ornate backdrop to the celebrated deceased in this one instance where a third-century patron dared to draw upon this challenging myth as *exemplum virtutis*.

Aphrodite's role, on the other hand, is primarily marked by her relationship to Adonis, her love of the hero, whom she hugs and kisses on some caskets, whom she bids farewell, and whom she desperately but vainly tries to rescue. She thus strongly encourages the viewer to also look at the story as an *exemplum maeroris*, like Ovid did when he compared his grief for Tibullus with that of Venus over Adonis (Ov. *Am.* 3.9.16). Her active role and passionate and demanding love of Adonis, which has irritated scholars as inconsistent with Roman decorum, explains her devastation at his death, but can happily be contained within the mythical realm.[84] Again, on the single example where she assumed portrait features, it was only in the central, strangely unemotional scene just described.

There is yet another aspect to her presence. As I have argued elsewhere, the frequent images of gods loving mortals – apart from Aphrodite these include Selene and Endymion, Dionysus and Ariadne, Mars and Rhea Sylvia, and even Hades and Persephone – may visualise the deceased's desire to somehow dwell in the vicinity of the gods, that their death may be sleep-like and/or guarded over by a caring divinity.[85] This desire is also expressed in epitaphs, where no specific gods are, however, mentioned.[86]

There is thus no need to assume that Aphrodite's passion and the physicality of her love were meant as a role model to be advertised to a Roman female audience, that she was an exemplar. Such a reading is discouraged by both a lack of precedents or parallels for such an understanding (which would have created the appropriate background of experience), and the adjustments deemed necessary in the single case where Aphrodite (and Adonis) actually did assume portrait features.

Meleager

Meleager sarcophagi are interesting here as they demonstrate the range of interpretations of this hero and his deeds even in a single medium and at the same time. Some 32 caskets show the Calydonian boar hunt (Fig. 3).[87] They differ in the prominence they award the deliberations preceding the hunt, but they all focus on the hunt itself, which is shown as a heroic deed with the hero fearlessly approaching the boar. Unlike the Adonis reliefs, and similar to Hippolytus sarcophagi, there is little indication of his death. Sometimes his death is not even alluded to and his victory is further enhanced by the depiction of the meal following the hunt on the lid, and/or real-world hunts on

---

84 Against a reading of the encounters between Venus and Adonis as reflections of or models for Roman gender relations proposed especially by Zanker 2003, Ewald 2005 and Russenberger 2011, see Borg 2015.

85 Borg 2016.

86 Peek 1955, nos. 613, 743, 770, 909, 1146, 1768, 1773, 1830; Moretti 1979, no. 1143; Peres 2003, 106–21, 141–8, 196–207, 217–32 (who notes that the point of living on among the stars or in Elysium is also proximity to the gods); *CIL* VI 26251 and 26282; *IG* XIV 1856.

87 Koch 1975, 7–16, 85–102 pls. 1–55; six sarcophagi imitating Asiatic sarcophagi from the second half of the third century can be added: ibid. 16–28, 102–5 pls. 56–63.

the short sides. There can be no doubt that he served here as *exemplum virtutis*, and it thus hardly comes as a surprise that the third-century sarcophagi which equipped the hero with portrait features kept the iconography largely unchanged.[88] In other cases, however, the dead hero and his mother's despair are depicted on the lid,[89] serving as a gentle reminder that even this great hero had to die.

However, we would be mistaken in generalising this message and imposing it also on the two other types of Meleager sarcophagi, which put his dead body centre stage.[90] On one group of over 18 caskets (Fig. 8), the return of Meleager's body to Calydon features most prominently, with his father leading the way and his equally desperate mother greeting them to the right; typically, Meleager's chariot, now only manned by his charioteer, is seen to the left of the group.[91] Other scenes are normally added and vary. On the left, several caskets show Apollo killing the hero, and some include Althaea's suicide on the right. Even though the chariot hints at Meleager's previous deeds, especially in the one instance where it is decorated with a Victory writing on a shield, and one example depicting him fighting before Pleuron, the key message is clearly death and despair, mitigated only by the care with which the hero is returned home, but aggravated where his mother's suicide is shown.

Fig. 8: Meleager sarcophagus showing the hero's body being returned to Calydon. Istanbul, Archaeological Museum 2100. Photo: W. Schiele 1967, neg. D-DAI-IST-67–18.

---

88 The only change consisted in moving the hero even more into the centre of the representation: Borg 2013, 172–3.

89 Lid with its sarcophagus: Koch 1975, cat. 8 pls. 10, 13, 82–3; isolated lids: cat. 80, 89, 102, 103, 107, 109; see also the mourning woman on a short side: ibid. cat. 21 pl. 52. Since the lids would have duplicated scenes if placed on one of the other types of Meleager sarcophagi, they must have belonged to the boar hunt type.

90 Similarly Newby 2014, 271–6; Russenberger 2015, 198–9; contra: Lorenz 2011; Lorenz 2016, 71–88.

91 Koch 1975, 28–38, 106–18 pls. 68–94; Koch and Sichtermann 1982, 164–5 with n. 37.

Fig. 9: Meleager-*conclamatio* sarcophagus. Paris, Louvre Ma 539. Photo: Mbzt, Creative Commons License.

The same applies to the second group of fifteen caskets[92] that display in the centre Meleager lying in state and being mourned by his parents and other figures in an iconography taken over from Roman "real life" *conclamatio* scenes (Fig. 9). It is flanked on the left by Althaea throwing the log into the fire on which Meleager's life hinged, and on the right by Meleager killing his uncles. Placed in different locations within the reliefs, the mourning Atalante normally features prominently, thus inviting identification with the bereaved. Not only is the narrative sequence of events disturbed in order to put the *conclamatio* centre stage. The flanking scenes both display the killing of kin, appropriately accompanied by Furies in some cases. We are presented with another example of death and destruction that leaves only grief behind.[93] It is consistent with this interpretation that epitaphs and the consolatory literature refer to the hero exclusively as *exemplum mortalitatis/maeroris*.[94]

Meleager sarcophagi are thus an excellent illustration of some of the observations made above. One and the same hero can serve as exemplum for different claims. Moreover, where he is used as *exemplum mortalitatis*, even contradictory versions of the story were used to express different ideas. The story according to which he is killed by Apollo is incompatible with the one used for the *conclamatio* sarcophagi, where his own mother kills the hero. While both groups put the death of the hero centre stage,

---

92 Koch 1975, 38–47, 119–29 pls. 95–113; Koch and Sichtermann 1982, 165–6; Lorenz 2011; Lorenz 2016, 71–88, with a list in n. 133.

93 Similarly Newby 2016, 298–300. Differently Lorenz 2011, 322, who thinks that Meleager is presented as a "formidable fighter", and protector of "the claims of his lover and wife". But as with Orestes' killing of his mother, I cannot see how the killing of kin can ever be perceived as an unambiguously positive act, and the furies seem to confirm this view; ditto Russenberger 2015, 198; Lorenz 2016, esp. 76–84, now wants to read all characters and scenes according to the *virtus* paradigm, and sees the four "cardinal virtues" embodied. Even Althaea killing Meleager by throwing the log into the fire becomes an unambiguous act of *iustitia*.

94 See example above.

the first group presents it as a fate caused by a god. The fighting in which he proved his *virtus* was a military campaign, to which the chariot and the escort of his comrades also draw attention. The mourning takes up different amounts of space, sometimes including his mother's suicide but sometimes relegated to a small part at the right-hand end of the relief or to the short sides. While death and mourning feature most prominently on these caskets, there is nothing that compromises the hero's *virtus*, making him an excellent *exemplum mortalitatis* with enough positive overtones to invite closer identification by those who felt so inclined.

On the *conclamatio* sarcophagi, some key aspects are changed. Mourning is the main theme in the centre, sometimes supplemented with scenes of mourning at a tomb on the front or a short side. Atalante is a prominent and unambiguously positive figure with whom any mourner, but especially a wife or female lover of the actual deceased could identify, and Katharina Lorenz has shown how she is used to draw the viewer into the mythical scene.[95] At the same time, the horror of death is taken to the extreme. Not only are more deaths added – that of Meleager's uncles. Meleager and his family are depicted, like Orestes, as entangled in a tragic fate that eventually even makes them kill their own kin. The message may be the mercilessness of Fate/fate, often lamented in epigraphs, but it still leaves them morally compromised, unsuitable as *exempla virtutis*. While Meleager is still a heroic figure, not every hero is also an exemplar. His usefulness as *exemplum mortalitatis* and *maeroris* is unaffected by this fact, as these do not necessarily involve any moral judgement.

Female Death

Female mythical protagonists serve a similar range of meanings as their male counterparts, although with different emphasis. One prominent role is that of mourners, which is in tune with the role of women in Roman society. The degree to which they invite identification by the viewer varies, however. Phaedra's often dramatic reaction to Hippolytus' departure (Fig. 2), for instance, highlights the fact that the myth is not just about Hippolytus as an *exemplum virtutis*, but that he will actually never come back, and thus is also an *exemplum mortalitatis*. Her love and grief underline the hero's desirability and the grief his death will cause,[96] but this does not turn Phaedra into a role model or positive figure.[97] Althaea is a somewhat more agreeable char-

---

95 Lorenz 2011, 319–22; she further assigns her the role of mitigating the levels of an *allegoria apertis permixta*. But as explained above, this concept is problematic.

96 Zanker 1999; Zanker and Ewald 2012, 92–3; Linant De Bellefonds 2013.

97 Differently the authors in the preceding footnote, but also Muth 2005, 280; contra Borg 2015. Phaedra receives portrait features only on a few Tetrarchic sarcophagi that radically change the iconography.

acter on those sarcophagi where Apollo does the killing, and possibly also on those where the cause of Meleager's death is left open. But she also adds another tragic death to the repertoire, and I see no room for reading her in any positive way on the *conclamatio* sarcophagi (Fig. 9). In contrast, Atalante is a figure easy to identify with, and so is Aphrodite to the extent that she is a loving woman desperate at her lover's death, as explained above.

The second prominent role assigned to women is that of a victim. Creusa/Medea sarcophagi put Creusa's (and Medea's children's) death centre stage, heightening the drama by including the marriage scene and pointing to the extent of her fall.[98] They may have been used primarily for women (and children?), as the subject and a cinerary urn from Ostia dedicated by a T. Flavius Carpus to his wife and daughter suggest, and again the story serves as *exemplum mortalitatis* and *maeroris*.[99] More often, women's deaths are presented with consoling overtones in that they are shown as sleeping beauties (Rhea Sylvia; Ariadne), or abducted by a god like Persephone (Fig. 4). In such cases, encomiastic elements are inherent in the story, as invariably they are worthy of the love of a divinity, and both Ariadne and Rhea Sylvia frequently obtain portrait features. On the second-century Persephone sarcophagi, however, this aspect is marginal, and only with changes in the overall composition and iconography is she given portrait features in the third century.[100]

But there are also slightly more active female role models such as Alcestis and Laodameia. The famous Alcestis sarcophagus from Ostia with its many portraits depicts the heroine on her deathbed (Fig. 10), but also claims the heroine's virtues as is occasionally done in epitaphs.[101] Two more Alcestis sarcophagi were dedicated to women, and it is plausible to assume that also the other 11 Alcestis sarcophagi were used for deceased females or a wife together with her husband.[102] Alcestis here obviously serves not just as *exemplum mortalitatis*, but also as *exemplum virtutis*, more precisely: as *exemplum pietatis*.[103] Laodameia, who committed suicide when her hus-

---

98 Gaggadis-Robin 1994; Zanker and Ewald 2012, 76–8, 354–7 no. 20 fig. 64; Russenberger 2015, 161–4; Newby 2016, 308–19.

99 A Creusa/Medea sarcophagus from a tomb found near Porta Maggiore contained three skeletons, but their age and sex were not determined: *NSc* 1911, 395–6 (E. Ghislanzoni); Herdejürgen 1996 143–4 no. 116 pl. 44.4; *Museo Nazionale Romano* I.8, 279–83 no. vi8 (L. Musso).

100 Newby 2011b; Borg 2013, 164–78; for the additional aspect of divine presence see above with n. 85.

101 Sarcophagus: Grassinger 1999, 227–8 cat. 76 pls. 75.2, 78.1–2, 79.1–2, 80–1, 84.6–7; cf. Newby 2014, 280–3, who draws the interesting parallel with Statius' way of projecting the deceased into the mythological realm; Newby 2016, 285–7 fig. 6.1. For epitaphs see e.g. *IG* XIV 1356 = Peek 1960, no. 393 (Rome); *IG* XIV 607 = Peek 1960, no. 463 (Sardinia).

102 Grassinger 1999, 110–28, 227–32 cat. 75–87 (a portrait on cat. 86, an inscription on cat. 75); Mucznik 1999, 25–79, esp. 36–52 (with an eschatological interpretation pp. 75–9); Newby 2011b, 194–6, 200; Zanker and Ewald 2012, (200–2, 306–10); Newby 2016, 275–6.

103 Against most modern accounts Bielfeldt 2005, 324 with n. 954, has observed that the Heracles scene does not show Alcestis' return but Admetus' eventual arrival in the underworld, and Zanker

Fig. 10: Alcestis sarcophagus of Metilia Akte and Junius Euhodus from Ostia. Photo: Jastrow (2006), Creative Commons License.

band fell before Troy, was suitable for the same end, and accordingly, both she and Protesilaos could be given portrait features on a casket from around 170.[104]

These female *exempla virtutis* may be fewer than those for deceased males, and they always include clear reference to death. Yet if my argument on male heroes above is accepted, the discrepancy appears already less dramatic. Given the frequent use of sarcophagi for married couples in the third century, one also wonders how often caskets were used in the same way in the second century. For instance, a Meleager sarcophagus from the Isola Sacra was dedicated by Berria Zosime to herself and her husband – in this sequence.[105] A late-second-century Meleager sarcophagus from Mausoleum R in the Vatican necropolis contained the skeletons of an adult and a child.[106] We may see here a similar attitude to that often found in epitaphs where the praise of a deceased woman or child consists in their relation to a husband or father with some achievement.

---

and Ewald 2012, 298 rightly note that none of the epitaphs referring to Alcestis mentions her return to life. Alcestis' return is only depicted on one sarcophagus front at the left hand corner and on one short side (Grassinger 1999, 231–2 no. 86 pls. 75.4, 83, 84.1–4; 229–30 no. 82 pls. 74.1, 85.4–5), and Zanker and Ewald 2012, 94, interpret it as referring to love of the husband for his wife, which proverbially can transcend death (cf. ibid. 201–2).

104 Robert 1919, 498–500 cat. 422–3. For a comparison in an epitaph see *CIL* X 5920, on which see Keegan 2008, 3–4 with transl. Again there is no indication that these sarcophagi symbolised apotheosis; they rather focus on the tragic departure: Zanker and Ewald 2012, 94–5, 392–6 no. 32 figs. 84–5; Bielfeldt 2005, 324, who observes that the protagonists appear both as surviving dependant and as deceased; Newby 2011b, 197–9.

105 D'Ambra 1988; Koch 1975, 126–7 cat. 130 pls. 114–45, and 48–50 on the subject of the meal after the hunt.

106 Koch 1975, 131 no. 146 pl. 120c; 121; the sex of these skeletons was not determined at the time.

Female *exempla virtutis*

However, more recently it has also become clear that some narratives were deemed suitable for women that previous scholarship had not considered. As Christian Russenberger has demonstrated, Amazonomachy sarcophagi (Fig. 11) were not all about the victorious Greeks, thus being a mythological equivalent to the battle sarcophagi and serving as *exempla virtutis* for a male audience, as has been the consensus so far.[107] At least sometimes, and possibly even typically, they were dedicated to girls and young women,[108] as is confirmed by the only preserved inscribed lid of an Amazonomachy sarcophagus, which was dedicated to 15-year-old Arria Maximina – together with a statue showing her as Venus.[109] The Amazons' death and desperation make them excellent *exempla mortalitatis* and *maeroris*, not least since Amazons, and Penthesilea in particular, had been admired for their bravery and beauty ever since archaic Greece.[110] The imagery thus also contains an element of praise that is reflected in some written sources. According to her epitaph, 20-year-old Marcia Helike, whose beauty equalled that of Venus in life, is said to have become even more beautiful and desirable to her husband in death.[111]

And yet, it is not necessarily only beauty but also *virtus* in the sense of courage in the face of adversity that may be compared. The *Laudatio Turiae* famously praises the deceased for avenging her parents' death (1.3), as well as for her courageous actions on behalf of her husband during the proscriptions, and is credited with *firmitas animae* (2.a and 15: firmness of mind), and *virtus* (2.6a and 19).[112] Emily Hemelrijk has collected similar descriptions of women and shown that Turia is not alone in such a role: Ovid urges his wife to intervene on his behalf while he is in exile.[113] Cicero praises his wife for similar interventions, and calls her as well as his daughter Tullia "more courageous than any man" (*fortiores … quam quemquam virum: Fam.* 14.7.2).[114] The epigraphic *Laudatio Murdiae* alleges that the deceased woman "was second to none

---

107 Russenberger 2015, 67–114.

108 Russenberger 2015, esp. 151–93, who draws on both a detailed analysis of the iconography and written evidence; for a similar suggestion see already Borg 2013, 170 with n. 51. As Russenberger notes, however, the sarcophagi were also suitable as "metaphors" for male death. Attic sarcophagi, however, do focus on Greek heroism, and so does a unique western exception, a sarcophagus in Toronto from Ostia: ibid. 342–4 fig. 157 cat. 13 pl. 19.2. Cf. on the sarcophagi more generally: Grassinger 1999, 129–94, 235–59 cat. 88–146, with Russenberger 2015, 17–64.

109 Russenberger 2015, 189–90, on *CIL* XIV 1839.

110 Arrigoni 1982, 58–9; Arrigoni 1981; Fantuzzi 2012, 267–79. For an argument that South Italian vases drew upon the motif in funerary contexts as well see Russenberger 2015, 239–97.

111 *IG* XIV 1838: Arrigoni 1981; Russenberger 2015, 190–2.

112 Kierdorf 1980, 33–48; Flach 1991; Hemelrijk 2004.

113 Hemelrijk 2004, 190–1, with further examples from literature; cf. also n. 117.

114 Cf. Grebe 2003, who seems to exaggerate the uniqueness of Terentia.

Fig. 11: Amazonomachy sarcophagus. Rome, Musei Capitolini 726. Photo: C. Rossa, neg. D-DAI-ROM-72.679.

... of courage, energy, and prudence in the face of danger" (*neque ulli cessit virtutis laboris sapientiae periculorum*).[115] Seneca responds to Livia's fictive objection that she is only a woman and cannot be expected to be as courageous as men:

> But who has asserted that Nature has dealt grudgingly with women's natures and has narrowly restricted their virtues (*virtutes*)? Believe me, they have just as much force (*vigor*), just as much capacity (*facultas*), if they like, for virtuous action (*Consolatio ad Liviam* 16, transl. J. Henderson).[116]

These examples most likely all come from the uppermost echelons of society, but their ideas are not limited to the upper class. In his *consolatio* to Abascanthus, the powerful *ab epistulis* of Domitian, Statius praised his recently deceased wife not only by admiring her beauty, charm and devotion to her husband in general, but by suggesting that she would have fought for him like a soldier or other brave man: "But if some formidable danger had summoned her to a larger role, she would gladly have confronted armed bands or lightning fire or the hazards of mid ocean for her man". She would have endured all sorts of inconveniences, "and, if the army allowed, even been fain to bear a quiver and shield her flank with Amazonian targe, so long as she might see you in the dust-cloud of battles" (Stat. *Silv.* 5.1.66–9; 130–2; trans. D. R. Schackelton Bailey).[117]

---

115 *CIL* VI 10230, with Hemelrijk 2004, 193–4; Lindsay 2004.

116 On female virtue in Seneca see Wilcox 2006, with pp. 79–80 on the passage. To be sure, since the first century BC, the term *virtus* can be used in the general sense of (moral) virtue (Thome 2002, 75–8; Mcdonnell 2003, 238–58), but except for the Seneca passage, which is more ambiguous, the contexts in these examples make it clear that courage is a key element of this female *virtus*.

117 Stat. *Silv.* 5.1.127–34. For comparisons with Amazons in the later literature see Russenberger 2015, 192–3. Cf. Gibson 2006, 104–5, 125–6, for other women enduring hardship and misfortunes for their husbands and even prepared to accompany their husbands on campaign and/or take up arms.

Fig. 12: Achilles sarcophagus of Metilia Torquata. Naples, Museo Archeologico Nazionale 124325. Photo: H. Koppermann, neg. D-DAI-ROM-62.847.

This kind of praise may help explain the choice of some other subjects for sarcophagi of girls or women. An enormous sarcophagus depicting Achilles' discovery on Skyros was dedicated to the senatorial girl Metilia Torquata (Fig. 12).[118] This episode is by far the most popular subject involving Achilles on Roman sarcophagi, appearing on a total of 23 Roman, and 6 Attic caskets found in Italy.[119] Grassinger and others have read them as male *exempla virtutis*, and there can be no doubt that the depictions hint at the hero's bravery and victory. On the Roman sarcophagi, the hero's entire pose is one of a warrior ready for attack, and in several examples, he has set his foot on a helmet, a pose of victory known from many other contexts including the victorious emperor and Victory herself.[120] Some reliefs further stress his masculinity by showing him entirely nude. One casket depicts his later fights on the short sides, while the lid of another depicted the ransom of Hector's body.[121] But these hints at his *virtus* and (ensuing) victories, which only become more prominent in the third century, are secondary to the main topic, which is his discovery among the daughters of Lycomedes.[122] Had *virtus* and victory been the primary intended message, other scenes would have been much

---

118 Sichtermann and Koch 1975, 5–6 no. 1 pls. 1–3; Rogge 1995, 133 cat. 19 pls. 26.2, 30.2, 31, 37.1, 38.3; Müller 1994, 106; Wrede 2001, 15 with n. 14. For Metilia Torquata, who was related to and possibly the daughter of M. Metilius Aquillius Regulus Nepos Volusius Torquatus Fronto, *cos. ord.* AD 157, cf. *CIL* IX 658; *PIR*[2] M 556; Raepsaet-Charlier 1987, 454 no. 549 stemma 27.

119 Grassinger 1999, 25–43, 196–204 cat. 4–26; Rogge 1995, 26–30, 43, 44–5, 125–6 cat. 4, 131 cat. 15, 134 cat. 21, 136–8 cat. 23–6.

120 Grassinger 1999, 41–2 with cat. 21 pls. 17.1, 25.2; cat. 24 pls. 17.2, 25.3.

121 Grassinger 1999, 196 cat. 4 pls. 4.1, 12.3–4; 35, 199–200 cat. 15 with p. 208 cat. 39.

122 Ditto Russenberger 2015, 416, but he concludes that the main theme was the "relationship between man and woman and the tragic farewell". Yet Achilles and Deidameia can hardly be understood as a paradigm of marital love as the hero is still shown half-dressed as a woman in most cases.

more suitable to express them. The choice of the discovery scene must therefore be motivated differently.

As Grassinger observed, the iconography of the daughters of Lycomedes has close parallels in scenes of rape and abduction:[123] From Deidameia and the other girls' point of view, his departure for Troy is a great loss, and so they can be taken as a visual hint at the fact that Achilles will not survive this departure for long. The event is in fact a major turning point in Achilles' life. Not only did Odysseus' trick of blowing the trumpet make him expose his real character – that of the hero and fighter – but in accepting this role, he also sealed his own fate as he knew he had to die young should he join the Achaeans in the fight against Troy. This consent to his own death is obviously another indication of his superior character, but also qualifies him as the prime *exemplum mortalitatis*, especially for a *mors immatura*, that he is in epitaphs and the consolatory literature.[124] As such, he was obviously suitable also for a girl, but the comparison may be taken further. On Metilia's as well as many other sarcophagi, Achilles is shown playing music with the daughters of Lycomedes on the short sides.[125] The implication therefore surely is that the deceased girl stood out among her peers in terms of both character and education, as Achilles did among the daughters of Lycomedes. He is depicted still in transformation from "girl" to (male) hero, a transformation that suggests the permeability of gender boundaries.[126] In light of the *virtus* discourse just discussed, the image may therefore also advocate bravery in the face of death for both sexes. If the much-discussed Albani sarcophagus showing Achilles receiving his new weapons, the second decisive moment in Achilles' acceptance of the inseparability of heroism and death, did indeed belong to a young woman, a similar choice was made for her.[127] As Müller concludes from these two examples and an epitaph from Thera comparing a girl or young woman to Achilles, the hero "was apparently regarded as a universal symbol of mortality, which could be applied to members of either sex."[128]

Scenes of Iulus Ascanius hunting in Africa were chosen for the burial of another girl, who was embalmed and fitted out with rich grave goods (Fig. 13).[129] On the left short side, the location is indicated by the personifications of a river and Africa. On

---

123 Grassinger 1999, 42–3.

124 Müller 1994, 103–6; Griessmair 1966, 89; cf. Statius, *Silv.* 2.6.30–1, praising a slave boy. For the epitaph see Peek 1960, 236–7 no. 417.

125 Grassinger 1999, cat. 21 pl. 14.1–2; cat. 17 pl. 14.3–4.

126 Gender boundaries have been much discussed in relation to the texts cited above (at nn. 112–116), and would merit further exploration. For sarcophagi see Birk 2011, which deserves separate discussion.

127 Müller 1994.

128 Müller 1994, 106; for the report on the skeleton see ibid., 1. For the epitaph see Peek 1960, 236–7 no. 417. On the various interpretations of the myth in literature and images see also Muth 1998, 151–85, whose ideas could be explored further for the funerary realm.

129 Dimas 1998, 130–2; Grassinger 1999, 91–8; 222 cat. 68 pls. 64–9; Galinier 2013, 101–3.

Fig. 13: Iulus Ascanius sarcophagus of a young girl. Rome, Museo Nazionale delle Terme 168186. Photo: H. Schwanke, neg. D-DAI-ROM-79.3940.

the front, the boy is leaving Dido and Aeneas on the left; he is seen on horseback in the centre, and the hunt is unfolding in front of him. Dido is shown like a Diana in hunting gear, suggesting that this kind of pursuit was not just for men. The only person actually hunting (apart from his anonymous male companions), however, is Iulus Ascanius, who is more similar in age to the deceased girl. Unlike the other examples discussed here, there is not even a hint of death present in this case. Moreover, we are dealing with a Roman myth, and the most likely point of comparison probably was the upbringing of the child and the noble character and status of its parents.[130] But like the Amazons and Achilles before, the hunting Iulus Ascanius and Dido in her hunting gear will also have hinted at the *virtus* of the girl, not suggesting that she was actually trained in hunting, or that she would have adopted male roles in society, but in more general terms as a courageous and confident individual.[131]

That such a reading is not arbitrary is demonstrated by an even more daring early third-century sarcophagus for six-year-old Octavia Paulina (Fig. 14). The girl is shown as a nude athlete throughout, crowning herself and with a palm of victory in the centre. On the left, she is being rubbed with oil, and wrestling with a boy; at the right, she is fighting a boy in a boxing match. Hardly did Paulina take part in any athletic competition of the kind we see in the relief, but the idea of superiority and victory in

---

130 Rogge 1995, 98; she doubts, however, the connection with the Cornelii, following Bordenache Battaglia 1983, 111–4 no. 3. Dimas 1998, 131, is reminded by the central scene of the riding protagonist of reliefs with *equites* on their horse and suggests an owner from this class. Birk 2013, 120.

131 For female *virtus* see also Birk 2013, 136–7, where she discusses sarcophagi of the third century showing Virtus as well as huntresses with female portraits. While she is certainly right in her claim that few if any virtues were monopolised by men (ibid., 115–56 on "Visualising Gender"), I find her terminology, contrasting the sex of the portrait with the gender of the figure's activity unhelpful as it suggests that the deceased was meant to be shown specifically with male characteristics rather than as being equal to men in certain regards.

Fig. 14: Athlete sarcophagus of Octavia Paulina, Milan, Torno Collection. Soprintendenza Archeologica della Lombardia no. AFS 9641: C. Rossa, neg. D-DAI-ROM-75.906.

competition was obviously considered important enough for her parents to commission this unique casket.[132]

Conclusion

These examples demonstrate that exempla could work at various levels of analogy. We would be in an infinitely better position to understand the details of how sarcophagus images may have been read, if we knew who was actually buried in these caskets, as the degree to which the deceased may have been identified with the mythical protagonists much depends on who they were. A male adolescent may have invited closer identification with Adonis (Fig. 6) or Endymion than an adult man or a woman, and a young woman may have been compared with Persephone (Fig. 4) more closely than an old lady or a man. Because of the well-known connection between hunting and warfare, a member of the military buried in a Hippolytus (Fig. 2) or Meleager-hunt sarcophagus (Fig. 3) may have identified with the hero more closely than the smith from Portus and his wife, who did not even have the opportunity to go hunting, let alone to go to war. Like the women and girls buried in Amazon or Achilles sarcophagi (Figs. 11–12), they would have read the hero's (and Atalante's) *virtus* in the wider sense the word had assumed in the imperial period as signifying general excellence, possibly involving also some degree of bravery in their own, probably rather mundane, lives and deaths.

Unfortunately, inscriptions or skeletal remains tell us only very rarely who the deceased were. But given the total number of known patrons from the second century, it is remarkable in how many cases gender and/or age of the deceased do not match

---

132 Huskinson 1996, 19, 21 no. 1.14 pl. 5.2; Amedick 1991, 132–3 no. 67 pls. 82–3, on the sarcophagus, and pp. 82–96, on *palaestra* sarcophagi in general; Dimas 1998, 152–62, 239 no. 84 pl. 12.3.

those of the mythical heroes.[133] We have already noted a number of instances in the previous section, and could add the depiction of the childhood of Dionysus deemed suitable for a one-year-old girl.[134] Of four inscribed Endymion sarcophagi, two were used for women, one for a couple but dedicated on the occasion of the wife's death, and only one for a young man.[135] No Persephone sarcophagus bears an inscription but of seven inscribed altars from the second century depicting her rape, four were dedicated to men, two to a couple, and only one to a single woman, suggesting similar practice for Persephone sarcophagi.[136] Accordingly, the myth is also sometimes evoked in epitaphs set up for deceased males.[137] Moreover, Ruth Bielfeldt has drawn attention to the fact that the images on sarcophagi were often intended, not only to speak about a single deceased person but about the wider group or family using the same tomb.[138]

Similar variation is found in literary exempla, where the gender and age of the deceased or the bereaved could, but by no means necessarily did, coincide with that of their mythical comparanda, and only in few instances is a closer comparison intended, e.g. where Apollo is mourning Linus in Ovid's elegy on Tibullus (3.8.23–4). Discrepancies are most frequent in *exempla maeroris*, where the mourning characters are, as on the sarcophagi, predominantly women even when a man is the grieving party,[139] but gender and age do not need to coincide in *exempla mortalitatis* either.

As in exempla more generally, analogies can obviously be pushed to various degrees,[140] and do not even necessarily require a positive evaluation of *any* element of the comparandum – just consider the Niobid sarcophagi.[141] On second-century sarcophagi, the point of comparison is often the poignancy of grief and the horror that is death, aggravated when it is premature and hits the young and innocent, or when it

---

133 Galinier 2013, rightly reminds us to keep in mind the varied conditions under which sarcophagi may be commissioned, chosen, and dedicated, but I hope the argument presented here shows that gender "discrepancies" may sometimes only exist in the mind of the modern beholder.

134 Matz 1969, 353–4 no. 201 pl. 210.1; Dimas 1998, 207.

135 Sichtermann 1992, nos. 27, 35, 79, 80; cf. Borg 2015, 85; Newby 2014, 269, for two of these examples with similar conclusions. Only one of these was reused for the burial of a woman, a certain Blera, in Late Antiquity, and may be dismissed as an ill judgement, simple incompetence, or neglect on the part of a late usurper.

136 Altars: Lindner 1984, 60–4 nos. 56–66 (her no. 58 is perhaps a second altar for a woman but it is lost and was never illustrated); Boschung 1987, 51 with n. 750.

137 E.g. *CLE* 1066 = *CIL* VI 6319; *CLE* 1219 = *CIL* VI 25871; *CLE* 1223 = *CIL* VI 25128. Cf. Newby 2011a, 306; Borg 2013, 177 with n. 76; Newby 2016, 276.

138 Bielfeldt 2003; Bielfeldt 2005, esp. 319–26; similarly Zanker and Ewald 2012, 40–3.

139 Newby 2014, 269, 274–5, for Statius and sarcophagi.

140 See already the conclusions by Koortbojian 1995, 9, that "the sarcophagi present analogies, not identifications: they do not merely equate the lives of those commemorated with the ancient stories but compel us to contemplate those lives in terms of the fundamental truths the myths reveal."

141 This aspect is overlooked by Gessert 2004, but also in the attempts noted above (nn. 96–97) to interpret the emotional (love) stories on second-century sarcophagi as reflections of a Roman value system.

hits several individuals at once. Alternatively it can be the peace and quiet achieved in death, the relief from all toil and hardship, and closeness to the divine. The potentially offensive parts of the stories remain securely contained within the realm of myth. They are part of the *ornatus* of the rhetoric, and they illustrate the human condition more generally, the tragedy, uncontrollability, and inescapability of death. Phaedra's love is inappropriate, more so her causing Hippolytus' death, but it is still love and she is already devastated when Hippolytus leaves. Althaea killed her son by throwing the log into the fire, but deeply mourns Meleager's death later on and eventually commits suicide. The death of Meleager, who is also shown killing his own uncles, and the tragic entanglements that brutally destroyed Orestes' family, can stand as *exempla mortalitatis* and *maeroris* without suggesting that the protagonists act as role models for a contemporary Roman; that the exempla are also exemplars.

The latter are not entirely absent during the second century, but often secondary or only implicit, able to be activated where the match is relatively close and a patron really wants to push for it. They become more clear-cut and more frequent from the late Antonine period onwards, and in particular in the third century when portrait identifications appear more widely. It has long been observed that the emotional depictions of *exempla mortalitatis* and *maeroris* such as the Creusa/Medea or Niobid sarcophagi disappear entirely. From the Meleager repertoire, only the hunting sarcophagi survive. Characteristically, Adonis sarcophagi also disappear from around the turn of the second and third centuries, and Russenberger has suggested that the encomiastic Hippolytus sarcophagi, which start to be produced only from the 180s and continue to be produced into the third century, are their successors and replacement.[142] This is also the time when Hercules sarcophagi become more popular. For other myths such as Hades and Persephone, Endymion and Selene, or the Amazonomachy, new iconographies were introduced in order to visually encourage identification and remove aspects (as far as possible) that were incompatible with an encomiastic, more direct comparison of hero and deceased.[143] The artists and patrons of Roman sarcophagi continued the creative process of using Greek myths as exempla for a range of different meanings and messages, adapting them to the desires of individuals and changing preferences over time. This process is what makes these myths excellent sources for our understanding of Roman ideology and values more broadly, and such exciting objects for study.

Acknowledgment: I would like to thank Beate Dignas and Lucy Audley-Miller, the organisers of the colloquium, on which this volume is based, for their kind invitation to contribute, and Lucy Audley-Miller for her corrections of my English and helpful comments on the text. All remaining errors are obviously my own.

---

142 Russenberger 2011, 157–8; Russenberger 2015, 402–3.
143 Newby 2011b; Borg 2013, 164–78.

Bibliography

Amedick, R. *Die Sarkophage mit Darstellungen aus dem Menschenleben* (Berlin, 1991).

Andreae, B. *Die römischen Jagdsarkophage.* Die antiken Sarkophagreliefs 1.2 (Berlin, 1980).

Arrigoni, G. Pentesilea e Marcia Elice. La bellezza dell'Amazzone come ricordo d'amore. *Archeologia Classica* 33 (1981), 253–272.

Arrigoni, G. *Camilla: amazzone e sacerdotessa di Diana* (Milan, 1982).

Balty, J. Franz Cumont et l'interprétation symbolique des sarcophages romains, à près de soixante ans des *Recherches*, in: *Iconographie funéraire romaine et société: corpus antique, approches nouvelles?*, edited by M. Galinier and F. Baratte (Perpignan, 2013), 7–27.

Balty, J. and J.-C. Balty. (eds.) *Franz Cumont. Recherches sur le symbolisme funéraire des Romains* (Rome, 2015).

Bielfeldt, R. Orest im Medusengrab. Ein Versuch zum Betrachter. *Mitteilungen des Deutschen Archäologischen Instituts, Abteilung Rom* 110 (2003), 117–150.

Bielfeldt, R. *Orestes auf römischen Sarkophagen* (Berlin, 2005).

Birk, S. Man or Woman? Cross-gendering and individuality on third century Roman sarcophagi, in: *Life, Death and Representation: Some New Work on Roman Sarcophagi*, edited by J. Elsner and J. Huskinson (Berlin, 2011), 229–260.

Birk, S. *Depicting the Dead: Self-representation and Commemoration on Roman Sarcophagi with Portraits* (Aarhus, 2013).

Blome, P. Zur Umgestaltung griechischer Mythen in der römischen Sepulkralkunst. Alkestis-, Protesilaos- und Proserpinasarkophage. *Mitteilungen des Deutschen Archäologischen Instituts, Abteilung Rom* 85 (1978), 435–457.

Blome, P. Der Sarkophag Rinuccini. Eine unverhoffte Wiederentdeckung. *Jahrbuch der Berliner Museen* 32 (1990), 35–68.

Blome, P. Funerärsymbolische Collagen auf mythologischen Sarkophagreliefs. *Studi Italiani di Filologia Classica* 10 (1992), 1062–1073.

Bordenache Battaglia, G. *Corredi funerari di età imperiale e barbarica nel Museo Nazionale Romano* (Rome, 1983).

Borg, B. E. *Der Logos des Mythos: Allegorien und Personifikationen in der frühen griechischen Kunst* (Munich, 2002).

Borg, B. E. *Crisis and Ambition: Tombs and Burial Customs in Third-century AD Rome* (Oxford, 2013).

Borg, B. E. Rhetoric and Art in Third-century AD Rome, in: *Art and Rhetoric in Roman Culture*, edited by J. Elsner and M. Meyer (New York, 2014), 235–255.

Borg, B. E. Eine Frage von Leben und Tod: Pathos und Leidenschaft auf den mythologischen Sarkophagen Roms, in: *IMAGO. Jahrbuch für Psychoanaylse & Ästhetik*, edited by M. Clemenz et al. (Gießen, 2015), 77–92.

Borg, B. E. Slumber under Divine Protection: from vague pagan hopes to Christian belief, in: *Bilder von dem Einen Gott. Die Rhetorik in monotheistischen Gottesdarstellungen der Spätantike*, edited by N. Hömke, G. F. Chiai and A. Jenik (Berlin, 2016), 263–288.

Borg, B. E. *Roman Tombs and the Art of Commemoration: Contextual Approaches to Funerary Customs in the Second Century CE* (Cambridge, forthcoming).

Boschung, D. *Antike Grabaltäre aus den Nekropolen Roms* (Bern, 1987).

Brandenburg, H. Meerwesensarkophage und Clipeus-Motiv. Jahrbuch des Deutschen Archäologischen Instituts 82 (1967), 195–245.

Brelich, A. *Aspetti della morte nelle iscrizioni sepolcrali dell'impero Romano* (Budapest, 1937).

Bright, D. F. *Elaborate Disarray: the Nature of Statius' Silvae* (Meisenheim a. Glan, 1980).

Brilliant, R. Roman Myth, Greek Myth. Reciprocity and Appropriation on a Roman Sarcophagus in Berlin. *Studi Italiani di Filologia Classica* 10 (1992), 1030–1045.

Cole, S. (ed.) *Cicero and the Rise of Deification at Rome* (Cambridge, 2013).

Coleman, K. Mythological Figures as Spokespersons in Statius' Silvae, in: *Im Spiegel des Mythos. Bilderwelt und Lebenswelt; Symposium, Rom 19.–20. Februar 1998*, edited by F. De Angelis, S. Muth and T. Hölscher (Wiesbaden, 1999), 67–80.

Courtney, E. *Musa Lapidaria. A Selection of Latin Verse Inscriptions* (Atlanta, GA, 1995).

Cumont, F. V. M. *Recherches sur le symbolisme funéraire des Romains* (Paris, 1942).

D'Ambra, E. A Myth for a Smith: a Meleager Sarcophagus from a Tomb in Ostia. *American Journal of Archaeology* 92 (1988), 85–100.

Dimas, S. *Untersuchungen zur Themenwahl und Bildgestaltung auf römischen Kindersarkophagen* (Münster, 1998).

Dowden, K. and N. Livingstone (eds.) *A Companion to Greek Mythology* (Malden, Mass., 2011).

Elsner, J. and W. Hung. Editorial. *RES: Anthropology and Aesthetics* (2012), 5–21.

Elsner, J. and J. Huskinson. Image and Rhetoric in Early Christian Sarcophagi: reflections on Jesus' trial, in: *Life, Death and Representation: Some New Work on Roman Sarcophagi*, edited by J. Elsner and J. Huskinson (Berlin, 2011), 359–386.

Elsner, J. Rational, Passionate and Appetitive, in: *Art and Rhetoric in Roman Culture*, edited by J. Elsner (New York, 2014), 316–349.

Elsner J. Review of Janine Balty, Jean-Charles Balty (ed.) *Franz Cumont. Recherches sur le symbolisme funéraire des Romains*. Bibliotheca Cumontiana – Scripta Maiora (BICUMA), 4 (Turnhout, 2015). Bryn Mawr Classical Review (2016), (http://bmcr.brynmawr.edu/2016/2016-06-38.html), last accessed 2017.

Esteve-Forriol, J. *Die Trauer- und Trostgedichte in der römischen Literatur untersucht nach ihrer Topik und ihrem Motivschatz* (Diss. Erlangen, 1962).

Ewald, B. C. Der Philosoph als Leitbild. Ikonographische Untersuchungen an römischen Sarkophagreliefs (Mainz, 1999).

Ewald, B. C. Rollenbilder und Geschlechterverhältnis in der römischen Grabkunst. 'Archäologische' Anmerkungen zur *Geschichte der Sexualität*, in: *Neue Fragen, Neue Antworten: Antike Kunst als Thema der Gender Studies*, edited by N. Sojc (Berlin, 2005), 55–73.

Ewald, B. C. Paradigms of Personhood and Regimes of Representation. *RES: Anthropology and Aesthetics* 61/62 (2012), 41–64.

Fantuzzi, M. *Achilles in Love Intertextual Studies* [online text] (Oxford, 2012).

Ferrari, G. The Ilioupersis in Athens. *Harvard Studies in Classical Philology* 100 (2000), 119–150.

Fittschen, K. Zum Kleobis und Biton-Relief in Venedig. *Jahrbuch des Deutschen Archäologischen Instituts* 85 (1970), 171–193.

Fittschen, K. *Der Meleager Sarkophag* (Frankfurt, 1975).

Fittschen, K. Der Tod der Kreusa und der Niobiden. Überlegungen zur Deutung griechischer Mythen auf römischen Sarkophagen. *Studi Italiani di Filologia Classica* 10 (1992), 1046–1059.

Fittschen, K. and P. Zanker. *Katalog der römischen Porträts in den Capitolinischen Museen und den anderen kommunalen Sammlungen der Stadt Rom, vol. 1: Kaiser- und Prinzenbildnisse* (Mainz, 1994).

Flach, D. *Die sogenannte Laudatio Turiae: Einleitung, Text, Übersetzung und Kommentar* (Darmstadt, 1991).

Gaggadis-Robin, V. *Jason et Médée sur les sarcophages d'époque impériale* (Rome, 1994).

Galinier, M. A vendre. Les sarcophages romains dans les ateliers, suggestions méthodologiques, in: *Iconographie funéraire romaine et société: corpus antique, approches nouvelles?*, edited by M. Galinier and F. Baratte (Perpignan, 2013), 81–115.

Gessert, G. Myth as Consolatio: Medea on Roman sarcophagi. *Greece and Rome* 51 (2004), 217–249.

Gibson, B. *Statius, Silvae 5* (Oxford, 2006).

Giuliani, L. Achill-Sarkophage in Ost und West: Genese einer Ikonographie. *Jahrbuch der Berliner Museen* 31 (1989), 25–39.

Grassinger, D. The Meaning of Myth on Roman Sarcophagi. *Fenway Court* (1994), 91–107.

Grassinger, D. *Die mythologischen Sarkophage: Achill, Adonis, Aeneas, Aktaion, Alkestis, Amazonen.* Die antiken Sarkophagreliefs 12.1 (Berlin, 1999).

Grassinger, D. Durch *virtus* und *labor* zu *gloria*, in: *Akten des Symposiums des Sarkophag-Corpus 2001*, edited by G. Koch (Mainz, 2007), 111–116.

Grebe, S. Marriage and Exile. Cicero's Letters to Terentia. *Helios* 30 (2003), 127–146.

Griessmair, E. *Das Motiv der mors immatura in den griechischen metrischen Grabinschriften* (Innsbruck, 1966).

Harkness, A. G. The scepticism and fatalism of the common people of Rome as illustrated by the sepulchral inscriptions. Transactions and Proceedings of the American Philological Association 30 (1899), 56–88.

Hekster, O. Propagating Power: Hercules as an example for second-century emperors, in: *Herakles and Hercules: Exploring a Graeco-Roman Divinity*, edited by L. Rawlings and H. Bowden (Swansea, 2005), 205–217.

Hemelrijk, E. A. Masculinity and Femininity in the Laudatio Turiae. *Classical Quarterly* 54 (2004), 185–197.

Herdejürgen, H. *Stadtrömische und italische Girlandensarkophage: Die Sarkophage des ersten und zweiten Jahrhunderts.* Die antiken Sarkophagreliefs 6.2.1 (Berlin, 1996).

Hoff, R. von den. "Achill das Vieh"? Zur Problematisierung transgressiver Gewalt in klassischen Vasenbildern, in: *Die andere Seite der Klassik: Gewalt im 5. und 4. Jahrhundert v. Chr. Kulturwissenschaftliches Kolloquium Bonn, Kunst- und Ausstellungshalle der Bundesrepublik Deutschland, 11.–13. Juli 2002*, edited by G. Fischer (Stuttgart, 2005), 225–246.

Hölscher, T. Mythen als Exempel der Geschichte, in: *Mythos in mythenloser Gesellschaft: Das Paradigma Roms; 3.Colloquium Rauricum, Augst, 1991*, edited by F. Graf (Stuttgart; Leipzig, 1993), 67–87.

Holub, R. C. *Reception Theory: A Critical Introduction* (London, 1984).

Hope, V. M. Death in Ancient Rome: a Source Book (London, 2007).

Hope, V. M. Roman Death: Dying and the Dead in Ancient Rome (London, 2009).

Huskinson, J. *Roman Children's Sarcophagi: Their Decoration and Its Social Significance* (Oxford, 1996).

Jauss, H. R. *Toward an Aesthetic of Reception* (Brighton, 1982).

Jauss, H. R. and E. Benzinger. Literary History as a Challenge to Literary Theory. *New Literary History* 2 (1970), 7–37.

Jongste, P. F. *The Twelve Labours of Hercules on Roman Sarcophagi* (Rome, 1992).

Junker, K. Römische mythologische Sarkophage. Zur Entstehung eines Denkmaltypus. *Mitteilungen des Deutschen Archäologischen Instituts, Römische Abteilung* 112 (2006), 163–188.

Junker, K. *Interpreting the Images of Greek Myths. An Introduction* (Cambridge; New York, 2012).

Kassel, R. *Untersuchungen zur griechischen und römischen Konsolationsliteratur* (Munich, 1958).

Keegan, P. Turia, Lepidus, and Rome's Epigraphic Environment. *Studia Humaniora Tartuensia* 9 (2008), 1–7.

Kierdorf, W. *Laudatio funebris: Interpretationen und Untersuchungen zur Entwicklung der römischen Leichenrede* (Meisenheim a. Glan, 1980).

Koch, G. *Meleager.* Die antiken Sarkophagreliefs 12.6 (Berlin, 1975).

Koch, G. and H. Sichtermann. *Römische Sarkophage* (Munich, 1982).

Koortbojian, M. *Myth, Meaning and Memory on Roman Sarcophagi* (Berkeley, 1995).

Koortbojian, M. Review of Jason et Médée sur les sarcophages d'époque impériale by Vassiliki Gaggadis-Robin. *American Journal of Archaeology* 100 (1996), 435–436.

Lattimore, R. *Themes in Greek and Latin Epitaphs* (Urbana, IL, 1942).

Létoublon, F. Homer's Use of Myth, in: *A Companion to Greek Mythology*, edited by K. Dowden and N. Livingstone (Malden, Mass., 2011), 27–45.

Linant de Bellefonds, P. Le 'motif de Phèdre' sur les sarcophages romains: comment l'image crée la vertu, in: *Iconographie funéraire romaine et société: corpus antique, approches nouvelles?*, edited by M. Galinier and F. Baratte (Perpignan, 2013), 65–79.

Lindner, R. *Der Raub der Persephone in der antiken Kunst* (Würzburg, 1984).

Lindsay, H. The "Laudatio Murdiae": its content and significance. *Latomus* 63 (2004), 88–97.

Livingstone, N. Instructing Myth: from Homer to the Sophists, in: *A Companion to Greek Mythology*, edited by K. Dowden and N. Livingstone (Malden, Mass., 2011), 125–139.

Lloyd, G. E. R. *Polarity and Analogy: Two Types of Argumentation in Early Greek Thought* (Cambridge, 1966).

Lorenz, K. Image in Distress? The Death of Meleager on Roman Sarcophagi, in: *Life, Death and Representation: Some New Work on Roman Sarcophagi*, edited by J. Elsner and J. Huskinson (Berlin, 2011), 309–336.

Lorenz, K. *Ancient Mythological Images and Their Interpretation. An Introduction to Iconology, Semiotics and Image Studies in Classical Art History* (Cambridge, 2016).

Matz, F. *Die dionysischen Sarkophage*. Die antiken Sarkophagreliefs 4.3 (Berlin, 1969).

McDonnell, M. Roman Men and Greek Virtue, in: *Andreia: Studies in Manliness and Courage in Classical Antiquity*, edited by R. M. Rosen and I. Sluiter (Leiden, 2003), 235–261.

Moretti, L. (ed.) Inscriptiones Graecae Urbis Romae, vol. 3 (Rome, 1979).

Mucznik, S. *Devotion and Unfaithfulness: Alcestis and Phaedra in Roman Art* (Rome, 1999).

Müller, F. G. J. M. *The So-called Peleus and Thetis Sarcophagus in the Villa Albani* (Amsterdam, 1994).

Muth, S. *Erleben von Raum – Leben im Raum: Zur Funktion mythologischer Mosaikbilder in der römisch-kaiserzeitlichen Wohnarchitektur* (Heidelberg, 1998).

Muth, S. Drei statt vier: Zur Deutung der Feldherrensarkophage. *Archäologischer Anzeiger* (2004), 263–273.

Muth, S. Im Angesicht des Todes: Zum Wertediskurs in der römischen Grabkultur, in: *Römische Werte als Gegenstand der Altertumswissenschaft*, edited by A. Haltenhoff et al. (Munich, 2005), 259–286.

Nagy, G. Mythological Exemplum in Homer, in: *Innovations of Antiquity*, edited by R. D. Hexter and D. Selden (New York, 1992), 311–331.

Newby, Z. Myth and Death: Roman mythological sarcophagi, in: *A Companion to Greek Mythology*, edited by K. Dowden and N. Livingstone (Malden, Mass., 2011a), 301–318.

Newby, Z. In the Guise of Gods and Heroes: portrait heads on Roman mythological sarcophagi, in: *Life, Death and Representation: Some New Work on Roman Sarcophagi*, edited by J. Elsner and J. Huskinson (Berlin, 2011b), 189–227.

Newby, Z. Poems in Stone: reading mythological sarcophagi through Statius' Consolations, in: *Art and Rhetoric in Roman Culture*, edited by J. Elsner (New York, 2014), 256–287.

Newby, Z. *Greek Myths in Roman Art and Culture. Imagery, Values and Identity in Italy, 50 BC-AD 250* (Cambridge, 2016).

Nock, A. D. Sarcophagi and Symbolism. *American Journal of Archaeology* 50 (1946), 140–170.

Peek, W. (ed.) Griechische Vers-Inschriften vol. 1: Grab-Epigramme, (Berlin, 1955).

Peek, W. (ed.) *Griechische Grabgedichte: Griechisch und deutsch* (Berlin, 1960).

Pekáry, T. Mors perpetua est. Zum Jenseitsglauben in Rom. Laverna (1994), 87–103.

Peres, I. *Griechische Grabinschriften und neutestamentliche Eschatologie* (Tübingen, 2003).

Platt, V. *Facing the Gods: Epiphany and Representation in Graeco-Roman Art, Literature and Religion* (Cambridge, 2011).

Raeck, W. *Modernisierte Mythen: Zum Umgang der Spätantike mit klassischen Bildthemen* (Stuttgart, 1992).

Raepsaet-Charlier, M.-T. *Prosopographie des femmes de l'ordre sénatorial (I.–II. siècles)* (Louvain, 1987).

Rawlings, L. Hannibal and Hercules, in: *Herakles and Hercules: Exploring a Graeco-Roman Divinity*, edited by L. Rawlings and H. Bowden (Swansea, 2005), 153–184.

Rees, R. The Emperor's New Names: Diocletian Jovius and Maximinian Herculius, in: *Herakles and Hercules: Exploring a Graeco-Roman Divinity*, edited by L. Rawlings and H. Bowden (Swansea, 2005), 223–239.

Ritter, S. *Hercules in der römischen Kunst von den Anfängen bis Augustus* (Heidelberg, 1995).

Robert, C. *Einzelmythen: Hippolytos – Meleager*. Die antiken Sarkophagreliefs 3.2 (Berlin, 1904).

Robert, C. *Einzelmythen: Niobiden – Triptolemos; ungedeutet*. Die antiken Sarkophagreliefs 3.3 (Berlin, 1919).

Rodenwaldt, G. *Über den Stilwandel in der antoninischen Kunst* (Berlin, 1935).

Rogge, S. *Die attischen Sarkophage: Achill und Hippolytos* (Berlin, 1995).

Russell, D. A. and N. G. Wilson. *Menander Rhetor* (Oxford, 1981).

Russenberger, C. Pathos und Repräsentation: Zum veränderten Umgang mit Mythen auf stadtrömischen Sarkophagen severischer Zeit, in: *Repräsentationsformen in severischer Zeit*, edited by St. Faust (Berlin, 2011), 136–171.

Russenberger, C. *Der Tod und die Mädchen: Amazonen auf römischen Sarkophagen* (Berlin; München, 2015).

Schmitz, C. "denn auch Niobe ...": die Bedeutung der Niobe-Erzählung in Achills Rede. *Hermes* 129 (2001), 145–157.

Schoonhoven, H. *The Pseudo-Ovidian "Ad Liviam de morte Drusi" (Consolatio ad Liviam, Epicedium Drusi). A Critical Text with Introduction and Commentary* (Groningen, 1992).

Sichtermann, H. *Späte Endymion-Sarkophage: Methodisches zur Interpretation* (Baden-Baden, 1966).

Sichtermann, H. *Apollon, Ares, Bellerophon, Daidalos, Endymion, Ganymed, Giganten, Grazien*. Die antiken Sarkophagreliefs 12.2 (Berlin, 1992).

Sichtermann, H. and G. Koch. *Griechische Mythen auf römischen Sarkophagen* (Tübingen, 1975).

Soffel, J. *Die Regeln Menanders fuer die Leichenrede in ihrer Tradition dargestellt. Hrsg., uebers. u. kommentiert* (Meisenheim am Glan, 1974).

Stilp, F. Autoreprésentation funéraire, entre mythe, art officiel et 'Berufsdarstellung', in: *Iconographie funéraire romaine et société: corpus antique, approches nouvelles?*, edited by M. Galinier and F. Baratte (Perpignan, 2013), 51–64.

Thome, G. *Zentrale Wertvorstellungen der Römer, vol. 1* (Bamberg, 2002).

Turcan, R. Les sarcophages romains et le problème du symbolisme funéraire, in: *Aufstieg und Niedergang der römischen Welt* 16.2 (Berlin, 1978), 1700–1735.

Turcan, R. *Messages d'outre-tombe: l'iconographie des sarcophages romains* (Paris, 1999).

Wilcox, A. Exemplary Grief. Gender and Virtue in Seneca's Consolations to Women. *Helios* 33:1 (2006), 73–100.

Willcock, M. M. Mythological Paradeigma in the Iliad. *The Classical Quarterly* 14 (1964), 141–154.

Willcock, M. M. Ad hoc Invention in the Iliad. *Harvard Studies in Classical Philology* 81 (1977), 41–53.

Wrede, H. Consecratio in formam deorum. *Vergöttlichte Privatpersonen in der römischen Kaiserzeit* (Mainz, 1981).

Wrede, H. *Senatorische Sarkophage Roms: Der Beitrag des Senatorenstandes zur römischen Kunst der hohen und späten Kaiserzeit* (Mainz, 2001).

Zanker, P. Phädras Trauer und Hippolytos' Bildung. Zu einem Sarkophag im Thermenmuseum, in: *Im Spiegel des Mythos. Bilderwelt und Lebenswelt*, edited by F. De Angelis and S. Muth (Wiesbaden, 1999), 131–142.

Zanker, P. *Die mythologischen Sarkophagreliefs und ihre Betrachter* (Munich, 2000).

Zanker, P. Discorsi presso la tomba. Le immagini dei sarcofagi mitologici: un linguaggio al superlativo, in: *Espacios y usos funerarios en el Occidente romano*, edited by D. Vaquerizo (Cordoba, 2002), 51–65.

Zanker, P. Die mythologischen Sarkophagreliefs als Ausdruck eines neuen Gefühlskultes. Reden im Superlativ, in: *Sinn (in) der Antike: Orientierungssysteme, Leitbilder und Wertkonzepte im Altertum*, edited by K.-J. Hölkeskamp (Mainz, 2003), 335–355.

Zanker, P. and B. C. Ewald. *Living with Myths: The Imagery of Roman Sarcophagi* (Oxford, 2012).

B. C. Ewald
Attic Sarcophagi

Myth Selection and the Heroising Tradition

Sarcophagi did not simply furnish the spaces in which they were put on display, but actively defined them in their specific quality. They did so through their particular choice of themes, their morphology and formal language, and they did so in concert with other elements of a tomb's architecture and decoration, as well as the rites and rituals that animated them. My contribution argues that the specific selection of mythological themes on Attic sarcophagi served to reinforce the specific spatial character of the tomb as a *heroon*: The sarcophagi's imagery, with its emphasis on heroic myth, was – among other things – designed to match the common designation of tombs as *heroa*, as well as the generous use of the *hero* title for deceased men, women and children. The habit of private heroisation, and the corresponding conceptualisation of the tomb as a *heroon*, provided a horizon of meaning that, to a certain degree, pre-determined the selection of myth as well as the rendering of individual mythical episodes. A specific idea of the tomb as a sphere of meaning, in other words, was already inscribed into the choice of themes and iconographies on Attic sarcophagi: "context" begins in the sarcophagus workshop. The highly anachronistic imagery of Attic sarcophagi, with its focus on male valour and virtue, has much to do with the retrospective mentality and the cultural tenets that are also evident in the literature of the so-called "Second Sophistic";[1] but it also should be interpreted against the background of the heroising tradition in the Greek East. The elaborate and immensely expensive Attic sarcophagi made "heroisation" available to everyone who had the necessary means. One could in fact say that the burial of a corpse in an elaborate Attic sarcophagus mimicked the fundamental operation involved in the act of heroisation: it segregated and hid away the body, then substituted it with a lasting, heroic narrative.[2]

My argument proceeds in three steps. Some introductory remarks serve to illuminate the broader context and the modalities of the production and reception of Attic sarcophagi. I then survey the specific theme selection found on them in the light of the heroising tradition in the Greek East. In order to give sharper contours to the phenomenon, I apply a comparative method: Attic sarcophagi and their rendering of mostly mythological themes are read in constant juxtaposition with Roman

---

1 Cf. Ewald 2004; Ewald 2012. Surveys of the "Second Sophistic": E.g. Anderson 1993; Swain 1996; Whitmarsh 2005. "Greek identity" under Roman rule: E.g. Veyne 1999; Veyne 2005, 163–257 (undercited); Whitmarsh 2010.
2 Cf. Pache 2004, 151–2.

https://doi.org/10.1515/9783110421453-010

sarcophagi, which alone show a comparably differentiated mythical imagery. The analysis demonstrates the existence of two distinct, yet open and interrelated "mythospheres", i.e. of two different thematic and discursive complexes. Some mythological figures and compositions "wandered" between East and West, and from one artistic medium or social group to another, while others did not. Each of these "mythospheres" had its own thematic preferences and focal points, as well as its blind spots and mechanisms of exclusion. Under the apparent chaos of the enormously varied and diverse imagery of sarcophagi in the West and East lies perhaps no perfect order (it does not quite amount to a discursive or semantic "system"), but certain meaningful structures and an internal logic are in evidence nonetheless. While there are several factors that determined the selection of myth on Attic sarcophagi, it appears that the differences that can be observed in the thematic orientation of Attic and Roman sarcophagi are inextricably linked to differing conceptualisations of the tomb as a sphere of meaning in East and West. In the case of Attic sarcophagi, their focus on heroic myth, though not exclusive, becomes readily apparent. The last part of the contribution then situates the Attic sarcophagi's imagery within contemporary practices and discourses about "heroisation" in the Greek East.

Attic Sarcophagi: an Introduction

Attic sarcophagi are plausibly believed to have been produced in Athens or its environs, from Pentelic marble, during the second and third centuries AD. They were very probably carved in the workshops that also produced decorative, "neo-Attic" sculpture for domestic decoration, such as table supports and small-scale ideal statues during the second and third centuries AD;[3] the Piraeus reliefs, famous for the quotations from the Amazonomachy on the shield of the Athena Parthenos shown on some of them, also belong in this context.[4] Through their references to famous Greek works of art (plainly evident in pieces such as the Varvakion Athena), the reliefs as well as the statues displayed a retrospective and "classicistic" orientation that is also apparent on the sarcophagi.

Even more so than the statuettes, which may have seen more of a local circulation,[5] Attic sarcophagi became highly successful items for export. They were used from

---

3 Table supports: Stefanidou-Tiveriou 1992. Ideal Sculpture: Stirling 2008; Stirling 2009. Neo-Attic workshops: Cain and Dräger 1994 (also discussing problems of definition of "neo-Attic" art); Fuchs 1999; Fittschen 2008.
4 Stefanidou-Tiveriou 1979 (with a date around the middle of the second century AD).
5 Sterling 2008; Stirling 2009. The Attic funerary reliefs, associated with the Athenian sculpture workshops of the first to third centuries AD, were also primarily produced for the local markets of Athens and Attica: von Moock 1998, 4–21.

Hispania in the west to Syria and Arabia in the east,[6] and they are often found in cities or regions that had long established trade relations with Athens, such as Ephesus, Palestine, the Cyrenaica, etc.[7] At their destinations, Attic sarcophagi often had a direct impact on the local sculpture workshops, which emulated Attic sarcophagi in both locally available and imported materials.[8] It has been estimated that ca. 65 % of Attic sarcophagi were produced for export, as compared to only 3 % of Roman sarcophagi and 15 % of those from Dokimeion (another workshop of upscale sarcophagi, located in Phrygia).[9] The production of "decorative" sculpture and in particular of these elaborate sarcophagi for export must have been profitable business in a city that otherwise relied heavily on the import of grain and goods from outside.[10] It has even been suggested that a small number of leading Athenian families may have been invested in the lucrative sculpture business;[11] this would have involved not only the carving and shipping of sarcophagi and other sculptures, but possibly also the quarrying of marble from Pentelicon.[12] The lively sarcophagus trade, however, only lasted as long as the differentiated economy that supported it, i.e. as long as the trade routes were not interrupted, and as long as the wealthy urban aristocracy that provided the clientele in the importing cities was thriving.[13] The end of this sarcophagus commerce came shortly after the middle of the third century AD, apparently several years before the sack of Athens by the Herulians in 267 AD.[14] Some smaller items, such as the decorative table supports and portraits, were produced after this date, but only in small quantities.[15]

How can we explain the extraordinary success of Attic sarcophagi? The evolution of the sarcophagi demonstrates how the workshops, in an apparently self-driven process of supply and demand, adapted to the emerging fashion of sarcophagus burial

---

6 Koch and Sichtermann 1982, 461–70; Koch 1989; Koch 2012a; Koch 2012b. Cf. Russell 2013, 169–78.

7 See Day 1942, passim, for an analysis of Athenian trade relations in the Roman imperial period.

8 Koch and Sichtermann 1982, 470–5; Koch 2012a; Koch 2012b; Papagianni 2016, 107–15.

9 Koch 2012b, 46–7. This is a downward correction from Koch's earlier estimate of 80–90 % of Attic sarcophagi being produced for export, cf. Ewald 2004, 265 n. 139; correctly also Papagianni 2016, 103 (ca. 40 % of Attic sarcophagi with Erotes were used locally, i.e. in Athens). It is not always easy to define where exactly "export" begins and production for the "local" market ends: outside Athens and its environs, outside the province of Achaea, or with the shipping of sarcophagi overseas?

10 Day 1942, 120–251, esp. 202–21.

11 Day 1942, 251.

12 The organisation and administration of the Penteli quarries during the period in question is uncertain, see Day 1942, 203–4; Pensabene 2013, 265–77 (268–9 on a possible involvement of Herodes Atticus). Also the brief discussion in Trimble 2011, 71.

13 Rodenwaldt 1952; Wiegartz 1965, 614–5; Wiegartz 1975, 251; also Stefanidou-Tiveriou 1993, 135, who points out the synchronicity between the end of the Attic production and that of Dokimeion.

14 Wiegartz loc. cit.; Stefanidou-Tiveriou 1993; also Day 1942, 252–61; Koch 2012b, dates the (possibly) latest known Attic sarcophagus, a Pelops sarcophagus in Athens (Oakley 2011, 93–5 no. 61), to ca. 260 AD.

15 Cf. Wiegartz 1975, 251; Stefanidou-Tiveriou 1992; 1993.

during the second century, and then gradually developed ever more successful iconographies catering to the hellenophile and heroising tastes of their elite clientele in the early third century.[16] In the process, the geographic range of the sarcophagus export business increased greatly.[17] By the early third century, Attic sarcophagi outperform other imports of comparable quality in the cities that also imported high-end sarcophagi from other workshops, in particular those produced in Dokimeion in Asia Minor. A recent estimate by G. Koch suggests that, in the city of Rome, only 10 of the ca. 80 imported Attic sarcophagi date to the second century AD, while ca. 60–70 examples date to the third century AD;[18] conversely, of the 41 sarcophagi imported to Rome from Dokimeion, 38 date to the second century, but only 3 to the third century. Similar observations were made by J. B. Ward-Perkins for the city of Tyre (Lebanon), which likewise imported Attic sarcophagi in significant numbers.[19]

The appeal of Attic sarcophagi lay in their Athenian origin as much as in their precious material and elaborate carving. At their places of destination, they stood out against the much simpler and often undecorated (though sometimes inscribed) sarcophagi from local production, as well as the (usually less elaborate) imports from other workshops. We may safely assume that many ancient customers and viewers, while lacking the fine-grained typological knowledge of modern sacophagus scholars, had at least a marginal understanding of the quality and the origin of a sarcophagus and its material. This, in any case, is suggested by a number of funerary inscriptions from Asia Minor. These inscriptions reveal a simple taxonomy and a scaled appreciation of sarcophagi, based on the various types of stone (ordinary, darker, or porous stone: μύλινος, πώρινος, vs. white marble or lighter stone: λευκόλιθος, λευκός), its origin (from Proconnesus, Dokimeion or local quarries) and the question of whether a sarcophagus was sculpted (κατάγλυφος, ἀνάγλυφος) or not.[20] Awareness of the fact that a sarcophagus was not only sculpted, but carved in Athens, and shipped all the way from there, must have also played an important role. This can be concluded from the fact that the so-called neo-Attic sculptures of the second and first centuries BC already displayed occasional inscriptions adding an Ἀθηναῖος to a sculptor's name, evidently as a marker of quality and origin.[21] While we do not have any sources on the *specific* motivations of the patrons of Attic sarcophagi, the success of the neo-Attic workshops leaves no doubt that there was a sufficiently large group of wealthy buy-

---

16 See, for example, the development of Attic sarcophagi with Achilles and Hippolytus: Ewald 2012.

17 Papagianni 2016, 106.

18 Koch 2012b, 47.

19 Ward-Perkins 1956; Ward-Perkins 1969.

20 Kubinska 1968, 58–60.

21 Day 1942, 155; cf. ibid 98–9; 103–4; 204–7; Cain and Dräger 1994, 818–9. Such inscriptions are lacking on the sarcophagi, perhaps because of their usually more private contexts of display, perhaps also because they were, much more so than the freestanding sculptures, easily recognisable as Attic works in their final settings.

ers in Italy and elsewhere that was very keen on art and artefacts produced in Athens. The retrospective thematic orientation of Attic sarcophagi was, as we shall see, particularly well matched to such expectations; it is not much of an exaggeration to say that the Athenian sarcophagus workshops partook in a broader marketing and selling of a Greek "cultural identity" that had become a profitable enterprise in the imperial period. Speaking in the broadest possible terms, the attraction of Attic sarcophagi must have been of a kind with that of the city's philosophical and rhetorical schools and the institution of epheby, which attracted young men from wealthy families from all over the Mediterranean. Given some partial correspondences between the places of origin of Athenian ephebes and the findspots of Attic sarcophagi, it is even possible that some of the men who had spent their ephebic year in Athens later imported Attic sarcophagi in their hometowns. Attic sarcophagi are particularly well suited to illustrate the fact that trade in antiquity usually amounted to more than the mere circulation of objects, and instead often implied a conscious exchange of ideas and ideologies, values and knowledge[22].

A number of interrelated changes to the design of Attic sarcophagi must have contributed to their extraordinary success during the late second and early third centuries AD. If we leave out of consideration possible external factors that may have given an advantage to the Attic sarcophagus workshops over their competitors (such as the relative proximity between the Penteli quarries and the Piraeus harbour, from where they must have been shipped[23]), it becomes clear that there were modifications to the sarcophagus design during the second and third centuries that made them ever more appealing to their elite customers. The introduction of the monumental *kline* lids depicting couples (or, more rarely, single figures) around 160 AD had afforded the female a highly representative position, one that reflected contemporary conjugal ideals as well as the significant social status of elite women at the time (Figs. 1; 3 a; 4 a-b; 7; 10; 11).[24] The relegation of the female to the sarcophagus lid, moreover, freed up the casket of the sarcophagus for imagery that was usually more male centred and heroising.[25] In addition, around the turn of the second to third century, the overall dimensions of the sarcophagi increase greatly, as do the number of figures and the depth of the carving. This aggrandising trend must have driven up prices for Attic sarcophagi further; they were now more assertively elite funerary monuments that contributed to an ongoing process of social differentiation, and even "polarisation", in the cities that imported them.[26]

---

22 Cf. the contribution by Draycott in this volume.

23 Russell 2011, 124; Russell 2013, 281.

24 Ewald 2011; Ahrens 2007, on the date of the introduction of *kline*-lids on Attic sarcophagi.

25 Ewald 2011.

26 Ewald 2004, 234; Wiegartz 1975, 249–51 offers some calculations about the prices for elaborate Attic sarcophagi, based on the relative cost of the marble and the labour of craftsmen. On the widening social gap in the importing cities in the Greek East see, for example, Woolf 1994, 124.

Fig. 1: Thessaloniki, Archaeological Museum Inv. 1794–96. Partial lack of finish on the lid of a 3rd cent. AD Attic amazonomachy sarcophagus. Not only the heads of the reclining figures and the less visible portions of the lid are not fully finished, but also the hand garland of the female figure as well as some folds of the garment and the frontal portion of the lid. (Photo: author).

It was, consequently, not merely the Athenian provenance of the sarcophagi or the quality of the marble that made them desirable. The sculpted (and presumably painted) imagery and elaborate architectural ornamentation of Attic sarcophagi must have accounted at least in parts for their attraction.[27] This is plainly evident from the fact that, unlike other centres of sarcophagus production (such as Assus, Ephesus or Proconnesus) the Attic workshops appear not to have been involved in the lively trade of so-called "Halbfabrikate"; i.e., of sarcophagi that were shipped in "quarry state", with only the basic decorative scheme (usually for garland decor)

---

[27] Wiegartz 1975, loc.cit. in fact suggested that the material of the sarcophagus would have only accounted for ca. 15 % of its final price (not including the additional cost for shipping and transport); the principal factor in establishing the value of an Attic sarcophagus would have been the immense labour involved in carving a monumental Attic sarcophagus. Differently, however, Ward-Perkins 1956, 15: "The cost of shipping one of these great marble sarcophagi from the quarries to its destination is nowhere recorded; but the skilled workmanship involved in carving it can have accounted for only quite a modest percentage of the whole." Salaries for skilled Attic craftsmen could be high: Cain and Dräger 1994.

roughed out.[28] Instead, they were shipped in an almost fully carved state, with emphasis on the front and one "main" small side, while the other small side and the back are executed more summarily; often, the characteristic ornament bands above and below the sculpted frieze were also not, or not entirely, finished.[29] Similar things can be said about the *kline*-lids, on which in particular the less visible portions (e.g., behind the reclining figures), but also details such as the folds of the garments, are sometimes left in a roughed-out state (Fig. 1). This partial lack of finish does not only concern sarcophagi that were shipped over wide distances, but also many pieces used in Athens herself. Usually, however, what needed to be added at the final destinations were principally the portraits of the reclining figures on the *kline* lids as well as occasional repairs made necessary by damage obtained during transport. In a number of cases, from both Athens and abroad, major reworkings of the sarcophagus lids with reclining figures can be observed. While it is sometimes not clear when exactly these modifications were carried out (upon arrival of the sarcophagus, or in connection with later re-use), they mainly include alterations to the typified and idealised representations of the reclining sarcophagus patron(s), i.e. the recipient(s) and/or dedicant(s) of a sarcophagus. Such reworkings can include the re-carving or removal of an entire figure, its transformation into a bundle of bookrolls, but also the addition of a *tabula* or other measures in order to create a proper space for an inscription[30] – a feature that Attic sarcophagi lack, unlike many of their counterparts in both the East and West. If the sarcophagi were already painted before they were sent on their way, or if this was done at their final destinations, is not known. While the above-mentioned statuettes from Attic workshops display abundant traces of painting, Attic sarcophagi seldom

---

28 Ward Perkins 1969; Koch and Sichtermann 1982, 476–97. However, blocks of Pentelic marble could also be traded and then carved locally into sarcophagi: Papagianni 2016, 110–1 pl. 61; Russell 2011, 135.

29 Cf. Rogge 1995, 15–6.

30 E.g. Ward-Perkins 1956; Rogge 1995, 17, no. 50 pl. 96, 1: Lid of an Attic sarcophagus from Trinquetaille in Arles, on which an (empty) tabula for inscription was added and the female figure was reworked into a male togate figure, while the male figure was removed. A similar case is a sarcophagus lid in storage at the National Museum in Athens (Inv. 3621); it shows a reclining female figure with garland in hand, but the upper body with the *chiton* appears to be re-carved so that it displays a wide *contabulatio* across the upper body (or a contabulated *stola*, as on the Proconnesian example in Palagia 2010, 435 fig. 4). – On the *kline* lid of a strigillated Attic sarcophagus in Athens, National Museum Inv. 1497, the female figure was reworked into a male figure, while the male figure was reworked into a bundle of book rolls (Goette 1991, 323–325 no. 4; Goette 1993, 108). On the Attic Dionysiac sarcophagus of Vitalius Restitutus in Thessaloniki (see n. 102; Papagianni, in Despinis et al. 2011, 333–8; Oakley 2011, 83–4 no. 41 pl. 32.2), the ornament band at the bottom of the sarcophagus was, as E. Papagianni points out to me, secondarily prepared for the inscription. This was probably done locally, after arrival of the sarcophagus at its destination, although it is of course not clear how much time had passed between the carving of the sarcophagus and the alterations made necessary by the inscription. Inscription on the battle sarcophagus of Q. Aemilius Aristides in Ephesus: Kintrup 2016, 109–12; 240–3 no. 87.

show the remnants of painting and gilding known from both the statuettes and many Roman sarcophagi. Be this as it may: in cases where the sarcophagi were exposed to the elements (as in the necropolis of Tyre, for example) any painted decoration would have deteriorated fairly quickly, and would have required occasional re-touching.[31]

Many questions surrounding the processes of ordering and shipping the sarcophagi remain. There are examples that suggest that the workshops were able to meet even extravagant customer choices, while in other cases, the figures on the *kline* lids appear to have been reworked only at the sarcophagi's final destinations. It is also difficult to say if, in the many cases in which the small or back sides are not fully carved (or are of considerably lesser quality), this fact takes into consideration the intended final placement of the sarcophagi, and if it does, how information about the final position of a sarcophagus within a tomb (or about details of the design) was transmitted from the customers to the distant workshop(s).[32] To J. B. Ward-Perkins, the summary carving of the back and one small side of many sarcophagi suggested that they were shipped in this state and only finished at their final destinations.[33] But his hypothesis of Attic craftsmen travelling from the "parent workshops" with their cargo, and finishing the sarcophagi on site, possibly even setting up "secondary workshops ... outside Greece" (e.g. in places such as Aquileia or Rome) has not resonated much with specialists in the field.[34] Interestingly, and for what it is worth, for Philostratus, writing in the second century AD, the type of practice suggested by Ward-Perkins is already a thing of the past. An illuminating passage in the *Vita Apollonii* (5.20) describes how the philosopher enters into a dialogue with a ship owner in Piraeus who is about to depart in order to sell his cargo of statues of the gods (in various materials) to buyers in the cities of Ionia.[35] In doing so, he contrasts the travelling craftsmen of yesteryear with the selling of finished Attic statues in his own time:

> But the image-makers of old behaved not in this way, nor did they go round the cities selling their gods. All they did was to export their own hands and their tools for working stone and ivory; others provided the raw materials, while they plied their handicraft in the temples themselves;

31 A recent scientific study of a Roman sarcophagus has produced evidence not only for the well-documented painting, but also for the subsequent re-painting of sarcophagi in antiquity: Siotto et al. 2014. Painting of Attic sarcophagi: Kintrup 1999, 6 with n. 34; Kintrup 2016, 91 n. 285; 249 no. 112 (traces of painting on an Attic battle sarcophagus in Jerusalem).

32 Russell 2011; Russell 2013, 285.

33 Ward-Perkins 1956, 13; cf. Rodenwaldt 1933, 182; Ward-Perkins 1969. For the Proconnesian workshops, Ward-Perkins 1969, 136, argues for the production of certain basic patterns which were designed to match the prevailing conditions of display in the cities that were the main importers – a middling position between the idea that sarcophagi were individual pieces made on order, and the assumption of a unified "mass production".

34 Ward-Perkins 1956, 15; Ward-Perkins 1969, 132–4, with the most recent, sensible discussion by Russell 2013, 281–5. However, the migration of Attic craftsmen, and their presence in Rome, are well attested for the late Hellenistic period (e.g., Cain and Dräger 1994, 817–20).

35 Day 1942, 205–6. Also Russell 2013, 313–6 on "production-to-stock".

but you are leading the gods into harbors and market places just as if they were wares of the Hyrcanians and of the Scythians – far be it for me to name these – and so you think you are doing no impiety? (5.20; Translation F. C. Conybeare)

However, Philostratus is referring here to the types of small-scale sculptures that have been attributed to the Attic workshops of the imperial period.[36] The sarcophagi were considerably larger and heavier, making their shipping and transport more challenging and costly, and "production-to-stock" less likely.

Who were the customers of Attic sarcophagi? Burial in a carved sarcophagus was always a marker of economic potency, even if it did not always correspond to actual social rank.[37] Due to their dimensions and elaborate carving, the cost for material and transport, as well as their prestigious origin, Attic sarcophagi must have been comparatively more expensive than sarcophagi manufactured locally, as well as most sarcophagi from other workshops. The sarcophagus inscriptions, though not at all frequent, clearly confirm the assumption of an elite client base that has sometimes left other traces in the archaeological record.[38] The less wealthy either ordered more modest funerary monuments, such as the Attic *stelai* without mythological decoration (e.g. Fig. 9 b), or, as mounting evidence from Asia Minor suggests, continued to practise cremation (which was overall the more economic rite) alongside the ever more popular inhumation.[39] The relative value and appreciation of Attic sarcophagi is also evident from their prominent placement within the tombs, in which they were often the element that contributed most decisively to a "hierarchisation"[40] of the tomb space. In the Meleager Heroon in Delphi, for example, a tetrastyle temple tomb named after the theme of the Attic sarcophagus found in it, the Attic piece is placed in the most

---

36 Philostratus' statement is (as already noted by Day 1942, loc. cit.) corroborated by several archaeological finds in Piraeus, such as the 1930/31 find of the neo-Attic so-called "Piraeus reliefs" (Stefanidou-Tiveriou 1979), dating to the second century AD, and the 1959 find of a group of late Hellenistic bronze and marble sculptures, which according to Fuchs 1999, 9–22, were pieces destined for export. Many of the late second and early third-century AD statues in the Athenian National Museum, including the Varvakion Athena, are indeed of the small scale implied by Philostratus, even if they appear to have circulated more locally (cf. Sterling 2008; 2009) than suggested by the passage quoted above.
37 In the case of Roman sarcophagi, patrons of widely differing backgrounds were among the customers: cf. Ewald 2015, 399–403 (with references); Mayer 2012, 100–65 (Roman sarcophagi and their use of myth as a "middle class" phenomenon). Unfortunately, there is, as of yet, no comprehensive, empirical analysis of sarcophagus inscriptions in the Roman Empire, which would provide the only reliable basis for any speculations regarding the sociology and possible motivations of sarcophagus patrons. Dresken-Weiland 2003 and, for the local sarcophagi of Thessaloniki, Nigdelis 2014, are important steps in the right direction.
38 Rogge 1995, 16–7; Kintrup 1999, 5–9; Ewald 2004, 234–6.
39 *Stelai*: von Moock 1998; Ewald 2004, 234. Continued practice of cremation in the East: Ahrens 2015.
40 Flämig 2007.

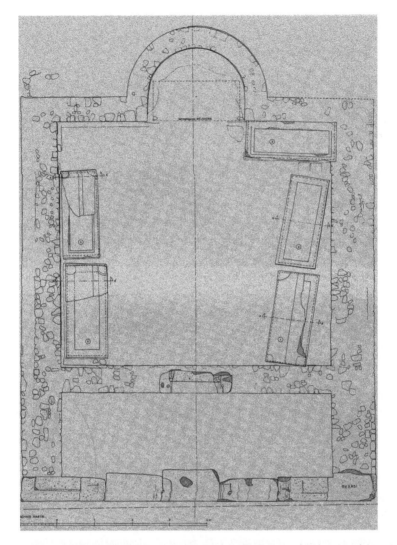

Fig. 2: Delphi, So-called Meleager Heroon, plan. The imported Attic sarcophagus was located in the apse opposite the entrance, while the local limestone sarcophagi were assembled along the walls (after: Flämig 2007, pl. 27).

prominent spot: an apse right opposite the entrance (Figs. 2–3 a–c).[41] Local limestone sarcophagi, either without decoration or with very shallow relief, line the remaining walls. The heroic imagery and splendour of the Attic sarcophagus was here the privilege of the patron or principal recipient of the tomb, and served to "naturalise" his

---

[41] Flämig 2007, 140–2 no. 17 pls. 27–31; Koch 1975, 140–1 no. 166 pl. 131 (on the sarcophagus, see here n. 139).

Fig. 3: a–c: Delphi, Museum. Attic Meleager sarcophagus with reclining female on the lid. From the so-called Meleager Heroon at Delphi. The sarcophagus depicts the Calydonian boar hunt (featuring Atalante) on the right, and a group consisting of Meleager, one of the Thestiadai, and again Atalante on the left (after: Koch 1975, pl. 131). The left small side shows a horse leading hero with spear, the right small side a hunter with spear and a female figure with not securely identified objects in both hands (Altheia receiving the message of the death of the Thestiadai?). Late 2nd cent. AD: (Photo: Inst. Neg. Rom 61.2948; small sides: Photo H. R. Goette).

Fig. 4: Tyre, Necropolis. Attic Achilles sarcophagus (a) and an Attic Hippolytus sarcophagus (b) in context. 3rd cent. AD. The sarcophagi were placed on funerary platforms in the open, together with other imported and locally produced sarcophagi (after: Chéhab 1968, pl. 1; 1985, pl. 97a).

or her elevated status. The lid of the sarcophagus shows a single figure, a reclining female, which suggests a woman as the recipient (and perhaps also patron) of this tomb; interestingly, the figure of Atalante is particularly emphasised on this sarcophagus.[42] Similar observations can be made for other tomb contexts in Greece, Asia Minor and beyond. The fact that Attic sarcophagi were carved on all four sides could also be used advantageously in their placement within a funerary precinct. In the necropolis of Tyre, for example, the main sides of the sarcophagi can serve as focal points of the open funerary precincts in which they were often placed on pre-existing funerary platforms, while the carved sides and backs were meant to impress other visitors to the necropolis (Fig. 4 a–b).[43]

Myth and Theme Selection on Attic vs. Roman Sarcophagi

The best way to make visible the specific thematic contours of Attic sarcophagi is from a comparative perspective, i.e. by contrasting them with Roman mythological sarcophagi, which alone show a similarly differentiated mythological repertoire. The sarcophagi from Asia Minor by contrast (and in spite of some punctual thematic overlap with both Roman and Attic sarcophagi), remain mostly non-mythological, and remain in their figural repertoire somewhat more closely attached to the established visual forms of public honorific modes; this is particularly evident in their representation of seated and standing, mantle-clad males and females.[44] The partial convergences and differences in the visual repertory of both centres of production that emerge from such a comparison appear significant, mainly because – as the sarcophagi themselves demonstrate – an iconographic exchange between Rome and Athens existed.[45] Differences can therefore not simply be written off with generalising references to local artistic traditions, accidents of preservation, or the accidental availability of iconographic models in the workshops of Rome and Athens – though all of these may have played a certain role.

---

42 see below, n. 143.

43 Ward-Perkins 1969; Chéhab 1968; Chéhab 1985. More recently on the necropolis of Tyre: de Jong 2010. On the import of Attic sarcophagi in the Roman provinces of the Near East, see Koch 1989; Koch 2012b. I intend to offer a more detailed discussion of the contexts of Attic sarcophagi elsewhere.

44 Cf. Wiegartz 1965; Koch and Sichtermann 1982, 476–557; Alexandridis 2014.

45 Ewald 2004. For detailed and instructive discussions of the complex iconographic cross connections between Roman and Attic sarcophagi, and the circulation of iconographic patterns, see Giuliani 1989; Kintrup 1999, 226–37 (battle and Amazonomachy); Russenberger 2015, 302–36 (Amazonomachy).

The Local Dimension of Myth in the Greek East

There are, of course, some obvious problems to such sweeping thematic comparisons, helpful as they may be, and these problems must be addressed at least briefly at the outset. For one, every sarcophagus was (just like a painted Greek vase or any other monument of a certain complexity) a semantic microcosm in itself, a sort of open system with manifold internal relations between the four sculpted sides. This simple fact, in principle, demands a close reading of each individual piece, which cannot be offered here. An added, and perhaps more important complication in such structural comparisons lies in the *local* dimension of Greek myth in Greece. Attic sarcophagi were produced, and in parts also used, in a region with a particularly dense mythical topography; Pausanias' book on Attica, for example, is a *staccato* of monuments, paintings, and sculptures with mythological decoration, and of the corresponding aetiologies. However, in the interpretation of sarcophagi, this additional layer of reference usually escapes us because the majority of them have been decontextualised. We are usually in no position to say if and how the local meanings of a myth may have resonated with the viewers of Attic sarcophagi, to what extent they may have been responsible for the choice of a particular theme, and how they would have factored into the "reading" of a given sarcophagus. There are, however, a few cases where we can at least speculate that the local significance of a myth may have played a significant role in the patron's decorative choices. The most obvious example is a sarcophagus in Corinth, depicting the Seven against Thebes on the front and the death of Opheltes on the right small side (Fig. 5 a-b).[46] Both myths resonated locally: the departure of the Seven against Thebes on the front was closely related to nearby Argos, in particular through the figures of Adrastos, Amphiaraus and Polyneikes. Opheltes (Archemoros), depicted on the right small side, was the baby son of the Nemean king Lykourgos; he was killed by a snake when his nurse, the Lemnian queen Hypsipyle, temporarily abandoned him in order to show Adrastos and his men the way to a spring. The subsequent funeral games for Opheltes were regarded as the founding act of the Nemean games, and a *heroon* in Nemea has been identified as that of the unfortunate child.[47] In his *Thebaid* (6.242–8), Statius mentions a shrine of Opheltes/Archemoros, decorated "with scenes of the child's brief life and death",[48] and Argive and Corinthian coins from the imperial period depict the death of Opheltes in variable (and often rather makeshift) iconography (Fig. 6).[49] Admittedly, the myth is also represented at other times and in other regions, for example on Apulian vases and on one of the second

---

46 Young 1922, 430–44; Oakley 2011, 39–41; 87–8 no. 50 pls. 36–9.
47 Pache 2004, 131–2, with convenient discussion of the full literary and archaeological evidence pertaining to Opheltes/Archemoros.
48 Pache 2004, 113.
49 Frazer 1898, 92 figs. 19–20; Pache 2004, 126–9 figs. 28–31.

century AD Spada reliefs from Rome.[50] But it seems almost inconceivable that the patrons of the sarcophagus from Corinth would *not* have been aware of the local references: the sarcophagus was found in the proximity of Corinth, only a few kilometres from the *heroon* of Opheltes in Nemea and not much further from the city of Argos. The choice of both myths, moreover, was highly unusual as far as the Attic sarcophagi go, and it does not appear to have been requested by customers who imported Attic sarcophagi from afar: as far as Opheltes is concerned, in addition to the example in Corinth, the myth is only found on two fragments in Athens.[51] As far as the theme of the front side goes, the sarcophagus offers (thus far) the only known representation of the myth in the Greco-Roman art of the imperial period.[52] While it seems plausible, then, to posit a local connection for the mythological décor of the Corinth sarcophagus, it is much more difficult to say just how exactly the local reference would have played into the interpretation of its imagery. One may speculate, for example, that the local popularity of Opheltes may have led to the choice of myth, with the allegorical message – the praise of heroic manliness and the evocation of the *mors immatura* of a child, soon to be heroised – remaining intact.

Many other myths represented on Attic sarcophagi were, in one way or another, either anchored in the cultic topography of Athens, Attica, and the provinces of Achaea and Macedonia as a whole, or depicted in famous and publicly accessible works of art. However, we are not able to establish if these local references and works of art had a direct impact on the iconography of Attic sarcophagi, to what extent customers were aware of the connections, and why they would have chosen one myth over another. That said, we do not find on Attic sarcophagi the types of *local* myths that were more narrowly concerned with Athenian autochthony and identity, such as Erechtheus/Erechthonios, Kekrops and his daughters, the hero Butes, or the contest of Athena and Poseidon over Attica.[53] Some of these (such as Erechthonios, and Athena/Poseidon) are in fact represented on the second and third-century coinage of imperial Athens, together with other mythological figures and groups (which often reference famous Athenian works of art) such as Athena Parthenos, Athena and Marsyas, Apollo Patroos, Eirene with the Ploutos child, Demeter, Zeus, Hermes, and Dionysus.[54] On the coins, we also encounter Heracles and Theseus in a number of episodes, in-

---

50 Pache 2004, 95–134; Oakley 2011, 39–40.

51 Oakley 2011, 39–40.

52 Oakley 2011, 52–4 (the only other possible representation of the myth, on an Attic sarcophagus from Aquileia, is too fragmented to be identified beyond doubt).

53 Cf. Ewald 2004, 266–7; von Mosch 1999. Local Athenian myth is at the centre of a recent exhibition in Frankfurt: Brinkmann 2016.

54 von Mosch 1999, 35–7 (Erechthonios); 29–30 (Athena/Poseidon as symbols of Athenian "philanthropy"). Von Mosch argues for an interpretation of the coin imagery as a sort of "panegyrical programme", in analogy to the praise of the city in epideictic rhetoric, in particular Aelius Aristeides' *Panathenaikos*.

Fig. 5: Corinth, Archaeological Museum Inv. 763–782/S 1021–1022. Attic sarcophagus depicting the 'Seven against Thebes' on the front, and the death of Opheltes on the right side. The figures on the front have been tentatively identified as (from left to right): two female figures, Amphiaraus, Adrastos, Parthenopaios, Tydeus, Kapaneus, Hippomedon, Polyneikes. The figures on the right small side are: a hero coming to Opheltes aid, Opheltes being strangled by the snake, Hypsipyle. Ca. 170–180 AD (Photos: H. R. Goette).

cluding the slaying of the Minotaur and the Marathonian bull. Other examples depict a victorious Themistocles on a trireme, and Miltiades with a captured Persian. Yet all of these mytho-historical figures and episodes play either no role, or only a very minor role, on Attic sarcophagi. Particularly striking is the reduced significance of Theseus, the great hero of the Athenian democracy, in the sarcophagi's imagery. We encounter him only as a secondary figure on the Hippolytus sarcophagi, usually on the back or the sides: in an encounter with Hippolytus and Phaedra, in the abandonment of Ariadne on Naxos, or in the context of his son's fatal chariot crash.[55] This is surprising

---

55 Rogge 1995, 75; 85–7; 90–1. In most of these contexts, Theseus appears to serve as a mythical place-holder for an unhappy father.

Fig. 6: Death of Opheltes on 2nd cent. AD coins from Argos (after: Pache 2004, figs. 28–29).

insofar as his statues and paintings were omnipresent in the Athenian cityscape, and he is explicitly mentioned in the west inscription on Hadrian's gate.[56] In a private funerary context, we find mention of Theseus in the inscription of a second-century AD funerary stele from Marathon, as a *tertium comparationis* for the heroised ephebe Paramonos (from Piraeus), who is called a "new Theseus".[57] Yet, the hero is only of a sharply reduced importance on Attic sarcophagi. Quite possibly, most of these peculiar thematic omissions relate to the fact that the décor of Attic sarcophagi had to be "hellenocentric" and heroic enough for their customers to be attractive, but not as narrowly "athenocentric" as to be inappropriate in the sarcophagi's final settings.

The sarcophagi that best fit the bill of private heroisation and simultaneous evocation of an Athens-inflected "Greekness" were, to judge by their numbers, Attic battle sarcophagi.[58] This was probably because the fighting of the Greeks at Troy, and later against the Persians (both represented on Attic battle sarcophagi) offered, on the one hand, highly topical and generic comparisons for heroic virtue in funeral orations such as Dio's *Melancomas* (29.14).[59] On the other hand, they could also take on a more "local" significance, by being used to exalt a specifically Athenian military prowess and naval superiority. Aelius Aristides for example, in his *Panathenaikos* (135), dwells at length on the battles at Marathon and Salamis as exemplifications of a specifically Athenian ἀρετή.[60]

---

56 *IG* II² 5185. Interpretation of the inscription, however, is controversial, cf. Adams 1989; Willers 1990.

57 von Moock, 1998, 171 no. 456.

58 Koch and Sichtermann 1982, 405–14; Kintrup 1999.

59 Cf. Ewald 2004, 262–3.

60 von Mosch 1999, 68, with reference to Touloumakos 1971, 59–60; also Saïd 2008.

Attic and Roman Sarcophagi: a Comparison of Themes

If we return, with such qualifications in mind, to a broader thematic and structural comparison, we find that the characteristics of Attic sarcophagi vis-à-vis their Roman counterparts can be summarised as follows:[61]

1. A reduced thematic spectrum, with only ca. 25 mythological episodes, distributed across ca. 1500 examples, as opposed to the ca. 60 themes on over 7000 Roman examples.[62] Several of these mythological themes on Attic sarcophagi are, moreover, preserved in only 10 or fewer examples (e.g. Heracles, Orestes, Odysseus, Pelops, Muses, Iphigenia in Aulis), or documented only in subordinate locations, i.e. the small or rear sides of Attic sarcophagi (e.g. Bellerophon, Orpheus, Leda).

2. A predominantly mythological outlook (exceptions will be discussed below); almost all of the so-called *vita humana* ("Menschenleben") scenes known from Roman sarcophagi are absent from the repertoire of Attic sarcophagi.[63] The relative absence of scenes evoking such concerns on Attic sarcophagi means that certain semantic realms are deliberately excluded. Among the motifs absent are those related to "work" and "profession" (rare also in Rome and to which, unsurprisingly, no symbolic value was attributed among the upper social strata that provided the customers of Attic sarcophagi), family life and values, references to magistratic activities (e.g. *"processus consularis"*) and formulaic praise of Roman virtues (as on Roman "military commanders' sarcophagi"), as well as symbolic representations of the patrons as "philosophers" ("men of letters") and Muses, or as lion hunters.[64] There are, consequently, also no combinations of myth and *vita humana* on the same side of a sarcophagus,[65] in contrast to the Roman examples, on which the two spheres can merge in a more or less organic fashion, without much concern about the categorical differences between them.[66] While Roman sarcophagi can align these heterogeneous visual elements along a single horizon

---

61 On the following, compare Koch and Sichtermann 1982, 366–475; Koch 1993, 97–112; Rogge 1995, 15; Oakley 2011, 60–2. The sketch provided here complements and in some details also corrects the one I gave in Ewald 2004.

62 See the statistics in Ewald 2004.

63 This category of *vita humana* is problematic even in describing Roman sarcophagi because myth and "Menschenleben" are often intertwined there, and the so-called scenes from human life are usually fictionalised to varying degrees.

64 On "vita humana" scenes on Roman sarcophagi, see Koch and Sichtermann 1982, 88–126; Amedick 1991; Reinsberg 2006.

65 Wiegartz 1975, 216 n. 306; Koch and Sichtermann 1982, 378.

66 The most pertinent example here is the Rinuccini sarcophagus, combining the hunting accident of Adonis with the *dextrarum iunctio* and sacrifice of a Roman military commander: Wrede 2001, 21–36; Zanker and Ewald 2012, 303–6.

of meaning in which myth and *"vita humana"* are conceived as commensurable, and even interchangeable to some degree, on the Attic examples, the two realms are kept separate. This is achieved mainly by relegating the (non-mythological) depiction of the deceased to the *kline* lids, thereby separating it from the mythological realm evoked in the sarcophagi's main reliefs. The almost total absence of so-called *vita humana* iconographies and any references to contemporary "daily life" and values gives the mythological main reliefs of Attic sarcophagi a decidedly "anachronistic" quality, to which I will return later.

3. The absence of most of the allegories of a *vita felix*, known from Roman sarcophagi, on the Attic examples. On Roman sarcophagi, the various *vita felix* themes dominate quantitatively at all times over the narrative mythological themes, even during the culturally particularly charged period under the late Antonines and Severans, which was the "heyday" of mythological sarcophagi. These *vita felix* ideas are most represented with Dionysiac themes and the marine *thiasos* in the second and early third centuries, followed by the massively popular bucolic themes, the seasons and the (less numerous) *vindemia* of cupids in the later third century. On the Attic sarcophagi, the only *vita felix* allegory that gained significant popularity are the Erotes, which are sometimes conflated with the Dionysiac theme in *vindemia* scenes.[67]

4. A strong preference for heroic, Homeric and Trojan war themes, and a particular interest in the figure of Achilles, who is depicted across a wide range of mythological episodes.[68] These include the ransom of Hector (Fig. 7), the mourning and lying-in-state of Patroclus, Achilles on Skyros (in several different compositions, Fig. 8), Achilles and Chiron, the forging of new weapons for Achilles and the hero arming himself in the presence of Thetis, etc. Achilles is followed in popularity by Hippolytus and Meleager in the Calydonian boar hunt (Figs. 3 a-c). In the third century, however, these different myths come to resemble one another, by being re-arranged into static *tableaux* that depict the protagonists in the company of other heroic, semi-nude hunters or warriors (Fig. 9 a); the latter are mostly shown in resting poses that emphasise the beauty and athleticism of the male bodies (see below).

5. A preference for classically stylised, "agonistic" battle scenes that depict naked (or almost naked) fighters in single combat. These include a variety of mytho-historical battles, which display a considerable amount of iconographic "cross-contamination": the Amazonomachy (Fig. 10), the Centauromachy, the battle at the ships at Troy (Fig. 11), the battle at the ships at Marathon (i.e. a Persian war episode), as well as a very popular, generic representation of battle whose identification as a fight between Greeks and Trojans is based solely on its occasional com-

---

67 On Attic sarcophagi with Erotes, see now Papagianni 2016.
68 Rogge 1995, 19–72; Ewald 2004, 237–40.

Fig. 7: Ioannina, Archaeological Museum Inv. 6176. Attic Achilles sarcophagus. The front side shows the ransom of Hector, with Priam kneeling before Achilles. On the left small side Achilles is being armed in the presence of Thetis, the right small side shows the lying-in-state of Patroclus. The kline lid depicts a reclining couple. From a tomb in Ladochori/Igoumenitsa, which contained several other sarcophagi. Late 2nd cent. AD (Photo: InstNeg Athen 1993/266 (von Eickstedt).

bination with other Trojan war episodes.[69] This deliberately "anachronistic" outlook differs markedly from the battle scenes on third-century Roman sarcophagi, which are set in the present, and which display hierarchical, centralised compositions that focus on the virtue of the protagonist.[70] There is also a telling difference in numbers: Attic battle sarcophagi were hugely popular, suggesting that they celebrate battle as a visual metaphor for heroic masculinity, while the much rarer Roman battle sarcophagi were probably connected to a circumscribed group of senatorial patrons of the late Antonine and early Severan periods, for some of whom the theme may even have had a biographical background.[71]

---

69 Koch and Sichtermann 1982, 378; 390–2; 405–14; Kintrup 1999, esp. 10–2; 157; Russenberger 2015, 299–336 (amazonomachy). Most scholars advocate an interpretation of the "generic" battle as the conflict between Greeks and Trojans, while Rogge 1995, 65 n. 329 is more cautious, pointing out that the "generic" battle can be combined with a number of different themes, including ones that are *not* related to the Trojan war. See now Kintrup 2016.

70 Koch and Sichtermann 1982, 90–2; Ewald 2004; Recently Faust 2012.

71 Wrede 2001, 21–4; 36–50.

Fig. 8: London, British Museum Inv. GR 1861.2–20.1, 20.3. Attic Achilles sarcophagus. The principal figures depicted on the front side are (from left to right): Diomedes, Odysseus, Achilles (seated, holding a helmet in his right; a lyre leans against his chair), Deidameia (seated, with nurse). The left small side shows Achilles receiving the new weapons from Thetis and Hephaestus, the right small side shows Achilles and Chiron. From from a tomb in Hierapytna (Crete), located between theatre and amphitheatre, where it was found together with a garland sarcophagus. Late 2nd cent. AD (Photo ©Trustees of the British Museum).

6. An almost exclusively male-focused conceptualisation of death as the heroic death of a warrior (καλὸς θάνατος), which is not found on the Roman sarcophagi, where we also encounter a number of mythological (and some non-mythological) images of the death of women and children.[72] This focus on heroic death is evident not only from the above mentioned Attic battle sarcophagi, but also from various scenes on the Achilles sarcophagi, such as the death and mourning of Patroclus, the ransom of Hector (Fig. 7) and the dragging and weighing of his body, the death of Achilles, as well as the recovery of a fallen hero's body, probably that of Achilles himself.[73] Exceptions to the emphasis upon the death of heroic warriors are the chariot crashes of Hippolytus and Oinomaos (the latter on the Pelops sarcophagi), both of them restricted to subordinate locations (the sides or backs of sarcophagi).[74] If the killing of the suitors on the front of two late second-century AD Odysseus sarcophagi should be seen in this context (i.e. as a "death

---

72 Ewald 2004, 239–40. On the Greek concept of a heroic death (καλὸς θάνατος), see Vernant 1992; Mirto 2012, 126–39; Pache 2009; Nagy 2013, 9–234 and passim (on the intricacies of heroic death and glory in Homeric epic and beyond).

73 Rogge 1995, 20–2; 59–63; 65–8; Oakley 2011, 49–52 (Polyxena sarcophagus in Madrid/Prado, with death of Achilles on the right small side and recovery of his body by Ajax on the back).

74 Rogge 1995, 86–7; 90–1; Oakley 2011, 46–9.

Fig. 9: (a) St. Petersburg, Ermitage Inv. A432. Attic Hippolytus sarcophagus, depicting Hippolytus together with Phaedra's nurse in the company of the hero's hunting companions (the appearance of the male bodies is enhanced by modern polishing). The left small side shows the chariot crash of Hippolytus, while the right small side depicts Phaedra and the nurse in the *gynaeconitis*. The back is decorated with a boar hunt. From a tomb on the Via Aurelia (near Cosa), which also included two Roman metropolitan sarcophagi (Hippolytus, Marsyas). It was found in 1853, together with fragments of the original kline lid, which appears not to be preserved. 2nd quarter of the 3rd cent. AD (Photo: after Rogge 1995, pl. 89,2).
(b) Athens, National Museum Inv. NM 1775. Attic funerary stele of Telesphoros. 2nd cent. AD (von Moock 1998, no. 278). The inscription reads: "Telesphoros the Meilesian, Son of Eukarpos, at the age of 26. I escaped the terrible war and returned unharmed, but I could not escape the Moira. Instead, I now lie here, leaving behind a child of 10 months as orphan. Alas!" (Photo: author).

Fig. 10: Thessaloniki, Archaeological Museum Inv. 283 (Kintrup 1999, no. 214). Attic sarcophagus with amazonomachy and reclining couple on the lid. The centre of the frieze is accentuated by a group of victorious Greek and Amazon. The back and small sides continue the theme of the front side. 2nd quarter 3rd cent. AD. The monumental sarcophagus ranks among the largest Attic examples (Photo: author).

myth") is doubtful and in any case difficult to decide.[75] If these sarcophagi were already equipped with the *kline* lids that come into fashion at the time (none of the examples have the lid preserved), the direct juxtaposition of the slaying of the feasting suitors on the sarcophagus with the reclining patrons on the *kline* lids above would, in any event, have created uncanny visual parallels between the two scenes – a fact that may have contributed to the early "fading out" of this theme. Unlike in Rome, Attic sarcophagi hardly depict any myths involving the death of women and children, with singular exceptions, such as the small sides of the already mentioned sarcophagus in Corinth (Fig. 5 b), showing the death of the child hero Opheltes, as well as a few more fragments of the same theme.[76] A small group of Attic Orestes sarcophagi shows the killing of Aegisthus and Clytemnestra in the centre of the front side, i.e. a myth that involves the violent death of a female. One of these examples, a now lost piece that is known only from eighteenth-century drawings, suggests that the myth could be combined with a *kline* lid depicting a couple (which, in this particular case, was later erased

---

75 Oakley 2011, 37–8.
76 Oakley 2011, 39–40.

Fig. 11: Thessaloniki, Archaeological Museum Inv. 1246 (Kintrup 1999, no. 218). Attic sarcophagus depicting the battle at the ships at Troy on the front and the left small side. The identification of the typified warriors and groups is uncertain; the central group may show the victorious Hector battling a Greek, while Achilles and Patroclus are standing in the ship. The right small side shows the seated Orpheus, the back the Caledonian boar hunt. The kline lid depicts a couple in a common scheme. Ca. 240–250 AD (Photo: author).

in favour of an inscription).[77] While the interpretation of the matricide of Orestes in a funerary context is controversial, the combination of a reclining couple on the lid with a mythical couple being killed in the main relief would have constructed a strong visual parallel between the two representations that must have influenced the understanding of this myth on Attic sarcophagi. There further exist a few fragments depicting the abduction of Persephone by Hades (an extremely common "death myth" on Roman sarcophagi, with over 100 examples), and of Oreithyia by Boreas; their attribution to an Attic sarcophagus workshop, however, is not beyond doubt.[78] An unusual Attic sarcophagus in Thessaloniki (Fig. 12) and a related fragment in Warsaw probably allude to the impending death of Iphigenia, but only in a rather indirect and subdued form which is characteristic of the

---

[77] Oakley 2011, 41–3; 89–90 no. 53.
[78] Oakley 2011, 61–2. (The Boreas/Oreithyia fragment may be a local imitation of an Attic sarcophagus).

Fig. 12: Thessaloniki, Archaeological Museum Inv. P116. Attic sarcophagus with preparation of the sacrifice of Iphigenia in Aulis (?). The figures on the fragmented sarcophagus front, framed by two corner figures, have been identified by Th. Stefanidou-Tiveriou as (from left to right): Talthybios, Odysseus, Diomedes, Achilles (seated), Orestes, Agamemnon (seated), Menelaos, Calchas, Artemis (with torch and bow), Iphigenia (seated, with sacrifical attendants behind her), Clytemnestra. Early 3rd cent. AD (Photo: author).

emotional "dampening" of the Attic sarcophagi's visual language.[79] In spite of the marked differences between Roman and Attic sarcophagi in their selection of death-related myths, and the latter's focus on male, heroic death, there is a clear synchronicity in their distribution, i.e. a matching preference for death-focused scenes from the mid/late-Antonine to the mid-Severan periods.[80]

7. The absence of depictions of Roman myths (e.g. Mars/Rhea Silvia, *Lupa Romana* and Romulus/Remus, Rape of Sabine women), of personifications of virtues, values, and concepts (*Genius Populi Romani, Genius Senatus, Virtus, Concordia, Pietas, Honos*), and of iconographies derived from Roman imperial art, such as the scenes of sacrifice and "*dextrarum iunctio*" used on the so-called Roman "military commander" sarcophagi ("Feldherrnsarkophage").[81] An interpretation of this phenomenon of "exclusion" would have to be complex and shall not be attempted here. Some of these iconographies (such as those found on "military commander" sarcophagi) were, for example, too closely tied to the specific situation of the Roman senatorial aristocracy to be generally suitable for the clients

---

79 Stefanidou-Tiveriou 1998 (with interpretation as scenes related to the sacrifice of Iphigenia); Oakley 2011, 24–6.

80 Ewald 2012, for an interpretation of this phenomenon, and the declining popularity of such themes during the third century.

81 Wrede 2001; Ewald 2003; Reinsberg 2006; also Ronke 1987. There appear to be single exceptions: a fragment of an Attic sarcophagus in storage at the National Museum at Athens (Inv. 2751) shows what appears to be a Roman-style sacrificial procession, with two *victimarii* (one of them with *limus* and shouldered axe) and bulls. Given the current state of publication and the fragmentary evidence, however, definitive judgments cannot be made.

of Attic sarcophagi, and they would hardly have matched the expectations for an Attic product. But it should be noted that some of the thematic exclusions found on Attic sarcophagi are not limited to the funerary realm. It corresponds, for example, to the absence of the portraits of Roman emperors in the imperial-period coinage of Athens (which, to complicate things further, appears to have been a privilege granted by the emperor), and to the general scarcity of Roman imperial iconographies and even toga statues in the Greek East.[82] In Greece and Asia Minor, the use of specifically "Roman" myths and iconographies is generally quite rare and usually limited to the representation of Roman officials and the context of the imperial cult. Examples include (but are not limited to) several reliefs from the south building of the Julio-Claudian Sebasteion at Aphrodisias (e.g. "Aphrodite and Anchises", "*Genius Senatus*", "*Roma*"), the Parthian monument at Ephesus, the Philopappos monument at Athens, as well as a number of cuirassed statues depicting the *lupa Romana* in relief, including an example from the Athenian Agora.[83]

8. No use of the tried and tested iconographies of Roman imperial art as templates for the re-modelling and re-patterning of mythical narratives on Attic sarcophagi. Even though this re-structuring of mythological narratives in accordance with Roman values and virtues is by no means a universal characteristic of Roman metropolitan sarcophagi, many Roman sarcophagi (Hippolytus, Bellerophon, Pelops, Alcestis) draw on models from Roman imperial art in their appropriations of the mythical material. The departure of Hippolytus for the hunt on Roman sarcophagi with Hippolytus and Phaedra, for example, is modelled on an imperial *profectio*; the encounter between Admetus and Heracles on the Alcestis sarcophagi resembles an imperial *adventus*.[84] This is not the case on Attic sarcophagi. The models for individual figures and compositions are instead often loosely inspired by a broad variety of locally available, mostly classical models,

---

82 Coinage: Day 1942, 137–8 ("autonomous coinage" as imperial privilege); von Mosch 1999, 22; Toga statues: Havé-Nikolaus 1998; cf. Price 1984, 170–206, esp. 184–5 (togate statues of emperors); Smith 1998. On issues of local "micro-identities", and the intensified engagement of Greek cities with their own past under Roman rule (and often encouraged by Rome), see the contributions in Whitmarsh 2010.

83 Sebasteion: Smith 2013, 123–307; Parthian monument at Ephesus: Hannestad 1988, 201–3; Cuirassed statues: Niemeyer 1968, 47–54; Philopappos monument: Flämig 2007, 123–7. The use of "official" Roman iconographies in the Greek East, moreover, often betrays considerable uncertainty with regard to antiquarian details such as dress and attributes (cf. Smith 2013, 193–5; Hannestad loc. cit.), and the imagery's exact "legal" range and implications (evident, for example, in the triumphal iconography of the Philopappos monument in Athens for aggrandising purposes).

84 In particular, Grassinger 1994, with the qualifications in Ewald 2012, 53–4; also Lewerentz 1995; Zanker and Ewald 2012, 344–50 (Hippolytus); 306–10 (Admetus).

Fig. 13: Rome, St. Maria Sopra Minerva. Tomb of Giovanni Alberini. Attic sarcophagus depicting Heracles wrestling the Nemean lion, in a scheme known from late archaic and early classical vase painting. The authenticity of the sarcophagus, with its unusally flat relief, has been doubted, but it probably is an Attic work from the 2nd cent. AD (Fittschen 1970/71) (Photo: Inst. Neg. Rom E54281).

including the Parthenon frieze and Attic funerary *stelai*.[85] A unique Attic sarcophagus in Rome, S. Maria sopra Minerva, even shows Heracles wrestling the Nemean lion, in a scheme known from late archaic and early classical Attic vase painting (Fig. 13).[86]

9. A "mnemonic", collective and retrospective dimension that is largely absent on the Roman examples, where even the occasional use of "Roman" myths (such as the encounter between Mars and Rhea Silvia) is highly "personalised". On the Attic sarcophagi, this mnemonic function is particularly evident on the battle sarcophagi. The battles depicted there, such as the defeat of the Persians at

---

85 Cf. Koch 1988; Oakley 2011, 61 and passim. A similar manner of processing the omnipresent classical models by the imperial period sculpture workshops in Athens can be observed in the unfortunately very fragmented second-century AD architectural friezes (from uncertain contexts) from Athens, which draw on classical figure types but combine them eclectically into new compositions: Despinis 2001; Lagogianni-Georgarakos 2004 (who rightly contrasts this approach with the more exacting mode of copying that is evident on the so-called Piraeus reliefs).

86 Fittschen 1970/71; Oakley 2011, 22–3 pl. 19. The choice of a late archaic (rather than classical) theme and iconography is remarkable, and clearly due to a patron's extravagant choice: Heracles was primarily a hero of the late sixth-century Athenian aristocracy; the popularity of the Nemean lion episode was already declining in the fifth century BC.

Marathon, did not only serve to magnify the virtues of the heroised sarcophagus patron, but had strong and well established collective and identificatory functions. The Amazonomachy (Fig. 10), the Centauromachy, the battles at Troy (Fig. 11) and against the Persians had long been charged with the familiar secondary meanings of Hellenic martial and cultural superiority.[87] The combination of the Centauromachy and the Amazonomachy on an Attic sarcophagus in London, for example, is one of several faint resonances of such well-established programmes.[88]

10. A comparably greater emphasis on the naked male body, and a de-emphasising of the visual discourse about heteroerotic longing and desire, so dominant on Roman metropolitan sarcophagi. This focus on the male body is particularly evident on third-century Attic sarcophagi with Hippolytus (Fig. 9 a), Achilles, and Meleager, which display static assemblies of semi-nude young men, sometimes gazed at by older men functioning as "internal" viewers and placeholders. Such compositional arrangements create a highly stylised homosocial aesthetic that has no exact equivalent in the Roman examples. The relevance of the specific mythological characters is greatly reduced in these examples, to the point where they are barely identifiable. In such cases, "meaning" is generated primarily on the level of poses, gestures, and bodies. Apart from creating a unique scopic dynamic, such compositions also reflect contemporary athletic ideals and a body-centred concept of elite *paideia*.[89] In the specific context of funerary commemoration, the flawless young males on the sarcophagi must have further evoked topical and diffuse ideas of the "eternal beauty" of heroised individuals.[90] Such ideas are made explicit, for example, in Aelius Aristides' funeral oration (*Or.* 31) for his deceased student Eteoneus, as well as in Dio Chrysostom's two orations (*Or.* 28; 29) on the deceased athlete Melancomas. Both honorands were, admittedly, young men. But the topical beauty and attraction of heroised individuals is, in my view, crucial for understanding some of the peculiarities of Attic sarcophagi, including the fact that youthful heroes must have often served as identificatory figures for males who had reached middle or old age, as indicated by the portraits of the reclining sarcophagus patrons on the *kline* lids.[91] In such cases, the discrepancy between youthful mythical protagonist and older sarcophagus patron was apparently of no

---

87 In particular, Castriota 1992.

88 Koch and Sichtermann 1982, 398; Walker 1990, 40–1 no. 45 pl. 18; Kintrup 2016, 255–7, no. 130.

89 Ewald 2004; Ewald 2011, 295–301 with further references.

90 "Eternal beauty": Wypustek 2013, 59–96; 177–200; cf. Nagy 2013, 387–414 ("sacred eroticism of heroic beauty"); also Pache 2004, 181 (on child-heroes): "Narratives of heroisation ultimately emphasised the youth and beauty of the victims, who become recipients of cult and objects of admiration and desire". For Aristides' praise of Eteoneus, see Wypustek 2013, 86; Jones 2010, 62.

91 The Achilles sarcophagi with seated older men at the corners in particular (e.g. Rogge 1995, 53–9 nos. 6. 42 pl. 52; Ewald 2004, 246) present the youthful hero in the centre as the object of (male, in this case) desire; for an ancient viewer, the hero at the centre of the composition may have reflected on

concern for the sarcophagus owners. One could also, in this context, cite the famous male Greek beauty contests, in which the contestants may well have struck poses similar to those found on the sarcophagi (e.g. Fig. 9 a), and which even featured competitions for older men.[92]

11. A sharply reduced range of emotional expression; this greater restraint is particularly evident in representations of grief and mourning. Extreme grief reactions, such as the suicide of Altheia and the lament of Meleager's sisters on the Roman Meleager sarcophagi, or the reactions of Creon and other bystanders on the Creusa/Medea sarcophagi, are either not found at all on Attic examples, or are greatly toned down and "muffled". Instead of the centrifugal, sweeping movements of female (and more rarely male) mourners on Roman sarcophagi, or the raging agony of the burning Creusa, we find quietly sobbing, contemplative figures with lowered heads – figures that appear as if under the influence of "tranquillisers".[93] Examples include the (already mentioned) myths of Achilles/Iphigenia (Fig. 12) and the mourning of Patroclus. The reduced spectrum in the articulation of emotions also concerns the depiction of mythological love stories. We do not find on Attic sarcophagi the gestures of tender affection used, in particular, on Roman sarcophagi depicting the final embrace of Venus and Adonis.[94] It is hardly only the different iconographic tradition that accounts for the somewhat cool and "academic" treatment of many myths on Attic sarcophagi. Rather, it appears that we are dealing with a differing cultural protocol regarding the expression of grief or emotions. On the Attic sarcophagi, we are probably confronted with a form of "Atticism", i.e. a preference for a visual idiom that was perceived as "plain" and "pure" by its viewers (in analogy to the "atticising" tendencies of the authors of the "Second Sophistic"[95]), and that eschewed excessive gestures aiming at the mobilisation of emotions – the kinds of visual "pathos-formulae" that had been developed in the context of Hellenistic art. Un-

---

the physical attributes of the presumed sarcophagus patron (and/or recipient) even if the latter was considerable older than the hero in the sarcophagus relief. This does not exclude the possibility that such sarcophagi may have also been commissioned by parents commemorating a deceased son, in which case the seated older males have served as identificatory figures for the father (or other male relatives), cf. Ewald 2011, 293 with n. 95.

92 Crowther 1985; Ewald 2011, 290–301.

93 Rare exceptions are sometimes made in female figures on Attic sarcophagi, in which strong emotional reactions are generally shown more commonly than in males; these exceptions are the figures of Hypsipyle rushing towards Opheltes (Fig. 5 b), as well as that of a servant on the sarcophagi depicting the death of Clytemnestra and Aegisthus (Oakley 2011, 90 no. 54 pl. 44.1).

94 Zanker and Ewald 2012, 207–12.

95 See, for example, Swain 1996, 43–64; Whitmarsh 2013, esp. 101–22; 186; 2010. The commonly used term "Second Sophistic", and what it may possibly encompass, is of course much contested (e.g. Whitmarsh 2013, 1–7; 188: "… an infelicitous term that carries a false implication that rhetoric's dominance was uncontested.")

surprisingly, then, the elite clientele of Attic sarcophagi seems to have cherished ideals of emotional moderation and self-control. On the Roman sarcophagi, on the other hand (which were used across a broader social spectrum),[96] the rendering of many myths displays an affective and "visceral" quality that was sought after probably because it was understood as an adequate expression of the emotional character and the intensity, strength and depth of spousal and, more generally, family relations. These were, in fact, the most central concerns on second and early third-century Roman sarcophagi.[97] In accordance with this new focus on the family unit and the affective ties between its members, the social framework of dying on Roman sarcophagi is usually that of the family, as opposed to the Attic examples, where death and mourning are usually related to the heroic condition.

12. The absence, on Attic sarcophagi, of most "love myths" which were so immensely popular in Rome, such as Selene and Endymion, or Venus and Adonis. The males (Endymion, Adonis) featuring in these myths are heroes of a different kind than most of those found on Attic sarcophagi: "soft" and passive, even suffering and dying, and at the mercy of a female deity (Selene, Venus) who plays the more active part. The impending death of the male heroes, who are sometimes shown in languid poses, only serves to intensify the overwhelming atmosphere of love, longing, and loss. It has long been noted that the use of such "love myths" on Roman sarcophagi is closely related in spirit to the use of myth in the literary genre of Roman erotic elegy, and that it also has antecedents in Roman Third and in particular Fourth Style wall painting. It further coincides with a broader turn towards the individual and a new focus on gender relations, to which an increasingly affective quality is ascribed.[98] While the Attic sarcophagi also commonly employ the type of the seated heroine longing for her hero (Deidameia, Hippodameia, Phaedra), also known on their Roman counterparts (Phaedra), the males are usually shown as erect, upright hunters or warriors. A remarkable exception is the depiction of the lyre- or kithara-playing Achilles on the small sides of a few Attic sarcophagi.[99] A related example in London shows him seated on the front side, in the presence of Deidameia and with a lyre leaning against his chair (Fig. 8).[100] The use of a lyre or kithara as attribute of a hero that clearly serves as a *leitfigur* of Attic *paideia* (the right small side shows him receiving athletic training from Chiron) is in contrast to the reclining males on the *kline* lids of Attic sarcophagi who commonly hold bookrolls alluding to their literary education. The lyre is more commonly found on Roman examples, where it characterises the female role within

---

96 Mayer 2012, 100–65.

97 See, for example, Ewald 2012 (with earlier literature).

98 See, for example, Koortbojian 1995; Muth 1998 (on Achilles and Deidameia); Ewald 2012 (with further references).

99 Rogge 1995, 31.

100 Rogge 1995, 131–2 no. 17 figs. 32.1; 37.2; 39.4.

a clear dichotomy of gender.[101] While the phenomenon should probably not be over-interpreted, it may indeed point to differing attitudes towards (and perhaps greater acceptance of) male music-making in the Greek East.

13. The relative scarcity of children's sarcophagi (i.e. of child-sized sarcophagi) and specifically child-related iconographies. The Attic sarcophagi with Erotes are an exception to this. These often appear to have been connected with women and children – as recipients, but in the case of women also as patrons.[102] This is in sharp contrast to Rome, where children's sarcophagi and specifically child-related iconographies, such as the *curriculum vitae* of a child, the funeral lament over a dead child (*conclamatio*), the childhood of Dionysus, Erotes in a variety of activities, etc., became popular during the second century AD. This development on Roman sarcophagi has to be seen in the broader context of the already mentioned "coming into focus" of family relations, and of an "intensification" and "emotionalisation" of these relations that is also evident in the above mentioned scenes of death and mourning on Roman sarcophagi.[103]

14. A lesser tendency to tailor the myths around the figures of the sarcophagus patrons than is usually the case on Roman mythological sarcophagi. The latter achieve this effect by making extensive use of a continuous narrative (i.e., the repetition of the protagonist(s) in several different scenes), and of portrait identifications with mythological figures. By re-orienting the entire narrative onto the protagonists, myth on Roman sarcophagi is related more closely to the sarcophagus patrons, and used more emphatically as a means of individual characterisation, than it ever is on the Attic sarcophagi. Accordingly, Roman sarcophagi of the early third century (the heyday of mythological portrait identifications) have a tendency to position the protagonists in the centre of the frieze, even if this runs

---

101 Ewald 1999, 124–6.

102 Papagianni 2016, 99–102, who convincingly argues that Attic adult sized sarcophagi with Erotes were often commissioned on occasion of the death of children, with a continued use for other family members in mind. Female patronage of sarcophagi with Erotes: an important (and, to my knowledge, thus far undiscussed) clue for the interpretation of such scenes comes from the inscription on the sarcophagus of Vitalius Restitutus in Thessaloniki (see n. 30) – a very rare case where the inscription offers information not only about the patron and recipient of a sarcophagus (and his social standing), but quite possibly also about the reasoning behind the choice of imagery. The sarcophagus, decorated with a Dionysiac *vindemia* featuring maenads and *erotes* on the front, and equipped with a *kline* lid, was purchased by Po(plia) Antia Damokratia "from their common toils" (ἐκ τῶν κοινῶν καμάτων) on occasion of the death of her husband, in order to commemorate his "beautiful soul" (καλῆς ψυχῆς) and his "sweetest children" (γλυκυτάτων τέκνων). The warm feelings Poplia had for her husband and her children were very likely condensed in the idyllic motif of the *vindemia* and the erotes, while the fight between griffins and centaurs on the back of the sarcophagus evokes a rather more martial and masculine ideal.

103 Dimas 1998, 200–12 and passim; also Ewald, 2012, for a broader interpretation of such scenes in the context of the development of Roman sarcophagi from the second to third centuries AD. On Roman children's sarcophagi in general, see Huskinson 1996; Dimas 1998.

against the internal chronology of the mythical episodes depicted (the "reading direction" on mythological sarcophagi can vary). Attic sarcophagi, by contrast, do not normally use portrait identifications with mythological figures, and also employ the technique of continuous narrative much more sparingly than the Roman examples. As a result, myth is not used to the same degree as a personal allegory, and the intended "reading" of the mythological friezes is often more open, and considerably less straightforward (e.g. Fig. 7). Moreover, instead of inserting the sarcophagus patrons into the mythological narratives, Attic sarcophagi usually separate the sphere of myth evoked on the body of the sarcophagus from that of the sarcophagus patrons portrayed on the lid (e.g. Figs. 4 a–b; 7; 10–11).[104] The lack of portrait identifications is, once again, not a phenomenon limited to the sarcophagi, but one that corresponds to the much greater popularity of mythological portrait statues in Rome and Italy in comparison with the Greek East.[105]

The comparison presented here, of the theme selection and narrative modes employed on both Attic and Roman sarcophagi, allows for a number of conclusions. First, it demonstrates that, in spite of the pronounced differences, a common, shared frame of reference existed. One could, in fact, argue that the attachment to a mythical idiom, though clearly greater in Athens than in Rome, is something that unites, rather than separates, Attic sarcophagi and their Roman counterparts. The parallels appear even stronger if we compare sarcophagus production from Rome and Athens to that from other workshops in Greece and Asia Minor. While some of these workshops did produce mythological sarcophagi, it is clearly the case that, overall, undecorated sarcophagi with inscriptions, sarcophagi with garland décor or with idealising representations of males and females in common mantle types prevailed elsewhere.[106] But within this shared mythological outlook of Attic and Roman sarcophagi, different thematic emphases and preferences are readily apparent. The point of greatest divergence between Attic and Roman sarcophagi lies in the almost complete lack of love myths and most *vita felix* allegories, so popular in Rome, on the Attic examples, as well as in the different conceptions of war, battle, and heroic masculinity. There are also considerable differences in the expression of grief and emotion, with the visual language of Attic sarcophagi showing a much cooler "emotional temperature". Partial correspondences and points of contact, by contrast, are found in the rendering of several mythological themes, above all in the boar hunt of Meleager (Fig. 3 a), which is represented

---

104 Cf. Wiegartz 1975; Wrede 1981, 45–6; Koch and Sichtermann 1982, 378, and the discussions of the phenomenon in Ewald 2004; Ewald 2011.
105 Wrede 1981, 44–54; Karanastassis 1986, 278–9.
106 See, for example, Stefanidou-Tiveriou 2014 (local sarcophagi from Thessaloniki with inscriptions); Isik 2007 (sarcophagi from Asia Minor with garland décor); Koch and Sichtermann 1982, 476–557; Waelkens 1982 (sarcophagi from Dokimeion); Wiegartz 1965; Alexandridis 2014 (sarcophagi from Asia Minor with figural decoration).

similarly in both Rome and Athens.[107] The discovery of Achilles on Skyros (popular in a variety of media throughout the imperial period) is also similar in both places at first, before its development on the Attic sarcophagi of the third century takes a completely different course from that seen on the Roman examples.[108] Isolated correspondences are also found in Orestes and Pylades' slaying of Aegisthus and Clytemnestra, comparatively rare on the Attic sarcophagi, as well as in the representation of the love-sick Phaedra on the Hippolytus sarcophagi (as well as of Hippodameia, who is represented in the same scheme on the Pelops sarcophagi).[109]

What are we to make of this specific selection of mythological themes and narratives on Attic sarcophagi – which has only been sketched in its broadest contours here – vis-à-vis their Roman counterparts? It is likely that a number of factors converged to create the specific thematic profile of Attic sarcophagi. As my comparison has shown, there are some fairly obvious analogies between the sarcophagus iconography and the contemporary rhetorical movement of "Atticism", as well as the retrospective and "classicistic" orientation of the authors of the "Second Sophistic".[110] There also must have been resonances between certain iconographies on Attic sarcophagi and important Athenian cultural rituals and institutions, such as the epheby.[111] The strong focus on the well-trained, naked male body as well as the "agonistic" character of the battles depicted on Attic sarcophagi further illustrate the importance of athleticism in the visual definition of elite masculinity.[112] Closely related to this cluster of deeply rooted Greek "culturemes" is the unique "homosocial" visual dynamic of Attic sarcophagi, which presents the male body as the subject of the male gaze.[113]

One of the most striking characteristics of Attic sarcophagi, however, is their preference for heroic myth. The various heroic themes related to Achilles and the Trojan War, as well as different battles are most clearly dominant within the repertoire of Attic sarcophagi. If one were to summarise in a succinct formula the thematic differences between Roman and Attic sarcophagi, one could say that Attic sarcophagi operate in a *heroic* mode of commemoration, while Roman sarcophagi operate in an *elegiac* mode. Many of the differences observable between sarcophagi from these different "centres of production" are a direct function of this heroising outlook, and its one-sided emphasis on the visual definition of masculinity.

---

107 Koch 1975; Koch and Sichtermann 1982, 161–6 (Roman); 399–402 (Attic).

108 Ewald 2011.

109 Oakley 2011, 41–3 (Aegisthus and Clytemnestra); Rogge 1995, 83–85; 112–114 (Phaedra). Also Linant de Bellefonds 2013.

110 The bibliography on the so-called "Second Sophistic" and related subjects is vast (cf. n. 1). Recent surveys and anthologies include Anderson 1993; Swain 1996; Goldhill 2001; Whitmarsh 2005; Whitmarsh 2013.

111 Ewald 2004, 242–7; Ewald 2011.

112 See, in particular, the studies of van Nijf 2001; van Nijf 2003; van Nijf 2004 (and Ewald 2011, for the reflection of such ideals on Attic sarcophagi).

113 Ewald 2011.

A problem that takes on a new shade of meaning if looked at from this perspective is the controversially discussed question of the relation between myth and *vita humana* themes on Attic sarcophagi. Scholars have long been aware that the Athenian sarcophagus workshops eschewed themes that were non-mythological. But, in addition to the historically grounded "battle at the ships at Marathon", there exist a few other scenes that are quite possibly *non*-mythological in nature.[114] They are relatively rare, and almost all of them pose problems in terms of interpretation, mainly because of their fragmented state. But the little that is preserved suggests that the dividing line between Attic and Roman sarcophagi may not have run neatly along the distinction between myth and *vita humana*. Interestingly, however, almost all of these (possibly) non-mythological themes are connected, just like most mythological ones, with the definition of "ideal"—that is, aristocratic and heroic—masculinity. They can, in other words, be attributed to the same semantic field of heroic manliness (proven in the hunt, athletics or combat) that also determines the selection and configuration of myth on Attic sarcophagi.[115]

One of these pieces is a fragmentary Attic sarcophagus in the Vatican (Fig. 14), found not far from the Mausoleum of Caecilia Metella on the Via Appia in Rome. It shows two groups of wrestlers or pancratiasts.[116] The heads of all of the figures on this piece, which was probably produced in the late second century, were reworked at some point; the head of the victor in the right-hand scene, who has handily defeated his opponent, displays the portrait features of a Roman male of the mid-third century AD. If the identification of the scene is correct (and this is by no means certain), it would be a non-mythological counterpart to the likewise relatively rare Attic Heracles sarcophagi; with these, it shares the paratactic arrangement of the fighters and their comparably muscular build.[117]

---

114 Koch and Sichtermann 1982, 378–82; also Wiegartz 1975, 196–7.

115 With respect to athletics, there are strong interferences with mythological themes, for instance in the *palaestra* scene on the small side of a Hippolytus sarcophagus in Apollonia (Rogge 1995, 149 no. 49 pl. 108.2; Ewald 2011, 298–9 fig. 8.15) as well as in the scene of Chiron educating Achilles in fist-fighting on the Achilles sarcophagi (Rogge 1995, 30). The representation of Hippolytus and his companions on third-century Hippolytus sarcophagi is also determined by athletic ideals, cf. Ewald 2011.

116 Himmelmann 1970, 14 n. 1; Wiegartz 1975, 197; Sartorio and Calza 1976, 178–81 no. 22 pl. 14.1 (compare the portrait of the victor on the right to that of Traianus Decius). Koch and Sichtermann 1982, 381 fig. 407 (date the relief to the late second century, but rightly notice the reworking of the heads in the third century); cf. Amedick 1991, 94. I have not studied this fragment in person. An Attic sarcophagus in Antakya, which depicts an athletic victor on one of the small sides (Wiegartz 1975, 196–7; Koch and Sichtermann 1982, 381 with n. 30) has likewise been discussed in this context. Athletic competitions are also depicted on a number of Roman sarcophagi: Koch and Sichtermann 1982, 124. On a scene possibly depicting Chiron who instructs Achilles in the art of fist-fighting, see Rogge 1995, 30 with n. 83 (with further bibliography on boxing and *pankration*).

117 Oakley 2011, 18–9 pls. 14–5 (Heracles wrestling Antaios).

Fig. 14: Rome, Musei Vaticani, Museo Gregoriano Profano. H 84cm, W 85cm. The two fragments, which were allegedly found ca. 150 m from the Mausoleum of Caecilia Metella on the Via Appia (in the general area of the Villa of Maxentius), have been attributed to an Attic sarcophagus of the 3rd cent. AD. The head of the pancratiast to the right was reworked into a Roman portrait head of the mid 3rd cent. AD; the heads of the group of wrestlers on the left appear to be either reworked or restored (*non vidi*). (after: Sartorio and Calza 1976, pl. 14,1).

More significant with regard to the myth/*vita humana* problem is the small group of high-quality Attic hunt sarcophagi of the first half of the third century AD. Their relationship with the mythological rendering of the hunting theme on the Hippolytus sarcophagi is so close that scholars have not been able to reach a consensus on the question of whether they are mythological or not.[118] A fragmented example in Gotha (Germany) is particularly suited to illustrate the group's proximity to the mythological sarcophagi, in particular the Attic Hippolytus sarcophagi: it shows the hunt on the front side (in analogy to the Budapest-Split hunt sarcophagus, and a fragment in Cyrene), while the left small side depicts a gathering of youths that greatly resem-

---

118 The group is represented by the Budapest-Split hunt sarcophagus as well as by fragments in Gotha (Germany) and Cyrene: Rodenwaldt 1952; Koch and Sichtermann 1982, 379; 397; Rogge 1995, 87 with n. 87; Rogge 1998 (with further references). Rodenwaldt 1952, 35–8 and Rogge loc. cit. plausibly advocate a non-mythological interpretation for the piece in Budapest (Rogge also for the other pieces of the group), while Koch (Koch and Sichermann 1982, 379; 397) points out that there are no other non-mythological Attic sarcophagi from the period in question.

bles similar compositions on the front side of third-century Hippolytus sarcophagi (Fig. 15).[119] The example demonstrates with great clarity how fluent the boundaries between mythological and non-mythological sarcophagi could be, governed as they were by the same values and viewing interests on the side of the patrons. The problem is, consequently, above all one of archaeological classification. But since verifiable mythological clues are missing, we may indeed be dealing with hunt sarcophagi that are non-mythological in nature. From their mythological counterparts, the Attic Hippolytus and Meleager sarcophagi, they differ mainly in the fact that they place even greater emphasis on the hunt itself. The Budapest-Split hunt sarcophagus, which (thanks to the effort of the specialists) represents the best-reconstructable example, even showed hunting scenes on all four sides. In contrast to the mythological hunt sarcophagi, where the prey is always a boar, here a whole series of different animals is hunted and presented "encyclopaedically", as it were. The small group of – possibly non-mythological – Attic hunt sarcophagi has little to do with the significantly more numerous and more martial lion-hunt sarcophagi from the city of Rome which, in their representation of the sometimes militarily armed lion-hunter, take up well-established image formulae from "official" Roman art.[120] Unlike the two-scene Roman lion-hunt sarcophagi, the Attic examples, as far as can be judged, also never include the patron's wife in the form of the figure of *virtus* in the image, as is occasionally the case on the Roman examples. This reflects, once again, the general tendency of the Attic sarcophagi to de-emphasise the female sphere in the main relief, and to relocate it to the *kline* lids with which the Attic hunt sarcophagi of the third century must have originally been furnished.

Fig. 15: Fragment of an Attic hunt sarcophagus in Gotha, Herzogliches Museum. First half 3rd cent. AD (Photo: Museum).

---

119 Fragment in Gotha: Rodenwaldt 1952, 38–40 figs. 8–9; Koch and Sichtermann 1982, 397; Rogge 1998, 203–4 fig. 91.3. On the Attic Hippolytus sarcophagi, see Rogge 1995, 73–118.
120 On Roman hunt sarcophagi, see Andreae 1980; Koch and Sichtermann 1982, 92–7; Blome 1998; Zanker and Ewald 2012, 222–9. On the hunt in antiquity, see the contributions in Martini 2000. On the heroising connotations of the boar hunt, see Scherrer 2000. Also Stefanidou-Tiveriou 2016; Tatas 2009, on the 'Reiterheros'.

The examples presented here may suffice to prove the point that, despite the clear dominance of mythological themes on Attic sarcophagi, it is, strictly speaking, not simply the absence or the much reduced significance of *"vita humana"* themes that distinguishes them from the Roman examples. Instead, they differ in the sense that they are directed more insistently at visually paraphrasing heroic masculinity, to which end they make recourse to an amalgam of mostly mythological, but quite possibly also a few non-mythological, themes. It is primarily in this semantic sphere of male heroism, that the boundaries between myth and *"vita humana"* become permeable, and that the otherwise relatively rigorous attachment to myth is punctured or partially abandoned. Also instructive in this context is the fact that the generic, heroising scheme of the horse-leading hero is found in both mythological (e.g. Figs. 3 b; 9 a) and non-mythological contexts, such as the Attic grave *stelai* (Fig. 9 b) or the decoration of tombs, such as the pediment of an imperial period example at Carystus (Euboea).[121]

If one now attempts to locate the specific thematic amalgam of Attic sarcophagi, at least in its broadest contours, within the larger context of Greek art, one quickly comes to the realisation that several (if not all) of these themes were already well established in the context of the funerary commemoration and heroisation of late Classical and Hellenistic rulers and local dynasts: painted or sculpted scenes of hunt and battle, antithetical groups of combatting animals and sometimes also representations of athletic competitions, to which can be added a limited selection of mythological scenes and depictions of banquets. In his discussion of Attic hunt sarcophagi, G. Rodenwalt already briefly pointed to a number of fourth-century BC monuments associated with royal or dynastic commemoration: the Nereid monument from Xanthus, the *heroon* at Gjoelbaschi/Trysa, as well as the hunt on the small (socle) frieze of the "mourning women" sarcophagus from Sidon.[122] The reliefs from the *heroon* at Gjoelbaschi do indeed depict a number of myths and themes later found on Attic sarcophagi: the Amazonomachy and the Centauromachy, Bellerophon and the Chimaera, the Calydonian boar hunt, the "Seven against Thebes", Odysseus' slaying of the suitors, as well as hunting and banquet scenes and an unidentified (but probably local and "historical") "battle at the ships".[123] Some of these myths – the "Seven against Thebes", and the slaying of the suitors – are, aside from the Attic sarcophagi, represented either very rarely or not at all in the art of the imperial period. In the case of the particularly popular Amazonomachy, one could also point to the friezes of the Mausoleum of Halicarnassus,[124] while hunt and battle scenes were used on a number of Macedo-

---

121 Goette 1994; Flämig 2007, 72 with n. 643 (with the correct interpretation).

122 Rodenwaldt 1952, 40–1; cf. Koch 1975, 72–5 (on the models of Attic Meleager sarcophagi). For a comprehensive survey of hunting scenes in the context of Greek funerary commemoration and heroisation, see Barringer 2001, 174–202 (with further references).

123 Bérard 1988; Oberleitner 1994, 19–61; Barringer 2001, 192–201; Barringer 2008, 171–202.

124 Fedak 1990, 71–4.

nian tombs.[125] Representations of athletic competitions are found in the reliefs of the coffered ceiling of the north peristyle of the mausoleum at Belevi; in this context, however, (and unlike on the sarcophagus fragment in the Vatican), they are usually understood not as a reference to the physical prowess of the deceased, but as an evocation of the funerary games held in his honour.[126] At the Belevi Mausoleum, the athletic contests are combined with Centauromachy scenes in the coffers of the other three sides of the peristyle, another theme occasionally found on Attic sarcophagi. Also relevant in this context is the sarcophagus that was discovered in the tomb chamber of this same monument. The lid shows the patron as a symposiast, resting on a thick cushion, while the sarcophagus itself is configured as a *kline* with a table and footstool in front of it.[127] In terms of their architectural semantic, the Attic sarcophagi with *kline* lids over mythological friezes can probably best be understood as hybrid "micro-*heroa*"[128] that point back towards such pre-existing, aristocratic or dynastic forms of funerary commemoration, and make them available for a wider circle of affluent customers – in analogy to the spreading habit of heroisation and the ever more inclusive use of the hero title from the late classical to the Hellenistic and Roman periods (see below). Although the Attic sarcophagi make no *direct* iconographic borrowings from any of the monuments discussed here, they tap into precisely this heroising and aggrandising commemorative tradition. Since *heroa* from the late classical and Hellenistic periods were still very much visible in the landscapes of Greece and Asia Minor, this referential link would have been ever-present and intelligible. Alongside such examples for the use of battle scenes in a dynastic funerary context, there existed of course many older *heroa* such as the ἱερὸν for Theseus, the walls of which were, according to Pausanias (1.17.2), adorned with paintings of the Amazonomachy and Centauromachy.[129]

---

125 Barringer 2001, 201.

126 Fedak 1990, 79–82; Webb 1996, 76–9 figs. 33–9.

127 Praschniker and Theuer 1979, 99–104; recent research suggests that the lid and the chest of the sarcophagus are indeed contemporaneous: Heinz and Ruggendorf 2002, 152–163.

128 For the columnar sarcophagi, Thomas 2011 has recently cast doubt on the interpretation of the type as *heroa* or "houses of the dead" and instead pointed out the parallels with public architecture (also Öğüş 2014) – a very reasonable proposition, since most of the figure types found on non-mythological sarcophagi from Asia Minor are also more closely related to the visual language of the public honorific than those on Roman and Attic sarcophagi. That said, the funerary inscriptions from Asia Minor suggest that the term *heroon* could be applied to tombs of widely differing types and even sarcophagi; there appears to have been no exclusive architectural typology of either tombs or sarcophagi associated with *heroa*, although the tombs themselves can display certain archaising features that are in line with their common perception as *heroa* (cf. Cormack 2004, with Ewald 2008).

129 Barringer 2008, 186; 192 (with further references and a discussion of the question of possible influences of the Theseion on the design of the Heroon at Gjölbaschi/Trysa). On the pertinent literary sources, see Zaccharini 2015.

The exalted commemorative mode of Attic sarcophagi does, of course, diverge significantly from the civic and "egalitarian" visual world of classical funerary reliefs from Athens, although the sarcophagus sculptors occasionally borrow isolated figure-types from the funerary reliefs.[130] A rare exception is the late-fourth-century BC "Callithea monument" in Piraeus which, in accordance with the origin of its patrons, may indeed have been inspired by monuments of Eastern dynasts. It consists of a naiskos with statues of the deceased that rises above a podium decorated with animal friezes and an Amazonomachy.[131] Generic, non-mythological battle scenes in the context of funerary commemoration are otherwise encountered primarily in the unfortunately extremely fragmentarily documented state tombs honouring the Athenian war dead of the fifth and fourth centuries BC.[132] It is entirely possible, although it cannot be proven, that the implicit analogy with the great Athenian war dead was intended by the patrons of the Attic battle sarcophagi. Much closer in date to the sarcophagi are a series of second-century AD friezes in imperial Athens, some of which depict battle scenes; while the provenance and original context of these friezes is uncertain, they do not appear to have been funerary in nature.[133] The heroising mode of commemoration employed on Attic sarcophagi finally also differs from the non-mythological imagery found on the near contemporary Attic grave *stelai* from the first to third centuries AD. While the grave *stelai* show, in individual cases, heroic figure-types and hunting scenes that are closely related to the sarcophagi (Fig. 9 b), their representation of the deceased is overall more strongly influenced by late classical, civic figure-types.[134] This makes plainly evident how the sprawling use of mythological, battle and hunting scenes for aggrandising, heroising purposes was a social phenomenon: the patrons of the imperial period Attic grave *stelai* belonged, as freedmen, craftsmen, and simple citizens, primarily to the social strata that could not afford elaborate and costly marble sarcophagi; the elite patrons of Attic sarcophagi, on the other hand, had the means to visually "naturalise" their status through monumental, mythological claims to outstanding valour and virtue.

---

130 For an iconographic study of classical funerary *stelai* from Athens and the civic ideology that informs them, see Bergemann 1997. Iconographical borrowings from funerary reliefs on the Attic sarcophagi (or more cautiously formulated, iconographic parallels) are, for instance, observable in the representation of Phaedra (Ewald 2011, 283–6; Linant de Bellefonds 2013), as well as in the configuration of the departure of a warrior on the sarcophagus with the "Seven against Thebes" (Fig. 5 a).

131 Fedak 1990, 103–4; Hagemajer Allen 2003, 211–3.

132 Hölscher 1973, 104–11; Stupperich 1977; Kurtz and Boardman 1971; most recently Arrington 2015.

133 Despinis 2001, with Lagogianni-Georgarakos 2004.

134 von Moock 1998, 55–83 (on the deceased as hunter, as on the stele of Artemidoros, see 80; 84 with n. 1002; 121 no. 205; compare also the "heroising" representational mode on the stele of Telesphoros, Fig. 9 b).

Attic Sarcophagi and the Practice of Heroisation

In the numerous funerary inscriptions from Asia Minor, the terms *heroon* and *mnemeion* are the ones used most frequently in order to designate tombs or funerary monuments of a variety of types.[135] I propose that the preference for heroic themes and the deliberate iconographic and thematic anachronisms on Attic sarcophagi correspond to the designation of tombs as *heroa*, and the ubiquitous use of the hero title in the Greek East.

This lavish use of the hero title in the context of private funerary commemoration, as well as the common nomination of tombs as *heroa*, characterises the end of a development that can safely be described as a successive widening of the range of recipients. This was by no means a linear process, but one with considerable regional variation, and with different co-existing and often interwoven strands of commemorative and heroising traditions – poetic and cultic, local and panhellenic, artistic, epigraphic and literary.[136] Nonetheless, the remarkable broadening of the use of the "hero" title over time remains one of its most striking characteristics. In the classical period, the "hero" title was most commonly used for generals who had fallen in the defence of their cities, for the alleged founders of cities and colonies as well as for outstanding athletes; they were heroised and honoured with intramural tombs, the establishment of cults and the celebration of athletic contests and games. In these contexts, "heroisation" usually meant a collective, public recognition of these individuals' outstanding virtue and valour, proven in war or athletics, and often resulting in their death.[137] But in the late classical and Hellenistic periods there already begins a process that can be described as a de-coupling of the bestowment of the "hero" title from violent death in battle, or even "military prowess"[138] in general. Heroic honours are applied to an ever wider circle of individuals, including politicians who had achieved diplomatic rather than military successes, as well as benefactors of cities and their children – that is, in the latter case, individuals whose public roles were

---

135 Kubinska 1968, 15–31; Cormack 2004. Flämig 2007, 19–20 seems overly sceptical and not convincing in the attempt to restrict the scholarly use of the term "*heroon*"; this is rightly noticed by Stefanidou-Tiveriou 2011, 352. The sarcophagi, often mentioned in combination with the *heroon* itself, are called (with some regional variation) σωρός, σωματοθήκη, θήκη, ληνός or λάρναξ, more rarely simply σκεῦον/σκεῦος: Kubinska 1968, 32–57; also the inscriptions in Cormack 2004; Nigdelis 2014, 93; Ahrens 2015. The Latin term *sarcophagus* was, though of Greek origin, used primarily in the Roman West, see epigraphische Datenbank Clauss s.v. "sarcophagum".

136 See in particular Jones 2010, for a concise discussion of the various aspects of "heroisation". Also Rusten 2014 (with regard to Philostratus' Heroikos), as well as the contributions in Meyer and von de Hoff 2010 for the archaeological material. For the significant regional variation of "heroisation" in the Hellenistic period, see Fabricius 1999; Fabricius 2010.

137 Jones 2010, 12.

138 Jones 2010, 48.

usually rather marginal. Furthermore, in the late Hellenistic and Roman periods, the bestowal of heroic honours and the establishment of a *temenos* and *heroon* for the deceased is ever more often carried out on private initiative, with private means and on private land.[139] It can also be jointly financed by the city and certain outstanding individuals, in what one would nowadays call a "public-private partnership".[140] While the building of a strategically located, intramural *heroon* remains a particular honour that depended on collective approval[141] and that permanently inscribed an outstanding individual into the broader religious and commemorative landscape of the polis, private heroisation remains unrestricted and independent of public sanctioning or the establishment of a collective cult. The death of male youths from aristocratic families continues to be a prime occasion for the building of *heroa*, but *heroa* can now be erected by individuals, families, burial clubs, and even slaves, and often during the lifetime of their patrons. In single cases, the honorific aspect can decidedly outweigh the funerary one: The combined *heroon-odeion* of Diodoros Pasparos in Pergamon for example was erected during the lifetime of the honorand in the first century BC and did not include his tomb, which was located elsewhere.[142] Women and even young girls, such as the 4-year old Marcia Egloge at Patara, are also among the recipients of *heroa*.[143] This could create considerable tensions and contradictions between the tomb occupants or dedicants and the architectural decoration of *heroa*, which did not offer a gendered iconography, but instead adhered to an established canon of heroic symbols, such as shields, horse-leading males, and so on. The *heroon* erected by Aurelia Ge for her parents and her deceased brother at Termessus, for example, was decorated with shields in relief, evoking an aura of martial valour and heroic masculinity that was in line with the conceptualisation of the tomb as a *heroon*, but that says little about its dedicant.[144]

An aspect that seems particularly relevant with regard to the situation in Athens, where Attic sarcophagi were produced, is the above-mentioned regional variation in

---

139 Hughes 1999; Jones 2010, 48–74.

140 Jones 2010, 48–65; Cormack 2004, 147–9 with Ewald 2008.

141 Cormack 2004, 37–49 (on intramural *heroa*).

142 Radt 1999, 248–54; Ewald 2008, 626. For the date of Diodoros Pasparos, see Jones 2000.

143 Cormack 2004, 88.266–7. The tomb was dedicated by Marcia Egloge's father Paideros, "the private secretary of Sextus Marcius Priscus, legatus pro praetore of the province of Lycia in the years 67–70" (266), and his wife Marcia Liberalis. Cormack suggests that the tomb's heroic décor may have reflected not on the recipient of the tomb, but the girl's father, cf. Ewald 2008, 629. The problem of finding adequate lexical and iconographic expression for the phenomenon of female heroisation already existed in the Hellenistic period: Fabricius 2010, 269. The Attic Meleager sarcophagus from the "Meleager-Heroon" at Delphi (see above, n. 41) depicts only a reclining female on the lid, which makes it possible that she was the main recipient of the tomb. The theme of the Calydonian boar hunt on the chest of the sarcophagus, if not understood simply as a general application of heroising imagery, was perhaps chosen because of the implied comparison of the tomb occupant with Atalante, who is represented twice on the front side (one time in an unusual central position).

144 Cormack 2004.

the use of the hero title. It appears that, in comparison with other cities in both mainland Greece and Asia Minor, Athens lagged behind in the business of private heroisation. This was probably because, as Christopher Jones suggests, out of "respect for
the traditional heroes".[145] The collective, identificatory functions of myth, as well as
the veneration of the Athenian war dead and local heroes, long stood in the way of
an unfettered instrumentalisation of heroic myth for personal storytelling of the kind
found on Roman sarcophagi. Whether the lack of portrait identifications with mythological figures, and the less "personalised" treatment of myth on Attic sarcophagi, has
something to do with this phenomenon, is difficult to decide. By the second and third
centuries AD, when Attic sarcophagi were produced, the situation in Athens appears
to have been very similar to that in other Greek cities, and the denomination of private tombs as *heroa* is also documented for Roman Athens.[146] A second-century AD
architrave with inscription from the Athenian Kerameikos, for example, mentions a
heroon that was dedicated, together with an (Attic?) sarcophagus (σωρός), by a certain Claudia Lyde Ventidia Claudiane for her son Aurelius Rufus;[147] another inscription
from Athens, dated to the second or third century AD, speaks of a "*heroon*" that had
been built by a certain Demylas, son of Preimos, and Zopyrus for themselves.[148] Very
similar epigraphic evidence comes from other Greek cities, in particular from Thessaloniki, where a large number of Attic sarcophagi have been found; they were used
alongside local and imported sarcophagi from a variety of workshops.[149] A fragmented
local sarcophagus with inscription, for example, mentions a *heroon* containing four
sarcophagi; a now lost sarcophagus inscription speaks of a *heroon* that was erected,
together with the sarcophagus, by a certain Annia Eutychis for herself while she was
still alive.[150]

The seemingly universal practice of heroisation does not simply provide a general
background for Attic sarcophagi and their theme selection, however. Attic sarcophagi
have also been found in the contexts of such *heroa*. A prominent example is provided
by a tomb in Messene: the so-called *Heroon* of the Saithidai (Fig. 16). It has the shape

---

145 Jones 2010, 21. According to Jones loc. cit., in Athens the term "'heroon' is not used for a family
tomb before about 200 BC.".
146 See also the statistics of *heros* inscriptions in the Hellenistic and Roman periods in Fabricius 2010,
262–3 fig. 1.
147 Stroszeck 2008, 300–2 plausibly argues against an older identification of the dedicant with the
wife of the archon of 143/44, Publius Aulius Vibellius from Marathon, and of that of the recipient,
Aurelius Rufus, with a sophist of the same name, mentioned by Philostr. *VS* 2.17. Cf. Flämig 2007, 213
no. I,1 pl. 11.3.
148 Stroszeck 2008, 302. The inscription also mentions that the brothers Zenas, Eisias, as well as
Demetria were granted access (ἐπίβασιν) to the Heroon.
149 Stefanidou-Tiveriou 2014.
150 Stefanidou-Tiveriou 2014, 12–5; 196–7 no. 64; 260–1 no. 181 (Annia Eutychis). See also 220–2
no. 109: *heroon* built by Ti. Claudius Lycus for himself, his wife and daughters while still alive, containing sarcophagi and statues (ἀνδριάντες).

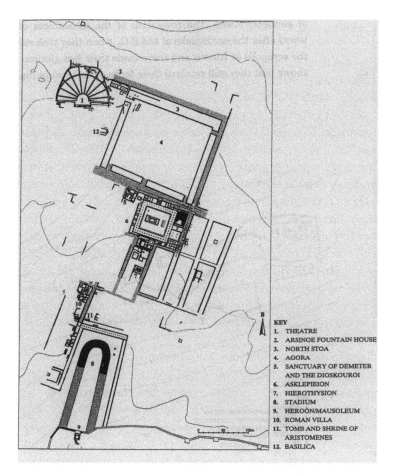

Fig. 16: Messene, plan. Stadium (8) and so-called Heroon of the Saithidai (9) (after: Themelis 2000, fig. 3).

of a prostyle temple tomb in the Doric order and is located off the longitudinal axis of a Hellenistic stadium-gymnasium complex, forming its southern end point.[151] The tomb is not, strictly speaking, intramural, as it uses parts of the city wall (partially removed for this purpose) as a foundation. But because of its prominent, elevated position, it would have dominated the stadium and the rites and competitions held therein, with the latter inevitably taking on the character of contests in honour of the tomb's inhabitant(s). Among the second-century AD sculptures found in the *heroon* is an *imago*

---

151 Themelis 2000, 102–13; Galli 2002, 22–4 (drawing a parallel between the Panathenaic Stadium at Athens and the Heroon at Messene); Flämig 2007, 175–6 no. 76 pls. 82–6 (with further bibliography and discussion of the excavator's identification of the tomb as *Heroon* of the Saithidai). On intramural tombs in general, see also Berns 2013.

clipeata with a bust in cuirass, as well as the *kline* lid of an Attic sarcophagus, showing a reclining figure. Identification of the recipient(s) of the *heroon*, which remained in use at least until the later second century AD, with the family of the Saithidai may be uncertain and controversial; but it is likely that the *heroon* served as the tomb of an outstanding individual or family who traced back its ancestry to one of the mythical heroes of the polis. Another important example for the use of an Attic sarcophagus in a *heroon* is the battle sarcophagus of the *eques Romanus* and *procurator Augustorum* (ἐπίτροπος τῶν σεβαστῶν) Q. Aemilius Aristides in Ephesus.[152] His sarcophagus was erected in the tomb of Claudia Antonia Tatiane, who is probably identical with the prominent Aphrodisian benefactress of the same name. An inscription from the tomb, dated to the year 204 AD through its mentioning of the *consules ordinarii*, and directly addressing Aemilius Aristides, states that the owner of the tomb, Cl. Antonia Tatiane, grants her "brother" (κύριέ μου ἀδελφέ) Aemilius Aristides a space (τόπον) in her *heroon*.[153] This was done, as is also noted, with the purpose of enabling the burial of Aristides' wife (κήδευσαί σε τὴν γυναίκα σου). If the battle sarcophagus did indeed also serve the burial of Aristides' wife (the tomb contained a further Attic Amazonomachy sarcophagus), it was possibly ordered with a view to Aristides' later burial in the same sarcophagus; the reclining male of a *kline* lid belonging to the battle sarcophagus carries his portrait.

Of particular interest in this context are the correspondences between the already-mentioned thematic anachronisms of Attic sarcophagi and the retrospective spatial character of contemporary *heroa*. Sarah Cormack in particular has described the numinous, archaising quality, as well as the fragile and permeable temporality of imperial period *heroa*, evoked by their setting, architecture and decoration.[154] The *heroa* of the imperial period were, on the one hand, monuments whose recent manufacture would have been apparent to many; on the other hand, they were designed to exude an aura of permanence, even of venerable age, and to become lasting elements of a city's sacred topography. One could also point in this context to Philostratus' *Heroikos*, an important source with regard to the thick web of associations surrounding hero tombs for the educated of the period. In this dialogue, the horizon of time collapses entirely in the vicinity of the tomb mound (κολωνός) of the hero Protesilaos (9.1), resulting in repeated encounters between hero and vinedresser. Through their deliberate thematic anachronisms, the Attic sarcophagi helped to construct *heroa* as spaces of chronolog-

---

152 Merkelbach and Nollé 1980, 97 no. 2204 A; Rudolf 1992 (fundamental publication); Rogge 1995, 16–7 n. 8 (further bibliography); Kintrup 1999, 107–12; Cormack 2004, 72; 135; 219–21; now Kintrup 2016, 109–12; 240–5 nos. 87, 90, who dates the sarcophagus to ca. 200 AD and the portrait of Aristides on the *kline* lid to ca. 220 AD.
153 Merkelbach and Nollé 1980, 85–6 no. 2121. On the emendation of τόπον instead of σωρόν in line 1 see Rudolf 1992, 29 with n. 104. A full translation of the inscription is given by van Bremen 1996, 227.
154 Cormack 2004, with Ewald 2008. Critically, but with limited attention to the tomb's cultural historical dimension, Berns 2013.

ical depth. Within the competitive social climate of the cities of the Greek East, this temporal dimension of *heroa* could prove advantageous, and serve as a means of legitimisation, in a number of ways. Intramural *heroa* in particular could, for example, make visible the age and pedigree of an aristocratic family. Aristocratic families made a point of tracing back their ancestry over many (as many as 40) generations, through fictive genealogies that connected them with a distant hero or heroised city founder (or other illustrious personality).[155] The heroic ancestry of the "leading families" in a city also seems to have played a role in the admission of cities to Hadrian's Panhellenion.[156]

In this context, we must briefly return to the already mentioned, mytho-historical battle scenes. They were anachronistic not only because they cultivated an "agonistic", classically stylised ideal of battle that was decidedly outdated and therefore well suited to furnish any *heroon*.[157] They were anachronistic also because the model of what it was to be a citizen (πολιτεύεσθαι) for the elite clientele of such sarcophagi in the cities of the East no longer included warfare, for the vast majority at least (unlike that of the citizen soldier of the classical period). Most of the wealthy customers of Attic sarcophagi would have been among the profiteers of the *pax Romana* – wealthy, to be sure, but without particular military ambitions. In instances where the reasoning behind the collective bestowal of heroic honours to members of the aristocracy is known (the honorific and consolatory decrees from the cities in Asia Minor are particularly informative in this respect), it is usually not because they had died in battle, but because of their moral goodness, patriotism, noble descent and virtues – in particular the φιλοτιμία they had proven through their public magistracies and their acts of munificence, generosity and magnanimity.[158] For Dio Chrysostom (31.161–62), writing in the later first century AD, "winning wars" is already a thing of the past, which he contrasts with the range of occupations left to his contemporaries under Roman rule: the ordering of the internal affairs of the polis, the bestowing of honours, the fulfilment of religious duties, the celebration of festivals, and so on. In a famous formulation in the same oration (31.125), he characterises the situation of his contemporaries as "peace and slavery" (εἰρήνη καὶ δουλεία).[159] And yet, in the realm of the visual, in the symbolic economy, the old connection between heroic valour and death in battle remains intact. The Attic battle sarcophagi relentlessly continue to construct battle as a "prime

---

155 Touloumakos 1971, 55–60; Meyer-Zwiffelhoffer 2003; Quass 1993, 67–76. Also Themelis 2000, 29.
156 Jones 2010, 68. See also the "genealogical bookkeeping" on Termessian tombs: van Nijf 2010, 166–174.
157 Ewald 2004, 260–3.
158 Quass 1993, 29–39; 44–56; Samellas 2002, 180–97 (consolation decrees). For the broader context, see also Touloumakos 1971; Meyer-Zwiffelhoffer 2003 (with references).
159 Meyer-Zwiffelhoffer 2003, 376–80; Veyne 1999; Veyne 2005, 215–39. Also Quass 1993, 196–346, on the liturgic offices and functions of the local aristocracies.

Fig. 17: Tyre, Necropolis. Attic battle sarcophagus. 3rd cent. AD. The kline lid shows a male with military attributes (sword, *vitis*?, rudder?), likely a military officer. (after: Chéhab 1985, pl. 93).

avenue to heroic status".[160] They offer "poetic" praises of elite masculinity, in a (usually) private setting, and in an exalted visual language that must, in most cases, have been quite detached from the actual circumstances in which an honorand had found his death. To a degree, and in spite of the differences in content, the diffusely heroising visual language of the sarcophagus reliefs matches the similarly vague, typified and moralising language of the honorific decrees.

This does not, of course, exclude the possibility that, in individual cases, there were deeper biographical connections between the patron and the battle imagery. P. Veyne has pointed out that, in the Barbarian invasions of the third century AD, Greeks fought and died alongside their Roman allies; they understood themselves as σύμμαχοι of the Romans.[161] It is indeed entirely possible that, in single cases, Attic battle sarcophagi may have served to commemorate military men. A mid-third-century AD example in Tyre (Fig. 17), depicting the "battle at the ships", appears to be such a case. The *kline* lid shows the reclining patron with a sword and another attribute (in addition to the obligatory book roll) that may either be a rudder or, as suggested by

---

160 Jones 2010, 38.
161 Veyne 2005, 212–213; 239–250.

M. Chéhab, the *vitis* of a *centurio*.[162] In the light of the very high number of Attic battle sarcophagi, however, such correspondences must have been the exception rather than the rule. Even the officer who was presumably buried in the sarcophagus at Tyre may not have fallen in combat, or in a naval battle. The primary message of the battle scenes was therefore not biographical, but metaphorical. They allowed patrons with the necessary means to convert real capital into "symbolic" capital, by celebrating the generic manly virtues that were universally understood as meriting heroisation: ἀρετή for sale.

Acknowledgment: I am, first and foremost, indebted to the editors for their invitation to the conference, as well as for their kindness, tact and patience in light of the late submission of the manuscript. I would also like to thank the friends and colleagues who provided photographs or copies of their publications, or who allowed me to consult, sometimes many years ago, their still unpublished works: J. Fabricius, H. R. Goette, C. Kintrup, J. Oakley, C. Pache, E. Papagianni, C. Russenberger, Th. Stefanidou-Tiveriou, L. Sterling, J. Stroszeck. Warm thanks are further due to the director (M. Lagogianni) and staff (E. Vlachogianni, Chr. Tsouli) at the National Museum at Athens for making accessible the sarcophagi in storage. The present article is based on material discussed in different chapters of a monograph on Attic sarcophagi (in preparation).

Bibliography

Adams, A. The Arch of Hadrian at Athens, in: *The Greek Renaissance in the Roman Empire*, edited by S. Walker and A. Cameron (London, 1989), 10–15.

Ahrens, S. Bemerkungen zur Ornamentik früher attischer Sarkophage. *Archäologischer Anzeiger* 2007:1 (2007), 29–42.

Ahrens, S. "Whether by Decay or Fire consumed …". Cremation in Hellenistic and Roman Asia Minor, in: *Death and Changing Rituals. Function and Meaning in Ancient Funerary Practices*, edited by J. R. Brandt, H. Ingvaldsen and M. Prusac (London, 2015), 185–222.

Alexandridis, A. Death and the City: Asiatic columnar sarcophagi in context, in: J. Osborne (ed.) *Approaching Monumentality in Archaeology* (Albany, 2014)

Amedick, R. *Die Sarkophage mit Darstellungen aus dem Menschenleben. 4. Vita privata.* Die antiken Sarkophagreliefs 1.4 (Berlin, 1991).

Anderson, G. *The Second Sophistic. A Cultural Phenomenon in the Roman Empire* (New York, 1993).

Andreae, B. *Die Sarkophage mit Darstellungen aus dem Menschenleben. 2, Die römischen Jagdsarkophage.* Die antiken Sarkophagreliefs 1,2 (Berlin, 1980).

---

162 Chéhab 1985, 559; Kintrup 1999, 399 no. 228 pl. 68. Linant de Bellefonds 1985, 30 n. 1 (as cited in Kintrup 1999, 399), on the other hand, recognises a rudder; similarly Kintrup 2016, 293 (rudder). I have not had the opportunity to study this sarcophagus in person. The *vitis* is found on the Attic tombstones of military men (*centuriones*): von Moock 1998, 59; 82 with n. 978 (nos. 85, 306, 486, 553).

Arrington, N. *Ashes, Images and Memories. The Presence of the War Dead in Fifth Century Athens* (Oxford, 2014).

Barringer, J. M. *The Hunt in Ancient Greece* (Baltimore, 2001).

Barringer, J. M. *Art, Myth and Ritual in Classical Greece* (Cambridge, 2008).

Bérard, C. La Grèce en barbarie. L'apostrophe et le bon usage des mythes, in: *Métamorphoses du mythe en Grèce antique*, edited by C. Calame (Geneva, 1988), 187–199.

Bergemann, J. *Demos und Thanatos: Untersuchungen zum Wertsystem der Polis im Spiegel der attischen Grabreliefs des 4. Jahrhunderts v. Chr. und zur Funktion der gleichzeitigen Grabbauten* (Munich, 1997).

Berns, C. *Untersuchungen zu den Grabbauten der frühen Kaiserzeit in Kleinasien* (Bonn, 2003).

Berns, C. The Tomb as a Node of Public Representation, in: *Deuxièmes rencontres d'archéologie de l'IFEA: La Mort dans la ville. Pratiques, contextes et impacts des inhumations intra-muros en Anatolie, du début de l'Age du Bronze à l'époque romaine, Nov 2011*, edited by O. Henry (Istanbul, 2013), 231–242.

Blome, P. Der Löwenjagdsarkophag Ludwig im Antikenmuseum Basel, in: *Akten des Symposiums 125 Jahre Sarkophagcorpus, Marburg 1995*, edited by G. Koch (Mainz, 1998), 1–6.

Borchardt, J. *Myra. Eine lykische Metropole in antiker und byzantinischer Zeit* (Berlin, 1975).

van Bremen, R. *The Limits of Participation. Women and Civic Life in the Greek East in the Hellenistic and Roman Periods* (Amsterdam, 1996).

Brinkmann, V. (ed.) *Athen: Triumph der Bilder. Eine Ausstellung der Liebieghaus Skulpturensammlung, Frankfurt am Main, 4. Mai bis 4. September 2016* (Petersberg, 2016).

Cain, H.-U. and O. Dräger. Die sogenannten neuattischen Werkstätten, in: *Das Wrack. Der antike Schiffsfund von Mahdia*, edited by G. Hellenkemper Salies et al. (Cologne, 1994), 809–829.

Castriota, D. *Myth, Ethos, and Actuality. Official Art in Fifth-century B.C. Athens* (Madison, 1992).

Chéhab, M. *Sarcophages à relief de Tyr* (Paris, 1968).

Chéhab, M. *Fouilles de Tyr: la nécropole*. Bulletin du Musée de Beirut 35 (Beirut, 1985).

Cormack, S. *The Space of Death in Roman Asia Minor* (Vienna, 2004).

Crowther, N. B. Male "Beauty" Contests in Greece. The Euandria and Euexia. *Antiquité Classique* 54 (1985), 285–291.

Day, J. *An Economic History of Athens under Roman Domination* (New York, 1942).

Despinis, G. *Hochrelieffriese des 2. Jahrhunderts n. Chr. aus Athen* (Munich, 2001).

Despinis, G. et al. *Κατάλογος γλυπτών του Αρχαιολογικού Μουσείου Θεσσαλονίκης* (Athens, 2011).

Dimas, S. *Untersuchungen zur Themenwahl und Bildgestaltung auf römischen Kindersarkophagen* (Münster, 1998).

Dresken-Weiland, J. *Sarkophagbestattungen des 4.–6. Jahrhunderts im Westen des Römischen Reiches* (Rome, 2003).

Ewald, B. *Der Philosoph als Leitbild: Ikonographische Untersuchungen an römischen Sarkophagreliefs* (Mainz, 1999).

Ewald, B. Sarcophagi and Senators: the social history of Roman funerary art and its limits. *Journal of Roman Archaeology* 16 (2003), 561–71.

Ewald, B. C. Men, Muscle and Myth. Attic Sarcophagi in the Cultural Context of the "Second Sophistic", in: *Paideia. The World of the Second Sophistic*, edited by B. Borg (Berlin; New York, 2004), 229–273.

Ewald, B. C. The Tomb as Heterotopia (Foucault's Heterotopies): heroization, ritual and funerary art in Roman Asia Minor (Review of S. Cormack 2004). *Journal of Roman Archaeology* 21 (2008), 624–634.

Ewald, B. C. Myth and Visual Narrative in the "Second Sophistic" – a Comparative Approach: notes on an Attic Hippolytos sarcophagus in Agrigento, in: *Life, Death and Representation. New Work on Roman Sarcophagi*, edited by J. Elsner and J. Huskinson (Berlin; New York, 2011), 261–307.

Ewald, B. C. Paradigms of Personhood and Regimes of Representation: some notes on the transformation of Roman sarcophagi. *RES: Anthropology and Aesthetics* 61/62 (2012), 41–64.

Ewald, B. C. Funerary Monuments, in: *The Oxford Handbook of Roman Sculpture*, edited by M. Sobocinski, E. Gazda and E. Friedland (Oxford, 2015), 390–406.

Fabricius, J. *Die hellenistischen Totenmahlreliefs: Grabrepräsentation und Wertvorstellungen in ostgriechischen Städten* (Munich, 1999).

Fabricius, J. Zwischen Konvention und Tabu. Zum Umgang mit Heroenehrungen in hellenistischen Poleis, in: *Helden wie sie: Übermensch – Vorbild – Kultfigur in der griechischen Antike. Beiträge zu einem altertumswissenschaftlichen Kolloquium in Wien, 2.–4. Februar 2007*, edited by M. Meyer and R. von den Hoff (Freiburg, 2010), 257–293.

Faust, S. *Schlachtenbilder der römischen Kaiserzeit: erzählerische Darstellungskonzepte in der Reliefkunst von Traian bis Septimius Severus* (Rahden, 2012).

Fedak, J. *Monumental Tombs of the Hellenistic Age. A Study of Selected Tombs from the Pre-classical to the Early Imperial Era* (Toronto, 1990).

Fittschen, K. Der Herakles-Sarkophag in S. Maria sopra Minerva in Rom, eine Arbeit der Renaissance? *Bullettino della Commissione Archeologica Comunale di Roma* 82 (1970–71), 63–69.

Fittschen, K. Über den Beitrag der Bildhauer in Athen zur Kunstproduktion im Römischen Reich, in: *Η Αθήνα κατά τη Ρωμαϊκή εποχή. Πρόσφατες ανακαλύψεις, νέες έρευνες*, edited by S. Vlizos (Athens, 2008), 325–335.

Flämig, C. *Grabarchitektur der römischen Kaiserzeit in Griechenland* (Rahden, 2007).

Frazer, J. G. *Pausanias's Description of Greece* (London, 1898).

Fuchs, M. *In hoc etiam genere graeciae nihil cedamus: Studien zur Romanisierung der späthellenistischen Kunst im 1. Jh. v. Chr.* (Mainz, 1999).

Galli, M. *Die Lebenswelt eines Sophisten: Untersuchungen zu den Bauten und Stiftungen des Herodes Atticus* (Mainz, 2002).

Giuliani, L. Achill-Sarkophage in Ost und West: Genese einer Ikonographie. *Jahrbuch der Berliner Museen* 31 (1989) 25–39.

Goette, H. R. Attische Klinen-Riefel-Sarkophage. *Athenische Mitteilungen* 106 (1991), 309–338.

Goette, H. R. Attische Klinen-Riefel-Sarkophage, in: *Grabeskunst der römischen Kaiserzeit*, edited by G. Koch and B. Andreae (Mainz, 1993), 107–110.

Goette, H. R. Der sogenannte römische Tempel von Karystos. Ein Mausoleum der Kaiserzeit. *Athenische Mitteilungen* 109 (1994), 259–300.

Goldhill, S. (ed.) *Being Greek under Rome. Cultural Identity, the Second Sophistic and the Development of Empire* (Cambridge, 2001).

Grassinger, D. The Meaning of Myth on Roman Sarcophagi. *Fenway Court* (1994), 91–107.

Hagemajer Allen, K. Becoming the "Other": attitudes and practices at Attic cemeteries, in: *The Cultures within Ancient Greek Culture. Contact, Conflict, Collaboration*, edited by L. Kurke and C. Dougherty (Cambridge, 2003), 207–236.

Hannestad, N. *Roman Art and Imperial Policy* (Aarhus, 1988).

Harris, W. H. and B. Holmes. *Aelius Aristides between Greece, Rome, and the Gods* (Leiden, 2008).

Havé-Nikolaus, F. *Untersuchungen zu den kaiserzeitlichen Togastatuen griechischer Provenienz: Kaiserliche und private Togati der Provinzen Achaia, Creta (et Cyrene) und Teilen der Provinz Macedonia* (Mainz, 1998).

Heinz, R. and P. Ruggendorf. Forschungen am Mausoleum von Belevi. *Jahreshefte des Österreichischen Archäologischen Instituts in Wien* 71 (2002), 149–176.

Himmelmann, N. *Sarkophage in Antakya*. Akademie der Wissenschaften und der Literatur. Abhandlungen der Geistes- und Sozialwissenschaft 9 (Mainz, 1970).

Hölscher, T. *Griechische Historienbilder des 5. und 4. Jahrhunderts vor Chr.* (Würzburg, 1973).

Hughes, D. Hero Cult, Heroic Honors, Heroic Dead: some developments in the Hellenistic and Roman periods, in: *Ancient Hero Cult*, edited by R. Hägg (Stockholm, 1999), 167–175.

Huskinson, J. *Roman Children's Sarcophagi: Their Decoration and Its Social Significance* (Oxford, 1996).

Işık, F. *Girlanden-Sarkophage aus Aphrodisias* (Mainz 2007).

Jones, C. Diodoros Pasparos Revisited. *Chiron* 30 (2000), 1–14.

Jones, C. *New Heroes in Antiquity: From Achilles to Antinoos* (Cambridge, MA, 2010).

de Jong, L. Performing Death in Tyre: the life and afterlife of a Roman cemetery in the province of Syria. *American Journal of Archaeology* 114:4 (2010), 597–630.

Karanastassis, P. Untersuchungen zur kaiserzeitlichen Plastik in Griechenland, 1. Kopien, Varianten und Umbildungen nach Aphrodite-Typen des 5. Jhs. v. Chr. *Athenische Mitteilungen* 101 (1986), 207–291.

Karanastassis, P. Untersuchungen zur kaiserzeitlichen Plastik in Griechenland, 2. Kopien, Varianten und Umbildungen nach Aphrodite-Typen des 5. Jhs. v.Chr. *Athenische Mitteilungen* 102 (1987), 323–428.

Kintrup, C. *Attische Sarkophage mit Schlachtszenen*. Microform (Marburg, 1999).

Kintrup, C. *Die Attischen Sarkophage. Amazonomachie – Schlacht – Epinausimachie*. Die Antiken Sarkophagreliefs 9.1,2 (Berlin, 2016).

Koch, G. *Die mythologischen Sarkophage. Meleager*. Die antiken Sarkophagreliefs, 12.6. (Berlin, 1975).

Koch, G. Zum Klassizismus auf attischen Sarkophagen des 2. und 3. Jhs. n. Chr., in: *Praktika tou XII Diethnous Synedriou Klassikes Archaiologias III, Athena 4–10 Septembriou 1983* (Athens, 1988), 155–160.

Koch, G. Der Import kaiserzeitlicher Sarkophage in den römischen Provinzen Syria, Palaestina und Arabia. *Bonner Jahrbücher* 189 (1989), 161–211.

Koch, G. *Sarkophage der römischen Kaiserzeit* (Darmstadt, 1993).

Koch, G. Einige allgemeine Überlegungen zur Problematik "Original-Kopie" bei den kaiserzeitlichen Sarkophagen, in: *Akten des Symposiums"Sarkophage der Römischen Kaiserzeit – Produktion in den Zentren – Kopien in den Provinzen", Paris, 2.–5. November 2005*, edited by G. Koch and F. Baratte (Wiesbaden, 2012a), 1–14.

Koch, G. Οι αττικές σαρκοφάγοι και η σημασία τους για την τέχνη της αυτοκρατορικής εποχής, in: *Κλασική παράδοση και νεωτερικά στοιχεία στην πλαστική της ρωμαϊκής Ελλάδας, Πρακτικά Διεθνούς Συνεδρίου, Θεσσαλονίκη, 7–9 Μαΐου 2009*, edited by T. Stefanidou-Tiveriou (Thessaloniki, 2012b), 35–56.

Koch, G. and H. Sichtermann. *Römische Sarkophage* (Munich, 1982).

Koortbojian, M. *Myth, Meaning, and Memory on Roman Sarcophagi* (Berkeley, 1995).

Kubinska, J. *Les monuments funéraires dans les inscriptions grecques de l'Asie Mineure* (Warsaw, 1968).

Kurtz, D. and J. Boardman. *Greek Burial Customs* (London, 1971).

Lagogianni-Georgarakos, M. Review of G. Despinis, *Hochrelieffriese des 2. Jahrhunderts n. Chr. aus Athen* (Munich, 2001). *Göttinger Forum Altertumswissenschaft* 7 (2004), 1147–1157.

Lewerentz, A. Zur Sepulkralsymbolik des Hippolytosmythos auf stadtrömischen Sarkophagen. *Boreas* 18 (1995), 111–130.

Linant de Bellefonds, P. *Sarcophages attiques de la nécropole de Tyr: une étude iconographique* (Paris, 1985).

Linant de Bellefonds, P. Le 'motif de Phèdre' sur les sarcophages romains: comment l'image crée la vertu, in: *Iconographie funéraire romaine et societé: corpus antique, approches nouvelles?*, edited by M. Galinier and F. Baratte (Perpignan, 2013), 65–79.

Martini, W. (ed.) *Die Jagd der Eliten in den Erinnerungskulturen von der Antike bis in die frühe Neuzeit* (Göttingen, 2000).

Mayer, E. *The Ancient Middle Classes: Urban Life and Aesthetics in the Roman Empire, 100 BCE–250 CE.* (Cambridge, Mass., 2012).

Merkelbach, R. and J. Nollé. *Die Inschriften von Ephesos. Inschriften griechischer Städte aus Kleinasien* (Bonn, 1980).

Meyer, M. and R. von den Hoff. (eds.) *Helden wie sie: Übermensch – Vorbild – Kultfigur in der griechischen Antike.* Beiträge zu einem altertumswissenschaftlichen Kolloquium in Wien, 2.–4. Februar 2007 (Freiburg, 2010).

Meyer-Zwiffelhoffer, E. Bürger sein in den griechischen Städten des römischen Kaiserreichs, in: *Sinn (in) der Antike. Orientierungssysteme, Leitbilder und Weltkonzepte im Altertum*, edited by K. J. Hölkeskamp et al. (Mainz, 2003), 375–402.

Mirto, M. S. *Death in the Greek World: From Homer to the Classical Age* (Norman, 2012).

Moock, D. W. von. *Die figürlichen Grabstelen Attikas in der Kaiserzeit: Studien zur Verbreitung, Chronologie, Typologie und Ikonographie* (Mainz, 1998).

Mosch, H.-C. von. *Bilder zum Ruhme Athens: Aspekte des Städtelobs in der kaiserzeitlichen Münzprägung Athens.* Nomismata 4 (Milan, 1999).

Muth, S. *Leben im Raum – Erleben von Raum* (Heidelberg, 1998).

Nagy, G. *The Ancient Greek Hero in 24 Hours* (Cambridge, Mass., 2013).

Niemeyer, H.-G. *Studien zu statuarischen Darstellung der römischen Kaiser.* Monumenta Artis Romanae, 7 (Berlin, 1968).

Nigdelis, P. Die Inschriften und ihr Inhalt, in: *Die lokalen Sarkophage aus Thessaloniki*, edited by T. Stefanidou-Tiveriou (Ruhpolding, 2014), 89–113.

Nijf, van O. Local Heroes: Athletics, festivals and elite self-fashioning in the Roman East, in: *Being Greek under Rome. Cultural Identity, the Second Sophistic and the Development of Empire*, edited by S. Goldhill (Cambridge, 2001), 306–334.

Nijf, van O. Athletics, Andreia and the Askesis-culture in the Roman East, in: *Andreia. Studies in Manliness and Courage in Classical Antiquity*, edited by R. M. Rosen and I. Sluiter (Leiden, 2003), 263–286.

Nijf, van O. Athletics and Paideia: festivals and physical education in the world of the Second Sophistic, in: *Paideia: The World of the Second Sophistic*, edited by B. Borg (Berlin, 2004), 203–228.

Nijf, van O. Being Termessian: local knowledge and identity politics in a Pisidian city, in: Whitmarsh 2010, 163–188.

Oakley, J. H. *Die attischen Sarkophage. Dritter Faszikel. Andere Mythen.* Die antiken Sarkophagreliefs 9.1,3 (Berlin, 2011).

Oberleitner, W. *Das Heroon von Trysa. Ein lykisches Fürstengrab des 4. Jahrhunderts v. Chr.* Zaberns Bildbände zur Archäologie 18 (Mainz, 1994).

Öğüş, E. Columnar Sarcophagi from Aphrodisias: elite emulation in the Greek East. *American Journal of Archaeology* 118:1 (2014), 113–136.

Pache, C. O. *Baby and Child Heroes in Ancient Greece* (Urbana, 2004).

Pache, C. O. The Hero Beyond Himself: heroic death in ancient Greek poetry and art, in: *Heroes: Mortals and Myth in Ancient Greece*, edited by S. Albermeier and M. Anderson (Baltimore, 2009), 88–107.

Palagia, O. Sculptures from the Peloponnese in the Roman Imperial Period, in: *Roman Peloponnese III. Society, Economy and Culture under the Roman Empire: Continuity and Innovation.* ΜΕΛΕΤΗΜΑΤΑ 63, edited by A. D. Rizakis and C. Lepenioti (Athens, 2010), 431–445.

Papagianni, E. *Attische Sarkophage mit Eroten und Girlanden* (Wiesbaden, 2016).

Pensabene, P. *I marmi nella Roma antica* (Rome, 2013).

Praschniker, C. and M. Theuer. *Das Mausoleum von Belevi*. Forschungen in Ephesos 6 (Vienna, 1979).

Price, S. R. F. *Rituals and Power. The Roman Imperial Cult in Asia Minor* (Cambridge, 1984).

Quass, F. *Die Honoratiorenschicht in den Städten des griechischen Ostens: Untersuchungen zur politischen und sozialen Entwicklung in hellenistischer und römischer Zeit* (Stuttgart, 1993).

Radt, W. *Pergamon* (Darmstadt, 1999).

Reinsberg, C. *Die Sarkophage mit Darstellungen aus dem Menschenleben. 3. Vita Romana*. Die antiken Sarkophagreliefs 1.3 (Berlin, 2006).

Rodenwaldt, G. Sarcophagi from Xanthos. *Journal of Hellenic Studies* 53 (1933), 181–213.

Rodenwaldt, G. Ein Attischer Jagdsarkophag in Budapest, *Jahrbuch des Deutschen Archäologischen Instituts* 67 (1952), 31–42.

Rogge, S. *Die attischen Sarkophage. Erster Faszikel. Achill und Hippolytos*. Die antiken Sarkophagreliefs 9.1,1 (Berlin, 1995).

Rogge, S. Weidmannsheil auf attischen Sarkophagen … nochmals zum attischen Jagd-Sarkophag Budapest-Split und verwandten Stücken, in: *Sarkophag-Studien, Band 1, Akten des Symposiums "125 Jahre Sarkophag-Corpus" Marburg, 4.–7. Oktober 1995*, edited by G. Koch (Berlin, 1998), 201–205.

Ronke, J. *Magistratische Repräsentation im römischen Relief: 1–3. Studien zu standes- und statusbezeichnenden Szenen* (Oxford, 1987).

Rudolf, E. *Der Sarkophag des Quintus Aemilius Aristides* (Vienna, 1992)

Russell, B. The Roman Sarcophagus "Industry": a reconsideration, in: *Life, Death and Representation. New Work on Roman Sarcophagi*, edited by J. Elsner and J. Huskinson (Berlin; New York, 2011), 119–147.

Russell, B. *The Economics of the Roman Stone Trade* (Oxford, 2013).

Russenberger, C. *Der Tod und die Mädchen: Amazonen auf römischen Sarkophagen* (Berlin, 2015).

Rusten, J. Heroicus Among the Works of Philostratus, in: *Heroicus Gymnasticus. Discourses 1 and 2*, edited and translated by J. Rusten and J. König (Cambridge, Mass., 2014), 5–98.

Saïd, S. Aristides' Uses of Myths, in: *Aelius Aristides between Greece, Rome and the Gods*, edited by W. V. Harris and B. Holmes (New York, 2008), 51–68.

Samellas, A. *Death in the Eastern Mediterranean (50–600 A.D.). The Christianization of the East: an Interpretation* (Tübingen, 2002).

Sartorio, G. and R. Calza. *La villa di Massenzio sulla via Appia: il palazzo, le opere d'arte* (Rome, 1976).

Scherrer, P. Der Eber und der Heros (Ktistes), in: *Altmodische Archäologie. Festschrift für Friedrich Brein*, edited by L. Dollhofer et al. (Vienna, 2000), 167–176.

Siotto, E. et al. A Multidisciplinary Approach for the Study and the Virtual Reconstruction of the Ancient Polychromy of Roman Sarcophagi. *Journal of Cultural Heritage* 16 (2014), 307–314.

Smith, R. R. R. Cultural Choice and Political Identity in Honorific Portrait Statues in the Greek East in the Second Century AD. *Journal of Roman Studies* 88 (1998), 56–93.

Smith, R. R. R. *The Marble Reliefs from the Julio-Claudian Sebasteion* (Darmstadt, 2013).

Stefanidou-Tiveriou, T. *Νεοαττικά. Οι ανάγλυφοι πίνακες από το λιμάνι του Πειραιά* (Athens, 1979).

Stefanidou-Tiveriou, T. *Τραπεζοφόρα με πλαστική διακόσμηση. Η αττική ομάδα. Δημοσιεύματα του Αρχαιολογικού Δελτίου* 50 (Athens, 1992).

Stefanidou-Tiveriou, T. Späte attische Sarkophage und das Ende der attischen Werkstätten, in: *Grabeskunst der römischen Kaiserzeit*, edited by G. Koch and B. Andreae (Mainz, 1993), 133–39.

Stefanidou-Tiveriou, T. Iphigenie in Aulis. Ein neuer Mythos im Repertoire der attischen Sarkophage, in: *Akten des Symposiums '125 Jahre Sarkophag-Corpus' 1995, Sarkophag-Studien 1*, edited by G. Koch (Mainz, 1998), 216–239.

Stefanidou-Tiveriou, T. Review of Flämig 2007, *Gnomon* 83 (2011) 348–54.

Stefanidou-Tiveriou, T. (ed.) *Die lokalen Sarkophage aus Thessaloniki* (Ruhpolding, 2014).

Stefanidou-Tiveriou, T. Der Annia-Tryphaina Sarkophag in Thessaloniki. Heroisierung und Selbst-darstellung, in: *Akten des Symposiums Römische Sarkophage, Marburg, 2–8. Juli 2006, Marburger Beiträge zur Archäologie Band 3* (Marburg, 2016), 95–102.

Stirling, L. M. Pagan Statuettes in Late Antique Corinth: sculpture from the Panayia Domus. *Hesperia* 77 (2008), 89–161.

Stirling, L. M. Recent Finds in Corinth and the Genre of Classicizing Attic Statuettes, in: *Actes du Xᵉ Colloque international sur l'art provincial romain. Les ateliers de sculpture régionaux: techniques, styles, et iconographie, Arles et Aix-en-Provence, 21–23 mai 2007*, edited by V. Gaggadis-Robin, A. Hermary et al. (Arles, 2009), 257–262.

Stroszeck, J. Römische Gräber und Grabbauten vor dem Dipylon, in: *Η Αθήνα κατά τη Ρωμαϊκή εποχή: πρόσφατες ανακαλύψεις, νέες έρευνες = Athens During the Roman Period: Recent Discoveries, New Evidence*, edited by S. Vlizos (Athens, 2008), 291–309.

Stupperich, R. *Staatsbegräbnis und Privatgrabmal im klassischen Athen* (Münster, 1977).

Swain, S. *Hellenism and Empire: Language, Classicism, and Power in the Greek World, AD 50–250* (Oxford, 1996).

Tatas, A. *Die figürlichen Grabstelen im römischen Thessaloniki* (MA thesis, Heidelberg 2009).

Themelis, P. G. *Heroes at Ancient Messene* (Athens, 2000).

Thomas, E. "Houses of the Dead"? Columnar sarcophagi as "micro-architecture", in: *Life, Death and Representation. New Work on Roman Sarcophagi*, edited by J. Elsner and J. Huskinson (Berlin; New York, 2011), 387–436.

Touloumakos, J. *Zum Geschichtsbewusstsein der Griechen in der Zeit der römischen Herrschaft* (Bonn, 1971).

Trimble, J. *Women and Visual Replication in Roman Art and Culture* (Cambridge, 2011).

Vernant, J.-P. A "Beautiful Death" and the Disfigured Corpse in Homeric Epic, in: *Mortal and Immortals. Collected Essays*, by J.-P. Vernant, edited by F. Zeitlin (Princeton, 1992), 50–74.

Veyne, P. L'identité grecque devant Rome et l'empereur. *Révue des études grecques* 112 (1999), 510–567.

Veyne, P. *L'empire greco-romain* (Paris, 2005).

Waelkens, M. *Dokimeion: die Werkstatt der repräsentativen kleinasiatischen Sarkophage: Chronologie und Typologie ihrer Produktion.* Archäologische Forschungen II (Berlin, 1982).

Walker, S. *Catalogue of the Roman Sarcophagi in the British Museum* (London, 1990).

Ward-Perkins, J. B. The Hippolytus Sarcophagus from Trinquetaille. *Journal of Roman Studies* 46 (1956), 10–16.

Ward-Perkins, J. B. The Imported Sarcophagi of Roman Tyre. *Bulletin du Musée de Beyrouth* 22 (1969), 109–45.

Webb, P. *Hellenistic Architectural Sculpture : Figural Motifs in Western Anatolia and the Aegean Islands* (Madison, WI, 1996).

Whitmarsh, T. *The Second Sophistic* (Oxford, 2005).

Whitmarsh, T. (ed.) *Local Knowledge and Microidentities in the Imperial Greek World* (Cambridge, 2010).

Whitmarsh, T. *Beyond the Second Sophistic. Adventures in Greek Postclassicism* (Berkeley, 2013).

Wiegartz, H. Review of Giuliano 1962. *Gnomon* 37 (1965), 612–617.

Wiegartz, H. Kaiserzeitliche Relief-Sarkophage in der Nikolaoskirche, in: *Myra. Eine lykische Metropole in antiker und byzantinischer Zeit*, edited by J. Borchardt (Berlin, 1975), 161–251.

Willers, D. *Hadrians panhellenisches Programm: archäologische Beiträge zur Neugestaltung Athens durch Hadrian.* Antike Kunst 16 (Basel, 1990).

Woolf, G. Becoming Roman, Staying Greek: culture, identity and the civilizing process in the Roman East. *Cambridge Classical Journal* 40 (1994), 116–143.

Wrede, H. *Consecratio in formam deorum: Vergöttlichte Privatpersonen in der römischen Kaiserzeit* (Mainz, 1981).

Wrede, H. *Senatorische Sarkophage Roms: Der Beitrag des Senatorenstandes zur römischen Kunst der hohen und späten Kaiserzeit.* Monumenta Artis Romanae 29 (Mainz, 2001).

Wypustek, A. *Images of Eternal Beauty in Funerary Verse Inscriptions of the Hellenistic and Greco-Roman Periods.* Mnemosyne Supplements 352 (Leiden, 2013).

Young, J. D. A Sarcophagus at Corinth. *American Journal of Archaeology* 26 (1922), 437–440.

Zaccharini, M. The Return of Theseus to Athens. *Histos* 9 (2015), 174–198.

Zanker, P. and B. C. Ewald. *Living with Myths. The World of Roman Sarcophagi* (Oxford, 2012).

Part III: **Wandering East, Wandering South**

Martin West
Gilgāmeš and Homer: The Missing Link?

This is an exercise in Neoanalysis. I am not going to prove anything, and it may be thought that I am merely spinning fantasies, building a house of cards. I hope that to some readers, at least, I shall seem rather to have constructed a useful and attractive hypothesis in the face of a puzzling problem.

The problem concerns the relationship of the Homeric epics to the poetic traditions of Mesopotamia, and especially to the greatest of Babylonian poems, the so-called *Epic of Gilgāmeš*. Most Homerists nowadays accept that the parallels between this poem and Homer are too striking to be fortuitous. I discussed them in detail in West 1997. The last chapter of that book was devoted to the whole problem of accounting for the interaction of Greek with west Asiatic poetries in and before the archaic age. I noted that within the whole broad current of what we may call "literary" influences *Gilgāmeš* stands out as a major source of inspiration, and specifically a version of *Gilgāmeš* similar to the one current in seventh-century Nineveh, the so-called Standard Babylonian Version. Many of the Homeric parallels are not just free-floating motifs but embrace whole scenic structures and sequences. It is noteworthy in particular that the episode in Tablet XII where the hero's dead friend returns from the underworld and they embrace appears to be reflected in the scene in *Iliad* 23.62–108 where Achilles sees Patroclus' ghost in a dream and tries to embrace it. Tablet XII is an appendage to the *Gilgāmeš* epic peculiar to the Standard Babylonian Version.[1]

In the same chapter of my book I suggested circumstances in which one or more Greek poets, perhaps from Cyprus, might have been taken to Nineveh and later returned with some knowledge of the poetry favoured in Assyrian court circles; or alternatively circumstances in which an Assyrian poet or poets might have migrated to the West and in the course of time become Hellenised and able to compose poetry in Greek hexameters. In any case I do not think we can avoid the assumption of bilingual poets – surely more than one bilingual poet. This is something paralleled in other cultures, and it often leads to the transference of themes from one national tradition to another. It happened in Western Europe in the Middle Ages, when there was considerable mobility of subject matter across linguistic boundaries. In the last century it happened in Uzbekistan, Tadjikistan, and northern Afghanistan, where bilingual singers introduced Iranian elements into Turkic oral poetry and on the other hand made what was originally Turkic epic popular among Iranian-speakers; and again in the Balkans, with poets who were bilingual in Serbo-Croat and Albanian, or Hungarian and Romanian.

---

[1] For the convenience of readers not well acquainted with the Babylonian epic I have provided a synopsis of it as an appendix to this chapter.

https://doi.org/10.1515/9783110421453-011

Another thing that most Homerists now accept is that the *Iliad* and *Odyssey* were not the work of the same poet.[2] But if that is so, how exactly could it come about that the poets of both epics were independently influenced by the same Babylonian poem?

There are several theoretical possibilities. The basic ones may be represented schematically as follows:

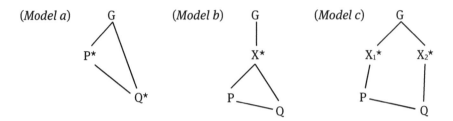

(Key: G = *Gilgāmeš*; X = unknown poet(s); P, Q = the poets of *Iliad* and *Odyssey*; * = bilingual poet.)

The first model is that the poets of the *Iliad* and *Odyssey* were both Assyrian immigrants, or Greeks who had spent prolonged periods among Assyrians, and so both independently had direct knowledge of *Gilgāmeš*. But it would seem an impossible coincidence that the two supreme epic poets of early Greece should both have belonged to the very small class of people having these unusual qualifications. In all probability we have to assume at least one stage of mediation between them and the Babylonian or Assyrian originals – mediation by at least one bilingual poet (model b), or by more than one (model c). The *Odyssey* poet in any case made much use of the *Iliad*[3] and may have taken some of the material we are interested in from the *Iliad*, though that cannot be true of all of it.

It is not enough to speak of a bilingual poet as intermediary. The mediation presupposes actual poetry by this poet or poets, composed in Greek and embodying the motifs from *Gilgāmeš* (and some other Mesopotamian texts) that were to reappear in Homer. So what was the subject of this poetry? It was presumably mythical narrative of some sort, but what was its theme?

Was it simply a Greek version of *Gilgāmeš*? We know that at an earlier period, in the later second millennium, there existed in Asia Minor versions or paraphrases of *Gilgāmeš* in other languages than Akkadian, in Hurrian and Hittite.[4] The assumption of a Greek version made in the eighth or seventh century would solve many of our problems. But the more one thinks about it, the less plausible that appears. How would

---

2 Those who are still not persuaded of this I urge to read West 2014, especially ch. 4.

3 See West 2014, 25–7, 70–6.

4 George 2003, 24 with literature.

the names Gilgāmeš, Enkīdu, and so on have been treated? They could not simply be transliterated; and no Greek shows any sign of having heard of these names before Aelian's mention of Gilgamos in the third century CE (*NA* 12.21). Could Greek names have been substituted? Perhaps for those two, but what about Humbaba, Ūta-napišti, and his boatman Ur-šanabi? What of the city of Uruk, or Mount Māšu with its scorpion-man gatekeepers? However anyone might try to Hellenise the story, it would inevitably have struck a Greek audience as a strange, alien tale that did not fit anywhere within the parameters of Greek mythology.

No, I think we have to postulate a poem or poems by a bilingual poet with *Greek* mythical subject matter, in the treatment of which he drew on motifs that he was familiar with from Akkadian verse. We may then suppose that one or more of his poems achieved some popularity and – directly or indirectly – influenced other Greek poets, including those of the *Iliad* and *Odyssey*. His poetry would be the missing link between *Gilgāmeš* and Homer.

Within the field of Greek myth, what would be a likely subject for this missing link? There is one subject that seems to me to stand out as pre-eminently suitable: the deeds of Heracles. Here is a mighty and violent hero of semi-divine parentage who, like Gilgāmeš, roams the earth wearing a lion skin and kills lions and monsters. He has a loyal comrade, Iolaos, who accompanies him through his earlier adventures. At a later stage, without Iolaos, he makes long excursions to remote lands, even to the ends of the earth, where he encounters the sun-god and crosses the outer waters in the sun's own vessel. Like Gilgāmeš again, he faces issues of life and death. He merits immortality if anyone does, but he does not achieve it, at any rate in the oldest accounts.

Certainly the figure of Heracles is not *derived* from that of the Babylonian hero; he must have been long established in Greek legend and popular belief, probably from the Mycenaean period. But there were enough points of similarity between him and Gilgāmeš to make it easy and natural for an Akkadian-trained poet to deploy *Gilgāmeš* motifs in telling his story.

Poetry about the adventures of Heracles must have been widely current before the *Iliad* and *Odyssey* were composed. This is evident from numerous allusions in both epics and in Hesiod and Archilochus: –

Il. 5.392–404, 11.689–693: he attacked Pylos, wounding gods and killing eleven of Neleus' twelve sons. Cf. [Hes.] frr. 33–35.

Il. 5.638–651, 20.145–148: he brought six ships against Troy and sacked it on account of Laomedon's horses. A sea monster chased him up the shore, but Athena and the Trojans built him a refuge.

Il. 8.362–369, 14.323–324, 15.639–640, 19.95–133: he was the son of Zeus, born to Alkmene in Thebes. Hera contrived that Eurystheus should be born first and have the kingship. He imposed labours on Heracles, using Kopreus to convey his messages to him. Zeus used to send Athena to help his son.

Il. 14.250–261, 15.18–30: after he sacked Troy, Hera persuaded Hypnos to put Zeus to sleep while she sent a storm against Heracles and drove him to Cos. Zeus brought him back to Argos.

Od. 8.224: he was a great archer, rivalling the immortals.

Od. 11.266–268: he was Zeus' son, born to Amphitryon's wife Alkmene.

Od. 11.601–627: he was in thrall to an inferior man who imposed hard labours on him. One of them consisted in going down to Hades to fetch Cerberus. Heracles succeeded in this with Hermes' and Athena's help.

Od. 21.24–30: Iphitos, son of Eurytos, came to Heracles' house with his fine herd of mares. Heracles violated the hospitality code by killing him and taking the animals.

Hes. *Theog.* 287–294: Heracles crossed Oceanus to Erytheia, killed Orthos, Eurytion, and Geryoneus, and drove Geryoneus' cattle back to Tiryns.

Hes. *Theog.* 313–318: with the help of Iolaos and Athena he slew the Lernaean Hydra that Hera had reared in her hatred of Heracles.

Hes. *Theog.* 327–332: he killed the Nemean Lion that Hera had reared and put there to ravage the works of men.

Hes. *Theog.* 526–532: with Zeus' blessing he killed the eagle that tormented Prometheus.

Archil. frr. 286–288 W.: as he crossed the river Euenos with his new wife Deianeira, the Centaur Nessos tried to rape her; Heracles killed him.[5]

These manifold allusions refer to many different adventures of Heracles and no doubt reflect several poems. Some of his exploits will have been treated singly in separate poems. From the sixth century we have the pseudo-Hesiodic *Shield*, which deals with a single episode in Heracles' career, his fight with the brigand Kyknos. The lost epic *Capture of Oichalia* also dealt with a single story. On the other hand the references in both the *Iliad* and the *Odyssey* to the labours imposed on Heracles by Eurystheus presuppose an extended account in which a whole series of adventures was narrated within the frame of the Eurystheus story. The poet who undertook to tell this story was committing himself to a major piece of composition, a poem that would stand out among the rest for its length and scope. And if a bilingual poet took up the subject and produced what we may call a "Gilgamising" version, it would have stood out even more by virtue of its original and affective qualities.

In what follows I endeavour to evoke a vision of what this hypothetical Gilgamising *Herakleia* might have looked like in outline. As the purpose of the hypothesis is to restore a missing link between the *Gilgāmeš* epic and the Homeric poems, I have

---

5 From sixth-century sources we may add [Hes.] *Scut.* and frr. 25.17–33, 26.32–3, 33a.22–35.7, 165.9–10, 229, 230, 248, 250, 263–5; Creophylus, *Capture of Oichalia*; Pisander, *Herakleia*; Stesichorus, *Geryoneis*, *Kerberos*, *Kyknos*; Ibycus *PMGF* 285, 298–300; numerous vase paintings.

made my construct out of elements that correspond on the two sides. The middle column displays my reconstructed (but still fragmentary) Heracles epic. The left-hand column shows, partly in quotation, partly in paraphrase, the relevant passages from the *Gilgāmeš* epic and one or two other Akkadian texts.[6] In the right-hand column will be found the Homeric passages which (according to the hypothesis) show the influence of the Heracles epic. The reconstruction is divided up into blocks, each followed by commentary. I recommend looking at the middle column first and then to left and right.

Babylonian/Assyrian sources	Hypothetical Heracles epic	Reflexes in Homer
[He who saw the Deep, the] foundation of the country, ... [Gilgāmeš, who] saw the Deep, the foundation of the country, [who] knew [...,], was wise in everything! ... who ... crossed the ocean, the wide sea, as far as the sunrise; who scoured the world-regions ever searching for life. (*Gilg.* I 1–4, 39–41.)	Tell me, Muse, of the man of mighty strength, Heracles, who performed many labours at the behest of Eurystheus, who travelled over many lands, who crossed the ocean as far as the sunset.	Tell me, Muse, of that man so versatile, who made many wanderings ... and many were the men whose towns he saw and whose mind he learned, many the pains that his heart suffered on the sea. (*Od.* 1.1–4.)
She is (number?) one, she is holy ... offspring of a god, daughter of Anu: for her ill will, her base counsel, Anu her father dashed her down from heaven to earth, for her ill will, her disruptive counsel. Her hair is loose, her private parts are stripped. She goes straight to the man who lacks a (protective) god. (Old Assyrian incantation.)	He was subject to Eurystheus because when he was due to be born, Zeus proclaimed that the man born that day would rule over all the peoples round about. Hera tricked him by making him confirm his statement on oath, and then delaying Heracles' birth till the day after Eurystheus'. Zeus was furious with Ate, whose victim he had been, and hurled her down from heaven. Now on earth she goes everywhere, doing harm to men. Eurystheus ordered Heracles to undertake a series of labours. In some of them he was assisted by his nephew Iolaos, for whom he had a particular affection.	*When Heracles was due to be born, Zeus proclaimed that the man born that day would rule over all the peoples round about. Hera tricked him by making him confirm his statement on oath, and then delaying Heracles' birth till the day after Eurystheus'. Zeus was furious with Ate, whose victim he had been. At once he seized Ate by the hair, and swore she should never return to Olympus. He flung her down from heaven, and she came to the world of men. Here she walks upon men's heads, doing them all harm.* (*Il.* 19.90–131; cf. 9.505–507.)

---

6 The translations from *Gilgāmeš* are from George 2003.

The poet began by stating his theme, with a general indication of its scope: "Tell me, Muse, of the man of mighty strength, Heracles, who performed many labours at the behest of Eurystheus." The poet who knew his *Gilgāmeš* could hardly forbear to add "the man who travelled over many lands, who crossed the ocean as far as the sunset". We may see a reflex of this in the opening verses of the *Odyssey*.

Before starting on the tale of Heracles' labours it was necessary to explain why he was under this obligation to a lesser man. It was the result of what happened at his birth. Zeus had proclaimed that the man born that day would rule over all the peoples round about. Hera tricked him by making him confirm his statement on oath; she then accelerated the birth of Eurystheus so that he was born that day, and delayed Heracles' birth to the next. The story is told in the *Iliad*, in the passage summarised in the right-hand column of the table. The *Iliad* poet is surely drawing directly on a Heracles epic.

He includes the detail that Zeus was furious with Ate for having overcome him. He seized her by the hair, swore she should never return to Olympus, and flung her down from heaven, and so she came to the world of men. This curious little piece of mythology is paralleled, not in extant versions of *Gilgāmeš*, but in another Akkadian poetic text, an Old Assyrian incantation against the malign goddess Lamaštu. The relevant passage is given in the left-hand column above. Anu the sky-god, father of the gods, being displeased with her for her ill will, her base counsel, threw her down from heaven to earth. She is a physically loathsome creature, and she goes straight to the man who lacks a protective god, bent on doing him harm.

Heracles is traditionally assisted in at least some of his exploits by his nephew Iolaos. Iolaos is especially mentioned in connection with the killing of the Hydra. But in art he appears in many other scenes as Heracles' companion, sometimes driving his chariot, often dressed as a warrior.[7] In the pseudo-Hesiodic *Shield*, in which Heracles fights an epic-style combat against Kyknos, Iolaos serves as his charioteer and dialogue partner. In the prologue of Euripides' *Herakleidai* he speaks with pride of having assisted him in most of his exploits: πόνων | πλείστων μετέσχον εἷς ἀνὴρ Ἡρακλέει (7, cf. 88). Pausanias says much the same in several places (1.19.3; 8.14.9; 8.45.6). Iolaos was probably a figure already given by Greek tradition, not an invention on the model of Gilgāmeš's friend Enkīdu, but our Heracles poet will have been struck by the parallelism and may have developed it.

---

7 See Maria Pipili, *LIMC* V (1) 686–96 s.v. "Iolaos" (and her succeeding article on his Etruscan form Vile, 696–701).

They stood marvelling at the forest (*where they had come to kill the monster Humbaba*), observing the height of the cedars ... the cedar was proffering its abundance, sweet was its shade, full of delight. [All] tangled was the thorny under-growth, the forest was a thick canopy, [...] cedar, *ballukku*-tree ... (*Gilg.* V 1–10.)	Heracles' first task was to kill and skin the lion that occupied the grove at Nemea. On coming to the grove they stood and admired its beauty and the tallness of the trees.	A wood grew luxuriant around the cave, alders and poplars and fragrant cypresses ... and round about soft meadows of violet and celery flourished ... There Hermes stood and admired it all. (*Od.* 5.63–75.)
Gilgāmeš kills lions: IX 18, cf. X 34 *etc.; wears a lionskin,* X 218.	After killing the lion Heracles clothed himself in its skin.	

The first of Heracles' labours was to kill the great lion that lived in the grove of Zeus at Nemea. The first and greatest exploit that Gilgāmeš undertakes with Enkīdu is to journey to the distant Cedar Forest and kill its monstrous guardian, Humbaba. On arriving at the forest they stand and admire its beauty. If our Heracles poet imitated the passage in describing the arrival of Heracles and Iolaos at the Nemean Grove, he might in turn have served as a model for the *Odyssey* poet when he describes Hermes' arrival at the island of Calypso: before finding her, he stands and admires the forest scenery.

After killing the Nemean Lion Heracles removes its skin and puts it on himself. Humbaba is nothing like a lion and does not have a skin that someone else could take over. But there are references elsewhere in the Babylonian poem to Gilgāmeš's having killed lions with Enkīdu, and at a later stage of the story, after he has left his city to go roaming over the steppe, he is clad in a lion skin.

Heracles goes on to kill or capture several other fierce creatures. These exploits do not correspond closely to those of Gilgāmeš, and as we cannot determine the exact sequence of events in our hypothetical Heracles epic, I pass over them.

Sennacherib sacked Babylon in 689 BCE *and diverted the Euphrates to wash away its remains.* (Royal inscriptions.)	After several more labours Heracles faced the task of cleaning out Augeas' stables. He achieved it by diverting the river Alpheios and/or Peneios.	*After the Trojan War Poseidon and Apollo diverted all the rivers of the Troad to wash away all traces of the Achaeans' fortification wall.* (*Il.* 12.10–33.)

This item of my reconstruction is particularly speculative: the cleansing of the stables of Augeias, king of Elis. Heracles succeeded in cleaning them out, according to most sources, by diverting the river Alpheios (Diod. Sic. 4.13.3), or the Peneios (Paus. 5.1.10), or both (Apollod. 2.5.5). In origin this does not seem to have been one of the labours ordained by Eurystheus, because Heracles appears in it as a workman hired by Augeias and expecting payment from him. It probably had its place in the body of heroic poetry centred on Elis and Pylos. But in later sources it is included in the cycle of Labours for Eurystheus, and it might have been so in our Gilgamising epic. If so, the poet might have embellished his description of the cleansing operation with motifs from his native traditions. He could have drawn on the account of the Flood in *Gilgāmeš*, Tablet XI. Also, if he was working after 689 BCE, he will have known that in that year Sennacherib destroyed Babylon and diverted the Euphrates to wash away its remains. In the *Iliad* there is a passage describing how, after the war was over, Poseidon and Apollo diverted all the rivers of the Troad to wash away every trace of the Achaeans' fortification wall. In previous studies I have shown that this Homeric account displays a series of features that seem to derive on the one hand from the Flood narrative in *Gilgāmeš*, on the other from the Assyrian royal propaganda about the destruction of Babylon as expressed in the inscriptions of Sennacherib and his successor Esarhaddon.[8] I suggest that these features might have been mediated by our Heracles poet's account of the cleansing of Augeias' stables.

My galloping steeds, my chariot-team, were plunging into the streams of their blood as into a river; the wheels of my battle-chariot, which lays low the wicked and the evil, were bathed in blood and guts. (Sennacherib's eighth campaign, Chicago Prism v. 78 ff.)	From Elis Heracles proceeded to Pylos and made war on it, fighting in a chariot. The enemy fell before him, and his horses charged ahead, trampling them, so that his chariot was all spattered with their blood.	He lashed the fair-maned horses with the whistling whip, and they ... quickly bore his swift chariot ... trampling corpses and shields. The axle below was all spattered with blood, and the chariot-rails hit by the spray from the horses' hooves and the wheel-rims. (*Il.* 11.531–537.)
(*Scorned by Gilgāmeš,*) Ištar was furious and went up to heaven. Ištar went weeping before her father Anu, Her tears flowing before Antu her mother. (*Gilg.* VI 80–83.)	Athena mounted his chariot beside him in place of Iolaos. (Cf. [Hes.] fr. 33.) Heracles, supported by Athena, wounded Hades, Hera and Aphrodite. Aphrodite went up to heaven and complained to Zeus and her mother Dione.	*Athena pushes Sthenelos out of Diomedes' chariot and takes his place as charioteer.* (*Il.* 5.835–840.) *Diomedes, supported by Athena, wounds Aphrodite, who goes up to heaven and complains to Zeus and Dione. Dione reminds her that similar things have happened before: Heracles wounded Hades and Hera at Pylos.* (*Il.* 5.330–404.)
Ištar demands Gilgāmeš's death. She sends the Bull of Heaven against him, but he and Enkīdu kill it. The gods take counsel and decide that Enkīdu must die. He wastes away. (*Gilg.* VI 92–VII.)	Aphrodite (supported by Hera and Hades?) demanded that Heracles be punished by death. Zeus would not allow that, but conceded that Iolaos be killed instead.	*Patroclus, fighting as Achilles' substitute, attacks Apollo, who warns him off. Soon he is killed.* (*Il.* 16.698–857.)

---

8 West 1995, 211–5 = 2011, 198–203; id. 1997, 377–80.

There are already allusions in the *Iliad* to Heracles' attack on Pylos. It was never part of the canonical cycle of Labours, but it might have been fitted in following the business with Augeias, as he and his kingdom of Elis played a role in Pylian saga (*Il.* 11.670–761). In some later accounts Heracles returned to Elis and made war on Augeias and killed him because he had refused to pay him for cleaning his stables; according to Apollodorus (2.7.2–3) his attack on Pylos followed on after this. A Hesiodic fragment (33.25–36) portrays Heracles as fighting at Pylos from a chariot. If our bilingual poet gave a similar account, this would have been a suitable context for the kind of blood-thirsty description of chariot fighting that we find on the one hand in Sennacherib's report of his eighth campaign below and on the other hand in the *Iliad* (above right). The Heracles epic could be the link between the two.

The same Hesiodic fragment represents Athena as assisting Heracles in the battle and apparently riding beside him on his chariot in place of Iolaos. This resembles the Iliadic episode where Athena displaces Sthenelos from Diomedes' chariot and takes his place to assist the hero. The parallel goes further, because earlier in that episode she has incited Diomedes to wound Aphrodite, who is also on the battlefield. Aphrodite goes up to heaven and complains to her parents, Zeus and Dione. Dione reminds her that similar things have happened before, at Pylos, when Heracles wounded Hades and Hera. It is evident that this episode in the *aristeia* of Diomedes, which stands out in the *Iliad* as something extraordinary, was modelled on an account of Heracles fighting against gods at Pylos. Hades and Hera are named as two deities whom he wounded. I suggest that we may add a third: Aphrodite. Her wounding by Heracles becomes in the *Iliad* her wounding by Diomedes, and when the poet refers to the Pylos precedent he does not include her among Heracles' victims precisely because he has transferred her to Diomedes.

The love goddess's flight to heaven and complaint to her parents comes from *Gilgāmeš*. The Babylonian love goddess, Ištar, made advances to Gilgāmeš, which he scornfully rejected. She was furious, went up to heaven, and complained to her parents Anu and Antu. Anu the sky-god corresponds exactly to Zeus, and Antu is the feminine of the same name, "Mrs Sky", just as Dione, who appears only here in Homer, is a feminine form of Zeus. This will all have stood in the Pylos narrative as told by our Heracles poet.

Ištar demands that Gilgāmeš be punished. She asks for the Bull of Heaven to be sent against his city of Uruk to kill him. The ferocious creature is duly sent, causing havoc in Uruk, but Gilgāmeš and Enkīdu are a match for it, and it is the one that is killed. This causes more outrage in heaven. The gods take counsel, and it is decided that one of the two heroes must forfeit his life. The choice falls upon Enkīdu. He is visited by a wasting sickness and dies after many days. I venture to suggest that some similar development in the Heracles epic brought Iolaos' life to an end. We can imagine that Aphrodite called for Heracles' death. His perpetual enemy Hera, whom he had also wounded, would certainly have supported her, and perhaps Hades did too. Zeus would not allow his mighty son to be eliminated – destiny had more in store for him – but conceded that Iolaos might die in his place.

This is an audacious conjecture, as there is nothing in the Greek tradition to support it. Iolaos somehow disappeared from the story in the course of Heracles' Labours, but no one tells us what became of him. How could this be, if my hypothetical epic had contained the story I am suggesting it contained? My answer must be that it was an oral epic, never written down; it was highly influential for a few decades, leaving its reflections in the *Iliad* and *Odyssey*, but it then went out of circulation and was forgotten. It cannot have been known to Pisander of Camirus, the author of the oldest Heracles epic known to later readers, because if he had used it many more of its Gilgamising elements would surely have remained in the later traditions about Heracles.

But my hypothesis, bold as it may be, is wonderfully fruitful, because it allows us to put in place a whole series of motifs that bridge the space between the *Gilgāmeš* epic's account of Gilgāmeš lamenting for Enkīdu and the *Iliad*'s account of Achilles lamenting for Patroclus.

He felt (Enkīdu's) heart, but it was not beating any more. He covered (his) friend, (veiling) his face like a bride, circling around him like an eagle. Like a lioness deprived of her cubs he kept turning this way and that. He was pulling out his curly tresses and letting them fall in a heap, tearing off his finery and casting it away. (*Gilg.* VIII 58–64.)	Heracles was overcome with grief, tearing his clothes and hair, laying his hands on Iolaos' chest and groaning like a lion whose cubs a huntsman has taken.	(*Achilles is overcome with grief:*) Seizing dust and cinders in both hands, he poured it over his head … the dark ash settled over his fair tunic. Stretched out in the dust he lay, tearing and spoiling his hair. … Peleus' son led them in the loud lament, placing his man-slaying hands on his friend's chest, groaning like a great bearded lion whose cubs a deer-hunter has stolen. (*Il.* 18.23–27, 316–319.)
"We it was who joined forces and climbed the mountain country, seized the Bull of Heaven and killed the Bull of Heaven, destroyed Humbaba, who lived in the Cedar Forest, killed lions in the mountain *passes*." (*Gilg.* X 31–34 = 128–131, 228–231.)	He recalled their past exploits together.	He turned this way and that, longing for Patroclus' manhood and strength, and all that he had endured and suffered with him, fighting against men and crossing the dreadful waves. (*Il.* 24.5–8.)
"Shall not I be like him and also lie down, never to rise again, through all eternity?" (*Gilg.* X 70–71.)	He realised that, like Iolaos, he himself must one day die.	"Not even Heracles escaped death … So I too, if a like fate is made for me, will be laid down when I die." (*Il.* 18.117–121.)

(*Enkīdu's ghost comes to Gilgāmeš*) They hugged each other, kissing one another, sharing thoughts and exchanging questions. (*Gilg.* XII 88–89.)	Iolaos' soul came to him in a dream and they conversed. He tried to embrace the soul, but it had no substance.	*Patroclus' soul comes to Achilles in a dream and they converse. He tries to embrace the soul, but it has no substance.* (*Il.* 23.62–107; cf. *Od.* 11.204–222.)

Achilles, like Gilgāmeš, (1) feels his dead friend's heart, (2) is like a lioness deprived of her cubs, (3) tears his hair and rends his clothes, (4) recalls their past exploits together, (5) realises that he himself must die. It is surely significant that he refers to Heracles as the paradigm. Gilgāmeš accepts that he must die just like Enkīdu; Heracles accepts that he must die just like Iolaos; Achilles accepts that he must die just like – not Patroclus, but Heracles. Finally the dead companion's ghost appears to the hero and they embrace.

Gilgāmeš roams over the steppe. After passing through the mountain from which the sun rises, he wants to cross the ocean, but is told that only the sun-god can cross it. (X 72–84.) *Gilgāmeš attacks the boat-man Ur-šanabi and prevails upon him to take him over the Waters of Death.* (X 92–170.)	Further wanderings brought Heracles to the ocean. He wrestled with Nereus and made him give advice on how to go further: he must use the sun's boat; there was no other. To obtain it he threatened Helios with his bow.	*Menelaus wrestles with Proteus to obtain information on how to move on.* (*Od.* 4.382–570.) *Circe, who is a daughter of Helios and lives by the sunrise, tells Odysseus he must sail across to Hades. 'Why, Circe, who is to guide me on this journey? No one has ever reached Hades by ship.'* (*Od.* 10.501–502.)
The tunnel through the mountain, guarded by two figures who hold up the sky, has already led Gilgāmeš to a shining garden of precious stones. There lives the divine alewife Šiduri. He asks her how to cross the sea to find the wise Ūta-napišti, who may have the knowledge he seeks. (IX 169–X 77.)	Having crossed the ocean he came to the garden of the Hesperides, where apples of gold grow. Here or nearby he met Calypso, the daughter of Atlas, who advised him on how to approach Atlas himself. He found Atlas holding up the sky.	*Circe and Calypso both resemble Šiduri in nature and function. Circe dispenses drinks and advises Odysseus on how to continue his journey to its furthest point. Calypso is located in the far west; she is daughter of Atlas, who knows all the sea's depths and holds the pillars of heaven* (*Od.* 1.52–53).
Ūta-napišti brings Gilgāmeš to the realisation that he cannot escape death. But he enables him to get a plant that restores youth. On his way home, however, it is stolen from him by a snake. (XI 207–307.)	He obtained the golden apples of immortality and set out for home. But on the way he was deprived of them by a snake.	*Calypso offers Odysseus immortality and can provide the food that would confer it, but he declines.* (*Od.* 5.135–136, 196–199, 208–209.)

Heracles' later labours take him to the far west, to the edge of the world and the sunset: the mirror image of Gilgāmeš's wanderings that bring him to the far east, beyond the sunrise. The Homeric parallels from this point on are to be found in the *Odyssey*.

Heracles' western adventures are alluded to in many early poets and logographers, and the tradition quickly became confused as the elements were differently selected and combined. Two distinct labours are involved: capturing the cattle of Geryon from Erytheia, and obtaining golden apples from the garden of the Hesperides. To reach Erytheia Heracles had to cross Oceanus, and he did so by borrowing or taking the sun's floating bowl. Somewhere close to the Hesperides' garden he had an encounter with Atlas and temporarily took over the task of holding up the sky. It is impossible to say quite how the story ran in our hypothetical epic. I would assume that Heracles did not make two separate journeys to the west. From Stesichorus (fr. 7 Finglass), Panyassis (fr. 12 West), and Pherecydes (fr. 16a Fowler) we can reconstruct the detail that he wrestled with Nereus, the shape-shifting Old Man of the Sea, just as Menelaus does with Proteus in the *Odyssey*, and obtained instruction from him on how he was to proceed. Nereus, I suggest, told him that to reach his goal he would need to cross the ocean. Heracles asked how he was to do that, just as Gilgāmeš, having come to the shining garden of Šiduri, asks her how to cross the sea to find the wise Ūta-napišti, and just as Odysseus, when Circe tells him he must cross over to Hades, asks how this can possibly be done: "No one has ever reached Hades by ship". Šiduri tells Gilgāmeš,

> There never was, O Gilgāmeš, a way across,
>> and since the days of old none who can cross the ocean.
> The one who crosses the ocean is the hero Šamaš [the sun-god]:
>> apart from Šamaš, who is there who can cross the ocean?
> The crossing is perilous, its way full of hazard,
>> and in between are the Waters of Death ... (*Gilg.* X 79–84.)

She then reveals that the boat that can cross these waters is nearby, and its boatman Ur-šanabi with it. He is identified as the boatman of Ūta-napišti, not of Šamaš, but if the only one who crosses the ocean is Šamaš, the boat ought to be the sun's boat, and we know that in the Old Babylonian version of the epic Gilgāmeš encountered Šamaš himself.[9]

Heracles got the sun's vessel by a show of violence, threatening Helios with his bow (Pherecydes fr. 18 F.). This corresponds to Gilgāmeš's violent approach to Ur-šanabi.

At Erytheia Heracles fought and killed the three-headed monster Geryon and his dog Orthos and made off with the cattle. I have not put this into my reconstruction because it does not seem to relate to anything in the *Gilgāmeš* epic or in Homer. The more

---

9 Meissner fragment: George 2003, 272–86.

significant episode for my purpose is the encounter with Atlas and the Hesperides. Already in Hesiod (*Theog.* 517–518) Atlas is located close to the singing Hesperides. In Pherecydes (fr. 17) he helped Heracles to get the golden apples. A scholiast on Euripides says that some identified the Hesperides as Atlas' daughters (Pher. fr. 16d; cf. Serv. *Aen.* 4.484).

No source says that Heracles met the particular daughter of Atlas who appears in the *Odyssey*, Calypso. I have constructed this encounter because Calypso the daughter of Atlas is curiously irrelevant to Odysseus' adventures; he is not going to have anything to do with Atlas. In folktale, when a wanderer in need arrives in the realm of a powerful male figure and encounters his daughter, she normally helps him to get what he wants from her father, or despite her father. Medea helped Jason to get the Golden Fleece in spite of Aietes; in the *Odyssey* Nausikaa helps Odysseus to get a favourable reception from Alkinoos, and the daughter of Proteus helps Menelaus to get what he needs from her father, the Old Man of the Sea. Calypso, therefore, may have been invented in order to facilitate someone's approach to her father Atlas; and the only person who ever visits Atlas in Greek mythology is Heracles.

Gilgāmeš, after crossing the steppe, comes to Mount Māšu at the sunrise. This immense massif rises up to heaven (IX 40). The entrance to the tunnel that goes through it is guarded by a scorpion-man and his wife, figures associated with the support of the sky; second-millennium seals show them standing or kneeling and holding the sky up on their heads and hands. They are the Babylonian counterpart to Atlas. After making his way through the tunnel, the ḫarrān Šamši or "path of the sun" (IX 138), Gilgāmeš finds himself in a place where the trees bear fruit of carnelian, lapis lazuli, and other precious stones. If this reminds us of the garden of the Hesperides where the trees bear apples of gold, the goddess Šiduri, who lives there by herself and helps Gilgāmeš to continue on his quest, reminds us both of Calypso and of Circe. When Šiduri is introduced at the beginning of Tablet X she is described as "veiled with a veil", *kutummi kuttumat*. Was it our bilingual poet who bestowed the name Calypso, which can be interpreted as the Veiled One, on the daughter of Atlas who was to receive and assist Heracles?

It is unclear what role Atlas played in the story. Heracles apparently needed to find him for some reason. In Pherecydes (fr. 17) he persuaded him to go and fetch him three of the apples while he relieved him temporarily of the burden of the sky. This does not look like the primary version, where presumably Heracles slew the dragon that guarded the apples and then plucked them for himself. Perhaps he needed some particular piece of knowledge or wisdom from Atlas, who as we read in the *Odyssey* (1.52–53) knew all the sea's depths. He would then correspond in function to the ancient sage Ūta-napišti whom Gilgāmeš was bent on finding.

Gilgāmeš was seeking the secret of eternal life; and the golden apples of the Hesperides have often been understood as the apples of immortality or of eternal youth, though there is actually no ancient authority for this so far as I can see. They resemble the apples of youth in Nordic myth that are guarded by the goddess Iðunn and eaten by the gods to stave off old age. There is also an Ossetic legend of a tree on which golden life-giving apples grow.[10] So was Heracles in his quest for the apples seeking for immortality, as Gilgāmeš was? There is never any such presumption in Greek tradition. He does in the end enter Olympus as an immortal, married to Hebe the personification of youth (*Od.* 11.602–603, [Hes.] *Theog.* 950–955, frr. 25.28–33, 229.7–13). But this seems to be a late development. It is not recognised by the poet of the *Iliad*, whose Achilles, as we have seen, takes Heracles as the paradigm of the great hero who could not avoid death.

There is another possibility. Gilgāmeš learns from Ūta-napišti that his search is in vain and that he cannot escape death. But as a reward for all his effort he is told a secret of the gods. At the bottom of the sea there grows a certain thorny plant that has the power of restoring youth. If he can dive down and pluck it, he may take it back with him to Uruk. If he cannot escape death, perhaps he can at least escape old age. Gilgāmeš ties stones to his feet, sinks down to the seabed, and succeeds in getting the plant. But in the course of his journey home, while he is bathing in a pool, a snake smells the plant and comes and carries it off (XI 273–307). That is why the snake can slough off its old skin and a human cannot. Gilgāmeš finally arrives back at his home city, disappointed of his hopes of escaping death. Versions of the myth of how we nearly got the elixir of youth but lost it to the snake were known to the Greeks. They appeared in Ibycus (*PMGF* 342), Sophocles (fr. 362), and Nicander (*Ther.* 343–358), whose scholiast calls it an ancient tale. Possibly our Heracles poet used the motif, telling how Heracles was robbed of the golden apples on his way home to Tiryns.

Odysseus does not seek immortality, but he could have had it, and it is when he is with Calypso that the opportunity is put before him. She is willing and able to make him immortal if he will stay with her. All he would have to do is change his diet from the food that he is served, which is such as mortals eat, to the ambrosia and nectar that she herself consumes (*Od.* 5.196–199).

In conclusion let me emphasise that I am not looking for a single solution to the whole question of Mesopotamian influences in the Homeric poems. They must have had many sources, which we can never fully trace.[11] I am only suggesting that the hypothesis of a vanished oral Heracles epic, constructed on something like the lines I have sketched, offers an economical way of accounting for a great deal.

So there is my house of cards. Blow it down who will. It is a frail structure, and I see no way of making it stronger. But I hope it may be found attractive enough to be let stand for the moment.

---

10 For the Nordic and Ossetic myths see West 2007, 159.
11 Cf. West 1997, 629.

Appendix: Synopsis of the *Epic of Gilgāmeš* (Standard Babylonian Version)

(Tablet I) Gilgāmeš is an outstandingly strong and handsome hero, but his overbearing behaviour as king of Uruk prompts the gods to create a counterweight to him, a man of the wild, Enkīdu. The news of this savage who lives at one with the animals comes to Gilgāmeš, who sends a prostitute to seduce him and bring him to town. After a week of continuous sex with her, Enkīdu finds that the animals are alienated from him.

(Tablet II) Enkīdu comes into Uruk. He wrestles with Gilgāmeš, who realises that he has met his equal. The two become firm friends. Gilgāmeš announces his intention of journeying to the Cedar Forest in faraway Lebanon to fight its monstrous guardian Humbaba. Enkīdu knows more about Humbaba than Gilgāmeš does, and tries to dissuade him.

(Tablet III) It is settled that Gilgāmeš will go and that Enkīdu will accompany him. Gilgāmeš asks his divine mother Ninsun for her blessing. She prays to the sun-god Šamaš to assist him and keep him safe. Then she gives the two heroes advice for their expedition, and they set out.

(Tablet IV) They make the journey. Each night on the way Gilgāmeš has a dream, and Enkīdu interprets it.

(Tablet V) They arrive at the Cedar Forest and admire it. Humbaba appears and addresses them with fearsome threats. To help them overcome him the sun-god sends violent stormwinds. Humbaba, beaten down, pleads for his life, but Enkīdu urges Gilgāmeš to kill him, and he does so. They fell some of the cedars to make a door for Enlil's temple in Nippur, take it down the Euphrates to Nippur, and return to Uruk with Humbaba's head.

(Tablet VI) The love-goddess Ištar, impressed by Gilgāmeš's manliness, offers herself to him, but he rejects her, pointing out how previous lovers of hers have come to bad ends. She is furious: she goes up to heaven, weeps before her parents Anu and Antu, and prevails upon Anu to let her deploy the Bull of Heaven against Uruk; otherwise she threatens to break open the underworld and let the dead pour out to overwhelm the living. The Bull causes havoc in Uruk, but Enkīdu and Gilgāmeš seize hold of it and kill it. This further enrages Ištar and she curses Gilgāmeš. Enkīdu answers her with a defiant insult. The people of Uruk acclaim Gilgāmeš's greatness.

(Tablet VII) The gods, however, have been conferring and have decided that one of the two insolent heroes must die. The choice falls upon Enkīdu. He has a dream vision presaging his arrival in the underworld, which he describes to Gilgāmeš. He wastes away over many days.

(Tablet VIII) Gilgāmeš laments him at length, recalling their exploits together, and arranges an elaborate funeral for him.

(Tablet IX) Distraught, troubled by the problem of death, to which he now realises that he himself will be subject, Gilgāmeš decides on a journey to see Ūta-napišti, the survivor of the Flood. The gods have granted Ūta-napišti eternal life at the ends of the earth, so perhaps he will be able to tell Gilgāmeš how to escape death. He comes to Mount Māšu, the mountain from which the rising sun comes out, and persuades the gatekeepers, a scorpion-man and his wife, to let him pass through the long, pitch-dark tunnel, "the path of the sun", that leads to the far side. After making his way through it for twelve leagues he comes out in a shining garden of precious stones.

(Tablet X) There he finds an isolated tavern. Its proprietress, Šiduri, does not like the look of this wild figure; she bars her door and takes refuge on the roof, until he explains who he is and why he is in such a dishevelled state. He asks her for directions on how to cross the sea to Ūta-napišti. She replies that those are the 'waters of death', and crossing them is unheard of. But Ūta-napišti's boatman is nearby, and Gilgāmeš induces him to take him in his boat. On completing the crossing he is received by Ūta-napišti and explains who he is and why he has come. The sage tells him he is wearing himself out to no purpose: death is everywhere and he cannot avoid it.

(Tablet XI) Gilgāmeš questions Ūta-napišti. Ūta-napišti relates the story of the Flood, which ended with the gods granting him eternal life. As for Gilgāmeš, if he wants immortality, he must first stay awake for a week. Gilgāmeš at once fails the test and falls asleep for a week. On waking he realises that there is nothing more to be done. Ūta-napišti directs the boatman to clean him up and take him home. But as a reward for all his effort he tells him where he can dive into the sea's depths to pluck an underwater plant that restores youth; if he cannot escape death, perhaps he can at least escape old age. Gilgāmeš obtains the plant, but as he continues his journey it is stolen from him by a snake. He arrives back in Uruk in the knowledge that his journey was in vain. – This was the original ending of the poem.

(Tablet XII) This supplementary tablet is an adaptation of the latter part of a Sumerian poem giving an alternative story of Enkīdu's death. His ghost returns through a hole made in the earth and describes to Gilgāmeš the horrors of the nether world.

Bibliography

George, A. R. *The Babylonian Gilgamesh Epic. Introduction, Critical Edition and Cuneiform Texts* (Oxford, 2003).

West, M. L. The Date of the Iliad. *Museum Helveticum* 52 (1995), 203–219.

West, M. L. *The East Face of Helicon. West Asiatic Elements in Greek Poetry and Myth* (Oxford, 1997).

West, M. L. *Indo-European Poetry and Myth* (Oxford, 2007).

West, M. L. *Hellenica. Selected Papers on Greek Literature and Thought.* Volume I: Epic (Oxford, 2011).

West, M. L. *The Making of the Odyssey* (Oxford, 2014).

Rana Sérida

Myth, Memory, and Mimesis

The Inaros Cycle as Literature of Resistance

People rely – consciously or not – on a complex combination of myth, memory, and mimesis which they use to tell stories, none more important than that of who they were and where they have been; who and where they are now and who they want to be; where they want to go and how they might get there.

(Selbin 2010, 46)

The *Inaros Cycle* is a group of stories chiefly from Greek and Roman Egypt[1] which are unique in their literary form and content, in comparison to Egyptian narrative traditions that predate this period. The stories are written in Demotic and re-tell the events of the seventh century BC, which was the last period of Egyptian history with native kings. At this time, Egypt was divided into princedoms, with Egyptians, Assyrians, and Kushites all fighting for control of Egypt.

The central figure of the stories is a certain prince named *Inaros of Athribis* and the stories relate his and his clan members' exploits. Inaros was an actual historical figure from Athribis in the Delta region, in northern Egypt, and in the stories he is described as the greatest warrior of the country. The many adventurous stories about him and his people constitute the largest connected group of narrative literature from ancient Egypt.[2] In the Tebtunis temple library in the Fayoum (second century AD) – the only surviving temple library, and the richest single source of literary material from ancient Egypt – these stories were housed side by side with other genres of texts, such as mythological, medical, priestly, and astrological, thus representing a substantial part of the native Egyptian literary tradition.[3] Against this background, the stories about Inaros have been classified as "historical" texts from Greco-Roman Egypt that reflect a native view on Egypt's past.[4] Furthermore, certain aspects of the texts have initiated a debate among scholars concerning whether Homer's epic influenced the development of the stories.[5] Few attempts have been undertaken so far to systematically

---

1 I.e. Ptolemaic period: 332–30 BC and Roman period: 30 BC-395 AD. The latest manuscripts of the *Inaros Cycle* date to the second century AD, the date of the manuscripts is further discussed below.

2 Ryholt 2004, 483–510.

3 On the contents and nature of the Tebtunis temple library see Ryholt 2005.

4 E.g. Ryholt 2009, 230–8.

5 E.g. Thissen 1999.

https://doi.org/10.1515/9783110421453-012

analyse the stories or establish their typology,[6] and even fewer have addressed the methodologies we can use to achieve this. This is a difficult task, not only due to the challenge involved in preparing the philological editions of the texts, but also to the very fragmentary state of the manuscripts, and the fact that many of the stories still remain unpublished.[7]

In this paper, I present my interpretation of the entire cycle within a context of collective action: as stories of resistance, composed and preserved by the Egyptian priesthood, in which myth, memory, and mimesis were important narrative strategies for fashioning an Egyptian collective identity. This approach is inspired by Eric Selbin's socio-political research on the power of story, in which three notions are at play: myth, memory and mimesis.[8] While myth refers to the stories through which people understand themselves and their history, memory is the continuous fusion of the past and present into a history that fulfils a social function in its cultural context. Mimesis is the process a certain group goes through when it seeks inspiration from another – ancestors, contemporaries, or people in distant places and times – in making fundamental and transformational changes in their society. Together, myth, memory and mimesis are powerful aspects of historical narrative, especially when those seeking change integrate cultural symbols, heroes and myths into the semantics of a heroic narrative in an attempt to exercise cultural dominance and legitimacy.[9] This characterisation of the cycle as *Resistance Literature* implies that the stories covertly encouraged political independence and cultural autonomy. At the same time, setting the stories of resistance in a bygone past would render any echoes of revolutionary thought inaudible to the unqualified ear, enabling the legends to endure for centuries. Thus, through storytelling, people can fashion and interpret their world. They can confront their past and their contemporary situations and envision their future and by which means this future will come about. Myth, memory and mimesis are concepts that can fruitfully be applied to the *Inaros Cycle*, where the character and attributes of Inaros were fashioned into a myth of an ideal Egyptian king. In creating this myth, the themes, protagonists and motifs that characterised Greek epic provided the tool that allowed the narratives to interact powerfully with their audience, placing Inaros and his legendary

---

6 References to text editions and discussions will be provided below. For an overview of studies and discussions on the cycle, see Sérida 2013, 111–9. See also Rutherford 2016 for the most recent discussion on the *Inaros Cycle* and Homeric influence.

7 In this respect, I am in a favourable situation, since the University of Copenhagen owns the majority of the material from the Tebtunis temple library, which includes a great amount of literature in the process of being published through an international research project (International Papyrus Carlsberg Project). I am particularly grateful to Prof Kim Ryholt for sharing his own findings and readings pertaining to the unpublished texts from the collection, which he is in the process of preparing for his study on Egyptian kings and historical narrative literature from Greco-Roman Egypt.

8 Selbin 2010, 48–73.

9 On collective memory as a cultural force, see: A. Assmann 2006; J. Assmann 2006.

armour on a par with Achilles and his shield, wrapping the compositions around epic references of honour, excellence and superiority in combat skills.

The *Inaros Cycle* is set in the seventh century BC, and the majority of the protagonists of the stories are actual historical figures from that period, including kings Taharqa, Assurbanipal and Necho. In order to better understand the function of the stories in their contemporary context (i.e. Greek and Roman Egypt), it is necessary first to have a glance at what took place during that part of Egyptian history, which was a period marked by political conflict, with Assyrians, Nubians and native kings all engaged in a struggle for power over Egypt.

Around the middle of the eighth century BC, the Kushite Empire expanded their territory into the south of Egypt, thus establishing the twenty-fifth dynasty in Egypt. At the same time, Egypt was experiencing decline and political instability and was divided into princedoms ruled by native Egyptians, which allowed the Nubians to keep expanding their territories beyond Thebes. When the Nubian king Piye came to power (c. 747–656 BC) he conquered more territories in middle and northern Egypt, including the historical capital city of Memphis. In reality, however, his authority only extended northward from Thebes up to the western desert oases, leaving the local princes in the northern Delta to act freely. Piye's successor, Shabaka, however, consolidated Nubian control over the entire country, including the Delta region, and established Thebes as the capital of his kingdom. Shabaka was able to maintain Egypt's independence from foreign powers for a while, but when his successor, King Taharqa, came to power, the Assyrian king, Esarhaddon (689–669 BC), invaded Egypt.[10]

Esarhaddon reorganised the political structure in the Delta and appointed local Egyptian princes as vassals of Assyria, including Necho of Sais and Pekrur of Per-Sopdu.[11] When Esarhaddon left Egypt, Taharqa fanned numerous revolts against the Assyrians. However, Esarhaddon died on his way back to Egypt, leaving it up to his heir, Assurbanipal (668–627 BC), to deal with the revolts. Taharqa was defeated and driven back to Thebes, but at some point Assyrian agents discovered that the fleeing king and some of the vassals in the Delta – including Necho of Sais and Pekrur of Per-Sopdu, – were plotting against him.[12] One query by Assurbanipal to the sun god, concerning the safety of his envoy from attacks by Necho and his allies, indicates that these rebels were considered a serious threat.[13]

---

10 For the twenty-fifth dynasty, see Nauton 2010; for the twenty-sixth dynasty, see Perdu 2010; for the Assyrian invasion in Egyptian literary tradition, see Ryholt 2004.

11 This is recorded in the *Annals of king Assurbanipal*: for the list of rulers, see Onasch 1994, 61–129, 147–54.

12 Detailed discussions of these events, the rebellion, and Inaros are described in: Ryholt 2004, 482–510; Holm 2007, 193–224. See also: Ryholt 2009, 230–8; Chauveau 2004, 39–46; Quack 2006, 499–505.

13 Ryholt 2004, 487 with further references.

As regards Inaros' identity and his involvement in these events, it only emerged a few years ago, from one of the unpublished stories of the cycle, that he was to be identified as the son of Bokennife and grandson of Petese, both of whom are known from Assyrian and Nubian sources: Inaros' grandfather, Petese, ruled Athribis during the Kushite invasion of King Piye (747–656 BC), and his father, Bokennife, ruled Athribis when the Assyrian invasion of King Esarhaddon (689–669 BC) took place.[14] The *Annals of Assurbanipal*, which document Bokennife as appointed vassal in Athribis, reveal that this name was later changed to what would appear to read the name of Inaros.[15] If this reading is correct, Inaros would have succeeded his father as ruler of Athribis during the reign of Assurbanipal. As Ryholt suggests, the attempted alliance against the Assyrians by Taharqa, Necho, and Pekrur probably took place when Inaros replaced his father, and included Inaros himself.[16]

As mentioned, the plot was discovered. Taharqa fled to Thebes, where he remained until his death, while Necho of Sais was captured and deported to Nineveh. Unexpectedly, Necho was pardoned and reinstated at Sais with his royal title and previous possessions, with the addition of new territories bestowed upon him as a gift, while the territory of Athribis was handed over to his son, Psamtik, who thus would have replaced Inaros. Subsequently, Tantamani, Taharqa's successor, marched north from Nubia and reoccupied Egypt as far as Memphis. According to the records, Necho was slain near Memphis, defending his territory, while Psamtik fled to Nineveh under Assurbanipal's aegis. Apparently, Pekrur escaped any punishment after his attempted revolt, since he appears at the head of a delegation at Memphis, offering Tantamani subjugation.[17] These references to Pekrur suggest that he held great political power in the Delta, which can explain his becoming one of the main heroes in the Inaros stories, placed on a par with Inaros and Necho.[18] Aside from that, we do not know much about Pekrur's fate, but we know that the Assyrians returned to Egypt in force, defeated Tantamani's army in the Delta and advanced as far south as Thebes, which effectively ended Nubian control in Egypt. Interestingly, one of the stories of the cycle claims that Pekrur was buried in Nubia, which could mean that Pekrur retreated to Nubia when Tantamani was defeated. At any rate, Psamtik was appointed his father's offices and territories and ultimately reunited Egypt under his sole control, consolidating the rule of the twenty-sixth dynasty of Egyptian kings. The fate of Inaros remains a mystery, along with many questions concerning his person: according to the stories, he was buried within the temple of Osiris at Busiris.[19] What

---

14 Ryholt 2004, 284–9.

15 Text: Onasch 1994, 37; restoration of Inaros' name: Quack 2006, especially 501–2.

16 Ryholt 2004, 486.

17 This is recorded on Tantamani's stela, which only mentions Pekrur's name and not anyone else from the delegation. Text and translation: Grimal 1981, 3–20, pls. I–IV.

18 Ryholt 2004, 487.

19 Quack 2006, 117–21.

remains certain, however, is that Egypt became a satrapy under the control of the Persian Empire in the sixth century BC, never to gain political independence again.

The earliest extant narrative about Inaros is, in fact, an Aramaic inscription on an Egyptian tomb wall from the fifth century BC.[20] The text is too fragmented to explore in detail, but it clearly conforms to the tradition found in the Demotic stories in several aspects: the historical setting of the text in the seventh century with the appearance of the same historical characters such as Inaros himself, Necho, and Taharqa; as well as the presence of 40 men who are undoubtedly Inaros' 40 warrior companions, who figure in the Egyptian versions as the *forty heroes, sons of gods, of the prince Inaros*.[21] The Aramaic version indicates that stories about the rebels were circulating as far back as 200 years after the heroes' lifetime and it is likely that the stories about Inaros were already circulating before the date of the Aramaic version, transmitted (presumably) orally from one generation to another before being recorded as narrative texts. Storytelling, thereby, constitutes an interactive narrative experience, allowing groups to share their experiences, knowledge and understanding of the world.[22] Subsequently, such legendary stories develop into traditional stories that are passed on through generations, ultimately becoming standard culturally shared narratives that have informative value.[23] At some point, the stories were collected, edited, and recorded in literary forms, and, consequently, they became source material for expressing a collective experience of the seventh century BC. There is, of course, no manner in which we can determine with any certainty the exact dates of these processes, but what can be said with certainty is that by the Greek and Roman periods, Inaros had become the most celebrated warrior hero in the Egyptian narrative tradition, and to this day, these stories remain our main source for his memory, constituting the largest connected group of narrative texts from ancient Egypt.[24]

In the second half of the twentieth century, some scholars considered the Inaros texts as involving "resistance" in some sense, but, unfortunately, none of these thoughts seem to have been put into print. This is also because, at the time, only a few of the stories of the cycle had been discovered and understood as a connected group. The full range of the Inaros texts has come to attention only through fairly recent work, most notably that of Kim Ryholt.[25] Nevertheless, Demotic literature (and

---

20 Latest text edition: Holm 2007, with further references. There are other examples of transmission such as the Aramaic story of Horus son of Pwensh, which is the earliest extant story about this magician about whom stories survive in Egyptian, suggesting that certain Egyptian narratives were known in a broader multicultural context. See for example: Porten 2004; Ryholt 2012. For other cross-cultural examples, see: Hoffmann 2009.

21 Hoffmann 2009, 216.

22 Egan 1995.

23 Bruner 1990.

24 Ryholt 2004, 491.

25 Ryholt 2004; Ryholt 2005; Ryholt 2009; Ryholt 2012.

literature thought to derive from Demotic) has been discussed as subversive or directed against the one or the other of Egypt's conquerors. Such texts include: the *Potter's Oracle* and *Oracle of the Lamb*, both prophetic texts about the demise of Egypt due to foreign rule, and the *Demotic Chronicle*, a text of the same nature that foresees the coming of a native hero who will ascend to the throne and restore an order in Egypt.[26] Along with the discovery of new texts of the *Inaros Cycle* follow the advances made within the approaches to literature and society, such as the model of myth, memory and mimesis, applied in the present study. Applying such new models of interpretation to the texts allows us to gain a better perspective on the development of ancient Egyptian literary traditions, themes and motifs, as well as an insight on the cultural context in which stories, such as the *Inaros Cycle*, were embedded.

Many of the Delta rulers who were appointed as vassals to Assyria figure in the *Inaros Cycle*, including Necho of Sais, Petubastis of Tanis and Pekrur of Per-Sopdu.[27] As a group, the stories are either set during Inaros' lifetime or after his death. In general, the stories that are set during Inaros' lifetime feature Inaros himself, Pekrur and Necho (the latter as reigning pharaoh), while the stories that are set after Inaros' lifetime take place during the reign of Petubastis and feature Inaros' own son, Pemu, as well as Pekrur, and Pekrur's son, Petechons. In this latter group of stories, the two young heroes, Pemu and Petechons, have leading roles.

In the stories, Inaros is referred to, among other epithets, as "king" (*nsw*), "good prince" (*rpꜥ nfr*) and "lord of the lance" (*pꜣ nb in-iw*) and his close ally, Pekrur, is referred to as "general" (*mr-mšꜥ*) and "chief of the east" (*pꜣ wr'Ꜣb.t*). Together, Inaros, Pekrur and Necho fight legendary battles against foreign powers, including Nubians, Assyrians and Persians. Inaros' son, Pemu, is commonly addressed with the epithet "young" (*šm*), and he and Petechons, Pekrur's son, appear as allies and great warriors themselves, who have key roles in the plots that are set after Inaros' death.

Predominantly, the stories involve the outbreak of some conflict that results in a great war: either civil wars between the clans or wars against foreign powers.[28] The battle scenes in the cycle form the longest sections of the stories and include extended and detailed accounts of warriors getting ready for combat, their armours, the battle formations, as well as the clashes on land and at sea. This aspect of the stories suggests that these scenes were an admired characteristic of the narratives and comprised the climax of the texts. In the stories, heroism and bravery are highly esteemed. The warriors embrace death as a *friend* and life as the *enemy*, and they express great distress if they are not allowed to engage in battle. Large parts of the combat scenes are dedi-

---

26 On the debate of the relations between Egyptians and Greeks in Egypt, and of the Egyptians' attitudes to various foreigners, see e.g. Milne 1928; Eddy 1961; Lloyd 1982; Johnson 1984.
27 For a detailed overview of the names of the Delta princes, written in Assyrian and their corresponding names in Egyptian, see Ryholt 2004.
28 For a comprehensive survey of the "traditional" and "non-traditional" literary aspects of the compositions from a diachronic perspective of Egyptian narrative traditions, see Sérida 2013, 114–20.

cated to describing the one-on-one combats between the warriors, frequently initiated with the adversaries cursing and insulting one another. Another important feature of the stories is that the warriors often overshadow the ruling pharaoh. Hardly any of the warriors obey the pharaoh's commands, which is an aspect that stands in opposition to the traditional image of the Egyptian pharaoh as singlehandedly defeating his enemies.[29]

In addition to these features of the cycle, the stories constantly emphasise the value and fame of Inaros' weapons. This is seen in light of the many stories that share the common theme of warriors contesting for the ownership of Inaros' weapons after his death. In one story, *Contest for Inaros' Armour*,[30] the hero's son, Pemu, and Inaros' nemesis, the general of Mendes, initiate a great civil war in Egypt after the latter had stolen Inaros' amour from Pemu. In another story, *Contest for Inaros' Diadem and Lance*,[31] Petechons, Pekrur's son, duels with a *kalasiris* to get hold of Inaros' diadem and lance.[32] With these motifs in mind, it would be safe to conclude that Inaros' armour, lance and diadem, i.e. heroic belongings, had an immense value and symbolic significance to his clan (this motif is discussed in detail further below).[33]

The many stories of the *Inaros Cycle* suggest that Inaros and his allies, Pekrur and Necho, were remembered for their significant role in resisting foreign domination in the seventh century BC. Their rebellion against the Assyrians apparently gave rise to a whole cycle of stories about their exploits, which survived as part of the native Egyptian narrative tradition for 750 years after their lifetime.

The Power of Myth[34]

Commonly, a myth is perceived as an untrue and fantastical story, or, "at best, myth might be read as historically based allegory or parable, meant to symbolise or convey meaningful information, albeit unreliably".[35]

In general, myths are dependent on society and culture: they help people process their surrounding world; they are arrived at collectively, as a combination of people's actual experiences and the lessons passed on to them as part of their community's collective memory; and they provide a means by which the complexity of the world

---

29 E.g. Ramses II's record *Battle of Kadesh*. The text is translated in Lichtheim 1976, 57–72.
30 Text edition: Hoffmann 1996. New translation: Hoffmann and Quack 2007, 59–87.
31 Text edition: Ryholt 2012, 89–102.
32 A *kalasiris* (gl-Sr) was one of the two classes in the Egyptian cast of warriors – the second being the *hermotybies*, mentioned in Diod.Sic. 1.94.
33 This aspect of Inaros' armour is discussed below within a context of mimesis. For a discussion that includes Egyptian symbolism, see Sérida 2013, 121–7.
34 I here focus on the uses of myth and not on terminology or definition.
35 Selbin 2010, 53.

can be organised into something simple and intelligible.[36] This communal and popular character of myths is what makes them so powerful[37] and defines "who and what becomes the stuff of legend".[38]

The Power of Memory

Memory is diverse and has many forms (social, cultural, collective, etc.). In collective memory, both social and cultural memories are at play, comprising factual claims about past events, which are held and shared by a certain group of people. Collective memories are communal and they are laden with emotions, thus, they embody an "archive of feelings"[39] in which all the possible pasts can be found.[40] These visions of the collectively experienced past are accordingly uncensored collective ideas of what actions are generally possible, permissible and desirable:[41] as such, they are uncanonical. When such uncensored visions are integrated into the "semantics of a heroic narrative",[42] they can become a powerful "cultural force"[43] in the struggle against oppression (i.e. resistance, rebellion and revolution).[44] Accordingly, those who control memory, or the "past", are in a position to control the present. Hence, the "most common battleground for the struggle over these memories are History and histories, often in popular culture"[45], where those seeking change deploy cultural symbols, heroes and myths, "as they attempt to exert cultural dominance and legitimacy".[46]

Seventh-century Egypt was marked by political turmoil and instability and this was the last period during which Egypt was ruled by native Egyptian kings. After this Egypt was constantly subjected to foreign domination: Persian domination (on two occasions), then Ptolemaic rule and, finally, it became a Roman province. Throughout these periods, the socio-political and cultural landscape of Egypt was constantly shifting. It is debatable to what extent Ptolemaic rule left room for Egyptian and Greco-Macedonian cultures to be exchanged, adapted and assimilated, but Roman

---

36 Selbin 2010, 54–5.
37 Brunk 2008, 4.
38 Selbin 2010, 58.
39 Quoted from Selbin 2010, 75, who quotes Cvetkovich 2003.
40 Selbin 2010, 60.
41 Tilly 1994, 247.
42 A. Assmann 2006, 218.
43 Lee and Yang 2007, 19.
44 Watson 1994, 9.
45 Selbin 2010, 61.
46 Selbin 2010, 61, quoting Whisnant 1995, 4.

policies, for sure kept Greek and Egyptian statuses apart.[47] Roman citizenship and class-enrolments were complicated by a series of rules and laws that, in modern day terminology, would be considered as prime examples of segregation and racism, which naturally increased ethnic consciousness.[48]

In light of the temple provenance of the *Inaros Cycle*, and the sole use of the Egyptian language in the texts, along with the attestations of the Egyptian priesthood as the source of knowledge about native Egyptian history in the Greek histories that have survived, it must have been this community that fostered the myth about Inaros (in its written form).[49] The Egyptian priesthood had for many centuries been a distinct class of society who, in their role as ritual experts, were believed to hold knowledge unavailable to ordinary humans, especially knowledge of the written, sacred word, through which they could influence almost every aspect of life, society, and even the course of history.[50] By the Roman period, this community had experienced a great decline in their power and influence: their numbers, wealth and political influence were efficiently reduced and restrained; their records and financial accounts were regularly scrutinised; they were prohibited from holding any other official titles than those related to divine service, and their previously automatic exemption from taxes and obligatory public services was abolished.[51] All these factors were, imaginably, a major setback for the priesthood that left room for a collective memory about "better times" to foster.

By the Roman period, this "willed nostalgia"[52] of an Egypt ruled by native kings had become a key element towards which an Egyptian self-image could be rooted and nurtured, embodying visions of everything possible, permissible and desirable, a time when legendary warriors fought and eliminated the very same powers that had once dominated Egypt. These stories, gradually, came to be seen as the "truth", residing in

---

47 For a discussion on the mix of cultures in Ptolemaic Egypt, see for example Sérida 2013, 88–94 with further references.

48 For a detailed overview with references, see Sérida 2013, 94–111.

49 Authorship and audience remains a heated subject in Egyptology, especially since none of the texts have ascribed composers. The common conception about Demotic stories remains that the texts were composed and in use mainly within temple contexts, see, for example, Tait 1992.

50 The archaeological and literary sources convey the same image. In Egyptian literature, for example, the literary function of the priest lies in the nature of his association to the god Thoth as his provider of effective magical knowledge: knowledge unavailable to ordinary humans. The priest utilises this wisdom righteously, for example to aid the king and country against threats. For a detailed overview of the literary construction of priestly identity, see Sérida 2013, 23–51.

51 E.g. the administrative texts reveal that 10 % of the population in Ptolemaic Fayoum were registered with priestly functions while, in comparison, a list of temples in the same region from AD 112 records 61 priests in Bakchias, 54 priests and 50 *pastophoroi* in Karanis, c. 50 priests and 40 *pastophoroi* in Tebtunis; see Clarysse and Thompson 2006, 195, and 188–90.

52 Geertz 2000, 22.

the intersection of myth and memory, ultimately "becoming a copy of the past".[53] The use of the Egyptian language in the *Inaros Cycle* was probably a very conscious choice that empowered the priesthood to preserve this *national* identity.[54] In this respect, they could conserve their traditional power (in the form of knowledge), but they would also become the only ones who held the power of transmitting that knowledge to their surrounding world.[55]

It is noteworthy that the *Inaros Cycle* is exclusively written in the native Egyptian script and language. Given the extensive size of the texts and number of stories, and the fact that these survived in the narrative tradition for over 700 years, it is surprising that these tales do not seem to have survived in Greek accounts.[56] A plausible explanation would be that the community of the priesthood consciously confined cultivating and transmitting the national history about Inaros to an exclusively Egyptian audience. As such, they can be seen as the actual revolutionaries who could challenge foreign occupation through cultivating a national myth about Inaros, the rebel, who kept Egypt free from foreign political and cultural dominance. Indeed: "while the collective memory endures and draws strength from its base in a coherent body of people, it is individuals as group members who remember".[57] We may also note, in this context, that, at roughly the same time when we see a peak in the number of surviving manuscripts relating to the *Inaros Cycle*, a violent riot occurred in Alexandria in AD 172, led by an Egyptian priest named Isiodorus. The rebellion, known as the *boukoloi* revolts (*boukoloi* usually translated "herdsmen"),[58] was rather powerful and would have ended with the conquest of Alexandria if the son of the Prefect of Egypt had not been summoned from Syria. He managed to divide the rebels and defeat them in several battles.[59]

---

53 For this aspect of collective memory, see Veyne 1983, 6.

54 Ryholt 2009, for example, discusses Egyptian historical literature from the Greco-Roman period in relation to three main periods of national trauma, namely the Hyksos era, the Amarna age, and the Assyrian invasion.

55 For the Egyptian priests and bilingualism, see for example Rémondon 1964.

56 For example, a story about King Sesostris does exist in both Demotic and Greek, see Ryholt 2010. For a survey of the exchange of motifs between Egyptian and Greek, and Egyptian heroes in Greek texts, see Sérida 2013, 99–103. To my knowledge, a Greek version of any of the stories from the *Inaros Cycle* is yet to be discovered.

57 Halbwachs 1980, 48.

58 For "boukoloi", see Rutherford 2000.

59 Capponi 2010.

"Myth and Memory is History in Ceaseless Transformation and Reconstruction"[60]

Our "repertoires of collective action" are essential tool kits for interpreting and constructing the world (present, past and future).[61] They comprise our collective culture, language, memory, symbols, common enemies and our shared experiences and understanding. In the *Inaros Cycle*, these repertoires of collective action are called upon when Inaros' character and attributes are concerned. Here, his entire being is seen in light of the most traditional notions of Egyptian culture: namely the ideology of kingship.[62]

Cosmologically, Egyptian society was established by the creator god as the norm for all other societies, where Egyptian kingship constituted the ideal form of governance. Even though the cosmos was strong, it was also vulnerable in all its aspects (divine, human, natural) and it had to endure repetitive rebirths to guarantee its strength and validity. During this process, it had to be persistently defended against the forces of chaos, which constantly surrounded it and threatened its existence. The king was the sole authority that safeguarded this process, through which he also ensured the survival of the community. His role in this perpetual process is well illustrated, for example in the depictions of his triumphs over the serpent of chaos (Apophis) in his journey through the hours of the night. In the earthly sphere, this process was reenacted by the king who defeated Egypt's enemies and made certain that her dominance was universally acknowledged. In this manner, he was repeating the divine pattern on earth. The dual and parallel activity of king and god was thus vital for the survival of the cosmos, and hence of Egyptian society. Amongst the living, the king was the main figure who maintained the required cultic links between humanity and the gods, accordingly guaranteeing the deities' own survival and at the same time instigating their benevolence towards Egypt and her people. It is against this background that Inaros' character and attributes can be understood, and the myth of an ideal native Egyptian king was born.

When Inaros ruled Egypt, so the legend goes, he accomplished many great things for the country and its people. Unpublished stories such as the *Inaros Epic*,[63] and

---

60 Tilly 1978, 43.
61 Swidler 1986, 273; Selbin 2010, 27.
62 For surveys, see for example: O'Connor and Silverman 1995, which deals with kingship in its official manifestations (titularies and their extensions) as well as the social and divine context (rhetorical developments and their contexts; the maintenance of order in a bounded cosmos etc.); Assmann 2001, especially chapter 3 for cosmography, the conception of the cosmic process, cosmos and time, and the relation between gods and the cosmos.
63 Being prepared for publication by Kim Ryholt. For preliminary remarks, see Ryholt 2004.

Inaros, Necho and Assurbanipal[64] describe how Inaros himself had campaigned in Assyria and waged war against the Assyrian king and defeated him. In the *Inaros Epic*, for instance, the notion of the dual aspect of king and god is most explicit in a scene where Inaros battles against a magical griffin, sent to the battlefield by King Esarhaddon, as the Egyptian and Assyrian armies face each other. Here, Inaros is explicitly referred to as "Horus the Great of Might" and the griffin as "Apophis".[65] The scene, accordingly, evokes the traditional representation of the god in his fight against the elements of chaos, symbolised by the giant snake Apophis. Thus, the stories portray a king who fulfilled his obligations, defending Egypt's borders and subjugating the earthly elements of chaos: elements that in the legends take the form of Nubians, Assyrians, Persians, Libyans and, on occasion, even Indians.[66] Accordingly, the historical *facts* in the cycle become reversed: rather than the Egyptians having been "vassals" of the Nubians, Assyrians or Persians, the myth portrays Inaros himself as the king who subdued every single one of these powers. This myth of *Inaros as God on Earth*, also served as an example of the possibilities that lay ahead, if the right indigenous man, knowledgeable of the native customs, had power over Egypt once more.

When the cycle addresses the civil wars of the seventh century BC, we find the same repertoires of kingship ideology at play. The tradition, as mentioned, stipulated that Egypt would suffer if her king failed to fulfil his obligations towards the gods. Accordingly the civil wars in Egypt are ascribed to a past where an incompetent king, who failed to maintain the cult of the gods, ruled Egypt. These stories are normally set after Inaros' death, with Petubastis as reigning pharaoh. Unwillingly, or due to his incompetence, this king frequently fails to maintain his traditional obligations towards the gods, causing the gods to rage and impose war and strife on Egypt as punishment. The *Contest for Inaros' Armour*, for instance, begins with Petubastis neglecting to sustain the ceremonies of the "Navigation of the god Osiris".[67] This infuriates Osiris, who then wishes to teach the Egyptians a lesson on the consequences of neglecting his cult. He subsequently sends daemons to Egypt to possess Inaros' son, Pemu, in Heliopolis, and Inaros' nemesis, General Wertiamunniut, in Mendes, with an unquenchable lust for war and strife. Possessed by the daemons, Wertiamunniut steals Inaros' armour from Pemu and the two leaders initiate a great civil war in Egypt over the possession of the armour. In addition to neglecting Osiris' cult, Petubastis also fails to sustain the cult of Amun in the *Contest for the Benefice of Amun*.[68] Here, a young priest feels entitled to the priestly stipend of Amun, which has gone to the king's son. He then joins forces with 13 "shepherds", interrupts the ongoing "ceremony of the crossing", and

---

64 Being prepared for publication by Rana Sérida.

65 Ryholt 2004, 494.

66 E.g. *Sarpot and Petechons* (see below).

67 Ryholt 2010, 80.

68 Text edition: Spiegelberg 1910; new translation: Hoffmann and Quack 2007, 88–107.

highjacks the bark of Amun. This, again, instigates a great civil war in Egypt for the return of the bark.[69]

Petubastis is subject to much critique in the *Inaros Cycle*: one opinion about him is expressed by Petechons, when he receives a call for help from the king, informing him that the young priest and his 13 shepherds had kidnapped Petubastis' son:

> He (i.e. Petechons) heard all the words, which it contained (i.e. the letter asking for his help). He raged like the sea. He fumed with rage as he said: "That fish-catcher of a man from Tanis, pit of *wrs*-plant of a man from Dep, Petubastis son of Anchhor, whom I cannot call 'King' (*bn-pwꜣy ḏd nꜣf pr-ꜥꜣ*). He honours me (only) when he seeks me in his misfortune. When he goes to celebrate the festivals of his gods, without there being war and strife against him, he never sends for me. I swear in the name of Sopdu, the Great of the East, my God: had not the Chief of the East, my father Pekrur, mentioned in that letter (the name of) Amun, the great God in the west of Upper Egypt, who is across from Thebes, one would not have let it (i.e. the letter) cross to Thebes (i.e. where Petechons is), and I would never have had to fight for the children of Tahor, daughter of Patjenef. But I do not want to be subject to the disgust of Amun against me (i.e. if he does not fight). My brothers (?) (and) my 56 (?) men of the East! My eight [priestly] colleagues [get on board! – So they prepared their] arms (i.e. for the trip to the) south of Thebes."
> (*Contest for the Benefice of Amun*, 13.12–24)

Aside from the obscure swearwords, which clearly are less than flattering, Petubastis is also described as a ruler unable to take up his own fights, and even his right to the title *king* is questioned. Furthermore, Petechons clearly states that the sole reason for his voyage to aid him is the fear of disrespecting the god, which, again, identifies Inaros' clan members as those who enjoy the favour of the gods. This myth of *The Gods' Fury* delivered an instrument through which the chaotic seventh century BC became intelligible, and, at the same time, it warned against the chaos that might ensue when power over Egypt fell into the wrong hands.

The cycle of stories about Inaros and his people re-organised the past into a collective myth: a myth at the root of which was the idyllic image of an ideal king. Inaros was "the son of Osiris Wennefer, King of the land, the *Kalasiris* and Lord of the lance."[70] He was a hero, known and famous worldwide: his name had been "heard in the districts of the entire world and in the horizon before Re, in the underworld before Osiris, and in Punt before Amun, because of his strength of might and marvel as a warrior".[71] Inaros had fought side by side with Pekrur, the general and chief of the East. Pekrur was the "Father of the bulls of Egypt", and the "Good leader of the *kalasireis*".[72] The two heroes had sons, Pemu and Petechons, both feared and famous warriors. Like his father, Pemu had fought against great powers: he singlehandedly crushed the As-

---

69 For "shepherd", Greek *boukoloi*, see note 58.
70 Ryholt 2010, 83.
71 Ryholt 2010, 82.
72 *Contest for the Benefice of Amun*, 11.9–12.

syrian army when it attacked Egypt in the reign of Petubastis, causing slaughter and destruction amongst them, thus saving Egypt from the humiliation of defeat:

ḫꜣ

> By Re-Horakhte, the Chief of the Gods, the Great God! [pharaoh] Petubastis on the [...] when the chief of Ashur Esarhaddon son of S[ennacherib came] to take Egypt from pharaoh Petubastis, I jumped in [/], I made considerable bloodbath (ḫꜣ) and destruction (wḫy). I caused him to return to the east.
> (*Contest for Inaros' Armour*, 5.6–9)

Although Pemu was "young" in age, he took much pride and honour in combat and in maintaining the reputation of his father and their clan, because, as the legend goes, "there is no warrior clan in Egypt like the clan of Osiris, King Inaros".[73] One example of Pemu's principled conduct with regards to his father's reputation is the abovementioned story of the *Contest for Inaros' Armour*, where the young Pemu honours his father by retrieving his stolen armour through exhibiting great combat skills against the man who had stolen it. This act is matched by Petechons, Pekrur's son, in the *Contest for Inaros' Diadem and Lance* where he defeats a *kalasiris* who had taken hold of Inaros' diadem and lance. Petechons himself was a gift bestowed by the gods to his father, a prince and mighty "Bull of Per-Sopdu," and the "Lion of the Eastern district".[74] This description is not far from his reputation outside of Egypt. In the story of *Sarpot and Petechons*, in which Petechons is campaigning in Assyria and meets the army of an Amazon queen en route, we are told of the petrifying stories about the prince that had reached the ears of Queen Sarpot: it was said that he had waged war against the king, and against the land of Assyria, and that he would fight with one chief today, and defeat another tomorrow; his combat skills were so great that even the gods could not help his opponent against him, and Sarpot, pleading to her gods, asks how she and her army ever will be able to defeat him.[75]

Such collectively held and shared memories could firmly forge an Egyptian identity. The memory of Inaros and his clan is powerful, pervasive and purposeful, lasting for more than 700 years after his lifetime, and laden with meaning. Storyteller(s) and audience(s) rely on memories to provide history and context, to "fill in the gaps, and construct a larger, more nuanced, often deeper, and unspoken tale than can be proffered".[76] In the *Inaros Cycle*, such hidden meanings, from which inspiration could be drawn, lie in the memory of "free ancestors". Such visions of liberated children and grandchildren are powerful tools for moving revolutionaries and constitute a deep structure upon which meaningful stories of resistance, rebellion, and revolution are

---

73 *Contest for Inaros' Armour*, 17.16–7.
74 *Contest for the Benefice of Amun*, 11.12–6.
75 *Sarpot and Petechons*, 2.22–5.
76 Selbin 2010, 65.

built.[77] The message is simple: if a native and beneficent king rules Egypt once more, she could be great again.

Mimesis: Epic Recollection

It is the conscious identification with and emulation of other people that has been particularly critical for resistance, rebellion and revolution.[78] The unique and unprecedented themes and motifs of celebrated warriors and their exploits, civil and external wars, sea battles and one-on-one combats that are so prominent in the *Inaros Cycle* have led some scholars to consider whether it had been produced under Homeric influence. Demotists have so far either entirely refused the idea or only cautiously suggested the possibility of Greek influence in the stories.[79] Such discussions have focused on narrative motifs or themes, but not many have considered the possibility of mimesis,[80] and even fewer have discussed *what* exactly it is that the stories imitate. In this regard, epic and its cultural context and function itself should be examined first, before drawing any conclusions concerning any narrative contents.

Epic may be characterised as tales of identity that convey extratextual meaning to those groups who recognise them as *our story*.[81] Epic is a saga of identity and, as such, a saga of "alterity".[82] This means that by creating unity (an "us"), epic simultaneously creates a contrast to and distance from other groups ("them").[83] From the onset of Hellenism in Egypt, Homer's epic constituted an important literary device by which Alexander the Great and the Ptolemies established a Greek group identity among non-Greek-subjects (i.e. alterity).[84] As Marincola states, "sometimes the literary echoes in a historian will have arisen from the fact that his subject was actually seeking to call up previous historical actors: the 'intertextuality' here was the doer's not the writer's (or at least not wholly the writer's)."[85] Hence, epic was an encyclopaedia for the Greeks to which they consciously reached for inspiration and recollection of their history and identity. The most obvious example that comes to mind is Alexander the Great's association with Homer and his heroes.

---

77 Benjamin 2003, 394.
78 Selbin 2010, 70.
79 Volten 1956; Tait 1992; Hoffmann 1996, especially 113ff.; Vittmann 1998; Thissen 1999.
80 Ryholt, for example, discusses with regard to *imitatio Alexandri* aspects of several of the Demotic narratives, including the *Inaros Cycle*; cf. Ryholt 2013.
81 Honko 1996, 21.
82 Connelly 1986, 225.
83 "Unity is impossible without alterity": Honko 1996, 21.
84 Finkelberg, 2011, 876.
85 Marincola 2010, 266.

Plutarch reports that Alexander thought of and called the *Iliad* a "viaticum of the military art", and that he kept Aristotle's recension of the poem lying with his dagger under his pillow (Plut. *Alex.* 8.2). Other sources relate that the first city the king visited on his campaign in Asia Minor was Troy, where he made a sacrifice and dedicated his armour to Athena. In exchange, he took down a display of arms said to date back to the Trojan War. He then sacrificed to Priam, king and ancestor of the Trojans, in order to appease his vengeful ghost because Alexander himself was a descendant of Neoptolemus, son of Achilles, who had killed Priam at the sack of Troy (Arr. *Anab.* 1.11.5). A parallel account adds that Alexander also made offerings at the tombs of the Achaeaen heroes and paid respect to Achilles, anointing his tombstone and running a race by it with his companions, as was the custom. He then crowned it with a wreath, pronouncing the hero "happy in having, while he lived, a faithful friend, and after death, a great herald of his fame." In Philostratus' *Heroikos*, set at the tomb of the first hero to fall in the Trojan War, Protesilaos, a dialogue between the spirit of the hero and the caretaker of his tomb is recorded in which the former reveals his insights about Homer, the Trojan War, its heroes, and their cults. In the text, the dead hero recalls how Alexander had made Achilles his ally in Troy while marching against Darius (Philostr. *Her.* 9.1–3). Accordingly, Alexander's victory could partially be ascribed to his heroic armour obtained from the temple of Trojan Athena, as well as his own heroic battle skills influenced by Homer. On a daily basis, the sources further recount, Alexander's tutor had found favour at the Macedonian court by identifying the members of the royal family with Homer's heroes. Alexander became Achilles, King Philip became Peleus, Achilles' father, and Alexander's tutor became Phoenix, the tutor of Achilles (Plut. *Alex.* 5). Our sources also liken Alexander's friend Hephaestion to Patroclus, who was Achilles' closest companion in the epic. When Hephaestion died on Alexander's campaign in the East, the king had mourned the death of his friend just as Achilles had mourned Patroclus in the *Iliad*: he cut off his hair over the body and sacrificed human flesh to the shade of his companion dragging an enemy leader behind his chariot around the walls of a city, in the same manner as Achilles had the dead Hector.[86]

Since Homer's epic ultimately functioned as an instrument of alterity for the Hellenic elite, representing perceptions of their "group identity, core values of their society, models of heroic conduct and human endeavor, and symbolic structures of history and mythology",[87] it is not surprising that Alexander's mimesis of the Homeric narrative and characters found its way into Egyptian historical narrativity, in order to tell a powerful story of their own. The notion of mimesis implies that patterns of behaviour or ideas (or emotions) move from person to person or group to group ("contagion").[88]

---

[86] Tutor: Plut. *Alex.* 5.5; Hephaestion: Arr. *Anab.* 7.14.2; Human sacrifice: Plut. *Alex.* 72.3.

[87] Honko 1996, 21.

[88] Selbin 2010, 67–8.

In mimesis, people adopt and adapt the actions of other people that have proven successful in causing changes in their society. As such, mimesis is a very powerful tool for generating socio-political change.

Mimesis: Rhetoric

The *Contest for Inaros' Armour* and the *Contest for Inaros' Diadem and Lance* share the common theme of being centred on Inaros' personal weapons, and it would be safe to assume that Inaros' heroic relics held great symbolic value to his clan members. The reason behind this emphasis evidently relates to its affiliation to such a distinctive warrior. In the *Story about the Living Inaros*,[89] which only survives in a single fragment, Inaros himself appears to be telling a story about his legendary armour. As he sits with his companions at a feast, he calls for his armour to be brought to him and then tells a story in which Egypt's neighbours in the "[East], West, North, and South", had all been turned into "vassals" (*bȝk*), every single one of them.[90] Although this scene is preserved in a fragmentary state, it is very likely that Inaros told a story about the role which his legendary armour had played in subjugating Egypt's enemies: a scene reminiscent of that described by his own son in the *Contest for Inaros' Armour*, mentioned earlier, in which the young prince causes havoc and destruction among the Assyrian army.

Not only does the symbolism of Inaros' armour echo the fame and value of Achilles' shield, the entire narrative technique of describing the suits of armour in the *Inaros Cycle* is unprecedented in any earlier stories from ancient Egypt. Here, the author gives the audience a visual perception of the entire armour's appearance: the material (gold, silver, etc.), the swords, the decorations of war motifs on the shields, and even the reaching for and putting on of each item.

Although a full description of Inaros' armour is not preserved in any manuscript, we get an impression of how it may have looked from the descriptions of his son's and Pekrur's armours in the *Contest for Inaros' Armour*. The portrayal of Pemu's armour is unfortunately much damaged. It begins with a detailed description from the moment the suit of armour was laid on a mat before the prince and each item he reaches for, until the suit is fully assembled. The scene occupies twenty lines on a page of an average of thirty lines, which is a rather long passage (12.25–13.17). The kilt was of first class byssus and decorated with precious stones. A part of the armour that covered Pemu from the navel to the thighs was made of gold and had rims of red leather. On his back, part of the armour was decorated with ten flowers in the centre, which were made of silver and gold. Further parts of the armour, which were also made of byssus, gold, and

---

89 Text edition: Ryholt 2010, 23–30.
90 *Story about the Living Inaros*, 7–10.

iron, including his helmet, are described. The undergarments were made of fine wool and other costly materials. His scale armour had strings of fine iron, and a decoration of war motifs. Further references are made to depictions of gods and goddesses of combat, which were the work of a "skilled artist". His shin guards were of silver and some of their parts were made of wool, and red leather was on a part that covered his feet. His sandals were braided, and red leather is mentioned again. The remaining lines are even more damaged, but some words are identifiable: leather, ebony, malachite, and gold with a reference to a lioness, presumably another figure on the armour.

The passage would have sounded more or less as the following much shorter description of Pekrur's armour, i.e. that of Inaros' closest companion:

> The Great of the East, Pekrur, came outside, girded with a suit of mail threaded with fine iron (*bnpy nfr*) (and) greaves of pure silver. He was armed with a battle sword (*sfy knkn*), measuring 45 [...] of iron, and his *hly*-sword (of) a man of the East, was of shiny steel from its hilt to its top. He was holding a lance [from] Arabia two thirds of which was [of wood?] and one of iron. A shield of gold was in his hand. The Great of the East, Pekrur, stood in the middle of the army of Egypt between the two [arrays] of shields (i.e. the two opponent groups). He spoke, in a high voice, crying out loudly: "Up, general Wertiamonniut! You're the opponent of General Pemu the young, the son of Inaros".
> *(Contest for Inaros' Armour, 18.22–31)*

This narrative device is unparalleled in earlier Egyptian fiction and is unique to the *Inaros Cycle*. It is a method of description referred to as *ekphrasis* in Greek, which is a rhetorical device that dramatically and vividly describes a visual work of art in a manner that relates more directly to the audience.[91] In the *Iliad*, *ekphrasis* is particularly used when Homer describes the shield of Achilles, going to great lengths in Book 18 in relating its complete shape and decoration, and how Hephaestus had made it.[92] It is this literary technique that was adapted to an Egyptian mode of describing weapons in the *Inaros Cycle*. A comparable episode in the *Iliad* is the scene where king Agamemnon is reaching for his armour:

> First he placed upon his legs the beautiful greaves linked
> With silver fastenings to hold the greaves at his ankles.
> Afterwards he girt on about his chest the corselet
> That Kinyras had given him once, to be a guest present. [...]
> Now there were ten circles of deep cobalt upon it,
> And twelve of gold and twenty of tin. And towards the opening
> At the throat there were rearing up three serpents of cobalt
> On either side, like rainbows, which the son of Kronos
> Has marked upon the clouds, to be a portent to mortals.
> Across his shoulders he slung the sword, and the nails upon it
> Were golden and glittered, and closing about it the scabbard

---

91 *Il.* 18. 478–608; Becker 1995.
92 Becker 1995.

Was silver, and gold was upon the swordstraps that held it.
And he took up the man-enclosing elaborate stark shield,
A thing of splendour. There were ten circles of bronze upon it,
And set about it were twenty knobs of tin, pale-shining,
And in the very centre another knob of dark cobalt.
And circled in the midst of all was the blank-eyed face of the Gorgon
With her stare of horror, and Fear was inscribed upon it, and Terror.
The strap of the shield had silver upon it, and there also on it
Was coiled a cobalt snake, and there were three heads upon him
Twisted to look backward and grown from a single neck, all three.
Upon his head he set the helmet, two-horned, four-sheeted,
With the horse-hair crest, and the plumes nodded terribly above it.
Then he caught up two strong spears edged with sharp bronze
And the brazen heads flashed far from him deep into heaven.
And Hera and Athene caused a crash of thunder about him,
Doing honour to the lord of deep-golden Mykenai.
(Hom. *Il.* 11.17–46).[93]

Mimesis: Epic Formula

In the *Iliad*, accounts of fighting have a purpose of their own: "it is not that epic attributes to the warriors a system of values that concords with their way of fighting; rather, they are depicted as fighting in a way that accords with their ethics".[94] Here, the heroes win glory and compete in the display of Homeric virtues, which include strength, skill, physical courage and fleetness of foot, as they slaughter their foes and demonstrate their qualities before their public, the other heroes on both sides, and, accordingly, establish their claim to relative rank.[95] The most important arena for exhibiting these virtues is the individual contest itself. In the *Inaros Epic*, several aspects of this epic formula are adopted. One example is in the *Contest for Inaros' Armour* where the heroes publicly display their combat skills before an audience. Here, one of the shepherds who has stolen the bark of Amun engages in a one-on-one combat with a descendant of Inaros, Minnemei, before the pharaoh and the entire army of Egypt:

> Then rose one of the 13 shepherds, saying, "I have come to you, you southerner, (you) Nubian, resin-eater of Elephantine!" He armed himself. He jumped ashore. He struck. He fought with Minnemei on the upper side of the bark of Amun from the first hour of the morning till the eighth hour of the evening, while pharaoh and the army of Egypt watched them as each displayed his combat skills, none of the two being able to defeat the other.
> *(Contest for the Benefice of Amun*, 15.20–16.2).

---

93 Tr. Lattimore (1951).
94 Lendon 2005, 28.
95 Lendon 2005, 24.

Another epic formula, which may also be noted in this scene, is how the encounter between the two warriors is initiated with the exchange of insults. This is also a very central aspect of single combats in the *Iliad*, where warriors not only compete in combat skills, but in insults as well.[96] In the passage above, the warrior insults Minnemeis' Nubian genealogy, in another episode, Petechons initiates the battle against his opponent with a much more elaborate insult: "you widow fornicator".[97]

Stripping the defeated party of his armour in the *Iliad* is a mode of proving one's worth through exceeding the opponent in combat and martial skills.[98] This principle is illustrated in the *Contest for Inaros' Armour*, where Pemu asks Wertiamonniut whether he had obtained Inaros' armour through the "might of his power" (*p3y⸗k nḫt.ṭ n nmṭy*) or through "surpassing [Pemu] in martial skills" (*tḳn n sbꜥ n mšs*).[99] If Wertiamonniut had fought against Pemu for the possession of the armour and established his superiority in combat, he would have been entitled to it:

> By Atum, the great god! When the armour is given to me, it will not be brought to Heliopolis without my having taken it through combat. It is because of it (i.e. the armour) that the lance is raised (i.e. war) and the army of the entire land recognises it (i.e. the fact). I shall go in the name of my lord Inaros and I (i.e. Wertiamonniut) shall take his armour to Heliopolis.
> (*Contest for Inaros' Armour*, 9.28–30)

As a result, when the war ends with Pemu's victory, Wertiamonniut acknowledges his own disgrace in Egypt by returning Inaros' armour to Pemu, along with his own ancestor's armour.[100] This code is also explicit in the *Contest for Inaros' Diadem and Lance*, where Inaros' heroic relics are returned to Petechons after a fight with a *kalasiris* in which the former's strength as a great warrior is established:

> He (i.e. Petechons) made battle (*knḳn*) with [the *kalasiris* … The moment] this happened, [the *kalasiris*] proceeded away from [him.] He [realised] that he had gained advantage over him in a skill of fighting. He, (i.e. the *kalasiris*) made a truce between himself and Petechons.
> (*Contest for Inaros' Diadem and Lance*, 9–12)

In the same manner as in the Homeric epic, the warriors of the *Inaros Cycle* fight in accordance with their ethics and set of belief. In *Sarpot and Petechons*, for instance, Petechons and the Amazon queen Sarpot fight around a principle in which they behold death as a companion and life as an enemy.[101] Here the warriors take pride in dying in the battlefield, which mirrors the attitudes with which the warriors in the Iliad enter battles: they have no fear of death, and rather see it as a welcome friend, as

---

96 On the competitive quality of insults and utterances before combat, see Martin 1989.
97 *Contest for Inaros' Armour*, 16, 15.
98 Lendon 2005, 23.
99 7, 8–9.
100 19.31; 25.23.
101 3.46.

opposed to life. Such is the depiction of death in the battlefield in the *Iliad*: "When a young man falls by the sword in battle, he may lie where he is and there is nothing unseemly; let what will be seen, all is honourable in death" (Hom. *Il.* 22.70–5).

There are many more aspects of the *Inaros Cycle* that echo epic formula, such as fighting under conditions agreed upon in advance, as the heroes are ranked one against another, the yearning always to be the best and preeminent above others, as well as the elaborate formal and informal assemblies of leading warriors that take place before the fights commence. All these aspects are echoed, in, for example, Pekrur's assigning opponents on the battlefield to each warrior, the lament of Monthbaal when the ninth hour approaches in the battlefield without him having fought against a single opponent, and the assemblies of the clans that take place before any battle begins in many of the stories.[102] However, the story must be tailored to both the physical environment and the mental tradition-morphology of its audience: ideals, values, social structures, etc.[103] The most alien motif in Egyptian narrative tradition is the tragic death of the hero. Even though heroes in the cycle embrace death as their friend, there is no actual "death scene" of the hero.[104] In the battle scenes, the warriors always retreat from killing their opponent for some reason or another. One example is in the *Contest for Inaros' Armour*, where Pemu has overpowered Wertiamunniut and has him firmly pinned to the ground with his foot. Just as Pemu raises his sword to strike Wertiamunniut, Monthbaal stops him because they have been established as the victors.[105] Accordingly, references to "bloodshed", "death" and "destruction" are commonly used in the stories as generalisations and never in explicit depictions because such notions of death and tragedy were simply too alien for adaptation. In *Petechons and Sarpot*, for example, Petechons and the Amazon queen chance upon each other in Assyria. When the queen sees the Egyptian army camped nearby, she sends her younger sister disguised as a man to spy on them. After finding out the intention and identity of Petechons, Sarpot prepares for battle against him. In the first clash between the armies, Sarpot and her female soldiers are so fierce that they cause much bloodshed and turmoil among the Egyptians and both armies then retreat to their respective camps. The next day, the two warriors meet on the battlefield and engage in a duel. They fight bravely and forcefully until nightfall:

> They set their lances before themselves. They cast their shields across their [shoulders]. [...] abuse, the language of warriors (i.e. they are insulting each other). They beheld death as a companion and life as an [enemy]. [...] duel. (So) skilled were their strikes, (and so) clouding their

---

102 E.g. *Contest for Inaros' Armour* 9.28–30.

103 Honko 1996, 52.

104 Heroes of Egyptian stories are hardly ever killed. Protagonists may pass away of natural causes, but those characters seldom play central roles in the stories in which they feature. Killing is limited to motifs of moral punishment, which especially occurs in relation to the punishment of adulterous women.

105 23.6–14.

blows [...] effort. They flew to the sky like vultures, they came down to the ground as [...] They began the attack as panthers. They were like [...] son of Sobek. The ground echoed [...] by the [...], by confusing, by striking, by jumping. No one gave the other way. [...] again. No one gave the other way. The fight [lasted from the] time of the first hour of the morning to the [... hour] of the evening.
(Sarpot and Petechons, 3.46- 4.5).

The two warriors then agree to take a break and continue fighting later. At some point during the combat, the two heroes see each other's faces, presumably as they take off their helmets, and fall instantly in love with each other:

She could not find a place on earth on which she was (i.e. she was beside herself) because of the great love that took hold of her (lit. entered). [At the moment] the prince [Petechons] himself [saw her] he did not find a place on earth on which he was.
(Sarpot and Petechons, 4.26–27).

Although the text is much damaged towards the end, it appears that at some point the two warriors join forces against an Indian king who is now attacking the Amazons, but the story breaks off at this point. The passages as a whole contain several epic concepts, the most interesting of which – aside from the notion of "Amazon" in itself, which is a direct reflection of the Egyptian understanding of the Greek *amazones,* which they conveyed as "land of women" (*t3 n shm.t*) – is the encounter of the heroes, Sarpot and Petechons and the love scene between the two, which is reminiscent of the motif of Achilles and the Amazon queen Penthesilea.[106] Penthesilea arrives at Troy and promises the Trojans that she will kill Achilles but Achilles eventually kills her with one blow through her breastplate. When he removes her helmet, he is so touched by her beauty that he falls in love with her instantly.[107] The differences between the Egyptian and Greek account lie in the endings of the stories: the Greek one has a tragic ending that is absent in the Egyptian version. Instead, the motif was re-formulated to fit Egyptian literary tradition: rather than dying, the Amazon queen joins forces with Petechons against the Indian king, thus providing the audience with the traditional happy ending of Egyptian narratives.

Some scholars understand the motif in *Sarpot and Petechons* as a story based on Alexander the Great and his exploits, thus placing Petechons on a par with Alexander the Great.[108] Although Alexander is also said to have met the Amazon queen Thalestris who, according to one tradition, stayed with him for thirteen days in order to conceive a child from him (e.g. Diod. Sic. 17.77; Str. 11.5), which is certainly reminiscent of the Sarpot/Petechons motif, it should be kept in mind that epic in itself constituted the main background against which the image of the warrior king was shaped: epic made

---

106 Ps.-Appollod. *Bibliotheca* 5.1 (second century).
107 Ibid.
108 See Ryholt 2013 for *imitatio Alexandri.*

the Greek past irreducibly past, and so rather than envisaging the past as the present, they tended rather to understand the present by means of the past. When a Greek sculptor wished to allude to the great wars between Greeks and Persians, he tended instead to depict the combat between the Greeks and Trojans or between Greeks and Amazons, mythic warrior-women, or the combat between the Greek Lapiths and the bestial Centaurs, themes elaborated from epic.[109]

Finally, there is the motif of the contest for Inaros' armour that shares similar patterns with book 5 in the *Posthomerica* of Quintus of Smyrna.[110] Here, after Achilles' death a feud between Odysseus and Telamonian Ajax begins for the ownership of Achilles' armour. The two warriors compete by giving speeches on who fought best to protect Achilles' body and thus is the bravest warrior after Achilles. The consensus turns out to be in favour of Odysseus, who then presents the armour to Achilles' son, Neoptolemus. The similarities in the Demotic and Greek texts lie in the value of the fallen hero's armour, the conflict concerning its ownership, and its return to the hero's son in the end. The means by which the armour is obtained is, on the other hand, very different. While the Greek episode applies one of the most important aspects of Greek culture as the means of retrieving the hero's weapon, i.e. rhetoric, the Egyptian story applies the principle of superiority in physical strength as the only way to regain the objects.

Conclusions

A few centuries after the Assyrian occupation of Egypt, stories about the men who attempted to resist the process began to emerge in written form. From the start, the stories appear to have been so popular that they were cross-culturally transmitted and found their way into Aramaic literature. Throughout the 700 years that followed, these tales evolved into great epics that constituted a fundamental part of the native Egyptian narrative tradition. These tales are the largest group of connected stories from ancient Egypt, known as the *Inaros Cycle*.

The community that had a significant role in fostering a collective memory about Inaros and his clan was the Egyptian priesthood, an elite literate social class, which, by the Roman period, had suffered great decline in power and influence. For them nostalgia towards an Egypt ruled by native kings became a key background against

---

109 Lendon 2005, 37.

110 The date of Quintus of Smyrna's *Posthomerica* is not definitely established. The current *communis opinio* is the third century, whereas the Demotic story dates to the second century, which raises the interesting question of the origin of the motif. At any rate, the parallelism is striking. See Maciver 2012.

which an Egyptian self-image could be formulated, in an attempt to resist cultural decline and maintain a national identity.

In order to tell a powerful story of their own, the authors of the stories adopted Greek epic recollection as an instrument of creating alterity, i.e. an *us*, as separated from *them*. The epic frame of reference also provided the authors of the cycle with new literary techniques, which allowed the texts to interact powerfully with their audience. For instance, *ekphrasis* facilitated placing Inaros and the symbolism of his warrior relics on a par with Achilles and his shield, while epic formula wrapped all the compositions around a context of honour and excellence in combat skills, voicing unity and bravery, where even death was a small price to pay for the protection of Egypt and its people. Naturally certain Greek narrative strategies were too alien for an Egyptian mindset, which meant that some aspects of Greek epic formula were not transformed into Egyptian motifs, while other motifs that were more relatable to the audience were adapted.

The result of this amalgamation of myth, memory and mimesis was an indigenous epic about Inaros, Pekrur, their sons Pemu and Petechons, and the pharaoh Necho. These men were the greatest men of Egyptian history by virtue of their status as the warriors, a category in their own right, who freed Egypt from foreign political and cultural dominance. Ultimately these visions were believed to be true, paving the way for the epic to become a popular source for Egyptian national history, which firmly established or consolidated Egyptian group identity and could, thus, covertly stimulate visions of free ancestors, and, hopefully, push towards resistance.

These stories were kept in temple archives and the priesthood was the source for gaining access to this indigenous history. In their capacity of being literate and bilingual, this community was the only one that could transmit the contents of the manuscripts to the outside world, which also conforms to their role as the source of information in Greek historical writing and to the existence of Egyptian narrative motifs in Greek texts. Accordingly, the priesthood was able to transfer their knowledge beyond the walls of the temple.

Considering the exclusively native Egyptian language and script of the *Inaros Cycle*, the extensive size of the texts and number of stories, and the longevity of the narrative tradition, it was likely a conscious choice that these tales did not travel to Greek ears. Rather than being their only *audience*, the priesthood community could have been involved in *transmitting* the stories to the outside world, but to *Egyptian* ears only. In this regard, this community could challenge foreign occupation through cultivating and transmitting the *National History* about Inaros, the rebel and freedom fighter of Egypt, and, in so doing, they would have been the inconspicuous *revolutionaries* of Greek and Roman Egypt.

Acknowledgment: I would like to thank Professor John Tait for his valuable input and for providing constructive feedback and comments for this paper.

Abbreviations

ÄAT Ägypten und Altes Testament
CdE Les cahiers Caribéens d'Égyptologie (Martinique)
Dem. Stud. Demotische Studien (Leipzig; Sommerhausen)
IFAO L'Institut français d'archéologie orientale du Caire
IBAES Internet-Beiträge zur Ägyptologie und Sudanarchäologie
MPER Mitteilungen aus der Papyrussammlung der österreichischen Nationalbibliothek
　　　Erzherzog Rainer
OLA Orientalia Lovaniensia Analecta (Louvain)
PdÄ Probleme der Ägyptologie (Leiden; Boston; Cologne)
PIHANS Publications de l'institut historique-archéologique néerlandais de Stamboul (Leiden)
SÄK Studien zur altägyptischen Kultur (Hamburg)
SAOC Studies in Ancient Oriental Civilisation (Chicago)

Bibliography

Assmann, A. Memory, Individual and Collective, in: *The Oxford Handbook of Contextual Political Analysis*, edited by R. E. Goodin and C. Tilly (Oxford, 2006), 210–224.
Assmann, J. *The Search for God in Ancient Egypt* (transl. D. Lorton; New York, 2001).
Assmann, J. *Religion and Cultural Memory: Ten Studies* (transl. R. Livingstone; Stanford, CA, 2006).
Becker, A. S. *The Shield of Achilles and the Poetics of Ekphrasis* (Lanham, MD, 1995).
Benjamin, W. On the Concept of History, in: *Selected Writings, Volume 4: 1938–40*, edited by H. Eiland and M. Jennings (transl. E. Jephcott; Cambridge, MA, 2003), 389–400.
Brunk, S. *The Posthumous Career of Emiliano Zapata: Myth, Memory, and Mexico's Twentieth Century* (Austin, 2008).
Bruner, J. *Acts of Meaning* (Cambridge, MA, 1990).
Capponi, L. Serapis, Boukoloi and Christians from Hadrian to Marcus Aurelius, in: *Hadrian and the Christians*, edited by M. Rizzi, Millennium-Studien 30 (Berlin; New York, 2010) 121–139.
Chauveau, M. Inarôs, Prince des rebelles, in: *Res severa verum gaudium: Festschrift für Karl-Theodor Zauzich zum 65. Geburtstag am 8. Juni 2004*, edited by F. Hoffmann and H.-J. Thissen (Leuven; Dudley, MA, 2004), 39–46.
Clarysse, W. and D. J. Thompson *Counting the People in Hellenistic Egypt*, II, *Population Registers (P. Count)*, Cambridge Classical Studies (Cambridge, 2006).
Connelly, B. *Arab Folk Epic and Identity* (Berkeley, 1986).
Cvetkovich, A. *An Archive of Feelings: Trauma, Sexuality, and Lesbian Public Cultures* (Durham, NC, 2003).
Depaw, M. Egyptianizing the Chancellery During the Great Theban Revolt (205–186 BC): a new study of limestone tablet Cairo 38258. *SÄK* 34 (2006), 97–105.
Eddy, K. *The King is Dead: Studies in Near Eastern Resistance to Hellenism 334–31 BC.* (Lincoln, Nebr., 1961).
Egan, K. Narrative and Learning: a voyage of implications, in: *Narrative in Teaching, Learning, and Research*, edited by H. McEwan and K. Egan (New York, 1995), 116–125.
Finkelberg, M. (ed.) *The Homer Encyclopedia*. Volume III (Singapore, 2011).
Geertz, C. Indonesia. Starting Over. *New York Review of Books* 47/8, (2000), 22–25.

Grimal, N. C. *Quatre stèles napatéennes au Musée du Caire. JE 48863–48866*, Mémoires 106 (Cairo, 1981).

Halbwachs, M. *The Collective Memory* (New York, 1980).

Hoffmann, F. *Der Kampf um den Panzer des Inaros. Studien zum P. Krall und seiner Stellung inner-halb des Inaros-Petubastis-Zyklus*, MPER Neue Serie 26 (Vienna, 1996).

Hoffmann, F. Die Entstehung der demotischen Erzählliteratur: Beobachtungen zum überlieferungs-geschichtlichen Kontext, in: *Das Erzählen in frühen Hochkulturen: 1. Der Fall Ägypten*, edited by H. Roeder (Munich, 2009), 351–384.

Hoffmann, F. and J. Quack. *Anthologie der demotischen Literatur* (Berlin, 2007).

Holm, T. L. The Sheikh Fadl Inscription in its Literary and Historical Context. *Aramaic Studies* 5/2 (2007), 193–224.

Honko, L. Epic and Identity: national, regional, communal, individual. *Oral Tradition* 11/1 (1996), 18–36.

Johnson, J. H. Is the Demotic Chronicle an Anti-Greek Tract?, in: *Grammata Demotika. Festschrift für Erich Lüddeckens*, edited by H. J. Thissen and K.-Th. Zauzich (Würzburg, 1984), 107–124.

Lee, C. K. and G. Yang. Introduction. Memory, Power and Culture, in: *Re-envisioning the Chinese Revolution: The Politics and Poetics of Collective Memories in Reform China*, edited by C. K. Lee and G. Yang (Washington DC, 2007), 1–20.

Lendon, J. E. *Soldiers and Ghosts. A History of Battle in Classical Antiquity* (New Haven; London, 2005).

Lichtheim, M. *Ancient Egyptian Literature*, II, *The New Kingdom* (Berkeley; Los Angeles; London, 1976).

Lloyd, A. B. Nationalist Propaganda in Ptolemaic Egypt, *Historia* 31 (1982), 33–55.

Lloyd, A. B. (ed.) *A Companion to Ancient Egypt* (Chichester; Malden, MA, 2010).

Maciver, C. A. *Quintus Smyrnaeus:' Posthomerica: Engaging Homer in Late Antiquity* (Leiden, Boston, 2012).

Marincola, J. The 'Rhetoric' of History: intertextuality, and exemplarity in historiographical speeches, in: *Stimmen der Geschichte: Funktionen von Reden in der antiken Historiographie*, edited by D. Pausch (Berlin; New York, 2010), 259–289.

Martin, R. P. *The Language of Heroes: Speech and Performance in the Iliad*. Myth and Poetics (Ithaca, 1989).

Milne, J. G. Egyptian Nationalism under Greek and Roman Rule. *The Journal of Egyptian Archaeology* 14 (1928), 226–234.

Naunton, C. Libyans and Nubians, in: *A Companion to Ancient Egypt*, I, edited by A. B. Lloyd (Chich-ester; Malden, MA, 2010), 120–139.

O' Connor, D. B. and D. P. Silverman (eds.) *Ancient Egyptian Kingship* (Leiden, 1995).

Onasch, H.-U. *Die assyrischen Eroberungen Ägyptens* I (Wiesbaden, 1994).

Perdu, O. Saites and Persians (664–332), in: *A Companion to Ancient Egypt*, I, edited by A. B. Lloyd (Chichester; Malden, MA, 2010), 140–158.

Porten, B. The Prophecy of Hor Bar Punesh and the Demise of Righteousness: an Aramaic papyrus in the British Museum, in: *Res severa verum gaudium. Festschrift für Karl-Theodor Zauzich zum 65. Geburtstag am 8. Juni 2004*, edited by F. Hoffman and H.-J. Thissen (Leuven; Dudley, MA, 2004), 427–466.

Quack, J. F. Inaros, Held von Athribis, in: *Altertum und Mittelmeerraum: Die antike Welt diesseits und jenseits der Levante. Festschrift für Peter W. Haider zum 60. Geburtstag*, edited by R. Rollinger and B. Truschnegg (Stuttgart, 2006), 499–505.

Rémondon, R. Problèmes du bilinguisme dans l'Égypte lagide (U.P.Z. I, 148). *Chronique d'Égypte* 39 (1964), 126–146.

Rutherford, I. The Genealogy of the Boukoloi: how Greek literature appropriated an Egyptian narrative-motif. *Journal of Hellenic Studies* 120 (2000), 106–121.

Rutherford, I. The Earliest Cross-cultural Reception of Homer? The Inaros narratives of Greco-Roman Egypt, in: *Greco-Egyptian Interactions: Literature, Translation and Culture, 500 BC – AD 300*, edited by I. Rutherford (Oxford, 2016), 23–37.

Ryholt, K. The Assyrian Invasion of Egypt in Egyptian Literary Tradition: a survey of the narrative source material, in: *Assyria and Beyond. Studies Presented to Mogens Trolle Larsen*, PIHANS 100, edited by J. G. Dercksen (Leiden, 2004), 483–510.

Ryholt, K. On the Contents and Nature of the Tebtunis Temple Library: a status report, in: *Tebtynis und Soknopaiu Nesos: Leben im römerzeitlichen Fajum. Akten des internationalen Symposions vom 11. bis 13. Dezember 2003 in Sommerhausen bei Würzburg*, edited by S. Lippert and M. Schentuleit (Wiesbaden, 2005), 141–170.

Ryholt, K. Egyptian Historical Literature from the Greco-Roman Period, in: *Das Ereignis: Geschichtsschreibung zwischen Vorfall und Befund*, IBAES 10, edited by M. Fitzenreiter (London, 2009), 230–238.

Ryholt, K. A Sesostris Story in Demotic Egyptian and Demotic Literary Exercises (O. Leipzig UB 2217), in: *Honi soit qui mal y pense: Studien zum pharaonischen, griechisch-römischen und spätantiken Ägypten zu Ehren von Heinz-Josef Thissen*, OLA 194, edited by H. Knuf, C. Leitz and D. von Recklinghausen (Leuven, 2010), 429–437.

Ryholt, K. *The Carlsberg Papyri 10: Narrative Literature from the Tebtunis Temple Library*, CNI Publications 35 (Copenhagen, 2012).

Ryholt, K. Imitatio Alexandri in Egyptian Literary Tradition, in: *The Romance between Greece and the East*, edited by T. Whitmarsh and S. Thomson (Cambridge, 2013), 59–78.

Selbin, E. *Revolution, Rebellion, Resistance. The Power of Story* (London; New York, 2010).

Sérida, R. *Cultural Identity and Self-presentation in Ancient Egyptian Fictional Narratives. An Intertextual Study of Narrative Motifs from the Middle Kingdom to the Roman Period*, PhD Thesis, University of Copenhagen (originally submitted as Salim, Rana, 2013).

Spiegelberg, W. *Der Sagenkreis des Königs Petubastis: nach dem Strassburger demotischen Papyrus sowie den Wiener und Pariser Bruchstücken*. J. C. Hinrichs, Demotische Studien 3 (Leipzig, 1910).

Swidler, A. Culture in Action: symbols and strategies. *American Sociological Review* 51/2 (1986), 273–286.

Tait, J. Demotic Literature and Egyptian Society, in: *Life in a Multi-cultural Society. Egypt from Cambyses to Constantine and Beyond*, Studies in Ancient Oriental Civilization 51, edited by J. Johnson (Chicago, 1992), 303–310.

Thissen, H.-J. Homerischer Einfluss im Inaros-Petubastis-Zyklus? *SÄK* 27 (1999), 369–387.

Tilly, C. *From Mobilization to Revolution* (Reading, 1978).

Tilly, C. Afterword. Political Memories in Space and Time, in: *Remapping Memory. The Politics of TimeSpace*, edited by J. Boyarin (Minneapolis, 1994), 241–247.

Veyne, P. *Did the Greeks Believe in Their Myths? An Essay on the Constitutive Imagination* (transl. P. Wissing; Chicago, 1983).

Vittmann, G. Tradition und Neuerung in der demotischen Literatur. *Zeitschrift für ägyptische Sprache und Altertumskunde* 25 (1998), 62–77.

Volten, A. Der demotische Petubastisroman und seine Beziehung zur griechischen Literatur, in: *Akten des VIII. Internationalen Kongresses für Papyrologie, Wien, 1955*, MPER Neue Serie 5 (Vienna, 1956), 147–152.

Watson, R. S. Memory, History and Opposition under State Socialism: an introduction, in: *Memory, History and Opposition under State Socialism*, edited by R. S. Watson (Santa Fe, 1994), 1–20.

Whisnant, D. E. *Rascally Signs in Sacred Places: The Politics of Culture in Nicaragua* (Chapel Hill, 1995).

Luke Pitcher

Death on the Nile: The Myth of Osiris and the Utility of History in Diodorus.

Egypt In Greco-Roman Historiography

For the student of wandering myths, the reception of Egyptian theology in Greece and Rome will always have unique attractions. There is no dearth of relevant material. The ancient world itself commented on Greek enthusiasm for information about Egyptian cult. So, for example, we find that the affable, if rather shady, Egyptian high priest Kalasiris, who is one of the central characters of Heliodorus' novel *Aethiopica*, explicitly remarks on this enthusiasm amongst the Greeks for the theological lore of his homeland, when talking about how he was received at Delphi:

> To begin with, our inquiries ranged over a variety of topics: one would ask me how we worship our native gods in Egypt, while another might ask me to explain why different races venerate different animals and what myth is attached to each case; and a third might enquire about the construction of the pyramids, and a fourth about the underground maze. In short, their questions covered everything there is in Egypt, for Greeks find all Egyptian lore and legend irresistibly attractive. (Heliod. *Aeth.* 2.27)

However, despite the wealth of coverage in such genres as the ancient novel,[1] extant Greco-Roman historiography offers, by and large, less than one might expect on the subject of Egypt and its religious practices. Herodotus announces his unwillingness to talk about divine matters as they pertain to Egypt beyond simply going through the names, except insofar as his narrative will constrain him to do so, justifying this policy with his conviction that "all men understand about them equally".[2] In the account of Egypt that follows, this policy holds. Herodotus comments in passing upon the Egyptian custom of not sacrificing heifers, since they are sacred to Isis;[3] upon a horned depiction of Isis that resembles the Greek Io;[4] upon the fact that Isis and Osiris (whom they say to be Dionysus) are the only gods that all the Egyptians revere alike;[5] upon the great temple of Isis at Busiris, and the fact that the goddess is to be identified with

---

1 Apart from Heliodorus, Apuleius' *Metamorphoses* is obviously a key text in this regard, especially the controversial Book Eleven. Fr. 19 of Petronius seems to allude to the rites of Isis observed at Memphis.
2 Hdt. 2.3.2. For Herodotus' tendency to suppose that Greek and foreign gods can be translated into one another, see Parker 1996, 159. Harrison 2000, 210–11 tabulates the equivalencies that Herodotus claims between Egyptian and Greek deities.
3 Hdt. 2.41.1. Hdt. 4.186.2 observes that the inhabitants of Cyrene share this reverence.
4 Hdt. 2.41.2.
5 Hdt. 2.42.2.

https://doi.org/10.1515/9783110421453-013

Demeter;[6] upon various alleged identities between the gods Horus, Isis, and Bubastis, and their Greek counterparts;[7] and upon the remarkable temple of Isis that Amasis built at Memphis.[8] He does not make any effort to handle the tales of the Egyptian deities as discrete stories.

Thucydides, in line with the usual tenor of his interests,[9] mentions the Egyptians rarely and Egyptian religion not at all. Xenophon's historiographical works are much the same. This lack of coverage was noted in antiquity.[10] Polybius' political narrative entails substantial coverage of Egypt, but Polybius displays little interest in matters of mythology or religion beyond the latter's usefulness as an instrument of social control.[11] He has, in general, a low opinion of what he sees as Egyptian national characteristics, although he is prepared to admit the possibility of individual exceptions: a grim narrative of deposition illustrates the savagery of Egyptians when roused to anger,[12] while Ptolemaios, a commander in Cyprus, is characterised as sensible and capable and "not at all Egyptian".[13] It is therefore unsurprising that Polybius shows no disposition to dwell on the country's mythological lore. The later extant narrative histories of Greece and Rome are perfectly happy to admit Egypt for the purposes of political coverage (notably, but not exclusively, in the treatment of Alexander the Great,[14] or of Roman politics during the period between Julius Caesar's almost fatal sojourn there after Pharsalus and the Battle of Actium).[15] They do not, however, usually discourse upon the nation's myths and early history in doing so, although Tacitus' account of Germanicus' tour in AD 18, which does speak a little about the monuments, is a partial and momentary exception.[16] Even Appian, who was himself from Alexandria and constructs the first half of his *Roman History* in such a way as to culminate with the Roman capture of Egypt, does not give his land's mythology an extended treatment

---

6 Hdt. 2.59.2 (with a glance back to this treatment at 2.61.1).

7 Hdt. 2.156.4–6. Cf. also Hdt. 2.144.2.

8 Hdt. 2.176.2.

9 Hornblower 1992.

10 Diod. Sic. 1.37.4: "Xenophon and Thucydides, who are praised for the accuracy of their histories, completely refrained in their writings from any mention of the regions about Egypt". This is an exaggeration – Thucydides, for example, covers an Athenian expedition to Egypt during the *pentekontaetia* (Thuc. 1.104, with Westlake 1950) – but not unduly so (*pace* Hornblower 1991, 163).

11 Polyb. 6.56.6–12 and 16.12.9–11.

12 Polyb. 15.33.10.

13 Polyb. 27.13.1.

14 The most notable extant treatment of Alexander's expedition to Egypt is that at Arr. *Anab.* 3.1–5. Arrian does mention in passing Alexander's sacrifices to Apis (3.1.4), the plans for the temple of Isis at Alexandria (3.1.5), and, at rather greater length, his visit to the oracle of Ammon at Siwah (3.3.1–4.5, with Brunt 1976, Appendix V).

15 Notable accounts include, but are not limited to, Caesar's own account of his arrival in Alexandria (Caes. *B Civ.* 3.106–12) and the *Bellum Alexandrinum* that is possibly the work of Hirtius (especially 1–33). Neither of these has anything to say about Egyptian mythology.

16 Tac. *Ann.* 2.59–60, with Pelling 2012 and Woodman 2015, 256–62.

in the extant stretches of his work. It is interesting to speculate as to what might have been found in the four books of his lost *Aegyptiaca*, although Appian, for all his conventional piety, is not especially interested in details of cult in the stretches of his work that remain to us.

Surviving historiography is, of course, an unreliable guide to the emphases of works no longer extant. Apart from the conjectural example of Appian, whom we have just mentioned, one has to consider the possibility of coverage in the historians whose oeuvres time has more comprehensively obliterated. In some cases, even the names of these individuals have perished. Jacoby, in his great collection of the fragmentary Greek historians, reserved a heading for anonymous writers on Egypt,[17] while some named historians, the titles of whose works suggest Egyptian preoccupations, remain, for us, little more than names: Ptolemaios the son of Agesarchos, who seems to have written a work about Ptolemaios IV Philopator in the early second century BC, is representative of the general dearth of information.[18] The incomplete attestation of these works makes it hard to derive from them a sense of their take (if any) on Egyptian mythology.

On the other hand, there is a beacon in the more general historiographical gloom. The topic of this article is a notable exception to the general tendency of (more or less) extant historiography not to discourse upon the mythology and early history of Egypt. In the first book of his work, Diodorus of Sicily, who wrote a universal history towards the end of the first century BC, sets out such a treatment on a lavish scale.

What led Diodorus to open his history in such a fashion? On this topic, as on many others, his narrator is more than happy to explain his reasoning:

> The first peoples which we shall discuss will be the barbarians, not that we consider them to be earlier than the Greeks, as Ephorus has said,[19] but because we wish to set forth most of the facts about them at the outset, in order that we may not, by beginning with the various accounts given by the Greeks, have to interpolate in the different narrations of their early history any event connected with another people. And since Egypt is the country where mythology places the origin of the gods, where the earliest observations of the stars are said to have been made, and where, furthermore, many noteworthy deeds of great men are recorded, we shall begin our history with the events connected with Egypt. (Diod. Sic. 1.9.5–6)

In the book that follows, Diodorus does indeed present a mythography and early history of Egypt. He includes an account of the geography of the land itself, its monuments and customs, its kings, and, most pertinent to our present theme, the gods and

---

17 *FGrHist.* 665. For a brief examination of Jacoby's methodology with regard to such geographically themed entries, see *BNJ* 83 Biographical Essay.

18 For Ptolemaios and his scanty fragments, see *BNJ* 161. For Agatharchides of Cnidus and Hecataeus of Abdera, two other lost Hellenistic historians whose works contained Egyptian material, see below.

19 *BNJ* 70 F 109, where the commentary is rightly cautious about Jacoby's wilder speculations as to the context in which Ephorus made this claim.

first men that arose there. Indeed, Diodorus addresses each of the topics about which Kalasiris' fictional audience consulted him at Delphi: the gods of Egypt;[20] the consecration of animals;[21] the construction of the pyramids;[22] and the labyrinth of Thebes.[23]

Looking at Diodorus

The question of what one does with this extensive material admits of various different answers. Until the last few decades, the dominant mode of Diodoran criticism was that of *Quellenforschung*. Diodorus was customarily analysed with an eye to retrieving his lost sources. Book One was no exception.

As is often the case with *Quellenforschung*, however, the labour was not straightforward. Diodorus does occasionally make explicit allusion, in the course of Book One, to various predecessors. In discussing the royal tombs at Egyptian Thebes, he notes that "Not only do the priests of Egypt give these facts from their records, but many also of the Greeks who visited Thebes in the time of Ptolemy son of Lagus and composed histories of Egypt, one of whom was Hecataeus, agree with what we have said".[24] In discussing the vexed question of the flooding of the Nile, he quotes, with qualified approval, the explanation given by Agatharchides of Cnidus,[25] having rejected, with varying degrees of detail, explanations by a variety of other authors.[26] Schwartz extrapolated from the reference to Hecataeus of Abdera in the passage about the royal tombs the theory that Hecataeus was the source for most of Book One;[27] the most recent Anglophone commentary on the book contends that it is "generally believed that

---

20 Diod. Sic. 1.11–12.

21 Diod. Sic. 1.83.

22 Diod. Sic. 1.63.2–64.14.

23 See n. 32 below. Diodorus also addresses the perennial question, which Kalasiris' Delphic audience goes on to ask (Heliod. *Aeth.* 2.28), of the Nile's sources (Diod. Sic. 1.37) and why it floods as it does (Diod. Sic. 1.38–41).

24 Diod. Sic. 1.46.8. Note that Diodorus does not actually state outright in this passage that Hecataeus of Abdera is his source for the description of the tomb of Osymandyas in chapters 47–9, *pace* Burton 1972, 3 ("the single passage which is attributed to Hecataeus by Diodorus himself") and 7 ("The most obvious passage is the description of the tomb of Osymandyas, which Diodorus explicitly says is drawn from Hecataeus"), although the hypothesis that the passage is so derived is a very probable one. This sort of glissade is, as we shall see, rather too common in the source-criticism of Diodorus.

25 Diod. Sic. 1.41.4–9.

26 "The early school" of Hellanicus, Cadmus, Hecataeus of Miletus (not to be confused with Hecataeus of Abdera) , and others (Diod. Sic. 1.37.3); Herodotus (1.37.4, 38.8–12); Ephorus (1.37.4, 39.7–130); Theopompus (1.37.4); Thales (1.38.2–3); Anaxagoras and Euripides (1.38.4–6); Democritus (1.39.1–6). It is unlikely that all, or even most, of these citations came at first-hand.

27 Schwartz 1885, although, as Burton 1972, 3, notes, the first person to attribute Book One to Hecataeus of Abdera was, in fact, G. J. Schneider (Schneider 1880).

Diodorus, employing the same technique here as in his later books, drew primarily upon Agatharchides of Cnidus for his geographical information, and upon Hecataeus of Abdera for the remainder of the book",[28] but goes on to demonstrate that the likely situation is much more complicated, and that much of the reasoning on which earlier investigations based themselves is rather tenuous.[29]

More recently, Diodoran criticism has focused to a greater extent on Diodorus' interests as a historiographer in his own right. Diodorus can, indeed, often be confused in his handling of his sources. So much is clear from his later narrative. On the other hand, over-eagerness to convict Diodorus of incompetence can also lead his interpreters into error.

Book One, in fact, is a case in point. Burton gives as a demonstration that Diodorus is "an inaccurate and uncritical excerptor using his sources without judgement, and occasionally duplicating events and information" and that he is "inept at selecting and collating his material", the assertion that "ch. 15.1 contradicts ch. 45.4".[30] In fact, a comparison of the two passages shows that in the first Diodorus notes that "they say" that Osiris was the founder of the Egyptian Thebes while explicitly acknowledging that there was no agreement about this and that some attributed the city's foundation to "a certain king". The second (again, with the addition of a cautious "they say") identifies that king as Busiris. Acknowledgement that different traditions exist would, in the case of, say, Herodotus, be adduced as evidence of methodological sophistication rather than ineptitude.[31] It is reasonable enough to note that Diodorus, in Book One, as later in his opus, is indeed fully capable of including two contradictory accounts of a matter without showing any awareness that he has done so. Burton is on surer ground when, for example, she observes the contradiction whereby the creator of the Egyptian labyrinth is named as Mendes or Marrus in one passage and Menas in a later one, with no acknowledgment of the variant tradition in either place.[32] But the assumption that variance or textual interest is *always* to be explained in terms of haphazard cutting and pasting on the part of Diodorus needs to be resisted, despite the occasions on which such an explanation is clearly correct.

The changing face of Diodoran criticism, from *Quellenforschung* to the inherent interest of Diodorus himself as an historiographer, can potentially affect how we handle his treatment of Egyptian mythology and history in Book One. Older treatments of

---

28 Burton 1972, 1–2.
29 Burton 1972, 2: "Unfortunately, comparatively little of the writing of either Agatharchides or Hecataeus has survived. Agatharchides is represented only by a few fragments and excerpts; while of the large portions of Book I generally assumed to have been borrowed by Diodorus from Hecataeus, much cannot be proved to have been so borrowed, and for the rest such proof as is possible depends upon a tenuous chain of reasoning with little or no means of verifying each step".
30 Burton 1972, 2.
31 Cf. also Rubincam 1989, 55, which notes 1.45.4 as one of a network of Diodoran cross-references.
32 Diod. Sic. 1.61.1–4 (Mendes or Marrus); 1.89.3 (Menas).

what the material in the book is aimed to achieve tend to focus on the ideologies of Diodorus' probable sources. So, for example, Oswyn Murray uses the book extensively in a study of Hecataeus of Abdera and pharaonic kingship.[33] With the upsurge of interest in Diodorus himself as a historian, albeit an occasionally haphazard one, other paths of investigation become viable. It is interesting to consider what the Egyptian material meant to Hecataeus of Abdera, or to Agatharchides. But the question of what it meant to Diodorus can be equally rewarding.

This becomes all the more apparent when one considers the exact location of Diodorus' guide to Egyptian myth within the economy of his work. Kenneth Sacks, in his recuperation of Diodorus as an organising (or, sometimes, disorganising) intelligence in his own right, correctly insists upon the importance for this operation of the preface to Book One.[34] This, however much it may owe to earlier historiography (and there are few historiographical prefaces which do not show evidence of some indebtedness to the tradition), illuminates what Diodorus is trying to achieve in the course of his history. The fact that Diodorus' treatment of Egyptian myth follows so hard upon the heels of this preface suggests that it is a reasonable strategy to interpret one in terms of the other. Historiographical precedent also indicates that this may possibly be a profitable pursuit. It is a recurring characteristic in the ancient historians that important and charismatic individuals described by the text echo, in their words, deeds, and motivations, the interests and preoccupations which the historian has already enunciated in the preface.

The primal example of this characteristic is Herodotus. Herodotus states at the beginning of his work the proposition that the fortunes of cities are ceaselessly mutable. He draws therefrom a moral for his own narrative strategy: "For the towns that were great of old have mostly become small, while those which were great in my time were formerly small. As I understand that human prosperity in no way abides in the same place, I shall make mention of both equally."[35] Later in Book One, the wandering statesman and sage Solon warns Croesus of Lydia that no man should be called prosperous until he is dead,[36] because the god has torn up by the roots many to whom he has formerly vouchsafed prosperity.[37] Sure enough, Croesus thereafter loses first his son,[38] and then his kingdom,[39] remembering Solon by name once he is strapped to a pyre.[40] While the kings who appear later in Herodotus do not play out the preoc-

33 Murray 1970.
34 Sacks 1990, 10–1.
35 Hdt. 1.5.4.
36 Hdt. 1.32.7.
37 Hdt. 1.32.9.
38 Hdt. 1.43.2.
39 Hdt. 1.86.1.
40 Hdt. 1.86.3.

cupations of the preface quite so blatantly, some of them do demonstrate an interest in travel and enquiry which can remind the reader of the Herodotean narrator.[41]

The historiographical tradition also warns us, however, that the interplay between the concerns enunciated by a history's prefatory material and the narrative that follows is not necessarily straightforward. Again, the case of Herodotus is instructive. Croesus does seem to learn a salutary lesson from Solon about the mutability of human fortune, and so becomes an advisor figure for Cyrus the Great once he is delivered from his pyre. On the other hand, Cyrus is killed and decapitated when he follows a later instance of Croesus' advice, as his son Cambyses is quick to point out when Croesus later attempts to rebuke him for unregal behaviour.[42] The exact interpretation of this sequence of events remains contested,[43] but certainly indicates a complex relationship between the generalities of the prologue and the playing-out of the actual history.

Comparable instances of such complexity may be multiplied from subsequent historiography as well. Sallust is a particularly instructive example. The narrator of the *Bellum Catilinae* is preoccupied with *gloria*, renown, and notes that this may be attained by deeds or by writing about the deeds of others, though the latter initially occupies a subsidiary position:

> both those who have achieved things and those who have written about the deeds of others are praised, and to me at least, although in no way does an equal glory attend upon the writer of deeds and the doer of deeds, however it seems to me surpassingly difficult to write history. (Sall. *Catil.* 3.1–2)

As the monograph progresses, however, the picture becomes more complicated: it is true that the glory of the agent outstrips the glory of the writer, but the example of Athens shows that a writer of sufficient talent can control the perception of a polity's valour. Athens was not, in fact, so very notable for achievements, but was sufficiently fortunate to have talented writers to celebrate its accomplishments.[44]

Is such a pattern detectable in Book One of Diodorus? Do we see the early narrative of Egyptian myth pick up the preoccupations of the preface, and do the generalities of the prefatory material remain as simple once the stories actually begin? The key figure, for such an investigation, is Osiris. In Diodorus's treatment of him, the Egyptian god-king takes on a central significance, as the individual most responsible for bringing the fruits of civilisation to his people. It will therefore be expedient to look at Diodorus' avowed intentions in his prologue, and then how, if at all, the narrative emphases in the historian's account of Osiris map on to those intentions.

---

41 Christ 1994.

42 Hdt. 3.36.3.

43 For treatments of Croesus as adviser, see for example Stahl 1975 and Grethlein 2010, 190–2.

44 Sall. *Catil.* 8.1–4, with Feeney 1994.

Diodorus on History

> For this reason one may hold that the acquisition of a knowledge of history is of the greatest utility for every conceivable circumstance of life. For (i) it endows (a) the young with the wisdom of the aged, while for (b) the old it multiplies the experience which they already possess; (ii) (a) citizens in private station it qualifies for leadership, and (b) the leaders it incites, through the immortality of the glory which it confers, to undertake the noblest deeds; (iii) (a) soldiers, again, it makes more ready to face dangers in defence of their country because of the public encomiums which they will receive after death, and (b) wicked men it turns aside from their impulse towards evil through the everlasting opprobrium to which it will condemn them. (Diod. Sic. 1.1.4–5)[45]

As the passage above demonstrates, Diodorus holds to a utilitarian view of history. History, for Diodorus, is directly profitable, in two ways. Firstly, it gives one the benefit of the experiences of others without obliging one to go to the trouble and effort of experiencing similar things directly oneself. This is what Diodorus means by saying that the young gain the wisdom of the old, while the experience of the old is multiplied. Secondly, history is an incitement to virtuous action. It carries the promise of immortal glory for those who achieve great things, through the memorialisation of their actions.

As noted above, the general tenor of this preface can readily be paralleled elsewhere in the classical historians or other ancient literature. The idea that the promise of eternal glory provided by literature is itself a spur to virtuous action appears in Cicero and others.[46] Nor is it unusual for writers of history in the ancient world to insist upon the profit that the reader can derive from engaging with it. Herodotus, to be sure, does not do so; the passages of Thucydides which might suggest such a possibility are still much debated;[47] and Xenophon is close-mouthed about what he thinks that historiography accomplishes. Polybius, however, is an exponent of history's utility, "since men have no readier corrective of conduct than knowledge of the past".[48] This shared utilitarian streak has made it traditional to stress the affinities between Polybius' proem and that of Diodorus.

More recent scholarship has pointed out that Diodorus and Polybius do not seem to view history as useful in exactly the same ways. Sacks argues that, whereas Polybius addresses himself to the improvement of the efficacy of statesmen and politicians through his *pragmatikē historia*, Diodorus is concerned only with what Sacks dubs "moral utility".[49] Diodorus, in Sacks' view, does not aim to demonstrate, by multiply-

---

45 The articulation here with parenthetical Roman numerals and letters is my insertion, to assist the examination of the articulation of Diodorus' argument which I undertake in the following paragraphs.
46 Cic. *Arch.* 29.
47 Raaflaub 2013, especially 6–7, and Stahl 2013, especially 314, are the latest contributions to this much-discussed question.
48 Polyb. 1.1.1, with Walbank 1972, 28 and McGing 2010, 66–8.
49 Sacks 1990, 25.

ing the reader's acquaintance with how possible lines of behaviour have panned out in the past, how the reader might increase his own success in the game of life. Rather, Diodorus aims to mould his readers, who do not necessarily have to be statesmen or generals, to an ideal of civic service by praising the goodly actions of men of old and blaming the bad actions of the reprobates.

Sacks posits rather too stark a dichotomy between the aims of Polybius and Diodorus. These aims are a little less monolithic than he implies. It is certainly true to say that Polybius envisages politicians and statesmen as his principal audience. At the outset of his work, he asserts that all historians "have impressed on us that the soundest education and training for a life of active politics [*pros tas politikas praxeis*] is the study of history".[50] Likewise, he is an overt advocate, as Diodorus is not, of the idea that being able to recognise repeating patterns in events can give one a competitive edge,[51] and goes to some trouble to include in his history practical and applicable information on topics which a budding general might find helpful, such as communication via fires,[52] calculating the areas of cities,[53] and practical siege trigonometry.[54] On the other hand, Polybius does at least acknowledge that some aspects of his history might have different sorts of application to different people, even if the improvement of future statesmen remains the primary agendum. Immediately after he stresses history's utility for those who envisage a life in active politics, he observes that history is also "the surest and indeed the only method of learning how to bear bravely the vicissitudes of fortune', in that it enables one "to recall the calamities of others",[55] which is obviously not a consideration that need apply only to statesmen.[56] Later in his work, he is also prepared to concede that pleasure, as well as utility, might be derived from consideration of the career of Scipio Aemilianus.[57]

Diodorus does not, in the main body of his history, provide anything that really resembles the wealth of practical information which Polybius lavishes upon his readership. There is no radical system of fire-signalling for him, or disquisitions upon the appropriate length of siege-ladders. But it must be conceded that the preface to Book One of the *Bibliothēkē sounds* as though the reader is going to derive a personal advantage from reading the Diodoran opus that is rather different from a simple incitement to civic virtue. While the first sentence of the history does claim that writers of universal history have helped the life of all (*ton koinon bion*), which would seem to bear out Sacks' point about Diodorus' interest in promoting the common weal, it goes on to say

---

50 Polyb. 1.1.2.
51 Walbank 1972, 58.
52 Polyb. 10.43–7.
53 Polyb. 9.26a.
54 Polyb. 9.18.5–9.
55 Polyb. 1.1.2.
56 A point well made at Walbank 1972, 58 and McGing 2010, 67.
57 Polyb. 31.30.1, with Walbank 1972, 40.

that such writers have achieved this happy result by providing readers with "a schooling, which entails no danger, in what is advantageous (*tou sumpherontos*)". The language of advantage and profit, of *to sumpheron*, seems to promise something more immediately beneficial to the individual reader than the second-order profit that would accrue to all through the exercise of civic virtue, even if the latter would be rather more true to the spirit of what Diodorus actually sets out to do later in his oeuvre. Moreover, Diodorus' emphasis in the preface to Book One on how reading history can *multiply* the experience of the reader does seem to suggest the promise of an augmentation to available and practical knowledge rather than reiterated insistence on what makes for a model citizen.[58] History is also described as "most excellent experience" (*kallistēn empeirian*) in that first sentence, and we may recall that "experience" is key to the benefits which it offers to young and old alike in the later passage quoted at the beginning of this section. Polybius and Diodorus are not quite so starkly differentiated in the promises they make for the utility of their respective histories after all.

All the same, Sacks' emphasis that Diodorus, simply by beginning his history with an appeal to the utility of historiography, is not necessarily just parroting Polybius when he does so, is salutary. In general, reading Diodorus as a *reaction* to Polybius and his ilk, rather than just an echo, proves to be a potentially interesting strategy.[59] Moreover, as we examine Diodorus' opening remarks, we continue to find up-endings of the emphases which we might incautiously expect: Diodorus' syntax is capable of springing surprises. One notes, for example, the sting in the tail of the tri-colon which concludes the passage cited above, veering off in a direction which the pattern Diodorus seems to be establishing does not lead us to expect. In each of the first two example-groups of history's utility – the audience of different ages which he mentions in clause (i), and the audience of citizens and leaders which he mentions in clause (ii) – Diodorus moves from an assertion of history's utility to the less well-endowed in a particular quality, to an assertion that history is equally helpful to those who already enjoy a measure of that quality. In clause (i), this is a movement from the young (who lack experience) to the old (who have experience) – both profiting from the vicarious experience that history brings. In clause (ii), the movement is from those private citizens who lack experience of leadership to those who already have such experience of leadership in their own right. When Diodorus begins his final pair of examples with the case of soldiers, one might reasonably expect, on the basis of how the relationship between (a) and (b) has worked in each of the two preceding clauses, that Diodorus' last target population will be those who already have the experience in which the soldiers are lacking (seasoned veterans, for example), but who can nevertheless find history

---

58 Marincola 2007, 26 nicely speaks of "vicarious instruction".

59 For more on the likenesses and disparities between the proems to Diodorus and Polybius, see Marincola 2007, 27 (on the differing ways in which they use the figure of Odysseus) and Sheridan 2010, 44–6 (on the differences between their conceptions of universal history). For a more general comparison of Diodorus and Polybius, see Sulimani 2011, 46–9.

profitable as well. In fact, Diodorus' last item supplies not escalation, but contrast. Whereas soldiers can be spurred on by the promise of glory, villains can be deterred by the possibility of everlasting opprobrium. After waving carrots consistently for several sentences, Diodorus disrupts the reader's complacency with a final flourish of the stick, all the more effective for its unexpectedness.[60] The flow of the argument is not, after all, as straightforward as one might suppose.

History for Diodorus, then, has utility through the provision of vicarious and applicable experience, and because it offers the spur of immortal glory (or infamy). Is it possible to detect such themes in his subsequent account of early Egypt? Above all, does it emerge in his treatment of Egyptian mythography?

Diodorus on Osiris

Diodorus' main account of the career of Osiris occupies chapters 13 to 22 of Book One. In this version, Osiris, although a son of Zeus, spends his time on earth like a successful mortal monarch. He is the first to convince mankind to desist from cannibalism by popularising the cultivation of wheat and barley.[61] He founds cities and temples,[62] and rewards innovators and technologists.[63] He gathers an army to share these improvements to the human lot with the remainder of mankind,[64] and curbs the Nile with dykes.[65] In fact, he "visited all the inhabited world and advanced community life by the introduction of the fruits which are most easily cultivated".[66]

By any standards, this is an impressive résumé, and one that has already attracted scholarly attention. Iris Sulimani, for example, has recently read the Diodoran Osiris as a "culture-hero", the first of several individuals whose careers the historian describes in thematically similar ways.[67] Osiris, with his own agricultural discoveries and support of other innovators, certainly fits into the pattern of Diodorus' on-going interest in the first discoverers of particular things, the theme of the *prōtos heuretēs*.[68]

For our present purposes, however, it is more germane to note that Osiris' career, as described in the first book of Diodorus' history, seems to fall in line with the historiographical pattern which we have already seen in operation in the text of Herodotus.

---

60 For history as a means to deter the wicked from bad behaviour through the promise of future infamy, compare Tac. *Ann.* 3.65.
61 Diod. Sic. 1.14.1, and cf. Sulimani 2011, 230–2.
62 Diod. Sic. 1.15.1–4 and Sulimani 2011, 265 (cities) and 280 (temples).
63 Diod. Sic. 1.15.5.
64 Diod. Sic. 1.17.1.
65 Diod. Sic. 1.19.5, and Sulimani 2011, 246.
66 Diod. Sic. 1.20.3.
67 Sulimani 2011, especially 64–5, and cf. Sacks 1990, 61.
68 On this, see also Ambaglio 1995, 90–2.

Once again, we find an exemplification of the emphases of the historian's proem in the behaviour of one of his important characters. In the preface, Diodorus gives examples of the sorts of achievements that history has spurred men on to make: "some of them have been induced to become the founders of cities... others have been led to introduce laws which encompass man's social life with security... many have aspired to discover new sciences and arts in order to benefit the race of mankind".[69]

One notes at once that these are the very deeds which Osiris and his wife Isis are depicted as achieving in the narrative that follows. We have already noted the descriptions of Osiris as a founder of cities and the account of the invention of agriculture. We might add Diodorus' portrait of Isis as a law-giver: "Isis also established laws, they say, in accordance with which the people regularly dispense justice to one another and are led to refrain through fear of punishment from illegal violence and insolence".[70] Not only do the preoccupations of the preface seem to play out in the story of Osiris' mortal life, but Osiris himself displays a self-conscious awareness of these preoccupations in his behaviour. Diodorus explicitly claims that a key motivation for the king in organising his campaign to civilise the world is not just his naturally beneficent cast of mind (*euergetikon*), but also his love of glory (*philodoxon*): "for he supposed that if he made men give up their savagery and adopt a gentle manner of life he would receive immortal honours [*timōn athanatōn*]".[71]

Osiris, then, shows himself to be the kind of self-reflexive protagonist to whom the prior tradition of historiography has accustomed us. Herodotus' Solon apprehends the importance which his author attributes to the inconstancy of human felicity, and instructs Croesus accordingly. Diodorus' Osiris seems to know that, if he plays by the rules that Diodorus' narrator has already set out in his preface, he can achieve his desire for eternal fame through conspicuous civic virtue.[72] Philanthropic achievement will be recognised by immortal glory. Sure enough, the narrative almost immediately seems to bear this theory out: "This did in fact take place, since not only the men of his time who received this gift, but all succeeding generations as well, because of the delight which they take in the foods which were discovered, have honoured those who introduced them as gods most illustrious".[73] Osiris, one of the most important figures in Book One, seems fittingly to demonstrate the principle of "moral utility" and how it works in action.

So far, the story of Osiris is reassuringly straightforward. We recall, however, that, in other historiography, the relationship between the claims of a preface and the sto-

---

69 Diod. Sic. 1.2.1.
70 Diod. Sic. 1.14.3.
71 Diod. Sic. 1.17.2.
72 For later explorations of this theme in Diodorus, see Sulimani 2011, 72. For the continuance of ethical judgments upon the agents in the narrative throughout the account of early Eastern history in the opening books of Diodorus, see Sartori 1984, 505 n. 70.
73 Diod. Sic. 1.17.2.

ries which might be taken to exemplify them sometimes turns out to be a little more complicated. Croesus, with his moment of revelation but, equally, his patchy subsequent record as an advisor, is as much a part of Herodotus as Solon. Does the Osiris of Diodorus show any similar tendency to complicate the broad claims of the preface?

On the whole, the career of Osiris does bear out the proposition that historiography serves a useful societal function by memorialising great achievements, making them available to subsequent generations, and so promoting good behaviour amongst those with an eye on their future glory. On the other hand, it also illustrates that such future fame may not necessarily be a straightforward transcription of achievement. The Osiris of Diodorus is admirable. But, because of Diodorus' tendency to stack up variant versions, his qualities are less a steady light than a kaleidoscope. This becomes clear once we appreciate the full complexity of the picture of Osiris (or Osirises) which the historian paints for us.

The *first* version of Osiris with which the Diodoran narrator presents us is not the human figure whose career we have examined above.[74] Rather, it is an Egyptian rationalisation of the sun:

> Now the men of Egypt, they say, when ages ago they came into existence, as they looked up at the firmament and were struck with both awe and wonder at the nature of the universe, conceived that two gods were both eternal and first, namely, the sun and the moon, whom they called respectively Osiris and Isis, these appellations having in each case been based upon a certain meaning in them. (Diod. Sic. 1.11.1)

Diodorus does not get on to the version of Osiris adumbrated earlier in this article until several paragraphs later, when he starts to deal with other gods "who, by reason of their sagacity and the good services which they rendered to all men, attained immortality, some of them having even been kings in Egypt. Their names, when translated, are in some cases the same as those of the celestial gods... "[75] This (originally) mortal Osiris has the lion's share of Diodorus' attention in the early stretches of Book One.

Quite apart from the possibility of conflation with a primaeval sun-god, however, the career of Osiris the king illustrates that posthumous reverence can also include elements of suppression and deception. According to Diodorus, the priests of Osiris originally resisted divulging the circumstances of the god-king's mortal end.[76] Once Isis has avenged the death of her husband at the hands of his impious brother Typhon, she ensures the robustness of his future cult through systematic deception:

---

74 Sulimani 2011, 159, notes that "the structure of the story of Osiris is exceptional" in comparison to that of the stories of the other culture-heroes with whom she is concerned, although she is inclined to minimise the significance of this difference.

75 Diod. Sic. 1.13.1.

76 Diod. Sic. 1.21.1.

summoning the priests group by group, she required of all of them an oath that they would reveal to no one the trust which she was going to confide to them, and taking each group of them apart privately she said that she was consigning to them alone the burial of the body ... (Diod. Sic. 1.21.6)

Isis ensures immortal honours for her husband via the multiplication of Osirises. Even though Diodorus can reveal the story of the deception, he obviously cannot undo its consequences, and notes its ramifications for present-day practice amongst the Egyptians.[77]

Osiris remains, then, a testament to the immortal glory which can be the meed of the successful philanthropist, and which history can help to mediate. But, in the creation and sustenance of his cult, he is also a testament to the obfuscation and chicanery which can attend upon the transmission of the past. His cult takes root to the extent it does thanks to Isis' deceptions. This instructional narrative, placed so close to the beginning of Diodorus' history, does not by any means undermine the themes set out in the proem. But it does show that memorialisation and its fruits are not necessarily straightforward in the winning. It can take care, attention, and (occasionally) lies to keep posterity on the right track.

If Diodorus is, indeed, using the story of Osiris to explore how the pursuit of an immortal reputation through great deeds can have its complexities and its hazards of reception as well as its straightforwardly laudable aspect, we may reasonably expect such themes to re-emerge later in his history. So, in fact, proves to be the case. In Book Two, for example, we meet the Assyrian king Ninus. One of Ninus' great ambitions is "to found a city of such magnitude, that not only would it be the largest of any which then existed in the whole inhabited world, but also that no other ruler of a later time should, if he undertook such a task, find it easy to surpass him".[78]

Ninus, then, is another man with his gaze trained firmly on posterity. The careful reader of Diodorus will already be aware, however, that architecture can potentially be an ambiguous way of memorialising one's reputation. It is true enough that (as we have already seen in the case of Osiris himself) founding cities can be good for one's reputation. But extravagant building projects run the risk of bad publicity. Diodorus' narrator records the popular notion that the architects of the pyramids were more deserving of admiration than the kings who commissioned them,[79] and notes the care taken by the later Egyptian king Sesoösis to ensure that his temples were built only with captive labour: "for this reason he placed an inscription on every temple that no native had toiled upon it".[80] Book Two, as well, gives indications for the diligent student that buildings, even if they endure, are not necessarily a reliable index of past

77 Diod. Sic. 1.21.9.
78 Diod. Sic. 2.3.1.
79 Diod. Sic. 1.64.12.
80 Diod. Sic. 1.56.2.

glory. Diodorus' narrator feels the need explicitly to argue against those who doubt the big numbers attached to accounts of bygone campaigns:

> Let these facts, then [i.e. Diodorus' comparative figures drawn from more recent military history] be a sufficient reply on our part to those who try to estimate the populations of the nations of Asia in ancient times on the strength of inferences *drawn from the desolation which at the present time prevails in its cities.* (Diod. Sic. 2.5.7)[81]

Surviving architecture, then, may well end up highlighting (to the foolish) the dismal present rather than the glorious past.

Sure enough, Ninus' bid for posthumous memorialisation turns out to be rather more haphazard than he envisages. Like Osiris, he owes one element of this memorialisation to a wife, Semiramis, who survives and reigns after him. Unlike Isis, Semiramis does not engage in active deception to assure her deceased husband's legacy, but her behaviour does set up a certain architectural irony. Diodorus is careful to record that, by his own day, the city on which Ninus spent so much effort has long been razed to the ground by the Medes. All that is now visible is the enormous mound which Semiramis raised to inter Ninus.[82]

Ironies of memorialisation accrete. Semiramis, it then transpires, is eager to surpass her husband's fame – something which Ninus did not anticipate (in the Greek, the terms in which Diodorus describes Ninus' vision of a ruler who might try to surpass him, *tōn metagenesterōn heteron epibalomenon*,[83] suggest that Ninus' first guess was not that that ruler would be female). To achieve this, Semiramis founds Babylon. Diodorus spends the next three chapters describing Babylon, a not inconsiderable investment of narrative time. Diodorus, to be sure, is freer with this sort of large-scale topographical description than some other Greek and Roman historians,[84] but the depth of coverage is still notable, even for him. Eventually, however, Diodorus reveals that, "as for the palaces and the other buildings, time has either entirely effaced them or left them in ruins; and in fact of Babylon itself but a small part is inhabited at this time, and most of the area within its walls is given over to agriculture".[85] Semiramis' crown jewel has ultimately fallen prey to time and depredation to almost as great an extent as that of her husband did.

---

81 To others, of course, depopulated ruins might suggest not that the wars of old were small but that they were especially vicious and destructive. Contrast Lucan 1.24–32, where the purportedly semi-abandoned state of Neronian Italy is seen as testimony to the magnitude of the Roman Civil Wars.
82 Diod. Sic. 2.7.2.
83 Diod. Sic. 2.3.1. The masculine gender, of course, predominates in such expressions, but a feminine could have been used if Ninus' suspicions had been sufficiently precise.
84 Compare, for example, the lavish description of Memphis at Diod. Sic. 1.50.3–51.2. By contrast, Appian's only such topographical set-piece of comparable length is the description of Carthage at App. *Pun.* 95–6.
85 Diod. Sic. 2.9.9.

Such observations do not invalidate the fact that, overall, Osiris and Isis, Ninus and Semiramis do all get the results they wanted. Even if their buildings have fallen down, and if some initial deception may have guaranteed the robustness of their posthumous adoration, Diodorus' history remembers their great deeds, and gives them the immortality for which they were hoping. All the same, we can see that Osiris establishes a pattern that repeats in the history that follows. Immortal glory is not necessarily assured by the particular actions that an historical agent thinks will bring it about.

Conclusion

The theme of this volume is "Wandering Myths". Amongst other things, it examines what factors determine the local interpretation of myths that have travelled some distance from their original homes. "Local" as it applies to Diodorus is, of course, a complex matter in and of itself. Writing in Greek, he acknowledges in his proem the status of Rome and his lengthy sojourn there, "for the supremacy of this city, a supremacy so powerful that it extends to the bounds of the inhabited world, has provided us in the course of our long residence there with copious resources in the most accessible form",[86] while also, at various points, emphasising his own Sicilian birthplace.[87] These multiple contexts are elegantly displayed in Book One, where Diodorus explains the shape of the Egyptian delta in terms of the shape of Sicily.[88]

As we have now seen, though, another valid context against which to read Diodorus' treatment of Egyptian myth in Book One of his history is prior historiography. In particular, it is helpful to recall the ways in which the Greek and Roman historians can use key stories in their works to bring into focus the claims which they make in their prologues and elsewhere. Diodorus argues that history is useful because it grants access to the past experiences of others and, in particular, because it is a spur to great achievements in that it offers the promise that such achievements will be remembered. The story of Osiris, the first extended narrative within the history, shows this process in operation. Osiris intelligently anticipates that philanthropic endeavour will enable him to achieve his ambition of eternal glory, and this turns out to be the case.

However, historiography also tends to use such paradigmatic narratives in a way which demonstrates the tensions and limitations of the broad claims made in the prefaces that precede them. Once again, Diodorus behaves as one might expect. Osiris does achieve his immortal fame, but the maintenance of his cult is due, at least

---

86 Diod. Sic. 1.4.4. For Diodorus and Rome, see Sacks 1990, 117–59.
87 For Diodorus and Sicily, see in particular Yarrow 2006, 116–8 and 152–6.
88 Diod. Sic. 1.34.1.

in part, to the prudent obfuscation and deceit of his wife. Not all of the god-king's subsequent reception turns out to be the fruit of his own unassisted achievements. Diodorus' deployment of Egyptian mythology, unusual though the subject is in extant Greco-Roman historiography, turns out to employ a rather familiar set of strategies. It explores the sweeping claims made by the preceding proem, and suggests the factors that might complicate their actual implementation.

The myth of Osiris is only a tiny portion of Diodorus' massive history. On the other hand, the prominent position which it occupies at the beginning of the work suggests the applicability of its themes to what comes later. Recent scholarship has increasingly uncovered the deep patterns in Diodorus' work, where themes from one part of the history may re-emerge later. Errietta Bissa, for example, has examined how the preoccupation with fiscal rectitude which first appears in the Egyptian narrative turns up again at subsequent points in the history.[89] In this article, we have seen how the pursuit of posthumous glory and its potentially surprising results, appearing first in the story of Osiris and Isis, soon re-emerges with interesting variations in the story of Ninus and Semiramis. It is not altogether unreasonable to suggest, then, that Diodorus' Osiris, and the narrative which he enacts concerning the potent and admirable but sometimes less than straightforward possibilities of memorialisation, have lessons for our reading of the rest of the *Bibliothēkē*.

Abbreviation

BNJ Brill's New Jacoby

Bibliography

Ambaglio, D. La 'biblioteca storica' di Diodoro Siculo. Problemi e metodo (Como, 1995).
Bissa, E. Diodorus' Good Statesman and State Revenue, in: Historiae Mundi. Studies in Universal Historiography, edited by P. Liddel and A. Fear (London, 2010), 56–70.
Brunt, P. A. Arrian. History of Alexander and Indica. Volume I (Cambridge, MA, 1976).
Burton, A. Diodorus Siculus. Book 1. A Commentary (Leiden, 1972).
Christ, M. Herodotean Kings and Historical Enquiry. Classical Antiquity 13 (1994), 167–202.
Feeney, D. Beginning Sallust's Catiline. Prudentia 26 (1994), 139–146.
Grethlein, J. The Greeks and Their Past. Poetry, Oratory and History in the Fifth Century BCE (Cambridge, 2010).
Harrison, T. Divinity and History. The Religion of Herodotus (Oxford, 2000).
Hornblower, S. A Commentary on Thucydides. Volume I. Books I–III (Oxford, 1991).

---

89 Bissa 2010, 61.

Hornblower, S. The Religious Dimension to the Peloponnesian War, or, What Thucydides Does Not Tell Us. *Harvard Studies in Classical Philology* 94 (1992), 169–197.

Marincola, J. Odysseus and the Historians. *Syllecta Classica* 18 (2007), 1–79.

McGing, B. *Polybius' Histories* (Oxford, 2010).

Murray, O. Hecataeus of Abdera and Pharaonic Kingship. *Journal of Egyptian Archaeology* 56 (1970), 141–171.

Parker, R. *Athenian Religion. A History* (Oxford, 1996).

Pelling, C. Tacitus and Germanicus, in: *Oxford Readings in Classical Studies: Tacitus*, edited by R. Ash (Oxford, 2012), 281–313.

Raaflaub, K. 'Ktēma es aiei': Thucydides' concept of "learning through history" and its realization in his work, in: *Thucydides Between History and Literature*, edited by A. Tsakmakis and M. Tamiolaki (Berlin; Boston, 2013), 3–21.

Rubincam, C. Cross-References in the 'Bibliotheke Historike' of Diodoros. *Phoenix* 43 (1989), 39–61.

Sacks, K. S. *Diodorus Siculus and the First Century* (Princeton, 1990).

Sartori, M. Storia, 'utopia' e mito nei primi libri della 'bibliotheca historica' di Diodoro Siculo. *Athenaeum* 62 (1984), 492–536.

Schneider, G. J. *De Diodori fontibus (Libr. I–IV)* (Weber, 1880).

Schwartz, E. Hekataeos von Teos. *Rheinisches Museum für Philologie* 40 (1885), 223–262.

Sheridan, B. Diodorus' Reading of Polybius' Universalism, in: *Historiae Mundi. Studies in Universal Historiography*, edited by P. Liddel and A. Fear (London, 2010), 41–55.

Stahl, H.-P. Learning Through Suffering? Croesus' Conversations in the History of Herodotus. *Yale Classical Studies* 24 (1975), 1–36.

Stahl, H.-P. The Dot on the 'I': Thucydidean epilogues, in: *Thucydides Between History and Literature*, edited by A. Tsakmakis and M. Tamiolaki (Berlin; Boston, 2013), 309–328.

Sulimani, I. *Diodorus' Mythistory and the Pagan Mission. Historiography and Culture-heroes in the First Pentad of the Bibliotheke* (Leiden, 2011).

Walbank, F. W. *Polybius* (Berkeley; Los Angeles; London, 1972).

Westlake, H. D. Thucydides and the Athenian Disaster in Egypt. *Classical Philology* 45 (1950), 209–216.

Woodman, A. J. Tacitus and Germanicus: monuments and models, in: *Fame and Infamy. Essays for Christopher Pelling on Characterization in Greek and Roman Biography and Historiography*, edited by R. Ash, J. Mossman and F. Titchener (Oxford, 2015), 255–268.

Yarrow, L. M. *Historiography at the End of the Republic. Provincial Perspectives on Roman Rule* (Oxford, 2006).

Rachel Wood
Wandering Hero, Wandering Myths?

The Image of Heracles in Iran

Introduction

On the edge of an ancient sacred site in Media, carved into the base of a mountain, a nude male figure reclines on a lion skin, his club, *gorytos* and quiver resting behind him. An accompanying inscription denotes the sculpture as a dedication made in 148 BC by Hyacinthus son of Pantauchus for the deliverance of Cleomenes, Seleucid governor of the Upper Satrapies. Four centuries later, in the first half of the third century AD, another rock relief was commissioned in Persis by the first Sasanian *Šāhanšāh*, Ardašir I, which seems to include among its weathered figures a small nude standing male holding up a club, a lion skin draped over his arm. The following discussion questions the relationship between Heracles iconography and any potential allusions to myth during the period between the commissioning of the two monuments mentioned above: the Seleucid Hyacinthus dedication at Bisotun in Media and the Sasanian relief of Ardašir I at Naqš-e Rajab in Persis; exploring the processes at work during the time of the Parthian Empire, a period for which few historical sources survive and the material record is itself sparse.[1]

While Heracles' image in Iran is a widely recognised phenomenon, this paper aims to explore whether traces of accompanying mythological narrative can be discerned in the visual representations. For example, did the lion skin retain the particular associations to a heroic mythical feat in mainland Greece? Or was the re-employment of the motif motivated by its function as an established signifier of the deity or hero, whether by referring to values or characteristics, or perhaps solely as an inseparable part of his visual representation? Despite the popularity of Heracles' image, his amenability to fit in with local *mores* and aspects of local divinities, and, most pertinently, his visual attributes bearing associations with his myth cycle, it seems there is little indication that stories of Heracles' exploits were taken up along with his image. In this instance, the visual signifiers once associated with myth – most notably lion wrestling and the lion skin – were removed from their specific narrative origins.

While this paper begins in Media and ends in Persis, the emphasis is on Elymais (modern Khuzestān in southwest Iran), where the majority of the relevant visual evidence was found, with a brief digression to the Seleucid capital at Seleucia on the Tigris in Babylonia and its neighbouring Parthian and Sasanian successor, Ctesiphon

---

1 Sinisi 2014.

https://doi.org/10.1515/9783110421453-014

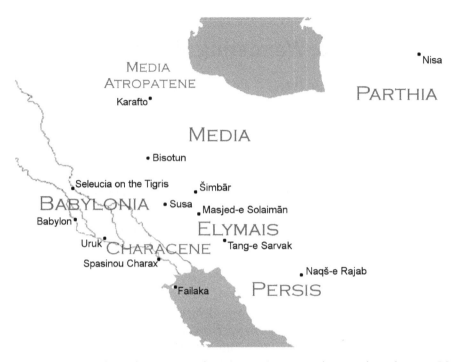

Fig. 1: Some sites of Heraclean iconography across ancient Iran and surrounds, 2nd century BC – 3rd century AD.

(Fig. 1).[2] Not only were these regions of Media, Babylonia, Elymais and Fars at the centres of the vast Achaemenid, Seleucid, Parthian, and Sasanian empires over the centuries, and pivotal to numerous trade networks, but from the second century BC to the third century AD the spheres of influence swayed remarkably, as Seleucid, Parthian, and rulers of Characene, Elymais, and Persis vied for territorial control. Aspects of Heraclean myth travelled from the Mediterranean as far as Central Asia before, during, and after this period, but the production and circulation of Heraclean iconography increased significantly after the Macedonian conquest.[3] The migration of these images presumably was facilitated not only through the movement of people telling stories and associating particular locations with myths from the Greek world, such as

---

[2] Relevant evidence from sites outside these regions is also included, such as from neighbouring Characene in the southwest and Parthia in the northeast. To follow the example of some previous works and divide studies by what we identify as culturally Iranian or culturally Semitic would be artificial in presuming impassable boundaries between the regions. Such a divide is predominantly the product of ethno-linguistic studies and historiographical burden, and interpretation in such terms would undercut the aim of studying the visual evidence in its own right, and the intention to elucidate cross-cultural themes.

[3] See West in this volume.

of Heracles at Aornos, but also was encouraged by the objects that those travellers brought with them and the subsequent commission of decorated objects in their new surroundings.[4] In light of the numerous attestations of Heracles' image across ancient Iran in various permutations, we might expect to find traces of his myths incorporated into Iranian art and folklore to explain his popularity and movement.

An alignment between Heracles and an Iranian divine being (*yazata*) – Vahrām in Parthian and Middle Persian, Verethragna in the Avestan language – has long been recognised in scholarship. Frequently the connection is discussed in terms of "translations", "religious syncretism", and "Hellenisation", the Iranian divinity expressed visually using the image of a Greek god.[5] Yet, despite much attention paid to the subject, there remain implications in the scholarship that there was a neat and consistent process leading to a common understanding of Heracles and Verethragna across the Near and Middle East and Central Asia, shared across territories and centuries. In addition, presumptions based upon the ethnicity and cultural attachments of the patron or craftsman of each instance are not necessarily helpful for understanding the on-going life and potential reinterpretations of the image. Inherent is a danger of oversimplification in references to "Heracles-Verethragna", creating a neat and linear story of syncretism and hybridisation whereby two clear identities become instantly inseparable and consistently synonymous.

Purposefully, therefore, this article is not intended as a comprehensive survey of "Heracles in the East", which could, and has, taken scholars in the space of a few paragraphs from Commagene and Syria to Bactria, Sogdia, and Gandhara.[6] Neither is it a search for all representations that could be categorised as Iranian, nor an attempt to account for the widespread popularity and adaptability of Heracles' image. Rather, the intention is to explore the question of the retention of myth, with reference to six sculptural depictions of Heracles iconography. In addition to the Hyacinthus dedication and the Sasanian royal rock relief mentioned above, the other case studies are a limestone lion wrestler and two rock-cut reliefs from sites across Elymais, and a bronze statue found at Seleucia on the Tigris. Each example contributes a different facet to how we might interpret visual signifiers of myth in Heracles iconography.

---

4 Arr. *Anab.* 4.28; see, for example, Heracles wrestling Achelous on an ivory dagger handle found in the Temple of the Oxus at Takht-e Sangin in Bactria (Dušanbe, National Museum of Antiquities of Tajikistan, Inv.Nr.M7249). For *interpretationes graecae* into Heraclean personae, see Hdt. 2.44 and Meg. fr.39.
5 De Jong 2003; Curtis 2007, 423. For the convenience of the reader, the Middle Persian transliteration will be rendered as Vahrām, while the Sasanian rulers of the same name will here be denoted by Bahrām.
6 See Downey 1969 on Heracles in the art of Assur, Dura Europus, Hatra, and Palmyra. More recently, see Kaizer 2000 on the Hatran and Palmyrene Heracles figures. For Heracles in Gandharan sculpture appearing as Vajrapani, companion of the Buddha, and Heracles as Orlagno or Eraklio in Kushan Bactria, see Carter 1995. For a recent summary of identifications of Verethragna in Iranian art, see Shenkar 2014, 159–63.

In such a task, we must strike a balance between engaging with comparanda and transposing observations drawn from external evidence onto our case studies, such as, notably, the first-century BC Artagenes-Heracles-Ares of Antiochus I in Commagene.[7] We must take care not to elide the processes and motivations identified in one context with those from another. We cannot apply one rule or model to all examples, but rather should consider each situation in its own right as far as is possible and be aware of the potential for multiple processes and multiple outcomes. In this way, we can interpret each image as an individual output dependent on its own context, rather than taking each image as testimony to a universal rule or "truth". The widespread popularity of Heracles' image across Eurasia is, however, a significant factor to consider in as much as it suggests there were certain traits in his projected character or image, or indeed, mythology, which appealed to varied cultures and levels of societies.

As already implied, studying the iconography of Greek (or any) gods in new locations presents numerous potential pitfalls for over-interpretation.[8] The images at hand can quickly be stretched beyond their capabilities by filling their caesuras with the testimony of material from different periods or regions, material that had very different patrons with different requirements. Such an approach can create the illusion of homogeneity, particularly by projecting later evidence onto earlier, more ambiguous, material. Similarly, in looking for explanations, we can tend to force all extant images to complement or fit nicely into the testimony provided by the textual and epigraphic evidence from elsewhere. Opposing suppositions, focusing either on the retention of the deity's original identity in its new cultural context, or the reverse, emphasising the deity's complete transformation, can over-emphasise distinctions between a Greek or an Iranian interpretation and enforce mutual exclusivity. Conflating any syncretistic features in the composition of an image with syncretism of the meaning of an image can confuse the task further. There is a constant difficulty in that even though these images seem ambivalent to us, it is not always clear that the patron or contemporary audience interpreted the images in numerous ways simultaneously.

Accompanying these issues of how and why Heracles' image was depicted in Iranian art are questions surrounding the role of images in the transmission of myth. We might assume that a figure so favoured in art, clearly holding local resonances for several centuries, would continue to hold some associated mythological narratives. Can we only usefully view images as a snapshot of one interpretation of a narrative, or can we say anything about their role in spreading and transforming mythology? Most of the case studies here are static monuments that were reinterpreted in their local vicinity over time and played a part in defining that locality, just as many of these

---

7 On Nemrud Dağı, see Brijder 2014. In Armenia under the Arsacid rulers in the first century BC, statues of Heracles were aligned with the god Vahagn, a dragon killer, who was linked also to Vahrām/Verethragna (Moses Khoranatsi, 2.12.14), see Downey 1969, 6; Russell 1987, 187–92.
8 On this issue see Adrych et al 2017.

monuments were attributed new origins, meanings and associated narratives over the centuries after the Islamic conquest.

In order to identify the retention of myth along with the image of Heracles, we would hope for an identifiable distinct action associated with his narrative repertoire. With Heracles, there is the added complication that a feature of his visual identification, the lion skin, was an intrinsic part of his associated mythology, the memento of his first labour set by King Eurystheus. Yet the presence of the lion skin in an image of Heracles does not attest to the sustained association of the image with that specific myth. As we shall see, distinguishing the representation of a Heraclean labour from a similar action is not always feasible. To summarise this problem more eloquently, we can turn to the five aspects put forward by the exponent of artistic independence from textual accounts of mythological narratives, Klaus Junker. Interpretation of an image of Greek myth, for Junker, involves consideration of the specificity of the figure, the presence of mythologemes (essential core themes), the historical environment, the communicative standpoint of the object based on its form and function, and the history of the particular motifs.[9]

For our wandering myths, we are faced with the added consideration of how the motifs were interpreted outside the Mediterranean and the assumed cultural divides between political spheres of influence. When the club is used in isolation on the reverse of a Seleucid coin minted in a workshop in Ecbatana or Susa, for example, it is assumed to be a reference to Heracles, but when the same motif appears in the architectural ornamentation of Mithradatkert/Old Nisa, a royal Parthian citadel in Turkmenistan, there is frequently the tendency to assume the meaning has changed, or is syncretised, to an Iranian alternative.[10] Heracles' image in an Iranian cultural context is assumed to really represent Verethragna, while in any Mesopotamian context he would be Nergal. As Potts observes, this issue of whether Heracles' image in Iran represents Heracles himself or an avatar of Verethragna has been an almost constant topic of debate.[11] Yet there remains the specific question of how those visual indicators that were integral to Greek myths of Heracles were reconceived in Iranian art.

Heracles, personally favoured by Alexander as mythical ancestor of the Argead dynasty, was a hero who became a god after performing extraordinary feats including an eastern *anabasis*, and thus was a fitting role model for the Macedonian ruler. Heracles' image was introduced to Iran on an official and far-reaching basis at the very beginning of Macedonian rule in the late fourth century on issues of Alexander.[12] Obverse types show the clean-shaven head of Heracles wearing a lion skin, whose facial features bear a strong resemblance to portraits of Alexander himself (Fig. 2–3). By also

---

9 Junker 2012, 128.

10 Invernizzi and Lippolis 2008, figs. 269–70. See also Heracles' inclusion among the Greek gods depicted on the ivory rhytons found at Old Nisa (Pappalardo 2010).

11 Potts 2015, 368.

12 Among other studies see Darbandi and Zournatzi 2008.

Fig. 2: Tetradrachm of Alexander, minted in Babylon, 17.19g, c. 325–323 BC, BM 1929,0811.98 (Courtesy of the Trustees of the British Museum).

Fig. 3: Drachm in the name of Alexander, minted in Babylon, 3.32g, c. 317–311 BC, BM 1986,0553.1 (Courtesy of the Trustees of the British Museum).

embodying physical strength and overcoming adversity, he was the perfect champion for Greco-Macedonian soldiers on campaign and those settled in the east, far from home.

Yet it is the particular conception of Heracles used in the Bisotun dedication that we find repeated in later Elymaean rock reliefs. These rock carvings show the subject bearded, with closely cropped hair, accompanied by club and lion skin, and holding a shallow round cup in front of his chest; not the clean-shaven young Heracles of the Alexander coins. These figures bearing their cups, however, are hardly references to the obstreperous and ungainly drunken Heracles of Greek myth and common in Hellenistic art of the Mediterranean. Reclining males holding a round cup became a common motif in Parthian art, particularly in the representation of rulers, and held connotations of grandeur, composure, and leisure rather than inebriated revelry.[13] Mechanisms of transmission independent from Alexander and Seleucid patronage are further suggested by the profusion of imagery of Heracles and other Greek subjects in the coroplastic assemblages from Babylonian and Elymaean sites where the hero was shown with various novel iconographic additions.[14]

---

13 See Vanden Berghe 1984, nos. 27 and 29; BM 1928,0716.76.
14 Recurring additions to the representation of Heracles in Babylonia and Susiana are a bulbous headdress and a baldric across his chest, found at Seleucia on the Tigris (Van Ingen 1939, pl.XVIII), Uruk (Ziegler 1962, figs. 329a-331), Failaka (Connelly 1990, 219, figs. 1, 60), and Susa (Martinez-Seĺve 2002, nos. 110, 113–19, 127–9).

Heracles' image and local myth

It is widely accepted that images, whatever their original designation or the intention of the patron or artist, can provide inspiration for later reinterpretation. Visual references to one myth can be reapplied to another, and monuments that did not make direct references to mythological narratives can be the focus around which a new collection of stories develops. It is in this way that we can view the recumbent nude and bearded Heracles Kallinikos holding a shallow cup in his left hand and lying on the outline of a lion, carved out of a low promontory at Mount Bisotun, near Kermānshāh in western Iran (Fig. 4). Behind, depicted in shallow relief and as if leaning against the rock, unrequired and discarded, are the hero's weapons: a club, a bow in its *gorytos*, and a quiver of arrows. Also carved in the background is an olive tree, as if offering the hero some welcome shade, and a stele inscribed with the dedication by Hyacinthus son of Pantauchus, referred to in the introduction to this article. The text, dedicated in 148 BC, makes explicit that it was Heracles Kallinikos who is depicted here as a reclining symposiast and bowman.

By the time of Seleucid rule, Bisotun (Old Persian *Bagastāna*, perhaps deriving from "place of the gods") had long been a sacred Iranian site, favoured by the

Fig. 4: Dedication of Hyacinthus son of Pantauclus, Bisotun (Copyright: the author).

Achaemenid Darius I as the place for his own rock relief that sits 150 m to the west and high above the Heracles relief.[15] The two images form a striking contrast: the image of a solitary reclining nude Greek god, carved almost in the round, the first addition to the site that we are aware of after the bas-relief of Darius carved three hundred and fifty years previously. Here we can see how the Seleucid elite participated in the traditions of Iranian rulers, by sharing in the same context of display, but did so distinctly in their own way according to their needs and iconographic traditions. The figure is just under one metre high from his elbow to head, raised above ground level yet close enough to be fully visible overlooking the main route from Babylon to Ecbatana. He further catches the eye of the passer-by since the sculptors cut into the corner of the promontory where the main thoroughfare encircles the edge of the mountain and skirts the plain.[16] In addition to profiting by the existing prestige and sanctity of the site, such a position was also very appropriate for the dedication to Heracles as protector of travellers.[17] The existing sacred character of this site may have facilitated the acceptance and appropriation of the image of Heracles into existing local narratives.

This question of how a previously foreign image became assimilated is vastly complex as there is huge potential for a range of responses. There is great potential for either the retention and reinterpretation of mythic elements, their simultaneous combination, and their inconsistent uptake or disposal. Yet, it is precisely this scope that makes the question of what one image, or one myth, means in another cultural environment, and its evolution over time, so fascinating. Although the inscription attests to the clear identity of the figure for the dedicator as Heracles Kallinikos, the interpretation of the figure by others over the succeeding centuries is open to further consideration. We have no evidence to confirm an established and recognised syncretism of Heracles with an Iranian divinity by 148 BC, but had the concept of Heracles already

---

15 Diod. Sic. 2.13.1–2, describes a mountain called Bagistanus that is sacred to Zeus, a park laid out by Semiramis where she commissioned a rock relief depicting herself with 100 spearmen. Diod. Sic. 17.110.5 mentions that Alexander diverted from the main road from Susa to Ecbatana to pass the region of Bagistane. From this reference and the discovery of a limestone Attic column base at the site, Luschey 1974 suggests that Alexander built a sanctuary of Heracles at Bisotun, but there is hardly the evidence to support this claim. See also Isidore of Charax, writing in the first century AD, who reports on an *agalma* and stele of Semiramis at the mountain city of Bagistana (*FGrHist.* 781 F(2)). Circulation of the name Bagistana in the Greco-Roman world adds doubt to the presumption that Tacitus mistook one as the other. Russell 1987, 191–2 suggests as an alternative solution that there was a confusion with Mount Sabalan. It is tempting to align the Gotarzes of Tacitus' narrative with the Gotarzes who dedicated a victory relief at Bisotun, although it is unknown whether that relief was dedicated by this Gotarzes or another ruler of his name. There was on-going sacred and royal activity at the site through to the Sasanian period, but no evidence has been found of a defined sanctuary or focus of worship.

16 The dedication presumably would have been painted, but there are no visible traces extant. Stronach suggested that the shallower lion relief was of a much earlier date, perhaps of the eighth century BC (referenced in Kleiss 1970, 133).

17 Boyce and Grenet 1991, 64 note that Verethragna also became a protector of travellers, hailed as *Panth Yazad*, "god of the road".

been accepted into popular Iranian culture? His image had, after all, been promulgated on coins of Alexander and the Seleucids over the preceding one hundred and eighty years. Any attempt to pinpoint a precise moment at which Heracles' image was adopted to represent an Iranian deity is both counterproductive and likely to remain guesswork. We can see a contemporary uptake of Heracles' image on the coins of Iranian dynasts, unlabelled but accompanied by Greek legends for the titles of the king, such as the walking figure on tetradrachms of the Arsacid Mithridates I minted at Seleucia on the Tigris soon after the Parthian conquest of the area c. 141 BC (only seven years after the Bisotun dedication), or the seated figure on the reverse of Characenean tetradrachms from c. 127 BC onwards (Fig. 5). Yet whether these Heraclean figures retained any association with the hero and his mythological canon remains unclear.

Fig. 5: Tetradrachm of Hyspaosines, Characene (Ashmolean Museum).

Heracles as presented at Bisotun does share similar qualities with Verethragna. His epithet, "Kallinikos" ("of beautiful victory"), was a common epithet of Heracles in the Mediterranean and is closely related to the character of Verethragna and the meaning of his Avestan name, "smasher of obstacles".[18] Verethragna's indomitable nature is reinforced in the *Vahrām Yašt* (Hymn to Verethragna) where he is hailed repeatedly as "best-armed of the heavenly gods".[19] Both deities are also connected to fertility, virility, and healing, as well as having a pugnacious aspect. Yet the established character of the Zoroastrian *yazata* Verethragna before the influx of Heraclean iconography with the Macedonian conquest, and before the Hyacinthus dedication at Bisotun is unclear. We can infer that Verethragna was venerated in the Achaemenid period, since he is one of the divine beings who had a day of each month named after him. Other references, however, are difficult to find. He is not, for example, mentioned among the gods named in the Persepolis Fortification Archive or other Achaemenid-period inscriptions.

Significantly, Tacitus' description of an Iranian myth of Heracles complements the Bisotun depiction of the resting archer god and provides a useful insight, whether or not we accept Herzfeld's association of Tacitus' "sanctuary of Heracles at Mount

---

18 For an introduction to Verethragna's role in Zoroastrianism, see Boyce and Grenet 1991, particularly 62–5.

19 *Yt*. 14 (translation available online at avesta.org).

Sambulos" with Bisotun.[20] Tacitus relates that the Parthian king Gotarzes II in AD 49 offered vows to the local gods at Mount Sambulos, among whom Heracles was prominent.[21] From Tacitus' account, we learn something more of the Heracles worshipped there. Through dream visitations, Heracles bids the priests there to leave horses with quivers full of arrows by his temple on certain nights. The horses return the next morning panting and with empty quivers. The following night, Heracles appears to the priests again and shows them his route, along which they find the bodies of his prey littering the forest. Paul Bernard argued that Heracles as a horseman and hunter was strange to the Greek understanding of the god, and therefore this was a local interpretation of Heracles that emphasises Iranian military virtues of archery and horsemanship.[22] While Bernard avoids making an identification with a local Iranian deity, it should be noted that patronage of hunting large animals is one remit of the Babylonian god Nergal.[23] Tacitus' reference can be understood as a gradual transformation by the late Parthian period, absorbing Heracles into a collection of local narratives. The attachment of local myth in western Iran to the figure of Heracles, or at least to a figure recognised by Tacitus as Heracles, could have been prompted or encouraged by the commission of images such as the Hyacinthus dedication. If so, this would indicate the potency of such images in shaping local attitudes and mythic narratives.

Art, Syncretism, and Myth: The Case of "Heracles-Verethragna"

"Accidentally found near the city boundaries" of Seleucia on the Tigris in 1984 was an 85.5 cm tall bronze statue of a heavily muscled nude male bearded figure with his right hand on his hip, his weight firmly on his right leg (Fig. 6).[24] He once wore a diadem or wreath, and his left arm is missing. On his left thigh is a Parthian inscription, while on the right thigh is the same text translated into Greek, both of which were added to the statue after the victory of the Arsacid king Vologases IV over the king of Mesene (Mešān/Characene), Mithridates, in AD 151.[25] The inscribed dedication records how the statue was taken from Mesene by the victorious Parthians and set up in the temple of the Iranian god Tir (Avestan Tištrya) in Seleucia on the Tigris, referred to in the

---

20 Herzfeld 1910, 190 n. 2; Herzfeld 1920, 46. See n. 13, above.

21 Tac. *Ann.* 12.13.

22 Bernard 1980.

23 See n. 27 below on a possible connection between Heracles and Nergal.

24 Al-Salihi 1984; Al-Salihi 1987.

25 For the full text of the inscriptions see Potter 1991, 278–9.

Greek inscription as "Apollo of the bronze gate".[26] Aside from the significant implications that this dedication holds for continued royal attention to the city alongside Ctesiphon, and to the vitality of Seleucia's religious infrastructure in the mid second century AD, replication of the Parthian inscription in the Greek language may suggest local recognition of the Greek hero and god, and the potential retention of aspects of his mythological cycle among the local community.[27]

The Parthian-period inscriptions on this statue are the first attestation of contemporaneous double meaning of the same image: the simultaneous "translation" of Heracles and Verethragna.[28] Yet another identity may have been attributed in its earlier Mesenian context, as Nergal.[29] There are clear stylistic similarities to Hellenistic sculp-

---

26 See Potter 1991, 285 on a connection between the apotropaic characters of Heracles, Nergal at Hatra, and this manifestation of Apollo, rather than Apollo Komaios, whose cult statue was taken from Seleucia on the Tigris by Lucius Verus in AD 165 (Amm. Marc. 23.6.24).

27 Other late Arsacid ceremonial inscriptions were also written in Parthian, such as that on the Bisotun Vologases relief (first to second century AD) or the Khwasak relief from Susa (AD 215), in contrast to the Greek inscriptions on the Mithridates and Gotarzes reliefs of the first century BC at Bisotun. Vologases IV's tetradrachms bore Greek legends, while his drachms bore both Parthian and Greek legends together. Parthian appeared on Arsacid coins after Vologases I (c. 51–78) (Haruta 2013, 783), at which time Greek legends on coins are mostly illegible. The inclusion of both Greek and Parthian inscriptions on this Heracles statue may, therefore, be typical of the contemporary epigraphic habit, or be indicative of a concern to communicate to a Greek-speaking section of Seleucia's population. Another aspect that should not be overlooked are the Achaemenid and Sasanian multi-lingual (tri- rather than bilingual) triumphal inscriptions. On some of Vologases IV's coins (AD 147–91) the ruler bears the Greek epithet "philhellenos", supporting the idea that there may have been an administrative policy of amenability towards the Greco-Macedonian population or, in the traditional view, that the Arsacid ruler was appreciative of Greek culture.

28 See Bernard 1990, 52–62 and Potter 1991, among others, on the question of the implications for the cult practice and religious beliefs in Seleucia on the Tigris from the translation of "the temple of Tir" to "the temple of Apollo", perhaps suggesting a pre-existing correlation between Tir and the Babylonian god Nabu. Apollo's more frequent Iranian counterpart, Mithra, (such as aligned in Antiochus IV's Commagenean dedications) demonstrates clearly the ineffectual nature of attempts to impose a consistent narrative of "religious syncretism".

29 Seyrig 1944; Al-Salihi 1987, 165–6; Potter 1991, 285. A Heracles figure appears on the reverse of coins of the first local ruler of Characene/Mesene, Hyspaosines (Aspasine) c. 127 BC. It is conceivable that the Seleucia statue represents the same patron of the dynasty as depicted on these coins, but there are significant differences in pose, hair, and he is without his club. The tetradrachms have Greek legends but do not label the figure on the reverse, who is seated on a rock, perhaps covered with a lion skin, and rests his club on his knee. It is commonly referred to that the chief deity of Mesene was Nergal. Nergal was a solar Babylonian deity, who also was invoked in times of war and plague and presided over the underworld. Nergal and Heracles shared an apotropaic protective aspect: in the Temple of Bel at Hatra, the niche containing a statue of Heracles was amended with a graffito invoking Nergal, "chief guardian of the gate" (Al-Salihi 1971; Al-Salihi 1973). The function of Heracles as apotropaic and as a guardian is also demonstrated in a late fourth- to early third-century Greek inscription from a cave complex at Karafto, c. 300 km north of Bisotun (*IGIAC* 75). An additional alignment with Mars/Ares has been noted not only in the inscription naming Heracles-Artagenes-Ares in Commagene, but also through the name

Fig. 6: Heracles-Verethragna, Seleucia on the Tigris, Iraq Baghdad Museum (Copyright: Centro Ricerche Archeologiche e Scavi di Torino).

of the planet Mars as Nergal in Babylonian astrology, and as Verethragna in Pahlavi (Gnoli 1989, 512). Strabo 15.2.14's reference (perhaps deriving from Nearkhos) to the Carmanians' sole worship of Ares has been taken by many to attest to the utmost importance of Verethragna in Achaemenid Carmania. Potter 1991, 285 infers a necessity to align Heracles, Nergal, and Verethragna in order to make sense of these attributes, to identify one specific god who was reinterpreted into different cultures. Heracles and Verethragna lack Nergal's solar aspect, although Verethragna may have shared a chthonic aspect, yet not to the extent of Nergal, who presided over the underworld. Verethragna is styled in the *Vahrām Yašt*: "who makes virility, who makes death, who makes resurrection, who possesses peace, who has a free way" (Yt. 14.28). Hdt. 2.43–4 on the Phoenician Heracles/Melquart. See below on Bel in Elymais. See Kaizer 2000 on the uncertainty surrounding the Palmyrene and Hatran identifications of the image of Heracles.

The religious communities of Mesene probably were diverse, yet little is known of the region in this period apart from the coins of the local rulers. While the kingdom was in southern Babylonia and therefore likely maintained veneration of Babylonian deities, Hyspaosines was perhaps of Arabian descent, and other Characenean rulers bear theophoric names deriving from Iranian as well as Babylonian gods (Tiraios and the Mithridates of the Seleucian bronze statue's inscription, and Attambelos and Abinergaos. On Characene, see Schuol 2000).

ture, and the statue is often referred to as a copy of Lysippus' "Weary Heracles" from the late fourth century BC.[30] Yet the only certain affiliated date for its production is the *terminus ante quem* of AD 151.

An attempt to reconstruct the pose of this statue is necessary for our discussion of the transmission of mythological narrative. The most common representation of Heracles in Iran, as seen on many terracotta figurines, shows him leaning on his club, sometimes with the lion skin draped over the lower arm, falling down behind the club.[31] His pose is different to that of the Farnese Heracles, who holds the apples of the Hesperides behind his back and droops his head in tiredness. Our Seleucian Heracles-Verethragna bears close affinity to the Heracles of the Villa Albani, who also has his right hand on his hip, very much at ease and hardly conveying exhaustion; with his left arm probably rested on his club that was draped with the lion skin.[32] His right leg appears to take the weight of his body, rather than forcing his hip outwards and thus displacing more weight onto the club. The Seleucian statue differs from the Albani type in that the hero's gaze is not directed to the floor, but outwards to his left. One reconstruction could place his left arm, in the manner of the Albani Heracles, extended outwards as the hero gazes at the Golden Apples in his hand, thus retaining the mythological reference.[33]

To more fully explore the potential perceptions of Heracles' image in Parthian Seleucia on the Tigris, it is also important to consider other representations of Heracles in circulation in the city that were perhaps in contemporaneous use, such as on seals

---

While it is conceivable that the Mesenian bronze was a cult statue, there is no strong evidence to support this. It could well have stood in the house of a wealthy patron as much as been on display in a public arena, whether the patron was Mesenian, Parthian, or a descendent of Greco-Macedonian settlers. See Invernizzi 1989, 99. Potter 1991 argues that the cult statue of Heracles/Nergal would have been a seated figure such as is depicted on Characenean coins, but I would argue that there is little indication that the coin iconography must replicate a cult statue, and the coin type is more likely dependent on the precedent and contemporary prevalence of seated and enthroned figures (usually identifiable as deities) on the reverse of coinage, such as the Seleucid Zeus Aetophorus and Apollo on the *omphalos*, and the Arsacid seated Tyche and archer.

Plin. *HN* 6.31.138; Gatier, Lombard and al-Sindi 2002. Bactrian heritage has been posited for Hyspaosines based on an inscription from Delos made by "Hyspaosines the Bactrian" just before 179 BC (*SEG* 36–733), and similarities in design between the reverse type of Hyspaosines' tetradrachms and those of Euthydemus of Bactria (r.c. 225–220 BC). The large gap of 65 years between the date of the Delian dedication and Hyspaosines' military activities in Babylonia in 124 BC makes this alignment tenuous but not inconceivable.

30 Al-Salihi 1987, 159 argues that traces of silver in the alloy indicate Babylonian production of the statue.

31 These are often referred to as drawing on the Albertini and Chiaramonti Heracles types, although with the addition of the baldric and sometimes a bulbous headdress (see n. 15, above).

32 Al-Salihi 1987, 160.

33 Bernard 1990, 5.

and as terracotta figurines.[34] It is notable that Heracles holding an apple has been identified among the Babylonian coroplastics of this period.[35] However, it is also possible that the left arm hung down by the side of the club and lion skin, hand empty, in the manner depicted in several terracotta figurines found in Babylonia.[36] In light of this evidence, let alone continued connections to Greco-Roman culture, both Heracles' appearance and identity are unlikely to have been unfamiliar in the Parthian context, and so a translation of the subject to Verethragna must not be perceived as a necessity for Parthian-period cognition of the bronze statue.

The statue type may have made an oblique visual reference to the mythological cycle of Heracles, presumably understood and wished for by the sculptor and patron, and clearly had not been disassociated from its Heraclean identity despite the additional identification with Verethragna. Whether the figure maintained its association with the myth for the Mesenian and later Parthian viewers is unknown, but here we can see how visual representations of Heracles that included indicators of myth were influential in defining representations of Verethragna. The statue probably only enjoyed a short period on display in its Seleucian setting since the city was destroyed by Avidius Cassius in AD 165.[37] It is to Elymais in the second century AD that we must turn for monuments that can tell us more about ongoing relationships with iconography of Heracles' myths in Iran.

The Lion Wrestler

Was a bearded, nude, lion wrestler always intended to represent Heracles, and always interpreted as such? Does the image necessarily refer to the same myth, holding connotations of a hero overcoming a set challenge designed to be his downfall, of the impermeable hide, of a creature terrorising the hills around Nemea? Even accounting for the existing local popularity of showing warriors defeating monsters and hunters killing large animals, which might contribute to the popular uptake of Heraclean iconography, this hardly fully explains the maintenance of features such as, for example, his nudity.[38] A generalised preference for images depicting warriors fighting creatures is also not a full explanation for the precise local formulations of Heracles' image and how it was employed. It is necessary to explore these in more detail and

---

34 For seals, see Invernizzi et al 2004, III, 3–14, pl. 1, colour pl. 1, and especially Ek 12: S6–9366. The majority of Heraclean seal impressions from Seleucia on the Tigris, however, only show his bearded head. For terracotta figurines, see Bernard 1990, fig. 14 and Menegazzi 2014, 79–81.

35 Van Buren 1930, no. 544 from Uruk now in the Ashmolean (1923.303), and no. 545 from Susa.

36 Menegazzi 2014, 1.G55, 59, 62.

37 Historia Augusta, *Vita Veri* 8.3.

38 De Jong 2003.

to question what connections to the specific mythological narrative of Heracles were maintained.

At the terraced sanctuary of Masjed-e Solaimān, in the foothills of the Zagros Mountains in Elymais, roughly one hundred kilometres east-south-east of Susa, were found several fragments of reliefs associated by the excavators with Heracles. One of these, now in the Šuš Museum, appears to show the hero in the midst of his first labour, grappling the Nemean lion (Fig. 7).[39] The statue was found in three pieces built into the Sasanian-period wall of the terrace outside the building designated, because of this statue, as a "temple of Heracles", although there is no trace of an original setting inside the building. It is one of two Parthian-period structures built along Babylonian temple-plans on the second-century BC western expansion of the sanctuary towards the crest of the hill. The extensive remodelling of the site in the second century, Parthian, and Sasanian periods and a modern cemetery have obscured attempts to identify any earlier occupation. The sanctuary, originally consisting only of a large open-air podium, and the small settlement to the south were in continuous use from at least the Seleucid period until the Sasanian period.[40]

The sculpture is over life-size at 2.40 m tall and has been variously dated to the first century AD through to the beginning of the third century AD. The lower half of the figure is carved in shallow relief, like the majority of sculpture from this site and rest of Elymais, but the torso and head are in the round.[41] Local additions to the typical iconography of Heracles in this sculpture include a torque around his neck and bracelets around his wrists. While the lack of dynamism and puny size of the lion may not suggest a particularly heroic struggle to our eyes, there are many precedents for this deliberate disregard for mimesis. In Neo-Assyrian art, for example, the lion-strangler figure is often much larger than the lion, thus emphasising the hero's strength. The animal fighter, often a king, was familiar to Mesopotamian and Iranian iconographic traditions, such as on a relief from the Palace of Sargon II in Khorsābād from the end of the eighth century BC (Fig. 8), where we can see the same pose of a hero gripping a small lion tucked under his arm.[42] This Khorsābād figure is usually identified as Gilgāmeš, the Sumerian hero, who was also part god. Just as Heracles

---

39 Ghirshman 1976. Many sculptural fragments were found at Masjed-e Solaimān, mostly limestone reliefs, showing male figures that the excavators wished to identify as Heracles, whether or not they were clothed, nude, bearded, unbearded, and whether or not a lion skin and club are present. The representation of a bearded man with closely cropped hair is a recurring motif in Iranian art of the Parthian period, however, and is not at all typical of how most male figures were represented. This has led to the identification of any such head as a head of Heracles, both at this site and at others, such as Failaka, often taken further as evidence of formal cult of Heracles (Connelly 1989).

40 Augé, Curiel, and Le Rider 1979.

41 Kawami 1987, 207 argues that the head is red-brown limestone and the body grey, so it is unlikely they belong together. The distinction between the two stones is difficult to discern by the naked eye, although it is clear that none of the breaks directly align.

42 Kawami 1987, 113.

Fig. 7: Limestone statue from Masjed-e Solaimān, Šuś Museum (Copyright: the author).

after his defeat of the Nemean lion, Gilgāmeš wore the skins of the pride of lions he killed, although his mortal prey lacked the defensive benefits of the Nemean lion's impermeable hide.[43] Problematic for our attempt to identify a specific myth is the fact that wrestling a lion was not a particularly distinct action in Iranian art belonging to the narrative of only one individual.[44]

Another example of a fighter tackling with his bare hands a smaller-scale lion can be found far closer in both chronological and geographical terms to the Masjed-e Solaimān sculpture than the Khorsābād relief. On the northwest face of a boulder at Tang-e Sarvak in eastern Khuzestān, fifty kilometres north of Behbahān, is a relief of a clothed man wearing a tall crown who grips a lion by the throat in his outstretched right hand. The accompanying inscription declares "this is the image of ... assuming

---

43 See West in this volume.

44 Downey 1969, 3–4 suggests the "transfer of symbolic force" between the Mesopotamian lion wrestler and Heracles.

Fig. 8: Lion-wrestler relief from the Palace of Sargon II, Khorsābād, Louvre AO 19862 (Copyright: Wikicommons Jean-Christophe Benoist).

the throne".[45] The protagonist's name was deliberately effaced but most probably pertained to a local dynast, perhaps an Abar-basi, who ruled in the area around AD 150.[46] Once again, the lion is raised up on its back legs and shown on a smaller scale to the victor. This composition, where the rearing lion is held at arm's length, is reminiscent of many such motifs in Achaemenid art, on cylinder seals and on the Persepolis reliefs of royal figures contending with real and fantastical creatures.[47] From this relief at Tang-e Sarvak we can see that the lion-wrestler motif was not monopolised or re-

---

45 Vanden Berghe and Schippmann 1985, fig. 11.

46 Henning 1952.

47 While the basic theme is similar, there are many variances between these depictions of Heracles and Achaemenid royal lion fighters. The Achaemenid heroes, like the Abar-basi relief, are fully

placed by the image of Heracles in Elymaean art, which suggests that the Heraclean figure had its own identity beyond that of the generic lion wrestler.[48]

The lion-wrestler motif is seen also in seal impressions on clay bullae from the Hellenistic period in Babylon and from Seleucia on the Tigris.[49] Once again, although to a lesser extent than in previous examples, the lion is smaller than real life, emphasising the extraordinariness of the hero, although this nude male figure is more dynamic and muscular than the previous example. There is real tension to this contest: the wrestler steps forward and leans down onto the rearing lion so that their bodies form a triangular composition. It should be noted, however, that depictions of nude male figures were very rare in Iranian and Mesopotamian art, particularly to represent a heroic figure.[50] Neither the generic appeal of lion wrestlers to this local audience, nor its limited use and patronage by Greco-Macedonian settlers and itinerant merchants fully explain the wide uptake of the Heraclean figure in Elymaean rock art of the second century AD.

Elymaean Repurposes

Heracles figures can be seen in two more Elymaean reliefs, where his image was reappropriated to suit local themes and without reference to his narrative cycle beyond the inclusion of his typical attributes, the club and lion skin. At both sites, the motif of holding a round cup in front of the chest was adopted, in the manner of the Bisotun Heracles, suggesting a local convention of the Heracles figure's representation. The first relief is at Šimbār (also called Tang-e Botān, "Valley of the Idols"), roughly 100 km northeast of Masjed-e Solaimān, perhaps dating to the beginning of the third

---

clothed, stand firmly upright, and hold the animal at arm's length while stabbing a dagger into its belly, and both the hero and monster are depicted in profile.

48 Heracles fighting the lion was also a popular motif in the art of Parthian Dura Europus (Downey 1969).

49 VA Bab 1823; Invernizzi et al 2004, III, pl. 1 Ek 16: S8–386. Another aspect to consider in discussing the popularity of Heracles figures, particularly those wrestling lions on seals and amulets, is raised by Faraone 2013's observations that a motif originally associated with a myth can have another function – that of apotropaic power. Images originating from mythological narrative can be employed for other reasons, and they are not necessarily indicative of sustained narrative understanding or the establishment of official cult practices.

50 See, for example, the victory relief of Anubanini of the Lullubi, from the third millennium BC. For a possible exception, see a cylinder seal in Berlin from the Ur III period (c. 2100 BC), VA 3605, where a long-bearded male figure, nude except for a loin-cloth, attacks a lion with a club, assisted by Ištar who holds the lion's tail.

century (Fig. 9).[51] Here, a long thin frieze was cut to form a deep recess in the rock, on which were carved twelve figures rendered in shallow relief. These figures are now badly weathered and their heads have been defaced. They seem to form five distinct groups seemingly directing the viewer from right to left, following the implied motion of their procession. In each of the first four groups, a nude male figure, wearing a diadem tied at the back of the head in large loops and flying ends, leans with his right arm on a club and holds his left hand in front of his chest, perhaps supporting a round cup on his fingers.[52] He is accompanied by a man wearing a knee-length ridged tunic and baggy trousers (although he has two companions in the second group). Each of these companions wears a roll of material over their left shoulder, suggesting a priestly function, and holds out the right hand to touch the figure in front.[53] Between each nude male figure and his accompanying priest is a small thin podium or altar, suggesting the naked figure was the object of worship in this region.[54] The relief seems to show successive generations of priests and their personal relationship with and veneration of the god, his guidance, and their attention to religious duties.[55] Among the Elymaean inscriptions above each altar that name the clothed figures is one that reads, "who is (keeper of) the altar of Bel".[56]

It therefore seems that we can assume that the relief depicts successive keepers, the altar, and Bel. This being so, the iconography of Heracles was employed to represent the Semitic god Bel rather than the Iranian Vahrām. Bel – "Lord" – was probably the head of the Elymaean pantheon, usually aligned with Zeus in the Classical literary sources, and is not known to bear resemblance to Heracles' characteristics or his associated myths.[57] Identifications of Zeus-Bel's image on coins of the Hellenistic and early Parthian period usually focus on enthroned and clothed male deities wearing

---

51 Dating according to Mathiesen 1992, 130 for Group I through comparison with the reliefs from Tang-e Sarvak, the Masjed-e Solaimān Heracles, and the Khwasak Stele from Susa (Irān-e Bastan Museum, Tehrān 844).

52 Vanden Berghe and Schippmann 1985, fig. 4.

53 Kawami 1987, 142–3.

54 Bivar and Shaked 1964, 269 note that there is a pestle and mortar in the hands of the priest in Group II. They argue that this would suggest the preparation of *haoma* and support a link of Elymaean religion to Zoroastrian ritual practice, but the identification is difficult to make out from photographs and drawings of the relief (see Vanden Berghe and Schippmann 1985, fig. 4 and pl. 13). The nomenclature of "fire altar" used to describe the small podia in this relief also presupposes a Zoroastrian interpretation for these reliefs.

55 Bivar and Shaked 1964, 287–90 on the phrase "taking the stool".

56 Bivar and Shaked 1964, 272. The Elymaean script is a form of Aramaic used in this region during the first and second centuries AD (Bivar and Shaked 1964, 266).

57 Antiochus III's death while plundering a temple in Elymais in 187 BC, referred to as a temple of "Zeus" (Diod.Sic. 28.3); "Bel" (Diod.Sic. 29.15; Strabo 16.1.18); and "Jupiter Elymaeus" (Justin 32.2.1–2). See also, Strabo 15.2.14, where Nearchus reports that the Carmanians worshipped a god of victory as their only god.

Fig. 9: Šimbar II (Copyright: L. Vanden Berghe).

a *polos*, rather than a nude figure holding a club.[58] The example of Šimbār speaks to the question of whether this image is a representation of a Semitic god or a translation of the honorific appellation "Lord" into the local language, just as "Bel" appears as a translation for Ahura Mazdā ("Wise Lord") in the Babylonian copy of Darius I's Bisotun inscription found in Babylon.[59] There has been an ongoing, somewhat proprietorial, debate concerning the character of Elymaean religion, its relationship to its Elamite forebear, and whether it can be regarded as belonging to the religions of its Iranian or Mesopotamian neighbours.[60] Perhaps the boundaries of categorisation between ancient religions were not so strict, or the relationships were more complex than might otherwise be assumed, as implied by a Bactrian document from the late fourth century where a "libation at the temple of Bel" is referred to alongside a reference to the Iranian wind deity, Vātu.[61]

The recurrence of a Heraclean figure at Tang-e Sarvak (Fig. 10) suggests that the image does refer to a major deity of the region, and not to discount the Šimbār relief as an anomaly, particularly since here he participates in commemorating the investiture of the local ruler.[62] On the south-eastern side of this gorge there are thirteen reliefs

---

58 See also Ba'altars on coins of Mazaios minted in Tarsus and Babylon.

59 Shaked and Naveh 2012, 261 n. 11. Hansman 1985, 245 prefers to see this "Lord" at Šimbār as a reference to an Elamite god.

60 Ghirshman 1976; Hansman 1985, 245; Henning 1952; Boyce and Grenet 1991, 45–8.

61 Shaked and Naveh 2012, 179–84.

62 Bivar and Shaked 1964, 269 assume the Šimbār frieze must have been carved on separate occasions over several decades due to the repetitive nature of the scenes. The action of adding to the frieze would thus form a ritual itself.

Fig. 10: Tang-e Sarvak I, from the west
(After Mathiesen 1992, fig. 15).

carved into four boulders along a track that was once a much-used route to the plain.[63] Carved into the north side of the boulder nearest the entrance to the valley, Rock I, is a two-metre tall nude male figure, probably dating to the end of the second century AD.[64] Over his outstretched left arm, which rests on a small club, hangs bunched material. It seems there was a round object in his right hand, held in front of his chest, perhaps the cup familiar from Bisotun, Šimbār, and the Orodes relief also at Tang-e Sarvak. To the right of this figure is another relief, perhaps added later but which joins this, where a figure with a roll of cloth over his shoulder approaches, his arm upraised towards the Heracles figure, a small stepped altar between them. Below left is a larger figure in a high tiara also holding up his right hand to the Heracles figure, labelled "this is the image of Orodes taking the throne".[65] The three reliefs create a complementary tiered image of king, priest, and god. Here we see how a very particular formulation of Heracles' image, holding a cup, was integrated into the local cult practice and playing a prominent role in the commemoration of the investiture of the local ruler.

The Iranian Heracles?

Near the Achaemenid capital Persepolis and the Sasanian capital of Istakhr is a series of four rock reliefs nicknamed Naqš-e Rajab. It is likely that the relief Naqš-e Rajab III was carved soon after Ardašir's investiture as King of Kings in AD 224, some seventy years after Vologases' inscriptions on the bronze statue found at Seleucia on the

---

63 Mathiesen 1992, 130–1 suggests Relief BS should be considered as the result of two separate commissions.
64 Mathiesen 1992, 145.
65 Bivar and Shaked 1964, 287; Vanden Berghe and Schippmann 1985, 60–5.

Tigris.[66] In this relief (Fig. 11), the king grasps a ribboned ring, held on the right by a larger figure, most likely representing Ahura Mazdā (MP Ohrmazd), to whom the king makes the common sign of deference by holding his hand to his mouth.[67] The ring signifies the personal bestowal of honour and approval on the king by the divinity, and thus the conferral of *farr* (Av. *khvarneh*, "divine glory"). In Ahura Mazdā's left hand is the *barsom*, a bundle of rods held by priests and worshippers during rituals in the presence of the sacred fire.[68] Between Ardašir and Ahura Mazdā stand two small figures that echo the composition of the larger pair.

The small figure on the right is a nude bearded male with a pudding-bowl haircut and wearing a torque around his neck (Fig. 12). In his right hand he holds out a stick. Rather than the even length of the *barsom* held by Ahura Mazdā above, this stick is wider at the top and seems to have knobbles like a club. Vanden Berghe's drawing depicts this stick as extending above the heads of the two figures with a peculiar circular sector end, which would be an interesting development of Heraklean iconography, but the weathering makes it difficult to be certain.[69] Under his left hand is a ridged column, which could be the crumpled lion skin. Weathering makes it too difficult to decipher whether the lion skin and club were recognisable as such or were reconfigured.[70] It seems, then, that Ardašir, proclaimed on his coinage as a "Mazdā-worshipper", included the image of a Greek god in one of the first public and permanent displays celebrating the divine approval of his rule and progeny in his Persian homeland.

---

66 Meyer 1990, 298. Daryaee 2010, 251 suggests this relief was commissioned earlier, upon Ardašir's investiture as king of Persis, thus perhaps explaining the anomalous iconography.

67 It is notable that although the figure identified as Ahura Mazdā is bodily larger than Ardašir, the king's *corymbus* (the ball of hair on his head, wrapped in silk) makes Ardašir the largest figure in the relief, in fact too large as the top of the *corymbus* is cut short.

68 To the left stands a page holding up a fly-whisk to the king and the diadem-wearing heir apparent, the future Šāpur I, who holds one hand to his mouth while his right (sword) hand is covered by his sleeve, two signs of deference. The identity of the two figures to the right of Ahura Mazdā is a subject of dispute. They face away from the scene and are separated from the rest of the relief by a pillar that supports a canopy over them. The figure furthest right wears a diadem around the rounded cap, the figure's hair falls in plaits over the shoulders, and it raises a hand to its mouth. This figure may be female, while the other is also beardless, but their short hair is hidden by an animal-headed cap (perhaps a lion's head). Identifications range from noble or royal women, to Ardašir's queen and a prince, to Anāhitā and, in the lion-headed cap, Mithra (Hinz 1969, 126). The idea that these two figures were part of a separate relief (Shenkar 2014, 51) is also an unsatisfying explanation due to the spatial constraints of the corner of the rock formation.

69 Hinz 1969, 122 tf.57 for a photograph of the relief before its restoration work and further weathering; Vanden Berghe 1984, fig. 9.

70 This separation of one image from its original meaning is not to suggest that lines of communication or cultural links with the Mediterranean world were severed entirely.

Fig. 11: Relief of Ardašir I, Naqš-e Rajab I (Copyright: the author).

The small figure on the left faces the Heracles figure and holds up his right hand in a gesture of respect. He wears a rounded tiara with a long ridged diadem and a knee-length belted tunic, and probably represents the eldest son of Šāpur I, Bahrām. Thus the king, Ardašir, faces the king of the gods, while the prince Bahrām faces his namesake, Vahrām (Middle Persian for the Avestan Verethragna). This relief attests to the continued legacy of Heracles' image in Iranian art, redeployed to depict an Iranian divine being, yet is there any correlation to a continued legacy of mythological narrative?

This representation is the only example of the image of Heracles employed in Sasanian rock reliefs (or, indeed, of any Greco-Roman divinity except Nike, shown on the spandrels of Tāq-e Bostān III) and probably the only representation of Vahrām in any form.[71] Allusions to Verethragna have been identified on Sasanian coins, such as the wings of a bird of prey included in the crown of another royal namesake, Bahrām II (r. AD 274–93), and on the crown of Peroz, whose name also means "victorious", (r. AD 459–84) after his release from Hephthalite captivity. These may be a reference

---

71 A late Sasanian column capital found at Tāq-e Bostān is generally referred to as depicting Verethragna, although there is little to support this identification.

Fig. 12: Detail, relief of Ardašir I, Naqš-e Rajab I (Copyright: the author).

to the Veregna bird of Verethragna, but may instead (or also) convey the possession of *khvarneh*.[72]

The choice of a nude male figure is striking since Zoroastrian sacred texts present so many other possible representations of Verethragna. By the time the oral tradition preserved in the Avesta was set down in the Sasanian period, there were ten manifestations of Verethragna who appeared to Zarathuštra. They are described in *Yašt* 14, the hymn to Verethragna: an impetuous wind, an armed warrior, an adolescent of fifteen, a bull with gold horns, a white horse with gold ears and muzzle, a virile camel, a boar, a ram, a wild goat, and a bird of prey – the Veregna bird.[73] His appearance, even when as a man, bears little resemblance to the material we've been looking at: rather than a bearded mature man, he is "running in the shape of a beautiful youth of fifteen, shin-

---

72 Curtis 2008, 140. Yt. 14.19–21.

73 Gnoli 1989, 511 notes that several of these incarnations were also applied to other divine figures, such as Tištrya (rain and fertility), Khvarneh (divine glory), and Vāyu (wind). This observation contributes to the doubt in identifying, for example, all wild boars in Sasanian art as avatars of Verethragna.

ing, clear-eyed, and thin-heeled"; or a man with a golden blade, not a club. Yet any comparison of the Zoroastrian descriptions with Sasanian or pre-Sasanian material is complicated by the nature of the scriptures, which were not fully codified until much later than the visual representations discussed here.[74]

Yašt 14 also describes Verethragna's qualities, which are similar to those of Heracles:

> I am the strongest in strength; I am the most victorious in victory; I am the most glorious in glory; I am the most favouring in favour; I am the best giver of welfare; I am the best-healing in health-giving. And I shall destroy the malice of all the malicious... the best-armed of the heavenly gods.[75]

Verethragna is the god "who makes virility, who makes death, who makes resurrection, who possesses peace, who has a free way." Somewhat unfortunately for our interests in this volume, there is little associated mythological narrative concerning Verethragna; the text focuses on praising his abilities. We might attempt to draw a faint analogy between the later Zoroastrian accounts of Verethragna binding Ahriman (Angra Mainyu) with Heracles' apotheosis since, after completing this seemingly impossible task, Verethragna was rewarded with elevation to the rank of Ameša Spenta (Bounteous Immortal).[76] This may bear loose similarity in narrative, but it is hardly a clear connection to Heracles' apotheosis. It seems that the visual conception and narratives surrounding Verethragna in Zoroastrian tradition or in Persian mythology were independent from any Heraklean associations, despite the similar qualities of the divinities and any earlier association between the two.[77] While we can see this one instance of Heracles' iconography used to represent Vahrām at Naqš-e Rajab, this type was then apparently abandoned.[78] Once again, this is a reminder that expectations of being able to discern continuity, consistency, and a logical chronological progression through the extant iconography can be misplaced.

---

74 The heterogeneity of Sasanian religion and its variances from what we would now recognise as Zoroastrian orthodoxy have been much discussed, such as Šāpur I's sponsorship of Mani, or evidence of ritual practices in caves, and the maintenance of image shrines.

75 Transl. available online at avesta.org.

76 Gnoli 1989, 513.

77 Melikian-Chirvani 1998, 186 suggests a resemblance between the Seven Labours of the Iranian hero Rostam in the tenth-century AD epic the *Šāhnāmeh* and Heracles, and attempts to identify the origin in the second to first century BC. Another loose similarity between the two heroes is that Rostam wears the head of his defeated foe, the Div-e Sepid (White Devil), as a helmet, and a tiger-skin cuirass.

78 A perceived abandonment of the Heracles image, whether intentional or not, could perhaps be supported by the re-use of Heracles' image into the terrace wall at Masjed-e Solaimān; yet this can hardly be taken as due to a purposeful rejection of Greco-Macedonian influences, since Verethragna was not represented elsewhere. It is also untenable to consider any connections to Greco-Roman culture as only legacies from the Macedonian conquest of the Achaemenid Empire in 331 BC rather than also influenced by contemporary contacts with the Mediterranean.

Concluding Thoughts

Mary Boyce went as far as to say that the popularity of Heracles in the Hellenistic period was a significant catalyst for the popularity of Verethragna, profoundly altering the character of the Zoroastrian divinity.[79] From an art-historical perspective, however, there is the significant problem that we have no certain attestations of the visual conception of Vahrām/Verethragna before the image of Heracles was widely dispersed and produced across Mesopotamia, Iran, and Central Asia. Despite the popularity of Heracles' image and the long-standing presence of Greco-Macedonian communities, it seems that the mythological repertoire of Heracles did not also become established in local traditions or integrated into ideas surrounding Verethragna. This is notwithstanding that the characters of the two divine beings (the associated virtues and values embodied by their personas) bear notable resemblance and that there are attestations of the alignment of their names with one image.

Images of Heracles in Iran continued to represent a virile warrior figure. He is often portrayed drinking, although in the sedate manner of a ruler rather than in the inebriated comic manner of Hellenistic sculpture. While the lion wrestler and lion hunter were established and familiar motifs in Iranian art, these had usually concerned fully clothed royal figures not nude deities, and there is no indication that the Parthian-period depictions of nude lion wrestlers refer to a Nemean beast. While the lion wrestler was a familiar motif with local resonances in visual tradition, the adoption of a nude male figure into the repertoire for gods and heroes was strikingly different. We can see the adoption of Heracles' image during the Parthian period into Elymaean religious practices; the association of Heracles with a local deity apparently so well established by the Sasanian period that the first ruler employed it to publicly display his dynastic succession; and the subsequent absence of Heracles' image to represent Vahrām/Verethragna. Heracles was plucked out of his mythological canon and his image retained to represent a local god, including visual references to that canon acting as his identifiers: the club and lion skin.

Heracles is the ultimate wandering hero in the material record of the ancient world, and yet, despite the movement of people in full knowledge of his stories and despite the existing local predisposition for the qualities he embodied, the retention of his mythological cycle is not recorded in either the visual or literary record of pre-Islamic Iran. There was a stronger vein of selectivity in the process of the adoption of Heracles' image into Iranian art than may have been recognised thus far. It would seem from this test case that something more than the movement of people and local predispositions for a subject is prerequisite for the persistence of myths.

---

[79] Boyce and Grenet 1991, 65.

Acknowledgment: With thanks to the Leverhulme Trust, the *Empires of Faith* project, and my colleagues at the British Museum and Wolfson College, Oxford.

Bibliography

Adrych, P., R. Bracey, D. Dalglish, S. Lenk and R. Wood. *Images of Mithra*, Visual Conversations in Art & Archaeology 1 (Oxford, 2017).

Al-Salihi, W. I. Hercules-Nergal at Hatra. *Iraq* 33 (1971), 113–115.

Al-Salihi, W. I. Hercules-Nergal at Hatra (II). *Iraq* 35 (1973), 65–68.

Al-Salihi, W. I. Mesene's Bronze Statue of "Weary Herakles". *Sumer* 43 (1984), 219–229.

Al-Salihi, W. I. The Weary Herakles of Mesene. *Mesopotamia* 22 (1987), 159–167.

Augé, C., R. Curiel and G. Le Rider (eds) *Terrasses sacrées de Bard-è Néchandeh et Masjid-i Solaiman: les trouvailles monétaires* (Paris, 1979).

Bernard, P. Héraclès, les grottes de Karafto et le sanctuaire du mont Sambulos en Iran. *Studia Iranica* 9 (1980), 301–324.

Bernard, P. Vicissitudes au gré de l'histoire d'une statue en bronze d'Héraclès entre Séleucie du Tigre et la Mésène. *Journal des Savants* (1990), 3–68.

Bivar, A. D. H. and S. Shaked. The Inscriptions at Shimbār. *Bulletin of the School of Oriental and African Studies* 27 (1964), 265–290.

Boyce, M. *A History of Zoroastrianism. vol. II. Under the Achaemenians* (Leiden, 1982).

Boyce, M. and F. Grenet. *A History of Zoroastrianism. vol. III. Zoroastrianism under Macedonian and Roman Rule* (Leiden, 1991).

Brijder, H. A. G. *Nemrud Dağı: Recent Archaeological Research and Conservation Activities in the Tomb Sanctuary on Mount Nemrud* (Boston, 2014).

Canepa, M. Bronze Sculpture in the Hellenistic East, in: *Power and Pathos: Bronze Sculpture of the Hellenistic World*, edited by J. M. Daehner and K. Lapatin (Florence, 2015), 82–93.

Carter, M. L. Aspects of the Imagery of Verethragna: the Kushan empire and Buddhist central Asia, in: *Proceedings of the Second European Conference of Iranian Held in Bamberg, 30th September to 4th October 1991, by the Societas Iranologica Europaea*, edited by B. G. Fragner et al. (Rome, 1995), 119–140.

Connelly, J. B. Votive Offerings from Hellenistic Failaka: evidence for Hercules cult, in: *L'Arabie pré-islamique et son environment historique et culturel.* Actes du colloque de Strasbourg, 24–27 juin 1987, edited by T. Fahd (Leiden, 1989), 145–158.

Connelly, J. B. Hellenistic Terracottas of Cyprus and Kuwait, in: *The Coroplast's Art. Greek Terracottas of the Hellenistic World*, edited by J. P. Uhlenbrock (New York, 1990), 94–101.

Curtis, V. S. Religious Iconography on Ancient Iranian Coins, in: *After Alexander. Central Asia before Islam*, edited by J. Cribb and G. Herrmann (Oxford, 2007), 413–434.

Curtis, V. S. Royal and Religious Symbols on Early Sasanian Coins, in: *Current Research in Sasanian Archaeology, Art and History. Proceedings of a Conference Held at Durham University, November 3rd and 4th, 2001, organized by the Centre for Iranian Studies, IMEIS and the Department of Archaeology of Durham University*, edited by D. Kennet and P. Luft (Oxford, 2008), 137–147.

Darbandi, S. and A. Zournatzi. (eds.) *Ancient Greece and Ancient Iran: Cross-cultural Encounters. 1st International Conference, Athens, 11–13 November 2006* (Athens, 2008).

Daryaee, T. The Fall of the Sasanian Empire to the Arab Muslims. From two Centuries of Silence to Decline and Fall of the Sasanian Empire: the Partho-Sasanian confederacy and the Arab conquest of Iran. *Journal of Persianate Studies* 3 (2010), 239–254.

De Jong, A. *Traditions of the Magi: Zoroastrianism in Greek and Latin Literature* (Leiden, 1997).

De Jong, A. Heracles. *Encyclopaedia Iranica* 12.2 (New York, 2003), 202–3.

Downey, S. B. *The Excavations at Dura-Europos. Final Report III.1.1: The Heracles Sculpture* (New Haven, 1969).

Duchesne-Guillemin, J. Art et religion sous les Sassanides. *Atti del convegno internazionale sul tema: La Persia nel Medioevo. (Roma, 31 marzo–5 aprile 1970)* (Rome, 1971), 377–388.

Faraone, C. A. Heraclean Labors on Ancient Greek Amulets: myth into magic or magic into myth?, in: *Mito y magia en Grecia y Roma*, edited by E. Suárez de la Torre and A. Pérez Jiménez (Zaragoza, 2013), 85–102.

Gatier, P.-L., P. Lombard, K. al-Sindi. Greek Inscriptions from Bahrain. *Arabian Archaeology and Epigraphy* 13 (2002), 223–233.

Ghirshman, R. *Terrasses sacrées de Bard-è Neìchandeh et Masjid-i Solaiman: l'Iran du sud-ouest du VIIIe s. av. n. ère au Ve s. de n. ère*, Mémoires de la délégation archéologique en Iran, 1 (Paris, 1976).

Gnoli, G. Bahram in Old and Middle Iranian Texts. *Encyclopaedia Iranica* 3 (New York, 1989), 510–513.

Hansman, J. The Great Gods of Elymais, in: *Papers in Honour of Professor Mary Boyce*. Acta Iranica 24 (Leiden, 1985), 229–246.

Haruta, S. Aramaic, Parthian and Middle Persian, in: *The Oxford Handbook of Ancient Iran*, edited by D. T. Potts (Oxford, 2013), 779–794.

Henning, W. B. Monuments and Inscriptions of Tang-e Sarvak. *Asia Major* (1952), 151–178.

Herzfeld, E. *Iranische Felsreliefs. Aufnahmen und Untersuchungen von Denkmälern aus alt- und mittelpersischer Zeit, von F. Sarre und E. Herzfeld* (Berlin, 1910).

Herzfeld, E. Am Tor von Asien (Berlin, 1920).

Hinz, W. Altiranische Funde und Forschungen (Berlin, 1969)

Invernizzi, A. Héraclès à Séleucie du Tigre. *Revue archéologique* 1 (1989), 65–113.

Invernizzi, A. and Lippolis, C. *Nisa partica: ricerche nel complesso monumentale arsacide, 1990–2006* (Florence, 2008).

Invernizzi, A., V. Messina, P. Mollo and A. Bollati. *Seleucia al Tigri: le impronte di sigillo dagli archivi 1. Sigilli ufficiali, ritratti 2. Divinità 3. Figure umane, animali, vegetali, oggetti* (Alexandria, 2004).

Junker, K. *Interpreting the Images of Greek Myths. An Introduction*, transl. A. and A. Snodgrass (Cambridge, 2012).

Kaizer, T. The "Heracles Figure" at Hatra and Palmyra: problems of interpretation. *Iraq* 62 (2000), 219–232.

Kawami, T. *Monumental Art of the Parthian Period in Iran* (Leiden, 1987).

Kleiss, W. Zur Topographie des "Partherhanges" in Bisitun. *Archäologische Mitteilungen aus Iran* 3 (1970), 133–169.

Luschey, H. Bisitun. Geschichte und Forschungsgeschichte. *Archäologischer Anzeiger* 89 (1974), 114–149.

Martinez-Sève, L. *Les figurines de Suse: de l'époque néo-élamite à l'époque sassanide* (Paris, 2002).

Mathiesen, H. E. *Sculpture in the Parthian Empire. A Study in Chronology* (Aarhus, 1992).

Melikian-Chirvani, A. S. Rostam and Herakles, a Family Resemblance. *Bulletin of the Asia Institute* 12 (1998), 171–199.

Menegazzi, R. *Seleucia al Tigri. Le terrecotte figurate dagli scavi italiani e americani* (Florence, 2014).

Meyer, M. Die Felsbilder Shapurs I. Mit 45 Abbildungen. *Jahrbuch des Deutsches Archäologischen Instituts* 105 (1990), 237–302.

Pappalardo, E. *Nisa Partica: i rhyta ellenistici* (Florence, 2010).

Potter, D. S. The Inscriptions on the Bronze Herakles from Mesene: Vologases IV's war with Rome and the date of Tacitus' 'Annales'. *Zeitschrift für Papyrologie und Epigraphik* 88 (1991), 227–290.

Potts, D. T. *The Archaeology of Elam. Formation and Transformation of an Ancient Iranian State*, 2nd ed. (Cambridge, 2015).

Rougemont, G. *Corpus Inscriptionum Iranicarum. Part II, Inscriptions of the Seleucid and Parthian Periods and of Eastern Iran and Central Asia. Vol. 1, Inscriptions in non-Iranian Languages. I. Inscriptions grecques d'Iran et d'Asie centrale* (London, 2012).

Russell, J. R. *Zoroastrianism in Armenia* (Harvard, 1987).

Seyrig, H. Héraclès-Nergal. *Syria* 24 (1944), 62–80.

Scarcia, G. Ricognizione a Shimbār. Note sull'Eracle iranico. *Oriens Antiquus* 18 (1979), 255–275.

Schuol, M. *Die Charakene: Ein mesopotamisches Königreich in hellenistisch-parthischer Zeit* (Stuttgart, 2000).

Shaked, S. and J. Naveh. *Aramaic Documents from Ancient Bactria (Fourth Century B.C.E.) from the Khalili Collections* (London, 2012).

Shenkar, M. *Intangible Spirits and Graven Images. The Iconography of Deities in the Pre-Islamic Iranian World* (Leiden, 2014).

Sinisi, F. Sources of the History of Art of the Parthian Period: Arsacid coinage as evidence for continuity of imperial art in Iran. *Parthica* 16 (2014), 9–59.

Soudavar, A. *The Aura of Kings: Legitimacy and Divine Sanction in Iranian Kingship* (Costa Mesa, 2003).

Van Buren, E. D. *Clay Figurines of Babylonia and Assyria*. Yale Oriental Series XVI (New Haven, 1930).

Van Ingen, W. *Figurines from Seleucia on the Tigris* (Ann Arbor, 1939).

Vanden Berghe, L. *Reliefs rupestres de l'Iran ancien: Bruxelles, Musées royaux d'art et d'histoire, 26 octobre 1983–29 janvier 1984* (Brussels, 1984).

Vanden Berghe, L. and K. Schippmann. *Les reliefs rupestres d'Elymaïde (Irān) de l'époque parthe* (Ghent, 1985).

Ziegler, C. *Die Terrakotten von Warka* (Berlin, 1962).

Katherine M. D. Dunbabin

The Transformations of Achilles on Late Roman Mosaics in the East

Achilles is ubiquitous in the arts of both Greece and Rome from the archaic period on-wards; the greatest of the heroes of the Trojan War has offered as attractive a subject to artists and their patrons as he did to poets.[1] In the later centuries of the Roman Empire his popularity enjoyed an extraordinary surge that lasted well into the Christian pe-riod; episodes of the Achilles saga are found in a very wide range of media at this time. On mosaics he is one of the most common of all mythological figures, comparable only to Heracles and the rather different case of Dionysus and his entourage. The stories of most other heroes – Perseus, Meleager, Bellerophon, for instance – have a single cen-tral episode, on which their representation in art most often concentrates, with only a few subsidiary incidents occasionally portrayed. In contrast, the Achilles saga offered a great variety of episodes for illustration, and it is on this variety and the different por-trayals of Achilles that I concentrate in this paper. My focus is on the Greek-speaking East, though examples from the western empire will be cited for comparison or con-trast where appropriate; the mosaics that I discuss run from the second century AD to the fifth or sixth. They share much of their iconographic material with works in other media, both contemporary and earlier, but the compositional freedom offered by a mosaic and the fact that almost all come from domestic contexts make them suit-able for discussion as a group.[2] As will be seen, the visual material reveals attitudes towards Achilles in Late Antiquity which are not always those that a casual observer might expect; the episodes of his story selected for illustration differ in a number of ways from those common at earlier periods. The ambivalence inherent in the charac-ter of the hero, frequently noted, lent itself to a wide range of different treatments; moreover some of the episodes handed down by tradition were inconsistent and even contradictory.[3]

The popularity of Achilles subjects in this period might most naturally be ascribed to the continuing role of the Homeric epics as the foundation of all education in Greek; the scenes might be regarded as expressive of the houseowners' desire to assert their

---

1 Kossatz-Deissmann 1981 collects the main scenes from the Achilles saga from all periods of Classi-cal Antiquity, listing 922 monuments. Earlier surveys in Bulas 1929; Kemp-Lindemann 1975; see also Bottini and Torelli 2006; Kossatz-Deissmann 2009.
2 I quote works in other media for comparison and parallels, but do not offer any comprehensive overview. Within the scope of this article it is not possible to discuss in more detail either finer regional variations and preferences among the mosaics in this area, or their chronological development.
3 For general overviews of the imagery of Achilles in Late Antiquity (especially on mosaics) see Delvoye 1984; Raeck 1992, 122–38; Ghedini 1997a; Ghedini 2001; Grassigli 2006; Ghedini 2009, esp. 42–9, 112–5.

https://doi.org/10.1515/9783110421453-015

devotion to Greek culture through the figure of the hero of the *Iliad*.[4] But while this element was undoubtedly always present, it is inadequate as an explanation of the roles that Achilles played in the art of the time. Very few of the Achilles scenes on mosaics show episodes that are actually derived from the *Iliad*; fewer still show him as the great warrior fighting before Troy. A number of monuments in various media, including one recently-discovered mosaic in Turkey, present a cycle of scenes constituting a biography of Achilles, and in these the Trojan episodes may play a part, but they seldom appear as independent subjects.[5] There is a tiny handful of mosaics, all from the West, that show the dragging of Hector, another handful with Priam before Achilles or the ransom of Hector.[6] Scenes of actual fighting are rarer still, in all media.

Far the most popular scene is the discovery of Achilles hidden among the maidens at the court of King Lycomedes on Skyros.[7] The story does not go back to Homer, perhaps not to any epic source. In its best-known form it is usually taken to have been introduced by Euripides in his *Skyrioi*; it is mentioned only briefly in the Hellenistic period, but became common among Roman poets of the first centuries BC and AD, and was treated in detail by Statius.[8] It also appeared in Roman art of the first century AD, for instance in a painting in the *Domus Aurea* and several at Pompeii, and was a favourite theme on sarcophagi, both Roman and Attic, in the second and third

---

4 Cf. Stefanou 2006, esp. 169–75. See for instance Leader-Newby 2004, 123–71 (esp. 125–41), on mythological scenes on silver plate in Late Antiquity as examples and demonstrations of *paideia*; Ewald 2004, 237–40, who concludes that the number and variety of Achilles scenes on Attic sarcophagi show "Achilles' enormous importance as a panhellenic hero and emblem of Attic *paideia*", and illustrate "the outstanding importance of Trojan themes in general and of Homer's *Iliad* in particular during the Second Sophistic".

5 Biographical cycles: below nn. 49–56; except on the Tensa Capitolina (n. 55), Trojan scenes are less prominent than those showing other aspects of Achilles' life. A more limited cycle composed entirely of Trojan scenes (pursuit and killing of Hector, ransom of Hector's body, plus Achilles and Briseis) appears on a brass jug now in Jerusalem, dating perhaps to the late fifth/early sixth century: Hengel 1982. For the mosaics at Haleplibahçe (Turkey) see below nn. 77–81.

6 The dragging of Hector on a fragmentary black-and-white mosaic from Ceccano, near Rome; one from the Vigna Brancadoro, now in the Vatican; and one from Nîmes, almost entirely restored: Stefanou 2006, 87–91; Kossatz-Deissmann 1981, nos. 611–13; possibly also on a very late mosaic from Santisteban del Puerto (Jaén): Kossatz-Deissmann 1981, no. 100; Ghedini 1997a, 253. A fourth to fifth-century mosaic in Faenza shows the ransom of Hector in the form of Priam before Achilles: Stupperich 1984, correcting the earlier interpretation of G. V. Gentili; one from Ulpia Traiana (Sarmizegetusa) is known only from a drawing. The rarer version of the ransom, with the weighing of Hector's body, appears on a mosaic from the late fourth-century villa at Tellaro: Voza 2003, 18–21, figs. 6–7; O. Touchefeu, "Hector", *LIMC* 4 (1988), 482–98, 483–4 no. 98 (with too early a date). See Ghedini 1997a, 253–6; Stefanou 2006, 92–107.

7 For a survey see Ghedini 2009, 84–90; ead. 1997a, 247–51; ead. 1997b; Muth 1998, 151–93.

8 Kossatz-Deissmann 1981, 58–69 (55–6 on the literary sources). Fantuzzi 2012, 21–97, examines the origins of the story and its treatment by both Greek and Latin writers down to the first century AD. For the story in Statius see Heslin 2005, ch.5.

centuries.[9] It is found, on our present knowledge, at least fifteen times on mosaics, distributed fairly evenly between eastern and western regions of the empire and the North African provinces.[10] One of the finest was found during the rescue excavations at Zeugma on the Euphrates, in the luxurious house known as the House of Poseidon; it dates from the first half of the third century AD.[11] The house is the grandest of those known at Zeugma, with mosaics in all the more public rooms, many of them with elaborate mythological scenes. The Achilles mosaic decorated a basin in a small fountain court, at the entrance to the huge triclinium; a thin veil of water covered it from a fountain spout at its centre (Fig. 1). Achilles in the centre brandishes a shield on his left arm, and clasps a spear in his right hand. He still wears woman's dress, now slipping off one shoulder and exposing his right leg; one foot has a woman's slipper, the other slipper is discarded beside him.[12] On the left side Deidameia hurries forward to restrain him, while her father Lycomedes, in royal robes and diadem, starts back beside her. Three other women, one probably Deidameia's nurse, and a bodyguard occupy the background. On the other side of Achilles, Odysseus, wearing his characteristic *exomis* and *pilos*, moves off to the right, but looks back at Achilles encouraging him to follow, and the head of a soldier blowing the trumpet can just be seen behind him. In the background are the columns of the royal palace.

A second example of the same subject has been found at Zeugma, of much the same date and similar in many respects: the entrance panel on the very fine triclinium mosaic in the House of Quintus, whose inner panel has the rare story of Theonoe and Leukippe.[13] Another version is found at Palmyra in the House of Achilles, as a panel set prominently in one portico of the small peristyle (Fig. 2).[14] It is badly damaged, but the iconography was generally similar to the Zeugma mosaics; the date is probably slightly later, the mid third century AD. The theme also appears, in simplified form with only Deidameia, Achilles, and Odysseus, on a mosaic from Kourion on Cyprus, which may date from the fifth century AD (Fig. 3); on one from Sparta it is

---

9 *Domus Aurea*: Kossatz-Deissmann 1981, no. 114; Pompeii paintings: ibid. nos. 107–113; Trimble 2002. Sarcophagi: Kossatz-Deissmann 1981, 61–4 nos. 128–165; Grassinger 1999, 25–43; Rogge 1995, 26–30, 99–102; Ewald 2004, 246–7. For possible Hellenistic prototypes (Athenion of Maroneia and/or Theon of Samos), see Kossatz-Deissmann 1981, nos. 105–6.

10 Ghedini 1997b, 691–2 n. 15, gives a list of 13 known to her at that date; some of them are questionable or too fragmentary to be deciphered. See also Kossatz-Deissmann 1981, 59–61 nos. 117–127; Muth 1998, 156 n. 575.

11 Abadie-Reynal 2002, 755–8; Önal 2002, 22–6; Darmon 2005, 1290–1; M. Önal, in Abadie-Reynal and Ergeç 2012, 67–72. The basin and fountain are later additions to the space: C. Abadie-Reynal, in Abadie-Reynal and Ergeç 2012, 235.

12 For the motif of the discarded slipper, found also on other examples of the theme in various media, see Balty 2013, 125–7.

13 Önal 2008, 268–70; M. Önal, in Abadie-Reynal and Ergeç 2012, 53–8; cf. Dunbabin 2010, with refs.

14 Balty 2014, esp. 37–44, updating the earlier study of Stern 1977, 15–22.

Fig. 1: Zeugma, House of Poseidon, fountain-basin. Mosaic of Achilles on Skyros. First half of 3rd century. Gaziantep, Zeugma Mosaic Museum. Photo Zeugma Archaeological Project, courtesy Kutalmiş Görkay.

reduced to two women, one of them nude, clutching at Achilles.[15] In the West the examples run from a small wall *emblema* from the House of Apollo at Pompeii (VI 7,23) to the magnificent scene from the main reception room of the great villa at Pedrosa de la Vega (La Olmeda) in northern Spain, certainly of the fourth century.[16] Two more unusual versions come from St-Romain-en-Gal in France and from Orbe-Boscéaz in Switzerland; both place Odysseus and the trumpeter on the roof of the palace, apart from Achilles and the maidens.[17] In western North Africa the scene occurs three times, at Thysdrus (El Djem) in Africa Proconsularis, and Tipasa and Caesarea (Cherchel) in Mauretania Caesariensis; on the last two it is combined with other episodes of the

---

15 Kourion: Michaelides 1987, 32–3 no. 33, pl. XIV. Ascribed there probably to the first half of the fourth century, which seems to me too early. Sparta: Kossatz-Deissmann 1981, no. 124.

16 Pompeii: Kossatz-Deissmann 1981, no. 122; Pedrosa de la Vega: Kossatz-Deissmann 1981, no. 121. Two others, at Santisteban del Puerto (Spain) and Keynsham (Britain), are more doubtful: Ghedini 1997b, 691–2 n. 15.

17 St-Romain-en-Gal/Ste Colombe: Kossatz-Deissmann 1981, no. 125. Orbe-Boscéaz: Paratte 2005.

Fig. 2: Palmyra, House of Achilles, Achilles on Skyros. Mid 3rd century. Central panel (in present state) 4.13 × 1.98 m. Palmyra Museum. Photo Archive Henri Stern, infographie Marc Balty (courtesy Janine Balty).

Achilles saga.[18] Finally, the scene can be identified on the fragments of a badly damaged mosaic at Ptolemais in Cyrenaica.[19]

The mosaics differ very widely in their style and composition, reflecting a time-span from the first century AD to (probably) the fifth, and a geographical diffusion from East, West, and South of the empire. They also differ in their iconography. On most of the western mosaics (apart from the early wall-mosaic from Pompeii) Achilles is nude, his female clothing discarded or reduced to a minimum; in the eastern examples he is still wearing women's dress, exposing no more than a leg or part of his chest. His body may lean to the left or the right, and the shield may still rest on the ground or be raised high in his left hand. The number of secondary figures, especially of the women, varies, as do their actions; Diomedes may be present with Odysseus; the setting differs. Despite all these variations, one or two basic iconographic schemes can be identified ultimately lying behind them, especially for the central characters, Achilles and Odysseus; the mosaicists draw on a common figurative stock, but use these ele-

---

18 El Djem: Kossatz-Deissmann 1981, no. 123; Russenberger 2002, 54–62. Tipasa: Kossatz-Deissmann 1981, no. 117; Raeck 1992, 124–6; Russenberger 2002, 62–9. Cherchel: Kossatz-Deissmann 1981, no. 118; Ferdi 1986; Raeck 1992, 127. For the other scenes on the two pavements see below, nn. 45–6.

19 Villa of Leukaktios: Mickocki 2004, 30, pl. X; Mikocki 2005; Kossatz-Deissmann 2009, add.13. The fragments had fallen from an upper storey, and the design was only partially recovered. It certainly contained a scene of the discovery on Skyros; Deidamia is identified by an inscription, the names [Achil]leus, Odysseus, and Diomedes survive, but not in place. Another figure, running from one side, is labelled Briseis (a mistake?); the entrance to an architectural structure is labelled *Parthenon*. Fragments of at least one other scene survived, perhaps part of the Skyros story.

Fig. 3: Kourion, Building of Achilles Mosaic, Achilles on Skyros. Perhaps 5th century. 3.85 × 2.37 m. Photo with the kind permission of the Director of the Department of Antiquities, Cyprus (courtesy Demetrios Michaelides).

ments freely to create something new each time.[20] The same schemes are identifiable also in other media, for instance in the painting of the *Domus Aurea* and on numerous sarcophagi, again with great variation in the way they are handled.[21]

An enormous amount has been written about Achilles on Skyros, and there have been many subtle readings of the varied composition of these scenes and the different messages that they may have conveyed in their specific contexts.[22] The fundamental sense of the Skyros episode is clearly the self-revelation of the hero, rejecting the life of soft luxury for that of manly virtue and his warlike destiny; but it can be tempered, to a greater or lesser degree, by the erotic elements: Achilles as the lover of Deidameia, who tries in vain to hold him back, or as the general object of female desire, surrounded and clutched by a bevy of maidens. In the eastern versions the ambivalent, feminine side

---

20 Ghedini 1997b, esp. 699, on iconographical variations and relations between different scenes.

21 *Domus Aurea*: above n. 9. Sarcophagi: above n. 9.

22 Ghedini 1997a; Muth 1998, 151–93, with especial emphasis on the mosaic from Pedrosa de la Vega and the three North African examples, from Thysdrus, Tipasa, and Caesarea/Cherchel; Russenberger 2002, refining the interpretation given by Muth. For the polysemy of the image, on mosaics and sarcophagi, see Balty 2013, with criticisms of the approach of Muth. Cf. also Trimble 2002, on paintings of the theme at Pompeii.

of the disguised Achilles is much more apparent; emphasis is placed on the transformation, the male body emerging from the female clothing. My concern in this paper is not with the specific way(s) in which viewers might have read any one of these scenes, nor with the message that each patron may have been wishing to convey, but with the flexibility of the scene and its potential to be adapted to so wide a range of meanings. Nevertheless, a central core persists through all the changes and variations, which allows the underlying story to be identified, and is essential if the image is to have any meaning at all.[23]

I return later to the question of the relationship between these scenes in art and the ways that the same subject is used in the literature of the time. But there is also a close relationship between the scenes found on the mosaics (especially in the East) and the contemporary theatre.[24] Several authors tell us that the Skyros episode was a favourite theme in pantomime, where the solo dancer presented each character in turn, both male and female. Libanios in his speech "On behalf of the Dancers", singles it out:

> the dancer displayed for you the many Lycomedian maidens, the work and tools of girls, and has represented Achilles playing the part of a maiden. Don't worry; he won't stop the dance at this point; Odysseus is coming to the door ..., and the son of Peleus is revealing what he really is instead of what he seems to be. (*Or.* 64.68).

It is noteworthy that the second Zeugma mosaic of Achilles on Skyros pairs it with the story of Theonoe and Leukippe, whose heroine, Leukippe, disguises herself as a man.[25] Theatre and domestic art belong to the same world and share the same interests, here especially in gender ambivalence, the relationship of sexes, the definition of "male" and "female", and the transformation of one to the other.

Other episodes that present Achilles primarily as lover are also popular on mosaics. The stage before his discovery on Skyros, while he was hiding among the maidens, appears on a fragmentary mosaic of the early third century from the so-called House of the Porticoes at Seleucia Pieria, the port of Antioch. A portico here contained a number of panels, on one of which Achilles and Deidameia are seated side by side, identified by their names above them (Fig. 4).[26] The same subject probably appeared on another fragmentary panel, from Nablus (Shechem) in Palestine, where inscrip-

---

23 This core might be confined to Achilles, Deidameia, and Odysseus, as at Kourion (above n. 15). Only on the mosaic from Sparta (above n. 15), where Odysseus is absent, does all notion of the underlying sense appear to have been lost, and the scene reduced to a titillating image.

24 I have discussed this at greater length in Dunbabin 2014.

25 Above n. 13. Cf. Dunbabin 2010, 425–6; Dunbabin 2014, 231–4; both with earlier references.

26 Levi 1947, 110–2, pl. XVIIIe. The plan of the building from which these panels come does not look like that of an ordinary house; Levi 1947, 116, suggests that it may have been a *palaestra* or gymnasium; Ghedini 1997b, 692, that it may have housed a corporation of athletes, corresponding to the athletic subjects found on a number of the mosaics from elsewhere in the building.

Fig. 4: Seleucia Pieria, House of Porticoes, Achilles and Deidameia. Early 3rd century. Photo Antioch Expedition Archives (neg. 4814), Department of Art and Archaeology, Princeton University.

tions give the names of Deidameia and Achilles; all that remains is the veiled head of Deidameia, above which a servant holds what appears to be another veil.[27] The theme is found occasionally in other media, for instance on an ivory *pyxis* of the fifth to early sixth century, probably of Syrian origin and now in Xanten, where Achilles is seated playing the lyre, with Deidameia standing affectionately beside him (Fig. 5 a). On the other side of the *pyxis*, continuing the narrative, is the scene of the discovery (Fig. 5 b).[28] The scene also formed part of a series of mosaic panels constituting a narrative sequence at Seleucia/Antioch; one panel showed an earlier episode with Thetis and Chiron, the rest were badly damaged, but the name Diomedes on one shows that

---

[27] Dauphin 1979; Talgam 2014, 56–9 fig. 84. Talgam dates it to the third quarter of the third century, perhaps too early.

[28] Stiftsmuseum Xanten, Inv. Nr. B 2: Volbach 1976, 72 no. 96; Weitzmann 1979, 236 no. 211; von Gonzenbach 1984, 306; Raeck 1992, 123–4; Grote 1998, 69–72. The discovery scene adds the detail of Deidameia holding out the baby Pyrrhus towards Achilles as he seizes the weapons. For the (very few) parallels on sarcophagi for this earlier scene of Achilles and Deidameia, see Levi 1947, 111.

Fig. 5: (a) Xanten, ivory pyxis with scenes of Achilles on Skyros. Achilles and Deidameia, approached by Odysseus with gifts. Probably 5th to early 6th century. © Stiftsmuseum Xanten, Photo Stephan Kube, Greven. (b) Xanten, ivory pyxis with scenes of Achilles on Skyros. Discovery of Achilles. Probably 5th to early 6th century. © Stiftsmuseum Xanten, Photo Stephan Kube, Greven.

it must have been the discovery scene.[29] A scene with Chiron also appeared at Nablus; I return later to it, and to the cycles of the education of Achilles.[30]

Of Achilles' other lovers, the story of Briseis is popular in both East and West. Sometimes, especially on earlier monuments, there is an evident intention to suggest to the viewer the Homeric story of the abduction of Briseis in *Iliad* 1 (327–56); but the details of Homer's account are never followed literally and are often lost sight of altogether. The focus is more on the romantic relationship between the two lovers and the sadness of their parting than on the wrath and injured pride of Achilles.[31] On a mosaic now in Malibu, of unknown but presumably Syrian origin, two heralds appear, evidently preparing to lead Briseis away, while Achilles is flanked by Patroclus and an old man who must be Phoenix, not mentioned at this point in the *Iliad*; Achilles rests one arm on a large lyre, and stares into the distance (Fig. 6).[32] On a third-century mosaic

---

29 Levi 1947, 112–5, pl. XVIIIf; either Thetis delivering the young Achilles to Chiron, or (more probably) receiving him from Chiron at the end of his education.

30 Below nn. 47, 49–56.

31 For the earlier history of the Briseis story in art see A. Kossatz-Deissmann, "Briseis" *LIMC* 3 (1986), 156–67; for its post-Homeric treatment in literature and the handling of the emotional relationship between her and Achilles in Latin poets, see Fantuzzi 2012, 99–185. For the mosaics and their relationship, or lack of it, to the Homeric text, see Stefanou 2006, 57–87.

32 Malibu, J. Paul Getty Museum 68.AA.12: von Gonzenbach 1975, with too early a date in the mid second century; Stefanou 2006, 60–4. The early third century seems to me more likely. The figures of Briseis and one of the heralds are badly damaged. Meyer 2002 interprets the mosaic as a literal render-

from the House of Aion at Antioch there is one herald, labelled as Talthybios, standing between Achilles and Briseis and preparing to lead her away (Fig. 7). Achilles holds his lyre in one hand, and stretches out the other towards Briseis; the two lovers gaze at one another sadly.[33] A similar composition appears on a mosaic in the late fourth-century villa at Carranque in Spain, where again Achilles and Briseis look sadly at one another. Between them stands a third figure, leading Briseis, but the damage he has suffered prevents easy identification.[34] Achilles leans here on a shield, not a lyre, and holds in his other hand what appears to be a tablet or diptych, a detail without parallel elsewhere in this scene.[35] On a fragmentary mosaic in the Casa dei Capitelli Ionici at Hierapolis in Phrygia, perhaps of the fifth century, the heads of three figures survive, two males labelled AIAS and PHOINIX, and an unlabelled female, presumably Briseis; a nude figure seated or reclining to the right must be Achilles.[36]

Scholars anxious to see in scenes such as these literal illustrations of the Homeric story have been puzzled by these divergences, and have argued over the precise episode illustrated: the Abduction of Briseis in *Iliad* 1, her return to Achilles in *Iliad* 19, or a "contamination" with elements taken from the Embassy in *Iliad* 9?[37] Achilles' lyre (one of his most characteristic attributes in art) has been taken to come from Book 9; neither Phoenix nor Ajax should be present at the Abduction, nor Briseis at the Embassy. In fact none of these scenes corresponds exactly to the Homeric account of any of these episodes, and the question is misconceived.[38] The mosaicists and their patrons were not concerned to re-tell Homer's account, but to illustrate the broad out-

---

ing of the scene of the embassy in *Iliad* 9, identifying the woman implausibly as Achilles' concubine Diomede and the second herald as Odios, two minor figures otherwise unknown to Roman art.

33 Levi 1947, 196, pl. XLIIIc; Stefanou 2006, 66–8. Compare another fragment from Antioch, with two heralds and part of Patroclus leading Briseis: Mosaic of Briseis' Farewell, Levi 1947, 46–9, pl. VIIIa; Stefanou 2006, 64–6.

34 Carranque: Fernández Galiano 1994, 205–7, who identifies the third figure as Ulysses returning Briseis to Achilles; Lancha 1997, 168–70 no. 83, with identification as the abduction of Briseis; Ghedini 2001, 66–7; Stefanou 2006, 69–77. The third figure is wearing a helmet, inappropriate for Odysseus/Ulysses, who almost always wears a *pilos*. He may be a herald, lacking his usual *caduceus*; I think it more likely that here it is a soldier who is taking Briseis away.

35 Lancha 1997, 170 suggests that this object might be a farewell present for Briseis, or a love poem, neither of which is convincing. If rightly identified as a tablet, it should be a letter, perhaps a message commanding the removal of Briseis. Clearly this has nothing to do with the text of the *Iliad*, at any point.

36 Zaccaria Ruggiu 2007, 235–44, who suggests a date after the earthquake of the late fourth century. At least one other figure was originally shown, probably Odysseus according to Zaccaria Ruggiu. The figured scene occupies a panel in a floor which also contained various animals, birds, and a pair of pancratiasts, set into the compartments of a geometric design.

37 E.g. Weitzmann 1954; Carandini 1965, 14–17; for a recent example of this approach see Meyer 2002 (above n. 32).

38 The subject of Achilles and Briseis appears on a number of other artworks from the Late Antique period, such as the engraved bronze bucket known as the Secchia Doria, or a bronze plaque in the British Museum (Carandini 1965); many repeat very similar iconographic motifs to those found on

Fig. 6: Unknown provenance, probably from Syria, mosaic of Achilles and Briseis. Probably early 3rd century. 217 × 227 cm. Malibu, J. Paul Getty Museum 68.AA.12. Photo J. Paul Getty Museum, Villa Collection, Malibu, California (Open Content).

line of the story and to present a picture of the emotional or dramatic experiences of the characters, in a way that fits the space to be decorated and the atmosphere that they wished to evoke.[39] Viewers would be familiar with the story, not only (if educated) from the *Iliad* and from its treatment by subsequent poets, but also from other

(some of) the mosaics, and show similar conflations of details from various stages of the story. For the iconographical history of the motif see Weitzmann 1954, who believed that these correspondences confirmed his theory (now outmoded) of the existence of an illustrated manuscript serving as archetype, in which all these episodes appeared separately; Carandini 1965, 13–19; contrast Simon 1967, who suggests that the version of the story of Briseis on the Secchia Doria is not derived from the *Iliad*, but reflects the way it might have been presented on the contemporary stage in a pantomime.

39 Another version of the Briseis story appears on the mosaic of the Seven Wise Men at Mérida (Spain), probably from the fourth century: Lancha 1997, 218–23, no. 106, pls. J, CII-CIII; Stefanou 2006, 77–87, both with earlier references. Here again it has proved impossible to identify satisfactorily the episode represented, but the context offers an explanation. The scene apparently serves to indicate the subject under discussion by the Wise Men seated above it – discussed for the moral qualities exemplified in the story as a whole, not for the exact details – and doubtless to encourage similar discussions among the assembled guests in the room.

Fig. 7: Antioch, House of Aion, mosaic of Achilles and Briseis. 3rd century. Excavation photograph in situ. Photo Antioch Expedition Archives (neg. 5600), Department of Art and Archaeology, Princeton University.

works of art, from presentations on the stage, and from numerous other contemporary references, to which I return later. We should not assume that any one of these was necessarily uppermost in the minds of creators or viewers, and all of them might introduce variants into the original Homeric account.

An extreme example of the detachment of the actors of the Briseis story from any narrative context can be seen on a mosaic from a house in Madaba (Jordan), dating probably as late as the first half of the sixth century (Fig. 8). Achilles and Patroclus stand frontally side by side, their names written above them in a barbarous Greek; Patroclus holds a spear, Achilles his lyre, both are nude, except for long cloaks. Beside Achilles is a woman, who must be Briseis, though the name is garbled (and half missing); above her head a pair of Erotes hold a crown.[40] There is no action, nor any attempt to tell a story; the characters are simply presented for the viewers' contemplation.

Other mosaics show a third of Achilles' love-episodes, entirely un-Homeric though at least partially derived from the epic cycle, Achilles and the Amazon queen Penthe-

---

40 Piccirillo 1989, 136–7; Piccirillo 1993, 76–7, pl. 32. The woman's name is given as *Eubre[...*; there was a lacuna on her other side which could have held the rest of the name. I have discussed the reading of the inscriptions on this mosaic in Dunbabin 2014, 237–9. A Byzantine (late sixth-early seventh century) silver plate now in the Hermitage has a similar array of three figures, probably to be interpreted as Briseis, Achilles, and Patroclus, presented to the viewer without identifiable action: Hengel 1982, 34, pl. XXIII.

Fig. 8: Madaba, mosaic of Patroclus, Achilles, and Eubre[...], before restoration. After Piccirillo 1989, fig. p.136, courtesy Studium Biblicum Franciscanum, Jerusalem.

silea.[41] On a mosaic from the Villa of Herodes Atticus at Eva/Loukou, in Arcadia, he holds her lifeless body in his arms, echoing the scheme of a well-known sculptural group (Fig. 9). The visual parallel was explicit; the mosaic occupied a panel in the portico of the peristyle, while an over-lifesized copy of the sculptural group stood nearby (Fig. 10).[42] Fragments show that there was a pendant sculpture on the other side of the peristyle with the so-called Pasquino Group, similar in composition to Achilles and Penthesilea; apparently it too was echoed in a panel of mosaic, which is not yet published. The Pasquino Group is usually identified as Menelaus with the body of Patroclus, but an alternative interpretation sees it as Ajax (or possibly Odysseus) with the

---

41 Cf. E. Berger, "Penthesileia", *LIMC* 7 (1994), 296–305; Ghedini 2001, 62–4; for the motif on sarcophagi see Grassinger 1999, 153–4; Ewald 2004, 254. For the literary tradition and the question of the way the theme of Achilles' love for the Amazon may have been treated in the *Aithiopis*, see Fantuzzi 2012, 267–86.

42 Spyropoulos 2006, 83–7, fig. 10; 136–7 (on the mosaic of the Pasquino group, not illustrated); 148, fig. 40; also Spyropoulos and Spyropoulos 2003; Spyropoulos 2012. The sculpture group probably dates to the mid second century; the Penthesilea mosaic appears to be substantially later, probably fourth-early fifth century. For the sculpture group and its reconstruction see E. Berger in *LIMC* 7 (1994), 303–4 nos. 59–67, with references; Gensheimer and Welch 2013.

Fig. 9: Eva/Loukou, Villa of Herodes Atticus, mosaic of Achilles and Penthesilea. Probably 4th to early 5th century. Photo courtesy George Spyropoulos.

body of Achilles.[43] With either interpretation, the contrast is poignant: Achilles holding the woman whom he has just killed and loved too late, balanced against either the recovery of the body of his friend or that of his own corpse. The further reflection of the two sculptures in the nearby mosaics is, to my knowledge, without parallel: a highly sophisticated visual play of allusions and echoes.

Two other versions of the Achilles and Penthesilea scene survive on mosaics, from different parts of the Roman world. At Apollonia in Epirus the scene (damaged) forms part of a wider composition of fighting Amazons, without apparently further focus on Achilles himself.[44] But at Caesarea/Cherchel in Mauretania Caesariensis it is one of three scenes, combined with Chiron teaching the young Achilles to play the lyre

43 For the Pasquino group see L. Kahil, "Menelaos", *LIMC* 8 (1997), 838 no. 32, with references; Ridgway 1990, 275–83, on the possible significance of the original (and of at least some of the replicas) as Ajax (or Odysseus?) with the body of Achilles. On the relationship between the two groups, also used as pendants in the Hadrianic Baths at Aphrodisias, at least in their Late Antique phase, see Gensheimer and Welch 2013, esp. 362–64.

44 Briefly mentioned in *Mosaïques de l'Albanie/Mozaike te Shqiperise*, Tirana 1974, 6, figs. pp. 22–6. A warrior slaying an Amazon on a mosaic at Complutum (Alcalá de Henares, Spain) is generally taken to show Achilles and Penthesilea, but the figures are not named, and the action is too general for specific identification (Fernández Galiano 1984, 16–19, 48–53; Ghedini 1997a, 259).

Fig. 10: Eva/Loukou, Villa of Herodes Atticus, sculptural group of Achilles and Penthesilea. Probably 2nd century. Photo courtesy George Spyropoulos.

and the Discovery on Skyros.[45] Achilles cradles the dying head of the Amazon more gently than in the other examples; a warrior to the left may be Thersites. The three panels at Cherchel appear selected, not just to tell the story of Achilles, but to convey a more pointed message: it was Achilles' education by Chiron that prepared him to make the decision to reject the life of luxury and to become the great warrior, but that also encouraged his more humane streak, the moment of pity and love in the midst of the fighting.

Several of the mosaics just discussed combine, like the Cherchel pavement, more than one episode from the Achilles saga. At Tipasa, also in Mauretania Caesariensis, two panels show the Discovery on Skyros below a scene from the education by Chiron.[46] The sequence on two eastern mosaics, at Seleucia/Antioch and at Nablus, is too damaged for reconstruction of the underlying programme, but both certainly included at least one scene with Chiron and one with the Skyros story.[47] It is not clear whether

---

45 Ferdi 1986; Ferdi 2006, 127–32, nos. 101–3, pls. XLIII, LXXXVIII–IX; she dates the pavement to the second half of the fourth century; Raeck 1992, 127; Muth 1998, 186–9. All three panels are damaged.
46 Raeck 1992, 124–6; Ghedini 1997a, 246–51; Muth 1998, 190–2; Russenberger 2002, 62–9; the upper panel showed Thetis retrieving Achilles from Chiron. A fragmentary panel below, with ships, may possibly have continued the sequence with a scene of Achilles' departure for Troy with the Greek fleet, but may have been unrelated in subject.
47 Seleucia: above nn. 26, 29. Nablus: above nn. 27, 30; below n. 62.

the selection of scenes on these mosaics was intended to constitute a coherent "biography" of the hero, or, like that at Cherchel, was limited to presenting pendants or bringing out a moral *exemplum*.[48]

A series of other monuments from Late Antiquity do present a biographical cycle of Achilles scenes starting with his birth, and illustrating in detail his childhood and education.[49] The great silver Achilles plate from the mid-fourth century treasure

Fig. 11: Kaiseraugst Treasure, Achilles plate. Central medallion with Achilles on Skyros, rim frieze with scenes of childhood of Achilles. Second quarter 4th century. Diam. 53 cm. Römermuseum Augst Inv. 62.1. Augusta Raurica, Photo Suzanne Schenker.

---

48 For scenes from the Achilles saga arranged as pendants in houses at Pompeii, see Ghedini 2009, 36–9.

49 See von Gonzenbach 1984, 301–7; Raeck 1992, 128–38; Ghedini 2009, 42–9; earlier Guerrini 1961 (who knows only a limited number of the monuments involved); Manacorda 1971, whose study is

from Kaiseraugst in Switzerland has ten separate scenes around the rim: his birth, his mother Thetis dipping him in the Styx to make him invulnerable, successive episodes of his education by the centaur Chiron, including his nourishment on the marrow of wild beasts, his training in hunting, athletics, but also in reading, then his delivery by Thetis to Lycomedes in the guise of a girl, and his life among the maidens, which includes the scene of Achilles playing the lyre for Deidameia. The final scene, the discovery on Skyros, occupies the central medallion, on a larger scale (Fig. 11).[50] No later episode is shown, and some scholars have argued that there may have been a companion plate, with the events from Troy; this is possible, but not necessary.[51] Other monuments with similar cycles show the same focus on the childhood scenes, but also include some later episodes.[52] On the "Capitoline puteal", the rim of a marble table of the fourth to fifth century in a thirteenth-century setting, successive episodes run from Achilles' birth and dipping in Styx, and his education by Chiron, to Skyros; there follow the duel with Hector and the dragging of Hector's body.[53] The ransom of Hector, which might be expected to conclude the sequence, is missing here; it forms the central scene on an early fifth-century series of rectangular dishes of *terra sigillata chiara* with moulded decoration from North African workshops, where the rim frieze shows again his birth, childhood, and education, as far as Skyros, as well as the wedding of his parents Peleus and Thetis (Fig. 12).[54] Fullest of all is the sequence on the decorative bronze cladding of a carriage in Rome known as the Tensa Capitolina, again clearly fourth-century.[55] This balances six scenes of Achilles' childhood, from the bath in Styx to Skyros (Fig. 13 a), against six of his deeds at Troy, which include

---

marred by his attempt to associate the Kaiseraugst plate with the emperor Julian, and to see the theme of the *paideia* of Achilles as an example of pagan propaganda against the Christians.

50 Von Gonzenbach 1984, 225–300; Leader-Newby 2004, 125–30. An inscription on the base gives the name of Pausilypos in Thessalonike, indicating that it may have been produced in the imperial silver workshops in that city. A similar scene of the discovery on Skyros forms the central medallion on the Achilles plate from the Sevso Treasure; but the rim frieze there has only the birth of Achilles, and is otherwise devoted to different subject matter, largely Dionysiac: Mundell Mango 1994, 153–80; Leader-Newby 2004, 130–7.

51 Raeck 1992, 132–4.

52 For a list see Ghedini 2009, 45. More limited sequences appear on other monuments, such as the Secchia Doria (above n. 38), and the brass jug in Jerusalem (above n. 5), but they lack the biographical element.

53 Rome, Musei Capitolini 64: von Gonzenbach 1984, 303–4; Dresken-Weiland 1991, 91–9, 346–8 Kat. 5, figs. 137–43; M. Cima, in Bottini, Torelli 2006, 152–5, who suggests that it may have been manufactured in Egypt.

54 Garbsch 1980; Von Gonzenbach 1984, 304–6; Garbsch and Overbeck 1989, 164–74, with earlier references; Raeck 1992, 128–31.

55 Ghedini 2009, esp. chs. II–III. Ghedini identifies the bronze sheets as cladding for a carriage for private transportation, with a date in the second quarter of the fourth century (17, 188). On a second frieze of smaller scenes ("ciclo piccolo") seven of the larger ones are repeated, and all but one of the Trojan scenes omitted.

Fig. 12: Dish (*lanx*) of terra sigillata chiara with moulded decoration from North African workshop, reconstructed on basis of several fragments. Central scene of Priam before Achilles, rim frieze of scenes from childhood of Achilles, at top marriage of Peleus and Thetis. Early 5th century. Drawing after Garbsch 1980, Abb. 1.

not only the canonical scenes of the duel and dragging of Hector and ransom of his body, but also two with the very rare story of his death at the hands of Apollo and Paris in the sanctuary of Apollo Thymbraeus and of Ajax and Odysseus rescuing his body (Fig. 13 b).[56]

The biographical cycles in the minor arts that concentrate on the childhood and education of Achilles clearly present him as model and ideal example.[57] In similar fashion rhetoricians and encomiasts in Late Antiquity quote the example of Achilles:

---

56 This version of the story of Achilles' death belongs to the legends of his love for Polyxena, found in various sources of the later Empire; cf. Ghedini 2009, 102–8; O. Touchefeu-Meynier, "Polyxene", *LIMC* 7 (1994), 431–5; Schwarz 1992; King 1987, 184–201. Ghedini hypothesises that there were two more scenes in the original sequence, now missing: one showing his birth, the other his apotheosis on the island of Leuke. For the traditional story of the death of Achilles see Burgess 2009.

57 See Cameron 2009, 11–19, who argues that the education for which the child Achilles is presented as a model should more properly be called *anatrophe* (nurture), rather than *paideia*. Cf. also Abbondanza 1996.

Fig. 13: (a) Tensa Capitolina, bronze panels with three scenes from life of Achilles: bath in Styx, delivery to Chiron, instruction in lyre-playing; below scenes from small frieze. After H. Stuart Jones ed., *A catalogue of the Ancient Sculptures preserved in the Municipal Collections of Rome. The Sculptures of the Palazzo dei Conservatori*, Oxford 1926, pl. 73. (b) Tensa Capitolina, bronze panels with three scenes from life of Achilles: Priam before Achilles, death of Achilles, Ajax with body of Achilles. Rome, Capitoline Museums. Second quarter of 4th century. After H. Stuart Jones ed., *A catalogue of the Ancient Sculptures preserved in the Municipal Collections of Rome. The Sculptures of the Palazzo dei Conservatori*, Oxford 1926, pl. 71.

Menander Rhetor for instance recommends the aspiring orator to compare the upbringing of a future emperor to that of Achilles, Claudian in his third panegyric on
the emperor Honorius has the young emperor listening to the precepts of his father
as eagerly as Achilles to those of the centaur.[58] Those who used or admired these objects – all designed for domestic use or exhibition – will have been encouraged by
them to think of the nature of the ideal education, such as they might have wished to
claim for themselves and their children, and on the nature of the perfect hero that it
should produce. But how far do the mosaics reflect these ideas? In the West, to our
present knowledge, very little. Despite the popularity in Pompeian painting of the
scene of Chiron instructing Achilles in lyre-playing, Achilles' education by the centaur appears only two or three times on mosaics in the West, mostly accompanying
the scene of the discovery on Skyros.[59] There is nothing here that adds up to a biography of the hero comparable to the cycles in the minor arts, or that shows a particular
focus on his early life and education.

In the East there is considerably more interest in this aspect of Achilles, especially
in the fourth and fifth centuries. A mosaic in the so-called Villa of Theseus (possibly
the palace of the governor?) in Nea Paphos on Cyprus shows his birth and first bath, as
on the Kaiseraugst plate and the Capitoline puteal; the date is probably fifth century
(Fig. 14).[60] The iconographic scheme resembles that used earlier for the birth of Dionysus, as well as the miraculous birth of Alexander. Thetis lies on the couch, with Peleus
on a throne beside her, while the baby is held out towards a basin by a woman labelled
Anatrophe, "nurture". Beside her, *Ambrosia* brings a jar of water, clearly the draught
which will render the child immortal; there is a conflation here between the mundane
scene of a baby's first bath and the story of Thetis dipping him in Styx, which appears
in the biographic cycles as a separate scene. On the other side, it is Achilles' mortal
nature which is in evidence; the three Fates stand watching with their book, spindle,
and scroll. At the bottom of the panel, under the feet of all the figures, flows the water
of Styx. At least two other panels, perhaps three, originally accompanied this scene,
in a layout typical of a dining-room, but only tiny fragments remain; it is tempting to
think that they may have contained further scenes from the Achilles saga, but this is
entirely hypothetical.

---

58 Menander Rhetor, *Peri epideiktikon* 371–2, pp. 82–3 Russell, Wilson. Claudian, *III Cons. Hon.* 60–
2. Greg. Naz. *Or.* 43 (*PG* 36, 509); all quoted, with other examples, by Cameron 2009, 13–14. Cf. also
Pavlovskis 1965, for further references.

59 See above nn. 45, 46, on the mosaics from Caesarea/Cherchel and Tipasa. For the well-known painting from the Basilica at Herculaneum showing Chiron teaching the young Achilles to play the lyre, often assumed to be based on the statue group in the Saepta in Rome mentioned by Pliny (*HN* 36.29),
see Kossatz-Deissmann 1981, nos. 50–51; for Pompeian paintings of the subject see ibid. nos. 52–4.

Fig. 14: Nea Paphos, Villa of Theseus, mosaic of birth of Achilles. 5th century. Photo courtesy of Demetrios Michaelides, with the permission of the Department of Antiquities, Cyprus.

The next episode, chronologically, in the saga, also appears on an eastern mosaic; a panel from Xanthus in Lycia, very crude in workmanship, has Thetis dipping the baby in a spring labelled *Pēgē* (Fig. 15).[61] The rest of the pavement has apparently nothing to do with Achilles; there is a larger panel with Meleager and Atalanta, busts of two personifications, *Eirene* and *Euprepeia*, both desirable qualities but rather incongruous in this context, as well as hunting scenes and other motifs in the panels of the geometric surround. It is hard to resist the conclusion that the mosaicist had only a very limited selection of models available in his repertory, from which to compose something that would satisfy the patron's desire for heroes. More coherent, apparently, was the mosaic from Nablus, where a damaged panel showed Chiron with a group of armed men labelled [*He*]*teroi*, perhaps Achilles with his companions. The next scene to the

---

Scenes of the education of Achilles by Chiron also appear occasionally on the sides of sarcophagi, as secondary subjects to the main scene of the discovery on Skyros: Grassinger 1999, 23–5; Rogge 1995, 30.
60 W. A. Daszewski, in Daszewski and Michaelides 1988, 72–6; Michaelides 1987, 44–5 no. 50, pl. XXXI.
61 From the House of Meleager: Manière-Lévêque 2012, 71–3. No date is proposed, but the mosaics are unlikely to be earlier than the fifth century.

Fig. 15: Xanthus, House of Meleager, mosaic showing Thetis dipping infant Achilles in Styx. Probably 5th century. 89 × 13 cm. Antalya Archaeological Museum. Photo KMDD.

right had Deidameia, so it looks as though there was a sequence here; a further panel continued to the left, though the subject cannot be recovered.[62]

In addition to his education with Chiron, Achilles' human tutor, Phoenix, also attracted attention. He appears in scenes of the abduction of Briseis, on the mosaic now in Malibu, and in the scene of the embassy to Achilles at Hierapolis; as seen above, in both mosaics the assembly of figures is un-Homeric.[63] Recent excavations at Sagalassus in Pisidia have revealed a building identified as the Library of Neon, built in the early second century; it was redecorated in the second half of the fourth with a mosaic whose (damaged) central panel shows Phoenix, Achilles (both identified by name), and a woman whose name does not survive (Fig. 16).[64] The remains of a shield against her leg, and a spear lying on the ground beneath, allow her to be iden-

---

62 Above n. 27; alternatively this may be an unusual version of the delivery of Achilles to Chiron, perhaps by his father Peleus: see Ghedini 1997a, 244–5; Talgam 2014, 56.

63 Above nn. 32, 36.

64 Waelkens 1993, 13–15, figs. 18–20; Waelkens et al. 2000. The figured panel bears the signature of the mosaicist Dioskoros. The building was destroyed by fire in the late fourth century, providing a secure *terminus ante quem* for the mosaic (Waelkens et al. 2000, 426). The figures of both Achilles and Thetis were largely destroyed, damage which the excavators believed was inflicted deliberately when the building was burnt; they assign this destruction, and that of the building itself, to Christian rioters attacking a building which represented the tradition of Greek *paideia*, and the images of a pagan deity and her semi-divine son (Waelkens 1993, 15; Waelkens et al. 2000, 436–7). I am grateful

tified as Thetis, providing arms to her son as he departs for the war.[65] The presence of the old pedagogue, especially on the floor of a library, illustrates the value attached at this time to the moral training that the pedagogue supplied to his young charge.[66]

A similar theme occurs on a mosaic from Amisos, modern Samsun, on the shore of the Black Sea; it shows the young Achilles with Thetis, both identified by name (Fig. 17).[67] Thetis sits in a mournful pose, her head resting on her arm; a sheathed sword rests on her lap, and a helmet sits on the rock beside her. Achilles is shown as a nude youth, much smaller than his mother; these cannot be the arms that she brings Achilles at Troy in *Iliad* 19, but must allude to his earlier departure for the war from Phthia. Thetis is evidently contemplating the fate of the boy who stands before her in the pose of the perfect athlete; the spear and shield that he holds show that

Fig. 16: Sagalassus, Library of Neon, mosaic showing Achilles, Phoenix, and Thetis. Second half of 4th century. Central panel 2.40 × 3.45 m. Photo courtesy Marc Waelkens.

to Marc Waelkens for a discussion of this question; he stresses (*per litteras*) that such a destruction is likely to have been an isolated incident rather than a coherent policy.

65 For the tradition of Thetis giving Achilles his armour before his departure for the war see Burgess 2009, 16.

66 Cf. Cameron 2009, 15–18.

67 Şahin 2005. Another inscription gives the name of the mosaicist, Orentes. There is no evidence for the date; Şahin suggests the first half of the third century on stylistic grounds, which may be confirmed by the surrounding geometric motifs. The association with Caracalla suggested in the discussion to Şahin's paper (p. 424) has no basis.

Fig. 17: Amisos, mosaic of Achilles and Thetis. Probably first half of 3rd century. Museum of Samsun. After Şahin 2005, fig. 2, courtesy of Derya Şahin.

he has already chosen the short-lived life of a warrior. There is no allusion here to the Skyros episode; on both these mosaics an alternative version of Achilles' departure for Troy may have been deliberately chosen, ignoring the more questionable story of his hiding in women's clothing on Skyros.[68] Around the central panel smaller panels have Nereids, Thetis' sisters, and busts of the Seasons who suggest the inevitable passage of time. A panel at the entrance, now destroyed, was much more unusual; it

---

[68] For attempts to dispute or deny the truthfulness of the Skyros episode, as unworthy of Achilles' heroic character, see e.g. Philostratus, *Heroic.* 45.8–46; Libanios, *Progymn.* 8, *Laud.* 3.5–6 (below n. 88); both quoted by Fantuzzi 2012, 63–4.

showed the sacrifice of a bull. Derya Şahin has suggested that the sacrifice is intended for Achilles, and that the allusion here is to the Achilles cult which we know persisted even into Late Antiquity on the northern shores of the Black Sea.[69] But the function of the building is not known, and the connection of the panel to the central scene is not clear. The emphasis on the relationship between Achilles and his mother and her awareness of the fate that hangs over him is characteristic of the interest in his early years and his formation as a hero.[70]

Another group of mosaics belongs on the borders of the Greco-Roman world. These are five panels, the product of illegal excavations and without known provenance; four have ended up in the Bible Lands Museum in Jerusalem, the fifth in a private collection.[71] Despite the lack of attested origin, the inscriptions are in the dialect

Fig. 18: Unprovenanced mosaic from region of Edessa. Patroclus and Achilles. H. 117.5 cm. Probably first half of 3rd century. Courtesy of the Bible Lands Museum, Jerusalem. Photography: M. Amar and M. Greyevsky.

---

69 For the cult of Achilles see Burgess 2009, esp. ch. 8; Hupe 2006, esp. 165–234.
70 Cf. Durán Penedo 2011.
71 Balty and Briquel Chatonnet 2000, 51–72.

of Aramaic characteristic of Edessa, modern Urfa in eastern Turkey, and identify them as coming from the region of Osrhoene or northern Syria. They all clearly belonged originally to a single pavement, probably arranged along the sides of a peristyle. Each panel contains between two to three figures, most identified by Edessene inscriptions above them; all belong to the Trojan story.[72] On one Patroclus and Achilles are seated on a couch, elegantly dressed, with Achilles playing his lyre (Fig. 18); a second has Briseis, led by a maidservant as though to her marriage and followed by another maid (Fig. 19). On the third, another servant (a nurse?) leads an unnamed female who must be Polyxena, escorted against her will to a pretended marriage with Achilles, but in fact to her death (Fig. 20);[73] the fourth shows Priam and Hecuba, also seated on a couch, with another maidservant apparently holding a scroll (Fig. 21). The fifth panel is now separated from the rest, but style and subject show that it belonged to the same group; it has the boy Troilus standing next to an altar. The scenes do not depict any specific episode of the story of Troy, and certainly do not constitute an illustration of the *Iliad* or of any other literary source. They offer a selection of the leading figures, presented to the viewers for their admiration, sympathy or marvel; the narrative element is confined to suggestions, that Briseis is perhaps escorted to a marriage with Achilles, or that news is brought to Priam and Hecuba, either of Troilus' death, or of the impending fate of Polyxena. The stories of Troilus and Polyxena are known in various Late Antique sources, but are very rare in Greco-Roman art of the Empire.[74]

Most of the Edessene mosaics known until recently come from tombs; the majority show funerary scenes or portraits of figures in local costume, identified by Aramaic inscriptions. Most are thought to date from the first half of the third century, when the kingdom of Edessa was enjoying a period of florescence, and they share a thoroughly unclassical style, very different from most of the mosaics of northern Syria and the adjacent regions. The Trojan panels just discussed share, more or less, the unclassical style, and probably date from the same period, but they most likely come from a domestic context.[75] They show that the wealthy inhabitants of Edessa or its region

---

72 Drijvers and Healey 1999, 211–3, nos. Cm3, Cm4, discuss the first three of these panels, with translation of some of the inscriptions; revised readings are given in Balty and Briquel Chatonnet 2000.

73 Cf. above n. 56.

74 O. Touchefeu-Meynier, "Polyxene", *LIMC* 7 (1994), 431–5; Schwarz 1992; A. Kossatz-Deissmann, "Troilos", *LIMC* 8 (1997), 91–4. See also Smith and Hallett 2015, on a (fragmentary) marble group of Troilus and Achilles from Aphrodisias, and its relation to other versions of the same scene, Hellenistic to early Imperial. The interpretation of Troilus as a mighty warrior, rather than a young boy, is found also in writers of the Imperial period such as "Dares the Phrygian" and Quintus Smyrnaeus.

75 Edessa mosaics: see references in Dunbabin 1999, 172–4; Drijvers and Healey 1999, 37–8, 160–90, with discussion of the inscriptions; Balty and Briquel Chatonnet 2000, 31–2. For another very striking mosaic with Edessene inscriptions, also without known provenance, with the scene of the creation of man by Prometheus, see Balty and Briquel Chatonnet 2000, 32–51. The dating of all these new panels of mosaic is based on the paleography of the inscriptions as well as on stylistic parallels with the Edessene mosaics known previously.

Fig. 19: Unprovenanced mosaic from region of Edessa. Briseis and maidservants. H. 115.5 cm. Probably first half of 3rd century. Courtesy of the Bible Lands Museum, Jerusalem. Photography: M. Amar and M. Greyevsky.

were familiar with the world of Greek mythology and saw it as appropriate decoration for their dwellings. This is not a display of adhesion to a foreign culture; the fact that they chose to identify the figures in their own language rather than Greek indicates that the stories and their heroes were acclimatised into the local culture. Balty and Briquel Chatonnet cite an excellent parallel from the same period in the Syriac translation of the *Hypomnemata* of the Christian apologist Ambrosius, which cites figures such as Achilles and Patroclus, Agamemnon and Briseis, Priam and Hecuba, as examples of the stupidity of pagan beliefs.[76] Familiarity with these themes may have been transmitted through literary sources and/or through art; one of the principal modes of transmission will have been the theatre, perhaps especially in the forms of musical performance and pantomime, less dependent on language.

More than 200 years later, Achilles appeared again on a mosaic from the region of Edessa, in very different form. This decorates the floor of a huge dwelling, a suburban villa or palatial residence, known as the Villa of the Amazons at Haleplibahçe just outside Edessa. The villa was discovered in 2005, and only preliminary publications are currently available.[77] I know as yet of no archaeological evidence for the chronology,

---

76 Balty and Briquel Chatonnet 2000, esp. 70–2.
77 Karabulut, Önal and Dervişoğlu 2011; for short summaries in English (with limited information about the Achilles mosaic), see M. Merola, "Turkish Delights", *Archaeology Magazine* 63.1, Jan-Feb 2015; M. Önal, "Edessa Mosaics", *Actual Archaeology Magazine Anatolia* 14, 2015, 82–4.

Fig. 20: Unprovenanced mosaic from region of Edessa. Polyxena and nurse. H. 111 cm. Probably first half of 3rd century. Courtesy of the Bible Lands Museum, Jerusalem. Photography: Ze'ev Radovan.

Fig. 21: Unprovenanced mosaic from region of Edessa. Hecuba and Priam, and a maidservant. H. 117. 5 cm. Probably first half of 3rd century. Courtesy of the Bible Lands Museum, Jerusalem. Photography: M. Amar and M. Greyevsky.

Fig. 22: Haleplibahçe, Villa of Amazons, Achilles mosaic, Thetis dipping infant Achilles in Styx. Probably late 5th to early 6th century. Photo KMDD.

Fig. 23: Haleplibahçe, Villa of Amazons, Achilles mosaic, meeting of young Achilles and Thetis. Probably late 5th to early 6th century. After Karabulut, Önal and Dervişoğlu 2011, pl. 24.

but the style of the mosaics indicates a date no earlier than the second half of the fifth century, and perhaps as late as the sixth.[78] There could hardly be a greater contrast with the earlier Edessene mosaics. Greek inscriptions are used, the style is elegant and sophisticated, similar to the best mosaics of that time in Syria and the surrounding region; in many places it is strongly classicising. Two of the mosaics have mythological subjects: a well-preserved pavement with hunting Amazons in a large hall at the back of the building, and the mosaic of the 33m-long entrance corridor. This, unfortunately, is much less well preserved, with only a strip of varying width along the top. That is enough, however, to show that here is what was previously missing: a mosaic with a biographical Achilles-cycle, a series of scenes of his early life, directly comparable to those used, a century or so earlier, in the minor arts such as the Kaiseraugst Plate and the Capitoline puteal. They include his birth, where the figure of a nurse, labelled *Trophos*, survives; Thetis dipping the baby in Styx (Fig. 22); the young Achilles greeting his mother (Fig. 23); at least two scenes with Chiron (there were doubtless others, now missing, in the central stretch), in one of which an extraordinarily classical Achilles wields spear and shield (Fig. 24 a-b). At the right end is Thetis again, between two maidservants, approached by a fragmentary Chiron, probably Achilles' return to his mother before the Skyros episode (Fig. 25). Below is one tiny fragment of the lower register – a helmet, and the name Odysseus, surely the discovery on Skyros. This leaves the question, what was shown on the rest of the lower register, which must have occupied as much space as the upper? We may assume that later episodes of the story were shown here: Briseis presumably, perhaps Penthesilea, who would have fitted well with the scenes of hunting Amazons at the other side of the building; probably the duel with Hector and the dragging of his body, and the Ransom: all scenes that are found elsewhere, despite the usual emphasis on the earlier parts of the story.[79] It is tantalising to consider whether it might have ended with the death of Achilles, perhaps immediately under the scene of his birth; as seen above, the story is very rare in Roman art, but ends the cycle on the Tensa Capitolina.[80] One fragment of the lower register does survive, right in the centre where the main entrance to the dwelling would have been; it shows two of the Fates, spinning the thread of his life (Fig. 26). The three Fates appear on the mosaic of the Birth of Achilles at Nea Paphos, and traditionally they sang at his parents' wedding, where they are shown on the North African *sig-*

---

78 A date in the second quarter of the sixth century has been suggested on the basis of certain parallels with the mosaics of the Great Palace in Constantinople. This should probably be widened, and a range from the second half of the fifth to the early sixth provisionally envisaged. The various mosaics in the villa do not appear all to be of the same dates, though the Amazon and the Achilles mosaics should belong together.

79 Cf. the jug in Jerusalem, above n. 5.

80 Above n. 56; Ghedini 2009, 102–8.

illata dishes.[81] Their central position at Haleplibahçe would have emphasised their dominion over the life of the greatest of heroes, the mortal son of the goddess; no one entering the building could have failed to understand the point.

By the date of this mosaic, Christianity was securely established as the religion of the empire. There is no hint of anything Christian in these mosaics, but we should certainly not think that they were inspired by any sort of crypto-pagan agenda. Pagans certainly still existed, but Edessa was very much a Christian city, for many centuries by this date, and whoever commissioned these mosaics as a very visible decoration for their sumptuous palace had no fear of disapproval and denunciation by the church authorities. The story of Achilles at the entrance would have impressed visitors with the cultured outlook of the occupants. This culture is not primarily literary: Homer is very distantly in the background, as he is in all references to the heroes of the Trojan War, but the episodes of Achilles' youth and childhood have nothing to do with Homer, and were described in numerous literary works of very varied origins and character. It is surely a misguided question to ask whether any specific literary work might have influenced the depiction of the subject in art; the range of possible sources is too great. It would be, for example, a pointless speculation to attribute aspects of the Achilles theme on western mosaics to the work of Statius;[82] still less can the art offer any solution to the debate over the existence of a lost Hellenistic *Achilleid*.[83] Well-educated patrons would be familiar with literary treatments of the theme (not only in surviving works or those we know of), and the images might prompt a display of literary erudition among guests who saw them. But the individual images and motifs also had a long history of their own in art, which itself affected both the way in which the artists portrayed a subject and its dissemination at all levels of society. In addition, the themes and stories of mythology had at all times a diffusion at levels of ephemeral culture which are now lost to us. In the later Empire, throughout much of the Greco-Roman world, they had become part of a common cultural heritage (the German *Bildungsgut*), communicated and made known in a wide range of different means and media: literature, contemporary as well as classical, art, theatrical performance, oratory, handbooks, and word of mouth.[84]

---

81 Above, n. 60. On the top side of the North African dishes (n. 54) is a group of three female figures who must be the Fates, attending the marriage of Peleus and Thetis; cf. Garbsch 1980, 156–8.

82 E.g. Lancha 1997, 308, 330–2. Heslin 2005, 169–72, believes the treatment of the story in the fourth-century cycles, for instance the dipping of the baby Achilles in the Styx or Thetis' role in delivering him to Chiron, to be influenced by Statius' *Achilleid*; he does not recognise that some of the monuments concerned are of eastern manufacture, less likely to be derived from a Latin source.

83 E.g. Weitzmann 1959, 54–9; Weitzmann 1984, 19–21, 86, 165–8, 192; for arguments against see Cameron 2009, 7–8.

84 I have discussed some of these questions, and their treatment in recent scholarship, in Dunbabin 2015.

Fig. 24: (a)–(b): Haleplibahçe, Villa of Amazons, Achilles mosaic, Achilles practising with arms under Chiron's tuition. Probably late 5th to early 6th century. After Karabulut, Önal and Dervişoğlu 2011, pls. 30–31.

Much more is at stake in the mosaics discussed in this paper than just the display of culture; mythology has been absorbed and domesticated to express the ideals and interests of contemporary society, independent of religious affiliation. Viewers could admire the marvellous childhood of Achilles, his early education under the watchful care of his tutor, his mother's tenderness and vain attempts to save him from his destiny; the decisive moment at Skyros, when he rejects the life of soft luxury and chooses

Fig. 25: Haleplibahçe, Villa of Amazons, Achilles mosaic, Thetis greeting Chiron. Probably late 5th to early 6th century. Photo KMDD.

Fig. 26: Haleplibahçe, Villa of Amazons, Achilles mosaic, fragment with two of the Fates. Probably late 5th to early 6th century. After Karabulut, Önal and Dervişoğlu 2011, pl. 25.

heroism and death, his various loves and complex relations with a number of women, his friendship for Patroclus. As we have seen, the Haleplibahçe mosaics may have included also the crowning episodes of his killing of Hector, and his reconciliation with Priam, and perhaps also his death; they certainly showed the ineluctable power of Fate. No one single message is being expressed here; there were many lessons that could be drawn from the story of Achilles, many different aspects that could be of interest, and educated viewers were surely encouraged to appreciate this diversity.

Achilles recurs constantly in the panegyrical and epigrammatic literature of Late Antiquity, as example and model with whom the objects of praise may be compared. More often than on the mosaics, it is the Achilles of the *Iliad* who is referred to, for his heroic deeds, but also for his negative qualities.[85] In the first half of the fifth century, for instance, the poet Kyros of Panopolis can praise no less a subject than the emperor Theodosius II, with the words: "You perform the heroic deeds of the son of Aiakos [i.e. Achilles], without his anger or his love" (*Anth. Gr.* 15.9). More than 100 years later in the mid sixth century, another Egyptian poet, Dioskoros of Aphrodito, has a hackneyed phrase which he recycles in a number of encomia and epithalamia: "You have outdone Achilles and brave Diomedes ...".[86] The mosaics offer a much broader and more nuanced picture of Achilles. Many of them could indeed serve as a vehicle for the self-representation of the patron; the viewer looking for a chance to pay a compliment could compare the patron's education, or that of his family, to that of Achilles, his musical culture, his beauty and attraction to women, his choice of the life of manly heroism, his invincibility, even his mother's care for her child. But the more elaborate and complex mosaics, with their many scenes, offered a stimulus to more profound meditations on the character of the hero: the inevitability of destiny and death, the failure of Thetis' attempt to give him immortality, the struggle between different elements in his nature, the warrior who is also a lover.

This multi-faceted Achilles provided inspiration for everyone of education, from the schoolchild to the professional orator and rhetorician. Several rhetoricians of the fifth and sixth century have left speeches or declamations of the type known as *Ethopoiai*: "What Achilles might have said when ... ." – when hearing the trumpet in the women's quarters, when dying on account of his love for Polyxena, when falling in love with the dead Penthesilea; or what Patroclus or Phoenix might have said to persuade Achilles to return to the fight, or Chiron on hearing of his pupil in the women's quarters.[87] In the fourth century, Libanios of Antioch has two balancing *progymnas-*

---

85 Cf. King 1987, 130: "Anger and belligerence thus remain Achilles' most prominent characteristics in late antiquity" – a judgement based principally on the epic sources, notably Quintus Smyrnaeus.
86 E.g. Encomium on Duke Callinicus, H5 (MacCoull 1988, 91–6), l.23; also in H21, l.22 (ibid. 88–91); H2 (ibid. 134–6).
87 E.g. Libanios 8, *Progymnasmata* 11, *Ethopoiai* 3, 4, 12, 13, 14, 15, 16, pp. 379–84, 401–12 Foerster (Gibson 2008, 364–71, 388–401); Prokopios of Gaza, *Opuscula rhetorica et oratoria* (ed. E. Amato, 2009), 46–9: *Or.* VII (= *Ethop.* 4, Phoinix); Dioskoros of Aphrodito, H 26, *Ethopoia* on Achilles and Polyx-

mata – model school exercises – on Achilles, one of praise, the other of blame; in one he defends Achilles' adoption of female disguise in Skyros, in the other he condemns it.[88] Myth was an unfailing source of material, and so long as the central kernel was recognisable one could use it as one wished; the appeal of Achilles was precisely that his story contained so many elements, sometimes contradictory. The rhetoricians' task was to bring out their subject's character with a special intensity, or to find a new way to present the familiar situation. The artists, and the patrons they worked for, used the material in the same way, and with similar versatility. Some aspects seldom appealed to them: heroic battles were less fitted to domestic decoration than stories of love, music, or of the ideal education. But the mosaics convey the strength of the hero's attraction and the range of interest in different aspects of his story, across a wide sweep of the East, and right up until at least the end of the fifth century; and new discoveries are constantly extending this picture.

Acknowledgment: I am grateful to Janine Balty, Kutalmiş Görkay, Demetrios Michaelides, Derya Şahin, George Spyropoulos, and Marc Waelkens for generously providing photographs and/or for helpful discussions. Thanks are also due to Elisabeth Maas (Xanten), Carolyn Ben-David (Jerusalem), Michele Mazeris (Princeton), Susanne Schenker (Augst), Carmelo Pappalardo and Fr. Massimo Pazzini (Jerusalem), for help with obtaining images and for permission to reproduce them here. Hasan Karabulut granted me access to the Villa of the Amazons at Haleplibahçe in 2012; I thank him, and Kutalmiş Görkay, for accompanying me there. I acknowledge with gratitude the continued support of the Social Sciences and Humanities Research Council of Canada for my research.

Bibliography

Abadie-Reynal, C. Les maisons aux décors mosaïqués de Zeugma. *Comptes rendus des séances de l'Académie des inscriptions et belles-lettres* (2002), 743–771.

Abadie-Reynal, C. and R. Ergeç. *Zeugma I, Fouilles de l'habitat (1): la mosaïque de Pasiphae*, Varia Anatolica 26 (Istanbul; Paris, 2012).

Abbondanza, L. Immagini dell'infanzia di Achille in età imperiale: continuità di un paradigmo educativo. *Ocnus* 4 (1996), 9–33.

---

ena (MacCoull 1988, 129–30); another, "What Achilles would have said when asking Thetis for his armour", (ibid. 130). Cf. Chorikios, *Decl.* 1 [X], and *Decl.* 2 [XII] (tr. D. Russell, Penella 2009, 74–86), contrasting speeches of Polydamas and Priam supporting and opposing the proposal of a marriage between Achilles and Polyxena. For a Latin *Ethopoiia* on the Skyros episode see Heusch 1997.

88 Libanios 8, *Progymnasmata* 8, *Laudationes* 3, Encomium of Achilles, 5–6, p. 237 Foerster (Gibson 2008, 220–9); 9, *Vituperationes* 1, Invective against Achilles, 5–7, p. 284 Foerster (ibid. 266–77).

Balty, J. Achille à Skyros: polysémie de l'image mythologique, in: *Iconographie funéraire et société: corpus antique, approches nouvelles?*, Collection Histoire de l'art 3, edited by M. Galinier and F. Baratte (Perpignan, 2013), 117–146.

Balty, J. *Les mosaïques des maisons de Palmyre*. Inventaire des mosaïques antiques de Syrie 2, Institut Français du Proche-Orient (Beirut, 2014).

Balty, J. and F. Briquel Chatonnet, Nouvelles mosaïques inscrites d'Osrhoène. *Fondation Eugène Piot. Monuments et mémoires publiés par l'Académie des inscriptions et belles-lettres* 79 (2000), 31–72.

Bottini, A. and M. Torelli. (eds.) *Iliade. Roma, Colosseo, 9 settembre 2006 – 18 febbraio 2007* (Rome; Milan, 2006).

Bulas, K. *Les illustrations antiques de l'Iliade* (Lwow, 1929).

Burgess, J. *The Death and Afterlife of Achilles* (Baltimore, 2009).

Cameron, A. Young Achilles in the Roman World. *Journal of Roman Studies* 99 (2009), 1–22.

Carandini, A. La secchia Doria: una "storia di Achille" tardoantica. Contributo al problema dell'industria artistica di tradizione ellenistica in Egitto. *Studi miscellanei* 9 [1963–1964] (1965), 4–45.

Darmon, J.-P. 'Le programme idéologique du décor en mosaïque de la maison de la Télétè dionysiaque, dite aussi de Poséidon, à Zeugma (Belkis, Turquie)', in: *La mosaïque gréco-romaine* IX, 2, edited by H. Morlier (Rome, 2005), 1279–1300.

Daszewski, W. A. and D. Michaelides. *Mosaic Floors in Cyprus* (Ravenna, 1988).

Dauphin, C. A Roman Mosaic Pavement from Nablus. *Israel Exploration Journal* 29 (1979), 11–33, pls. 1–8.

Delvoye, C. Éléments classiques et innovations dans l'illustration de la légende d'Achille au Bas-Empire. *L'Antiquité classique* 53 (1984), 184–199.

Dresken-Weiland, J. *Reliefierte Tischplatten aus theodosianischer Zeit*, Studi di Antichità Cristiana 44 (Vatican City, 1991).

Drijvers, H. J. W. and J. Healey. *The Old Syriac Inscriptions of Edessa and Osrhoene. Texts, Translations and Commentary* (Leiden, 1999).

Dunbabin, K. *Mosaics of the Greek and Roman World* (Cambridge, 1999).

Dunbabin, K. The Pantomime Theonoe on a Mosaic from Zeugma. *Journal of Roman Archaeology* 23 (2010), 413–426.

Dunbabin, K. Mythology and Theatre in Mosaics of the Graeco-Roman East, in: *Using Images in Late Antiquity*, edited by S. Birk, T. M. Kristensen and B. Poulsen (Oxford, 2014), 227–252, pls. 26–27.

Dunbabin, K. Image, Myth, and Epic on Mosaics of the Late Roman West, in: *Images for Classicists*, edited by K. Coleman (Cambridge, MA, 2015), 39–65, figs. 3.1–3.14.

Durán Penedo, M. Mosaicos con la iconografía de Thetis, madre de Aquiles, en Turquía y en otros enclaves del Imperio, in: *XI. Uluslarası Antik Mozaik Sempozyumi 16–20 Ekim 2009 Bursa, Türkiye – 11th International Colloquium on Ancient Mosaics, October 16th-20th, 2009, Bursa Turkey* (Istanbul, 2011), 363–379.

Ewald, B. Men, Muscle, and Myth: Attic sarcophagi in the cultural context of the Second Sophistic, in: *Paideia. The World of the Second Sophistic*, edited by B. Borg (Berlin; New York, 2004), 230–275.

Fantuzzi, M. *Achilles in Love. Intertextual Studies* (Oxford, 2012).

Ferdi, S. Le légende d'Achille sur une mosaïque de Cherchel, in: *Iconographie classique et identités régionales*, Bulletin de correspondance hellénique suppl. 14, edited by L. Kahil, Chr. Augé, P. Linant de Bellefonds (Athens, 1986), 207–14.

Ferdi, S. *Corpus des mosaïques de Cherchel*, Études d'antiquités africaines (Paris, 2005).

Fernández Galiano, D. *Complutum II. Mosaicos. Excavaciones arqueológicas en España* (Madrid, 1984).

Fernández Galiano, D. The Villa of Maternus at Carranque. *International Colloquium on Ancient Mosaics* V, *Bath 1987*, Journal of Roman Archaeology suppl. 9 (Ann Arbor, 1994), 199–208.

Garbsch, J. Spätantike Keramik aus Nordafrika in der prähistorischen Staatssammlung. Ein spätantiker Achilles-Zyklus. *Bayerische Vorgeschichtsblätter* 45 (1980), 155–160.

Garbsch, J. and B. Overbeck. *Spätantike zwischen Heidentum und Christentum* (Munich, 1989).

Gensheimer, M. and K. Welch. The Achilles and Penthesileia Statue Group from the Tetrastyle Court of the Hadrianic Baths at Aphrodisias. *Istanbuler Mitteilungen* 63 (2013), 325–377.

Ghedini, F. Achille "eroe ambiguo" nella produzione musiva tardo antica. *Antiquité tardive* 5 (1997a), 239–264.

Ghedini, F. Achille a Sciro nella tradizione musiva tardo antica: iconografia e iconologia. *Atti del IV colloquio dell' associazione italiana per lo studio e la conservazione del mosaico, Palermo 1996*, (Ravenna, 1997b), 687–704.

Ghedini, F. Achille nel repertorio musivo tardo antico tra tradizione e innovazione, in: *Actes du VIIIème colloque international pour l'étude de la Mosaïque antique et médiévale, Lausanne 6–11 octobre 1997*, edited by D. Paunier and Chr. Schmidt (Lausanne, 2001), 58–73.

Ghedini, F. Achille a Sciro, in: *Le immagini di Filostrato Minore. La prospettiva dello storico dell'arte*, Antenor Quaderni 3, edited by F. Ghedini, I. Colpo and M. Novello (Rome, 2004), 17–26.

Ghedini, F. *Il carro dei Musei Capitolini. Epos e mito nella società tardo antica*, Antenor Quaderni 13 (Rome, 2009).

Gibson, C. (ed.) *Libanius's Progymnasmata: Model Exercises in Greek Prose Composition and Rhetoric. Translated with an Introduction and Notes* (Atlanta, 2008).

Giuliani, L. Sarcofagi di Achille tra Oriente e Occidente: genesi di un' iconografia, in: *Tre figure. Achille, Meleagro, Cristo*, edited by M. L. Catoni (Milan, 2013), 13–46 [trans. and revision of 'Achill-Sarcophage in Ost und West', *Jahrbuch der Berliner Museen* 31, 1989, 25–39].

von Gonzenbach, V. Ein neues Briseismosaik. *Colloque de la mosaïque grecque et romaine II, Vienne 1971* (Paris, 1975), 401–408, pl. CXCIII.

von Gonzenbach, V. Achillesplatte, in: *Der spätrömische Silberschatz von Kaiseraugst*, edited by H. Cahn and A. Kaufmann-Heinimann (Derendingen, 1984), 225–307.

Grassinger, D. *Die mythologischen Sarkophage I, Achill, Adonis, Aeneas, Aktaion, Alkestis, Amazonen*, Die Antiken Sarkophagreliefs 12.1 (Berlin, 1999).

Grassigli, G. L. L'ultimo Achille. Per una lettura dell' Achille tardoantico, in: *Iliade. Roma, Colosseo, 9 settembre 2006 – 18 febbraio 2007*, edited by A. Bottini and M. Torelli (Rome, 2006), 124–137.

Grote, U. *Der Schatz von St Viktor: Mittelalterliche Kostbarkeiten aus dem Xantener Dom* (Regensburg, 1998).

Guerrini, L. Infanzia di Achille e la sua educazione presso Chirone. *Studi miscellanei* 1 [1958–1959] (1961), 43–53, pls. XLX–XXII.

Hengel, M. *Achilleus in Jerusalem: Eine spätantike Messingkanne mit Achilleus-Darstellungen aus Jerusalem*, Sitzungberichte Heidelberg 1982.1 (Heidelberg, 1982).

Heslin, P. J. *The Transvestite Achilles. Gender and Genre in Statius' Achilleid* (Cambridge, 2005).

Heusch, C. *Die Achilles-Ethopoiie des Codex Salmasianus: Untersuchungen zu einer spätlateinischen Versdeklamation* (Paderborn, 1997).

Hupe, J. (ed.) *Der Achilleus-Kult im nördlichen Schwarzmeerraum vom Beginn der griechischen Kolonisation bis in die römische Kaiserzeit*, Internationale Archäologie 94 (Rahden, 2006).

Karabulut, H., M. Önal and N. Dervişoğlu. *Haleplibahçe Mozaikleri. Şanlıurfa/Edessa* (Istanbul, 2011).

King, K. *Achilles. Paradigms of the War Hero from Homer to the Middle Ages* (Berkeley; Los Angeles, 1987).

Kemp-Lindemann, D. *Darstellungen des Achilleus in griechischer und römischer Kunst* (Bern; Frankfurt, 1975).

Kossatz-Deissmann, A. Achilleus. *Lexicon Iconographicum Mythologiae Classicae* I (1981), 37–200.

Kossatz-Deissmann, A. Achilleus. *Lexicon Iconographicum Mythologiae Classicae Suppl. 2009* (2009), 2–15.

Lancha, J. *Mosaïque et culture dans l'Occident romain (Ier–IVe s.)* (Rome, 1997).

Leader-Newby, R. *Silver and Society in Late Antiquity. Functions and Meanings of Silver Plate in the Fourth to Seventh Centuries* (Aldershot, 2004).

Levi, D. *Antioch Mosaic Pavements* (Princeton, 1947).

MacCoull, L. *Dioscorus of Aphrodito. His Work and his World* (Berkeley; Los Angeles, 1988).

Manacorda, M. *La paideia di Achille* (Rome, 1971).

Manière-Lévêque, A.-M. *Corpus of the Mosaics of Turkey* II, *Lycia. Xanthos, part 2. The West Area* (Istanbul, 2012).

Meyer, H. Vom Herold Odios und der schönwangigen Diomede: Neues zur Ikonographie der Briseïssage und dem Themenrepertoire römischer Sarkophagwerkstätten. *Boreas* 25 (2002), 159–165, pl. 27.

Michaelides, D. *Cypriot Mosaics* (Nicosia, 1987).

Mickocki, T. New Mosaics from Ptolemais in Libya. *Archeologia Warsaw* 55 (2004), 19–30, pls. I–X.

Mickocki, T. The Achilles Mosaic from the Villa with a View in Ptolemais (Libya). *Archeologia Warsaw* 56 (2005), 57–68, pls. I–IV.

Mundell Mango, M. *The Sevso Treasure, Part One*, Journal of Roman Archaeology Suppl. 12 (Ann Arbor, 1994).

Muth, S. *Erleben von Raum – Leben im Raum. Zur Funktion mythologischer Mosaikbilder in der römisch-kaiserzeitlichen Wohnarchitektur* (Heidelberg, 1998).

Muth, S. Eine Kultur zwischen Veränderung und Stagnation. Zum Umgang mit den Mythenbildern im spätantiken Haus, in: *Epochenwandel? Kunst und Kultur zwischen Antike und Mittelalter*, edited by F. A. Bauer and N. Zimmermann (Mainz, 2001), 95–116.

Önal, M. *Mosaics of Zeugma* (Istanbul, 2002).

Önal, M. Die Mosaiken im Triclinium des 'Kointos-Hauses' in Zeugma, in: *ΠΑΤΡΙΣ ΠΑΝΤΡΟΦΟΣ ΚΟΜΜΑΓΗΝΗ. Neue Funde und Forschungen zwischen Taurus und Euphrat*, Asia Minor Studien 60, edited by E. Winter (Bonn, 2008), 263–273, pls. 35–37.

Paratte, C.-A. Les mosaïques de la villa gallo-romaine d'Orbe-Boscéaz (Canton de Vaud, Suisse), in: *La mosaïque gréco-romaine* IX, 1, edited by H. Morlier (Rome, 2005), 209–225.

Pavlovskis, Z. The Education of Achilles, as Treated in the Literature of Late Antiquity. *Parola del Passato* 20 (1965), 281–297.

Penella, R. (ed.) *Rhetorical Exercises in Late Antiquity. A Translation of Choricius of Gaza's*, Preliminary Talks and Declamations (Cambridge, 2009).

Piccirillo, M. *Chiese e mosaici di Madaba* (Jerusalem, 1989).

Piccirillo, M. *The Mosaics of Jordan* (Amman, 1993).

Raeck, W. *Modernisierte Mythen. Zum Umgang der Spätantike mit klassischen Bildthemen* (Stuttgart, 1992).

Ridgway, B. *Hellenistic Sculpture* I. *The Styles of ca. 331–200 B.C.* (Madison, 1990).

Rogge, S. *Die attischen Sarkophage* I. *Achill und Hippolytos*, Die antiken Sarkophagreliefs 9.1.1 (Berlin, 1995).

Russell, D. and N. Wilson *Menander Rhetor, edited with translation and commentary* (Oxford, 1981).

Russenberger, Chr. Achill im Wohnraum der Kaiserzeit: Liebhaber, Krieger, Musterknabe. *Hefte des Archäologischen Seminars der Universität Bern* 18 (2002), 53–73.

Şahin, D. The *Amisos* Mosaic of Achilles. Achilles Cult in the Black Sea Region, in: *La mosaïque gréco-romaine* IX,1, Collection de l'école française à Rome 352, edited by H. Morlier (Rome, 2005), 413–426.

Schwartz, G. Achill und Polyxena in der römischen Kaiserzeit. *Mitteilungen des Deutschen Archäologischen Instituts, Römische Abteilung* 99 (1992), 265–299, pls. 75–79.

Simon, E. Review of Carandini 1965. *Byzantinische Zeitschrift* 60 (1967), 127–129.

Smith, R. R. R. and C. H. Hallett. Troilos and Achilles: a monumental statue group from Aphrodisias. *Journal of Roman Studies* 105 (2015), 124–182.

Spyropoulos, G. *Η Έπαυλη του Ηρώδη Αττικού στην Εύα/Λουκού Κυνουρίας* (Athens, 2006).

Spyropoulos, G. Η Βίλα του Ηρώδη Αττικού στην Εύα/Λουκού Κυνουρίας. *Arkhaiologia, Peloponnesos* (Athens, 2012), 292–295.

Spyropoulos, G. and T. Spyropoulos. Prächtige Villa, Refugium und Musenstätte. Die Villa des Herodes Atticus im arkadischen Eua. *Antike Welt* 34.5 (2003), 463–470.

Stefanou, D. *Darstellungen aus dem Epos und Drama auf kaiserzeitlichen und spätantiken Bodenmosaiken* (Münster, 2006).

Stern, H. *Les mosaïques des maisons d'Achille et de Cassiopée à Palmyre*, Institut français d'archéologie de Beyrouth, Bibliothèque archéologique et historique 101 (Paris, 1977).

Stupperich, R. Achill in Faenza. *Boreas* 7 (1984), 261–268.

Talgam, R. *Mosaics of Faith. Floors of Pagans, Jews, Samaritans, Christians, and Muslims in the Holy Land* (Jerusalem, 2014).

Trimble, J. Greek Myth, Gender, and Social Structure in a Roman House: two paintings of Achilles at Pompeii, in: *The Ancient Art of Emulation: Studies in Artistic Originality and Tradition from the Present to Classical Antiquity*, edited by E. Gazda (Ann Arbor, 2002), 225–248.

Volbach, W. F. *Elfenbeinarbeiten der Spätantike und des frühen Mittelalters*, 3rd ed. (Mainz, 1976).

Voza, G. *I Mosaici del Tellaro. Lusso e cultura nel sud-est della Sicilia* (Syracuse, 2003).

Waelkens, M. The 1992 Season at Sagalassos. A preliminary report, in: *Sagalassos II. Report on the Third Excavation Campaign*, Acta Archaeologica Lovanensia Monographiae 6, edited by M. Waelkens and J. Poblome (Leuven, 1993), 9–41.

Waelkens, M. et al. The Sagalassos Neon Library Mosaic and its Conservation, in: *Sagalassos V. Report on the Survey and Excavation Campaigns of 1996 and 1997*, Acta Archaeologica Lovanensia Monographiae 11/A, edited by M. Waelkens and L. Loots (Leuven, 2000), 419–447.

Weitzmann, K. *Greek Mythology in Byzantine Art* 2nd ed. (Princeton, 1984).

Weitzmann, K. Observations on the Milan Iliad. *Nederlands kunsthistorisch Jaarboek* 5 (1954), 241–264 (= *Classical Heritage in Byzantine and Near Eastern Art*, London 1981, II).

Weitzmann, K. *Ancient Book Illumination* (Cambridge, MA, 1959).

Weitzmann, K. (ed.) *Age of Spirituality. Late Antique and Early Christian Art, Third to Seventh Century*. Catalogue of Exhibition at the Metropolitan Museum of Art, November 19, 1977 through February 12, 1978 (New York, 1979).

Zaccaria Ruggiu, A. *Regio* VIII, *insula* 104. Le strutture abitative: fasi e trasformazioni, in: *Hierapolis di Frigia* I, *Le attività delle campagne di scavo e restauro 2000–2003*, edited by F. D'Andria and M. P. Caggia (Istanbul, 2007), 211–256.

Robert Parker
Epilogue

What are wandering myths? Of myth, no prudent person will attempt a definition. It seems to be a concept applied to certain types of story, but not for the same reason in every case; that there is a real essence that could be isolated is not clear. One of the difficulties emerges when Lane Fox intriguingly introduces, but then dismisses, El Dorado, the gilded man from the country in which gold was so abundant as to be used for body-décor, as a possible example of a "myth" that, very unusually, has an identifiable origin. This is after all not, or not initially, a myth, he argues, because "the first tellers, I presume, and the first explorers, certainly, believed that El Dorado existed". But the first tellers of the myths of Amazons and of what Lane Fox describes as the "new myth" of Christ believed that Amazons and Christ existed: even if one modern usage and indeed one ancient usage associates "mythical" with "unreal", many ancients accepted as true many of what we loosely classify as their myths. Perhaps "wandering stories" is a more workable category; but in what follows I shall revert to "myths" in obedience to normal usage.

Whether myths or stories, "wandering" can be understood in several ways. One type is a myth that is originally set in one place but comes to be retold in a new setting and possibly with a new set of characters. This is the form Lane Fox has in mind when he speaks of the Near-Eastern Succession in Heaven and related myths being taken up by Euboeans, applied to Greek gods and given new locations in the Greek world: the story of Zeus' birth, which came eventually to be relocated in myriad places, is indeed a paradigm case of such re-housing. But a myth that is told in places other than its place of origin is surely also a wandering myth even if names and locations remain unchanged; it was in this way that Greek stories became central to Roman and later European culture. A by-form of the first type is the story that sprouts offshoots in new locations: the paradigm case here is that of the *Nostoi* and *Flight from Troy* stories, old narrative mainlines from which branch lines were constantly led off as different cities sought connection with the age of heroes. The myths have not wandered, but new places have been brought within their network. A little different again is the case discussed by Lane Fox when a people takes its own myths abroad and discovers new foreign locations for them, as when Alexander and his troops discover traces of Dionysus' and Heracles' history and journeys in Bactria and India. Lane Fox points out that for Alexander's men these are "home thoughts when abroad", a reassuring process not of "othering" but of "saming". Here the story has in a sense wandered, but it has

https://doi.org/10.1515/9783110421453-016

not acquired a new clientele, unless we believe the ancient sources who assure us that locals too saw these traces of Dionysus and Heracles.[1]

The present book is hospitable to all these forms of myths that wander. Greece is the fulcrum of the book, and one broad distinction might be between myths that, perhaps, arrived in Greece and others that went out from it. The problems raised by imports and exports are in many ways very different. Ancient Near-Eastern influence on Greek myth has been a classic theme of scholarship at least since the decipherment of Hittite and the publication of what was then known as the Song of Kumarbi, now re-named Song of Going Forth, early in the twentieth century. More recently possible connections between the Epic of Gilgamesh and Homer have been energetically discussed, amid much else. But the postulated relation is always difficult and complex, however plausible. Characters in Greek myth never bear the same names as their putative Near-Eastern originals; individuals motifs and even sequences of motifs may show striking similarities, but always accompanied by divergences that are little less striking. The dates and places where contact may have occurred are uncertain, as are the human agents involved, powerfully though Lane Fox has argued for the busy Euboeans as the bees who distribute the narrative pollen. The prior state of Greek myths about the gods before contact with the Near-Eastern tradition is another unknown: one cannot suppose that the Greeks told no stories about the reign of Zeus and its antecedents before word reached them of the Succession in Heaven recounted in the Hittite poems. Gritty questions about whether, when and how influence occurred have always to be faced, and can scarcely be resolved with enough confidence to give a firm basis for asking in detail, as one can when the answers to these questions are clear, how the recipients used and adapted borrowed myths for their own purposes.

The two papers in this volume operating in this area are strikingly different in approach. Rutherford sets the Hesiodic Succession in Heaven in the context of numerous surviving (and more lost?) Sumerian, Akkadian, Hurrian, Hittite, and other mythological traditions, already "travelling" and influencing one another in the second millennium BC; the Hesiodic myth surely belongs somewhere within that jigsaw, but too many pieces are missing to allow it to be located with any precision. West by contrast explains the postulated influence of Gilgamesh through a hypothesis of dazzling simplicity: a single Heracles epic by a Greek poet familiar with Gilgamesh, which introduced "Gilgamising" motifs to the Greek epic tradition. The need to multiply bilingual poets is strikingly reduced by the postulate of such an, unfortunately lost, intermediary. "There is my house of cards. Blow it down who will", he concludes, engagingly.

---

1 The same issue of "take up" applies in an opposite way to Lane Fox's example of the Indian myth of Pandaia heard by Megasthenes and added by him to the long list of Heracles' loves. It does not enter the Greek repertoire of stories about the hero.

The third study of a myth imported to Greece is spared these hair-raising uncertainties, not least because if takes us down more than half a millennium, to Diodorus writing in the late first century BC. Diodorus of Sicily, the Euhemerising historian, recreates the Egyptian god Osiris as a mortal king, a culture-hero with an alert eye to his own posthumous reputation. A myth is certainly here imported to Greek historiography, as again later to Greek philosophy in Plutarch's *On Isis and Osiris*. Whether one can also speak of a myth, as opposed to a divine figure, being imported to Greek religion, as opposed to Greek literature, is less clear: Greek enthusiasts for the enormously popular cults of the Egyptian gods asserted that their appeal lay not in myths but in displays of present power.[2] What we clearly observe is the drastic re-modelling to which Diodorus subjects the myth, to make it, as Pitcher shows, part of a suitable programmatic opening to his universal history.

As noted above, the export of myths from Greece, unlike imports to it, is in the main easily and unambiguously observable: stories, names included, were carried on the flood tide of the prestige of Greek culture, as well as by their intrinsic narrative appeal. The case is a little different with Sérida's argument that the Inaros cycle, the most extensive set of tales around a single theme surviving in Egyptian demotic literature, has been influenced by Greek epic, Homer above all. The claim is that aspects of Homeric style and themes have been applied to completely new subject matter; what has wandered is not a myth or a character or set of characters but a poetic manner. But questions can arise even with known characters and stories. No iconographic image in the ancient world was more widely diffused than that of the club-bearing, lion-skin-clad muscle man known to us as Heracles. But, in the wanderings of that type across central Asia and beyond, for how long was Heracles Heracles? Were the familiar myths still attached to it, Wood asks, or had a quite different divine personality entered into it? The decoration of the Polyxena sarcophagus found in the Granikos River plain (NW Anatolia) and the stone-built tomb chamber at Kızılbel in the Milyad north of Lycia poses different problems, but no less serious. That the sacrifice of Polyxena is figured on sides A and B of the former (datable c. 510–460 BC) is not in doubt, even if Sides C and D are more problematic. But the human remains found within it are, inappropriately, of a male (re-use?). Still worse, "the ethno-linguistic identity of the owners of the Polyxena sarcophagus" (Draycott) is unclear. Of the many scenes painted on the walls of the Kızılbel tomb some are recognisable (decapitation of Medusa; ambush of Troilus; departure of a hero, perhaps Amphiaraus), others that are less clearly so[3] are not necessarily mythological. But, again, the cultural context is very unclear if we acknowledge with Draycott that the Milyad is not ethnically Lycian at this date. These are striking instances of the reception of Greek myths in Achaemenid Anatolia – but by whom? They have recently been joined by the myth of Geryon on the painted tim-

---

2 Diod. Sic. 1.25.4; cf. Aristid. 45.15.
3 Draycott tentatively identifies an "exposure of Andromeda".

bers of the Tatarlı Tomb in Phrygia, a long way indeed from Geryon's mythical home in the far West.[4]

"Who?" the recipients of Greek myth were in Etruria is not in doubt, the Etruscans. But de Grummond's essay reveals startling aspects of the "How?". She argues that the figures apparently named as Achle, Uhuze, Velachtra, Ethun and Mezntie on an Etruscan mirror (c. 300 BC) are Achilles and Odysseus, the Etruscan Ethun and Velachtra, and the Mezentius so notorious from Virgil. As a preparation for this unexpected juxtaposition she offers a delightful review of some of the many instances of novel mythology found on other mirrors, where for instance the Trojan horse can be named Pecse = Pegasus or the Minotaur slain by Hercle = Heracles. But, she argues, these apparent anticipations of Trimalchio-style mythology (Petronius, *Satyricon*, 52.1–2, 59.3–5) are not that, the muddle of the semi-educated, but rather evidence for a vibrant oral story-telling culture in which themes and characters split, mutate and re-combine in kaleidoscopic ways: on the mirror in question, "Achle may have been preparing to go out on the battlefield to avenge the death of the son of Mezntie". Intoxicating vision!

The remaining contributors were less troubled by gaps in our knowledge and contexts of reception that can only be guessed. A partial exception is the study by Scheer. Why Pausanias records the foundation of Paphos in Cyprus by Agapenor of Tegea in Arcadia on his way home from Troy is at first sight obscure: if such a tradition existed in early epic, it has left little trace, and the linguistic links between Arcadia and Cyprus so familiar to modern philologists were unknown to the ancients. But Scheer lays bare a plausible context in the second century BC: the Ptolemaic general of Cyprus was an Arcadian with literary interests, a leading Paphian family was naming its sons Agapenor, and international diplomacy was energetically reviving or devising ancient connections of kinship. Myths continued to travel, then: the underground mythical root system that had long connected mainland Greece with innumerable places in the Aegean and beyond could always send up new shoots.

Scheer is required, successfully, to engage in a detective exercise. But we all know why Greek myths were available to Apulian painters, Pompeian decorators, Roman and Attic sarcophagus makers and late antique mosaicists: they had become shared cultural capital, the central imaginative resource diffused through many media across the whole range from high to popular culture. These are not so much travelling myths as myths that have arrived and undergone naturalisation. Two contributors stress the autonomy that the imported myths enjoy as stories, independent of the medium through which they are received. Giuliani shows that the Apulian vase painters are not depicting such and such a myth as shown on the tragic stage, but such and such a myth in itself, as a story (even if their and the viewer's knowledge of it is likely to come from tragedy). More broadly, Dunbabin insists that the efflorescence of scenes in late antique art depicting a whole range of incidents from the life of Achilles, with

---

4 Summerer and Kienlin 2010.

a paradoxical new emphasis on Achilles the lover, cannot be traced back to particular sources: the "themes and stories of mythology... had become part of a common cultural heritage (the German Bildungsgut), communicated and made known in a wide range of different means and media: literature, contemporary as well as classical, art, theatrical performance, oratory, handbooks, and word of mouth." She shows incidentally how Achilles appears, labelled in Aramaic, in mosaics probably of the third century from Osrhoene, and continues to flourish under Christianity: here we see travel not in place but between cultures.

For those contributors who treat the uses of myth in very particular decorative contexts, the questions to be asked are about the uses to which they are put and the selections that are made, the emphases chosen. Lorenz reveals the art of "juxtaposition" of complementary or contrasting scenes in Roman wall painting. Borg and Ewald study the uses of myth in, respectively, the equally spectacular Roman and Attic sarcophaguses of the imperial period: both see the selections as designed to provide exempla, but (to summarise rich discussions crudely) Borg finds more (though decreasing) use of *exempla mortalitatis* and *maeroris*, Ewald a dominant stress on "heroic masculinity".

Why do myths wander? The phenomenon of Greek genealogical myth spreading its tentacles to embrace almost all the peoples of the world was explained by Bickerman in his classic article "Origines Gentium":[5] Greeks fitted every people they met into their own frame of understanding, their own genealogical myth. So Persians for instance were made descendants of Perseus to bring them within a comprehensible Greek worldview; this was a form of Lane Fox's "saming". The association of Persians with Perseus is also an instance of the "creative misunderstanding" stressed by Lane Fox, the kind of do-it-yourself understanding of foreign names that probably made Iasonia, Jason shrines, out of Iayezana, west Iranian "places of worship". A form of the so-called "interpretatio graeca" also operated here, as foreign figures resembling Greek were assimilated to them: there were forty-three different Heracleses, according to Varro (Serv. ad *Aen.* 8. 564), "since all those who were valiant were called Heracles"; a god Lycurgus apparently emerges in Arabia because Dionysus' Thracian foe of that name lent his myth and name to the Arab god Shai 'al Qaum, who "doesn't drink wine" (another foe of Dionysus, therefore).[6] The Greeks themselves were probably responsible for most such interpretations and extensions. But many Greek myths thriving among peoples who were not, or not originally, Greek have been met in these pages; there were also innumerable extensions and reapplications within the Greek world, as when the Cypriots discovered their Arcadian connections through Agapenor. The huge cultural prestige of Greek culture, and within it of the special time, the age of heroes, are crucial factors here: to know the myths was a mark of education for an

---

5 Bickerman 1952.
6 See Parker 2017, 51 n. 72.

individual, to have mythical ancestors was a community's patent of nobility. In particular circumstances the claims involved could become more pointed and political.

In a contribution on heroic myth in the Sebasteion at Aphrodisias to the conference that underlay this book, however, R. R. R. Smith began by stressing that, first and foremost, prior to any political or sociological meanings, the myths appealed as stories; they satisfied the profound human craving and need for narrative. Giuliani speaks of Attic tragedy as "a most powerful cultural engine generating a constant output of new myths"; its uptake in Apulia reveals the human passion not just for stories but for new stories. One example among many might be the myth of Iphigeneia among the Taurians, which has the extra interest of being a further candidate for Lane Fox's (extremely) short list of myths with an identifiable origin, in this case the poet Euripides. Euripides' plot builds, it is true, on an existing myth and characters, and probably could not have survived had it not done so, but is none the less a new creation. Euripidean invention though it was, it enjoyed huge success, and in Roman Anatolia even acquired one of the classical functions of older myths as a charter for cities.[7] Part of the myth's appeal derives, no doubt, from its dramatisation of the opposition between Greek and barbarian, but more from its narrative and emotional power: the pathos of the unrecognised brother and his sister, the near disaster of his sacrifice, the happy ending, the relationships that it makes so effective (brother to sister; buddy to buddy), also its exoticism. Dunbabin like Smith opposes a reductionism that confines the role of myth to one of cultural decoration or ideological underpinning. "Much more is at stake in the mosaics", she writes, "... than just the display of culture: mythology has been absorbed and domesticated to express the ideals and interests of contemporary society, independent of religious affiliation." And Lane Fox stresses that "it is quite untrue that myths can take roots only in societies with a social structure similar to the one in which they originate. Myths from the Greek poleis were taken up and adapted in the very different social structures of early Rome and Etruria".

Doubtless such an "autonomy of the imagination" approach can be extended too far; and, as so often, to speak of "myth" in general may obscure crucial distinctions: would, say, theogonic myth perform the same functions, or appeal to the same audience, as, say, Euripides' Iphigeneia myth? But, at bottom, it seems that to understand why myths wander one must understand why societies need stories and to what extent the stories that a society needs or can accept are society-specific, socially constrained. To the extent that they are not so constrained, and to the extent that they can overcome language barriers, nothing is more natural than that myths should wander – as indeed this volume shows that they do.

---

7 Burrell 2005; for a comprehensive study Hall 2013.

Bibliography

Bickerman, E. J. Origines Gentium. *Classical Philology* 47 (1952), 65–81.

Burrell, B. Iphigeneia in Philadelphia. *Classical Antiquity* 24 (2005), 223–256.

Hall, E. *Adventures with Iphigenia in Tauris: A Cultural History of Euripides' Black Sea Tragedy* (New York; Oxford, 2013).

Parker, R. *Greek Gods Abroad* (Oakland, 2017).

Summerer, L. and A. Kienlin. (eds.) *Tatarlı: renklerin dönüşü/The return of colours/Rückkehr der Farben* (Istanbul, 2010).

Index

A

Abar-basi   343
Abascanthus   196
Abdera   311–314, 326
Abinergaos   338
Acestes   l
Achaea/Achaeans   211, 223, 271–272, 298
– Achaean heroes   296
Achaemenid   39, 60, 328, 337, 343
– Anatolia   399
– Asia Minor   23, 25, 29, 62
– conquest   23, 41
– Empire, xiv   23–24, 39–41, 351
– heroes   343;
– royal lion fighters   343
Achilleis (Statius)   176
Achilles   xxi, 32–33, 38–40, 48, 107–109,
    174–176, 181, 197–199, 227–229, 241–242,
    274–275, 296, 302–305, 357–391,
    400–401; *see also* Achle and Aciles
– Iphigenia   237
– mosaic   359, 362, 385, 388–389
– sarcophagi   197, 200, 229
Achle (αχle)   95, 107–109, 111, 118, 119, 121,
    400
Achmemrun   100–101
Achuvisr   118
Aciles   102–1044, 107, 118
Actaeon   9
actors   136, 139, 141, 149, 368
Acuphis' kingdom   xxxv, xxxviii
Adados   11
Adana   11
Adanos   11
Addu   6
Admetus   193, 234
Adonis   xxxviii, 153, 171, 187–189, 200, 205,
    226, 237, 238, 393
Adrastos   222, 224
Adriatic   xlix
Aegae, Cilicia   xxxv
Aegae-Vergina   xl
Aegean   xxxvi, xxxviii, xliii, 6, 60, 400
Aegisthus/ Aigisthos   138, 139, 231, 237, 241
Aegyptiaca   311
Aelian   267

Aelius Aristides   223 n.53, 225, 236, 257, 260
Aeneid   xlix–l, 98, 117, 120
Aeneas   xlviii–l, 116, 117, 119, 148, 151, 153,
    155, 199, 205, 393
Aethiopica (Heliodorus)   309
aetiologies   13, 19, 222
Aetolians   xlix, 176
Aetolos   98
Aevas   100–101
Afghanistan   265
Africa   3, 198. See also North Africa
Africa Proconsularis   360
Agamemnon   33, 74, 76, 85, 102, 147, 233, 383
– conquering Cyprus   79
Agapenor (in Cyprus)   xv, 72–73, 75–79, 81–87,
    89–91
– of Tegea in Arcadia   400–401
– Agapenorids   81, 83, 86
Agatharchides of Cnidus   311–314
Agesarchos   311
Agoratis   81
Ahhiyawa   5, 17
Ahura Mazdā   346, 348
Aiakos   129, 390
Aietes   277
Aigipan   15
Aineia   xlviii
Ainos   xlix
Aion   366, 368
Aisepus River   30
Ajax/Aias   100, 102, 104, 113, 118, 147, 229,
    366, 369, 370, 374–375
Akarum   xxxvi
Akkadian   266, 267, 269–270, 398
Alalu   7
Alba Longa   116
Albanian   265
Albani Heracles   339
Albani sarcophagus, Rome   198
Albertini and Chiaramonti Heracles types   339
Alcestis   193, 194, 206, 234
Alcmaeon   180
Alcyone   181
Aleas   87
Aleppo   xlii, lii–liii, 6, 11, 18

Alexander the Great   xxxv–xxxvi, xxxix–xli,
    l–lii, 184, 185, 295, 296, 302, 310, 331, 332,
    334, 335, 397
Alexandra   75, 90
Alexandria   79–80, 144, 290, 310, 354
– Alexandrian scholars   79
Alixentr (Paris-Alexander)   102–3; see also
    Elchsntre
Alkinoos   53, 277
Alkmene   267
Al Mina   xliii
Alpheios river   271
Alses   102
Alsir   102–3
Althaea   176, 190–192, 202, 219, 237
Amarynthos   xlv
Amasis   310
Amazon (South America)   li
Amazonian mountains (Asia Minor)   xxxix
Amazonian targe   196
Amazonomachy   202, 210, 221, 227, 228, 231,
    236, 245–147, 252
Amazons,   xxxviii–xli, l–liii, 195, 196, 199–200,
    231, 302–303, 369–371, 383, 385, 386,
    388, 389, 391, 397; see also Amezan
– queens   xxxix, 35, 294, 300–302, 362
Ambrosia   376
Ambrosius   383
Amezan   xxxviii
Amisos   379–380
Ammon   310
Amphiaraus   45, 50–52, 59, 61, 62, 118, 132,
    133, 222, 224, 399
Amphidamas   xiii
Amphipolis   xxxvi
Amun   292–294, 299
Amymone   162
Anāhitā   348
Anatolia   xii–xiv, liii, 1–9, 11–13, 15, 17–21, 30,
    37, 40, 42, 59, 62
Anatrophe   376
Anaxagoras   312
Ancaeus   72
ancestors/ancestry   29, 48, 252, 253, 282, 331,
    402; see also genealogy mythical
Anchas   156
Anchhor   293
Anchises   xlviii, 155–156

Andromache   xlviii, 36–38, 41, 60–61, 126,
    128, 181
Andromeda   55, 57–58, 61, 68, 166
Annales school   26
Annals of Assurbanipal   283 n.11, 284
Annia Eutychis   250
Antioch   xlvi, lii, 363, 366, 368, 390
– House of Aion   366, 368
Antiochus I   330
Antiochus III   345
Antiochus IV   337
Antonines   227–228
Antu   272, 273, 279
Anu   7, 11, 13, 269, 270, 273, 279
Anubanini of the Lullubi   344
Aornos   329
Aphrodisias   69, 234, 252, 258, 259, 370, 382,
    393, 395, 402
Aphrodite   xix, xliii, xlix, 12–13, 75, 78–81, 84,
    100, 153, 155–157, 162, 171, 187–189, 193,
    272–273
– sanctuary/temple at Paphos   72, 76, 81–82,
    86, 88
– Anchises   234
– Paphia   xv, 78, 84–87
– Venus   155, 156
Apis   310
Apollo   33, 48, 126, 148, 149, 159, 160,
    162–164, 191, 193, 201, 271, 272, 337, 339,
    360
– Lykeios   156
– Patroos   128, 144
– Thymbraeus   374
Apollodorus   15–16, 75, 85, 271, 273
Apollonia   370
Apollonis, Queen   144
Apollonius Rhodius   xxxix, 80, 146
Apophis   291, 192; see also snakes and griffins
Appian   310, 311, 323 n.84
Apuleius   309
Apulia/Apulian vase painters   xvi, 112, 113, 125,
    126, 139–141, 222
Apzuwa (Mesopotamian Apsu)   8
Aquileia   216, 223
Arab god Shai 'al Qaum   401
Arabia   211, 298, 401
– Arabian descent   338
Aramaeans   xliii

Aramaic   345, 40
– inscriptions   285, 382
– literature   303
– story of Horus son of Pwensh   285
Arbela   20
Arbinas (Lycian dynast)   59
Arcadia/Arcadians   xiv–xv, 71–78, 80–83,
    86–88, 91, 121, 369, 400–401; *see also*
    Tegea
Arcadocypriot dialect   73
Archemoros   222
Archilochus   xix, 267–268
Arctinus of Miletus   32
Ardašir   327, 347–349
Ares   156, 157, 338
Argead dynasty   331
Argonautica   146
Argos   xxxv, xlviii, 5, 46, 82, 88–89, 222, 223,
    225, 268
Ariadne   146, 147, 161, 162, 189, 193, 224
Ariatha   99
Aricia   113
Arimoi   15
Aristion   81
Aristobulus   xxxvi
Aristophanes   14
Aristotle   xxxiii, xxxviii, 77
Arles   165, 166, 215, 261
Armenia   xxxvi–xxxvii, 330
Armenos   xxxvii
Arria Maximina   195
Arrian   42, 296, 310
Arsacid (Parthian dynasty)   330, 337
– Mithridates I   335;
– Vologases IV   336
Arsuz   xlii, 20
Artagenes-Heracles-Ares   330
Artemis   xxxvi, xlvii, 35–36, 126, 128, 147, 233
– Artemis Tauropolos   xxxvi
Arycandus River   60
Arzawa   5–6, 18
Ascanius   115–117, 119, 120
Asinius Pollio in Rome   145
Assur, Iraq   18, 329
Assurbanipal   283, 284, 292
Assyria/Assyrians   xix, xliii, liii, 20, 22, 266,
    281, 283–284, 286–287, 290, 292–294,
    297, 301, 307, 355
– occupation of Egypt   303

– immigrants   266
– incantation   269, 270
– king Ninus   322
– poet   265
– royal propaganda   272
Atalanta   102, 377
Atalante   191–193, 200, 219, 221, 249
Ate   269, 270
Ateleta   102–3
Athena   13, 23, 77, 87, 156, 258, 267, 268, 272,
    273, 296
– Alea   83
– Parthenos   210, 223
– Pallas   98
Athenaeus   180
Athenodorus of Cana   11
Athens   xlvi, li–liii, 30, 74, 90, 210–213, 215,
    221, 223–224, 233–235, 240–241, 247,
    249–251
athletes and athletic competitions   157,
    199–200, 242, 245, 246, 248, 259, 363, 373
Athribis, northern Egypt   281, 284
Atlas   8, 11, 275, 277
Atreus   138
Atropates   xxxix
Attis   xxxv
Atticism   237, 241
Auge   87
Augeias   271–273
Augustus   70, 148, 181, 207
– Augustan state art   153, 157
– *clipeus virtutis*   177
Aulus Vibenna   147
Aurelia Ge   249
Aurelius Rufus   250
Australasia   3
Avesta   329, 349, 350; *see also* Zoroastrianism
Avidius Cassius   340
Avle   120
Avle Vipinas (Etruscan warrior)   119, 120
Avl Tarchunus (Etruscan Tarchon)   110
Azerbaijan   xxxix

B
Baal   xliv, 9–11, 13, 16
– identified with Seth   17 n.65
– Baal S.apanu   11, 16–17
– Ba'altars   346 n.58

Babylon/Babylonians   4–5, 265–267, 269, 271,
    272, 277, 323, 327–328, 332, 334,
    336–340, 344, 346, 355
Bacchae   xxxv
Bactria   xxxv, xli, 329, 339, 397
– Bactrian document   346
Bagistana/Bagistane/Mt. Bagistanus   333,
    334 n.15; *see also* Bisotun.
Bahrām II (Sasanian king)   349
Baitylos   11
barbarians   311, 402
Barlaam and Jehoshapat legend   xli–xlii
Battle of Actium   310
Battle of Alalia   118
Bayindir   42, 44, 63
Bel   337, 338
– Bel and Iranian Vahrām   345
– temple   337
– translation for Ahura Mazdā   346; Bel and
    Iranian Vahrām, 345
Belevi Mausoleum   246, 257, 260
Bellerophon   44–45, 53, 55, 69, 146, 207, 226,
    234, 245, 357
Benoît de Sainte-Maure's *Roman de Troie*   176
Berossos   11
Berouth "in Byblos"   11
Biga River/plain (Hellespontine Phrygia)
    30–32, 38–39; *see also* Granicus
bilingual, *see* language
birds   14, 100, 349, 350, 366
Bisotun/Bisitun,
– reliefs and dedications   327, 332–337, 344,
    347, 354
Bithynians   30
Black Sea   xxxix–xl, 3, 6, 379, 381
boars   117, 171, 186, 187, 189, 244, 350; *see
    also* Calydonian boar hunt
Bodhisattva   xli
Boeotia   xlv, 12
Boghaz-Köy (Hittite capital)   4
Bogota   xxxiv
Bokennife (father of Inaros)   284
Boreas   232
Borysthenes river   xxxix
boukoloi ("herdsmen")   290, 305, 307
boys   50, 132, 199, 379
Brahmins   xxxvii
Brides   xxxviii, 35–36, 68, 274; *see also*
    marriage and wives

Briseis   358, 365, 368, 378, 382, 383, 386
British history   li
Brutus   186
Bubastis   310
Buddha   xli, 329
Bulgaria   xxxviii
bulls   48, 98, 100, 233, 293, 350, 381
– Bull of Heaven   272–274, 279
– Bull of Per-Sopdu   294
Burkert, Walter   ix, xxxiii, 6
Busiris, Egypt   284, 309, 313
Buthrotum (Butrint)   xlix–l
Byblos   10–11, 19

C
Cacu/Cacus   95, 119–121
Cadmus   15, 312
Caecilia Metella   242, 243
Caelius Vibenna (brother of Aulus Vibenna)
    147
Caere/Cerveteri, Etruria   115, 118, 119
Caesarea/Cherchel   360, 362, 370, 376
Caile Vipinas   120
Calchas   233
Callimachus   79–80
Callisthenes   xxxvi
Callisto   147
Callithea monument   247
Calydon   190
Calydonian boar hunt   189, 219, 227, 232, 245,
    249
Calypso   271, 275, 277, 278
Cambyses   315
Camillus   186
Campania   150
Campus Martius, Rome   145
Çanakkale   68
Canosa   128, 130
Caracalla   379
Caria   xxxiv
Carmania, Persian/Sasanian province   338,
    345
Carranque, Spain   366
Carthaginians   146 n.13, 148
Carystus   245
Caspian Sea   xxxix–xl
Cassiopeia   58
Cato   116, 117, 119

cattle   14 n.50
– of Geryon   24, 276
– of the Sibai   xxxvii
Caucasian epic   xxxviii
caves   xliv, 15, 271, 337, 351
Cecrops   xlvi, 223
Celaenae   24
Centauromachy   29, 227, 236, 245, 246
centaurs   239, 303, 376; *see also* Nessos and
     Chiron
Central Asia   328, 329, 352, 353, 355, 399
centurions   255
Cephallenia   xlix
Cerberus   184, 268
Chalcidice   xlviii
Chalcis   xiii
Characene/Mesene   328, 335, 337
– rulers   338
chariots   xlviii, 8, 50–51, 129, 190, 192, 270,
     272, 273, 296
– charioteer   44, 50, 105, 190, 270, 272
– chariot-team   272
Charun (Etruscan demon of death)   147 n.18
Cherchel   360, 361, 371, 372, 392
Chiaramonti Heracles types   339
child/children   7–8, 11–12, 32, 38, 51, 58,
     81–82, 85–86, 102, 106, 129, 132, 141, 173,
     175, 180–182, 194, 199, 222, 223, 229–231,
     239, 248, 302, 390; *see also* boys and girls
– Achilles   374
– Epiur   100
childhood,   xxi, 201, 239, 372–374, 387
Chimaera   44, 47, 55, 245
China   xxxviii
Chios   xlix
Chiron   227, 229, 238, 242, 258, 364, 365, 371,
     373, 375–378, 386, 387, 390
– Chiron teaching   370, 388
Chiusi   118
Choma/Hacimusalar, Lycia   42
Christ   315, 325, 397
Christians/Christianity   xli, xlvi–xlvii, 305, 357,
     373, 387, 395; *see also* Manicheans
– Christian rioters   378
– Christian sarcophagi   173
Chrysaor   44, 47
Cicero   174, 186, 195, 204, 316
Cilicia   xxxv, xliii, xlvi, 11, 14–15, 17–18
Circe   149, 275–277

Civita Castellana (Falerii)   99
Claudia Antonia Tatiane   252
Claudia Lyde Ventidia Claudiane   250
Claudian   376
Clazomene   24
– sarcophagus   48
Clearchus of Soloi   77
Cleisthenes   xlvi
clementia   161
Cleomenes, Seleucid governor   327
Cleopatra Eurydice   xl
Cleopatra VII   xxxiii
Clymene   181
Clytemnestra   85, 231, 233, 237, 241
Cnidus   311–313
Codex Sabaiticus   75
coins   xxxv, xlix,
– depicting death of Opheltes   222–223, 225,
– depicting Heraclean figures   331, 334, 335,
     337, 338, 345, 346, 348
colonies/colonisation   liii, 30, 32, 248;
– Arcadian colonisation myth, Cyprus   72
– Greek colonisation in Cilicia   18
combat   xliv, 10, 116, 227, 242, 255, 286, 294,
     298, 300, 302–3
comedy   134–137
comic iconography   134
Commagene   329–330, 337
Commodus   185
concordia   160, 161, 177, 233
concubines   11, 36
– *hetairai*   xxxviii
Conference Tomb   144
connectivity   xiv, 18, 52, 62
consolatio   178–182, 193, 196; Roman
     consolatory texts, 184; decrees, 253
contemptor divum   117
Contest for Inaros' Armour   292, 294, 297–301
Contest for Inaros' Diadem and Lance   287,
     294, 297, 300
Contest for the Benefice of Amun   292–294,
     299
Coptic   xli
Corinth   129, 222–224, 231, 261, 262
– Corinthians in Italy   xlvii
– coins   222
– sarcophagus   223
Corycian Cave in Cilicia   15
Corycus   15–19

corymbus 348
cosmogony, early Greek 16
craftsmen 213 n.26, 247, 329; Epeios the
  craftsman, 98
Creon 129, 130, 237
Creophylus 268
Crete/Cretans xliii–xliv, xlvi, xlix, l, lii, 18, 77,
  229
– Cretan seer Epimenides 16
– Cretan Zeus xliv
Creusa 173, 179, 182, 193
– Creusa/Medea 180, 202
– Creusa/Medea sarcophagi 193, 237
Crimean peninsula xxxix
Croatia xlvii
Croesus 181, 314, 315, 320, 321
Ctesiphon 327
cult xiii, xxxvi, xlii, xlv, xlvii, 1, 16, 87, 89, 223,
  248, 249
– of Achilles 381
– Aphrodite of Paphos 81, 296, 311, 321, 322,
  324
– Aphrodite of Tegea 86
– Egyptian 292, 296, 311, 339
– Heracles 341 n.39
– Hittite 18
– Imperial Roman 234
– Osiris 292, 321, 322, 324
– Ptolemaic ruler cult 82
– Venus and Mars domestic cult images 154
Cumae xliv, xlvii, 12
cupids 147 n. 15, 148, 151, 153, 154, 156, 157,
  160, 227
Curetes 176
Cycnus xlv
Cydonia xlix
Cyprus/Cypriots xii, xiv–xv, xxxviii, xliii–xliv,
  xlvi, xlviii, l, lii, 6, 44, 52, 71–91, 353, 359,
  362, 376, 377, 400
– Arcadocypriot dialect of ancient Greek 73
– Cypriot Aphrodite xliv
– Cypriot and Arcadian traditions 80
– hellenisation of Cyprus 72
– kings of Salamis 78
– royal traditions 79
– syllabic script 76
Cyrenaica 211, 361
Cyrene 80, 82, 243, 257, 309
Cyrsilus of Pharsalus (Thessalian officer) xxxvi

Cyrus the Great 315
Cythnus 74
Cyzicus 30–32, 144

D
daemons/demons 57, 147 n.18, 292; see also
  Div-e Sepid.
Dagan 10–11, 19
Dagon/grain 11
Daoist myths xlvi
Dardanos 37
Dareios Painter 132
Dares the Phrygian (*De excidio Trojae*) li, 176,
  382 n.74
Darius I 334, 346
Darius III 296
Daskyleion 30, 32, 37, 39–40, 63, 65, 68
death,
– good death (καλὸς θάνατος) 229
– hero's tragic death (as foreign motif) 176
– of Achilles 303, 374
– of Atreus 138
– of women and children on Attic sarcophagi
  229, 231
– waters of 275, 276, 280
Deianeira 268
Deidameia 197, 198, 229, 238, 359, 362–365,
  373, 378
deities xliii, 5, 9, 16–17, 22, 273, 291, 327, 330,
  335, 339, 346, 355; see also divinities
– ancient semitic 11
– pagan 378
– primeval 9
– primordial 14
– solar Babylonian 337
– tutelary 9
– deity-lists 11. See also divinities.
Delhi xxxvii
Delian League 30, 78
Delphi 33, 126–128, 217–219, 249, 309, 312
Delphyne (she-dragon) 15
Demarous 11
Demeter 5, 223, 310
Demokrates 81
Demotic stories 285, 289; narratives, 295
Demylas 250
Dep, Egypt 293
Derrida, Jacques 28
Diagoras of Rhodes 14

Diana xlvii
Dictys of Crete (*Ephemeris belli Trojani*) li, 176
Dido 149, 151, 153, 199
Didymateiche/Didyon Teichos 30
Diesptr 104
Dio Chrysostom 236, 253
– *Melancomas* 225
Diodoros Pasparos 249
Diodorus vi, xx, 309, 311–325, 399
– Diodorus' treatment of Egyptian myth 324
Diomedes xix, 108, 229, 233, 272, 273, 361
Dione 272, 273
Dionysius Halicarnassus 116–119, 121
Dionysus xxxv, xxxvii, 5, 161, 162, 189, 201,
       223, 239, 309, 357, 376, 397, 398, 40
– Dionysiac vindemia 227, 239
Dioskoros of Aphrodito 390
Div-e Sepid (White Devil) 351
divinities xxxvii, 44, 171, 174, 193, 325, 348,
       351
Dodona 114
Dokimeion xxxv, 211, 212
Domitian 196
Domus Aurea 358, 359, 362
Dorian xlvi
dragons 15, 57, 277
– dragon killer 330
– dragon-slaying myths 16
dream 265, 275, 279
Drusus Nero 181
Dura Europus 329, 344

E
Ea 7–9, 14, 19, 22
eagle 158, 268, 274
earth 7–8, 11–14, 40, 90, 126, 267, 269, 270,
       280, 291, 292, 302, 319
Ecbatana xxxvi, 331, 334
Echedoros xlv
Echemus 72
Echetime 78–79, 81, 86
Echetimon 79
Echo 181
Edessa, Turkey 382, 383, 387, 392
Egypt/Egyptians xx, xxxvi, 6, 17, 19, 74, 79,
       82, 281, 283–295, 300, 303, 304, 307,
       309–312, 321, 322, 326, 399
– collective identity 282, 294
– cast of warriors 287
– god-king 315

– and Greeks in Egypt 286
– historical literature 282, 290, 307
– national characteristics 310
– national history 304
– priesthood xix–xx, 282, 289, 290, 303
– self-image 289, 304
– theology 309
Eirene 223, 377
ekphrasis 298, 304–5
El 10–11, 13
Elchsntre 100–101
El Djem 360, 361
El Dorado xxxiv, 397
Elephantine 299
Eleusis 123
Elinai 100–101, 113
Elioun 11
Elis 271–273
Elmali 41, 63, 65, 67–69
Elos/Kronos 11
Eltarra 9
Elus/Kronos 11
Elymais 327–329, 338, 340, 341, 345, 354
– Elymaean inscriptions 345
– pantheon 345
– religion and religious practices 345, 346,
       352
– rock reliefs 332, 344
Elymian Segesta,
– adoption of Trojan ancestry xlix
Endymion 189, 200–202, 207, 238
Enkīdu xix, 267, 270–275, 279, 280
Enlil's temple 279
envoys xxxix, 87–88, 121, 283
Eos 181
Epeios xlviii–xlix, liv, 98
Ephesus 211, 214, 215, 234, 252
Ephialtes 14
Ephorus of Cyme 311, 312
Epirus xlviii, 156, 370
Epiur 100–101
Eratosthenes 75, 80, 89
Erechtheus/Erechthonios 223
Eretria xlv–xlvi
Erigone 181
Erinyes 12
Eriphyle 51, 132
erotes 211, 227, 239, 368
Erytheia 268, 276

Esarhaddon   272, 283, 284, 292
eschatological interpretations   178, 180
– message   184
Esquiline Hill   115, 116, 144
Ethiopia/Ethiopians   57, 74
– hero Memnon   38
Ethopoiai   390
Ethun   95, 111, 112, 118, 400
Etruria/Etruscans   xxxiv, xlvii, 48, 95–121, 123,
   400, 402
– Ethun and Velachtra   400
– founder hero Tarchon   118
– goddess   156
– goddess of Victory   100
– mirrors   97, 100, 104, 106, 107, 109, 111, 118,
   122, 155, 156, 400
Etule   98
Euadne   181
Euagoratis   79, 86
Euboea/Euboeans   xlii–xlvi, liii, 245,397, 398
– travellers   xii–xiii
Eubre   368, 369
Euenos, river   268
Eukarpos   230
Eunike   81
Euphrates   10, 271, 272, 279, 359
Euprepeia   377
Eurasia   3, 330
Euripides   xxxv, xlvii, 277, 312, 358, 402
– *Andromache*   126
– *Herakleidai*   270
– *Hippolytus*   xlviii
– *Iphigenia in Tauris*   126, 128
– *Medea*   129
– *Skyrioi*   358
– *Trojan Women* and *Hecuba*   32
Eurystheus   xix, 267–272, 331
Eurytion/ Eurytos   268
Eve   12
Exekias   35
– *exemplum/exempla*
– *maeroris*   xvii, 181, 189, 192, 193, 202, 401
– *mortalitatis*   vi, xvii, 50, 169, 180, 181, 183,
   187, 188, 191–193, 201, 202, 401
– *virtutis*   vi, xvii, 169, 171, 182–186, 190, 192,
   193, 195
– *virtutis*, female   194, 195
– *deificationis*   184
– *pietatis*   193

F
Failaka/Phylake island   xxxvi, 341
Faliscans   96
Farnese Heracles   339
Fate/fate   192
Fates   376, 386, 389
Fayoum   281
festivals   x, 6, 116, 117, 253, 259, 293
Flood   272, 280
Foucault, Michel   26
France   li
François Tomb   144, 166
Furies   132, 191, 293

G
Gaia   10, 12
games   248
Gandhara/Gandharan sculpture   329
Ganymede Painter   113
gardens   xlvi, li, 67, 275–277
Ge   12
gender   xiv, xviii, 37–38, 41, 44, 50, 61, 63, 69,
   149, 160, 198–201, 204, 238, 239, 249
– ambivalence   363
– boundaries   198
– gender identity   xiv, 28
– female   69
– masculine   323
– permeability of   198
– gender relations   238
– gendered iconographies   38, 249
– gendering in memorial practices   37
– multi-gender burials   38
genealogy/genealogies   xiv, 11–12, 71, 253,
   300, 307; *see also* kinship fictive
genitals   12, 57
Genius Populi Romani   233
Genius Senatus   233, 234
Gens Iulii   148, 157
Gergis   38
Germanicus   310, 326
Geryon   24, 276, 399–400
Geryoneis/Geryoneus   268
ghosts   33, 129, 275, 280, 296, 306
giants   xliv, 8, 12
– giant Aloeadae Otus   14
Gilgāmeš   vi, xviii–xix, 5, 122, 265–280, 341,
   342, 398
– Gilgamising elements   274

– Gilgamising epic   272
– Gilgamising *Herakleia*   xviii, 258
– motifs   398
– version   268
girls   xviii, xxxvii, 33–35, 58, 60, 195, 197–201, 249, 363, 373
Gjölbaschi/Trysa   245–246
Glastonbury Tor   xlvii
globalisation   ix
Gnaeus Gellius   120, 121
goats   xxxvi, 21, 350
god-king   325
gods, *see also* deities
– generations of   10, 17
– vanishing gods   5
golden apples   275, 277, 278, 339
Golden Fleece   277
Golgi, Cyprus   44, 72
Gondwana   3
Gordium   42, 59
gorgons   24, 47, 299
Gospel stories   xlvii
Gotarzes   334
– reliefs   337
Gotha   243, 244
Graeci   xlv
Graia   xlv
Granicus Plain   23, 30
– River   399
Greco-Macedonian communities   352
– settlers   344
Greek culture   xv, 140, 358, 399, 401
– in opposition to Persian   39
– influence on Etruscan   105
– influence on Indian tradition   xxxvii
– in Egyptian context   303
– western   140
Greek East   xviii, 209, 210, 222–225, 234, 239, 240, 248, 253
Greek Drama   xlviii, 142
griffins   239, 292
Guido delle Colonne   li
Gürses   60
gymnasium   134, 136, 363

H
Hacimusalar   42, 68
Hadad   11

Hades   5, 129, 174, 179, 189, 202, 232, 268, 272, 273, 275, 276
Hadrian   255, 261, 305
– Hadrian's gate, Athens   225
– Hadrian's Panhellenion   253
Haleplibahçe   358, 383, 385, 387–391
– Villa of Amazons   385, 388, 389
Halieutica by Oppian   15
Halimedes   51
Harmonia   51
Harpy Monument   32, 60
Hatra   329 n.6, 337 n.26, 338
Hattic   4–5
heaven   xlii–xliv, xlvi, 5, 8–9, 11 n.37, 14, 269, 270, 272, 275, 277, 279, 299, 397, 398
Hebat   8
Hebe   278
Hecataeus of Abdera   311–314
Hector   36, 38, 53, 173, 175, 197, 227–229, 296, 358, 373, 374, 386, 390
Hecuba   32–33, 36, 85, 382–384
Hedammu   8, 14
Hekate   5
Helen   55, 100, 102, 113, 148, 149
Helena   102–3
Helenus   xlviii, l
Helike, Marcia   195
Heliodorus   309
Heliopolis   292, 300
Helios   205, 207, 275, 276
Hellanicus   79, 312
Hellenisation   viii, liii, 72, 90, 225, 212, 265, 267, 329
Hellespontine Phrygia   30–31
Hephaestion   296
Hephaestus   98, 108, 229, 298
Hephthalite   349
Hera   112, 156, 185, 267–270, 272, 273, 299
Heracles   xix–xxi, xxxvii, xlv, 163, 166, 183, 184, 186, 234, 235, 267, 278, 327, 329–332, 334–342, 351, 352, 398–401; *see also* Hercle and Hercules
– in Bactria and India   397
– in Gandharan sculpture   329
– in Iran   327, 331
– sanctuaries in Iran   34–35, 341
– Kallinikos   333, 334
– Nergal   339
– Verethragna   329, 336, 338

– Heraclean figure 335, 344, 346
Herakleia xviii, 268
heralds 365, 366
Hercle (Etruscan Hercules) 99–101, 104, 400
Hercules 120, 121, 171, 172, 184–186
– life of 162, 163
– sarcophagi 202
Hermes 15–16, 22, 156, 207, 223, 268, 271
Hermes (Eratosthenes of Cyrene) 80
Hero x
Heroon/-oa xviii, 44, 209, 245, 246, 248–253, 259
– of Opheltes at Nemea 222, 223
– of the Saithidai at Messene 250, 251
Herodes Atticus 211, 257, 369–371, 395; *see also* Villa of Herodes Atticus
Herodotus xx, 46, 74, 106, 309, 312–316, 319–321
heroes xiii, xv, xviii–xxii, 44, 50, 103, 104, 106, 171, 176, 177, 180–192, 197, 198, 200, 224, 225, 235–238, 248, 259, 261, 285, 295, 296, 299, 301, 302, 331–333, 340, 341, 344, 351, 352, 357, 387
– age of 397, 401
– culture-hero 319, 399
– Egyptian heroes in Greek texts 290
– Homeric hero 87
– panhellenic 358
– wandering xiii–xv, 71, 76, 86–88
– heroines 193, 363
heroisation vi, xviii, 209, 210, 212, 236, 245, 246, 248, 250, 254–255
– female 249
– private 209, 225, 249, 250
– heroised ephebe 225
Herulians 211
Hesiod vii, xix, 11–15, 18–19, 22, 267, 277
Theogony xliii, 4, 10, 12–13, 21
Hesiodic fragment 273
Hesiodic *Naupaktia* xlviii
Hesiodic divine succession in heaven myth xiii, 13, 16, 398
Hesperides 275–277, 184, 339; Hesperides' garden, 276
heteroerotic 236
Hierapolis, Phrygia,
– Casa dei Capitelli Ionici 366
Hierapytna 229
Hippodameia 238, 241

Hippolytus xlvii–xlviii, 171, 183, 186, 192, 200, 202, 212, 224, 227, 229, 230, 234, 236, 242
– sarcophagi 172, 187, 189, 224, 241–244
Hippomedon 224
Hisarlik 38
Hispania 211
historiography 311, 313, 315–326, 399
– Greco-Roman historiography vi, xx, 309, 325
Hittites/Hittite
– cults and myth xiii xlii–xliv, 4–19, 398
– comparison with Hesiod's Theogony 12–13
– Hittite-Hurrian language 266
– myth 7, 10, 13, 16
– texts, xlii 5, 11
Hiyawa in Cilicia 18
Homer vi–vii, xxxix, l, 14–15, 98, 175, 265–280, 295, 296, 387, 398, 399; *see also* *Iliad* and *Odyssey*
– Homeric epics xiii, xix, xxi, 72, 77, 88, 146, 261, 265, 268, 357
– Neoanalysis 265
– stories 156, 365, 366
Homeric Hymn to Demeter 5 n.9
Homerists 265, 266
Homonoia 161
homosocial aesthetic 236, 241
Honos 233
hoplites 53
Horace 145
horses xxxix, xlvii–xlviii, 48, 50–51, 53, 56, 97–98, 102, 186, 199, 219, 272, 336, 350
– winged 44
Horus 17, 310
Humbaba 267, 271, 274, 279
Hundred-Handers 12
Hungarian 265
hunting 38, 150, 151, 153, 171, 172, 186, 187, 189, 190, 198–200, 219, 226, 227, 230, 242–245, 247, 274, 336, 373, 377, 386
– hunting dogs 9
Hupasiya 15
Hurrian 4–5, 9, 17, 266, 398
– bilingual 5
Hurrian-Hittite, see Hittites
– Hurrian Tessub 7
Hyacinthia festivals xlvi
Hyacinthus son of Pantauchus 327, 329, 333, 335, 336
hybridisation hybridity, ix, 329

Hydra   270
Hyksos   290
Hylas   146, 181
Hypnos   268
Hypomnemata   383
Hypsipyle, Lemnian queen   222, 224, 237
Hyrcanians   217
Hyspaosines   335, 337–339

I

Iapetos   11–12, 17
Iasonia festivals/Iayezana "places of worship"
   xxxvi–xxxvii, 401
Ibycus   268, 278
identity
– cultural   ix, xviii, xxiii, 65, 213, 257, 259
– ethno-linguistic   31, 35, 61, 399
Ikaria   xxxvi
Ikaros   xxxvi, li
Ikaros island   li
Iliad   xviii–xix, xxi, 162, 163, 181, 184,
   265–268, 270, 272–274, 278, 280, 296,
   298–301, 358, 365–367, 379
Ilioupersis   32
Ilioupersis Painter   126, 128
Illuyanka   14–16
immortality   186, 267, 275, 277, 278, 280, 316,
   321, 324, 390
– immortal honours   xx, 320
Inara   15
Inaros   xix, 281–287, 289–294, 297–301,
   303–304
Inaros of Athribis (historical figure), 281
Inaros-Petubastis-Zyklus   306-7
India   xxxvii, 292
– Indian king   302
– Indian myth of Pandaia   398
Indigenisation   ix
Indo-European   3
Indo-Iranians   4
Ino-Leucothea   xlvii
Iodasphes   xli
Iolaos/Iolaus   xix, 267–275, 270–272, 274,
   275; Iolaus/Vile, 99
Ionia   xlvi, 18, 24, 30, 39, 216
Iðunn, Nordic goddess   277
Iphigenia   xlvii, 33–34, 126–128, 226, 232,
   233, 402–3
Iphitos   268

Iran   vi, 327, 331, 333, 339, 340, 352, 353
– pre-Islamic   352
Iranian   xxxvii, 265, 328, 329, 336, 346
– art   xxi, 329–331, 341, 342, 349, 352
– deities/divinities   334, 335, 329, 345, 349
– dynasts   335
Iraq   353, 354
iron race   12
Ischia   xliii–xliv
Isidore of Charax   334
Isinda   60
Isis   xx, 309, 310, 320–325, 399
Islamic conquest   331
Isola Sacra   194
Ištar   20, 272, 273, 279, 344
Italian Marches   xlvii
Iulus Ascanius   198–199
Iuventus   102, 104, 118

J

Japan   xlvi
Japeth   17
Jason   xxxiv, 146, 204, 206, 277; *see also*
   Iasonia
Jauss, Robert   177, 178
Jebel Aqra   xlii–xliii
Jehoshaphat   xli–xlii
Jerusalem   216, 358, 369, 373, 381, 383, 384,
   386
Jordan   368
Joseph of Arimathea   xlvii
Julius Caesar   310
Jung, Carl   114
Junius Euhodus   194
Jupiter   116, 117
Justin's *Epitome of Trogus*   xlix

K

Kaiseraugst Plate   373, 376, 386
kalasiris   287, 294, 300
Kalasiris, Egyptian high priest   293, 309, 312
Kapaneus   224
Karaburun II Tomb   41–42
Karhuha   9
Kastorion of Soloi   77
Katakekaumene, area of Lydia   19
Kazakhstan   xxxix
Kerberos *see* Cerberus
Kekrops, *see* Cecrops

Kerényi, Carl   95, 114
Ketos   57–58; Ketos/Kraken, 55
Khorsābād   341, 343
Khuzestān   327
kings   xvi, xx, 72, 81, 112, 119, 286, 289, 293,
    296, 314, 320, 335, 341, 348
– ideal Egyptian   xix, 282
– native   281, 283, 289, 303
– neo-Hittite   xlii
– pre-Greek Cypriot   76
– kingship in heaven   xiii, 3–19
– Sassanian "King of kings" (Šāhanšāh)   327
kinship   xv, xlix, 87–88, 400; see also
    genealogy
Kinyras   76, 80–81, 83, 86, 298
Kizilbel Tomb, Lycia   xiv, 23–24, 29, 41–42,
    45–48, 50, 59–61, 399
Kizöldün Tumulus, Lydia   31
Kizzuwatna   6, 17
Klytemnestra, see Clytemnestra
Kopreus   267
kore   35, 123
Kouretes   xliv
Kourion   359, 360, 362, 363
Kouros   xliv
Kraken   57; see also Ketos
Kreonteia   129
Kronos   xliv, 11–14, 22, 298
Kubaba   9
Kumarbi   xliv, 7–9, 11, 13–14, 19–20, 398
Kurunta   9, 16
Kushan Bactria   329
Kushites   281
– Kushite Empire   283
– invasion of Egypt   284
Kyknos   268, 270
Kypros   74, 80
Kyros of Panopolis   390

L
Laconian vase painting   52
Ladochori/Igoumenitsa   228
Lagaria   xlviii
Lamaštu   270
LAMMA   9, 14
language   viii, xxxv, 31, 173, 261, 266, 290,
    291, 301, 318, 383
– bilingual   xviii, 265–268, 273, 277, 304, 337,
    398

– Cyriot and Greek dialect   73, 74, 81
– dialect akin to Latin   100
– Egyptian language   289, 290
– Etruscan   110, 111
– Greek creative misunderstanding of Levantine
    worshippers   xxxviii
– Greek-speakers   xliv, xlvi, 23, 30–31, 39, 337,
    357
– Iranian speakers   265
– monoglot Greeks   xxxv
– multi-lingual Achaemenids and Sassanians
    337 n.27
– polyglot missionaries, misunderstanding   xli
– Sanskrit-speakers   xxxvii
– Syriac   383
– translation   vii, xxxviii, 4–5, 75, 337, 346, 394
Laodameia   193
Laodike   xv, 83–87
– historical   84
La Olmeda   360
Laomedon   148, 159, 160, 163
Lasa Thimrae   100
Late Bronze Age   xlii–xliii, 3, 6, 10
Latium   xlvii, 96
Laucie Mezenties   95, 115
laudatio funebris   180
Laudatio Murdiae   195
Laurasia   3
Lausus, son of Mezentius   116, 117
Lavinium   116
Leander   x
Lebanon   212, 279
Leda   158–161, 226
Ledra, Cyprus   81
Lefkandi   xlv
legends; see also myth
– El Dorado   xxxiv
– Egyptian legendary stories   285–286,
    288–289, 291–292, 309
– Etruscan historical legend   148
– Heracles in early Greek legend   267
– Latin legend   112
– Legend-myth   95
– Ossetic legend   278
– Trojan   xlix
– legendary rulers of Britain   li
Lernaean Hydra   268
Lesbos   18
Leucas   xlix

Leucothea xlvii

Leuke (island) 00 n.12, 374 n.56

Leukippe 359, 363

Levant xxxviii, xlii, xlvii, 6, 8, 10, 16, 18, 52

Levant and east Cilicia xliii

Levantine xlvi

Lévi-Strauss, Claude 26

Libanios of Antioch, *On behalf of the Dancers*
  363

– *Progymnasmata* 390, 391

Library of Alexandria 79

Library of Asinius Pollio in Rome 145

Libya 292, 394

Limyra, Lycia 44, 46, 60

Linus 201

Lions xxi,117, 267, 271, 274, 333, 341–344

– lion cubs 274, 275

– hunt 46, 48, 60

– hunters 226, 352

– lion skin 185, 267, 271, 327, 331, 332, 337,
  339–341, 344, 348, 352, 399

– wrestlers 340, 343–344, 352

– lioness 274, 275, 298

Livius Andronicus xlix

Livy 116, 117, 119, 121

lotus 52

Lubarna xliii

Lucan 323

Lupa Romana 233, 234

Luqorcos 100, 102

Luwian 4, 8–9, 15–17

– Anatolian route of transmission xiv

– neo-Hittite inscriptions xlii

Lycaon 181

Lycia 32, 41–42, 44–46, 50, 59–60, 249, 377,
  399

– Lycian king 53, 55

– myth 53

– Lycians 30, 48, 50, 55

Lycomedes 108, 197, 198, 358–359, 363, 373

Lycophron, *Alexandra* 74–75, 80

Lycourgus/ Lycurgus

– Thracian king 146, 401

– grandfather of Agapenor 72

– Nemean king 222

Lydia 18–19, 31, 37, 44, 314

Lykourgos, *see* Lycourgus/Lycurgus

Lysippus 339

M

Macedon/Macedonia xlvi, xlviii, 223

– Macedonians xxxvi, xxxix, xl–xli, 245, 296,
  33; *see also* Greco-Macedonians

Madaba, Jordan 368, 369

magic 129, 354

– magician 285 n.20

Magna Graecia 96, 107, 140

maidens 47, 358, 360, 362, 363, 373

maids/ maidservants 154, 158, 382–386

male Greek beauty contests 237

Malibu 365, 378

Mani xli–xlii, 351

Mania 37

Manichaeans xli

Marathon 225, 227 n.5, 236, 242, 250 n.147

Marathonian bull 224

Marduk 6, 115

Mari, Syria 6, 10

Mark Antony xxxiii, 184

marriage 35, 36, 38, 40, 60, 77, 373, 382, 386,
  387 n.81, 391 n.87; see also *matrimonium*

Marrus/Mendes 313

Mars 153–155, 157, 158, 189, 235 n.9

– planet 338

Marsi (Italic tribe) 121

Marsyas 121, 223, 230

masculinity 197, 205, 228, 240–242, 245, 249,
  254, 401

Masjed-e Solaimān sanctuary, Elymais 341,
  342, 344, 345, 351

masks xvi, 125, 130, 136, 138, 139; comic, 134,
  136

Mater Matuta xlvii

matrimonium 160

Mauretania Caesariensis 360, 370, 371

mausoleum 194, 246

– of Caecilia Metella, Rome 242, 243

– of Halicarnassus 245

Maxentius 243

Meda xl

Medea 38, 128–130, 165, 173, 177, 277

Medes 323; Media, xxxix, 327, 328

Medius of Larissa (Thessalian officer) xxxvi

Medusa 44–47, 61, 70, 113, 399

Megales, prophet 120, 121

Megasthenes (*Indica*) xxxvii, 398

Meleager 112 n.51, 171, 172, 176, 177, 181,
    189–192, 194, 202, 219, 227 n.4, 236, 237,
    240, 244, 357, 377
– Heroon at Delphi 217–219
– sarcophagi 172, 189–191, 194, 244, 200
Meliai-Nymphs 12
Melicertes xlvii
Memnon 181
Memphis xxxvi, 283, 284, 309, 310, 323 n.84
Menander Rhetor 186, 376
Menas 313
Mende, Chalcidice xliv
Mendes xliv, 287, 292, 313
Menelaus 76, 100 n.12, 233, 275–277, 369;
    see also Menle
Menle (Etruscan Menelaus) 100–101
Menrva 99
Mešān/Characene 336
Mesene 336–338, 353, 355
– Mesenian 339, 340
Mesopotamia 4, 6, 9, 21, 122, 265, 352, 353
– Mesopotamian xviii, 8, 278, 331, 341
– art 344
– narratives 6
– texts 266
Messene, Greece 250, 251
Messina xliii, li
Metapontum xlviii
Metilia Akte 194
Metilia Torquata 197, 198
Metis 12
Mezentius xvi, 95–121, 400
Mezntie 95–121, 400
Micos 102
Miletus 32
Milo 174
Miltiades 224
Milyad 41–42, 46, 60–61, 399
Mine 100
Minerva 144
Minnemei 299
Minos 98–99, 129, 130, 181
Minotaur 99, 224, 400
Mithra 337, 348
Mithradatkert/Old Nisa 331
Mithridates 336–338
Moira 230
Mongolia xxxviii
Mons Kasion 8

monsters 8, 16, 47, 52, 120, 176, 271, 267,
    340, 344
Monte Iato 144
Monthbaal 301
Morgantina 144
mortals ix, 16, 180, 186, 278, 298, 387
– gods loving mortals 189
mothers 13, 35–36, 58, 80–81, 87, 106 n.28,
    108, 138, 148, 173, 176, 181, 187, 191, 272,
    379, 381, 386, 388, 390
Mount Bisotun 333
Mount Etna 15
Mount Hazzi xlii–xliii, 8, 15–16, 18
– Mount Hazzi/Kasios xlii
Mount Ida 155
Mount Kanzura 7, 13
Mount Kasion, see Mount Hazzi
Mount Māšu 267, 277, 280
Mount Sabalan 334
Mount Sambulos 336
Mount S.apanu 10–11, 16
Muses 226, 269, 270
Mycenae 138
Mycenaean Greeks 5, 18, 73, 89–91, 267
Mysia/Mysians 30, 38, 66–67
myth; see also legends, story telling
– anthropogenic 12
– diffusion xiii, xxxiii, li, 3, 140, 387
– dragon-slaying 16
– early Levantine 6
– founder stories xlviii, 23, 25, 38, 45, 71, 72,
    75, 77, 85, 87, 118, 248, 253, 313, 320
– Greek (wandering) vii, xi, xiv, xlix, lii, 95–97,
    100, 105, 169, 176, 202, 331, 332, 398–
– hypothetical proto-Syrian 17
– making meaning/sense of myth 23, 25, 39,
    62, 177–179
– myth as resistance literature 381–387
– myths of divine succession in heaven 3–19
– mytho-spheres 210
– national myth 290, 310
– non-mythological themes 24, 34, 44, 221,
    227, 229, 242, 244, 245, 247
– Nordic myth 277
– oral transmission of myth 95, 100, 105, 106,
    121
– proto-Phoenician 12, 17
– Roman myths 95, 118, 146, 199, 233–235
– sociological meanings of myth 402

– theogonic   402
mythologemes   95, 114, 331
myth-ritual pattern, common   14
Mytilene/*muwatalla*   18 n.73

N
Nablus   363, 365, 371, 377, 392
Naevius, Gnaeus   xlix
Naples   xii, liii, 126, 150, 152, 154, 158–160, 165, 197
Naqš-e Rajab, in Persis   327, 347, 349–351
Narcissus   xlv–xlvi, 146, 162
Nart Sagas   xxxviii, 26
Nausikaa   277
Naxos   224
Nea Paphos, Cyprus
– Villa of Theseus   376, 377
Nearkhos   338
Necho of Sais   283–287, 292, 304
Pekrur of Per-Sopdu   283
Nemea   222, 223, 271, 340
Nemean Games   222
Nemean lion   xxi, 235, 268, 271, 341, 342, 352
Nemi   xlvii–xlviii, l
Nemrud Daği   330
Neo-Assyrian   341
Neo-Hittite   xliii–xliv, 18
Neon   378, 379
Neoptolemus   xlviii, 35–36, 126–128, 296, 303
Nereid monument   245
Nereids   108, 380
Nereus   275, 276
Nergal   331, 336–338
Nerik, Anatolia   14, 16
Nestor   108, 176
Nicander   278
Nike   52, 349
Nikokles, king of Paphos   79
Nile   312, 319
Nineveh   265, 284
Ninos   xx
Ninsun   279
Ninus   322–325
Niobe   38, 58, 175, 180, 181, 207
Niobids   175, 179, 180, 201, 202, 182
Nippur   7, 279
Nireus   181
Nonnus   15–16
North Africa   359, 360, 373, 374, 386, 387

Nostoi   74, 136, 141, 397
novel, ancient   309
Nubia/Nubians   xix, 57, 283, 284, 286, 292, 299
– Nubian sources on Inaros   284
Numicus river   116
nurses   106, 132, 222, 229, 230, 382, 384, 386
Nyktimos   75
Nysa   xxxiv–xxxv

O
oath   269, 270, 322
Oceanus   268, 276
Octavia Paulina   199–200
Odios   366
Odysseus   xlvii, l, 95, 108–111, 118, 226, 229, 233, 245, 275–278, 303, 318, 359, 361, 363, 365, 366, 369, 370, 374, 375
Odyssey   xviii, xlix, 50, 266–271, 274–277
Oenotrians   xlviii
Oinomaos   229
Old Man of the Sea   275–277
Old Paphos   72, 75, 90; *see also* Palaepaphos
Olumbros   11
Olympia   29
Olympus   184, 269, 270, 278
omphalos   126
On behalf of the Dancers, Libanios   363
Opheltes   222–225, 237;
    Opheltes/Archemoros, 222
Oplontis   148
Oppian   15–16
oracle   114
– Oracle of Ammon   310
– Oracle of the Lamb   286
– Potter's Oracle   286
Orbe-Boscéaz, Switzerland   360
Oreithyia   232
Orestes   xlvii, 102, 126, 127–128, 161, 173, 177, 192, 226, 231–233, 241
Orestikon, Argos   xlviii
Origines, Cato   117, 119
Orodes   347
Oropus, Attica   xlv
Orpheus   109 n.36, 129, 130, 226, 232
Orthos   268
Orvieto   95, 98
Osiris   xx, 17, 284, 293, 294, 309–325, 399
– Osiris Wennefer   293

Ossetic myths   278
Ostia   193–195
Osymandyas, tomb of   312
Ouranos   11–12
Ovid   116, 117, 119, 121, 145, 181, 189, 195
– *Elegy on Tibullus*   201
Oxus   xli, 329

P

Pactolus   181
Paeonians   xlviii
pagan/pagans   xxii, 387
– beliefs   383
– propaganda   373
Pahlavi   338
Palaepaphos   72–73, 75, 90; *see also* Old
   Paphos
Palatine   148
Palestine   xlii, 211, 363
Palistin   18
Palmyra   329, 338, 359, 361
– House of Achilles   359, 361
Pamphylia   50, 60
Pan   15, 77
Panathenaikos, Aelius Aristides   225
Pandaia   xxxvii
Pandora   12–13
pantomime   136, 363, 367, 383
Panyassis   276
Paphos   xv, 72–88, 400
– kings of   76, 79, 81
Paramonos   225
Parion   30–32
Paris/Alexander   55, 100, 102, 118, 148, 149,
   156, 161
Parma   xlii
Parthenopaios   224
Parthia   327–329, 331, 332, 334, 336–337,
   339, 341, 352
– Parthian Seleucia   339
Pasquino Group   369, 370
paternity, dual   11
Patina, Syria   xlii
Patjenef   293
Patroclus   xix, 38, 108, 147, 163, 173, 181, 228,
   229, 232, 237, 265, 272, 274, 275, 365, 368,
   369, 381–383, 390
patrons   xiv, xvi–xvii, 147, 183–185, 187, 188,
   202, 217, 218, 221–223, 235–237, 239, 240,
   244, 246, 247, 249, 254, 255, 329, 330,
   336, 339, 340, 344, 390, 391
– clientele   211, 212, 238, 253
– female patronage   239
– patron's wife   244
– patroness   157
– Seleucid patronage   332
– senatorial   228
Pausanias   xv, 72, 76, 83–85, 87–88, 222, 246,
   270, 271, 400
Pava Tarchies   110
pax Romana   253
peace   40, 115–117, 119, 120, 202, 338, 351
– peace and slavery   253
– treaty   118
Pecse   400
Pedrosa de la Vega, Spain   360, 362
Pegasus   44, 47, 400
Pēgē   377
Pekrur of Per-sopdu   283, 284, 286, 287, 293,
   294, 297, 298, 301, 304
Pelasgian Argos   88
Peleus   108, 296, 363, 374, 376, 387
Pelopeia   138
Peloponnese   xlviii
– Peloponnesian Greeks   73
– theoroi   88
Pelops   211, 226, 229, 234, 241
Pelusium   17
Pemu, son of Pekrur   286, 287, 292–294, 297,
   300–301, 304
Peneios   271
Pentelicon, Attica   211
– Pentelic marble   210
– quarries   213
Penthe, Amazonian queen   368
Penthesilea   xxxviii, xl, 35, 195, 302, 369–371,
   386
Pentheus   146
peplos   76, 83–88
pseudo-Aristotle   76, 83
Pergamioi   xlix
Pergamon   xlix–l, 86–89, 144, 249, 260
Pergamus   xlviii
Perikles   44, 46
Peroz, the crown of   349
"persea" (Mimusops) plant   xxxvi

Persephone   5, 174, 178, 179, 189, 193,
    200–202, 232
– sarcophagus   179, 201
Persepolis   335, 343, 347
Perseus   xxxiv–xxxvi, 44–48, 57–59, 357, 401
Persia/Persians   30, 39–40, 46, 62, 74,
    224–225, 227, 235, 236, 286, 292, 303,
    401; see also Achaemenid
conquest of Asia Minor   24, 31, 42, 44, 59–60
– domination   288
– Persian Empire   39, 285
– geneaology   46
– Persian Gulf   xxxvi
– homeland   348
– kings   xli
– mythology   351
Persis   46, 327, 328, 348
Peshawar   xxxv
Petechons   286, 287, 292–294, 300–302, 304
Petese   284
Petronius   309, 400
Petubastis of Tanis   286, 292–294
Phaedra   148, 171, 173, 186, 192, 224, 230,
    234, 238, 241, 247
Phaeton   162, 173, 181
Pharsalus   310
Pherecydes   276, 277
Philip IV   xl, 296
Philo of Byblos   10–11, 19
Philoctetes   180
Philomela   181
Philopappos monument   234
Philostephanos of Cyrene   80, 82
Philostratus   216, 217, 260, 380
– Heroikos   252, 296
Phineus   112, 180
Phlyax Vases   136
Phoenicia/Phoenicians   xliii–xliv, xlix, 10–11,
    18–19, 74
– myths   10, 13
Phoenix   108, 296, 326, 365, 366, 378, 379,
    390
Phoinix   366
Phrygia   xxxv, 24, 31, 42, 211, 366, 400
– Phrygian Corybantes   36
– Phrygian costume   156
– Gordium   42
– king   121
Phrygians   30, 38, 121

Phthia   108, 379
pietas   160, 161, 177, 233
Pilonicos   100, 102
Pindar   40, 52
– Victory ode for Diagoras of Rhodes   14
Piraeus   216, 217, 225, 247
Pisander of Camirus   268, 274
Pisidia   378
Piye, Nubian king   283, 284
plague   163, 164, 337
Pleuron   190
Pliny the Elder   xxxvi, 145, 376
Ploutos   223
Plutarch   296, 399
Pluto   5 n.9
Poplia Antia Damokratia   239
Polybius   xx, 82, 310, 316–318
Polydorus   xlix
Polykrates   82, 88
Polyneikes   222, 224
Polyxena   32, 34–36, 40, 48, 50, 60, 374 n.56,
    382, 384, 390, 391
Polyxena Sarcophagus   xiv, 23–24, 29–34,
    37–41, 44, 50, 59–60, 399
Pompeii/Pompeians   xvi, 143–164, 358,
    360–362
– Casa dell'Amore Punito   154
– Casa del Citarista   150–154, 156, 159, 160
– Casa dell'Efebo   154
– Casa delle Vestali   157, 158
– Casa di Octavius Quartio/Loreius Tiburtinus
    163
– Casa di Sirico, Pompeii   157
– Casa di Virinius Modestus   157
– House of Apollo   360
– House of Octavius Quartio   162
– House Regio IX   151
– Villa of Terzigno   162
Porticus Octaviae, Rome   145
Poseidon   44, 148, 149, 159, 160, 162–164,
    223, 271, 272, 359, 360
Posthomerica of Quintus Smyrnaeus   xx, 303
Praeneste/Praenestines   96, 100, 102–105,
    107, 118
Prajapati   xxxvii
Preimos   250
Priam   53, 55, 85, 112, 118, 175, 296, 358, 374,
    375, 382–384, 390, 391

Priests   1, 76, 81,126, 289, 290, 292, 293, 304,
    312, 321, 336, 345, 347, 348
princes   48, 50, 77, 281, 283, 285, 286, 294,
    297, 302, 348
princesses   xl–xli, 32–36, 48
processus consularis   226
Procne   181
Proconnesus   32, 212, 214
– marble quarries   31, 40, 215
– workshops   216
Prometheus   12, 268, 382
Propertius   181
prophecy   7, 100, 114, 119, 120
– prophets   109, 110, 114, 19–121
Protesilaos   xlviii, 194, 296
Proteus   275–277
Psamtik   284
Pseudo-Hesiodic Shield   268
Pseudo-Ovid   181
Pseudo-Scylax   xlix
Ptolemaic kingdom in Cyprus   xv, 79–80
– dynasty   88
– ruler cult   82
– strategos   79
Ptolemaios IV Philopator   310–311
Ptolemaios of Megalopolis   xv, 81–83, 86, 88
Ptolemais in Cyrenaica   361, 394
Ptolemies   80, 82–83, 89, 295
Ptolemy I Soter (of Lagus)   312
Ptolemy IV   82
Publius Aulius Vibellius   250
Publius Fannius Synistor   165, 166
Punt   293
Purifying a House Ritual   14 n.50
Purulli-festival (Hittite)   14
Pwensh   285
Pylades   126, 161, 241
Pylian saga   273
Pylos   267, 272, 273
Pyrgi, Italy   xlvii
Pyrrhic dance   35–36
Pyrrhus   35, 38
– Neoptolemus   36

Q
Q. Aemilius Aristides   252
queen   xl, li, 57, 301; *see also* Amazon
– queen of Kanesh story   5
Quellenforschung   313

Quintilian   174, 175
Quintus Smyrnaeus   xx, 303, 306, 382, 390
Quirinius, governor of Syria   xxxiii
Quito, Ecuador   xxxiv

R
races of gold, silver, bronze and iron   12
ram   350
Ramses II   287
rape   xl, 174 n.26, 179, 198, 201, 233 n.7, 268
Remus   233
Rhadamanthys   129
Rhea   11
Rhea Sylvia   189, 193
Rhodes   14
Rig Veda   xxxvii
Rinuccini sarcophagus   187, 226
rites   rituals, ix–x, xlii, lii, 6, 19, 36, 63, 95,
    106, 209, 251, 309 n.1, 346, 348
river god   116
– personification of a river   198
Robert, Louis   xxxiv, xxxix, li
Roma   234
Roman de Troie (Benoît de Sainte-Maure)
Romanian   265
Romanisation   ix, 170
Rome   vii, xi, xvii–xviii, xxxiv, xlvii, xlix–l, 122,
    123, 148, 163–167, 184–186, 203–206, 212,
    234–235, 238–244, 256, 257, 259, 260,
    353–355, 375, 376, 392–395, 402
– Rome's Trojan kinship   xlix–l
Romulus and Remus   116, 233
Rutuli (Italic tribe)   116

S
Sabines   121, 233 n.7
sacrifice   8, 12, 14, 32–33, 48, 58, 146, 148,
    160, 226, 233, 296, 381, 402
– sacrificed cow   136
– human flesh   296
Saepta, Campus Martius   145
Sagalassus   378, 379
Sais, Egypt   283, 284, 286
Salamis, Cyprus   74, 76–78, 83, 88, 225
Sallust   315
Šamaš (sun god)   276
Samnites   145
Samos   39, 359
Sanchuniathon (Phoenician author)   10, 12–13

Sandas/Santas (Luwian deity)   18
Sappho   35–36
Šāpur I   348, 349, 351
Sardinian Sea   118
Sargon II   341, 343
Sarpot, Amazonian Queen   292, 294, 300–302
Sasanian Empire   xxi, 327–329, 334, 347, 349–353
– Sasanian art   350
– capital   347
– coins   349
– religion   351
– rock reliefs   329, 349
– rulers   327, 329
Satrapies   xxxix–xl, 30, 285, 327
– satrapal building projects   32
Satyricon, Petronius   400
Sauska/Ishtar   8
Scaean Gate   l
Scandinavia   li
Scione   xlviii
Scipios, the   186
scorpion-men   267, 277
scribes   104, 105, 110–111
Scythians   xl, 217
– Scythian arrowheads   xl
Sea god   6–10, 12–14, 16–17, 19; *see also* Old Man of the Sea and *Song of the Sea*
seals   339, 340, 344
sea-monster   14
– Hedammu   8
Secchia Doria   366, 367, 373, 392
Second Sophistic, the   xviii, 209, 237, 241, 358 n.4
Segesta, Sicily   xlix–l
Seha-River Land   18
Seki Plain   42
Selene   189, 202, 238
Seleucia   327, 329, 332, 335–338, 340, 344, 347, 371
– Seleucia/Antioch   364, 371
– Seleucian Heracles-Verethragna   339
Seleucia Pieria,
– House of the Porticoes   363–364
Seleucids   85, 328, 335
– Seleucid capital   327
– coin   331
– elite   334
– governor   327

– Hyacinthus dedication   327
– period   34
– rule   333
– Zeus Aetophorus and Apollo   339
Seleucus   xxxvii
semen   7, 13
Semiramis   xx, 323–325, 334
Semitic   4, 12, 16, 328, 345, 346
Seneca   196
Sennacherib   271–273
Serbo-Croat   265
serpents   57, 291, 298; *see also* snakes
Servius (*Vergilii Aeneidem commentarii*)   277, 401
Sethlans (Etruscan craftsman god)   98, 112
Seven against Thebes expedition   132
Seven Wise Men   367
Severan   227, 228
sex   xii, xxxv, xxxvii–xxxix, 41, 193, 194, 198, 199, 363
Sextus Marcius Priscus   249
Shabaka, Nubian king   283
Shai 'al Quam (Arab god)   401
shepherds   15, 150, 155, 292, 293, 299
Sibai of South India   xxxvii
Sicily   xii, xlii, xlvi, xlix, li, 123, 142, 144, 311, 324, 399
Sidon   37, 245
Šiduri   275–277, 280
Silver (son of Kumarbi)   9
silver race   12
Silvia, Rhea   116, 235
Šimbār   344, 346, 347
Siphnian Treasury   29
sirens   24, 47, 60
Siwah, oracle of Ammon   xxxvi, 310 n.14
Sky (Hittite god)   13
sky-god (Anu)   270, 273
Skyros   197, 227 n.4, 241, 358, 360–363, 365, 371–373, 380, 386, 388, 391
slaves   xxxviii–xxxix, 134, 249
– slave boy   198
– slavery   253
snakes   7–8, 14, 19, 129, 185, 222, 224, 275, 278, 280, 299; *see also* serpents
– Apophis   17
– Illuyanka   5
Sogdia   xli, 329
soldiers   159, 196, 316, 318, 319, 366

Solinus   121
Solon   314, 315, 321
song   xlii–xliii, 106
Song of Coming/Going Forth, xiii   4, 7, 12, 16
Song of Hedammu   8
Song of Kumarbi   7
Song of LAMMA   9, 14
Song of Release   5
Song of Silver   9
Song of the Sea   10
Song of Ullikummi   6, 8, 13
Sopdu, (Egyptian god of the sky)   293
Sophocles   32, 278
Sophoniba (Carthaginian heroine)   146
Spain   360, 366, 367
Spanish conquistadors   xxxiv, xli
Sparta   xlvi, 148, 149, 359, 360, 363.
sphinxes   24, 47
stag   9
Statilii   115, 116
Statius   173, 176, 181, 182, 193, 196, 222, 358, 387
Stesichorus   xlvii, 268, 276
Sthenelos   272
storm god   4, 7, 9–10, 12, 15, 17–18
– gods   8
Storm-god   6–7
story-tellers   71, 294
– storytelling   107, 147, 282
Strabo   xlv, 30, 38, 75, 79, 144, 338, 345
St-Romain-en-Gal, France   360
Styx   373, 375, 376, 378, 385–387
Sumerian   7, 9, 16, 280, 341, 398
sun   5, 8, 109, 151, 267, 275–277, 280, 283, 321
sun-god   14, 267, 275, 276, 279, 321
Suppiluliuma   xliii
Susa   331, 332, 334, 337, 340, 341, 345
swans   158, 159, 161
Switzerland   373
symposiasts   246, 333
syncretism   329, 330
Syria   xii, xxxiii, xli–xlii, xliv, liii, 3–11, 13, 15, 17, 19, 52, 211, 290
– Syrian   xiv, 6, 9–10, 17–18
– Syrians   xliii, 364, 365

T
Tacitus   76, 81, 310, 334–336
Tadjikistan   xxxv, 265

Tages   109
Taharqa, Nubian king   283–285
Tahor   293
Tahta, King   xlii
Taita, kingdom of   18
Talthybios   233, 366
Tang China   xlvi
Tang-e Botān, Valley of the Idols, Iran   344
Tang-e Sarvak, Iran   342, 343, 346, 347, 354
Tanis   286, 293
Tantalus   129, 130, 181
Tantamani   284
Tāq-e Bostān III   349
Taranto   132, 133, 136, 138
Tarchon   109, 120, 121
Tarhundaradu of Arzawa   18
Tarhunt   7
Tarhunta   xlii
Tarpalli, tarpanalli   7–8
– Tarpanalli-Narratives   7
Tarquinia   118, 144
Tarsos   18
Tatarlı Tomb   24, 400
Taseos   100, 102
Tasmisu/Suwaliya   8
Tasmisu/Suwaliyat   7, 13
Tatarlı Tomb, Phrygia   24, 400
Tauris/Taurians   126, 127, 161, 402–403
Taurian Artemis   xlvii
Tebtunis Temple Library   281, 282, 307
Tegea, Tegeans   xv, 75, 83–88, 400
– descendants of Agapenor   83
– envoys   86
– Tegeans' isopoliteia embassy   87
Tekke Peninsula   42
Telamonian Ajax   303
Telephus   87–88, 102, 180
Telesphoros   230, 247
Tellaro   358, 395
Tell Tayyinat   xlii–xliii
Temple of the Oxus   329;
Tensa Capitolina   358, 373, 375, 386
Termessus   249
Terzigno   148, 156, 159, 161–167
Tessub   8–9, 14
Tetrarchic sarcophagi   171, 192
Teukros   76–78
– Teukrians   38
T. Flavius Carpus   193

Thalestris, Amazonian queen   xxxix
Thalna   100–101, 156
Theban cycle   145
Thebes   51, 132, 222, 267, 283, 284, 293, 312
– Seven against   224, 245, 247
Thebes, Egypt   283, 293, 312
Themistocles   224
Theodosius II   390
Theonoe   359, 363
Theopompus of Chios   79
theorodokoi   88, 90
Thera, xlvi   182, 198
Thermodon river   xxxix
Thersites   371
Theseus   99, 147, 223–225, 246, 376, 377
Thespiae   xlv
Thessalian   xxxvii
Thessalonike   214, 215, 217, 231–233, 239,
    240, 250, 261, 373
Thestiadai   219
Thetis   108, 109, 118, 181, 227–229, 364, 365,
    373, 374, 376–380, 385–387, 390, 391
Thoth   10, 289
Thrace   15, 112, 130
– Thracian   401
– Coast   xlix
– groups   30
– kingdom   xxxix
Thucydides   1, 72, 310, 316
Thyestes   138
Thysdrus (El Djem)   360, 362
Tiberius   181
Tibullus   181, 189, 201
Tigris River   7, 329, 332, 335–340, 344, 348
Timades Painter   34
Tinia   100
Tipasa   360–362, 371, 376
Tir   336, 337
Tiraios   338
Tiryns   268, 278
Tištrya   350
Titanomachia   15
Titans   11–14
Tiverios, Michalis   xlv
Tomba François   122, 147, 149, 163
Tomb of the Blue Demons   57
trade   xviii, 17, 185, 213, 214; traders,
    merchants
tragic costumes   129, 132, 142

tragic iconography   125, 141
Trajan   184
travellers   xiii, 106, 329, 334
– travelling Corinthians   xlvii
– travelling craftsmen   xxxiv, 216
– Euboans   xii–xiii, xlii–xlvi, liii, 397, 398
– travelling Greek poets   59
– travelling heroes and travelling myth   xii–xiii,
    xxxiii–xxxv, xliv–xlv, xlvii–xlviii, 400
– travelling singers   6
trees   xxxiii, xxxvi, 136, 271, 277, 278
– ballukku-tree   271
– cedars   271, 274, 279
– laurel   126
– leafless   33
– olive   333
– palm   126
Trimalchio-style mythology   400
Triptolemus   129
Troad   23, 30, 35, 37–38, 271, 272
– Troad and Hellespontine Phrygia   31
Troezen   xlvii–xlviii
Troilus   45–46, 48, 50, 61, 382, 399
Trojan(s)   xiii, xlviii–l, 32, 98, 116, 145–148,
    227, 228, 267, 296, 302–3
– ancestry   xlix
– Athena   296
– Horse   xlviii, 53, 97–98, 400
– War   xv, 23, 39, 41, 48, 55, 71–72, 84, 100,
    149, 228, 241, 296, 357–358; 373
Trophos   386
Troy   xlviii–xlix, 36, 38–39, 72–73, 76, 147,
    148, 176, 198, 225, 267, 268, 296, 373,
    379–380
Trysa   44, 60
Tullia   195
Turan   100–101, 156
Turia   195
Turkey   xii, 18, 358
Turkic   265
Turkmenistan   331
Turnus   116, 117
Tuscania   110
Tüse   60
twins   xlix
Tyche   339
Tydeus   224
Typhon   xliv, 10, 12, 14–17, 19, 321

tyrant 117, 119–120
– Luwian *tarwani* 6 n.18
Tyras xxxix
Tyre 212, 220, 254
– necropolis 216, 221
Tyrrhenian 33, 121

U
Ubelluri 8
Ugarit 4, 6, 10, 17
Ugaritic 5–6, 8–9, 12–13, 19
– Ugaritic and Phoenician Myths 10
Uhuze 95, 111, 119, 400
Ullikummi 8–9, 13–14, 19
underworld 5, 7–8, 14, 105, 129, 131, 140, 174, 193, 265, 279, 293, 337, 338
Underworld Painter 128
Unqi, land of xlvi
Ura 17
Ur-šanabi 267, 275, 276
Uruk 267, 273, 278–280, 332, 340
Ūta-napišti 267, 275–277, 280
Uzbekistan 265

V
Vahagn 330
Vahrām 329, 349, 351
– Vahrām/Verethragna 330
– Vahrām Yašt 335, 338
Vajrapani 329
Vanth 147
Varro l, 105, 401
Varvakion Athena 210, 217
Vātu (Iranian wind deity) 346
Veii, Etruria 120
Velach 111
Velachtra 95, 400
– Etruscan *velaxtra* 111
Venus 146, 148, 149, 152–155, 157, 158, 160, 161, 189, 195, 237, 238
– Venus Genetrix 148
Veregna bird of Verethragna 350
Verethragna 329, 331, 334, 335, 337, 338, 340, 349–353
– hymn to 335, 350
Veritus 104
Via Appia 242, 243
Via Aurelia 230
Vibenna, *see* Vipinas brothers

Victoria 102–104, 118
Victory 190, 197
Vile (Etruscan Iolaus) 99
Villa Albani, Rome 339
Villa Giulia, Rome
– Villa Giulia mirror xv, 95–113, 121
Villa of Herodes Atticus, Eva/Loukou 369–371
Villa of Maxentius, Via Appia 243
Villa of Publius Fannius Synistor, Boscoreale 148
Vinalia festival 116, 117
vindemia 227, 239
Vipinas brothers 95, 120, 121; *see also* Cacu and Avle
Virbius xlvii
Virgil xvi, xlix–l, liv, 95, 112,117–120, 145, 400 ; *see also* Aeneid
Virgin Mary xlvii
virtus 104, 160, 161, 177, 186, 187, 192, 195, 197, 199–200, 233, 244
Vita Apollonii 216
vita felix 227
vita humana 226, 227, 242, 245
Vitalius Restitutus 215, 239
vitis 254, 255
Volnius 105
Vologases I 337
Vologases IV 337 n.27, 347
Volterra, Italy 57
votives xv, 84, 87–88
– votive pillars 151, 154, 157
Vulci 100–101, 109, 110, 122, 144, 147

W
war 33, 40, 116, 118, 176, 200, 240, 248, 253, 272, 273, 294, 300, 303, 337, 379
– civil war 72, 286, 292, 293, 295
– war motifs, decorations of 297, 298
warriors xxxviii, 11, 44, 50–51, 53, 55, 60, 98, 104, 107, 120, 121, 150, 197, 227, 229, 238, 247 n.130, 270, 286, 287, 293, 299–304, 380, 390
– warrior clan 294
– warrior companions 285
wedding, see marriage
Wertiamonniut 292, 298, 300–301
wives xx, xl, 11, 38, 86, 138, 181, 187, 192–195, 200, 277, 280, 323, 325
Wolfgang Petersen 176

women   xviii, xxi, xl–xli, 32, 36–37, 40, 50–51,
    55, 61, 84, 107, 108, 149, 150, 162, 182, 193,
    195–197, 200–201, 209, 221, 229, 231, 239,
    249, 359–361, 366, 368, 370, 376, 378,
    390 adulterous, 301 n.104
– bird   47
– elite women   213
– "land of women"   302
– as patrons   239
– role in Roman society   192, 193
– royal   85, 348
workshops,
– coin   331
– sarcophagi   210–212, 216–217, 221, 240, 250
– vase painting   139
wrestlers   199, 242–243, 279, 344
– lion wrestler   342

X
Xanthos   64, 67–68, 260, 394
Xanthus   l, 44, 59–60, 64, 245
– House of Meleager   377, 378

Xenagoras   80
Xenophon   xxxix, 30, 310, 316

Y
Yamm   8–10, 16
Yašt (hymn to Verethragna)   350, 351

Z
Zagros Mountains in Elymais   341
Zarathuštra   350
Zelach   111
Zelachtra   111, 118
Zeugma   359–360, 391–392, 394
– House of Poseidon   359–360
– House of Quintus   359
Zeus   xliii, 5, 10–13, 15–16, 20, 29, 100, 158,
    161, 175, 181, 184, 267–273, 397, 398
– Zeus-Bel   345
Zimri-Lim (king of Mari)   6
Zopyrus   250
Zoroastrianism   335, 345, 350–353
Zosime, Berria   194

Lightning Source UK Ltd.
Milton Keynes UK
UKHW051342280121
377755UK00002B/10